NORTH AMERICAN GAELS

MCGILL-QUEEN'S STUDIES IN ETHNIC HISTORY
SERIES ONE: DONALD HARMAN AKENSON, EDITOR

24 The Development of Elites in Acadian New Brunswick, 1861–1881
Sheila M. Andrew

25 Journey to Vaja
Reconstructing the World of a Hungarian-Jewish Family
Elaine Kalman Naves

MCGILL-QUEEN'S STUDIES IN ETHNIC HISTORY
SERIES TWO: JOHN ZUCCHI, EDITOR

1 Inside Ethnic Families
Three Generations of Portuguese-Canadians
Edite Noivo

2 A House of Words
Jewish Writing, Identity, and Memory
Norman Ravvin

3 Oatmeal and the Catechism
Scottish Gaelic Settlers in Quebec
Margaret Bennett

4 With Scarcely a Ripple
Anglo-Canadian Migration into the United States and Western Canada, 1880–1920
Randy William Widdis

5 Creating Societies
Immigrant Lives in Canada
Dirk Hoerder

6 Social Discredit
Anti-Semitism, Social Credit, and the Jewish Response
Janine Stingel

7 Coalescence of Styles
The Ethnic Heritage of St John River Valley Regional Furniture, 1763–1851
Jane L. Cook

8 Brigh an Orain / A Story in Every Song
The Songs and Tales of Lauchie MacLellan
Translated and edited by John Shaw

9 Demography, State and Society
Irish Migration to Britain, 1921–1971
Enda Delaney

10 The West Indians of Costa Rica
Race, Class, and the Integration of an Ethnic Minority
Ronald N. Harpelle

11 Canada and the Ukrainian Question, 1939–1945
Bohdan S. Kordan

12 Tortillas and Tomatoes
Transmigrant Mexican Harvesters in Canada
Tanya Basok

13 Old and New World Highland Bagpiping
John G. Gibson

14 Nationalism from the Margins
The Negotiation of Nationalism and Ethnic Identities among Italian Immigrants in Alberta and British Columbia
Patricia Wood

15 Colonization and Community
The Vancouver Island Coalfield and the Making of the British Columbia Working Class
John Douglas Belshaw

16 Enemy Aliens, Prisoners of War
Internment in Canada during the Great War
Bohdan S. Kordan

17 Like Our Mountains
A History of Armenians in Canada
Isabel Kaprielian-Churchill

18 Exiles and Islanders
The Irish Settlers of Prince Edward Island
Brendan O'Grady

19 Ethnic Relations in Canada
Institutional Dynamics
Raymond Breton
Edited by Jeffrey G. Reitz

20 A Kingdom of the Mind
The Scots' Impact on the Development of Canada
Edited by Peter Rider and Heather McNabb

21 Vikings to U-Boats
The German Experience in Newfoundland and Labrador
Gerhard P. Bassler

22 Being Arab
Ethnic and Religious Identity Building among Second Generation Youth in Montreal
Paul Eid

23 From Peasants to Labourers
Ukrainian and Belarusan Immigration from the Russian Empire to Canada
Vadim Kukushkin

24 Emigrant Worlds and Transatlantic Communities
Migration to Upper Canada in the First Half of the Nineteenth Century
Elizabeth Jane Errington

25 Jerusalem on the Amur
Birobidzhan and the Canadian Jewish Communist Movement, 1924–1951
Henry Felix Srebrnik

26 Irish Nationalism in Canada
Edited by David A. Wilson

27 Managing the Canadian Mosaic in Wartime
Shaping Citizenship Policy, 1939–1945
Ivana Caccia

28 Jewish Roots, Canadian Soil
Yiddish Culture in Montreal, 1905–1945
Rebecca Margolis

29 Imposing Their Will
An Organizational History of Jewish Toronto, 1933–1948
Jack Lipinsky

30 Ireland, Sweden, and the Great European Migration, 1815–1914
Donald H. Akenson

31 The Punjabis in British Columbia
Location, Labour, First Nations, and Multiculturalism
Kamala Elizabeth Nayar

32 Growing Up Canadian
Muslims, Hindus, Buddhists
Edited by Peter Beyer and Rubina Ramji

33 Between Raid and Rebellion
The Irish in Buffalo and Toronto, 1867–1916
William Jenkins

34 Unpacking the Kists
The Scots in New Zealand
Brad Patterson, Tom Brooking, and Jim McAloon

35 Building Nations from Diversity
Canadian and American Experience Compared
Garth Stevenson

36 Hurrah Revolutionaries
The Polish Canadian Communist Movement, 1918–1948
Patryk Polec

37 Alice in Shandehland
Scandal and Scorn in the Edelson/Horwitz Murder Case
Monda Halpern

38 Creating Kashubia
History, Memory, and Identity in Canada's First Polish Community
Joshua C. Blank

39 No Free Man
Canada, the Great War, and the Enemy Alien Experience
Bohdan S. Kordan

40 Between Dispersion and Belonging
Global Approaches to Diaspora in Practice
Edited by Amitava Chowdhury and Donald Harman Akenson

41 Running on Empty
Canada and the Indochinese Refugees, 1975–1980
Michael J. Molloy, Peter Duschinsky, Kurt F. Jensen, and Robert J. Shalka

42 Twenty-First-Century Immigration to North America
Newcomers in Turbulent Times
Edited by Victoria M. Esses and Donald E. Abelson

43 Gaelic Cape Breton Step-Dancing
An Historical and Ethnographic Perspective
John G. Gibson

44 Witness to Loss
Race, Culpability, and Memory in the Dispossession of Japanese Canadians
Edited by Jordan Stanger-Ross and Pamela Sugiman

45 Mad Flight?
The Quebec Emigration to the Coffee Plantations of Brazil
John Zucchi

46 A Land of Dreams
Ethnicity, Nationalism, and the Irish in Newfoundland, Nova Scotia, and Maine, 1880–1923
Patrick Mannion

47 Strategic Friends
Canada-Ukraine Relations from Independence to the Euromaidan
Bohdan S. Kordan

48 From Righteousness to Far Right
An Anthropological Rethinking of Critical Security Studies
Emma Mc Cluskey

49 North American Gaels
Speech, Story, and Song in the Diaspora
Edited by Natasha Sumner and Aidan Doyle

North American Gaels

Speech, Story, and Song in the Diaspora

EDITED BY
NATASHA SUMNER AND AIDAN DOYLE

McGill-Queen's University Press
Montreal & Kingston · London · Chicago

ISBN 978-0-2280-0378-6 (cloth)
ISBN 978-0-2280-0379-3 (paper)
ISBN 978-0-2280-0517-9 (ePDF)
ISBN 978-0-2280-0518-6 (ePUB)

Legal deposit fourth quarter 2020
Bibliothèque nationale du Québec

Printed in Canada on acid-free paper that is 100% ancient forest free (100% post-consumer recycled), processed chlorine free

This book has been published with the help of a grant from the Canadian Federation for the Humanities and Social Sciences, through the Awards to Scholarly Publications Program, using funds provided by the Social Sciences and Humanities Research Council of Canada. Funding was also received from from the Anne and Jim Rothenberg Fund for Humanities Research at Harvard University, from the National University of Ireland, and from the College of Arts, Celtic Studies, and Social Sciences, University College, Cork.

Funded by the Government of Canada | Financé par le gouvernement du Canada | Canada | Canada Council for the Arts | Conseil des arts du Canada

We acknowledge the support of the Canada Council for the Arts.

Nous remercions le Conseil des arts du Canada de son soutien.

Library and Archives Canada Cataloguing in Publication

Title: North American Gaels : speech, story, and song in the diaspora / edited by Natasha Sumner and Aidan Doyle.
Names: Sumner, Natasha, editor. | Doyle, Aidan (Lecturer in Irish), editor. | Nilsen, Kenneth E., 1947–2012, honoree.
Series: McGill-Queen's studies in ethnic history. Series two ; 49.
Description: Series statement: McGill-Queen's studies in ethnic history. Series two ; 49 | This book is dedicated to the memory of Professor Kenneth E. Nilsen, who held the Sister Saint Veronica Chair in Gaelic Studies at St Francis Xavier University in Antigonish, Nova Scotia, for twenty eight years before his death in 2012. | Includes bibliographical references and index.
Identifiers: Canadiana (print) 20200275143 | Canadiana (ebook) 20200275410 | ISBN 9780228003793 (paper) | ISBN 9780228003786 (cloth) | ISBN 9780228005179 (ePDF) | ISBN 9780228005186 (ePUB)
Subjects: LCSH: Irish literature—History and criticism. | LCSH: Scottish Gaelic literature—History and criticism. | LCSH: Folk literature, Irish—History and criticism. | LCSH: Folk literature, Scottish Gaelic—History and criticism. | LCSH: Irish—Canada—History. | LCSH: Scots—Canada—History. | LCSH: Irish—United States—History. | LCSH: Scots—United States—History. | LCGFT: Festschriften.
Classification: LCC PB1306 .N67 2020 | DDC 891.6/209—dc23

This book was typeset by True to Type in 10.5/13 Sabon

Contents

Foreword

In 1983, with the support, moral and financial, of the late Hon. Allan J. MacEachen, MP, St Francis Xavier University was awarded one of the ethnic chairs funded by the Canadian Department of Multiculturalism. Ken Nilsen was the successful applicant for the Sister Saint Veronica Chair in Gaelic Studies.

It was my privilege to welcome Ken to join me in the effort to enhance the quality and scope of our small Celtic department. For the next two decades his intelligence, industry, and integrity, hallmarks of the true scholar, inspired respect and gratitude among students, faculty, and the numerous local tradition bearers he valued and treated with such courtesy.

This memorial volume will, I hope, serve to give due honour to a fellow traveller in the pursuit of *veritas*, and a truly good and faithful servant of StFX.

Sister Margaret MacDonell
PhD Harvard '69

Acknowledgments

The editors would like to thank the following institutions and people: Harvard University; the National University of Ireland; University College, Cork; Mark Abley, our editor at McGill-Queen's University Press, for his help and support in the publication of this work; Matthew Kudelka for copy editing the text; our indexer, Eileen O'Neill; and last but not least, the contributors.

NORTH AMERICAN GAELS

North American Gaels

Natasha Sumner and Aidan Doyle

Irish and Scottish Gaelic have been spoken in North America since the earliest days of colonization, yet knowledge of the lengthy history of Gaelic speakers – or Gaels – on the North American continent is hardly widespread. Indeed, a survey conducted of the Canadian or American public – or, for that matter, among members of any university Humanities division – would likely register surprise that Scottish Gaelic was the third most widely spoken language in Canada at the time of Confederation (1867), or that the United States was home to hundreds of thousands of Irish speakers around the same time.[1] One does not need to look far to discover a reason for the general lack of awareness of these once sizable diasporas: despite numerous accounts of Irish and Scottish emigration to North America, historical scholarship of the first three quarters of the twentieth century often contained little or no information on the linguistic background of the immigrants. (This absence is particularly notable in sources pertaining to the Irish.) Moreover, Irish and Scottish Gaelic texts were, and to some extent continue to be, all but invisible in reference works about, and canonical anthologies of, the multi-ethnic literature and folklore of North America.[2]

That North American Gaels were long overlooked by historians, folklorists, and literary anthologists is lamentable but to some extent understandable. Then, as now, very few academics possessed the requisite language skills to make informed judgments about Gaelic literature and culture, and other topics of inquiry held sway among Gaelic scholars. As a result, few collections, translations, or studies of North American Scottish Gaelic narrative, and none of Irish narrative, were published before the final quarter of the last century.[3] Fortunately, interest has been growing since the 1970s, and considerable work has been done over the past fifty years to elucidate Canadian and American Gaels' history, culture, and language use. Much of the effort has been exerted by North American-born or -resident academics,[4] but the topic is gaining in popularity among scholars with less obvious personal connections to the regions in question. It is a promising sign that in 2014, several papers on North American topics were given at a large conference in Dublin dedicated to "Litríocht na Gaeilge ar fud an Domhain" (Irish-language Literature throughout the World), which resulted in two published volumes of essays.[5] These volumes can be added to a growing number of articles and books pertaining to diasporic Gaels that have lately appeared.[6] In October 2017, another step forward was taken with the Harvard Symposium on North American Gaelic Literature – the first academic event specifically designed to consider North American Irish and Scottish Gaelic literature in tandem.[7] Even with increasing scholarly activity, however, the Irish and Scottish Gaelic diasporas in Canada and the United States remain understudied, and they continue to receive little recognition outside of the fields of Irish, Scottish, and Celtic Studies.[8]

This book represents a concerted effort to advance the study of the Gaelic diasporic experience, drawing together research by established and emerging scholars on aspects of Irish and Scottish Gaelic narrative in North America. Our choice to explore the Irish and Scottish Gaelic diasporas in the same volume was deliberate. Although the two are usually considered separately, the modes of literary and oral expression in both languages are closely related. However, rather than conflating ethnic groups – as in the Canadian census's failure to distinguish between the Gaelic languages after 1941, or the early twentieth-century US Census's grouping of Celtic languages together with English – we have divided the book into two sections, focusing first on Irish Gaels, and then on Scottish Gaels.[9] The division encourages the reader to view each group as unique and cohesive. The cultural and experiential similarities of Irish and Scottish Gaels are nonetheless evident when the two are presented alongside each other, and we hope the juxtaposition will lead to a deeper understanding of these diasporic communities and their place in North American history, literature, and culture. The chapters in each section progress chronologically from early literature to recent literature and folklore, in which order they are introduced below.

The book is dedicated to the memory of Professor Kenneth E. Nilsen, who held the Sister Saint Veronica Chair in Gaelic Studies at St Francis Xavier University in Antigonish, Nova Scotia, for twenty-eight years before his death in 2012. As the first chapter illustrates, Ken Nilsen had a deep knowledge of both Irish and Scottish Gaelic, and he worked tirelessly to document the languages, literatures, and lived traditions of North American Gaels across the eastern United States and the Canadian Maritimes. His work was deeply influential and highly deserving of honour, and it is referenced frequently by our contributors. We regret the loss of a kind, generous, and erudite scholar and of the wealth of further research that his untimely death prevented him from completing.

A SHARED CULTURAL HERITAGE

Irish and Scottish Gaelic narrative traditions are grounded in a shared cultural heritage. Until the seventeenth century, the North Channel (Sruth na Maoile) separating Ireland and Scotland did not act as a barrier to population movement and cultural exchange; rather, this well-traversed thoroughfare facilitated a network of connections within a Gaelic cultural zone that stretched from County Cork in the south to Sutherland and Caithness in the north. Without overemphasizing the unity of Gaelic-speaking people or the fixity of their social practices, it can generally be said that during the late medieval period (ca. 1200–1600), Gaels across Ireland and Scotland shared a similar social structure and cultural institutions.[10] Of greatest relevance here is that learned Gaels often trained in the same professional schools and that, despite dialectal differences among spoken Irish and Scottish Gaelic, they shared a common literary language (Classical Gaelic).[11] Poetry was the most elevated literary form, and among the elite it served as a vehicle primarily for public rather than private expression. The preeminent poets acted as diplomats and advisers to chieftains, and their compositions were directly relevant to statecraft.[12]

The connection between Ireland and Scotland weakened in the half-century following the defeat and departure overseas of the foremost Gaelic nobility in Ulster in 1607 and the plantation of their forfeited lands in 1609. As patrons of the arts in both regions subsequently came under more stringent government control, the centuries-old learned institutions were shuttered and the shared Classical Gaelic literary tradition waned.[13] Coming to prominence in its place were modern vernacular Irish and Scottish Gaelic traditions.

Professional poets faded into obsolescence, yet poetry remained the principal mode of literary expression throughout the seventeenth to nineteenth centuries in both Ireland and Scotland, and poets from a range of social backgrounds earned wide renown among speakers of the same vernacular. In these now separate but broadly parallel traditions, poems were generally set to recognizable tunes and transmitted orally, in manuscripts, and eventually in print, and poetry continued to function not simply as a vehicle for personal expression, but also as a mode of public communication.[14] Emigrant and diasporic poets brought their skills to bear on new subject matter, in both the homeland and the so-called "new" world, where Irish and Scottish Gaelic poetry functioned as a means of connecting members of a community and affirming their shared social values.[15]

In addition to poetry, prose narrative circulated orally among Irish and Scottish Gaelic-speaking emigrants, and there is a certain degree of overlap in the recorded folk tale corpuses. For instance, both Irish and Scottish Gaels in North America told stories about the legendary hero Fionn mac Cumhaill, who was a popular figure in late medieval and early modern manuscripts; Ken Nilsen collected some of these.[16] A short fairy story he collected in Scottish Gaelic – "Di-luain, Di-màirt" (Monday, Tuesday), printed in Catrìona NicÌomhair Parsons's chapter – evidences not only a shared tradition but also the importance of the diasporic folklore record. The story reflects a standard Irish and Scottish Gaelic ecotype of international tale type ATU 503; uniquely, however, it is the only collected Scottish Gaelic version in which the fairies' song (beginning "Di-luain, Di-màirt") is accompanied by a melody – the same one commonly associated with it in Ireland.[17]

Despite a large degree of cultural similarity, it should be stressed that in terms of national and ethnic identity, Irish and Scottish Gaels diverged considerably after the turn of the seventeenth century and into the present day. The most striking difference had to do with religion. Irish Gaels largely remained Catholic after the Reformation, and religion gradually ousted language as a marker of Irish identity.[18] In the Scottish Highlands, by contrast, while Protestantism took hold in a majority of regions, some prominent kindreds maintained their adherence to Catholicism, and religious affiliation did not predominate over "traditional 'ethnic' understandings" of what it meant to be a Gael.[19] More universal was the identification with Britishness that emerged in the late eighteenth and nineteenth centuries and permeated all social levels.[20] When the Celtic Revival movement arose in the late nineteenth and early twentieth centuries, some of those at its forefront sought to draw Irish and Scottish Gaels together again; however, by that time there were fundamental differences in their political and social interests.[21] There is little evidence that during the period of emigration, Irish and Scottish Gaels perceived any great kinship with each other: Sruth na Maoile had come to divide rather than unite. It is in hindsight that we reflect upon their persistent cultural similarities in their new North American environment.

IRISH GAELS

We have limited documentary evidence of the earliest Irish Gaels to set foot in North America, but we know they were present in English, French, and Spanish colonies in the sixteenth to eighteenth centuries, both as colonial settlers and as indentured servants transported to Virginia, Maryland, and elsewhere.[22] From the mid-eighteenth century, Irish Gaels flocked to the fishing grounds adjacent to Newfoundland's Avalon Peninsula in large enough numbers to necessitate the appointment of Irish-speaking priests in the colony.[23] Irish-speaking priests could also be found in New Brunswick and Nova Scotia, as well as Massachusetts, New York, and Pennsylvania in the eighteenth and early nineteenth centuries, although no records have been preserved in the language.[24] Irish Gaels fought on both sides of the American War of Independence (1775–83), and some in the British army appear to have settled in Canada afterward.[25]

The first half of the nineteenth century saw the arrival of many Irish-speaking immigrants to the United States and Canada, but as Ken Nilsen noted, most of them "left nearly no trace of their linguistic presence."[26] This is because, although many were monolingual, they were rarely literate in Irish. The lack of early newspapers or public notices in the language has thus rendered them all but invisible to historians.[27] However, as in earlier centuries, it is possible to deduce their presence from their regions of origin and from references to the spoken language. Departing for the most part during the downturn in the United Kingdom's economy that followed the Napoleonic Wars (1803–15), these migrants sought economic advancement in a new land.[28] In the United States, they augmented Irish populations in Maryland, Pennsylvania, New York, and Massachusetts, and they could also be found in other regions.[29] In present-day Canada, they settled not only in the Atlantic provinces but also farther west in Ontario and Quebec.[30] References are extant to numerous Irish speakers working in mills in Maine and as labourers in the construction of the American capitol buildings, the Erie Canal in New York, and the Rideau Canal in Ontario.[31] Many of the newcomers were Irish-speaking Catholics. This we know from documented proselytizing in Irish on behalf of Protestant organizations in New Brunswick in the 1830s and in Massachusetts, New York, Pennsylvania, and Ohio in the late 1840s and 1850s.[32]

Emigration greatly increased during and after the great Potato Famine (1845–48), which struck the Irish-speaking regions of Ireland particularly hard. It is estimated that from 1845 to 1855, more than two hundred thousand Irish speakers arrived in the United States and more than twenty thousand in Canada.[33] Less well off than earlier emigrants, most of these left "more out of panic or despair than calculated ambition," and a portion of them received assistance to relocate to North America.[34] Departures from Ireland remained high through the remainder of the century, such that by the 1890s the United States may have been home to four hundred thousand Irish speakers.[35] They settled in large numbers in the northeastern United States, including in Portland, Maine; Boston and Springfield, Massachusetts; New York City; and along the Schuylkill River in Pennsylvania; they also ventured farther afield to places like Cleveland, Ohio; Butte, Montana; and Minneapolis–Saint Paul, Minnesota.[36] A considerable number of Irish speakers could also be found in Montreal, Quebec. Although emigration slowed in the twentieth century, people from Gaeltacht areas have continued to arrive to the present day.[37]

The degree of intergenerational transmission of Irish in North America is difficult to determine, given the lack of early documentation. Presence of the language has been attested at relatively late dates in regions of concentrated Irish settlement. For instance, it appears to have been spoken in Newfoundland and New Brunswick until around the beginning of the twentieth century;[38] a small number of regular speakers could still be found in Portland, Maine, in the 1980s and '90s;[39] and it continues to be spoken by some in the Boston area.[40]

However, the longevity of the language in such regions appears to have had more to do with a steady influx of Irish-speaking immigrants than with transmission from one generation to the next. While considerable research remains to be done, only scattered cases of transmission are presently known.[41] It therefore seems that while Irish was – and in some places continues to be – used as a private language among Irish-born speakers, many did not see a need to pass it on to their children. As Ken Nilsen has noted, this is comprehensible. Irish received no institutional support whatsoever until very recently; English was thus the language of advancement in North America.[42]

Irish Literature and Print Media

Although the majority of early Irish-speaking immigrants to North America were likely not literate in Irish, some not only were in the habit of writing but also brought their manuscripts with them. Manuscripts survive that are known to have circulated in Canada in the eighteenth and nineteenth centuries, and Donncha Rua Mac Conmara is believed to have composed poetry during a period of residence in St John's, Newfoundland, in the 1740s–50s before returning to County Waterford.[43] Pádraig Ó Liatháin traces the evidence for Donncha Rua's presence on the island and details the local knowledge he left us in the second chapter of this book. Although Donncha Rua is the earliest author of whom we are aware in North America, there must certainly have been others whose works did not survive.

Irish manuscripts circulated in the United States as well, and Galway native Maitias Ó Conbhuí spent thirty years compiling an Irish dictionary in Philadelphia, which remained unfinished at his death in 1842.[44] In her chapter, Nancy Stenson conducts a linguistic study of two relatively unknown manuscripts written by North Connacht emigrants, with a view to providing a fuller picture of nineteenth-century Irish. Tony Ó Floinn, for his part, takes a new approach to a well-known figure: Pádraig Phiarais Cúndún, the earliest Irish-language poet of whom we are aware in the United States. Cúndún's extant compositions have survived both in manuscript and in oral memory, and his letters home to Ballymacoda, County Cork, contain descriptions of daily life and working conditions in Utica, New York, in the years 1825–55. Ó Floinn investigates these letters in an effort to determine to and for whom Cúndún was writing.

A new era in Irish literature in North America began in 1851, when the *Irish-American*, a weekly newspaper published in New York City, printed a poem that Nilsen describes as "probably the first original composition in Irish to be published in the United States."[45] It has a mere three verses, describing a tavern in Manhattan. The style is that of the poetry of Ireland in the eighteenth and nineteenth centuries, the only difference being the location: Duane Street in New York. In the second half of the nineteenth century, the more politicized Irish Americans began to take an interest in their linguistic heritage. This enthusiasm found an outlet in Irish language societies, which were established across the United States beginning in the 1870s, and some newspapers began publishing material in Irish.[46] In this collection, Tomás Ó hÍde addresses the best-known of these, the Brooklyn Philo-Celtic Society's *An Gaodhal* (The Gael), providing a transcription and translation of a folk tale that appeared in that journal in 1890–91, and Matthew Knight traces the history of Irish-language content in the *Irish Echo*, launched by the Boston Philo-Celtic Society in 1886. Early publishing endeavours in Irish dovetailed with other efforts to curb the trend of language loss among immigrant Gaels and their progeny, including the provision of Irish classes in cities with large Irish populations and the establishment of a Chair of Gaelic (i.e., Irish) Language and Literature at the Catholic University of America in Washington in 1896.[47] As William Mahon recounts in his chapter, an innovative teaching method emerged in 1909: Irish instruction by correspondence with the aid of phonograph records. The three phonograph courses he discusses exemplify American revivalists' use of modern technology to advance their cause.

A number of scholars have pointed out that the language revival movement in the United States provided inspiration and funding for the activities of the Gaelic League in Ireland.[48] One would expect the Irish in Canada to have taken note as well, founding organizations and journals for speakers and learners of Irish there. Only one periodical in Canada had an Irish-language section, however: a monthly magazine called *The Lamp*, published in Hamilton, Ontario, in the 1870s, no copies of which appear to have survived.[49] Even so, the American publications circulated in Canada, connecting Canadian Irish Gaels to their more numerous southern counterparts. As Nilsen noted in 2002, the first five original poems in the *Irish-American*'s Gaelic column, which was introduced in 1857, were submitted by two men residing in present-day Ontario.[50] That the revival movement also resonated among some in Newfoundland is suggested by the recollection of a former student of St Bonaventure's College in St John's that the school's sixth president not only belonged to a Society for the Preservation of the Irish Language, but also taught the language in the 1870s.[51] In a posthumously published essay, Nilsen posited that closer inspection would likely reveal a Canadian counterpart to the American language revival movement.[52]

The late nineteenth- and early twentieth-century American Irish-language press printed songs, poetry, and prose extracted from manuscript and print sources, as well as correspondence and original poetic compositions.[53] Original verse turns up in archival records and oral tradition, as well. The composers generally followed the conventions they had been used to in Ireland, adapting them to new settings. At times, one can also discern the influence of the English-language emigrant ballads of the day, many of which were translated into Irish. Principal subjects included the Irish language and the British occupation of Ireland, and less frequently, we find poems in which the author laments the fate of the emigrant and pines for the former home and comrades. There is disappointingly little in the extant poetry that gives us much insight into the daily lives of Irish immigrants in North America, however. A rare exception is the composition "Amhrán na Mianach" (The Mining Song), which describes in detail the reality of working conditions for immigrants to Butte, Montana, in the nineteenth century. Ciara Ryan draws our attention to the copy of "Amhrán na Mianach" that is preserved, along with several other poems, in the papers of another inhabitant of Butte, Seán "Irish" Ó Súilleabháin. Her chapter traces the personal history of this Beara-born poet and song collector, based on close examination of his papers in the Butte-Silver Bow Archives.

While a few Irish-language plays were written and staged in New York City in the late nineteenth and twentieth centuries, very little prose emerged from North America.[54] The scarcity of prose can be ascribed to the widespread lack of literacy in the language, even during the revival period. Yet, as emigrants sailed west from Ireland and occasionally returned, their experiences found their way into memoirs and influenced twentieth-century prose fiction published in Ireland. For instance, Micí Mac Gabhann's recollections of prospecting for gold in Yukon in the 1890s, narrated to folklore collector Seán

Ó hEochaidh, were published posthumously in 1959 in the celebrated autobiography *Rotha Mór an tSaoil* (The Great Wheel of Life).[55] In his chapter, Pádraig Ó Siadhail examines three novels from the 1920s–'30s in which part of the action takes place in Canada, allowing us a glimpse of the impact of emigration and return migration on Ireland.

Irish Folklore

In the late nineteenth and early twentieth centuries, Irish revivalists in Ireland and overseas encouraged the collection of stories and songs from the oral tradition. Folk tales appeared among other Irish-language content in the American journals, as Tomás Ó hÍde discusses,[56] and song collections like that of Seán "Irish" Ó Súilleabháin were compiled from written and oral sources as well as personal recollection. No large-scale, systematic folklore collecting was ever done among Irish speakers in North America, however, and many narrative traditions have undoubtedly been lost due to limited intergenerational transmission of the language and inadequate collecting. The most concerted collecting effort was made by Ken Nilsen in New England in the late twentieth century, and his articles about the Irish community in Portland, Maine, contain samples of the Irish-language folklore he encountered.[57] Following in his footsteps, collectors for the Boston and the Irish Language project are currently gathering oral histories of present-day Irish speakers in Greater Boston.[58]

SCOTTISH GAELS

Comparable to the Irish, while some of the earliest Scottish Gaels to arrive in North America came as adventurers, others had little choice in the matter, like the Highland prisoners forced to labour in Virginia and New England in the 1650s.[59] Emigration to Gaelic-speaking settlements in Georgia and upper New York and along North Carolina's Cape Fear River began around the 1730s. As many as fifty thousand Scottish Gaels may have settled in the Cape Fear region by the outbreak of the War of Independence (1775–83).[60] Although Highland emigrants then shifted their principal destinations northward, Gaelic continued to be spoken in North Carolina at least until the Civil War (1861–65).[61] Elsewhere in the United States, the language does not appear to have continued as a community language past independence, although it is estimated that more than thirty-five thousand speakers lived in the country in 1910. These largely resided in major urban centres like New York City, Boston, and Chicago.[62]

The first significant influx of Scottish Gaels into present-day Canada began with the arrival of the *Falmouth* and the *Annabella* at Isle St-Jean (Prince Edward Island) in 1770 and the *Hector* at Pictou, Nova Scotia, in 1773.[63] For the most part, these newcomers were economic migrants seeking to escape rising rents and better their lot; the same could be said of the group of immigrants who arrived in Glengarry County, Upper Canada (Ontario), via New York's Mohawk Valley after the American War of Independence.[64] Most of the Gaelic-speaking settlers who arrived in the latter decades of the eighteenth century, and the large influx at the beginning of the nineteenth century, were individuals of some means who sought to emulate the success of their countrymen overseas; these settled mainly in Glengarry County, Prince Edward Island, eastern Nova Scotia, and Cape Breton Island.[65] From around 1815 to 1840, tens of thousands of emigrant Scottish Gaels were victims of the Highland Clearances, evicted from properties slated for agricultural "improvement" and enticed or even assisted to relocate to Canada; thousands more were assisted to emigrate during the great Potato Famine, which reached Scotland in 1846. These early to mid-century migrants settled in existing communities of Highlanders, as well as new regions farther afield, including the Eastern Townships of Quebec, southwestern Ontario, and Manitoba's Red River Valley.[66] Scottish Gaelic speakers also settled in Newfoundland's Codroy Valley after failing to find suitable landholdings in Nova Scotia.[67] After Confederation, in the late nineteenth and early twentieth centuries, Gaelic-speaking immigrants went to the prairie provinces, Ontario, and the Eastern Townships. Migration within North America was also very common at this time, and a considerable number of Canadian Gaels migrated to industrial cities in Canada and the northern United States for temporary or permanent employment.[68] After the Second World War, immigrant Scottish Gaels tended to settle in major cities.[69]

In some places, the language may not have survived longer than a generation or two, as appears to have been the case among Irish speakers in North America. However, the situation was vastly different in rural regions, where large groups of people from the same area emigrated and settled together. These new communities acted as magnets for later emigrants hoping to retain their familiar way of life. The density and relative isolation of these settlements was such that intermarriage was common among Scottish Gaels, enabling lengthy intergenerational transmission of the language. This happened in Prince Edward Island, Nova Scotia, and Glengarry County, just as it had earlier in Cape Fear. Glengarry County continued to receive Gaelic-speaking settlers into the early nineteenth century and did not lose its last native speaker until 2001.[70] Prince Edward Island, the eastern mainland of Nova Scotia, and Cape Breton constituted an even larger Gaelic cultural zone. In the mid-nineteenth century, they were the most prominent Gaelic-speaking region outside of Scotland. In 1901 they were likely home to more than fifty thousand speakers, although by then the language was beginning to decline everywhere except in Cape Breton. Cape Breton remained a Gaelic-speaking hub into the early twentieth century, and a small but engaged population of native speakers continues to reside there.[71] Sporadic language revitalization efforts were undertaken in Cape Breton and elsewhere in Nova Scotia throughout the twentieth century, and more sustained efforts are now under way with the support of the provincial Oifis Iomairtean na Gàidhlig (Office of Gaelic Affairs), established in 2006.[72]

Scottish Gaelic Literature and Print Media

Three decades after Donncha Rua Mac Conmara is thought to have been in Newfoundland, Kintail-born poet Iain mac Mhurchaidh (John MacRae) is said to have composed poetry in North Carolina. Iain, who likely emigrated in 1774 and died around 1780, is among the earliest Scottish Gaelic poets in North America about whom we know anything.[73] Others include Mìcheal Mór MacDhòmhnaill (Michael MacDonald) of South Uist, who arrived on Cape Breton via Prince Edward Island in 1775, and to whom a poem about his first winter there is attributed; Anna NicGillìosa (Anna Gillis) of Morar, who settled in Glengarry County in 1786, and to whom a poem in praise of her new locale is attributed; Calum Bàn MacMhannain, who described setting out to sea from Skye, the hardship he was fleeing, and his impressions of Prince Edward Island, to which he arrived in 1803; Ailean "a' Ridse" MacDhòmhnaill (Allan "the Ridge" MacDonald), who left the Braes of Lochaber for Nova Scotia in 1816 and there composed several poems; and the most prolific of the early emigrant poets, Iain MacIlleathain (John MacLean) of Tiree, known colloquially as the Bard MacLean, who relocated to Nova Scotia with his young family in 1819.[74] The Bard MacLean's most famous poem, "Òran do dh'Aimearaga" (A Song for America), reflects the difficulties he faced upon arrival, while his later poetry shows him to have adapted well, finding his place within a thriving Gaelic community.

While we are fortunate to know about these and other early emigrant poets, particularly in comparison with the dearth of knowledge about early Irish-language poets, the record for literary activity in North America before the second quarter of the nineteenth century is poor. Often only one or two of a poet's works survive, due in part to a lack of written sources. Although literacy in Scottish Gaelic was beginning to rise in the late eighteenth century as a result of the evangelical movement's emphasis on universal access to scripture, which coincided with the appearance of the earliest published collections of secular Gaelic verse in Scotland, much poetry continued to circulate orally rather than in print.[75] The Ossianic controversy over the authenticity of James Macpherson's Gaelic-inspired epics prompted the collection of such poetry in Scotland, often by clergymen, but no similar oral collecting appears to have taken place at that time in North America.[76] We are thus largely reliant on later transcriptions in manuscript and print sources, as well as relatively recent oral collecting at home and abroad, for our knowledge of eighteenth- and early nineteenth-century Scottish Gaelic literature in the United States and Canada.[77]

Of the poets named above, sizable repertoires exist only for Ailean "a' Ridse" and the Bard MacLean, due in both cases to exceptional circumstances. The Bard MacLean was literate in Gaelic, unlike most of his fellow emigrants. He had been the poet to the Laird of Coll prior to emigrating (an honorary rather than professional appointment at that point), and he brought two manuscripts with him to Nova Scotia, one of which he compiled himself. In this book, Robert Dunbar discusses the Bard MacLean's own and later efforts to preserve and transmit his compositions, and examines the relationship between written and orally collected versions. Ailean "a' Ridse," on the other hand, was well-known as a poet and *seanchaidhe* (tradition bearer), but he was not a compiler of manuscripts. We owe the written record of his compositions to his son, also a poet, who was encouraged to collect them by the Bard MacLean's grandson, Alasdair MacIlleathain Sinclair (Alexander Maclean Sinclair).[78]

The interest of later generations in the active preservation of their families' language and narrative traditions has helped ensure the survival of a great deal of material from Atlantic Canada over the past couple of centuries. Nearly two hundred Nova Scotian Gaelic poets have been identified, including Scottish- and Canadian-born individuals, who composed on themes including emigration and longing for home, criticism and praise of the landscape, and aspects of community life.[79] Significantly less material survives from regions in which intergenerational transmission of the language was less prolonged. However, in their oral tradition, Atlantic Gaels sometimes preserved compositions originating in other parts of North America that had been carried north and east by travellers. Beginning in the nineteenth century, books and periodicals also aided the transmission and preservation of Gaelic literature.[80]

The earliest North American publications in Scottish Gaelic were religious tracts for the use of Presbyterian congregations. The first of these, *Searmoin Chuaidh a Liobhairt ag an Raft-Swamp* (Sermons at Raft-Swamp) by Rev. Dùghall Crauford (Dugald Crawford), originally of Arran, was printed at Fayetteville, North Carolina, in 1791.[81] This was apparently followed a few decades later by an edition of *Dàin Spioradail* (Spiritual Verses) by Rev. Pàdraig Grannd (Peter Grant), printed by the same press in 1826.[82] The language was declining in the United States by the early nineteenth century, but no Gaelic press yet existed in the new heartland of Atlantic Canada. When Rev. Seumas MacGriogair (James MacGregor), the first Gaelic-speaking Presbyterian minister appointed to Nova Scotia, published a collection of his own religious poetry in 1819, the book was printed in Glasgow.[83] Publishing in Canada soon followed, however. The first Gaelic books printed by presses in Pictou, Nova Scotia, and Charlottetown, Prince Edward Island, in 1832 were of a religious nature, as were the first Gaelic books printed in Toronto and Montreal in 1835 and 1836. The first Catholic text was printed in Pictou in 1836.[84]

Secular Gaelic publications had begun appearing more regularly in Scotland by then. In fact, a year before he emigrated, the Bard MacLean published a collection of poetry, some of which was his own, in Edinburgh.[85] The first Gaelic book both written and published in North America was *Companach an Òganaich* (The Youth's Companion) by Alasdair MacGillebhrath (Alexander MacGillivray), printed in Pictou in 1836.[86] Prose also began to circulate in periodicals like *An Teachdaire Gaelach* (The Highland Messenger) and *Cuairtear nan Gleann* (Visitor of the Glens), published in Glasgow in the 1830s and '40s, which inspired similar ventures in Gaelic Canada. Material from *An Teachdaire Gaelach* was reprinted in the *Prince Edward Island Times* in 1836, and a short-lived bilingual periodical, *Tourist of the Woods / Cuairtear nan Coillte*, appeared in Kingston, Ontario, in 1840–41.[87] Other periodical publications followed, the most important of which were the *Casket*, an initially bilingual weekly newspaper launched in Antigonish, Nova Scotia, in 1852, and *Mac-Talla* (Echo), printed in Sydney, Cape Breton, from 1892 to 1904. These are referenced by several authors in this collection. *Mac-Talla* features prominently in Michael Linkletter's chapter, which investigates the sometimes contentious relationship between the periodical's editor and Alasdair "a' Ridse" (Alexander "the Ridge" MacDonald), son of Ailean "a' Ridse." *Mac-Talla* also figures in Tiber Falzett's chapter, which showcases the periodical's role in fostering a sense of community among Scottish Gaelic speakers across great distances, much like the Irish-language periodicals.[88] In an exploration of the networks maintained by migrant Canadian Gaels in the Boston area, Falzett presents Prince Edward Island-born Murchadh MacLaomuinn (Murdoch Lamont)'s letters to *Mac-Talla*, sent from Quincy, Massachusetts, seeking half-forgotten passages of Canadian Gaelic verse. Lamont received responses from as far away as Vancouver, and he went on to publish a collection of poetry in Quincy in 1917.

As large concentrations of Gaelic speakers amassed in cities in the late nineteenth and early twentieth centuries, cultural organizations formed in the United States and Canada.[89] In his chapter, Michael Newton explores the work of Alasdair Friseal (Alexander Fraser), an essayist in Toronto who worked to promote Scottish Gaelic language, literature, and history in cultural organizations and in his publications. The founders of the cultural organizations were undoubtedly influenced by the Irish revival movement taking place in many of the same cities, and like their Irish counterparts, a few organizations succeeded in offering language classes.[90] However, the most significant advances in Gaelic education took place in rural Nova Scotia: St Francis Xavier University in Antigonish began teaching Scottish Gaelic in 1891, and a Gaelic College was established in St Ann's, Cape Breton, in 1938 to offer summer courses.[91] Books also continued to be published in Scottish Gaelic in late nineteenth- and early twentieth-century Nova Scotia and Prince Edward Island, including several literary collections and genealogical studies by Alasdair MacIlleathain Sinclair.[92]

Scottish Gaelic Folklore

Members of the cultural organizations and subscribers of *Mac-Talla* were encouraged to collect songs and stories from the oral tradition, and some were published. Collecting by experienced folklorists began in 1937 with John Lorne Campbell and Margaret Fay Shaw's visit to Nova Scotia to investigate the song tradition.[93] Others followed, among the most notable of whom were Harvard Celtic professor Charles Dunn, who collected in Nova Scotia, Ontario, and Quebec in the 1940s–60s; Helen Creighton, who collected in Nova Scotia in the 1940s–60s; and St Francis Xavier University Celtic professor Calum MacLeod, who recorded and published Nova Scotian Gaelic stories and songs in the 1950s.[94] MacLeod's successor at St Francis Xavier University, Sr Margaret MacDonell, also gathered folklore in her native Cape Breton, and she secured a grant from the Canadian Multicultural Directorate that enabled systematic collecting to be undertaken.[95] In the resultant project, John Shaw recorded more than two thousand items of oral narrative in Cape Breton from 1977 to 1982, which are now archived at St Francis Xavier University.[96] A sizable collection was also made by the late Jim Watson in Cape Breton,[97] and Ken Nilsen collected among Scottish Gaelic speakers in mainland Nova Scotia and Boston.[98] Although much less work was done outside of Nova Scotia, we can note, in addition to Charles Dunn's material, Margaret Bennett's collections from Newfoundland's Codroy Valley and the Eastern Townships of Quebec and material collected by Gordon MacLennan in Saskatchewan, Ontario, and Prince Edward Island.[99]

Our final three chapters investigate Scottish Gaelic oral traditions. Kathleen Reddy examines religious apocrypha collected in Scotland and Cape Breton, using the Canadian material to help elucidate attitudes toward apocrypha among Catholic and Presbyterian tradition bearers. Lorrie MacKinnon also highlights the connection between Gaelic Scotland and North America, detailing a visit paid by renowned Barra tradition bearer Annie Johnston to Nova Scotia and Boston in 1954. Likely on the advice of John Lorne Campbell, Johnston collected folklore in Cape Breton; this collection is now housed in Campbell's archive on the Isle of Canna. Catrìona Parsons's chapter concerns another important but little-known folklore collection. In an appropriate conclusion to this memorial volume for Ken Nilsen, Parsons has selected and translated nine items that Nilsen collected between 1979 and 1995 from Danny Cameron, one of the last speakers of mainland Nova Scotian Gaelic, then living in the Boston area. Nilsen published a selection of Cameron's folklore in the *Casket*.

STUDYING NORTH AMERICAN GAELS

It is hoped that this book will generate forward momentum in the study of Irish and Scottish Gaels in North America. At present, the scholarly corpus is somewhat unbalanced, far more work having been done on Scottish Gaels' history, language, literature, and lore. This is understandable, given the much larger corpus of primary material available for study. While Irish and Scottish Gaels began arriving on the North American continent around the same time, periods of mass migration and the social circumstances of many of the immigrants differed, which affected not only their settlement patterns but also the retention of their language and narrative traditions. Scottish Gaels began migrating overseas in large numbers earlier than Irish Gaels did. Many of the Highlanders who arrived in the late eighteenth and early nineteenth centuries were reasonably well off. Facing a worsening economic situation at home, they migrated with their friends and relatives, secured land in rural areas, and reconstituted a Gaelic-speaking society abroad that was perpetuated by their descendants. When less fortunate Highland immigrants arrived later, there were established Gaelic-speaking settlements that they could join. Scottish Gaels thus set out with the expectation of retaining their culture in the new land. Most Irish Gaels had no such solace. By the mid-nineteenth century when mass Irish emigration began, large areas of contiguous tracts of land were no longer easy to come by, and poverty-stricken famine immigrants could hardly have acquired them in any case. They primarily went to cities, and although Irish appears to have been spoken in neighbourhoods of dense Irish settlement, the urban environment was less conducive to intergenerational transmission of the language. Had widespread literacy occurred for Irish in the early to mid-nineteenth century, as it did for Scottish Gaelic, copious stories, songs, and recollections might have been preserved despite the limited use of the language among descendants. That not being the case, we owe much of the modest store that survives to the late nineteenth-century Irish revival movement. The piecemeal folklore collecting that has been carried out since sheds additional light on the Irish North American experience.

Considerable work remains to be done to establish a more complete picture of the Irish language in the United States and Canada. Our contributors demonstrate the value of examining extant print and manuscript sources, and further investigation is needed to elucidate both the American corpus and the smaller Canadian one. Additional desiderata include an edited collection of North American Irish-language writings and a comprehensive scholarly treatment of the same. Irish oral narrative also remains under-researched, and there could be considerable benefit in studying developments in the Irish oral and literary traditions in comparison with their better evidenced Scottish Gaelic counterparts. With regard to the Scottish Gaelic corpus, while the literature and lore of the Canadian Maritimes have been studied for more than a century, the experiences and narrative traditions of Scottish Gaels in other regions of the United States and Canada warrant greater attention than they have thus far received.

The inadequacies in the scholarly record writ large are replicated, to some extent, in this book, which might be seen to reflect the scholarly landscape as it is, rather than as we wish it were. While we strove to be as inclusive as possible, soliciting chapters focusing on both literature and folklore and investigating primary sources across a broad geographic and temporal range, we could not address every aspect of the Gaelic North American experience in the limited space available. One area of deficiency, the interactions between Gaels and peoples of Indigenous and African ancestry in North America, has received attention elsewhere from Pádraig Ó Siadhail and Micheal Newton.[100] Additional omissions include contemporary language policy and activism, as well as non-linguistic forms of expression such as music, dance, and material culture. We anticipate that topics not addressed here will form subjects of investigation in future conferences and publications dedicated to the study of North American Gaels.

NOTES

1 Dembling, "Gaelic in Canada," 11; Miller, *Emigrants*, 580; Nilsen, "Irish in Nineteenth-Century New York," 59–60.
2 Several scholars have noted these omissions. See Kallen, "Irish," 31; Kennedy, *Gaelic Nova Scotia*, 28–9; McMonagle, "Finding," 140; Newton et al., "Past and Future Celt," 10; Newton, "Highland Canon Fodder," 149; Newton, *Seanchaidh*, 9–12; Nilsen, "An Ghaeilge," 262; Nilsen, "Irish in Nineteenth Century New York," 56–7; Nilsen, "Thinking of Monday," 6–7.
3 Collections of Irish-language literature and folklore from seventeenth- to twentieth-century North America are still lacking, although a literary anthology on the theme of emigration appeared in 2008: Ní Dhonnchadha and Nic Eoin, *Ar an gCoigríoch*; and Pádraig Ó Siadhail's 2005 book of short stories, *Idir Dha Thír*, explores the lives of Irish immigrants in Canada.
4 See, for instance, scholarship in this book or cited in this chapter by Margaret Bennett, Cyril Byrne, Jonathan Dembling, Danny Doyle, Robert Dunbar, Tiber Falzett, F.G. Foster, Bradford Gaunce, Michael Kennedy, Matthew Knight, Michael Linkletter, Margaret MacDonell, Lorrie MacKinnon, William Mahon, Michael Newton, Kenneth Nilsen, Tomás Ó hÍde, Pádraig Ó Siadhail, Catrìona Parsons, Effie Rankin, Kathleen Reddy, John T. Ridge, Ciara Ryan, John Shaw, Nancy Stenson, and James Watson.
5 Nic Congáil et al., *Litríocht na Gaeilge*.
6 Regarding Scottish Gaels, see, for example, Michael Newton's collection, *Seanchaidh na Coille*; John A. MacPherson and Michael Linkletter's collection, *Fògradh, Fàisneachd, Filidheachd*; and several histories by James Hunter including, most recently, *Set Adrift Upon the World*. The most substantial recent publication on the Irish side is Danny Doyle's monograph, *Míle Míle i gCéin*.
7 The editors organized the Harvard Symposium on North American Gaelic Literature with the generous support of the Weatherhead Center for International Affairs' Canada Program and the Department of Celtic Languages and Literatures at Harvard University. Versions of several essays in our collection were presented and discussed there, including those by Robert Dunbar, Tiber Falzett, Michael Linkletter, Michael Newton, Pádraig Ó Liatháin, Pádraig Ó Siadhail, and Ciara Ryan.
8 On the ideological barriers in other academic disciplines to the consideration of Celtic language–speaking peoples' history, literatures, and cultures as separate from, equally valid as, and relevant to the study of anglophone history, literature, and culture(s), see Newton et al., "Introduction: Past and Future Celt."

9 Dembling, "Gaelic in Canada," 204; Dembling, "Celtic Languages," 232.

10 For a detailed consideration of the relationship between Gaelic Scotland and Gaelic Ireland during this period, see McLeod, *Divided Gaels*.

11 Whether all regions of Scotland adhered to precisely the same literary and intellectual norms is unclear; ibid. 6.

12 See Breatnach, "The Chief's Poet," 51–60.

13 McLeod, *Divided Gaels*, 194–6, 219. The Classical Gaelic literary tradition survived longer in Scotland than in Ireland. The last poems composed in the shared literary language date to the early eighteenth century.

14 With regard to Scottish Gaelic poetry, see MacInnes, "Panegyric Code." The social context and artistic conventions for Irish-language poetry of the period, while not identical, were broadly similar.

15 See Dunbar, "Poetry," 25 on the place of poetry in Scottish Gaelic culture in Scotland and the diaspora.

16 Ken Nilsen collected Irish narrative about Fionn and his warriors from Pat Malone of Portland, Maine; see Nilsen, "Collecting," 70–3; and Nilsen, "Thinking of Monday," 12–13, 16. More than twenty such items were recorded in Scottish Gaelic in Cape Breton; see Shaw, "Observations," 81.

17 Nilsen, "Nova Scotia Gael," 91.

18 Caball, "Faith," 131–7; Ó Tuathaigh, "Gaelic Ireland," 24.

19 McLeod, *Divided Gaels*, 199.

20 Multiple factors contributed to Scottish Gaels' identification with Britishness, including religion among Protestants and imperial warfare among Highland regimental soldiers and their families. See, for example, Colley, *Britons*; Newton, "Jacobite Past."

21 For instance, Patrick Pearse proposed that "the dwellers on the two sides of Sruth na Maoile have in many things common traditions, and to a large extent common problems. Why not then … an *entente cordiale* between the Gael of Scotia Major and the Gael of Scotia Minor?": Pearse, "Reciprocity," 7. Pearse was responding to a similar recommendation put forth in *Guth na Bliadhna* (Glasgow); see O'Leary, *Prose Literature*, 387. Looking further back, the work of eighteenth- and nineteenth-century Irish and Scottish Gaelic scholars in copying, editing, and translating Gaelic literature from both regions might be noted. However, ideological differences are perceptible among these earlier scholarly elites. For instance, Rev. Norman MacLeod (Tormod MacLeòid, 'Caraid nan Gàidheal'), a strong supporter of Highland literature who also preached in Ireland and collaborated on an Irish edition of the psalms, had no hesitation in differentiating between the moral qualities of the Irish and Highland inhabitants of Glasgow: "the

conduct of the Highland population [is] far superior to that of the Irish" (Parliamentary Papers 1841, VI, quoted in Kidd, "Tormod MacLeòid," 120–1). At the popular level, moreover, it is worth noting that the term *Albanach* in Ulster Irish denotes not a Scottish person, but a Presbyterian. This is how a prominent early twentieth-century Donegal writer summed up the situation in his community, referring to his Irish-speaking Protestant neighbours: "Ach sa tír s'againne is ionann Albanach agus Protastúnach, is cuma cen tír arb as é. Agus is ionann Gael agus Caitliceach" [But in our country *Albanach* is synonymous with Protestant, no matter where the person is from. And *Gael* is synonymous with Catholic] (Ó Grianna, *Nuair a Bhí Mé Óg*, 143). When it came to feelings of kinship, religion far outweighed language.

22 Kallen, "Language," 102–3, 105; McMonagle, "Finding the Irish Language," 138; Miller, *Emigrants*, 143–4; Nilsen, "Celtic Languages," 376–7. Goodwife Glover, who was hanged for witchcraft in Boston in 1688, is the most famous representative of the latter category. A contemporary account of her trial indicates that she spoke Irish, but no evidence survives to confirm or contest the nineteenth-century speculation that she was an indentured servant. See Mather, *Memorable Providences*, 7; Hogan, "Myth."

23 Byrne, "Irish Language," 2–4; Foster, "Irish in Avalon," 3–4; Nilsen, "An Ghaeilge," 262–9. Evidence also exists for Irish translators in court cases in eighteenth-century Newfoundland; see Byrne, "Irish Language," 3.

24 Kallen, "Language," 105; Nilsen, "Irish Language in the U.S.," 471; Nilsen, "An Ghaeilge," 266, 270, 272.

25 Nilsen, "Irish Language in the U.S," 471; Nilsen, "An Ghaeilge," 269.

26 Nilsen, "Irish Language in the U.S." 471–2.

27 Nilsen, "Irish Language in New York," 253.

28 McMonagle, "Finding the Irish Language," 137.

29 Nilsen, "Celtic Languages," 377.

30 McMonagle, "Finding the Irish Language," 139; Nilsen, "An Ghaeilge," 269–76.

31 Nilsen, "Celtic Languages," 377; Nilsen, "An Ghaeilge," 275.

32 Nilsen, "Irish Language in New York," 257; Nilsen, "A' Ghàidhlig," 97; Ridge, "Hidden Gaeltacht," 15–17. The proselytizers were likely converts themselves.

33 Miller, *Emigrants*, 297, 580; Nilsen, "Irish in Nineteenth Century New York," 59–60; Nilsen, "Celtic Languages," 378. Danny Doyle documents references to the Irish language in Canada in the late nineteenth century in *Míle Míle*, 169–78.

34 Miller, *Emigrants*, 132, 295–6.
35 Nilsen, "Irish Language in New York," 254.
36 Doyle, "Remaking of Irish America," 224; McGowan, "Irish Language," 5; Nilsen, "Thinking of Monday," 7.
37 Nilsen, "Celtic Languages," 378.
38 Doyle, *Míle Míle*, 246; Foster, "Irish in Avalon," 10; Nilsen, "An Ghaeilge," 269, 272.
39 Nilsen, "'The language,'" 301. Irish continued to be used as a working language on Portland's docks until the 1960s: Nilsen, "Irish Language in the U.S.," 473.
40 Nilsen commented on the use of the language in Boston in the 1990s and early 2000s in "Celtic Languages," 378; and in "Irish Language in the U.S.," 473. Cumann na Gaeilge i mBoston (The Irish Language Society of Boston) continues to operate in the city, and Irish can still be heard at events that draw a considerable Irish-born crowd, such as the annual Féile na gCurrachaí (Currach Festival) in South Boston. See also Vaughan, "Landscapes," 60–1.
41 Given that Irish is thought to have been a dominant language in St John's, Newfoundland, until the early nineteenth century, it seems likely that intergenerational transmission occurred there; see Vaughan, "Landscapes," 62. In a paper titled "Irish Language Survival in Canada: Many Questions, Few Answers," presented on 29 June 2011 at the *Celts in the Americas* conference at St Francis Xavier University, Peter Toner used 1901 census data to show intergenerational transmission in the Canadian Maritimes; see also Doyle, *Míle Míle*, 183–7, 236; and Gaunce, "Challenging the Standard Interpretation." Lesa Ní Mhunghaile similarly demonstrated intergenerational transmission in the Ottawa Valley in a paper titled "The Prevalence of the Irish Language in Eastern Ontario during the Nineteenth Century: Evidence from the 1901 Canadian Census," presented on 24 February 2014 at University College, Dublin. See also Mac Aonghusa, "Reflections," 712; and McMonagle, "Finding," 145. In the United States, Nilsen uncovered a few cases of intergenerational transmission of Irish in New York City in the post-Famine period, and John T. Ridge has noted others; see Nilsen, "Irish Language in New York," 258; and Ridge, "Hidden Gaeltacht," 17. Proinsias Mac Aonghusa also states that the language was passed on to a second generation on Beaver Island in Lake Michigan, although he does not indicate a source: "An Ghaeilge," 19–20.
42 Nilsen, "'The language,'" 333–4; Ihde, *Irish Language*, x; Callahan, "Irish Language," 21–2.

43 Regarding the surviving manuscripts, see Nilsen, "An Ghaeilge," 266–9, 273, 274, 278–9; Ó Macháin, "Imirce agus Filleadh," 111–14, 133–4.

44 Ó Macháin, "Imirce agus Filleadh," 134–8; Mac Aonghusa, "An Ghaeilge," 16–17.

45 Nilsen, "Irish Gaelic Literature," 200.

46 Ní Ghabhann, "Gaelic Revival"; Nilsen, "Irish Language in the U.S.," 472–3.

47 Blenner-Hassett, "Brief History," 13; Mac Aonghusa, "An Ghaeilge," 21, 24–5. Irish was also taught at the University of Notre Dame in the early 1870s: Linkletter, "Early Establishment," 146.

48 See e.g. Ní Ghabhann, "The Gaelic Revival," para. 16; Uí Chollatáin, "Athbheochan Thrasatlantach," 283–93.

49 Nilsen, "An Ghaeilge," 278. Later, in the 1950s and '60s, Dublin-born Pádraig Ó Broin published two journals in Toronto, *Irisleabhar Ceilteach* and *Teangadóir*, which included material in English, Irish, Scottish Gaelic, and Manx; see Ó Siadhail, "*Irisleabhar Ceilteach*."

50 Nilsen, "Irish Gaelic Literature," 202–3.

51 Foster, "Irish in Avalon," 9; Furlong, "1875–1880," 69.

52 Nilsen, "An Ghaeilge," 279.

53 Nilsen, "Irish Gaelic Literature," 202, 205–7, 213–14.

54 Ibid., 213–14.

55 Ibid., 216. Mac Gabhann's book appeared in translation in 1962 as *The Hard Road to Klondike*. Desmond Bell's documentary film of the same title was released in 1999.

56 See also Nilsen, "Irish Gaelic Literature," 214.

57 Nilsen, "Thinking of Monday"; Nilsen, "The Language"; Nilsen, "Collecting," 69–73.

58 The Boston and the Irish Language project is sponsored by Cumann na Gaeilge i mBoston and housed at the University of Massachusetts, Boston's Healey Library. Videos, transcriptions, and translations are available online: http://blogs.umb.edu/archives/ohc/boston-and-the-irish-language.

59 Hartley, *Ironworks*, 198–202. Gaels also arrived in America as prisoners following the failed eighteenth-century Jacobite uprisings; see Newton, *We're Indians*, 67, 71; Nilsen, "Celtic Languages," 379.

60 Kelly, *Carolina Scots*, 81; Kennedy, *Gaelic Nova Scotia*, 20.

61 Newton, "In Their Own Words," 7–14; Nilsen, "Celtic Languages," 379.

62 Bumsted, *People's Clearance*, 67; Newton, "Becoming Cold-Hearted," 65.

63 Bumsted, *People's Clearance*, 56–7; MacKay, *Scotland Farewell*, 62, 89–103. Lucille Campey tells the stories of the Scottish immigrants in Prince

Edward Island and Nova Scotia in *"A Very Fine Class of Immigrants"* and *After the Hector*.

64 Bumsted, *People's Clearance*, 62–3, 67; Campey, *Scottish Pioneers*, 17–21; Hunter, *Dance*, 75, 80–1; MacDonell, *Emigrant Experience*, 7–8, 15; McLean, *People of Glengarry*, 84–7.

65 Campey, *Scottish Pioneers*, 21–33, 70–1; Nilsen, "A' Ghàidhlig," 92–3.

66 Nilsen, "A' Ghàidhlig," 93–4. Regarding the Quebec settlers, see Bennett, *Oatmeal*, 2–8, Campey, *Les Écossais*, 77–110 and Little, "From the Isle." For Highland settlers in Southwestern Ontario, see Campey, *Scottish Pioneers*, 98–108, 113–25, 130–7, 144–50. James Hunter tells the story of the Red River settlement in *Set Adrift Upon the World*; see also Campey, *Silver Chief*, 77–142.

67 Bennett, *Last Stronghold*, 34–5.

68 Bennett, *Oatmeal*, 24, 286; Campey, *Silver Chief*, 154–5; Nilsen, "A' Ghàidhlig," 100–1.

69 Nilsen, "A' Ghàidhlig," 101.

70 Campey, *Scottish Pioneers*, 69; Dunbar, "Poetry," 22; McLean, *People of Glengarry*, 152, 213–16; Rod McDonald, "'Talk to me in the Gaelic before I go': Alec McDonald, who died last month at age 96, was a rare breed in Ontario," *Toronto Star*, 1 December 2001, M13.

71 Dembling, "Gaelic in Canada," 207; Kennedy, *Gaelic Nova Scotia*, 58–61, 71–5, 114–15; Nilsen, "Celtic Languages," 380.

72 Dembling, "Gaelic Revival," 19–31; Graham, "Marginalization," 661–3, 665–9; McEwan-Fujita, "Gaelic Revitalization Efforts," 169, 170–82.

73 MacDonell, *Emigrant Experience*, 26–9; Dunbar, "Poetry," 26, 30; cf. Newton, "In Their Own Words," 14–24. Newton questions the authorship of all four extant poems said to have been composed by Iain mac Mhurchaidh in North Carolina. That he was a poet is not in doubt, however; poems that he composed in Scotland are extant, and it seems likely that he would have continued his art in America, regardless of whether he authored the poems in question. Newton suggests in "Unsettling" that one of the poems may have been composed by a woman in the Carolinas in the same period (151). Regarding additional surviving Gaelic verse from the United States, see Newton, "Scottish Gaelic Poetry"; and Newton, *We're Indians*.

74 Dunbar, "Poetry," 26–7, 35, 46, 66; MacDonell, *Emigrant Experience*, 57–9, 68–71, 105–13, 131–3; Newton, *Seanchaidh*, 517, 519–20, 522–3. Effie Rankin has edited the poetry of Ailean "a' Ridse" in *As a' Bhràighe / Beyond the Braes*.

75 The two earliest Scottish Gaelic poets to publish collections of their poetry

were Alasdair mac Mhaighstir Alasdair in 1751 and Donnchadh Bàn Mac an t-Saoir in 1768.

76 Meek, "Pulpit," 110–11; Newton, "In Their Own Words," 3–4. Newton suggests various potential reasons for the lack of oral collecting in North Carolina. Conditions in the Canadian Maritimes would hardly have been conducive to oral collecting during the early period of settlement.

77 Dunbar, "Poetry," 26; Newton, "In Their Own Words," 4.

78 Dunbar, "Poetry," 26; Rankin, *As a' Bhràighe*, 10–11.

79 Dunbar, "Poetry"; Kennedy, *Gaelic Nova Scotia*, 127; Shaw, "Brief Beginnings."

80 MacDonell, *Emigrant Experience*, 16–17; Newton, *Seanchaidh*, 25–6.

81 Meek, "Pulpit," 97–8; Newton, "In Their Own Words," 4–5.

82 Dunn, *Highland Settler*, 75. If this book was printed, it appears that no copies survived; see Newton, "In Their Own Words," 6.

83 Nilsen, "Some Notes," 127. MacGregor arrived in Nova Scotia in 1786.

84 Ibid., 127, 129–30, 131; Dunn, *Highland Settler*, 171n5. In 1832, Domhnull Mathanach (Donald Matheson)'s *Laoidhean Spioradail* (Spiritual Hymns) was reprinted in Pictou and a translation of William Dyer's *Christ's Famous Titles* was reprinted in Charlottetown. In 1835 a Toronto press reprinted the Gaelic translation of the Church of Scotland's Shorter Catechism. In 1836 in Montreal, Pàdraig Grannd's *Dàin Spioradail* and Dùghall Bochanan (Dugald Buchanan)'s *Laoidhean Spioradail* were reprinted, and in Pictou, Raonull MacRaing (Ranald Rankin)'s *Iùl a' Chrìostaidh* (The Christian's Guide) was reprinted.

85 The Bard MacLean's *Orain Nuadh Ghaedhlach* (New Gaelic Songs) was published in Edinburgh in 1818. His second book, a collection of his own religious verse, was published in Glasgow in 1835. See Nilsen, "Some Notes," 127–8, and Robert Dunbar's article in this book.

86 Dunn, *Highland Settler*, 75–7.

87 Nilsen, "Some Notes," 130–1; Newton, *Seanchaidh*, 83.

88 See also Newton, "Becoming Cold-Hearted," 72.

89 Newton, "Gaelic Literature," 354; Newton, *We're Indians*, 266.

90 Linkletter, "The Early Establishment," 148; Newton, "Becoming Cold-Hearted," 93, 101, 106.

91 Nilsen, "A' Ghàidhlig," 99. Scottish Gaelic was also taught at Dalhousie University in Halifax from 1907: Linkletter, "The Early Establishment," 149.

92 Nilsen, "Sinclair, Alexander MacLean," 950–1.

93 See Campbell, *Songs*.

94 See Creighton and MacLeod, *Gaelic Songs*; MacLeoid, *Bàrdachd*; and

MacLeoid, *Sgialachdan*, translated as MacLeod, *Stories*. Dunn's recordings can be streamed online; visit the website for the Harvard Celtic Folklore Collection, https://celtic.fas.harvard.edu/harvard-celtic-folklore-collection. These are discussed in Innes and Hillers, "Mixed-Media Folklore Trove."

95 Nilsen, "A' Ghàidhig," 102. See MacDonell and Shaw, *Luirgean Eachainn Nìll*.

96 See the online database Gaelstream / *Sruth nan Gàidheal*, www.gaelstream.stfx.ca. John Shaw has also edited collections of Cape Breton folklore including *Blue Mountains*, *Brìgh an Òrain*, and *Tales until Dawn*.

97 See Watson and Robertson, *Sealladh gu Taobh*; and several articles in *Am Bràighe*, a Cape Breton-based cultural journal, and *An Rubha*, the magazine of the Nova Scotia Highland Village Museum.

98 Nilsen, "Recording."

99 Bennett, *Oatmeal*; Bennett, *Last Stronghold*. Gordon MacLennan also collected in Nova Scotia. His material is held at the Canadian National Museum of History.

100 This topic is referenced in connection with an Irish-language novel in Ó Siadhail's chapter. For more comprehensive treatments, see chapters by Ó Siadhail and Newton, among others, in Morton and Wilson, *Irish and Scottish Encounters*. See also Newton, *We're Indians*; and Newton, "Did You Hear." In present-day Nova Scotia, collaboration between Gaelic and Mi'kmaq language and cultural advocates was recently prompted by the 2015 Truth and Reconciliation Commission of Canada, resulting in the *Aonach / Mawiomi*: Sharing Our Paths symposium in October 2016, as well as a series of MAGIC (Mi'kmaq, Acadians, and Gaels of Inverness County) gatherings in 2017 and 2018; see "Mi'kmaq and Gaels to Reconnect Shared Histories and Experiences," News and Events, Cape Breton University, 7 October 2016, https://www.cbu.ca/news-events/story/mikmaq-and-gaels-to-reconnect-shared-histories-and-experiences; Anne Farries, "MAGIC Event Celebrates History, Friendship and Reconciliation," *Inverness Oran*, 29 August 2017; Anne Farries, "MAGIC Là Buidhe Bealtain," *Inverness Oran*, 8 May 2018.

BIBLIOGRAPHY

Bennett, Margaret. *The Last Stronghold: The Scottish Gaelic Traditions of Newfoundland*. Edinburgh: Canongate, 1989.

– *Oatmeal and the Catechism: Scottish Gaelic Settlers in Quebec*. Edinburgh: John Donald; Montreal and Kingston: McGill-Queen's University Press, 1998.

Blenner-Hassett, Roland. "A Brief History of Celtic Studies in North America." *Publications of the Modern Language Association of America* 69, no. 4, pt. 2 (1954): 3–21.

Breatnach, Pádraig A. "The Chief's Poet." *Proceedings of the Royal Irish Academy* 83, Section C: Archaeology, Celtic Studies, History (1983): 37-79.

Bumsted, J.M. *The People's Clearance: Highland Emigration to British North America, 1770–1815*. Edinburgh: Edinburgh University Press, 1982.

Byrne, Cyril. "Irish Language in Newfoundland." In *Proceedings of the First North American Congress of Celtic Studies*, ed. Gordon MacLennan, 1–8. Ottawa: Chair of Celtic Studies, University of Ottawa, 1988.

Caball, Marc. "Faith, Culture, and Sovereignty: Irish Nationality and Its Development, 1558–1625." In *British Consciousness and Identity: The Making of Britain, 1533–1707*, ed. Brendan Bradshaw and Peter Roberts, 112–39. Cambridge: Cambridge University Press, 1998.

Callahan, Joseph. "The Irish Language in Pennsylvania." In *The Irish Language in the United States: A Historical, Sociolinguistic, and Applied Linguistic Survey*, ed. Thomas W. Ihde, 18–26. Westport and London: Bergin and Garvey, 1994.

Campbell, John Lorne. *Songs Remembered in Exile: Traditional Gaelic Songs from Nova Scotia Recorded in Cape Breton and Antigonish County in 1937*. Aberdeen: Aberdeen University Press, 1990.

Campey, Lucille H. *After the Hector: The Scottish Pioneers of Nova Scotia and Cape Breton 1773–1852*, 2nd ed. Toronto: National Heritage Books, 2007.

– *Les Écossais: The Pioneer Scots of Lower Canada, 1763–1855*. Toronto: National Heritage Books, 2006.

– *The Scottish Pioneers of Upper Canada, 1784–1855: Glengarry and Beyond*. Toronto: National Heritage Books, 2005.

– *The Silver Chief: Lord Selkirk and the Scottish Pioneers of Belfast, Baldoon, and Red River*. Toronto: National Heritage Books, 2003.

– *"A Very Fine Class of Immigrants": Prince Edward Island's Scottish Pioneers 1770–1850*, 2nd ed. Toronto: National Heritage Books, 2007.

Colley, Linda. *Britons: Forging the Nation, 1707–1837*, 2nd ed. New Haven: Yale University Press, 2005.

Creighton, Helen, and Calum MacLeod. *Gaelic Songs in Nova Scotia*. Ottawa: Department of the Secretary of State, 1964.

Dembling, Jonathan. "Celtic Languages in the 1910 US Census." *Proceedings of the Harvard Celtic Colloquium* 20–1 (2007): 232–47.

– "Gaelic in Canada: New Evidence from an Old Census." In *Cànan agus*

Cultar / Language and Culture: Rannsachadh na Gàidhlig 3, ed. Wilson McLeod, James E. Fraser, and Anja Gunderloch, 203–14. Edinburgh: Dunedin Academic Press, 2006.

– "The Gaelic Revival in Nova Scotia." *Proceedings of the Harvard Celtic Colloquium* 18–19 (2006): 11–33.

Doyle, Danny. *Míle Míle, i gCéin: The Irish Language in Canada*. Ottawa: Borealis Press, 2015.

Doyle, David Noel. "The Remaking of Irish America." In *Making the Irish American: History and Heritage of the Irish in the United States*, ed. J.J. Lee and Marion R. Casey, 213–54. New York: NYU Press, 2006.

Dunbar, Robert. "The Poetry of the Emigrant Generation." *Transactions of the Gaelic Society of Inverness* 64 (2004–6): 22–125.

Dunn, Charles. *Highland Settler: A Portrait of the Scottish Gael in Cape Breton and Eastern Nova Scotia*. Toronto: University of Toronto Press, 1953.

Foster, F.G. "Irish in Avalon: An Investigation of the Gaelic Language in Eastern Newfoundland." In *Languages in Newfoundland and Labrador*, 2nd ed., ed. H.J. Paddock, 2–13. St John's: Department of Linguistics, Memorial University, 1982.

Furlong, Martin W. "1875–1880." *The Adelphian* 4, no. 1 (1907): 68–71.

Gaunce, Bradford. "Challenging the Standard Interpretation of Irish Language Survival in the Diaspora: The New Brunswick Case Study." MA thesis, University of New Brunswick, 2014.

Graham, Glenn. "Marginalization, Resilience, Integration: Reconstructing and Globalizing Canada's Celtic Fringe Island Region of Cape Breton." *Journal of Canadian Studies / Revue d'Études Canadiennes* 52, no. 3 (2018): 650–90.

Hartley, E.N. *Ironworks on the Saugus: The Lynn and Braintree Ventures of the Company of Undertakers of the Ironworks in New England*. Norman: University of Oklahoma Press, 1957.

Hogan, Liam. "The myth that Goodwife Glover, the Irish woman executed for witchcraft in Boston in 1688, was an 'Irish slave.'" *Medium*. 1 September 2017, https://medium.com/@Limerick1914/the-murder-of-goodwife-glover-in-boston-and-the-politicisation-of-her-death-two-centuries-later-via-90ab171fe576.

Hunter, James. *A Dance Called America: The Scottish Highlands, the United States, and Canada*. Edinburgh: Mainstream, 1994.

– *Set Adrift upon the World: The Sutherland Clearances*. Edinburgh: Birlinn, 2015.

Ihde, Thomas W., ed. *The Irish Language in the United States: A Historical,*

Sociolinguistic, and Applied Linguistic Survey. Westport and London: Bergin and Garvey, 1994.

Innes, Sìm, and Barbara Hillers. "A Mixed-Media Folklore Trove: Celtic Folklore Collections in Harvard Libraries." *Proceedings of the Harvard Celtic Colloquium* 31 (2012): 173–208.

Kallen, Jeffrey L. "Irish as an American Ethnic Language." In *The Irish Language in the United States: A Historical, Sociolinguistic, and Applied Linguistic Survey*, ed. Thomas W. Ihde, 27–40. Westport and London: Bergin and Garvey, 1994.

– "Language and Ethnic Identity: The Irish Language in the United States." In *Language across Cultures*, ed. Liam Mac Mathúna and David Singleton, 101–12. Dublin: Irish Association for Applied Linguistics, 1984.

Kelly, Douglas. *Carolina Scots: An Historical and Genealogical Study of Over 100 Years of Emigration*. Dillon: 1739 Publications, 1998.

Kennedy, Michael. *Gaelic Nova Scotia: An Economic, Cultural, and Social Impact Study*. Halifax: Nova Scotia Museum, 2002.

Kidd, Sheila. "Tormod MacLeòid: Àrd-chonsal nan Gàidheal." In *Glasgow: Baile Mòr nan Gàidheal*, ed. Sheila Kidd, 107–29. Glasgow: Department of Celtic, Glasgow University, 2007.

Linkletter, Michael. "The Early Establishment of Celtic Studies in North American Universities." *Proceedings of the Harvard Celtic Colloquium* 29 (2011): 138–53.

Little, J.I. "From the Isle of Arran to Inverness Township: A Case Study of Highland Emigration and North American Settlement, 1829–1834." *Scottish Economic and Social History* 20, no. 1 (2000): 3–30.

Mac Aonghusa, Proinsias. "An Ghaeilge i Meiriceá." In *Go Meiriceá Siar. Na Gaeil agus Meiriceá: Cnuasach Aistí*, ed. Stiofán Ó hAnnracháin 13–30. Baile Átha Cliath: An Clóchomhar, 1979.

– "Reflections on the Fortunes of the Irish Language in Canada, with some Reference to the Fate of the Language in the United States." In *The Untold Story: The Irish in Canada*, ed. Robert O'Driscoll and Lorna Reynolds, 711–18. Toronto: Celtic Arts of Canada, 1988.

MacDonell, Margaret. *The Emigrant Experience: Songs of Highland Emigrants in North America*. Toronto: University of Toronto Press, 1982.

MacDonell, Margaret, and John Shaw, eds. and trans. *Luirgean Eachainn Nìll: A Collection of Folktales told by Hector Campbell*. Stornoway: Acair, 1981.

MacInnes, John. "The Panegyric Code in Gaelic Poetry and Its Historical Background." *Transactions of the Gaelic Society of Inverness* 50 (1976–78): 435–98.

MacKay, Donald. *Scotland Farewell: The People of the Hector*. Toronto: McGraw-Hill Ryerson, 1980.

MacLeod, C.I.N., trans. *Stories from Nova Scotia*. Antigonish: Formac, 1974.

MacLeoid, Calum Iain M. [C.I.N. MacLeod], ed. *Bàrdachd a Albainn Nuaidh*. Glaschu: Gairm, 1970.

– ed. *Sgialachdan a Albainn Nuaidh*. Glaschu: Gairm, 1969.

MacPherson, John A., and Michael Linkletter, eds. and trans. *Fògradh, Fàisneachd, Filidheachd: An t-Urr. Donnchadh Blàrach (1815–1893) ann am Mac-Talla / Parting, Prophecy, Poetry: Rev. Duncan Blair (1815–1893) in Mac-Talla*. Sydney: Cape Breton University Press, 2013.

Mather, Cotton. *Memorable Providences Relating to Witchcrafts and Possessions*. Boston: R.P., 1689.

McEwan-Fujita, Emily. "Gaelic Revitalization Efforts in Nova Scotia: Reversing Language Shift in the 21st Century." In *Celts in the Americas*, ed. M. Newton, 160–86. Sydney: Cape Breton University Press, 2013.

McGowan, Lynn. "The Irish Language in America." In *The Irish Language in the United States: A Historical, Sociolinguistic, and Applied Linguistic Survey*, ed. Thomas W. Ihde, 3–7. Westport and London: Bergin and Garvey, 1994.

McMonagle, Sarah. "Finding the Irish Language in Canada." *New Hibernia Review* 16, no. 1 (2012): 134–49.

McLean, Marianne. *The People of Glengarry: Highlanders in Transition, 1745–1820*. Montreal and Kingston: McGill-Queen's University Press, 1991.

McLeod, Wilson. *Divided Gaels: Gaelic Cultural Identities in Scotland and Ireland, c. 1200–c. 1650*. Oxford: Oxford University Press, 2004.

Meek, Donald. "The Pulpit and the Pen: Clergy, Orality, and Print in the Scottish Gaelic World." In *The Spoken Word: Oral Culture in Britain 1500-1850*, ed. Adam Fox and Daniel Woolf, 84–118. Manchester: Manchester University Press, 2002.

Miller, Kerby A. *Emigrants and Exiles: Ireland and the Irish Exodus to North America*. New York and Oxford: Oxford University Press, 1985.

Morton, Graeme, and David A. Wilson, eds. *Irish and Scottish Encounters with Indigenous Peoples*. Montreal and Kingston: McGill-Queen's University Press, 2013.

Newton, Micheal. "'Becoming Cold-Hearted like the Gentiles around Them': Scottish Gaelic in the United States 1872–1912." *e-Keltoi: Journal of Interdisciplinary Celtic Studies* 2 (2003): 63–131.

– "'Did You Hear about the Gaelic-Speaking African?': Scottish Gaelic Folklore about Identity in North America." *Comparative American Studies* 8, no. 2 (2010): 88–106.

– "Gaelic Literature and the Diaspora." In *The Edinburgh History of Scottish Literature*, vol. 2, ed. Susan Manning, Ian Brown, Thomas Owen Clancy, and Murray Pittock, 353–9. Edinburgh: Edinburgh University Press, 2007.

– "Highland Canon Fodder: Scottish Gaelic Literature in North American Contexts." *e-Keltoi: Journal of Interdisciplinary Celtic Studies* 1 (2016): 147–75.

– "In Their Own Words: Gaelic Literature in North Carolina." *Scotia: Interdisciplinary Journal of Scottish Studies* 25 (2001): 1–28.

– "Jacobite Past, Loyalist Present." *e-Keltoi: Journal of Interdisciplinary Celtic Studies* 5 (2003): 31–62.

– "Scottish Gaelic Poetry in the USA." In *Celtic Culture: A Historical Encyclopedia*, vol. 1, ed. John T. Koch, 381–2. Santa Barbara: ABC-CLIO.

– "Unsettling Iain mac Mhurchaidh's Slumber: The Carolina Lullaby, Authorship, and the Influence of Print Media on Gaelic Oral Tradition. *Aiste* 4 (2014): 131–54.

– *We're Indians Sure Enough: The Legacy of the Scottish Highlanders in the United States*. Auburn: Saorsa Media, 2001.

Newton, Micheal, ed. *Seanchaidh na Coille / Memory-Keeper of the Forest: Anthology of Scottish Gaelic Literature of Canada*. Sydney: Cape Breton University Press, 2015.

Newton, Micheal, Robert Dunbar, Gearóid Ó hAllmhuráin, and Daniel Williams. "Introduction: The Past and Future Celt." In *Celts in the Americas*, ed. M. Newton, 5–17. Sydney: Cape Breton University Press, 2013.

Nic Congáil, Ríona, Máirín Nic Eoin, Meidhbhín Ní Úrdail, Pádraig Ó Liatháin, and Regina Uí Chollatáin, eds. *Litríocht na Gaeilge ar fud an Domhain*, 2 vols. Baile Átha Cliath: *Leabhair*Comhar, 2015.

Ní Dhonnchadha, Aisling, and Máirín Nic Eoin, eds. *Ar an gCoigríoch: Díolaim Litríochta ar Scéal na hImirce*. Indreabhán: Cló Iar-Chonnachta, 2008.

Ní Ghabhann, Gillian. "The Gaelic Revival in the U.S. in the Nineteenth Century." *Chronicon* 2 (1998) 6: 1–34, https://www.ucc.ie/research/chronicon/nigh2fra.htm.

Nilsen, Kenneth E. "A' Ghàidhlig an Canada: Scottish Gaelic in Canada." In *The Edinburgh Companion to the Gaelic Language*, ed. Moray Watson and Michelle Macleod, 90–107. Edinburgh: Edinburgh University Press.

– "An Ghaeilge in Oirthear Cheanada." In *Séimhfhear Suairc: Aistí in Ómós don Ollamh Breandán Ó Conchúir*, ed. Seán Ó Coileáin, Liam P. Ó Murchú, and Pádraigín Riggs, 262–79. An Daingean: An Sagart, 2013.
– "Celtic Languages in North America," s.vv. (1) Irish and (2) Scottish Gaelic. In *Celtic Culture: A Historical Encyclopedia*, vol. 1, ed. John T. Koch, 376–81. Santa Barbara: ABC-CLIO, 2006.
– "Collecting Celtic Folklore in the United States." In *Proceedings of the First North American Congress of Celtic Studies*, ed. Gordon W. MacLennan, 55–74. Ottawa: The Chair of Celtic Studies, Ottawa University, 1988.
– "Irish Gaelic Literature in the United States." In *American Babel: Literatures of the United States from Abnaki to Zuni*, ed. Marc Shell, 188–218. Cambridge, MA: Harvard University Press, 2002.
– "Irish in Nineteenth-Century New York." In *The Multilingual Apple: Languages in New York City*, ed. Ofelia García and Joshua A. Fishman, 53–69. Berlin: Mouton de Gruyter, 1997.
– "The Irish Language in New York, 1850-1900." In *The New York Irish*, 252–74, ed. Ronald H. Bayor and Timothy J. Meagher, 252–74. Baltimore: Johns Hopkins University Press, 1996.
– "Irish Language in the U.S." In *The Encyclopedia of the Irish in America*, ed. Michael Glazier, 470–4. Notre Dame: University of Notre Dame Press, 1999.
– "'The language that the strangers do not know': The Galway Gaeltacht of Portland, Maine, in the Twentieth Century." In *They Change Their Sky: The Irish in Maine*, ed. Michael C. Connolly, 297–339. Orono: University of Maine Press, 2004.
– "The Nova Scotia Gael in Boston." *Proceedings of the Harvard Celtic Colloquium* 6 (1986): 83–100.
– "Recording Scottish Gaelic Folklore and Oral History in the United States." *Scotia: Interdisciplinary Journal of Scottish Studies* 27 (2003): 22–33.
– "Sinclair, Alexander MacLean." In *Dictionary of Canadian Biography*, vol. 15, ed. Ramsay Cook and Réal Bélanger, 949–51. Toronto: University of Toronto Press, 2005.
– "Some Notes on Pre-*Mac-Talla* Gaelic Publishing in Nova Scotia (With References to Early Gaelic Publishing in Prince Edward Island, Quebec, and Ontario)." In *Rannsachadh na Gàidhlig 2000: Papers Read at the Conference "Scottish Gaelic Studies 2000," Held at the University of Aberdeen, 2-4 August 2000*, ed. Colm Ó Baoill and Nancy R. McGuire, 127–40. Aberdeen: An Clò Gaidhealach, 2002.
– "Thinking of Monday: The Irish Speakers of Portland, Maine." *Éire-Ireland* 25, no. 1 (1990): 6–19.

Ó Grianna, Séamus. *Nuair a Bhí Mé Óg*. Corcaigh: Cló Mercier, 1979 [1942].

O'Leary, Philip. *Prose Literature of the Gaelic Revival, 1881–1921: Ideology and Innovation*. University Park: Pennsylvania State University Press, 1994.

Ó Macháin, Pádraig. "Imirce agus Filleadh Lámhscribhinní na nGael." In *Litríocht na Gaeilge ar fud an Domhain*, vol. 1, ed. Ríona Nic Congáil, Máirín Nic Eoin, Meidhbhín Ní Úrdail, Pádraig Ó Liatháin, and Regina Uí Chollatáin, 109–54. Baile Átha Cliath: *Leabhair* Comhar, 2015.

Ó Siadhail, Pádraig. *Idir Dha Thír: Sceitsí O Cheanada*. Belfast: Lagan Press, 2005.

– "*Irisleabhar Ceilteach* 1952–1954 agus *Teangadóir* 1953–1960: Innéacs." Comhar*Taighde* 3 (2017): 2–27.

Ó Tuathaigh, Gearóid. "Gaelic Ireland, Popular Politics and Daniel O'Connell." *Journal of the Galway Archaeological and Historical Society* 34 (1974): 21–34.

Pearse, Patrick. "Reciprocity." *An Claidheamh Soluis* 7, no. 37 (1905): 7.

Rankin, Effie, ed. *As a' Bhràighe / Beyond the Braes*, 2nd ed. Sydney: Cape Breton University Press, 2005.

Ridge, John T. "The Hidden Gaeltacht in Old New York: Nineteenth Century Preaching in the Irish Language." *New York Irish History* 6 (1991–92): 13–17.

Shaw, John. "Brief Beginnings: Nova Scotian and Old World Bards Compared." *Scottish Gaelic Studies* 17, ed. Donald MacAulay, James Gleasure and Colm Ó Baoill. *Festschrift for Professor D. S. Thomson* (1996): 342–55.

– "Observations on the Cape Breton Gàidhealtachd and Its Relevance to Present-Day Celtic Studies." In *Proceedings of the First North American Congress of Celtic Studies*, ed. Gordon W. MacLennan, 75–87. Ottawa: Chair of Celtic, University of Ottawa, 1988.

Shaw, John, ed. and trans. *The Blue Mountains and Other Gaelic Stories from Cape Breton / Na Beanntaichean Gorma agus Sgeulachdan Eile à Ceap Breatainn*. Montreal and Kingston: McGill-Queen's University Press, 2007.

– *Brìgh an Òrain / A Story in Every Song: The Songs and Tales of Lauchie MacLellan*. Montreal and Kingston: McGill-Queen's University Press, 2000.

– *Tales Until Dawn / Sgeul gu Latha: The World of a Cape Breton Gaelic Story-Teller*. By Joe Neil MacNeil. Kington and Montreal: McGill-Queen's University Press, 1987.

Uí Chollatáin, Regina. "Athbheochan Thrasatlantach na Gaeilge: Scríbhneoirí, Intleachtóirí, agus an Fhéiniúlacht Éireannach." In *Litríocht na Gaeilge ar fud an Domhain*, vol. 1, ed. Ríona Nic Congáil, Máirín Nic Eoin, Meidhbhín Ní Úrdail, Pádraig Ó Liatháin, and Regina Uí Chollatáin, 277–309. Baile Átha Cliath: *Leabhair*Comhar, 2015.

Vaughan, Jill. "Landscapes of the Irish Language: Discursive Constructions of Authenticity in the Irish Diaspora." *Irish Journal of Applied Social Studies* 16, no. 1 (2016): 56–76.

Watson, James, and Ellison Robertson, eds. *Sealladh gu Taobh: Oral Tradition and Reminiscence by Cape Breton Gaels*. Sydney: University College of Cape Breton Art Gallery, 1987.

1

Kenneth E. Nilsen (1947–2012): *Gaisgeach nan Gàidheal* (Champion of the Gaels)

Natasha Sumner

Ken Nilsen was a highly respected scholar whose deep commitment to the teaching and preservation of Celtic languages and cultural traditions left a lasting legacy. From his early forays into language learning as a youth in Brooklyn, New York, Ken set out to seek the Celtic tongues in their native and diaspora milieux, earning a PhD in Celtic Languages and Literatures from Harvard along the way, and becoming the first holder of the Sister Saint Veronica Chair in Gaelic Studies at St Francis Xavier University (StFX) in Antigonish, Nova Scotia. A quintessential public scholar, his dedication to the Irish and Scottish Gaelic-speaking communities in New England and the Canadian Maritimes was evident not only in his involvement in regional language and cultural organizations, but also in the incredible effort he made to document local speakers' oral traditions, and in the lasting connections he forged with tradition bearers and other members of the language-speaking communities. He was widely beloved for his kindness, his humility, his conviviality, and his genuine interest in people's traditional culture, which he practised alongside them. Although Ken's untimely passing in April 2012 weighs heavily upon his many friends and colleagues, both within and beyond academia, his legacy lives on. In the spirit of his work as a folklore collector, this chapter traces his academic journey through the recollections of those whose lives he touched along the way.

POLYGLOT

Ken's remarkable talent for learning languages was apparent to anyone who interacted with him in Irish, Scottish Gaelic, Welsh, or Breton – all of which he spoke fluently; however, it sometimes came as a surprise that the earliest "second" language he acquired was not a Celtic one. I owe the story of Ken's initial study of language acquisition to his wife Moireach, who relates that when Ken was very young – four or five years old – a relative from Norway came to stay with his family in Bay Ridge, Brooklyn. His parents had a Norwegian–English dictionary, and Ken watched as one adult or another referred to it while trying to converse. After observing this process for some time, Ken realized that all one would have to do to speak with the relative without the aid of the dictionary would be to learn everything in the book! Another story about Ken's boyhood quest to learn Norwegian tells how, around the age of twelve, he acquired a record of Norwegian phrases. This he played constantly through the night on a stereo he set up in the bedroom he shared with his brother Ron. It worked, to some extent, for both Ken and his slightly irritated brother: Ron can repeat the recording to this day, although he admits that he does not really know what it means.[1]

Michael Connolly of Portland, Maine, Ken's former student and friend for over three decades, explains Ken's acquisition of Norwegian slightly differently. "The story is told," Michael says, "that Ken's father wished for his son to become competent in Norwegian, whereupon Ken's mother agreed, but with the stipulation that he should also learn Irish from her side of the family."[2] Perhaps this version is more fable than fact, but Ken did indeed have Irish-speaking relatives: his grandmother's brother, James Cullinan, was among the last Irish speakers in Co. Tipperary.[3] Growing up, Ken studied Irish in classes organized by Cumann Bhreandáin (The St Brendan Society) in Brooklyn, Cumann na Gaeilge (The New York Gaelic Society) in Manhattan, and Conradh na Gaeilge (The Gaelic League) in the Bronx, and sought out Irish-language books in Keshcarrigan Bookshop, an Irish-interest bookstore in lower Manhattan.[4] In the summer of 1966 he visited Ireland for nearly two months, several weeks of which were spent at Coláiste Bhríde (St Brigid's College) in Rannafast in the Donegal Gaeltacht (Irish-speaking region).[5] As a young man, he was well integrated in New York's Irish community: he regularly attended cultural events; he spoke Irish with local immigrants, like Mike

Curran and Cole Connelly, the Connemara-born owners of a Brooklyn bar; and he even served as president of the now-defunct Cumann na Gaeilge in Manhattan in 1967–68.[6]

Ken's interest in both Norwegian and Irish was sparked by family heritage, but he was always interested in other languages. He majored in French at Brooklyn College, City University of New York, graduating *cum laude* in 1969. In this language, too, he maintained fluency throughout his life. Thelma Snyder, who has served as administrative assistant for the Department of Celtic Studies at StFX since 2002, recalls that Ken "loved languages and always made an effort to speak to me in my first language of French."[7] Indeed, it seems his linguistic interest was boundless. As Moireach Nilsen remarks, "I knew Ken spoke at least seven languages fluently, but when I was sorting his papers I found his exercises and lectures in Sanskrit! He was even able to get along in Mi'kmaq."[8]

HARVARD MAN

Upon graduating from Brooklyn College, Ken was awarded a Fulbright Fellowship to study in Ireland; instead, he elected to accept a Harvard University Graduate Prize Fellowship to pursue doctoral studies in the Department of Celtic Languages and Literatures. He found himself in an academic department chaired by Charles W. Dunn, whose wide-ranging interests and love of languages paralleled Ken's own. Under Dunn's guidance, Ken studied the medieval and modern Celtic languages, receiving additional tuition in the Celtic Studies Summer School at the Dublin Institute for Advanced Studies. Dunn can also be credited with nurturing Ken's interest in Celtic folklore and dialectology; the Harvard professor is well known today for the fieldwork he conducted among Canadian Scottish Gaelic speakers, and he encouraged his students to take up the mantle.[9] In a 2003 article, Ken recalled that "in his Celtic 100 classes at Harvard, Charles Dunn used to exhort his students to go out into the neighborhoods of Boston, such as Dorchester and Somerville, to meet and interview speakers of both Irish and Scottish Gaelic."[10]

In 1970, in the course of his studies, Ken was awarded the AM degree, qualifying him to pursue advanced research. With the aid of a Harvard travel grant, he spent the 1972–73 academic year in the North Connemara region known as Bun a' Cruc, northeast of Sraith Salach (Recess) at the foot of the Maumturk Mountains, where he lived in the home of Pádraig and Máire Seoighe (Patrick and Mary Joyce) in the village of Doire Bhéal an Mhárna (Derryvealawauma).[11] There he forged close friendships, perfected his pronunciation, and conducted fieldwork for his dissertation, which was to be a linguistic dialect study of the Irish of that region.[12]

Upon returning from Connemara to write up his findings, Ken took on the role of instructing Modern Irish and Early Welsh in the Celtic Department. Among his Welsh students was Joseph Nagy (then an undergraduate, and now the Henry L. Shattuck Professor of Irish Studies at Harvard), who says the course "was inspiring and a very deft alternation between Modern and Middle Welsh, done in that very persuasive but gentle way of his."[13] Virginia Blankenhorn (now an Honorary Fellow at the University of Edinburgh) comments on the methodology of the Irish course, stating that "Ken's ambition was to help us learn the complicated sound-system of Irish and get us speaking like natives. Our textbook … was Tomás de Bháldraithe's *The Irish of Cois Fhairrge, Co. Galway*; and in order to read it, we first had to learn how to decipher the International Phonetic Alphabet. It was all pretty hard-core."[14] A natural instructor, Ken's methods in his earliest courses were innovative and intensive.

Virginia further notes that "Ken was always on the lookout for native Irish speakers, and there were plenty of those in the Boston area."[15] Ken's efforts to seek out native speakers, whether in Connemara or America, led him to develop such flawless pronunciation that even the Connemara-born mistook him for their countryman. Peigí Ní Chlochartaigh of Brookline, MA, recalls her confusion the first time she met him because she thought he must be from her home region, but she could not place him: "Bhí aithne aige ar Loch Conaortha, mo bhaile dhúcha[i]s, ach ní raibh aon aithne agamsa airsean, an dtuigeann tú? Agus bhí canúint Chonamara [aige], agus bhí a fhios aige cén t-ainm a bhí ar an ngadhar a bhí ag mo dheartháir! Bhí an-spraoi aige – bhí an-chraic aige, mar a déarfá – agus chuir mé aithne air" (He knew Loughaconeera, my home place, but I didn't know him, you know? And he spoke Connemara Irish, and he knew the name of my brother's dog! He was great fun – he was great craic, as they say – and I got to know him).[16] Indeed, Ken and Peigí became *buanchairde* (perpetual friends), as she puts it.

He also honed his pronunciation of other Celtic languages while at Harvard. He practised Welsh with three native speakers, Eirug Davies,

Dic Driver, and Rod Bowen, whom he used to meet at a pub in Cambridge; they too became his friends, and said Ken was able to speak Ceredigion Welsh like a natural.[17] Years later, living in Nova Scotia, Scottish Gaelic speakers would comment on the impeccable accent he began to acquire in that language during his time at Harvard.

Ken was a conduit for both linguistic and cultural transmission at this time. He had gotten to know the great Connemara Irish *sean nós* (old style) singer Joe Heaney (Seosamh Ó hÉanaí) in Brooklyn, and helped to bring him to Harvard as the Vernam Hull lecturer in February of his graduating year. Ken later noted, "I am very happy that I requested at the time that the performance be recorded. We have as a result a recording of about an hour and a half in length."[18]

In 1975 Ken submitted his dissertation, "The Phonology and Morphology of the Irish of Bun a' Cruc, Sraith Salach, Co. Galway," for which he was awarded a PhD in Celtic Languages and Literatures.

WANDERING SCHOLAR

The years between 1975 and 1984, when Ken took up the call to the Celtic Department at StFX, were lean ones. For nearly a decade, he drove throughout New England teaching at different colleges, planting "seeds of interest in Celtic languages" to the extent that he became known as "Johnny Apple Seed."[19]

Harvard

Ken held part-time positions at Harvard University for this entire period, working first as a preceptor in the Department of Celtic Languages and Literatures (1975–77) and then as an instructor in Celtic at the Extension School (1977–84). (He would later go on to teach in the Summer School as well.) William Mahon (now an emeritus lecturer at Aberystwyth University) began his graduate studies in the Department of Celtic in 1976 and recalls that Ken "peppered his lectures with anecdotes (from his own experience) that provided insights into the Gaeltacht culture of the time (Doire Bhéal a' Mhárna was still without electricity)."[20] He had a knack for making learning come alive, as was the case for Margo Griffin-Wilson, who now teaches Irish at the University of Cambridge (UK) and in the Harvard Summer School. She shares that

> Ken made the structure of Irish visible and intelligible, and he had a gift for bringing challenging texts within our reach. We read *Caoineadh Airt Uí Laoghaire* (The Lament for Art O'Leary) that year, line by line, and the rhythms of the lament and Ken's recitation drew me in … [His] knowledge of Irish was exceeded only by his desire to share it, and he shared it with many. He taught Irish in the Harvard Summer School for years, and students gravitated to his courses. Now, when I teach Irish in the Harvard Summer School … I always think of Ken Nilsen. He is irreplaceable, but the memory of his teaching inspires me.[21]

In fact, Ken's Harvard courses were such a draw that it was not unheard of for students to repeat them, as Michael Connolly learned in 1979 in the "phenomenal" Extension School course in which he first met Ken. Then a graduate student at Boston College, Michael is now a professor at St Joseph's College in Standish, Maine. He states: "Speaking with others in the class during breaks, I discovered that most had taken this same class multiple times … Ken brought humor and passion into the classroom and he became for me a model of what a teacher, in the full sense of that word, should be."[22]

Regional Colleges

In the interim between Ken's doctoral graduation and his appointment at StFX, he also taught at Westfield State College (Westfield, MA), Elms College (Chicopee, MA), Cape Cod Community College (West Barnstable, MA), Boston College (Newton, MA), and the Taft School (Watertown, CT).

Catherine Shannon (emerita professor of history, Westfield State University) describes how Ken came to teach at Westfield and Elms, and the considerable impact his courses had:

> I met Ken Nilsen through the American Conference of Irish Studies in the late 1970s and was very impressed with his knowledge of and commitment to teaching the Irish Language in the Boston area … A few years later when Westfield State College received a generous federal Ethnic Heritage Grant to develop Irish Studies curricula, I reached out to Ken to teach two courses for the pro-

> gram, which was multi-disciplinary in nature. Initially he taught … a beginning course in Irish and a course in Irish Folklore, and they were fully subscribed. The Irish Language course was taught on the Elms College campus in Chicopee, which was a convenient location for members of the County Kerry Diaspora in the area. Ken was a very engaging and enthusiastic teacher and motivated his students, both traditional undergraduates as well as adult learners, to continue on with their Irish language studies … Three decades later, Irish language courses are still being taught at the Elms College, and this is an important aspect of Ken's living legacy to the Irish community in the Springfield area.[23]

Ken offered support and encouragement to students and the wider Irish heritage community in western Massachusetts; he also presented them with rare opportunities for cultural immersion. Catherine goes on to recall the time he brought Joe Heaney for a three-day visit, during which time the *sean-nós* singer not only visited Ken's classes but also gave two well-attended public performances. Ken presented Irish learners at Westfield and Elms with another unique opportunity in the early 1980s, when he organized a summer Irish language school for them in Dingle in the Kerry Gaeltacht.[24]

Ken's students at Cape Cod Community College similarly benefited from his enterprising approach and overseas connections when, in the summers of 1983 and 1984, he designed summer Irish language and folklore courses for them on Inis Meáin (Inismaan) in the Aran Islands. His co-instructor, Nóirín Ní Nuadháin, describes the memorable experience Ken was able to create:

> We both taught Irish (Gaeilge) in the morning and in the afternoons, we would walk around the island, sing Gaelic songs or dance, and some days we visited a well-known personality on the island. These visits were unique, and I do not think that any other students ever had access to the people's houses and lives that we had during those two summers … The American students saw the remnants of a way of life that is long gone.[25]

In addition, Ken taught Irish in Boston College's Evening Division from 1982 to 1984, and at Taft School.[26]

Cumann na Gaeilge i mBoston

Ken was heavily involved in Cumann na Gaeilge i mBoston (The Irish Language Society of Boston) during his time in New England, and William Mahon notes that he was the "most eminent and dynamic Irish language teacher" the society had at the time.[27] William recalls that in 1978 and 1979, Cumann na Gaeilge students were early beneficiaries of Ken's innovative Irish summer courses. These were co-sponsored by Cumann na Gaeilge i mBoston and Comharchumann na nOileán (Tír an Fhia) (The Islands' Co-operative [Teeranea]) and took place in Cois Fharraige and Trá Bháin (Trabane) in Connemara.[28] This region was a natural location, given the heritage of many people of Irish descent in the Boston area.

Ken served as vice-president of Cumann na Gaeilge i mBoston from 1979 to 1984. In those days the Cumann would hold *feiseanna* (language and music competitions), and former president Peigí Ní Chlochartaigh tells us that Ken was both instrumental in starting these, and an eager participant.[29] The *feiseanna* have not been held for the past several years, but they are remembered fondly.

After moving to Nova Scotia, Ken returned regularly to Boston. Peigí says that during these southern sojourns the Cumann would often organize Laethanta Gaeilge (Irish Language Days) and invite him "as the guest teacher, because [the students] would never get his like again."[30]

Further Education Courses

A couple of years after completing his doctorate, Ken began teaching evening Scottish Gaelic courses in Cambridge through Massachusetts's Adult Education Program. He published an account of the first night:

> The course was advertised and, lo and behold … quite a crowd showed up. A number of them were seniors, and I surmised that they might well be native speakers of Gaelic … As it turned out, [they] were … natives of Cape Breton who had been living in Boston for many decades … they came to my class hoping to learn to read Gaelic. And, indeed, some did learn to read Gaelic and continued to attend the course over the next few years.[31]

Ken also taught an evening Welsh course in Cambridge.[32]

Public Scholar

It is a mark of respect for Ken's stature as a scholar that he served as the representative for the United States at the UNESCO Meeting of Experts on Celtic Cultures in Dublin in the fall of 1981.[33] During the "lean years" he had minimal time for research, writing academic articles, or presenting at conferences;[34] however, his impact within the communities to which he belonged cannot be underestimated. In his efforts to make academic knowledge about Celtic languages and cultures accessible to their broader heritage communities, he embodied the concept of the "public scholar."

Ken's public was widespread. Some will remember him from further education courses or cultural events in their communities. Others will know him from his radio interviews and television appearances. Beginning in 1966, he was interviewed numerous times on Raidió Éireann, Raidió na Gaeltachta, BBC Radio nan Gàidheal, and the Canadian Broadcasting Corporation (CBC). In 1983 he appeared as the sole interviewee on the Raidió Teilifís Éireann (RTÉ) television program *Eadrainn*, and he subsequently appeared in documentaries featuring Irish, Scottish Gaelic, and Breton topics.[35]

In addition to his activities in New England, Ken maintained contact with the New York Irish community, teaching at Laethanta Gaeilge, giving public lectures, and visiting Irish classes in his hometown.[36] New York *Gaeilgeoir* (Irish speaker) Conn Mac Aogáin recalls meeting him on one such visit in the early 1980s as a Columbia undergraduate: "[I] had begun studying Irish formally at the now defunct Gaelic Society of New York [Cumann na Gaeilge]. Ken would occasionally visit New York to socialize with students of the Irish Language, including one time when he brought along an elderly woman who was his primary informant in a study he had done on the Irish of North Connemara who was then visiting the United States."[37] This was Mary Joyce.

Not only did Ken keep in contact with the Joyces in the years following his dissertation research, he paid them yearly visits, and, as Conn describes, he introduced them to other North American students of the language.[38] He also formed and maintained lasting connections with others in Ireland. Michael Connolly remarks: "Wherever and whenever I travelled in Ireland over the years, but especially in … County Galway, the name Ken Nilsen came up frequently and always with great admiration and respect both from those who knew him personally … or even from those who had never met Ken but were familiar with him from his many interviews on Raidió na Gaeltachta."[39] The following was shared by Gearóid Denvir, professor emeritus of Modern Irish, National University of Ireland, Galway, who met Ken at the Harvard Celtic Colloquium in the early 1980s:

> One of my most abiding memories of Ken is a short few days' visit with us in our family home in the Connemara Gaeltacht which included a tour of what I call my hidden Conamara, away from the trodden tourist trails. I still remember Ken that day standing at the site of Cúirt an tSrutháin Bhuí [The Court of the Yellow Stream] in the islands of West Connemara and almost communing with Colm de Bhailís, the nineteenth-century poet who composed the famous poem/song of the same name in this exact spot … Our book learning, he said, came alive there in a most human way.[40]

Whether in the North American diaspora or overseas via radio and television, Ken sought to bring Celtic cultures alive to others, regardless of their academic proclivity, just as his friends had done for him.

DEPARTMENT CHAIR

In 1984 Ken moved to Antigonish County, Nova Scotia, shifting from a largely Irish to a predominantly Scottish Gaelic heritage environment. In September of that year, he became the first holder of the Sister Saint Veronica Chair in Gaelic Studies at StFX.[41] Sr Margaret MacDonell served as chair of the Celtic Department at the time he took up his position, but in 1986 that responsibility became his. He had the singular task of expanding the department and, as the number of students grew, of securing a second instructor, Catrìona NicÌomhair Parsons, in 1993. A third full-time position was created in 2001 with the endowment of the Ben Alder Chair in Celtic Studies, held by Michael Linkletter.[42] The daily language of the department was Gaelic.

As student numbers increased, so did the course offerings. An Honours program was instituted that led to a full four-year set of courses, including instruction in early Celtic literature and civilization, Scottish Gaelic and Irish literature, and Scottish Gaelic, Irish, and Welsh language. In fact, under Ken's leadership, StFX became the only North American university to offer four years of Scottish Gaelic language instruction.[43] An MA program, which had existed in the past, was also reinstituted.

Throughout his years at StFX, Ken engaged in activities designed to facilitate and increase the use of Gaelic on an everyday basis not only among the students but also in the community. To this end, from 1987 to 1989, he conducted a Còmhlan Còmhraidh (Conversational Group) with invited Gaelic speakers, and in 1987 he also instituted a weekly lunchtime Bòrd na Gàidhlig (Gaelic Table) for students, faculty, and the public, which has continued. Goiridh Dòmhnullach (Jeffrey MacDonald) recalls that as a student in the late 1980s, he attended Bòrd na Gàidhlig in the Student Union Building cafeteria; it would later move to the Celtic Department in Immaculata Hall.[44] In 1991, Làithean Gàidhlig (Gaelic Language Days) were put in place twice and then three times a year, to which the public was invited; as Ken related in a 2006 interview with former student Liam Ó Caiside, "bithidh suas neo lethcheud neo trì fichead às a h-uile h-àite ann an Albainn Ùir a' tighinn gu na clasaichean a bhios againne air na làithean sin" (upward of fifty or sixty from every place in Nova Scotia come to the classes we have on those days).[45] In 1995, Ken helped establish the StFX Gaelic Summer Scholarship, which has since sent more than twenty students to Scotland for summer language study. Each year, the student Celtic Society has held a concert to raise funds for this purpose.[46] Then in 2000–01, with the aid of a grant from Industry Canada, he undertook the StFX Gaelic Digital Project, in the course of which thirty recordings from the StFX Cape Breton Folklore Collection were digitized for the benefit of learners and speakers. Ken selected the recordings, gave background material on each, wrote brief lessons, and made transcriptions for each one.[47]

In addition to a busy teaching and extracurricular schedule, as well as the administrative responsibilities of chairing a department, Ken remained academically engaged. He maintained his involvement with the American Conference for Irish Studies (ACIS) after leaving the United States, and in 1988 he chaired the organization's Irish Language Committee.[48] Catherine Shannon states: "I always looked forward to those occasions when Ken would come down from Canada for the summer or when he came to the ACIS meetings. I still recall our last meeting in New York City when he was a key-note speaker at the national ACIS [2007] and when we were able to catch up over a 'jar or two' at a local hostelry."[49] Ken was a regular presenter at conferences of the North American Association of Celtic Language Teachers

(NAACLT), and he served as the organization's president in 1998. He was an at-large member of the Celtic Studies Association of North America (CSANA) executive committee in 1989 and 1990 and was responsible for the Scottish Gaelic section of the CSANA Bibliography (1983–88).[50] He also got involved with the Canadian Association of Irish Studies, serving as the Irish language editor for the *Canadian Journal of Irish Studies* from 2005 to 2009,[51] and he was active in Celtic academia overseas, joining the Advisory Board of the University of Glasgow's Digital Archive of Scottish Gaelic / Dachaigh airson Stòras na Gàidhlig project in 2007.[52]

During his tenure at StFX, Ken also took on the formidable task of organizing three conferences. In 1992, he hosted the Annual Meeting of CSANA, which featured a poetry reading by acclaimed Scottish Gaelic poet Sorley MacLean; it was the first time the conference had been held in Canada. He hosted the NAACLT Annual Conference in 1997, and in July 2008 he brought Rannsachadh na Gàidhlig, the major biennial Scottish Gaelic research conference, to StFX. The latter attracted a large attendance, and Rob Ó Maolalaigh (professor of Gaelic and vice-principal and head of the College of Arts, University of Glasgow), who was invited to give a plenary lecture, remembers the event very positively: "This legendary conference was one of the best RnaG conferences yet and the first and only conference so far to be held outwith Scotland. Ken was a superb and generous host and we all came away with very fond memories of the university and of the Gaels of Nova Scotia."[53]

Ken edited the proceedings of the 2008 Rannsachadh na Gàidhlig conference, published his research in essay collections and journals, and authored regular columns intended for Gaelic learners in the Antigonish *Casket* and the Halifax-based magazine *Celtic Heritage*. *Suas leis a' Ghàidhlig* (1987–96, 2008–10) in the *Casket* presented primarily short folklore items drawn from his fieldwork with Antigonish Gaelic speaker Danny Cameron, while Gaelic Notes (1995–2003) in *Celtic Heritage* addressed points of grammar and pronunciation that tend to cause confusion. A persuasive writer – and not only in scholarly and pedagogical contexts – Ken was also awarded several grants that enabled him to pursue his research. For instance, in the 2004–05 academic year he received both an Ireland Canada University Foundation (ICUF) Fellowship and an Irish American Cultural Institute / National University of Ireland, Galway (NUIG) Fellowship, which allowed him to spend a sabbatical at NUIG as a Visiting Research Fellow. In addition, in each of the five academic years between 2008–09 and 2012–13, Ken was able to secure an instructor of Irish Gaelic for the Department of Celtic Studies through the ICUF, allowing him to direct more attention elsewhere.

Under Ken's leadership the Celtic Department flourished, and the visibility of Gaelic increased at StFX and in the wider region. Ken became department chair at a decisive moment in the efforts to maintain and enhance the future of Gaelic language and culture in Nova Scotia, and there is no doubt that his work had an enabling effect in the resurgence of Gaelic. One significant example of progress during his time may be given. With the help and encouragement of the provincial Oifis Iomairtean na Gàidhlig (Office of Gaelic Affairs), the university's Department of Education added Gaelic as a teachable subject – a first in North America – and in 2008–09 hired Oighrig Nic Fhraing (Effie Rankin) to teach Gaelic pedagogy.[54] Prospective secondary school teachers of Gaelic no longer need to go to Scotland to gain accreditation, and several alumni of the Celtic Department have graduated from the Gaelic-accredited B.Ed. program. The program recently received a sizable bequest from the estate of Neil and Marianne MacLean; Neil was a frequent visitor to the Celtic Department Gaelic Days that Ken instituted.

FOLKLORE COLLECTOR

Ken's greatest contribution to the study, and living legacy, of Celtic languages and cultures is the fieldwork he undertook with native speakers, primarily in the diaspora. His personal archive of videotaped interviews conducted with North American speakers of Irish, Scottish Gaelic, Welsh, and Breton contains several hundred hours of material, and it is undoubtedly the largest such archive on the continent. He also recorded many speakers of Celtic languages on his numerous trips to Ireland, Scotland, Wales, and Brittany, and he videotaped events throughout New England and Nova Scotia at which the languages were spoken.

The United States

From the time Ken arrived in Massachusetts in 1969, he interviewed many Irish speakers throughout the American northeast. The oral history and traditions of many Irish immigrants to the Boston area, most of whom are no longer living, are contained in his folklore collection. Peigí Ní Chlochartaigh recalls one recording in particular that he made with her sister Bríd and a few other people: "D'inis sí an scéal dó, an Gobán Saor, agus bhí muid ag caint ar – pisreogaí agus rudaí" (She told him the story of the Gobán Saor, and we were talking about superstitions and things).[55] When Ken's teaching took him farther afield, he took advantage of the opportunity to seek out and record speakers in other parts of Massachusetts. Catherine Shannon remembers,

> During his time at Westfield and the Elms, Ken engaged in considerable outreach to those in the local Irish diaspora who were Irish speakers from both Kerry and Mayo. He used interviews with them to illustrate various aspects of his Folklore and language courses. The opportunity to speak Irish and to tell stories of their homeland in Kerry, especially those from the Dingle area and the Blasket Islands, was greatly appreciated by those he interviewed and recorded. These interviews are an important source in documenting the living links that were kept up by Irish speakers with the culture of their home land and place.[56]

By the mid-1970s, Ken was also recording Scottish Gaelic speakers around Boston. Many of these he met through his evening courses, as well as through the Cape Breton Gaelic Club of Boston, which was still very lively more than thirty years after its founding in 1940 by economic migrants from Nova Scotia.[57] Others he encountered by happenstance, as he shared in his article, "Recording Scottish Gaelic Folklore and Oral History in the United States":

> One day in 1976 when I was teaching at Harvard, I was in the Celtic Department office for my office hours. The telephone rang and the woman on the line asked if there was someone at the department who could give her the correct spelling of *Ciad Mìle Fàilte.* I suspected from her pronunciation of the words that she was a native speaker. We had an interesting conversation in which we each proceeded to see how much Gaelic the person at the other end of the line had. The final result was that Mrs. MacDougall invited me to her house to have dinner and meet with some Cape Breton Gaelic speakers … This was just the first of many visits for me to the MacDougall home. Mrs. MacDougall

> was quite willing to be tape-recorded and enjoyed answering my questions about Gaelic.[58]

Designing a questionnaire similar to Heinrich Wagner's in his *Linguistic Atlas and Survey of Irish Dialects*, Ken recorded a valuable collection of words, phrases, and terminology from Elizabeth MacDougall, a very small portion of which he shared in the article referenced above.

Ken's publications give us glimpses of the riches he had accumulated in his fieldwork with Celtic language speakers. Several of them feature material he collected from Danny Cameron, who grew up in Antigonish County.[59] From Danny he recorded "the most extensive collection known to [him] of mainland Nova Scotia Gaelic."[60] Moreover, Danny told him much about Antigonish and the surrounding area before he ever set foot there.

In total, Ken recorded more than one hundred hours of material from thirty-nine Cape Bretoners, two mainland Nova Scotians, and eight Hebrideans in greater Boston, New York, New Jersey, and Maine.[61] He also distributed questionnaires to try to gauge the size of Boston's Scottish Gaelic-speaking community (an estimated two to three hundred in the mid-1980s).[62]

After moving to Nova Scotia in 1984, Ken began passing through Portland, Maine, on thrice-yearly trips to Boston. He would stop for the night there, staying with Michael Connolly.[63] It was from Michael that Ken learned about Portland's sizable Connemara Irish-speaking population, as Michael relates:

> He seemed skeptical at first, as he knew much about similar populations in New York City, Boston, Springfield, among others. So finally, around 1984, I convinced him to travel to Portland for a meeting I had arranged with nearly fifty Irish speakers ... That morning before attending this impressive gathering, I took Ken to see one older individual that I knew would not be attending. This was Pat Malone of Stetson Court in the Saint Dominic's Parish of Portland's West End ... Pat had emigrated from his native Ros an Mhíl (Rossaveal), County Galway, shortly after the Anglo-Irish War and Irish Civil War ... After a lengthy interview that morning and an even lengthier interview a few months later, Ken declared with joy and amazement that we had discovered a true *seanchaí* (storyteller) and one of the very best native Irish speakers in America.[64]

Over the next couple of decades, with Michael as his liaison and cameraman, Ken set out to record as many as possible of the Irish speakers Michael had identified.[65] They interviewed at least one person every time Ken passed through town, and Michael says, "Everybody really enjoyed Ken because ... nobody had ever come into their home for the purpose of speaking Irish ... They were very, very pleased whenever he did that."[66] Although it was a race against time, Ken succeeded in interviewing sixteen Irish speakers in Portland – some of them more than once – and six people who were regularly in contact with local Irish speakers.[67] Material from several of these speakers appears in print.[68]

On his trips back and forth, Ken would also attend Irish-language events in Boston, and he continued to record there. During a 2008 visit he encountered, and interviewed, Irish poet and novelist Jackie Mac Donncha. Cumann na Gaeilge i mBoston, under the leadership of Peigí Ní Chlochartaigh, had invited Jackie and *sean-nós* singer Joe John Mac an Iomaire over from Ireland for a poetry reading and performance in West Roxbury. Ken's reputation preceded him: Peigí had been singing her learned friend's praises, and Jackie was a bit nervous about meeting an eminent scholar. His remarks well illustrate Ken's ability to put interviewees at ease, and the affection people often felt for him afterward:

> Pé ar bith cén náire nó cúthaileacht a bhí orm, sciorr sé díom mar sciorrfadh uisce de lacha, tar éis cúpla nóiméad ag caint le Ken Nilsen. In achar an-ghairid thuig mé go raibh Ken Nilsen mar dhuine againn féin. Ní raibh aon éirí-in-áirde ná postúlacht san Ollamh seo chor ar bith: ní raibh aon ghoití ná gaisce. Bhí sé ag labhairt mar dhuine dínn féin. Agus chomh maith leis sin, bhí sé líofa san teanga a bhí agamsa ón gcliabhán! ... Thuig mé ag an bpointe sin an fáth a raibh Ken in ardmheas ag Peigí agus ag an gCumann. Bhí mé in éad leis na scoláirí a raibh sé de ádh orthu bheith dá múineadh ag an bhfear.
>
> Dúirt sé liom go mba mhaith leis agallamh a chuir orm, mura mhiste liom ... Tháinig sé le na ghléas taifeadta ar an lá a bhí socraithe againn. Níor thosaigh sé ar an agallamh go ceann tamaill. Muid ag caint faoi rudaí éagsúla i dtosach. Thuig mé go raibh sé do mo chur ar mo shuaimhneas i ngan fhios dom fhéin.
>
> Ní cuimhin liom go barainneach cé na ceisteanna a chuir sé orm an lá sin, ach bhí a bhformhór faoi Chonamara, áit ar chaith

sé féin tréimhsí: na daoine, a dtréithe, a gcuid amhráin agus a gcuid béaloidis. Léigh mé cúpla dán as mo leabhar dó. Chuir sé an-áthas air go raibh Joe John Mac an Iomaire, duine de amhránaithe móra Chonamara, beo beathach ós a chomhair ag casadh amhráin dó.

... Bhí lé ar leith aige leis an nGaeilge. Go deimhin d'fhéadfá a rá go raibh Ken Nilsen chomh Gaelach leis na Gaeil. ... Nuair a chuir Peigí glaoch orm in Aibreán na bliana 2012 agus dúirt liom go raibh Ken básaithe, ghoin sé mo chroí, cé nár chaith mé ach píosa de dhá lá leis. Bhí an tionchar sin aige ar dhaoine.[69]

Whatever worry or shyness I felt slipped away from me, as water would slip off a duck, after a couple minutes talking to Ken Nilsen. In a very short time I understood that Ken Nilsen was just like us. There wasn't any uppitiness or self-importance in this Professor at all: he wasn't conceited. He was speaking like one of us. And what's more, he was fluent in the language I'd had from the cradle! … I understood immediately why Ken was highly respected by Peigí and the Cumann. I was jealous of the students who were lucky enough to be taught by him.

He told me that he'd like to interview me, if I wouldn't mind … He came with his recorder on the agreed-upon day. He didn't start the interview for a while. We were talking about different things at first. I understood unconsciously that it was to put me at ease.

I don't remember precisely what questions he asked me that day, but most of them were about Connemara, where he himself had spent some time: the people, their traits, their songs and their folklore. I read a couple of poems from my book for him. It made him very happy that Joe John Mac an Iomaire, one of the great Connemara singers, was there in the flesh singing for him.

… He had a remarkable affection for the Irish language. You could certainly say that Ken Nilsen was as Gaelic as the Gaels … When Peigí called me in April 2012 and told me that Ken had died, it stung my heart, even though I only spent part of two days with him. He had that effect on people.

In addition to Irish and Scottish Gaelic speakers, Ken was interested in documenting the experiences and speech of Welsh and Breton speakers in the United States; however, his publications only give tantalizing hints of his work with these populations. A memorate he collected from a Welsh speaker in Pennsylvania in the 1970s appeared in an essay published ten years later, and Eirug Davies of Cambridge recalls him collecting from others in New England.[70] In the 1980s, moreover, he began to interview Breton restaurant workers in Manhattan,[71] and his comments in a 2006 publication suggest that his recordings contain valuable oral historical information: "In the 1960s–80s Breton speakers could be found in New York's French restaurants as busboys, waiters, *maîtres d'hôtel*, barmen, and owners. New York's Brittany du Soir, the Café Brittany, and Café des Sports had principally Breton-speaking staff and owners, mostly natives of the Gourin–Roudaouallec–Langonned region. Some Breton speakers have claimed that they learned French while working in New York's French restaurants."[72]

The Celtic Countries

Although based in North America, Ken collected in Ireland, Scotland, Wales, and Brittany as well. In an article derived from his dissertation research he noted:

> I have collected a good deal of traditional lore in [Bun a' Cruc]: tales, songs, proverbs, placenames, prayers, etc. Máire Seoighe [Mary Joyce] has preserved a number of charms (*araidheadchaí*) that are still used when needed. She and others in [Bun a' Cruc] still keep up many of the traditional calendar customs, including the lighting of a bonfire on St. John's Eve … On June 23, 1982, I videotaped Mrs. Seoighe's performance of the ceremony.[73]

Other of his essays contain references to material he collected in the Scottish Hebrides in the 1970s and '80s.[74] He also gathered a good deal of Breton material during a sabbatical in Brittany in 1990–91, and he returned there later that decade with Antigonish filmmaker Peter Murphy. Peter recalls that as they travelled around filming segments for the documentary *Finisterre*, Ken expressed interest in seeking out Breton speakers: "We'd be walking in the supermarket … and he'd say, 'He's a Breton speaker.' And he'd go up and talk to them, and he was always right … And when we'd go for a bed and breakfast … he'd always find a Breton[-owned] BnB … and he'd chat with the owners."[75] Some of these conversations appear in the film, and an interview from Ken's Breton research punctuated a lecture that Conn Mac Aogáin attended at the American Irish Historical Society in Manhattan. Conn recalls: "In this presentation [Ken] showed a video of a folklore collection interview with an elderly woman in Plougastel in Brittany providing a rich commentary on all aspects of the interview, the informant and the social/spatial context."[76]

Canada

In the nearly thirty years Ken spent in Nova Scotia he interviewed numerous individuals, primarily in Cape Breton. He began this work immediately upon his arrival, as his former student at StFX, Lodaidh MacFhionghain (Lewis MacKinnon), relates:

> Nuair a chuala Coinneach gu robh a' Ghàidhlig aig bràthair mo sheanmhar Dùghall, rinn e céilidh air taigh mo phàrantan is chlàraich e Dùghall is m'athair 's a' Ghàidhlig is mo mhàthair 's an Fhraingis ... Gun an t-suim a ghabh Coinneach anns a' Ghàidhlig aig Dùghall cha bhiodh sion air a chlàrachadh dhen a' Ghàidhlig bhriagha mhóir a bh'aige. Chan e dìreach Dùghall am fear-labhairt dùthchasach ionadail a-mhàin a chlàraich Coinneach. Thuig mi nuair a ràinig e am Baile Mór ann an 1984, chaidh Coinneach mun cuairt air an t-siorramachd gus an luchd-labhairt dùthchasach mu dheireadh a chlàrachadh.
>
> When Ken heard that my granduncle was a Gaelic speaker, he visited my parents' home [in Inverness, Cape Breton] and recorded Dougald and my father in Gaelic and my mother in French ... Without the interest Ken took in Dougald's Gaelic, there would be no recordings of his deep, beautiful Gaelic. And Dougald wasn't the only native Gaelic speaker in the area that Ken recorded. I understand that when he arrived in Antigonish in 1984, Ken went around the county to record any remaining native Gaelic speakers.[77]

Doing this work, Ken formed close connections with Nova Scotia's Gaelic speakers and became an important member of the community, not only encouraging language speakers and learners, but also telling their stories and singing their songs – often after averring, "Chan eil guth agam" (I can't sing).[78]

Ken Nilsen interviewing Dan Allan Gillis of Broad Cove, Inverness County, Cape Breton, in 1995. Photo by Peter Murphy.

Like Charles Dunn at Harvard, Ken encouraged his StFX students to seek out native speakers and "to get out into the field" and collect from them.[79] In 1995–96 he organized and directed a project that provided institutional support for them to do so. In the Gaelic Video Project, conducted in conjunction with Peter Murphy of Seabright Video, a team of students helped Ken interview twenty-eight Cape Breton Gaelic speakers on videotape.[80] Participants have fond memories of the experience. Recalling a day on the road in Cape Breton with Ken and Peter, Will Lamb says: "We visited two or three people in nursing homes, then went … to speak to Anna MacKinnon, a great younger Gaelic speaker (in her early 60s then) with Barra connections … It was a meaningful, special day for me and my first experience of fieldwork with Gaelic speakers."[81]

Shawn McDaniel also describes time spent in the field with Ken as a StFX student. On one unforgettable trip, they visited a woman from Judique in a nursing home in Port Hawksbury:

> At first, she was understandably shy, but Ken's genuine curiosity, and well-placed compliments, soon had her speaking "more Gaelic than she had in ages." She recounted how for many years she

> lived alone in Halifax, where … she would record herself singing Gaelic songs, some of which were composed by locals in Judique, as well as other ubiquitous tunes like "Gun chrodh gun aighean" (Without cattle or heifers) … Her demeanor changed dramatically by the time we left, and Ken emphasized to her just how wonderful her Gaelic and her voice were.

Shawn comments more generally, as well, on Ken's manner when collecting in Nova Scotia:

> I will always recall with great fondness Ken's giddiness when informants gifted us exceptional lore, songs, or constructions (which he would subsequently rave about in the car ride back to Antigonish, or wherever our next stop was). And I will certainly never forget the incredulous look he would shoot my way … when other people around would do loud laundry or receive – and take! – phone calls while we were recording. "Such is life," he would often say.[82]

Comparing Ken with the renowned Scottish folklore collector Calum Iain MacLean, Rob Ó Maolalaigh comments: "Just like Calum Iain before him, and in Sorley MacLean's memorable words about his much cherished brother, Ken was never more content than when he was amongst Gaels, 'a' beothachadh na cuimhne aosda / le coibhneas is le spòrs' [kindling ancient memory / with kindness and fun]."[83] Celtic languages and their oral traditions were his greatest passion, and he generously shared this with his students, inspiring many to join him in his important work gathering, elucidating, and supporting the languages, traditions, and history of native speakers.

The Collection

Ken's wife Moireach, entrusted as she was with the care and disbursement of her husband's collection, has been confronted with an awesome task. She explains:

> Ken's collection spans approximately forty-five years. In his limited spare time, he had indexed parts of it himself and occasionally had student assistants index as well. He copied many fragments or complete recordings from various media to audio cassettes, VHS and DVD. He transcribed and cross-referenced and annotated hun-

> dreds of hours of interviews. Ken used the material as a teaching aid and topics for articles and published submissions … He was really looking forward to semi-retirement and to a time when he could immerse himself in his collection and write.[84]

It was vitally important to him that the privacy of the people he interviewed be respected and that their contributions be used with discretion, always mindful of their lives, their families, and their communities. In effect, Moireach says, "he insisted that these be the first and final deliberations before any part of a transcription or recording be shared publicly."[85] The Danny Cameron material, and possibly the Cape Breton collection, will find a home at StFX, while the Irish and other Celtic material is destined for Harvard.

MENTOR

The respect Ken's former students have for him and the gratitude they express is striking. He was a dedicated mentor to many individuals who went on to become writers, performers, educators, and language activists – and he was very proud of their accomplishments. In turn, they remember him as an exceptional instructor who captivated classes, and who treated them with respect inside and outside the classroom. As Will Lamb notes, he was capable of being "open to his students in a way that is rare today," understanding how to be friendly yet professional at the same time.[86]

For many, it is Ken's generous encouragement that stands out. He inspired his students to push beyond the limits of their knowledge, and he took great care to provide the tools they would need to do so. This is inherent in Shawn McDaniel's assertion that "I could not have had a more astute and involved mentor." Shawn (now an assistant professor of Romance studies at Cornell University) says that upon arriving at StFX, "during my first year of studies, Ken would frequently bring me unsolicited mixed tapes of Gaelic interviews, video recordings, songs, and books." And if students found their confidence had exceeded their level of understanding, Ken was happy to help. Shawn continues that on the night before his first solo fieldwork trip, when "it suddenly dawned on me that I really had no idea what fieldwork was about, what kinds of questions to ask, or how to even ask them," one phone call to Ken set him on the right path, and "my session … the next day was wonderful."[87]

Others explain how Ken's unique use of oral traditions in language instruction appealed to them. Kathleen Reddy notes that "Ken's [advanced] Gaelic class was a treat. Our class texts were transcriptions of Gaelic stories Ken personally collected from Danny Cameron … These were supplemented with Nova Scotian Gaelic songs and poetry … [Through these] we were not only being introduced to Gaelic language and idiom, but [also] to local oral history, Gaelic storytelling conventions and cultural practices."[88] Will Lamb adds that this "was such a fresh way of learning the language and classes were always a pleasure, even when they were challenging. Ken was the only Gaelic instructor I had who drew from folklore in this way, and – for me at least – it was such an effective way of learning: absorbing the language and the culture together."[89] Indeed, this was a feature of his teaching even in his graduate student days at Harvard, as Virginia Blankenhorn illustrates:

> One of my great memories of his introductory Irish course was the day he came to class with a bunch of [*sean-nós*] LPs under his arm, which he proceeded to play for us. It will sound a bit grandiose to say this, but I can truthfully swear to you that that class changed my life, as I have spent the past fifty years, nearly, pursuing my interest in the songs I heard for the first time that day.[90]

Grandiose-sounding or not, it is a familiar refrain. Lodaidh MacFhionghain, now a Gaelic poet and CEO of Nova Scotia's Office of Gaelic Affairs (OGA), recognizes that Ken's courses were foundational for "iomadh duine … a tha an sàs ann an leasachadh cànan agus cultur 's an là an diugh an Albainn Nuaidh" (many people … who are now involved in Gaelic language and cultural development in Nova Scotia) – himself included.[91] Goiridh Dòmhnullach, a Gaelic singer, storyteller, and OGA field officer, similarly remarks that Ken "had a profound effect on my life," opening his eyes to the traditions of his people.[92] Students also went on to pursue careers in research and teaching, like Will Lamb, now a senior lecturer in Scottish ethnology at the University of Edinburgh, who comments that "Ken was the most formative Gaelic and ethnology teacher I had. Without him, I simply wouldn't be where I am … I am forever indebted to him."[93] Kathleen Reddy notes that Ken "was instrumental in my own journey to Gaelic fluency and my career path"; she trained and worked as a

Gaelic instructor in Scotland for several years, returning to StFX to teach Gaelic after Ken's passing.[94] As another former student, Joseph Windsor, adds, Ken "pushed his students to grow, to learn, to be better, and as a result, we did."[95]

The story Lindsay Milligan Dombrowski has chosen to share well illustrates Ken's impact as a mentor, and brings a fitting close to this commemoration:

> I was nearly a year into my first proper university job, as a lecturer, when I first had the opportunity to teach undergraduates about my passion: Gaelic education ... That Friday afternoon, I stood in front of a hundred or so soon-to-be elementary school teachers, who peered down at me in a manner that was wholly intimidating. I took a breath, turned on the PowerPoint, and began with a photo of Ken.
>
> I told them about my first class at St. Francis Xavier University, and how my professor's eyes burst with excitement and enthusiasm for Celtic languages. I told them about how he began by saying, "You have the privilege to learn this language. You now have a responsibility to it." I told them truthfully about how, at nineteen years old, I leaned in on my little wooden seat in Immaculata Hall and bought into each word that came out of this man's mouth. Ken's passion created my passion; it brought me to Scotland and brought me to that lecture theatre, where I had the privilege to teach others about Gaelic.
>
> ... Later that afternoon I settled into a seat on a train to go home ... I opened Facebook on my phone to pass the time, maybe to boast to the world about how well my lecture had gone, and I felt gratitude to Ken. I scrolled through my newsfeed. There was a post. The date was 13 April 2012.[96]

Today, not far from Immaculata Hall, a tree grows. It is an oak tree – held by the Gaels for millennia as a symbol of wisdom and strength – planted in honour of Ken by his students and colleagues. It is a fitting memorial for a man who spread his roots so widely and influenced so many.

APPENDIX

It has long been a tradition among Gaelic poets to mark the passing of important individuals in poetic lament. Given the important role Ken played in the diasporic Irish and Scottish Gaelic communities, it should come as no great surprise that he was memorialized in this way. Included below is one of the poems composed in his memory, with a translation by its author.

Do Choinneach Nilsen, M'Oide

Lodaidh MacFhionghain

"Tha agam ri falbh a-nist, a laochain"
Tha thu 'cagarsaich 'nam chluas
"Sgìths orm a-nist … fhuair mi mo leòr dheth
'S e an t-àm a th'ann …"

Is fhad 's a tha fìor bhròn d'fhàgail
a' bualadh ar cridheachan an Di-haoine seo
Le truime do chall,
Tha fhios'm gu robh agad ri falbh
Cha ruig thu leas a dh'fhulaing tuilleadh, a shàr-laoich;

Ach mar a bhios mi 'meamhrachadh air an dìleab
A thug thu dhuinn,
Tha mi 'dol beagan air chall
Ann an teagamh
Ag aideachadh nach eil mi comasach
A' cur ás àicheadh gu bheil mi deiseil airson a' chòrr dhen sgrìob
Ás d'aonais;

Mar a dh'ionnsaich mi bhuat;
Bho do chainnt, fhios, dhòigh, mhodh
Mar a dhéilig thu ri ar seann daoine prìseil,
M'athair is bràthair mo sheanmhar 'nam miosg

Le meas, suairceas, gasdachd,
Chuir thu ri togail a' rathaid
Far a b'urrainn dha na Gàidheil creidsinn a-rithist
Ann an luach an cànain is an cultair

Le do làmhan caoimhneil fhéin
Thug thu air flùr beag brisg ar muinntir fàs
Is a' bhuaidh a th'agad
Connadh anam' airson ghinealaichean;

Mu dheireadh thall tha mi 'tuigsinn
Fhad 's a tha mi 'faicinn do ghàire leathainn mhiarailtich
Is tu 'dòirteadh gloine fhìon mhath' is a 'gabhail a' bhìdh'
As fhèarr leat
Thall thairis air an taobh eile
A' seanchas is a' gabhail naidheachdan is ri horo gheallaidh
Anns na teagannan Ceilteach uile
Ro oidhcheannan gun stad;

A' gàireachdainn is a' coimhead orm
Far a chluinneas mi do ghuth ag ràdhainn,
"Na biodh cùram ort.
Bidh sibh-se dìreach taght,' 'ille,
Nach robh fhios agad gu robh agam ri falbh
Los gum biodh sibhse 'tuigsinn
Gur ann a-nist an t-àm agaibh-se
A' bhratach a ghiùlain nas àirde fhathast?"

To Ken Nilsen, My Mentor
Lewis MacKinnon

"I have to go now, little hero"
You whisper in my ear,
"I am tired ... I've had my fill ...
It is time ..."

And while the true sadness of your departure
Strikes our heart on this Friday
With the weightiness of your loss
I know that you had to go away
You needn't suffer more, oh great hero;

But as I reflect on the legacy
You gave to us,
I am a little lost in doubt,

Admitting that I am not capable
Denying that I am ready for the remainder of the journey
Without you;

Oh, how I learned from you,
From your speech, knowledge, way, approach
How you dealt with our treasured elders
My father and granduncle amongst them;

With kindness, gentleness, respect
You contributed to the building of the road
Where Gaels could again believe
In the merit of their language and culture

By your own kind hands
You made the little brittle flower of our people grow
And your impact
The soul fuel for generations

At last I understand
As I see your broad wondrous smile
As you pour a good glass of wine and enjoy
Your favourite meal
Over yonder on the other side
Talking and telling stories and making merry
In every Celtic language
Through nights that have no end

Laughing and looking at me
Where I hear your voice saying,
"Don't worry,
You'll all be just fine, boy,
Didn't you know that I had to go away
So that you would understand
That it is now your time to shoulder
The flag that much higher still?"

NOTES

I must first acknowledge Catrìona NicÌomhair Parsons's contribution to this memorial chapter. Ken's colleague for many years, Catrìona provided much of the information about Ken's time at StFX, and spoke with Moireach [Marty] Nilsen, who kindly shared additional details. Catrìona and Moireach, I am truly grateful. I also wish to thank everyone who contributed their memories. There are almost certainly others who would have liked to contribute, and who would have had valuable information to add. I regret that I could not contact more people or share every story that was offered. I extend my deepest gratitude to Dr Ken Nilsen for his invaluable scholarship, his important work with North American Celtic-language communities, and the excellent foundation in Celtic Studies that I, along with so many others, received from him at StFX. I now teach many of the same courses Ken first taught me, and I am often reminded how influential he was in shaping the course of my life.

1 Moireach Nilsen in conversation with Catrìona NicÌomhair Parsons, 5 June 2018.

2 Statement sent by email from M. Connolly to the author, 8 July 2018.

3 Nilsen, "Priest," 193; cf. Nilsen, "James Cullinan," 153–4.

4 Nilsen, "James Cullinan," 150; email from M. McShane to the author, 28 May 2018.

5 Nilsen, "James Cullinan," 150.

6 Uí Chollatáin, "Nilsen, Ken"; Claire Foley in conversation with the author and Michael Connolly, 11 July 2018. Originally from Kilchreest, Co. Galway, Claire lived in Brooklyn for three years before moving to Portland, Maine. She and Ken used to reminisce about life in Brooklyn. She passed away in January 2020.

7 Email from T. Snyder to the author, 4 May 2018.

8 Moireach Nilsen in conversation with Catrìona NicÌomhair Parsons, 5 June 2018.

9 See the Charles William Dunn Collection, Celtic Department Audio Collection, acquisition nos. 1378 and 1379, Widener Library; see also Dunn, *Highland Settler*.

10 Nilsen, "Recording," 22.

11 Nilsen, "Some Features," 91, 104n1.

12 Ken described how he chose that particular location and his arrival there in "Some Features," 91–2.

13 Joseph F. Nagy in conversation with the author, 28 February 2019.

14 Statement sent by email from V. Blankenhorn to the author, 20 June 2018.

15 Ibid.

16 Peigí Ní Chlochartaigh in conversation with the author, 2 May 2018; translated by the author.

17 Moireach Nilsen in conversation with Catrìona NicÌomhair Parsons, 5 June 2018; Eirug Davies in conversation with the author, 23 March 2019.

18 Nilsen, "Living Celtic Speech," 92–3; "Joe Heaney at Harvard 2/8/75: Irish Songs and Stories," Celtic Department Audio Collection, acquisition no. 3609, Widener Library.

19 Obituary for Kenneth (Ken) Edward Nilsen, C.L. Curry Funeral Services, Antigonish, Nova Scotia, http://www.clcurry.com/obituaries/70052, accessed 12 July 2017.

20 Statement sent by email from W. Mahon to the author, 9 May 2018.

21 Statement sent by email from M. Griffin-Wilson to the author, 7 August 2018.

22 Statement sent by email from M. Connolly to the author, 8 July 2018.

23 Statement sent by email from C. Shannon to the author, 5 September 2018.

24 Ibid.

25 Statement sent by email from Nóirín Ní Nuadhain to the author, 13 July 2018. Now retired, Nóirín lectured in the Teaching of Irish at St Patrick's College, Dublin City University.

26 Peigí Ní Chlochartaigh in conversation with the author, 2 May 2018.

27 Statement sent by email from W. Mahon to the author, 9 May 2018.

28 Ibid.

29 Peigí Ní Chlochartaigh in conversation with the author, 2 May 2018.

30 Ibid.

31 Ken Nilsen, "Ais-éiridh na Gàidhlig – Gaelic Revival," *Chronicle-Herald*, 14 February 1999, C2; reprinted in Nilsen, "A Reminiscence," 337–8.

32 Eirug Davies in conversation with the author, 21 November 2018.

33 UNESCO, "Meeting of Experts on Celtic Cultures (Dublin, 17–19 November 1981): Final Report," Annex 1, p. 3. Paris: 22 January 1982, CC-81/CONF.606, UNESCO Archives.

34 Ken's primary research concentration at this time – collecting oral traditions – is discussed in a later section of this chapter.

35 *Eadrainn*; Feiritéar, *Pádraig Feiritéar* (televised on RTÉ); MacLeod, *Na h-Eilthirich* (televised on BBC Alba); Murphy, *Finisterre* (televised on BravoTV).

36 See, for example, "Irish Language Day"; "Conference in Irish, About Irish."

37 Statement sent by email from C. Mac Aogáin to the author, 17 December 2018.

38 Nilsen, "Some Features," 92.

39 Statement sent by email from M. Connolly to the author, 8 July 2018.

40 Statement sent by email from G. Denvir to the author, 16 July 2018.

41 Regarding the history of Celtic Studies at StFX, see Nilsen, "A Brief History," and the Department History page online: http://www2.mystfx.ca/celtic-studies/department-history.

42 Professor Linkletter now heads the StFX Celtic Department, having succeeded to the Sister Saint Veronica Chair.

43 Ó Caiside, "Agallamh," 5.

44 Statement sent by email from G. Dòmhnullach to the author, 14 July 2018.

45 Ó Caiside, "Agallamh," 5; translated by the author.

46 The Antigonish Gaelic Choir, originally founded by Sr St Veronica and which Catrìona directed during her tenure, took active part in these concerts.

47 These items were drawn from the Cape Breton Gaelic Folklore Collection, gathered by Dr John Shaw over the years 1977–82; see Nilsen, "A' Ghàidhlig," 102. The full digitization of the collection began in 2005 and resulted in the online database Gaelstream / *Sruth nan Gàidheal* (www.gaelstream.stfx.ca).

48 *American Conference for Irish Studies Newsletter*, 1.

49 Statement sent by email from C. Shannon to the author, 5 September 2018.

50 Matonis, *Celtic Studies Bibliography*, 55–60; Matonis and Rittmueller, *Celtic Studies Bibliography*, 77–82.

51 "Obituary: Ken Nilsen," 6.

52 Statement sent by email from R. Ó Maolalaigh to the author, 8 August 2018.

53 Ibid.

54 Email from Catrìona NicÌomhair Parsons to the author, 25 March 2019.

55 Peigí Ní Chlochartaigh in conversation with the author, 2 May 2018.

56 Statement sent by email from C. Shannon to the author, 5 September 2018.

57 Nilsen, "Nova Scotia Gael," 88, 90; and "Recording," 22. The Cape Breton Gaelic Club still meets on the third Sunday of each month at the Canadian American Club in Watertown.

58 Nilsen, "Recording," 27.

59 See Nilsen, "Collecting"; "Gaelic Place-Names"; "Nova Scotia Gael"; "Priest"; and "Recording." For selections of Danny's material from Ken's *Casket* column *Suas leis a' Ghàidhlig*, see Catrìona NicÌomhair Parsons's chapter in this volume.

60 Nilsen, "Recording," 26.

61 Ibid., 23. He stresses the importance of these recordings as linguistic records: "The dialects spoken by many of my Nova Scotia informants represent dialects that originated in parts of mainland Scotland where Gaelic is no longer spoken" (24).

62 Nilsen, "Nova Scotia Gael," 88.
63 Michael Connolly in conversation with the author and Claire Foley, 11 July 2018.
64 Statement sent by email from M. Connolly to the author, 8 July 2018.
65 Nilsen, "Thinking of Monday," 9.
66 Michael Connolly in conversation with the author and Claire Foley, 11 July 2018.
67 Nilsen, "'The language,'" 301.
68 Nilsen, "Collecting," 69–73; "'The language'"; and "Thinking of Monday."
69 Statement sent by email from J. Mac Donncha to the author, 24 May 2018; translated by the author.
70 Nilsen, "Collecting," 57; Eirug Davies in conversation with the author, 21 November 2018. Eirug was present when Ken recorded a man in Southborough, MA. Ken also recorded Eirug on more than one occasion.
71 Email from W. Mahon to the author, 17 August 2018; Statement sent by email from C. Mac Aogáin to the author, 17 December 2018.
72 Nilsen, "Celtic Languages," 384.
73 Nilsen, "Some Features," 103. Several collected items are included in his doctoral dissertation; see Nilsen, "Phonology," 191–290.
74 Ken referenced a story he collected in South Uist in 1970 in "Priest," 177. He referenced collecting in Berneray in the mid-80s in "Recording," 31.
75 Peter Murphy in conversation with the author, 21 August 2018.
76 Statement sent by email from C. Mac Aogáin to the author, 17 December 2018.
77 Statement sent by email from L. MacFhionghain to the author, 31 July 2018; translated by L. MacFhionghain.
78 Statement sent by email from S. McDaniel to the author, 15 June 2018; translation by S. McDaniel.
79 Nilsen, "Nova Scotia Gael," 92–3.
80 Nilsen, "A' Ghàidhlig," 103; Peter Murphy in conversation with the author, 21 August 2018. Fourteen of the interviews were conducted by Ken.
81 Statement sent by email from W. Lamb to the author, 30 June 2018.
82 Statement sent by email from S. McDaniel to the author, 15 June 2018.
83 Statement sent by email from R. Ó Maolalaigh to the author, 8 August 2018; translation by R. Ó Maolalaigh.
84 Moireach Nilsen in conversation with Catrìona NicÌomhair Parsons, 5 June 2018.
85 Ibid.
86 Statement sent by email from W. Lamb to the author, 30 June 2018.
87 Statement sent by email from S. McDaniel to the author, 15 June 2018.

88 Statement sent by email from K. Reddy to the author, 20 July 2018.
89 Statement sent by email from W. Lamb to the author, 30 June 2018.
90 Statement sent by email from V. Blankenhorn to the author, 20 June 2018.
91 Statement sent by email from L. MacFhionghain to the author, 31 July 2018; translated by L. MacFhionghain.
92 Statement sent by email from G. Dòmhnullach to the author, 14 July 2018.
93 Statement sent by email from W. Lamb to the author, 30 June 2018.
94 Statement sent by email from K. Reddy to the author, 20 July 2018. Kathleen taught Gaelic at StFX from 2013 to 2016. She is now a PhD candidate at the University of Glasgow.
95 Statement sent by email from J. Windsor to the author, 22 May 2018.
96 Statement sent by Facebook Messenger from L. Milligan Dombrowski to the author, 2 May 2018.

BIBLIOGRAPHY

American Conference for Irish Studies Newsletter (Winter 1988).

"Conference in Irish, About Irish." *Irish Literary Supplement: A Review of Irish Books* 4, no. 1 (1985): 4.

Dunn, Charles W. *Highland Settler: A Portrait of the Scottish Gael in Cape Breton and Eastern Nova Scotia*. Wreck Cove: Breton Books, [1953] 1991.

Eadrainn. Radio Teilifís Éireann, 26 July 1983.

Feiritéar, Breandán, dir. *Pádraig Feiritéar 1856–1924*. 1998.

"Irish Language Day." *Irish Literary Supplement: A Review of Irish Books* 2, no. 1 (1983), 4.

MacLeod, Bill, dir. *Na h-Eilthirich*. BBC Alba, 1999.

Matonis, Ann, ed. *A Celtic Studies Bibliography for 1983–1985*. Philadelphia: Celtic Studies Association of North America, 1987.

Matonis, Ann, and Jean Rittmueller. *A Celtic Studies Bibliography for 1986–1988*. N.p.: Celtic Studies Association of North America, 1990.

Murphy, Peter, dir. *Finisterre: Celtic Spain and France*. SeaBright Productions, 2000.

Nilsen, Kenneth E. "A Brief History of the Department of Celtic Studies, Saint Francis Xavier University, Antigonish, Nova Scotia." *Journal of Celtic Language Learning* 2 (1996): 78–80.

– "Collecting Celtic Folklore in the United States." In *Proceedings of the First North American Congress of Celtic Studies*, ed. Gordon W. MacLennan, 55–74. Ottawa: Chair of Celtic Studies, Ottawa University, 1988.

- "The Gaelic Place-Names of Mainland Nova Scotia – A Preliminary Survey." *Ainm: Bulletin of the Ulster Place-Name Society* 4 (1989–90): 220–3.
- "A' Ghàidhlig an Canada: Scottish Gaelic in Canada." In *The Edinburgh Companion to the Gaelic Language*, ed. Moray Watson and Michelle Macleod, 90–107. Edinburgh: Edinburgh University Press, 2010.
- "Celtic Languages in North America," s.v. (5) Breton. In *Celtic Culture: A Historical Encyclopedia*, ed. John T. Koch, vol. 1, 383–4. Santa Barbara: ABC-CLIO, 2006.
- "James Cullinan and Some Items of South Tipperary Seanchas." In *Atlantic Currents: Essays on Lore, Literature and Language / Sruthanna an Aigéin Thiar: Aistí ar Sheanchas, ar Litríocht agus ar Theanga*, ed. Bo Almqvist, Críostóir Mac Cárthaigh, Liam Mac Mathúna, Séamus Mac Mathúna, and Seosamh Watson, 150–62. Dublin: University College Dublin Press, 2012.
- "'The language that the strangers do not know': The Galway Gaeltacht of Portland, Maine, in the Twentieth Century." In *They Change Their Sky: The Irish in Maine*, ed. Michael C. Connolly, 297–339. Orono: University of Maine Press, 2004.
- "Living Celtic Speech: Celtic Sound Archives in North America." In *6th Annual Conference of the North American Association for Celtic Language Teachers: The Information Age, Celtic Languages, and the New Millenium* [*sic*], ed. Richard F.E. Sutcliffe and Gearóid Ó Néill, 89–94. Limerick: Department of Computer Science and Information Systems, University of Limerick, 2000.
- "The Nova Scotia Gael in Boston." *Proceedings of the Harvard Celtic Colloquium* 6 (1986): 83–100.
- "The Phonology and Morphology of the Irish of Bun a' Cruc, Sraith Salach, Co. Galway." PhD diss., Harvard University, 1975.
- "The Priest in the Gaelic Folklore of Nova Scotia." *Béaloideas* 64–5 (1996–97): 171–94.
- "Recording Scottish Gaelic Folklore and Oral History in the United States." *Scotia: Interdisciplinary Journal of Scottish Studies* 27 (2003): 22–33.
- "A Reminiscence." *Proceedings of the Harvard Celtic Colloquium* 31 (2012): 337–41.
- "Some Features of the Irish of Bun a' Cruc, Recess, Co. Galway." *Proceedings of the Harvard Celtic Colloquium* 3 (1983): 91–106.
- "Thinking of Monday: Irish Speakers of Portland, Maine." *Éire-Ireland* 25, no. 1: 3–19.

"Obituary; Ken Nilsen." *Canadian Association for Irish Studies Newsletter* 26, no. 2 (Autumn 2012): 6.

Ó Caiside, Liam. "Agallamh: Coinneach Nilsen aig Naomh FX / An Interview with Ken Nilsen of Saint Francis Xavier University." *An Naidheachd Againne: The Newsletter of An Comunn Gàidhealach, America* 23, nos. 2–3 (2006): 5.

Uí Chollatáin, Regina. "Nilsen, Ken (1947–2012)." In *Ainm.ie: An Bunachar Náisiúnta Beathaisnéisí Gaeilge*. Fiontar: Ollscoil Chathair Bhaile Átha Cliath, 2018. https://www.ainm.ie/Bio.aspx?ID=3063.

ARCHIVAL COLLECTIONS

Celtic Department Audio Collection. Widener Library, Harvard University.

United Nations Educational, Scientific and Cultural Organization (UNESCO) Archives, Paris. UNESDOC: UNESCO Digital Library. https://unesdoc.unesco.org/ark.

Irish Gaels

2

"An tan do bhidh Donchadh Ruadh a tTalamh an Éisg" (The Time That Donncha Rua Was in Newfoundland): An Eighteenth-Century Irish Poet in the New World

Pádraig Ó Liatháin

Kenneth Nilsen was, in many ways, a pioneering scholar, and although it is to the great regret of this writer that I did not make his acquaintance, many of his publications have inspired me to reassess received opinions of Irish literacy and literary activity in the eighteenth and nineteenth centuries.[1] With specific attention to the diasporic community, Professor Nilsen was gradually building an ever more convincing case for the copying and transmission of Irish-language literature in North America at this time. His efforts contributed to an emerging scholarly interest in vernacular sources that has cast new light on diasporic Irish-language communities and lent greater awareness to their participation in literary composition and transmission. Due, in part, to his work, it is becoming increasingly clear that Irish-language literature was not only brought across the Atlantic Ocean in manuscript form and later added to, but also newly begun in the New World.

I wish to build upon some of Professor Nilsen's broad findings in this field in an examination of eighteenth-century Irish poet Donncha Rua Mac Conmara's transatlantic poetry. Donncha Rua was among the more accomplished Irish-language poets of his time, and his poetry provides some of the earliest references in Irish to life in Newfoundland.[2] Nilsen himself cautiously suggested that Donncha

Rua's knowledge of the fishing outpost may have been second-hand, rather than derived from personal experience: "Ceaptar go raibh an file Donncha Rua i dTalamh an Éisc roimh 1750, má bhí sé ann riamh ach sin scéal eile" (It is thought that the poet Donncha Rua was in Newfoundland before 1750, if he was ever there, but that is another story).[3] I trace below the argument for Donncha Rua's presence in Newfoundland and present new supporting evidence. Donncha Rua's works indicate that he had a deep familiarity with the island, and manuscript sources and documented biographical accounts add further support to the theory that he resided there for a time. Indeed, it seems virtually certain that during a mid-eighteenth-century sojourn in Newfoundland, Donncha Rua composed the earliest extant pieces of Irish-language literature on the island.

DONNCHA RUA MAC CONMARA

Donncha Rua Mac Conmara (1715?–1810) was a peripatetic multilingual poet who wrote predominantly in Irish.[4] Due to the nature of life in eighteenth-century Ireland under British rule, and the officially marginalized status of the Irish language and its literature at that time, it can be difficult to piece together definitive biographies of contemporary Irish-language literary figures.[5] In this particular case, we are dependent upon gleanings from manuscripts in which Donncha Rua's poems appear and on published sources in which there are references to, and discussions of, his life and works. The former date from 1756 to ca. 1860 and the latter from the early nineteenth century to the present day.

Virtually all nineteenth- and twentieth-century commentators maintained that the poet was born in east County Clare, near Cratloe, although I can find no conclusive evidence for this. According to folklore sources stretching back into the nineteenth century, he studied in Rome to become a priest but never completed his studies.[6] I have not found any documentary evidence to confirm Donncha Rua's presence in any of the four Irish colleges in Rome, but it is possible that he studied in one of them without leaving any record behind.[7] Around half of those who attended the Irish colleges on the continent never completed their degrees, and probably never intended to do so. They would have attended because it was the only opportunity for higher learning available to Irish Catholics.[8] Indeed, it seems very possible that Donncha Rua received a university education, as a close reading of his work suggests he possessed a deeper knowledge of the

Classics than most of his contemporaries. For example, the second half of the narrative in "Eachtra Ghiolla an Amaráin" (The Adventure of a Luckless Fellow) is heavily informed by book 6 of Virgil's *Aeneid*.[9] Donncha Rua also later wrote an elegy in Latin as a mark of respect for his friend and fellow poet Tadhg Gaelach Ó Súilleabháin, who died in 1795.[10] He would have been around eighty years old at the time. That his own death occurred in 1810 is clear from an obituary notice in the *Freeman's Journal* of 5 November of that year, which states that he died "in the 95th year of his age" at Newtown, near Kilmacthomas, Co. Waterford.[11]

The manuscript sources present clear evidence of his presence in the vicinity of County Waterford from 1756 until his death, during which time he composed elegies for local figures, and satires, as well as a pass (a testament of learning) for a scholar under his tutelage to move freely around the province.[12] The only other location expressly emphasized in his work, or in scribal copies of his work, is Newfoundland, where folk memory holds that he worked and resided for a time.[13]

In 1933, Risteard Ó Foghludha, the most recent editor of Donncha Rua's poetry, posited that he was in Newfoundland sometime between 1745 and 1755.[14] The manuscript sources appear to support the notion that Donncha Rua went abroad during this period: there is no evidence of him in Ireland between the years 1745, the date of composition of the "Eachtra,"[15] and 1756, when we find the earliest version of his poem "As I Was Walking One Evening Fair," copied in Cork.[16] In addition to the conspicuous gap in manuscript evidence, local knowledge contained within Donncha Rua's poems and recently unearthed documentary evidence strongly suggest that Ó Foghludha's intuition was accurate: Donncha Rua did spend time in Newfoundland in the mid-eighteenth century.

POETRY WITH CONNECTIONS TO NEWFOUNDLAND

Donncha Rua is the earliest known author to refer to Newfoundland by its Irish name, Talamh an Éisc (the fishing grounds), a toponym in use by speakers of the language in Ireland to this day.[17] Three of his poems evidence clear connections with Talamh an Éisc, and they can all be read in extant eighteenth-century manuscripts: "Bánchnoic Éireann" (The Fair Hills of Ireland), the macaronic composition "As I Was Walking One Evening Fair," and "Fáilte Aodh Uí Cheallaigh go Talamh an Éisc" (Hugh O'Kelly's Welcome to Newfoundland). One further poem, the mock epic "Eachtra Ghiolla an Amaráin," describes a transatlantic voyage to the New World, but there is no mention within the poem of Newfoundland; rather, the generic *Sasana Nua* (New England / America) is the stated destination.[18] Even so, a possible connection can be traced in the name of the captain of the ship, Captain Allen, for we know that New Ross merchant James Napper owned an independent commercial boat whose captain in 1742 – a man called Allen – requested permission to sail to St John's.[19] However, this tenuous link does not merit further consideration, and I will not dwell on "Eachtra Ghiolla an Amaráin" here. "As I Was Walking One Evening Fair" and "Fáilte Aodh Uí Cheallaigh go Talamh an Éisc," on the other hand, contain depictions of life in Newfoundland, and "Bánchnoic Éireann" is expressly linked with Newfoundland by the scribe who copied one of its earliest versions, and who was personally acquainted with the poet.

"As I Was Walking One Evening Fair"

The earliest attestation of this macaronic composition is in a manuscript written in 1756.[20] It was copied by an anonymous scribe in Cloyne, County Cork. A port village on the southeastern coast of Ireland, Cloyne had strong connections with Newfoundland in the eighteenth century. This makes it probable that the poem – which narrates an episode on the island – was composed in Newfoundland and, due to its popularity, quickly made its way to Ireland, where it spread. I include Ó Foghludha's version of the text below: [21]

As I was walking one evening fair
Is me go déidheanach i mBaile Sheáin,
  [And I lately in St John's,]
I met a gang of English blades
Is iad dá dtraochadh age n-a námhaid;
  [Being exhausted by their enemies;]
I sang and drank so brisk and airy
With those courageous men of war –
'S gur bhinne liom Sasanaigh ag rith le foiréigean
'S gurbh iad clanna Gaedhal bocht a bhuaidh an lá.
  [And sweeter to me would be Englishmen running swiftly / and the unfortunate Gael having won the day.]

I spent my money by being freakish
Drinking, raking and playing cards –
Cé ná raibh airgead agam ná gréithre
Ná rud san tsaoghal acht nídh gan áird;
[Although I had neither money nor possessions / or anything at all in the world;]
Then I turned a jolly sailor,
By work and labour I lived abroad,
Is bíodh ar mh'fhallaingse gur mór an bhréag san
Is gur beag den tsaothar a thuit lem láimh.
[And upon my word that's a great lie / for little is the amount of work that I did.]

Newfoundland is a wide plantation,
'Twill be my station before I die;
Mo chrádh go mb' fhearra dham bheith in Éirinn
Ag díol gártaeirí ná ag dul fén gcoill:
[Alas but I would rather be in Ireland / selling garters or wandering the woods:]
Here you may find a virtuous lady,
A smiling fair one to please the eye –
An paca straipeanna is measa tréithe
'S go mbeiread féin ar bheith as a radharc.
[The worst pack of harlots / and may I be far from the sight of them.]

Come, drink a health, boys, to Royal George,
Our chief commander - nár órduigh Críost [not ordered by Christ],
Is aitchimís ar Mhuire Mháthair
É féin 's a ghárdaí do leagadh síos;
[And we appeal to mother Mary / to strike down him and his guards;]
We'll fear no cannon nor loud alarms
While noble George shall be our guide –
'S a Chríost go bhfaiceadsa iad dá gcárnadh
Ag an mac so ar fán uainn ag dul don bhFraingc.
[And by Christ may I see them being routed / by the exiled son going to France.][22]

The poem was quite evidently composed with both a bilingual, and simultaneously, a monolingual audience in mind, the bilingual audience being speakers of Irish and English, and the monolingual audience being speakers of English only. In fact, the meanings conveyed are quite different in both languages throughout the poem. In the first stanza, we are told that the speaker was drinking late into the night in *Baile Sheáin*, or St John's, the capital of Newfoundland. Partaking in the revelry were Englishmen – "blades" and "courageous men of war" – whose company the English-language passage suggests he was happy to share: "I sang and drank so brisk and airy"; however, in the Irish language he says he would rather the English soldiers be routed by the Gael. This seems mere wishful thinking designed to amuse the Irish-speaking audience, but it chimes with the Jacobite sentiments of the final stanza.

The second stanza is more concerned with the daily life of the speaker, although the tone is ironic and mirthful, designed to amuse the audience. This includes descriptions of gambling and working, although in reality his motto seems more akin to "play hard and hardly work." The speaker implies that he has a tendency to throw away his money rather fecklessly, and in the Irish language he pokes fun at his own laziness and reluctance to do the hard physical work that a demanding, financially rewarding stay on the island would require. Again, in English, he contradicts himself, implying that although he was once a lost soul, coming to Newfoundland and engaging in honest work made him a happier man. The Irish-speaking bilingual listener understands, of course, that this is not true.

The remaining two stanzas are particularly relevant, as they refer specifically to two matters: Newfoundland itself, and British rule of the island. In this and other poems, Donncha Rua is far from complimentary about local life. The narrator would rather be in Ireland, no matter what that might entail. Neither work nor play in Newfoundland seems to satisfy him. He is also far from laudatory when speaking about the women of St John's: "Here you may find a virtuous lady, / A smiling fair one to please your eye – / An paca straipeanna is measa tréithe / 'S go mbeiread féin a bheith as a radharc" (The worst pack of harlots and may I be far from the sight of them). This sort of bawdy talk seems particularly suitable to a tavern, where men would gather away from the presence of women, but all the same, it suggests an added layer of dissatisfaction with the speaker's current location.

Though not recognized as an official British colony until 1824, the Treaty of Utrecht in 1713 ensured that the island was in the possession of Britain.[23] In the final stanza, the speaker pretends to venerate King George III, while in reality, he is sorely lamenting the British monarch's presence on the throne, and he prays for the king's downfall. "Royal George" is not a ruler of the true faith – "nár orduigh Críost" (not ordered by Christ) – and the speaker wishes for a Jacobite rebellion led by Bonny Prince Charlie to overthrow him: "'S a Chríost go bhfaiceadsa iad dá gcárnadh / Ag an mac so ar fán uainn ag dul don bhFraingc" (And by Christ may I see them being routed / by the exiled son going to France). Notwithstanding the failures of the Jacobite uprisings, there is no sense, in this or other poems, of Donncha Rua having lost hope for a change in British rule and a return to a Catholic monarch. Ultimately, as in works such as "Eachtra Ghiolla an Amaráin" and "Bánchnoic Éireann," at the poem's end we see a Jacobite sting in the tail, as if all roads lead to this inevitable conclusion. The message is subtly yet strongly delivered: intended as words to the wise (i.e., the Irish-speaking audience), the Jacobite sentiment is hidden behind the poet's use of English, so as not to draw unwanted attention upon the messenger. In fact, the message becomes more powerful by the juxtaposition of two culturally and politically opposed languages and the contradictory sentiments they convey. This poem is subversive, as is much of Donncha Rua's verse, which should not be forgotten even while we appreciate the insouciant surface humour that somewhat obscures the ironic delivery.

"As I Was Walking One Evening Fair" is perhaps the best known Irish-language macaronic work, certainly in the eighteenth century,[24] and it is difficult not to be cognizant of its potential value to the Irish in Newfoundland at this time. Although most of the Irish fishermen who went abroad would have been native speakers of Irish, the spread and importance of the English language in Ireland was growing, and we can assume a fair amount of bi- or multi-lingualism. These men, although they had more individual freedom than back in Ireland, were still migrating to an island under British rule. A literary work like this, which pokes fun at the status quo within the safe space of a language that those in authority would not have understood, seems highly appropriate to the social and geographical context of mid-eighteenth-century Newfoundland. As noted above, the location and date of the earliest copy also accord well with the theory that it was composed there. While these factors do not conclusively prove that Donncha Rua was in Newfoundland, they support the much stronger internal evidence of the next poem.

"Fáilte Aodh Uí Cheallaigh go Talamh an Éisc"

The earliest extant copy of "Fáilte Aodh Uí Cheallaigh go Talamh an Éisc" dates from 1786.[25]

Of all Donncha Rua's works, this poem exhibits the greatest knowledge of daily life in Newfoundland. I give here the first verse with translation:

Ar maidin indé bhí camadán scéil
Ag gaige gan chéill dá leathadh idir mhná
Go bhfeaca sé Aodh Ó Ceallaigh go tréith
I dTalamh an Éisc 'n-a mhangaire smáil,
Lag marbh sa *stage* gan tapa ina ghéig
Ó tharraint an éisc is an tsalainn de ghnáth
Is Sasanach méith dá lascadh ar a thaobh
Ó bhaitheas go féar is do b'aindeis mar phágha.[26]

Yesterday morning there was a crooked story
By a foolish fop, being circulated amongst the women,
That he saw Aodh Ó Ceallaigh [Hugh O'Kelly]
In Newfoundland, a weak and filthy pedlar,
Half dead on the stage without strength in his limbs
From dragging fish and salt
And a fat Englishman whipping him
Up and down, and [moreover] his pay was pathetic.

Having spent time in Newfoundland with the eponymous Aodh Ó Ceallaigh, the speaker relates hearing idle gossip in Ireland denigrating Ó Ceallaigh's character and work ethic, and he feels honour-bound to defend him. The speaker goes on to expound Ó Ceallaigh's best traits: he is a fine man to have by your side in a faction fight, good company to his friends, and generous in the buying of drink. He is a willing, honest labourer, and heroic and hardy at sea: "Is tapa do théigheann i *shallop* de léim / Is na flaithis ag séide seachtmhain nó lá, … / A ghlaca ba tréan ar *halyard* nó ar *mainsail*" (He swiftly goes into a shallop with a leap / While the heavens are blowing a week or a day, … / His hands were strong on halyard or mainsail).[27] Moreover, Ó

Ceallaigh is a man of action who would take no backward step in the presence of any Englishman (although this is not a political poem by any stretch of the imagination): "Do chnagfadh sa tsúil éan-tSasanach reamhar / Is rachadh le fonn i sparainn le namhaid" (He would smite in the eye any fat Englishman / And would stand his ground against any enemy).[28] He is portrayed as a true man of the people and is even credited with having fought for better wages for the migratory fishermen: "do neartaigh sé an *wage* i dTalamh an Éisc" (he strengthened the wage in Newfoundland).[29]

While written in Irish, the poem uses strategically placed English words. Mostly these are seafaring terms. Some are well-known, such as *mainsail* and *halyard*, while others are less so, such as *shallop*, which is defined in *The Newfoundland Dictionary of English* as "a large, partly decked boat, rigged with lug sails and used in the cod and seal fisheries," and *seine*, which is "a large vertical net placed in position around a school of fish, the 'foots' drawn together to form a bag, and hauled at sea or in shallow water near the shore."[30] We also find words in the poem that refer specifically to the drying and salting of cod in Newfoundland. For instance, the *stage* referenced in line 5 is "an elevated platform on the shore with working tables, sheds, etc. where fish are landed and processed for salting and drying, and fishing gear and supplies are stored."[31] Elsewhere, Donncha Rua refers to a *flake*, which is "a platform built on poles and spread with boughs for drying codfish on the foreshore": "An té chasfadh le hAodh bheith ag tarraint an tséine, / Nó i mbarra na fléice..." (He who would come across Aodh pulling the seine, / Or at the top of the flake ...).[32] It is doubtful that these words would have been widely understood in Ireland at the time; I have found no sources to indicate that they were in use in contemporary Hiberno-English.[33]

It is difficult to postulate any reason for Donncha Rua to have composed this poem in defence of Ó Ceallaigh had he not known him personally and spent time in his company. If so, it would seem that the poem was composed after Donncha Rua had returned to live in Ireland, and the date of the earliest extant copy accords with this supposition. Moreover, the poem displays a familiarity with, and a practical knowledge of, aspects of life and work on the island of Newfoundland. Significantly, this composition also contains the earliest written examples of the toponym Talamh an Éisc that I have found; it appears in five of the six verses. Although Talamh an Éisc was gradually accepted as the Irish-language toponym for Newfoundland, there were differing versions throughout the early to mid-eighteenth century in Irish-language literature. It is notable that the version Donncha Rua employed was also that which ultimately prevailed in common usage from the middle of the eighteenth century until the present day. As I have suggested elsewhere, this usage further indicates his familiarity with the island.[34] The internal evidence of "Fáilte Aodh Uí Cheallaigh go Talamh an Éisc" thus strongly suggests that Donncha Rua spent time in Newfoundland.

"Bánchnoic Éireann"

This poem is Donncha Rua's best known and most popular work, and it is of greater literary quality than either "As I Was Walking One Evening Fair" or "Fáilte Aodh Uí Cheallaigh go Talamh an Éisc" (although their documentary value is unquestionable). The earliest known copy of "Bánchnoic Éireann" was transcribed in 1786 by the scribe and schoolmaster Labhrás Ó Fuartháin.[35] One of the subsequent earliest copies is preserved in a manuscript in the University of Manchester's John Rylands Library, which was written around 1821 by Tomás Ó hAthairne. Only recently discovered, this copy is particularly remarkable for the scribal note it contains at the foot of the page: "an tan do bhidh Donchadh ruadh a ttalamh an éisg do canadh an laoi-si leis" (the time that Donncha Rua was in Newfoundland he composed this work).[36] The same manuscript contains a second copy of "Bánchnoic Éireann" with this scribal note: "slán beannocht dhonchadh mhacnamara chuin na h-éireann an uair do bhí se a n-oilean an eisg" (Donncha Mac Conmara's farewell blessing to Ireland when he was in Newfoundland).[37] These written sources are the first to explicitly state that Donncha Rua lived and composed poetry in Newfoundland. They represent contemporary evidence heretofore unknown to scholars of the poet's sojourn on the island and of the history of Irish language and settlement there.

Ó hAthairne was a poet, teacher, and scholar of Irish and Latin who copied the manuscript in Stradbally, Co. Waterford, and who knew Donncha Rua personally.[38] Seán Pléimeann (John Fleming) (1814–1896), who gathered and collated local information on Donncha Rua in the nineteenth century, comments on the poet's relationship with Ó hAthairne: "During the last years of his life he [Donnchadh Ruadh] was a constant visitor at the house of the Clancys, gentlemen farmers, in old Kill, in the parish of Kill, county of Waterford. At this house too, Thomas Harney [Tomás Ó hAthairne], of Stradbally, then a youth, was also a visitor."[39] Glossing a work by Ó hAthairne in a manuscript, the prominent nineteenth-century Irish scholar Standish Hayes O'Grady also explains that both Donncha Rua and Ó hAthairne availed of the generosity of Rody Clancy as a literary patron: "These verses are addressed by Harney to Rody Clancy, a strong farmer, who used to extend great hospitality to the rhymers of the country. Donnchadh Ruadh lived with him some time, and afterwards Harney [lived with him]."[40] Ó hAthairne therefore ought to be considered a reliable authority on the subject of Donncha Rua's presence in Newfoundland.

With this in mind, we can examine the portrayal of Newfoundland in the poem, which opens thus:

> Beir beannacht óm chroidhe go Tír na hÉireann,
> Bánchnuic Éireann Óighe,
> Chum a mhaireann de shíolrach Ír is Éibhir
> Ar bhánchnuic Éireann Óighe
> An áit úd nur bh'aoibhinn binnghuth éan
> Mar shámhchruit chaoin ag caoine Gaedhal,
> Mo chás a bheith míle míle i gcéin
> Ó bhánchnuic Éireann Óighe.[41]

> Take a blessing from my heart to Ireland,
> The fair hills of pure Ireland,
> where the descendants of Ír and Éibhear live
> on the fair hills of pure Ireland,
> the place where the sweet voices of the birds would be beautiful
> As a soothing harp lamenting the Gael,
> Woe is me to be one thousand miles away
> From the fair hills of pure Ireland.

Here the speaker wistfully expresses his homesickness while in an environment of lesser beauty "míle míle i gcéin / ó bhánchnuic Éireann Óighe" (a thousand miles from the fair hills of pure Ireland). The overriding theme throughout is one of exile, and the underlying sentiments are those of loneliness and dissatisfaction at his current plight.

The speaker then describes his far-off home as a land of milk and honey: "a cuid meala agus uachtar gluaisid 'n-a slaoda" (her honey and cream flow in swathes).[42] Her soil is fertile (echoing the older bardic theme of abundance as an outcome of the successful marriage of the ruler to his land[43]), and in a nod to his more familiar environs, he praises, in several versions of the text, the river Suir (Ireland's third longest river, which flows into the sea at Waterford) for its vigorous flow: "uisce na Siúire ag brúcht 'na shlóigh" (the waters of the Suir flowing vigorously).[44] This portrayal of Ireland contrasts pointedly with the depiction of Newfoundland. Ireland is a place in which even the worst mountain is more beautiful than the landscape now surrounding him: "is fearr ná an tírse díogh gach sléibhe."[45] The comparative lack of livestock on the island is also mentioned: "ní fhaicim a gcóraid ag gabhóil san taobh so / … ní fhaicim a mbólacht dá treór chum féir ann" (I do not see herds in these parts / … I do not see cattle driven to pasture).[46] This is a historically accurate assessment, as the soil was relatively poor and livestock were scarce; making a living in Newfoundland could not be achieved by means of extensive farming, but rather by the prosecution of the fishing industry.[47] For many Irish people who migrated from the southeast of Ireland, Donncha Rua included, the lack of arable land would have represented a big change. Taking Donncha Rua's temporary residence in Newfoundland as now firmly established, the harsh contrast with and poignant longing for the homeland in "Bánchnoic Éireann" leave us with little wonder that he returned to Ireland.

The popularity of "Bánchnoic Éireann" has stood the test of time, perhaps due to the universality of its patriotic sentiment and exilic narrative. Set to an air of captivating and majestic beauty, it seems to have resonated with audiences and readerships from the beginning to the present day, appearing in multiple manuscripts and literary anthologies, and on traditional music recordings.[48] Unbeknownst to the majority of people presently familiar with the poem, however, is the fact that it was almost certainly composed in a different land, albeit with its gaze firmly fixed across the Atlantic.

CONCLUSION

There is little cause to doubt that Donncha Rua Mac Conmara spent time in Newfoundland and composed poetry there; his position as the earliest recorded Irish-language author in Newfoundland is now secure. The harsh climate and challenging living conditions in early Newfoundland settlements were not conducive to the preservation of paper, and the earliest extant copies of Donncha Rua's Newfoundland poems appear in manuscripts written in Ireland. Remarkably, however, two manuscripts written in Newfoundland in the eighteenth and nineteenth centuries, which Professor Nilsen described in a posthumously published essay, have survived to this day.[49] These offer indisputable evidence of the existence and continuity of an Irish scribal tradition in Newfoundland from the mid-eighteenth to the mid-nineteenth century at least. One can only imagine what has been lost, and hope that neglected or yet undiscovered scribal notes may shed further light.

Considered in the context of the broader Irish manuscript tradition, the production of Irish-language literature in Newfoundland, although perhaps little-known, fits neatly into the wider narrative attested by the presence of eighteenth- and nineteenth-century Irish-language manuscripts in North American libraries today.[50] Professor Nilsen not only recognized the importance of these North American manuscripts, he also rediscovered and catalogued a number of them.[51] In so doing, he brought to light several examples of diasporic Irish-language literacy in the United States and eastern Canada. From his and others' recent work, it is becoming ever clearer that the transatlantic trajectory of Donncha Rua and his texts was not *sui generis*; rather, the migratory paths between Ireland, Europe, and North America were well frequented, and the Irish language and its literature travelled far and wide. In firmly establishing Donncha Rua Mac Conmara's position as a Newfoundland poet, *tá súil agam, sa mhéid seo, go bhfuil cloch curtha agam lena charn* (I hope, in this contribution, to have added a stone to Ken's cairn).

NOTES

I am very grateful to the editors for their valuable suggestions during the editing process. I am also grateful to the Dublin City University Faculty of Humanities Conference Travel Scheme, which allowed me to travel to Newfoundland in May 2018, and to the Faculty Journal Publication Scheme, which allowed me to undertake research in the Burns Library, Boston College, in July 2018.

1 I am thinking particularly of articles relating to the spoken and literary presence of the Irish language from New England to Newfoundland. I will not concern myself here with evidence of the spoken language. See Nilsen, "Three Irish Manuscripts," "Mícheál Ó Broin," and "An Ghaeilge."

2 Donncha Rua Mac Conmara was during his lifetime, and remains, primarily known as Donncha Rua (Red-Haired Donncha]. This was a privilege afforded to well-known poets in the tradition. The best known examples

from his own era are Seán Clárach (Mac Domhnaill) (1691–1754), Tadhg Gaelach (Ó Súilleabháin) (1715–95), and Eoghan Rua (Ó Súilleabháin) (1748–84).

3 Nilsen, "An Ghaeilge," 262–3.

4 Ó Flannghaile, *Eachtra*; Ó Foghludha, *Donnchadh Ruadh*; Ó Liatháin, *Eachtra*, 9–23.

5 Ó Cuív, "Irish Language," 390–1.

6 Ní Chrotaigh, "Beatha Donnchadh Ruadh," 141–2.

7 I have examined Fenning, "Clerical Recruitment," "Documents," and "Irishmen"; Hanly, "Records"; Kearns, "Archives"; Martin, "Archives"; Millett, "Archives."

8 O'Connor and Lyons, *Strangers to Citizens*, 48–52.

9 For further consideration of the links between "Eachtra Ghiolla an Amaráin" and the *Aeneid*, see Ó Liatháin, *Eachtra*; "Roinnt Tagairtí do Virgil," 178–95; and "Dialogues," 229–43. For a consideration of Donncha Rua and Classical learning in eighteenth-century Irish-language literature generally, see O'Higgins, *Irish Classical Self*, 53–98.

10 A copy of this elegy can be found in an early nineteenth-century manuscript, JRL Gaelic Ms. 134, which has not been catalogued. My thanks are due to Dr Úna Nic Éinrí who provided me with a photocopy of Donncha Rua's poetry from this manuscript.

11 "Irish Bard," *Freeman's Journal*, 5 November 1810, 4.

12 Discussions of "Pas Risteard Rábach Mac Gearailt," "Eachtra Shéamais Grae," and other compositions can be found in Ó Foghludha, *Donnchadh Ruadh*, 15–18. For further information on sources see Ó Liatháin, *Eachtra*, 9–23.

13 See, for example, Ó Flannghaile, *Eachtra*, 9–10; and Ó hEochaidh, "Mac Uí Dhomhnaill," 98.

14 Ó Foghludha, *Donnchadh Ruadh*, 15.

15 See, for example, JHL Ms. De hÍde 18, 72.

16 See RIA Ms. 23 A 16, 14–16.

17 For discussions of the origins, meaning, and usage of this toponym, see Ó Liatháin, "Roinnt Tagairtí do Thalamh an Éisc."

18 Ó Liatháin, *Eachtra*, 41.

19 Ó hEadhra, *Na Gaeil*, 189. While "Eachtra Ghiolla an Amaráin" does not concern Newfoundland, it is particularly interesting from a historical and socio-economic point of view for its depiction of the preparations involved and the hardships endured on a transatlantic voyage; indeed, it is the best eighteenth-century account of such matters in the Irish language, notwithstanding its fictive qualities. (The poem is an unusual take on an *aisling* [a

political vision poem], and not meant to be taken literally; it describes a voyage to the Underworld in the manner of Virgil's Aeneas.) Other voyage accounts include, in English, James Orr's "Song Composed on the Banks of Newfoundland" and "The Passengers" (see Carpenter, "From Ulster," 65–74); and Thomas, *Newfoundland Journal*. For a French account, see Conan and Cabon, *Avanturio*.

20 RIA Ms. 23 A 16, 14–16.
21 Ó Foghludha, *Donnchadh Ruadh*, 36. There are no critical editions of these Newfoundland poems in modern scholarship. I intend to rectify this in the near future.
22 Ibid., 36. All translations of the poetry in this chapter are my own.
23 O'Flaherty, *Old Newfoundland*, 60–1, 138–41.
24 Mac Mathúna, *Béarla*, 194–5. For examples of similar works from the eighteenth and nineteenth centuries, see Ó Muirithe, *An tAmhrán Macarónach*.
25 JHL Ms. De hÍde 18, 184–5.
26 Ó Foghludha, *Donnchadh Ruadh*, 37.
27 Ibid., 38.
28 Ibid., 38.
29 Ibid., 38. See Kirwin, Widdowson, and Story, *Dictionary*, s.v. "wage": "comb wages man, one indentured or engaged on wages for a period in the fishery."
30 Ibid., s.vv. "shallop" and "seine."
31 Ibid., *Dictionary*, s.v. "stage."
32 Ó Foghludha, *Donnchadh Ruadh*, 38. Kirwin, Widdowson, and Story, *Dictionary*, s.v. "flake."
33 Dolan, *Dictionary*.
34 Ó Liatháin, "Roinnt Tagairtí do Thalamh an Éisc."
35 JHL Ms. De hÍde 18, 66–7. Little is known of Ó Fuartháin apart from his manuscripts. For an account of these, see Ó Súilleabháin, "Scríobhaithe," 281–2.
36 JRL Gaelic Ms. 134.
37 Ibid.
38 For a discussion of Ó hAthairne and his works, see Ó Macháin, "Filíocht Athairneach I," 152–64; and "Filíocht Athairneach II," 165–75.
39 Quoted in Ó Macháin, "Filíocht Athairneach I," 155.
40 Cambridge University Library Ms. Additional 6558, quoted in de Brún and Herbert, *Catalogue*, 76.
41 Ó Foghludha, *Donnchadh Ruadh*, 31.
42 Ibid., 32.
43 Breatnach, "Lady," 321–6.

44 Ó Flannghaile, *Eachtra*, 78. Ó Foghludha's edition does not contain this line, but it is in the earliest manuscript version (JHL Ms. De hÍde 18, 67).
45 Ó Foghludha, *Donnchadh Ruadh*, 31.
46 Ibid.
47 Mannion, *Irish Settlements*, 30–2.
48 I am currently working on an edition of the text. For manuscript copies see, for example, JHL Ms. De hÍde 18, 66–7, and JRL Gaelic Ms. 134; for anthologies, see e.g. Ó hAodha, *Óir-chiste*, 28–33; and Breathnach, *Fíon*, 110–11; and for contemporary traditional music recordings, see e.g. Skara Brae, *Skara Brae*; and de Búrca, *Sioscadh na Gaoithe*.
49 Nilsen "An Ghaeilge," 266–9. The manuscripts are Macarten's Seminary Ms. B, transcribed by William Hawe, and the Michael Herbert Ms. in the Burns Library, Boston College. Éamonn Ó hÓgáin earlier discussed Ms. B in "Scríobhaithe," 412, 687.
50 There remain Irish-language manuscripts in North American repositories that have yet to be catalogued. For a discussion of those that have been catalogued, and to gain an insight into their origins, transmission, and procurement, see e.g. Buttimer, "Catalogue," 105–23; Buttimer, *Catalogue*, 7–15; Mahon, *Catalogue*, 1–15.
51 Nilsen, "Three Irish Manuscripts," "Mícheál Ó Broin," and "An Ghaeilge."

BIBLIOGRAPHY

Breathnach, Mícheál, ed. *Fíon na Filidheachta*, 2nd ed. Baile Átha Cliath: Comhlucht Oideachais na hÉireann, 1947.

Breatnach, R.A. "The Lady and the King: A Theme of Irish Literature." *Studies: An Irish Quarterly Review* 42, no. 167 (1953): 321–6.

Buttimer, Neil. "A Catalogue of Irish Manuscripts in the Boston Athenaeum." In *Folia Gadelica*, ed. Pádraig de Brún, Seán Ó Coileáin, and Pádraig Ó Riain, 105–23. Cork: Cork University Press, 1983.

– *Catalogue of Irish Manuscripts in the University of Wisconsin–Madison*. Dublin: Dublin Institute for Advanced Studies, 1989.

Carpenter, Andrew. "From Ulster to Delaware: Two Poems by James Orr about an Eighteenth-Century Emigrant Voyage." In *New Perspectives on the Irish Diaspora*, ed. Charles Fanning, 65–74. Carbondale: Southern Illinois University Press, 2000.

Conan, Jean, and Bernard Cabon. *Avanturio Ar Citoien Jean Conan a Voengamb. Les Adventures Du Citoyen Jean Conan De Guigamp*. Montroules: Editions Skol Vreizh, 1990.

De Brún, Pádraig, and Máire Herbert. *Catalogue of Irish Manuscripts in Cambridge Libraries*. Cambridge: Cambridge University Press, 1986.

Dolan, Terence. *Dictionary of Hiberno-English*. Dublin: Gill and Macmillan, 2014.

Fenning, Hugh. "Clerical Recruitment 1735–1783, Documents from Windsor and Rome." *Archivium Hibernicum* 30 (1972): 1–20.

– "Documents of Irish Interest in the *Fondo Missioni* of the Irish Archives." *Archivium Hibernicum* 49 (1995): 3–47.

– "Irishmen Ordained at Rome, 1698–1759." *Archivium Hibernicum* 50 (1996): 29–49.

Hanly, Rev. John. "Records of the Irish College, Rome, under Jesuit Administration." *Archivium Hibernicum* 27 (1964): 13–75.

Kearns, Rev. Conleth O.P. "Archives of the Irish Dominican College, San Clemente, Rome." *Archivium Hibernicum* 18 (1955): 145–9.

Kirwin, William J., J.D.A. Widdowson, and G.M. Story. *Dictionary of Newfoundland English*. Toronto: University of Toronto Press, 2006.

Mac Mathúna, Liam. *Béarla sa Ghaeilge: Cabhair Choigríche: An Códmheascadh Gaeilge / Béarla i Litríocht Na Gaeilge 1600–1900*. Baile Átha Cliath: An Clóchomhar, 2007.

Mahon, William. *Catalogue of Irish Manuscripts in Villanova University, Pennsylvania*. Dublin: Dublin Institute for Advanced Studies, 2007.

Mannion, John J. *Irish Settlements in Eastern Canada: A Study of Cultural Transfer and Adaptation*. Toronto: University of Toronto Press, 1974.

Martin, F.X. "Archives of the Irish Augustinians, Rome: A Summary Report." *Archivium Hibernicum* 18 (1955): 157–63.

Millett, Benignus, O.F.M. "The Archives of St Isidore's College, Rome." *Archivium Hibernicum* 40 (1985): 1–12.

Ní Chrotaigh, Eibhlín. "Beatha Donnchadh Ruadh Mac Conmara (Téacs de Pháipéar a Léigh Eibhlín Ní Chrotaigh do Connradh na Gaeluinn i bPortláirge Oichdhe [*sic*] Dé Luain an 19adh Lá de Mhárta 1928)." *Decies* 59 (2003): 141–50.

Nilsen, Kenneth E. "An Ghaeilge in Oirthear Cheanada." In *Séimhfhear Suairc: Aistí in Ómós don Ollamh Breandán Ó Conchúir*, ed. Seán Ó Coileáin, Liam P. Ó Murchú, and Pádraigín Riggs, 262–79. An Daingean: An Sagart, 2013.

– "Mícheál Ó Broin agus Lámhscríbhinní Gaeilge Ollscoil Wisconsin." *Celtica* 22 (1991): 112–18.

– "Three Irish Manuscripts in Massachusetts." *Proceedings of the Harvard Celtic Colloquium* 5 (1985): 1–21.

O'Connor, Thomas, and Mary Ann Lyons, *Strangers to Citizens: The Irish in Europe, 1600–1800*. Dublin: National Library of Ireland, 1998.

Ó Cuív, Brian. "Irish Language and Literature." In *A New History of Ireland*, vol. 4: *Eighteenth-Century Ireland, 1691–1800*, ed. T.W. Moody and W.E. Vaughan, 374-423. Oxford: Clarendon Press, 1986.

O'Flaherty, Patrick. *Old Newfoundland: A History to 1843*. St John's: Long Beach Press, 1999.

Ó Flannghaile, Tomás. *Eachtra Ghiolla an Amaráin, or The Adventures of a Luckless Fellow and Other Poems*. Dublin: Sealy, Bryers and Walker, 1897.

Ó Foghludha, Risteard. *Donnchadh Ruadh Mac Conmara 1715–1810*. Baile Átha Cliath: Oifig Díolta Foillseacháin Rialtais, 1933.

Ó hAodha, Séamas. *Óir-chiste*. Baile Átha Cliath: Comhlucht Oideachais na hÉireann, 1922.

Ó hEadhra, Aodhán. *Na Gaeil i dTalamh an Éisc*. Baile Átha Cliath: Coiscéim, 1998.

Ó hEochaidh, Seán. "Mac Uí Dhomhnaill." *Béaloideas* 27 (1959): 74–98.

O'Higgins, Laurie. *The Irish Classical Self: Poets and Poor Scholars in the Eighteenth and Nineteenth Centuries*. Oxford: Oxford University Press, 2017.

Ó hÓgáin, Éamonn. "Scríobhaithe Lámhscríbhinní Gaeilge i gCill Chainnigh 1700–1870." In *Kilkenny: History and Society*, ed. William Nolan and Kevin Whelan, 405–36. Dublin: Geography Publications, 1990.

Ó Liatháin, Pádraig. "Dialogues des Morts: A Subversive Representation of Hades in an Eighteenth Century Manuscript." In *Non-Violent Resistance: Counter-Discourse in Irish Culture*, ed. Agnes Maillot and Jennifer Bruen, 229–43. Oxford: Peter Lang, 2018.

– *Eachtra Ghiolla an Amaráin*. Indreabhán: Cló Iar-Chonnacht, 2018.

– "Roinnt Tagairtí do Thalamh an Éisc i Litríocht na Gaeilge ón Ochtú agus ón Naoú Céad Déag." *Éigse* 38 (2013): 94–103.

– "Roinnt Tagairtí do Virgil i Litríocht na Gaeilge." In *Saoi na Féile: Aistí ar Litríocht Ghaeilge an Ochtú hAois Déag in Onóir do Úna Nic Éinrí*, ed. Stephen Newman, Breandán Ó Cróinín, and Liam Ó Paircín, 178–95. Baile Átha Cliath: Coiscéim, 2018.

Ó Macháin, Pádraig. "Filíocht Athairneach I." *An Linn Bhuí* 7 (2003): 152–64.

– "Filíocht Athairneach II." *An Linn Bhuí* 8 (2004): 165–75.

Ó Muirithe, Diarmaid. *An tAmhrán Macarónach*. Baile Átha Cliath: An Clóchomhar, 1980.

Ó Súilleabháin, Eoghan. "Scríobhaithe Phort Láirge 1700–1900." In *Water-*

ford: History and Society, ed. William Nolan and Thomas P. Power, 265–308. Dublin: Geography Publications, 1992.

Thomas, Aaron. *The Newfoundland Journal of Aaron Thomas, Able Seaman in H.M.S. Boston: A Journal Written during a Voyage from England to Newfoundland and from Newfoundland to England in the Years 1794 and 1795, Addressed to a Friend*, ed. Jean M. Murray. London: Longmans, 1968.

Wright, Joseph. *The English Dialect Dictionary, Being the Complete Vocabulary of All Dialect Words Still in Use, or Known to Have Been in Use during the Last Two Hundred Years*. Oxford: Oxford University Press, 1961.

MUSIC RECORDINGS

Skara Brae. *Skara Brae*. Dublin: Gael Linn, 1971.

De Búrca, Nan Tom Taimín. *Sioscadh na Gaoithe / The Whispering Wind*. Conamara: Cló Iar-Chonnacht, 2014.

ARCHIVAL COLLECTIONS

James Hardiman Library (JHL), National University of Ireland, Galway.

John Rylands Library (JRL), University of Manchester.

Royal Irish Academy (RIA), Dublin.

Russell Library (RL), Maynooth University.

3

Vernacular Irish Orthographies in the United States

Nancy Stenson

The dearth of written Irish from the eighteenth century to the late nineteenth-century Gaelic revival is well-known, a result of the collapse of the Gaelic elite and its literary traditions during the Penal period. The anglophone education system, which focused on producing literacy in English, exacerbated the loss of Gaelic intellectual traditions. Promotion of English literacy was already an important feature of the eighteenth-century hedge schools, and the establishment of a national education system in the 1830s largely ignored the Irish language altogether until the founding of the Irish Free State in the 1920s. Writing in Irish continued to a limited degree during this period of decline, but for many who did not have access to the literary traditions of the past, the only option was a home-grown orthography based mainly on that of English. Several publications in recent years have provided documentation of some of these texts.[1]

Occasional samples of such writing have appeared in the North American context as well, in the hands of descendants of Irish-speaking immigrants from previous generations. In the spirit of Ken Nilsen's seminal work on the Irish and Gaelic of North America, and in homage to him, this chapter examines and compares the orthographies of two such manuscripts. The first, a story presumably written by the mid-nineteenth-century immigrant it originally belonged to, has been published previously.[2] The second is an unpublished diary kept by the great-great-grandfather of the current owner. Each is written in an idiosyncratic script of the author's invention, clearly based on English spelling, but without full consistency of usage within either manuscript. The goal here is to compare the scripts with an eye to determining both the range of variation between them and their adequacy in capturing the phonological patterns of Irish, as well as to identify which phonological features appear to be most salient to an Irish speaker with literacy skills only in English.

The manuscript previously published and described under the title *An Haicléara Mánas* is in a North Galway dialect, the presumptive author, Patrick Lyden, having been born in 1832 in a village just on the isogloss identified by T.S. Ó Máille that runs along the railway line from Galway to Clifden.[3] The area is no longer Irish-speaking, but the language of the text reflects features of both South Connemara and Mayo Irish, as would be expected from a dialect area located between the two. The story is a farcical tale of high jinks among migrant labourers in mid-nineteenth-century Connemara, although it appears to have been written toward the end of the author's life, perhaps in the first quarter of the twentieth century, sometime after Lyden had immigrated to the United States. It will be referred to as H in what follows.

The unpublished diary (hereafter G) was written by William Gormley, whose descendants have made it available to the author.[4] Gormley identifies himself in the manuscript, and the date 1847 appears several times (possibly 1849 on one occasion). His descendants recall few details about his background but have provided the following information: Gormley was born in Ireland and emigrated during the Famine, according to relatives, apparently settling in Ohio and raising a family there; his birthplace and original family home may have been in County Mayo or North Galway – descendants are uncertain, and some have also mentioned Clare, although that seems to have been based less on personal knowledge than on general information about the origins of the family name. A North Connacht origin is mostly consistent with the language of the text. Before he emigrated, Gormley was reportedly a schoolteacher somewhere in the southwest of Ireland. Most of the diary is in Irish, with a few passages in English. It consists primarily of prayers and religious reflections, but also contains digressions into Irish history and mythology. It has not been fully deciphered, but enough of the meaning is clear to permit some preliminary comparisons of the two orthographies.

Both texts contain very little punctuation, and capitalization of initial letters is limited and apparently random, with certain letters favouring capitalized forms regardless of where in the sentence (or even word) they appear. Division of sentences is therefore not always clear and must be guessed from context. Additionally, the hands are sometimes difficult to interpret, as graphemes are often ambiguous; for instance, it is often difficult to distinguish between **u** and **ee**, **i** and **e**, **R** and **K**, and so forth. Vowels are particularly troublesome. Also, as both manuscripts are quite old and written in pencil, numerous smears and torn pages obscure parts of the text. Nevertheless, both are interpretable to the extent that their patterns of spelling, as well as their inconsistencies, can be discerned.

GENERAL OBSERVATIONS

Direct borrowings of English spellings (for words that sound similar to the Irish word being represented) appear occasionally, although, perhaps surprisingly, they are relatively rare. A few clear-cut examples are the following. (Orthographic representations throughout will be presented in bold font and standard Irish spellings in italic.)

G:	**may**	*mé*	I, me
	down	*domhan*	world
	Own	*Eoin*	John (the Baptist)
	angle	*aingeal*	angel
H:	**raw**	*rá*	saying
	(**le**)**high**	*le haghaidh*	for
	van	*bhean*	woman
	amask	*i measc*	among
	green	*grinn*	fun

Other borrowing by both authors of uniquely English spelling conventions is also seen in occasional spellings such as **ie** for /i:/ and **i** or **y** for the diphthong /ai/:

	G			H	
piesa	*píosa*	piece	**an tiece**	*an t-aos*	the folk
miden	*maighdean*	Virgin	**ibrah**	*oibre*	work (genitive)
vy	*bheidh*	will be	**y**	*uaidh*	from him

as well as in the regular use of **ck** for /k/ in post-vocalic position:

	G			H	
Padrick	*Pádraig*	Patrick	**hanick**	*tháinig*	came
ylackin	*ghlacfainn*	I'd accept	**backach**	*bacach*	lame
aspuck	*easpaig*	bishop	**glick**	*glic*	clever

In H, where examples of this spelling pattern are very common, intervocalic **k** is often doubled: **suckker** *socair* (quiet), **wackkah** *bhfaca* (saw [interrogative form]). Initially, **c** is the most common choice for velar stops, but it is sometimes replaced by **k** when followed by a front vowel, where in English orthography a **c** would normally be pronounced as /s/, e.g., **ke(a)** *cé* (who) (G, H), **kees** *cíos* (rent) (G, H). The manuscripts occasionally vary in minor ways, as in the case of *minic* (often), which appears as **minik** in G but **minick** in H.

The widespread English convention of using double consonants following a short vowel is also found in a few words from G, **obber** *obair* (work), **tappy** *tapaidh* (fast), and **lubby**, which remains undeciphered. H contains more than two dozen such examples, among them **hussee** *thosaigh* (began), **madden** *maidin* (morning), **thoffon** *tafann* (barking), and **faddah** *fada* (long).

Unsurprisingly, given the improvised nature of the orthographies, both manuscripts contain inconsistencies in the spellings of words that appear multiple times in the texts. Examples from G include the spellings **teave/tiove** for *taobh* (side), and **dulan/delin** for *d'fhulaing* (suffered). Multiple spellings are very frequent in H; a few examples are **a tees/a tiece** *an t-aos (óg)* (the [young] folk), **prindeesach/printeechach** *printiseach* (apprentice), and **sagarth/sogarth** *sagart* (priest). The word *focal* (word) has seven different spellings in H. The most common is **fuckle**, but **fuckkall, fuckkle, fuckel, fockl, fockul**, and **fockel** each appear more than once. Most such variations are best attributed to the ambiguities of English spellings, but other alternative spellings may reflect actual pronunciation variations, for example, **rove/roh** for *raibh* (was), or **hussah/hussee** *thosaigh* (began). Reduced pronunciations may explain variants such as **cho, choh, choo** *chuaigh* (went), or spellings like **bul** *buail* (hit) (also appearing as **bool, voul, boel**), all from H.

That spellings do reflect pronunciations is clear from words that show phonological processes of the writers' dialects that are not represented in standard Irish orthography. Epenthesis in clusters with sonorants is robustly represented, for example, **gurramma** *gorma* (blue), and **mullag** *mbolg* (belly) in H; **dareg** *dearg* (red), and **maruve** *marbha* (dead) in G; and **anim** (G) / **annam** (H) *ainm* (name) in both. Several examples in H confirm the phonological shift of /n/ to /r/ following a consonant, as in **crick** *cnoic* (hills), **graus** *gnás* (custom), and **crittaulee** *cniotálaí* (knitter). In G, however, the **n** remains written, as in **mna** *mná* (women) and **gnas** *gnás* (custom), leaving open the question of whether these spellings reflect the author's native pronunciation, something he picked up teaching in the southwest, or a knowledge of the classical spelling of such words. An example of metathesis also appears in G: **aspalode** *absalóide* (absolution [gen.]); there is no evidence for or against the process in H.

Other features of the orthographies include more idiosyncratic attempts to convey Irish pronunciations with spelling patterns not found or not widespread in English itself, by using the alphabet in creative ways to capture the necessary distinctions. The spelling system that emerges from examining the texts will be described in greater detail in the following sections, beginning with the patterns used for vowels.

SHORT VOWELS

Short vowels are relatively straightforward, as most correspond approximately to an English short vowel and use similar spelling conventions. More often than not, spellings of short vowels are identical to both standard Irish orthography and the corresponding English vowel, as shown in Table 1. The focus in what follows will be on stressed vowels only; unstressed vowels vary considerably more, according to the surrounding consonant environments. Any vowel may be found in unstressed position, for example, G: **hugedar** *thugadar* (they gave), **shinsher** *sinsear* (elder), **oalish** *eolais* (knowledge [gen.]), **obor** *obair* (work)], **eshun** *eisean* (he, him); H: **ahas** *áthas* (happiness), **vunther** *mhuintir* (people, family), **hanick** *thánaic* (came), **posove** *pósadh* (was married), and **hlachtfur** *shlachtmhar* (attractive), although **a** is by far the most common in H and to a lesser degree in G for unstressed vowels.

These are the usual representations of short stressed vowels, but variations can be found. Sometimes the standard Irish spelling is

Table 1
Short vowels

	G			H		
/a/	**tallive**	*talamh*	land	**daga**	*dtaga*	come (subjunctive)
	mahim	*maithim*	I forgive	**wallah**	*abhaile*	homeward
	ylac	*ghlac*	accepted	**wackathu**	*an bhfaca tú*	did you see?
/e/	**ele**	*eile*	other	**ellah**	*eile*	other
	brehunes	*breithiúnas*	judgement	**berth**	*beirt*	two people
	lesh	*leis*	with him	**derenach**	*deireanach*	last
/i/	**shin**	*sin*	that	**rinnah**	*rinne*	did
	inish	*inis*	told	**dimmidur**	*d'imíodar*	they went
	hit	*thit*	fell	**vick**	*[a] mhic*	son (vocative)
/o/	**soles**	*solas*	light	**obber**	*obair*	work
	olk	*olc*	bad	**cossee**	*cosaí*	feet
	bobel	*bpobal*	people	**docctoor**	*dochtúir*	doctor
/u/	**cur**	*cur*	putting	**cur**	*cur*	putting
	hug	*thug*	gave	**huggam**	*chugam*	to me
	dulen	*d'fhulaing*	suffered	**gull**	*dhul*	going

replaced by a different vowel in the manuscripts, as in **moc** *mac* (son) (G) and **moggah** *magadh* (joking) (H), reflecting an English convention that represents /a/ with **o** in words like *box.* The ambiguity in the pronunciation of short back vowels in Connacht Irish can also be seen in spellings of **u** where standard Irish has **o** and vice versa: G **dum** *dom* (to me) and **dol** *dul* (going), or H **fuckle** *focal* (word) and **hussee** *thosaigh* (began).

One common strategy in H, not reflected in the table, is the use of **h** word-finally following a short vowel. Examples include **yeenah** *dhéanamh* (doing), **thussah** *tusa* (you), **faddah** *fada* (far, long), **wallah** *abhaile* (homeward). It is not universal – cf. **faultha** *fáilte* (welcome), **tiera** *tíre* (country [gen.]) – but occurs more commonly than not, including in certain monosyllables, where even long vowels sometimes are followed by **h**: **moh** *mo* (my), **nah** *na* (the [pl.]), **goh** *go* (that [complementizer]), **keah** *cé* (who?).

Occasionally in both texts, a spelling normally reserved for long vowels is used to represent a short one, such as **creadem** *creidim* (I believe) in H and **clough** *cloch* (stone) in G. Such cases, however, are relatively uncommon, and on the whole, short vowels bring no major surprises.

Table 2
Long vowels

	G			H		
/a:/	**sasu**	*sásamh*	satisfying	**daug**	*d'fhág*	left
	faltie	*fáilte*	welcome	**faultha**	*fáilte*	welcome
	grasta	*grásta*	grace	**rawtee**	*ráite*	said
	laher	*láthair*	location	**bawn**	*bán*	white
/e:/	**meal**	*mbéal*	mouth	**beal**	*béal*	mouth
	fean	*fein*	self	**fean**	*féin*	self
	geur	*géar*	sharp	**greanah**	*gréine*	sun (gen.)
/i:/	**ree**	*rí*	king	**tee**	*tí*	house (gen.)
	deelish	*dílis*	loyal	**eehah**	*oíche*	night
	Fisdin	*Faoistín*	Confession	**calleenee**	*cailíní*	girls
/o:/	**stor**	*stór*	treasure	**oag**	óg	young
	moran	*mórán*	much	**stroak**	*stróic*	tore
	doyeanty	*dódhéanta*	impossible	**soarth**	*sórt*	sort
	or	*ór*	gold	**ore**	*ór*	gold
	foulem	*foghlaim*	learning	**olem**	*fhoghlaim*	learning
	counee	*cónaí*	residence	**poes**	*pós*	marry
	do	*dó*	to him	**yow**	*dhó*	to him
/u:/	**inshud**	*ansiúd*	yonder	**foon**	*fonn*	desire
	brehunes	*breithiúnas*	judgement	**dooradur**	*dúradar*	they said
	tul	*[an] t-úll*	[the] apple	**woonah**	*mhúineadh*	teaching
	mureel	*múraíl*	shower	**duel**	*dúil*	desire
	tnu	*tnúth*	longing	**fuentach**	*fiúntach*	respectable

LONG VOWELS

In general both manuscripts tend to distinguish long vowels and diphthongs from short vowels by the use of digraphs, although the practice is considerably less consistent in G. The authors' choices for representing long vowels are not always the same, nor are they internally homogeneous (any more than are standard Irish or English orthographic representations of given vowels). Spelling practices for long vowels are summarized in Table 2.

The two texts differ noticeably in their representation of the long low back vowel /a:/, which in G is almost always written as **a**, indistinguishable from the corresponding short vowel. In H, however, a digraph is normally used, either **aw** or **au.** In a few cases, H as well as G uses the single vowel **a**, as in **tha**, *tá* (is). Several words are thus written identically in both texts – **bra** *breá* (fine), **hanick** *tháinig* (came) –

and the name *Pádraig* appears in G as **Padric(k)** and in H as **Paric(k)**, but this is relatively rare. The other back vowels in G are likewise not always differentiated from their short counterparts. Although /u:/ is usually written with the digraph **oo** in H, and occasionally with **ue** (especially in final position but also medially, as the table shows), it is normally represented simply by **u** in G, with just the occasional alternative spelling: **yeanue** *dhéanamh* (doing), **dourt** *dúirt* (said). Similarly, the usual representation of /o:/ in G is simply **o** (very occasionally **ou**); in contrast, H represents /o:/ most often as **oa.** However, **oe** is also common in H, for example, **toeg** *tóg* (build), **coel** *ceol* (music), and in both texts *beo* (alive) is written **boe.** This is the only such spelling in G, however, in contrast to H.

Greatest commonality is found in the front vowels, especially /e:/, which is usually spelled **ea** in both texts (a spelling that doubles as a diphthong, described below, and sometimes as /i:/, noted above). The pronoun *sé* (he) appears very frequently in both texts, always as **shea.** They part company, however for the pronoun *mé* (I, me), which is **mea(h)** in H, but **may** in G. The phoneme /i:/ in G often shares with H the spelling **ee,** but one also finds the simple spelling **i** for /i:/ about 30 percent of the time. In H, alternative spellings for /i:/ are all digraphs. *T(h)aobh* (side) appears as **tiove/hiove** in both texts, and *píosa* (piece) is spelled **piesa** in G and **piecah** in H, probably under influence of English *piece*. The digraph **ie** is also used in H in a number of other words (e.g., **ariest** *arís* [again]), and *dhíbirt* (banish) in G appears as **yeabert** despite the more common use of this digraph for /e:/.

Finally, the English convention of identifying long vowels (and diphthongs) with a final silent **e** (*fine, Eve, came, tune, lone*) is represented to varying degrees in both manuscripts. In H we find roughly three dozen words using this convention, among them **more/vore** *mór/mhór* (big), **shere** *siar* (westward, back), **shule** *siúil* (walk), and **breagadore** *bréagadóir* (liar). Most of these involve the back vowels, **shere** being the only example of a front vowel (and the only token, as the word is usually spelled **shear**). The same spelling is used in several cases instead of **au/aw** to represent long /a:/ but never the so-called "long a" of English (/ej/, as in *name*): **wane** *amháin* (one), **ale** *fháil* (getting), **scudane** *scadáin* (herring). A number of words ending in **-ve** do not represent preceding long vowels, but seem to use the final **e** as a means of avoiding a final **v: rove** *raibh* (was), **gurave** *gcomhaireamh* (counting), **live** *libh* (with you). In only one case of such spelling in H does the final **e** seem meant to be pronounced: **shine** *sin é* (that's it).

In contrast, G uses this "long vowel" convention only rarely. Of approximately the same number of such spellings that have been deciphered, only a few follow the English orthographic conventions used in H, and all uses (long vowels, including Irish **á,** final **v** avoidance) are attested: **dove** *dóibh* (to them), **shude** *siúd* (yonder), **more** *mór* (big), **clane** *clann* (family), **Eve** (Eve), **rove** *raibh* (was), **yeanuve** *dhéanamh* (doing). But more than two thirds of words spelled with a final **e** following a vowel + consonant sequence in G use the spelling to represent two syllables, with a stressed (short or long) vowel and final schwa: **tege** *tuige* (why), **fade** *fada* (far), **dine** *duine* (person), **corle** *comhairle* (advice), **Mure** *Muire* (Mary).

DIPHTHONGS

Irish diphthongs rely on some of the same digraphs used for long vowels in both texts, resulting in grapheme ambiguity, although actual words are rarely ambiguous. The diphthong /iə/ is most commonly spelled as **ea** in both manuscripts. And /uə/ is usually written **ou** in G, but alternates in H between **ou, oa,** and **oo** with approximately equal frequency.

	G			H		
/iə/	**blean**	*bliain*	year	**bleana**	*bliana*	year (gen.)
	shead	*siad*	they	**shead**	*siad*	they
	tearna	*tiarna*	lord	**ceal**	*ciall*	sense
/uə/	**voul**	*bhuail*	beat	**voul**	*bhuail*	beat
	nour	*nuair*	when	**noar**	*nuair*	when
	four	*fuair*	got	**boochalee**	*buachaillí*	boys

Suas (upward) alternates between **ou** and **oa** in both texts, but in other vocabulary **oa** is the primary spelling in H, **ou** in G. In both texts, the use of these digraphs represents long vowels more often than diphthongs.

The derived diphthongs /au/ and /ai/ show both overlap and similar variation in the two texts, as indicated on page 101.

Both texts favour **ow** as the spelling to represent /au/, although H contains several tokens of **au** and occasionally **ou** for this diphthong.[5] G has only one or two examples of **ou** for /au/, often in alternation with **ow** in other tokens of the same word, as in *labhair*, shown above. There are no unambiguous uses of the sequence **au** to represent /au/

	G			H		
/au/	**down**	*domhan*	world	**gown**	*gabhainn*	[cattle]-pound
	dowel	*diabhal*	devil	**powal**	*poll*	hole
	lowr	*labhair*	spoke	**lowerth**	*labhairt*	speaking
	lour	*labhair*	spoke	**ourdoo**	*ordú*	order
	doul	*diabhal*	devil	**baurd**	*bord*	table
/ai/	**viden**	*mhaighdean*	Virgin	**iree**	*éirí*	rising
	line/lign	*Laighean*	Leinster	**clirah**	*cladhaire*	coward
	lighd	*laghad*	least	**viledore**	*veidhleadóir*	fiddler
	eye	*aghaidh*	face	**igh**	*aghaidh*	face
	foy	*faigh*	get	**Thieg**	*Tadhg*	Tadhg
	deiry/dery	*d'éirigh*	rose	**clie**	*claí*	wall

in G, where the deciphered examples of **au** usually represent a long low vowel, or occasionally a short vowel or schwa. However, enough words containing the sequence remain undeciphered that examples of **au** for /au/ could yet emerge.

The representations of /ai/ vary considerably more, although examples of this diphthong are relatively infrequent in both texts. Both occasionally use the single vowel **i** followed by a consonant plus **e** or another vowel, following the English convention. This is more common in H. The English sequence **igh** is more common in G, as shown by several examples above, but is used in H only for *aghaidh* (face) and *le haghaidh* (**lehigh, leahigh**) (for). The primary representation of /ai/ in H is **ie**, largely due to multiple occurrences of the name *Tadhg*, though it is also found in several other words. This spelling for the diphthong is not found in G, although **e(i)** appears for /ai/ once in **deiry** *d'éirigh* (arose) (in other examples it represents /i:/ or /e:/). Given the existence of variation in the pronunciation of the initial vowel of *éirigh*, and the uncertainty regarding G's dialect origins, however, the intended phonetic representation of this spelling cannot be taken as absolute. G also spells *aghaidh* as **eye,** another clear borrowing from English.

CONSONANTS

In one sense the consonant orthography is more straightforward than that of the vowels, in that the consonant symbols in both manuscripts match those of standard Irish (and English) orthography in point and

Table 3
Consonant quality

	Letter		Broad			Slender	
G:	p	**papa**	*Pápa*	Pope	**paccee**	*peacaí*	sins
	b	**ban**	*bain*	take	**banee**	*beannaithe*	blessed
	d	**down**	*domhan*	world	**dowel**	*diabhal*	devil
	d	**fada**	*fada*	far, long	**maden**	*maidin*	morning
	n	**clan**	*clann*	family	**clane**	*clainne*	family (gen.)
	l	**tul**	*[an] t-úll*	apple	**capull**	*capaill*	horse (gen.)
	c	**cree**	*croí*	heart	**cree**	*cré*	clay
	g	**garey**	*gáire*	laughing	**galley**	*gealaí*	moon (gen.)
H:	b	**bee**	*buí*	yellow	**beer**	*b'fhíor*	was true
	m	**mannee**	*mbannaí*	bonds	**mannee**	*meanaí*	awls
	m	**mannam**	*m'anam*	my soul	**thannam**	*t-ainm*	name
	t	**tiggah**	*tuige*	why?	**tithim**	*titim*	falling
	d	**deer**	*daor*	expensive	**deer**	*[i] dtír*	ashore
	l	**mallah**	*mála*	bag	**mallah**	*mbaile*	village
	ch	**chunnie**	*choinnigh*	kept	**chunneal**	*chinéal*	kind, type
	g	**sagarth**	*sagart*	priest	**gark**	*gcearc*	hen

manner of articulation. On the other hand, neither writer makes any systematic effort to represent the distinction between palatalized and velarized consonant phonemes (slender and broad consonants) of Irish. Although this distinction is usually marked by orthographic vowels in standard Irish spelling, broad and slender consonants are only marginally distinguished in the texts, as the ambiguous graphemes of Table 3 indicate.

Not surprisingly, the most visible orthographic distinction found in both manuscripts is the differentiation of broad and slender **s**, where a comparable phonemic (and spelling) distinction exists in English. Both authors rely on the English convention of spelling the alveopalatal sibilant as **sh**. In H, **sule** *súil* (eye) versus **shule** *siuil* (walk) illustrates this distinction clearly; in G, **soles** *solas* (light) versus **inesh** *inis* (island). In both manuscripts, the distinction is widespread but not universal; thus we also find **sackead** *seaicéad* (jacket) and **hashadar** *sheasadar* (they stood) in H and **shinsear** *sinsear* (elder) in G, with only the first palatal marked orthographically. Both texts avoid marking palatalization before a consonant, as in **skeal** *scéal* (story) (H) and **iska** *uisce* (water) (G).

What appear to be some efforts to show other consonant quality distinctions can also be detected, especially in H, where both **v** and **w** can represent lenited **b/m** (in G, only **v** is used). In many cases in H, **w** indicates a broad consonant (**wan** *bhán* [white], **awallah** *abhaile* [homeward], **wallach** *i bhfolach* [hidden]) and **v** a slender one (**van** *bhean* [woman], **verth** *bheirt* [two people], **veal** *bhéal* [mouth]). But many exceptions can be found as well: **v** is almost as frequent as **w** for broad consonants: **vuill** *bhfuil* (is [dependent form]), **vaur** *bharr* (top), **vunther** *mhuintir* (people). *Mhór* [big] appears as both **wore** and **vore.** On the other hand, **v** is almost always the choice for a slender consonant; **w** is used only once in this context, **weich** in one token of the place name *Tóin na bhFiach.*

Similarly, a distinction between **th** and **t** in H can seem tantalizingly like an attempt to distinguish consonant quality in many cases: **thiee** *tuí* (thatch) and **theel** *tsaoil* (life [gen.]) contrast with **tee** *tí* (house [gen. and dative]) and **truer** *triúr* (three people). This makes sense, in that representations of Irish English in literature often use the sequences **th** and **dh** to represent the dental pronunciation of /t/ and /d/ in that variety of English. But each spelling is found representing one of the two slender consonants in **tithim** *titim* (falling), and there are many other cases that contraindicate a firm pattern. Apart from a few proper names spelled in the English way (*Athens, Thebes*), Irish spellings of **th** in G are limited to just three deciphered words: **thaher** *[an] t-athair* (the father), **narth** *neart* (plenty), and **basthu** *baisteadh* (baptism), and four undeciphered ones: **neaghneeth, lathna, leather**, and **thig** – possibly *tuig* (understand).

Vowels often seem at first to match quality of adjacent consonants; almost all examples of slender /p′/, /m′/, and /d′/ in H are followed by **i** or **e**, as in standard Irish orthography, and all examples of broad /p/, /m/, and /d/ are followed by **a, o,** or **u.** One occurrence of *buí* (yellow) as **buee** in H suggests an attempt at preserving such a pattern, but again, neither writer is entirely consistent; **bee** is in fact the more frequent spelling for *buí* in H (as well as for *bí* [be]), and similar divergences can be found with other consonants, as the table shows. Finally, sporadic use in H of the English **VCe** (Vowel+Consonant+e) pattern may be intended to suggest palatalization in examples like **tallure** *táilliúir* (tailor), **sidure** *saighdiúir* (soldier[s]),[6] and **yune** *dheamhain* (demon [voc.]). But these cases are rare; in G, they are non-existent.

Another set of Irish phonemic consonant distinctions that is essentially ignored by both authors is the pattern of tense and lax sonorant consonants, reflected by double versus single spellings in standard Irish orthography. Most Connacht dialects, of which the authors of these texts were apparently both speakers, retain a distinction between tense and lax in the palatalized (slender) consonants but not in the velarized (broad) ones. Thus the standard spellings of pairs like *buile* (madness) and *buille* (a blow) reflect a pronunciation difference in the two lateral phonemes. Apart from the example of **tallure** for *táilliúr,* mentioned above, which could be argued to represent palatalization of the **ll** orthographically, no differentiation is found in the manuscripts' spellings for these consonants. Thus, in H, not only does the **mallah** represent both broad and slender consonants in *mála* (bag) and *mbaile* (village), but the same **ll** represents the tense palatal consonant in **ballee** *b'fhàillí* (neglected). A similar spelling ambiguity from G can be seen in **ille** *uile* (all) and **kille** *Cille,* part of the name *Colm Cille.* A similar example from G showing identical spellings for tense and lax nasals can be seen in the pair **orin** *orainn* (on us) versus **vleen** *bhlain* (year). Such examples are limited in both texts, but to the extent that (near) minimal pairs exist, they clearly rely on the same spelling conventions.

MUTATIONS

Another salient characteristic of Irish consonant orthography is the system of writing initial consonant mutations in such a way as to show both the actual pronunciation and the original citation form of the mutated consonant. Thus, lenited consonants are marked with a following **h**, signalling the pronunciation change, but the original consonant remains as well. The consonant pronounced in eclipsis is placed before the citation consonant, again leaving the relationship between forms clear. Such subtleties are absent from both texts, but mutations are shown to the extent that the English orthography offers symbols for the new pronunciation. Table 4 summarizes the use of mutations in the two manuscripts. Words illustrating each mutation are chosen from those that occur in both citation form and with a mutation. Both spellings are provided in the table, separated by a colon. The standard orthography is that of the mutation.

It is clear that the two authors followed the same strategy of replacing the citation form of the initial consonant with the pronounced consonant of the mutation (more similar to the spelling conventions of Welsh than of Irish), and did so in nearly identical ways, with few

Table 4
Initial mutations

	Lenition					
	Standard mutation G			*Standard mutation H*		
p:ph	*Phádraig*	**Padrick:Fadrick**	Patrick	*phós*	**poes:foes**	married
b:bh	*bhaisteadh*	**bastu:vastu**	baptism	*bhuí*	**bee:wee**	yellow
m:mh	*mhór*	**more:vore**	big	*mhúineadh*	**moonah:voonah**	teaching
f:fh	*Fhlaithis*	**flahish:lahish**	heaven	*fhearr*	**farr:arr**	better
t:th	*thiarna*	**tearna:hearna**	lord	*tharraing*	**tarran:harrant**	pull(ing)
d:dh	*dhia*	**dea:yea**	God	*dhearg*	**darag:yarag**	red
s:sh	*shíl*	**sheel:heel**	thought	*sheas*	**shass:hass**	stood
c:ch	*chuid*	**cud:cud**[1]	portion	*chur*	**cur:chur**	putting
g:gh	*ghluais*	**gloash:yloach**	move	*ghualainn*	**goolen:yoolen**	shoulder
	Eclipsis					
p:bp	*bpobal*	**pobel:bobel**	people	*bpoll*	**poul:boul**	hole
b:mb	*mbliana*	**bleana:mleana**	year (gen.)	*mbainis*	**banish:mannish**	wedding
f:bhf	*bhFlaithis*	**flahish:vlahish**	heaven	*bhfuair*	**four:vour**	got
t:dt	*dtáinig*	**hanick:danic**	came	*dtógfadh*	**toeg:dochach**	would lift
d:nd	*ndia*	**dea:nea**	God	*ndúirt*	**duarth:nuarth**	said
c:gc	*gcléir*	**clear:glear**	clergy	*gcladach*	**cladach:gladach**	shore
g:ng	*nglanfadh*	**glanegh:glanegh**	would clean	*ngar*	**gar:ngar**	near

[1]Since lenition of **c** is never marked initially in G, both *cuid* and *chuid* are written identically

exceptions. In H, as previously noted, lenited **b** and **m** and eclipsed **f** vary between use of **v** and **w**, whereas in G, only **v** is used. The least consistent representations of consonant mutations are in the velars, as is to be expected, since English (and therefore its orthography) lacks the velar fricatives that arise from lenition in Irish. H marks lenition of **c** as **ch**, but only erratically in initial position. Not only are many words beginning with **c** left unmarked for lenition, but **ch** is used more than a few times in non-lenition contexts. In contrast, G almost never marks lenition of initial **c** at all. In post-vocalic contexts, both texts show fairly consistent lenition orthographically, but with different strategies. H relies on the standard Irish spelling **ch** in all environments (as in **dochtoor** *dochtúir* [doctor], ***boochallee*** *buachaillí* [boys], and **backach** *bacach* [cripple]), whereas G consistently uses **gh** post-vocalically (**degh** *deich* [ten], **creaghive** *críochaibh* [boundaries], **bought** *bocht* [poor]). The use of **gh** in G can also signal the post-vocalic **th** of standard spelling on occasion, as in **mogh** *maith* (good) and **vanegha** *bheannaithe* (blessed). Only one example of eclipsed **g** as **ng** is found in H, and none in G, where underlying **g** in eclipsis environments is consistently left as **g**, leaving it uncertain whether the writer actually pronounced the initial nasalization or not, although the default assumption must surely be that he did, and merely failed to mark it orthographically.

CONCLUSION

The two manuscripts show a fairly high degree of similarity in the orthographic choices their authors made, as well as in the phonological features of Irish that they failed to represent, whether this was by choice or forced by the limitations of the English orthographic system that formed the basis for their spellings. Consonants and short vowels are represented very similarly whenever comparable phonemes exist in English, long vowels and diphthongs to a lesser degree, with variations in the orthographic choices readily traceable to variations in English orthography. Only where it was necessary to improvise spellings for forms without an English counterpart (most notably some of the long vowels) did the authors' choices sometimes differ.

H seems to show somewhat more sensitivity to phonological distinctions of Irish, however erratically they are represented in the written text. Differentiation of long and short vowels is more consistent than in G, and there is somewhat greater consistency in attempting to represent initial mutations, as in his use of **ch**, at least sometimes, to write a lenited **c.** Some possible attempts to represent phoneme distinctions for consonant quality can be detected in H that have no analogues in G; these include the use of **v** for slender lenited labials (in contrast with **v/w** variation for the broad series), frequent use of **th** to represent (broad) dental /t/, and perhaps even his occasional use of English spelling conventions to reflect the palatal quality of tense sonorants, as in *táilliúir*, written as **tallure**. Although these spellings are quite infrequent, G reflects noticeably less effort to capture these distinctions at all. The fairly regular representation of final short vowels with a following **h** is a feature unique to H and without precedent in English orthography, and its intent is not clear, but it may be assumed to reflect a perception on the author's part of some difference between unstressed final vowels in Irish and English.

In contrast, G contains a few more spellings that seem to be full and direct borrowings from English words, and relies marginally more on a variety of sequences directly traceable to English conventions; this includes the use of a greater number of spelling choices in general (e.g., for the diphthong /ai/). It is tempting to view this tendency as reflecting a more conscious awareness of English orthographic variation, which would be consistent with his having been a teacher, but the effect is small and only suggestive. On the other hand, G's preference for **ou** to represent the diphthong /uə/ and occasionally long /o:/ has no obvious precedent in English orthographic conventions. Again, consistency is elusive.

Two curious spelling patterns seem to suggest a possibility of some acquaintance with Irish orthography on the part of both writers. In H, the word *teach* (house) is always spelled in the standard way, **teach** (although *isteach* [inward] never is, appearing instead as **istach, astach**, or **stach**). In G, the use of **mh** to represent lenited **m** occurs frequently in the words *naomh* (saint) (**nomh**) and *naofa* (holy) (**nomha, nomhfa**), and once in **nomhan** *ndomhan* (world). It is hard to imagine how one might arrive at these spelling sequences based only on knowledge of English spellings. One may also cite here G's use of **n** after a consonant (if in fact he spoke a dialect where it would be pronounced as /r/), and H's use (albeit erratic) of **ch** to represent lenited **c.** But no other indications of literacy in Irish are evident in either text.

Notwithstanding the differences between the authors' choices, some individual idiosyncrasies, and the internal variations of both manuscripts, the two texts show a remarkable similarity in the spelling choices their authors made, even down to their inconsistencies and the phonological distinctions they ignore. With only a few exceptions, most variant spellings within the two manuscripts fall within the conventional spelling options available to English orthography. Given English literacy on the part of both writers, variations such as that between **c, k,** and **ck** (always in appropriate contexts), for instance, or between **ee** and **ie** for /i:/, are unsurprising and even to be expected. Apart from a few distinctions, such as the tense/lax sonorant phonemes, both authors, but especially H, go to impressive lengths to capture phonological distinctions that the English spelling system, having no need for such distinctions, is quite unequipped to handle. Where they fail, context usually is sufficient to establish the intended meaning. In some respects, the most difficult challenges for interpretation of each text lie with the difficulty of deciphering the hands themselves; once that has been resolved, and barring a few quirks in each text, the spelling falls into place without undue difficulty.

NOTES

1 See, for example, Ó Fiannachta, "Do Lochtuiv" and several sermons published in *Éigse*: Ó Fachtna, "Seanmóír"; Ó Dúghaill, "Seanmóir"; O'Sullivan, "A Sermon." Longer texts include Mahon, *Doctor Kirwan's Catechism*; and Stenson, *An Haicléara Mánus*.
2 Stenson, *An Haicléara Mánus*.
3 Ibid.; Ó Máille, *Úrlabhraíocht*.
4 The family has at present no plans for publication of the diary.
5 Most of the time **ow** represents a diphthong (usually /au/, but sometimes /uə/). Twice in H the spelling represents /o:/, in multiple tokens of **yow** for *dhó* [to him], shown in Table 2, and once in **crow** for *cródha* [brave, hardy]. In G there are no clear cases of **ow** for /o:/.
6 **Sidure** appears four times in H; twice it can be assumed to represent a singular, but two occurrences are found following **naw** *na*, which can only be interpreted as the plural article.

BIBLIOGRAPHY

Mahon, William J., ed. and trans. *Doctor Kirwan's Irish Catechism*, by Thomas Hughes. Cambridge, MA: Pangur, 1991.

Ó Dúghaill, Gréagóir, ed. "Seanmóir ar an Troscadh." *Éigse* 15, no. 2 (1973): 131–9.

Ó Fachtna, Anselm, ed. "Seanmóir ar Pháis ár dTiarna Íosa Chríost," by Michael Meighan. *Éigse* 12, no. 3 (1968): 177–98.

Ó Fiannachta, Pádraig, ed. "Do Lochtuiv na Tangan." *Éigse* 12, no. 1 (1967): 1–28.

Ó Máille, T.S. *Úrlabhraíocht.* Baile Átha Cliath: Comhlacht Oideachais na hÉireann, 1928.

O'Sullivan, Donal, ed. "A Sermon for Good Friday by Father Michael Walsh of Sneem." *Éigse* 4, no. 3 (1944): 157–72.

Stenson, Nancy, ed. *An Haicléara Mánas: A Nineteenth-Century Text from Clifden, Co. Galway*. Dublin: Dublin Institute for Advanced Studies, 2003.

4

Pádraig Phiarais Cúndún in America: Poet without a Public?

Tony Ó Floinn

During the 1980s and '90s, on periodic trips between Nova Scotia and Boston, Professor Nilsen stopped in Portland, Maine, to record previously undocumented Irish speakers on video and audiotape. These recordings, and Nilsen's subsequent articles about Portland's Irish-speaking population, are among his most important contributions to the study of the Irish in North America.[1] In his work with these people, Nilsen was helping to answer questions that have surfaced frequently in recent decades: what happened to the substantial numbers of native Irish speakers who reached the shores of North America, especially those who arrived before the twentieth century? What were their linguistic and cultural fates, and how were these manifested? Describing the researcher's challenges, he notes that the "vast majority of undocumented Irish speakers, some of whom never learned English and most of whom never belonged to a language movement, remain unknown to historians," and that only "diligent probing will yield occasional traces of their existence."[2]

The situation of the poet Pádraig Phiarais Cúndún contrasts with that of many of his emigrant countrymen. Around 1826, Cúndún settled with his young family in Deerfield, Utica, in New York State.[3] As Nilsen asserts, Cúndún is "perhaps the most notable Irish monoglot speaker to arrive in this country." Indeed, "his letters and poems, written in upstate New York to his neighbours in Ballymacoda, County Cork, represent the most important body of pre-famine writing in Irish from the United States."[4] The question of to and for whom Cúndún was writing takes on added significance subsequent to his migration. This chapter presents an overview of the various publics that Cúndún had, or may have had, during his time in Utica, highlighting some particularly noteworthy aspects.[5]

DEFINING THE POET'S PUBLICS

We are not wholly ignorant of the audience for Cúndún's poems and songs prior to his departure from Ballymacoda.[6] He gives us certain indications in this regard in some of his compositions. For instance, it is difficult to surpass "Tórramh an Bhairille" (The Wake of the Barrel) in its expression of the affection he had for the community where he was born and lived for half a century:

Seolfad teastas ar shlóighte Bhaile
Mhac Óda mhaiseamhúil mhúinte:
Leóghain lannmhar cheólmhar cheannasach
chródha chalma chómhachtach,
Treóin do chleachtas gach ló gan lagarach
ól go flaitheamhail flúirseach;
Is mór an t-aiteas go deó bheith eatortha
ar thórramh an bhairille á dhiúgadh.

I will send forth a testament to the multitudes
of beautiful, well-mannered Ballymacoda:
Fierce, vigorous, commanding,
valiant, brave, powerful lions,
Mighty men who were in the habit every day without weakening
of drinking generously, liberally;
It's a great joy to be amongst them
at the wake of the barrel being drained.[7]

Scenes like the above suggest the sort of occasions at which Cúndún's compositions could have been transmitted orally.[8] Fragments of folklore collected in the twentieth century tend to support the likelihood of oral transmission of Irish-language poetry at such social occasions, as does the proportion of native Irish speakers in the Ballymacoda region in the early decades of the nineteenth century.[9]

Around 1826 Cúndún left his beloved community and turned his face toward a new and very different world. He appears to have initially felt he had arrived into a wilderness, not just in terms of his physical surroundings, as reflected in his reference to "coillte is crannaibh is gairbhthin mhóra / ... / ainmhithe allta ag amhastrach chómhraic" (woods, trees and extensive rough terrains /... / savage animals bellowing for a fight), but also in terms of the cultural atmosphere of his new home, as reflected both in the inhabitants' predominant language and in their religious practices: "Foireann na tíre ... / Cré ná Paidir ní cantar go deó leó" (The natives of this land ... / Neither Creed nor Pater is ever said by them).[10] However, the loss of direct access to his native constituency in the short term did not discourage his creative instincts or his urge to communicate, and in the medium term he developed new publics.

Attempting to reconstruct Cúndún's publics at this remove is undoubtedly problematic, but attention to language allows for a certain degree of clarity. While conclusive evidence does not exist, it has been widely accepted – as expressed by Nilsen above, for example – that Cúndún could not read, write, or speak English before or subsequent to his arrival in America.[11] We may therefore make the working assumption that his post-1826 audiences were restricted to Irish speakers locally and those literate in Irish farther afield (primarily correspondents in the Ballymacoda region), as well as those in contact with the latter orally. I will first consider Cúndún's Ballymacoda public,[12] and then his potential Irish American public.

LIMITATIONS

Some of the limitations at play in this attempt to characterize Cúndún's various publics are significant and restrict the insights possible. Chief among these limitations is the poet's missing correspondence. Some of the letters he sent to east Cork are known to be missing, as are all of the letters he received from correspondents in Ireland. The existence of others cannot be ascertained; for instance, he might have sent letters to recipients in Ireland and North America to which no references survive.

LETTERS AND POEMS HOME: THE BALLYMACODA PUBLIC

That Cúndún imagined a public for himself in Ballymacoda is evident from the opening lines of the poem that accompanied his first letter home: "Slán cuirim libh go stát chine Scuit, / a cháirde gan chlis 's a chómharsain" (Greetings I send to you in the land of the race of Scota [the Irish], / my faithful friends and neighbours).[13] The letter dates to 1834 and was sent to Pártholán Suipéal. In it, Cúndún explains why he did not write earlier:

> Do scríbhfinn chúghad fadó roimhe seo, acht an talamh so do ghlacas, ní raibh aguinn acht beagán airgid an tan do ghlacas é, acht do fuaireas cáirde chum na coda eile an oiread sin do dhíol gacha bliaghain, air feadh seachd mblíaghna, agus mar a mbeidheadh sé díolta go h-uile an t-am sin, an talamh agus an t.airgiod do bheith scartha liom, agus d'eagla 'ná tiocfadh liom sin do dhéanadh, níor mhaith liom scríobh chúghat, a maoídheamh an nídh ná beidheadh agam. Atá sé uile díolta anois agus mar sin is féidir liom scéal fírinneach lúthgháireach do luadh.[14]

> I would've written to you long before this, but this land that I took, we only had a small amount of money when I took it, but I got credit for the other part [on condition] of paying a certain amount every year over seven years, and if it wasn't fully paid I would lose the land and money; for fear that I wouldn't succeed in doing that, I didn't want to write to you, boasting of what I mightn't have. It's completely paid now and so I can pass on joyful accurate news.

This should not be taken to mean that he received no news of his relatives, neighbours, and friends in east Cork and that they received none of him, but rather that such news and greetings were most likely exchanged indirectly. That this did indeed occur is also evident in the letter: Cúndún notes the death of a neighbour in Ballymacoda, and inquires into the veracity of the news that Suipéal's brother drowned in Newfoundland.[15]

Intermediaries, Addressees, and Indirect Referents

While generalized and reasonably accurate assertions can be made about the audience for a particular poet's work based upon headings, internal evidence, and scribal copies, the survival of Cúndún's letters offers us a rare opportunity to construct a more detailed depiction (see Appendix A). A tripartite picture of his publics emerges in which varying roles can be seen. The first group comprises the intermediaries in and around Youghal, County Cork, to whom he sent the letters to be passed on to the addressees. In the second group are the ultimate recipients of the letters. The final group comprises people to whom he sent greetings and more detailed messages indirectly, or those who were discussed in greater depth in the letters. I have carried out initial research on those in the first two groups with a view to ascertaining who they were and where they lived; this has not yet been done for the third group.

The four intermediaries include Bartholomew Pack and Mark Hudson – both likely to have been members of the Church of Ireland and agents of the local landlord, Lord Ponsonby – as well as Daniel Murphy and John Russell, the Roman Catholic parish priests of Youghal and Cloyne respectively (see Appendix B, Group 1). What relationship, if any, Cúndún had with this quartet during his time in Ballymacoda is not evident from the letters. What is apparent is that the intermediary system was not fully reliable. To deal with this, Cúndún adopted a practice of occasionally listing the letters he had sent and inquiring if they had been received.[16] This has proven helpful in identifying his addressees.

All seven addressees of the letters resided in the Ballymacoda area (see Appendix B, Group 2), including two who apparently never received letters sent to them in 1834: Míghcheál Ó Eichíaruinn, who held twenty-one acres in Yellowford with his wife Margaret, and Seághan Cúndún, who, although he cannot be identified with any certainty, appears not to have been a close relative. Both Pártholán Suipéal, who held about four acres in East Clonard, and Mícheághal Ó Glasáin, with a more substantial holding of forty-three acres in Lisquinlan, received letters in 1834; these townlands are situated to the east and west of Cúndún's former farm in Shanakill, Ballymacoda. Séamas Mac Gearailt, the captain of a sand-lighter as well as a poet and scribe in his own right, received a letter in 1837. Tomás Ó Briain received letters in the late 1840s, and Tomás Stac in the early 1850s; they may have lived in the townlands of Ballypherode and Redbarn respectively.

It is notable that while two or more letters to each of Pártholán Suipéal, Tomás Ó Briain, and Tomás Stac survive, the dates are clustered in each case with no evidence to suggest that the individual correspondences lasted over Cúndún's two decades of letter writing. Given that he sent greetings to a large number of friends and neighbours, it is possible that some may have been inspired to write without first having received a letter; Tomás Stac, for example, may have followed this pattern. One other feature that stands out is the apparent lacuna between the letters of 1837 and 1848; the dates of Cúndún's poetry exhibit a similar pattern, with a poem in 1840 but none again until 1847. The 1840 composition "Óm chroidhe mo scread a' teacht go cruaidh" (My cry comes keenly from my heart) likely explains the caesura as it is a lament for his wife Maighréad, who was some fifteen years his junior and not yet fifty at the time of her death.[17] The tenor and themes of his 1847 poem "Is truagh san treabha chlanna Míleadh thréan" (That is wretched, the tribes of the descendants of mighty Míle)[18] and an 1848 letter in which he writes "Guidhim tú scéala do chur chugham cionnus mar atá na barraí in Éirinn i mbliana" (I beseech you to send me news of how the crops are in Ireland this year)[19] lead to the conclusion that it was another tragedy, the Great Famine, that prompted him to take up the pen again.

The final and largest group in Ballymacoda – those to whom Cúndún sent greetings or messages, or who received an honourable mention or otherwise – are listed in Appendix B, Group 3. The level of detail ranges from mere names to short descriptions to lengthy accounts. In the first two letters sent in 1834, he makes a particular effort to send greetings to many of his neighbours and friends, an approach that can also be observed in his only surviving letter from 1849, albeit to a lesser extent.

Cúndún's references to others illustrate his continued involvement with the Ballymacoda community. His mention, in an 1837 letter to Séamas Mac Gearailt, of the grief of Pártholán Suipéal's mother upon Cundún's departure is a reminder that the sorrow associated with emigration was not confined to those who were leaving.[20] The sorrow occasioned by the deaths of his wife's sister, the children of Ruisdeárd Ó Muirighthe, and the children of Seághan Ó Bruadair exemplifies the impact of the high mortality rate not only on the public locally, but also on those farther afield, the geographical separation clearly not reducing the emotional impact.[21]

In addition to empathy, the references contain criticism, as in the 1854 letter to Tomás Stac in which Cúndún expresses his disapproval of Séamas Mac Gearailt for working with the Irish Society for Promoting the Education of the Native Irish through the Medium of Their Own Language.[22] He also harshly criticizes Diarmaid Sdúndún, whom he blamed for the loss of his farm in Shanakill, Ballymacoda; the extended vituperative vilification of Sdúndún in his 1852 letter subsequent to receiving news of Sdúndún's death demonstrates that in this case, he neither forgot nor forgave.[23] Not everyone who received Cúndún's communications in Ballymacoda was fully at ease with transmitting his criticism publicly, however, despite the fact that he had no compunction in making such comments. One manifestation of such reluctance is the excision by certain scribes of a number of lines in which he gives vent to his unvarnished opinions in "Aiste na nIarthar" (Poem of Faraway Places), one of his most popular works.[24]

Declining Correspondence Home

Cúndún's contact with his Ballymacoda public may be divided into three distinct periods: the early years (1834–40), the middle to later years (1847–54), and the last years (1855–57). In the early years, he sent greetings to more people and mentioned more news from his native locality than in the middle to later years, with this declining to nothing at all in the last years. He composed and sent home more poems in the early years, and far more copies were made of these than of the poems from the middle to later years. It is likely that the poems composed in the last years were never sent home.[25]

When considering the decline in correspondence in the middle to later years, Cúndún's relatively advanced age on reaching America should be taken into account. He was almost fifty years old when he settled in Deerfield, Utica.[26] By the mid-1830s many of his peers would have been in or around sixty; by the mid-1840s, seventy; and by the mid-1850s, eighty. Inevitably then, the number of survivors in his own age cohort, those with whom he would most likely be in greatest contact, would have declined at a sharpening rate throughout these decades. In tandem with this, an increasing fraction of the younger age groups would have had little or no memory of him or his family.

An intriguing question thus emerges: did the changing nature of Cúndún's public in Ballymacoda affect his written compositions? The period 1847–56 saw an even split between poems and letters from his pen, but if one takes into account that three of these poems were written in 1856, the year before his death, a bias toward letter-writing during the period 1847–54 becomes apparent. Could this change have been due to a decline in the number of poems sent to him, as well as his awareness of the decline of such activity in Ballymacoda during the Famine decade and thereafter? Toward the end of one of his last compositions, Cúndún says "sin críoch ar mo sheanchas daoibh" (that's the end of my account for you), prompting the further question as to whom he was addressing, for it would appear that this and the two other poems composed in 1856 never crossed the Atlantic.[27]

A PUBLIC IN AMERICA?

An absence of letters or poems in Cúndún's hand destined for American recipients and a similar lack of eyewitness accounts makes characterizing his American public a more challenging task. We are almost entirely dependent on limited references in his surviving letters to Ireland, as can be seen from Appendix B, Group 4. In light of the size of his household and the proximity of his three cousins' households, the existence of an Irish-language community on a day-to-day basis in Deerfield, Utica, must be considered quite likely. This could then have extended into a language network, given the number of east Cork individuals named as prospering in the greater Utica area. To these can be added the potential presence of at least some other Irish speakers from outside east Cork. If it were already an established habit of his in Ballymacoda, it is not inconceivable that Cúndún would have recited or sung old and new compositions in his new homeland, be it solely for his own household or at gatherings of the extended family and at social occasions such as weddings and funerals.

Whether the putative public outlined above functioned in this way or whether it even existed is difficult to determine. It is also important to recognize that if the Irish-speaking community described above did exist, most of the members would have been bilingual to some extent; even the primary language used in the households of two of Cúndún's cousins, Seághan Cúndún and Máire Cúndún, is uncertain, given that no mention is made of the native tongue of their spouses, who hailed from counties Wexford and Monaghan respectively.[28] That the community itself was not fully rooted is illuminated by Cúndún's news in his 1849 letter to Tomás Ó Briain that Máire Cúndún and her husband sold their land in Utica in order to purchase a larger but much cheaper holding farther west.[29]

Conspicuously absent from Cúndún's poems and letters from America are social occasions involving alcohol; indeed, Sunday mass is the only gathering mentioned.[30] The gatherings described in Ballymacoda's taverns apparently had no equivalent in his life in Utica, thus reducing the prospects for oral transmission of poems and songs. Whether this reflects a change in cultural practice by this class of emigrant, or merely reflects a lack of suitable opportunities, it is tempting to interpret it as a significant transformation in the poet's own life.

Cúndún's reference to one individual in particular, Mighcheáll Ó Néill, evidences communication with at least one person outside the Utica area: "Atá sé céad míle síar ó dheas uaim, a mbaile mór d'á ngoirthear Albainídh, a stát Nuadh York. Cuirimíd scéala chum a chéile go minic" (He's a hundred miles southwest of me, in a big town called Albany in New York State. We send news to each other frequently).[31] In the absence of further evidence, concrete conclusions about a wider network cannot be made, but the likelihood that there were more such correspondents cannot be discounted – and given Cúndún's proclivity to include poems in his letters to Ireland, it is not unreasonable to suggest that he may have done likewise in his missives to North American locales.[32]

At the end of the previous section, the question arose of what public, if any, Cúndún's last poems may have had. Ironically, during the last years of his life antiquarian and nascent revivalist interest in the Irish language in North America started to coalesce, typically in urban areas in the east. At this remove, it appears that linking the more rural native Irish speakers of Cúndún's ilk, or the increasing numbers of poorer and less literate native speakers, together in a society bound by language use was not among their goals.[33] However, shortly after Cúndún's death, his son Piaras made the manuscript NYPL MssCol 1773 available to the *Irish-American* newspaper, which published two of his poems in 1858.[34] This act, and the *Irish-American*'s description of "Mr. Pierce Condon" as being "of South Brooklyn," suggest that Cúndún's son was aware of emerging Irish-language activities. The *Irish-American* began publishing Irish-language material in 1851; one wonders if he, or indeed others, may have passed such material on to his father.[35]

Publication of Cúndún's work did not cease with the two poems that appeared in the *Irish-American* in 1858. Later that same year the *Nation* published a number of his poems.[36] Then between 1908 and 1910 Risteárd Ó Foghludha published extracts from Cúndún's letters and poetry, accompanied by an extended essay, in the *Gaelic American*,[37] and in 1932 Ó Foghludha published *Pádraig Phiarais Cúndún 1777–1856*, the most comprehensive edition of Cúndún's works to date. Modern Irish-language scholarship continues to engage with Cúndún's works and their reception, as exemplified by recent essays by Seán Ó Duinnshléibhe.[38] Kerby Miller's use of translated extracts in his seminal study *Emigrants and Exiles*, published in 1985, brought Cúndún to the attention of a wide English-speaking readership, a trend that was continued by Neil Buttimer in his 2012 exposition of Cúndún's references to the Great Famine.[39]

CONCLUSION

Although Pádraig Phiarais Cúndún may initially have felt he had arrived into a wilderness, his voice did not remain submerged under the burden of isolation. Rather, it sprang forth to reclaim a public centred on Ballymacoda, and possibly one centred on Deerfield, Utica. Much has clearly been lost, depriving us of a great deal of documentary evidence, but the fraction that has survived suffices to give us a reliable insight into some of the people with whom Cúndún corresponded. Moreover, surviving evidence gives us sufficient hints to suggest the inclusion of other individuals and networks in our picture of his publics.

While this goes some way toward addressing the experience of one native speaker who reached the shores of America, it would appear not to address one of the underlying and perplexing factors in the challenge described by Nilsen in the opening paragraph: even allowing for the very low levels of literacy in Irish among emigrant native speakers up to and during the Great Famine, the dearth of letters and other writings in Irish is pronounced. Given the exceptional nature of Cúndún's output, consideration of the converse question may shed light on this striking absence: what are the reasons that prompted Cúndún not only to continue to compose poems in Irish, but also to correspond in Irish, rather than having a relative or neighbour write letters for him in English, a strategy used by many of his fellow native speakers?

Whatever the answers to these questions, it seems that the act which uprooted Cúndún from his native community and natural constituency was the very one which opened up a wider public in Irish for his work in the first hundred years or so after his death, and a much wider public still in succeeding decades as awareness also spread to English-speaking publics in his native and adopted homes. Considering the following exhortation to the writings he sent home, it is surely no exaggeration to claim they have travelled farther and for longer than he ever foresaw:

Go h-Éire a sgríbhinn sgíord go tapadh treórach,
Ná déin do sgíth go ttíghir asteach go h-éochuill.

Mo gheuga gaóil is príomh mo sheana chomharsan
Tabhair léir a laói mo mhíle beanacht dóibh sin.[40]

Fly to Ireland, my missive, swiftly, directly;
do not rest till you come into Youghal.
To my relations and, importantly, my old neighbours,
clearly give effusive greetings from me, my poem.

APPENDIX A

Surviving Sources of Cúndún's Letters

Pádraig Phiarais Cúndún (PPC) to Pártholán Suipéal (PS), 1834
- TC Ms. T vii, 59–67
- RIA Ms. 24 B 27, 229–31 (the final third of the letter only is given here)

PPC to Míghcheál Ó Glasáin (MÓG), 1834
- TC Ms. T vii, 35–49
- RIA Ms. 24 B 27, 208–22 (the final third or so of the body of the letter is omitted)
- NLI Ms. G 849, 33–3 / 62–57 (pages of the manuscript numbered twice)

PPC to PS, 1837
- TC Ms. T vii, 69–70
- RIA Ms. 24 B 27, 233–4

PPC to Séamas Mac Gearailt (SMG), 1837
- This may comprise fragments from more than one letter.
- TC Ms. T vii, 67–8 (Part 1), 70–1 (Part 2)
- RIA Ms. 24 B 27, 231–2 (Part 1), 235–8 (Part 2)

PPC to Tomás Ó Briain (TÓB), 1848
- Ó Foghludha, *Pádraig Phiarais Cúndún*, 79–84

PPC to TÓB, 1849
- Ó Foghludha, *Pádraig Phiarais Cúndún*, 85–92

PPC to Tomás Stac (TS), 1851
- Ó Foghludha, *Pádraig Phiarais Cúndún*, 92–4

PPC to TS, 1852
- CCCA Ms. G 6, 3–7

PPC to TS, 1854
- Ó Foghludha, *Pádraig Phiarais Cúndún*, 100–4

APPENDIX B

Intermediaries, Addressees, and Indirect Referents

The first and second lists (intermediaries and addressees) do not aim to be an exhaustive unearthing of available information about these individuals; rather, they represent an initial attempt to shed light on their location and roles in East Cork. The third and fourth lists record the other people Cúndún mentions in East Cork and North America as a first step in establishing their identities and illuminating the links mentioned. Additional insights will undoubtedly emerge from further research into these individuals and their connections.

Group 1: Intermediaries

1 Marcus Hutson, intermediary for a letter to Míghcheál Ó Eichíaruinn (not extant) (PPC to PS, 1834; PPC to MÓG, 1834).
This would appear to be the same Mark Hudson who held sixty-nine acres in the townland of Knockmonalea East in 1833 (TAB, County Cork, Clonpriest (Cloyne Priest) parish, Knockmonalea East). It seems he was a member of the Church of Ireland and of the Hudson family in the vicinity of Youghal. The family was likely related to the Hudsons who owned an estate in Glenville, Co. Cork (Landed Estates Database, Hudson [Glenville]).

2 Dómhnall Ó Murchú, intermediary for a letter intended for Míghcheál Ó Glasáin (PPC to PS, 1834).
Daniel Murphy is recorded as the Roman Catholic parish priest for Youghal in 1837–38 but he is absent from the 1849 *Thoms* listing for the Diocese of Cloyne and Ross: *Complete Catholic Registry*, 378; *Thom's*, 339–40. Ó Foghludha states that he appears in Canon Sheehan's *My New Curate* as "Daddy Dan": *Pádraig Phiarais Cúndún*, xiv.

3 Pártholán Peaic, intermediary for a letter intended for Seághan Cúndún (PPC to PS, 1834; PPC to MÓG, 1834).
Bartholomew Pack was an agent for the landlord, Lord Ponsoby. He resided in Strand House, Youghal, in 1824 but was no longer there in 1846: Ó Foghludha, *Pádraig Phiarais Cúndún*, xiv; *City of Dublin*, 324; *Slater's*, 337. Brady records that Bartholemew Pack was admitted to the benefice of Tullagh in the Diocese of Ross in 1823 but resigned in 1828:

Clerical and Parochial Records, 564. A Revd Barthw. Pack is listed as holding fourteen acres in the townland of Cornaveigh close to Youghal in 1828: TAB, County Cork, Ardagh parish, Cornaveigh.

4 Seághan Ruiséal, intermediary for a letter intended for Pártholán Suipéal (PPC to MÓG, 1834).

Though linked by Cúndún to Youghal, no priest of that name is listed there. However, a John Russell is listed as the Roman Catholic parish priest of Cloyne, which borders Ballymacoda to the southwest, in 1837–38 and 1849: *Complete Catholic Registry*, 378; *Thom's*, 339–40; *Slater's*, 340.

Group 2: Addressees

5 Pártholán Suipéal: received PPC to PS, 1834 and PPC to PS, 1837.

Barthw Supple is listed as holding about four acres in the townland of East Clonard in 1833: TAB, County Cork, Clonpriest (Cloyne Priest)] parish, East Clonard.

6 Míghcheál Ó Eichíaruinn: named in PPC to PS, 1834 and PPC to MÓG, 1834, as the intended recipient of a letter which may have never arrived.

Michael Ahern and Margaret Ahern are listed as holding twenty-one acres in Yellowford in 1834: TAB, County Cork, Kilmacdonogh parish, Yellowford.

7 Seághan Cúndún: named in PPC to PS, 1834, and PPC to MÓG, 1834, as the intended recipient of a letter that never arrived.

Pádraig Phiarais Cúndún passed on a message to Seághan Cúndún in a letter to Séamas Mac Gearailt in 1837 (see no. 40 below). No evidence in the letters or poems suggests that Seághan Cúndún was a close relative. There are two entries under the name John Condon in townlands close to each other in 1833 – a thirty-acre holding in Lower Ballinvarig and a thirty-four-acre holding in Youghal Park: TAB, County Cork, Clonpriest (Cloyne Priest) parish, Ballinvarrig Lower and Youghal-park (Parkeneig). However, there are at least ten other entries under the same name in East Cork. None of these are in the parishes of Kilmacdonogh or Ightermurragh.

8 Mícheághal Ó Glasáin: received PPC to MÓG, 1834.

This letter contained the poem "Aiste na nIarthar," which was addressed to Ó Glasáin. Cúndún sent him greetings in the 1848 and 1849 letters to Tomás Ó Briain: Ó Foghludha, *Pádraig Phiarais Cúndún*, 80, 90. Michael Gleeson is listed as holding about forty-three acres in Lisquinlan in 1833: TAB, County Cork, Ightermurragh (Ightermorrough) parish, Lisquinlan. There are two entries in Griffith's *General Valuation* under the name Michael Gleeson in Lisquinlan: one holding is about forty-three acres while the other is about fifty-three acres (154). While both entries may relate to the same individual, they may also be father and son.

9 Séamas Mac Gearailt: received PPC to SMG, 1837.

Mac Gearailt composed a lengthy response to "Aiste na nIarthar," and a small number of manuscripts in his hand survive: Ó Conchúir, *Scríobhaithe Chorcaí*, 256n181; see, e.g., RIA Ms. 24 B 27, 238–50. Cúndún criticized him fiercely in a letter to Tomás Stac in 1854: Ó Foghludha, *Pádraig Phiarais Cúndún*, 100–1. Jas Fitzgerald held four acres in the townland of Finisk in 1833. He also operated a boat that transported sand and was a Bible teacher for the Irish Society at various times, including the mid- to late 1820s and around 1848: TAB, Clonpriest (Cloyne Priest) parish, Finisk (Fanisk); de Brún, *Scriptural Instruction*, 244–5.

10 Tomás Ó Briain: received PPC to TÓB, 1848, and PPC to TÓB, 1849.

This may be the same Tomás Ó Briain to whom Cúndún sent greetings in his 1834 letter to Mícheághal Ó Glasáin (see no. 29 below). Though Ó Foghludha links Tomás Ó Briain with Mountcotton, a Thomas Brien is listed as holding about sixty acres in the nearby townland of Ballypherode in 1834, while Griffith's *General Valuation* lists a holding of thirty-seven acres under the same name and townland: Ó Foghludha, *Pádraig Phiarais Cúndún*, xviii; TAB, County Cork, Kilmacdonogh parish, Ballyperode; Griffith, *General Valuation*, 35.

11 Tomás Stac: received PPC to TS, 1851, PPC to TS, 1852, and PPC to TS, 1854.

Cúndún sent greetings to Tomás Stac in an 1834 letter to Pártholán Suipéal: TC Ms. T vii, 65. Thomas Stack was a Bible teacher for the Irish Society from the mid-1820s and appears to have been active until the early 1850s at least: de Brún, *Scriptural Instruction*, 460–1. A holding of about twenty-eight acres is listed under the names John and Thos Stack in the townland of Redbarn in 1833: TAB, County Cork, Clonpriest (Cloyne Priest) parish, Redbarn. Griffith's *General Valuation* has no entries for either name in Redbarn, but does list a holding of about thirty acres in the neighbouring townland of Pillmore under the name John Stack (19).

Group 3: Persons in Ballymacoda who received greetings or news or were otherwise mentioned

12 Mother of Pártholán Suipéal: PPC to PS, 1834.
"Is 'na hainm do stiúireóchainn an litir seo, ach d'eagladh gur éag sí. Do bhí buairt mhór uirthe an tan do bhíodhmair-ne a fágbháil Éireann." (I would have addressed the letter to her but for fear that she had died. She was very upset when we were leaving Ireland): TC Ms. T vii, 61.

13 Ruisdeárd Ó Muirighthe: PPC to PS, 1834: TC Ms. T vii, 65.
PPC to PS, 1837: TC Ms. T vii, 69.
See no. 37 below.

14 Seághan Ó Bruadair (1), Seághan Ó Bruadair (2): PPC to PS, 1834.
"Chum an dá chSeághan Ó Bruadair" (to the two Seághan Ó Bruadairs): TC Ms. T vii, 65.
PPC to PS, 1837: TC Ms. T vii, 69.
See no. 37 below.

15 Pádraig Héad: PPC to PS, 1834: TC Ms. T vii, 65.

16 Mighcheál Héad: PPC to PS, 1834.
"Do chualadh go bhfuair Mighcheál Héad bás, is och liom a bhás go deimhin; do bhí mé chum scríobh cuige an tan do chuala é" (I heard that Mighcheál Héad died – I sincerely regret his death; I was about to write to him at the time I heard it): TC Ms. T vii, 65.

17 Dáibídh Ó Néill: PPC to PS, 1834.
"Ó'n Rubhán" (from an Rubhán [*sic*]): TC Ms. T vii, 65.

18 Muiris Líghe: PPC to PS, 1834.
"An táilúir beól bhínn" (the sweet-voiced tailor): TC Ms. T vii, 65.

19 Muiris Ó Laochadh: PPC to PS, 1834.
"Ó Eóchaill" (from Youghal): TC Ms. T vii, 65.

20 Mighcheál Galldubh: PPC to PS, 1834.
"Ó Eóchaill" (from Youghal): TC Ms. T vii, 65.

21 Uillíam Óg Ó Donomháin: PPC to PS, 1834.
"An dochtúir ó Eóchaill" (the doctor from Youghal): TC Ms. T vii, 65.
PPC to MÓG, 1834.
"A nEóchaill" (in Youghal): TC Ms. T vii, 47.

22 Féilim Mac Cárrtha: PPC to PS, 1834.
"Ó Eóchaill" (from Youghal): TC Ms. T vii, 65.

23 Tomás Mac Ciúghadh: PPC to PS, 1834.
"Ó Árd Suileach" (from Ardsallagh): TC Ms. T vii, 66.

24 Peattair Ó Néill: PPC to MÓG, 1834.
"An tEaguilseach diadha, deadh shomplach .I. Peattair Ó Néill" (and the pious exemplary churchman, i.e., Peattair Ó Néill): TC Ms. T vii, 47.

25 Mártan Ó Cruadhluídhe: PPC to MÓG, 1834: TC Ms. T vii, 47.

26 Muiris Ó Laocha: PPC to MÓG, 1834.
"A nEóchaill" (in Youghal): TC Ms. T vii, 47.

27 Uillíam Stúndún: PPC to MÓG, 1834.
"Bhóthar an champa" (of Bóthar an Champa [*sic*]): TC Ms. T vii, 47.

28 Uillíam mac Dhaibhídh mac Gearailt: PPC to MÓG, 1834: TC Ms. T vii, 47.

29 Tomás Ó Néill: PPC to MÓG, 1834.
"Chum Tomás Ó Néill dá ngoirmís Toimín thomáis óig" (to Tomás Ó Néill who we used to call Toimín Thomáis Óig): TC Ms. T vii, 48.
PPC to TÓB, 1849.
"Chum Tomás Ó Néill is chum Pilib Ó Néill" (to Tomás Ó Néill and to Pilib Ó Néill): Ó Foghludha, *Pádraig Phiarais Cúndún*, 90.

30 Tomás do Baradh: PPC to MÓG, 1834.
"Ó Chíll Chríodáin" (from Kilcredan): TC Ms. T vii, 48.

31 Maitias Ua Doinnléith: PPC to MÓG, 1834.
"Ó Ghort an sciobóil" (from Barnfield): TC Ms. T vii, 48.

32 Muiris Ó hAongusa: PPC to MÓG, 1834.
"Ó Bhaile Mhicíaith" (from Ballymakeagh): TC Ms. T vii, 48.

33 Seághan Dlúth Ó Bríain: PPC to MÓG, 1834.
"Chum Seághan Dlúth Ó Bríain etc. Chum a mhic Tomás Ó Bríain fá seach" (To Seághan Dlúth Ó Bríain etc. To his son Tomás Ó Bríain in turn): TC Ms. T vii, 48. This may be the

Tomás Ó Briain named above as a recipient of letters from Cúndún.

34 Séamas Ó Cochláin: PPC to MÓG, 1834: TC Ms. T vii, 48.

35 Muiris Ó Ciosáin: PPC to MÓG, 1834: TC Ms. T vii, 48.

36 Toirdhéalbhach Ó Maghamhna: PPC to MÓG, 1834: TC Ms. T vii, 48.

37 Mother of Maighréad Nic Carrthaigh: PPC to PS, 1837.
"Níor nochtas fós dam mhnaoi gur éug a máthair. Do bhithin gur ghlac sí ró bhuadhartha bás a deirbhshéur, bás chlainne chSheághain Uí Bhruadair agus bás chlainne Ruisdeáird Uí Mhuirighthe." (I haven't yet revealed to my wife that her mother died as she took the death of her sister, the death of Seághan Ó Bruadair's children and the death of Ruisdeárd Ó Muirighthe's children very badly): TC Ms. T vii, 69.

38 Sister of Maighréad Nic Carrthaigh: PPC to PS, 1837: TC Ms. T vii, 69.
See no. 37 above.

39 Bhailtéar (Mac Gearailt?): PPC to SMG, 1837.
"Acht do h-innsiog dam gur fhágbhuis an Fhanuisg agus go ndeachais go Cosdubh le Bhailtéar" (but I was told that you left Finisk and that you went to Cosdubh [*sic*] with Bhailtéar): TC Ms. T vii, 67.

40 Pádruig Brún: PPC to SMG, 1837?
"Labhair lé Seághan Cúndún agus abair leis go bhfuil fear ann-sa mbaile seo, Útica, fear dá ngoirthear Éamon Brún, bráthair fogus do bhean chSheághain Cúndún. Atá sé a ccaidreamh liom-sa, búisdéireacht do leanan sé ... Ímpídhean sé air cSeághan agus air a mhnaoi, scéala do chur chum a dhearbhráthar .I. Pádruig Brún, agus a rádh leis scríobh chuige." (Speak to Seághan Cúndún and tell him that there's a man in this town, Útica, who is called Éamon Brún, a brother-in-law of Seághan Cúndún's wife. He's good friends with me; butchery is what he's doing ... He beseeches Seághan and his wife to pass a message to his brother, i.e., Pádruig Brún, and to tell him to write to him): TC Ms. T vii, 70.

41 Wife of Seághan Cúndún: PPC to SMG, 1837?: TC Ms. T vii, 70.
See no. 40 above.

42 Tomás Cúndún: PPC to SMG, 1837?

"Tabhair mo bhithnniochd dom' dhearbhráthair .I. Tomás Cúndún, agus abair leis gan smuaíneamh air theachd annso. Atá obair na h.áite seo ró chruaidh dho, no mádh thagan bídheadh mairg air" (Pass my greetings to my brother, i.e., Tomás Cúndún, and tell him not to think of coming here. The work in this place is too hard for him, for if he comes he will regret it): TC Ms. T vii, 70.

43 Seán Mac Pádraig Uí Fhinn: PPC to TÓB, 1849: Ó Foghludha, *Pádraig Phiarais Cúndún*, 90.

44 Pilib Ó Néill: PPC to TÓB, 1849: Ó Foghludha, *Pádraig Phiarais Cúndún*, 90.

See no. 29 above.

45 Diarmuid Ó Cruadhlaoich: PPC to TÓB, 1849: Ó Foghludha, *Pádraig Phiarais Cúndún*, 90.

46 Tomás Hárbhí: PPC to TS, 1851.

"Is maith liom go maith é: duine uasal macánta" (I like him well: he is an honest gentleman): Ó Foghludha, *Pádraig Phiarais Cúndún*, 90.

PPC to TS, 1852.

"An duine uasail" (the gentleman): CCCA Ms. G 6, 7.

47 Mairgréud Stac: PPC to TS, 1852.

"Do sgribh Mairgréud do dearbhshúr leitir chugham ... Adubhairt si liom go bhfuil triur dod chlainn inghean anois aMeiricea agus is maith do riniotar san" (Mairgréud, your sister, wrote a letter to me ... She told me that three of your daughters are in America now and it's good that they did so): CCCA Ms. G 6, 3.

PPC to TS, 1854.

"Do scríbh aon dem ingheanaibh dhá leitir gonuig do dheirbhshiúr Mairghréad: ní bhfuaireamair freagra ar bith fós; is eagal linn ná fuair sí ceachtar díobh." (One of my daughters wrote two letters to your sister Mairghréad: we didn't get any answer yet; we fear that she didn't receive either of them): Ó Foghludha, *Pádraig Phiarais Cúndún*, 100.

48 Seaghan an Sgadain: PPC to TS, 1852.

"Do bhí cómharsa dhom ... ar an Seanacoill. ... ní itdheasac sé an sgadán ar aón chlárr le buachaill is cailín do bhíoch aige" (I had a neighbour ... in Shanakill ... he wouldn't eat the herring at the same table as the boy and girl who used to work for him): CCCA Ms. G 6, 3–4.

49 Diarmaid Sdúndún: PPC to TS, 1852 .

"Do chuala gur éag an baodhaltach … .i. Diarmaid Sdúndún" (I heard that the betrayer died … i.e., Diarmaid Sdúndún): CCCA Ms. G 6, 5–7. This was the person blamed by Cúndún for the loss of his farm in Shanakill and, consequently, for his need to emigrate.

50 Séaghan Sdúndún: PPC to TS, 1852.

"Atá … séaghan a dhearbhráthair cómh olch … leis an mbaoghaltach" (Seaghán, his brother … is as evil … as the betrayer): CCCA Ms. G 6, 6.

Group 4: North American persons mentioned

51–61 Maighréad Nic Carrthaigh (wife) and children (all): PPC to PS, 1834.

"A táimse … dá fhaisnéis duit go bhfuilim féin, mo bhean, agus mo chlann, gan easbadh bídh, éaduig, 'ná sláinte; gan beárrnadh air bith an aon dam bhuídhin fós" (I'm … informing you that I myself, my wife and my children, are not lacking in food, clothing nor in health – no gap whatsoever in my brood yet): TC Ms. Tvii, 61.

PPC to MÓG, 1834: TC Ms. Tvii, 46.

PPC to PS, 1837: TC Ms. T vii, 69.

Maighréad Nic Carrthaigh (wife): PPC to PS, 1837: TC Ms. Tvii, 69.

See no. 37 above.

Children (all): PPC to SMG, 1837?

"Deichneamhar clainne … Atá mór-sheisior bainionaicc orrtha sin, mar atá triúr do thugas liom ó Éire agus ceathrar ó thángadh go hAmerica" (ten children … There are seven girls among them, three of whom I took with me from Ireland and four since I came to America): TC Ms. Tvii, 71. In 1821 the ages of Cundún's children were: Piaras, 9; Eibhlin, 8; Caitlín, 2; Maighréad, 1: Ó Foghludha, *Pádraig Phiarais Cúndún*, ix.

PPC to TÓB, 1848.

"Tá mo mhuinghín iomlán i nDia go bhfuil sibh uile i sláinte mhaith: tá mo mhuinntirse uile mar sin" (I place my complete trust in God that you are all in good health: all my kin are likewise): Ó Foghludha, *Pádraig Phiarais Cúndún*, 79.

PPC to TÓB, 1849: Ó Foghludha, *Pádraig Phiarais Cúndún*, 85.

PPC to TS, 1854: Ó Foghludha, *Pádraig Phiarais Cúndún*, 100.

Piaras Cúndún (son): PPC to TS, 1854.

"Tá Piaras, mo mhac, go maith" (My son, Piaras, is well): Ó Foghludha, *Pádraig Phiarais Cúndún*, 100.

Daughter: PPC to TS, 1854: Ó Foghludha, *Pádraig Phiarais Cúndún*, 100.

See no. 47 above.

62 Seághan O Néill: PPC to PS, 1834.

"Agus gur ab aon díobh Seághan Ó Néill ó Eachamhín. Do chuala go ttáinigh sé amach. Ó, is truaigh ná táinigh sé an am an so" (and that one of them is Seághan Ó Néill from Eachamhín [*sic*]. I heard that he came out. Oh, it's a pity he didn't come here in time): TC Ms. T vii, 62.

63 Seághan Cúndún (first cousin): PPC to PS, 1834.

"Clann dearbhrathar m'athar – Atá trí feirmeacha breághtha talmhan aco, teóra lem' chuid talmhansa. Atá Seaghan Cúndún pósda lé bean o chonntaé lochgarmain, atá dís mhac agus inghean aco." (My father's brother's children – they have three fine farms of land, close to my own land. Seághan Cúndún is married to a woman from County Wexford, they have two sons and a daughter): TC Ms. T vii, 64.

PPC to PS, 1837: TC Ms. vii, 69.

PPC to TÓB, 1849.

"Féach Séan is Piaras Cúndún, is iad atá gan uireasbha annso. Tá seacht mbó is fiche ag Seán Cúndún, agus cheithre chapaill." (Look at Seághan and Piarais Cúndún who are without want here. Seághan Cúndún has twenty-seven cows and four horses): Ó Foghludha, *Pádraig Phiarais Cúndún*, 85.

64 Wife of Seághan Cúndún: PPC to PS, 1834: TC Ms. T vii, 64.

See no. 63 above.

65 Máire Cúndún (first cousin): PPC to PS, 1834.

"Clann dearbhrathar m'athar ... Atá Máire Cúndún pósda lé fear ó chonntaé Mhanachán, a ccúige Uladh ... Atá feirm thalmhan aco an san mbaile céadhna 'na bhfuilimíd-na, atá dís mhac agus dís inghean aco." (My father's brother's children … Máire Cúndún is married to a man from County Monaghan in Ulster … they have a farm of land in the same locality as we're in, they have two sons and two daughters): TC Ms. T vii, 64.

PPC to TÓB, 1849.

"An fear do bhí ag Máire Chúndún do dhíol sé a chuid talmhan bliain ó shoin … agus do cheannuigh sé céad is trí fichid acra ar dalaer an t-acra" (Máire Cúndún's husband, he sold his land a year ago … and he bought one hundred and sixty acres at a dollar an acre): Ó Foghludha, *Pádraig Phiarais Cúndún*, 92.

66 Husband of Máire Cúndún: PPC to PS, 1834: TC Ms. T vii, 64. See no. 65 above.

PPC to TÓB, 1849: Ó Foghludha, *Pádraig Phiarais Cúndún*, 92. See no. 65 above.

67 Piaras Cúndún (first cousin): PPC to PS, 1834.

"Clann dearbhrathar m'athar … Níor phós Píaras fós, atá sé féin agus an cailín beag martraighthe agus Seághan Ó Cealladh a tteannta chéile" (My father's brother's children … Piaras has not married yet – he himself and the little disabled girl and Seághan Ó Cealladh are together): TC Ms. T vii, 64.

PPC to TÓB, 1849.

"Féach Séan is Piaras Cúndún, is iad atá gan uireasbha annso … Tá sé bó déag is fiche agus sé chapaill ag Piaras Cúndún" (Look at Seághan and Piarais Cúndún who are without want here … Piaras Cúndún has thirty-six cows and six horses): Ó Foghludha, *Pádraig Phiarais Cúndún*, 85.

68 The little disabled girl (Cúndún) (first cousin): PPC to PS, 1834: TC Ms. T vii, 64.

See no. 67 above. This is a translation of "an cailín beag martraighthe," a description that is imprecise with regard to both age and the nature of the disability in question, but which most likely served to fully identify her to the letter's addressee. Implicit in the context in which the girl or young woman is mentioned is that she is a sister of Piaras, Seághan, and Máire Cúndún, and a first cousin of Pádraig Phiarais Cúndún.

69 Seághan Ó Cealladh: PPC to PS, 1834: TC Ms. T vii, 64. See no. 67 above.

70 Seághan Suipéal: PPC to PS, 1834.
"Cuir chúgham scéala cad is corr dod' dhearbhrathair Seághan Suipéal, óir do chualamair gur báthag é a ttalam an éisg" (Send news to me about what befell your brother, because we heard that he drowned in Newfoundland): TC Ms. T vii, 65.

71 Mighcheáll O Néill: PPC to PS, 1837.
"An litir úd do chuiris chúgham níor thárlaidh liom an teachdaire .I. Mighcheáll O Néill. Atá sé céad míle síar ó dheas uaim, a mbaile mór d'á ngoirthear Albainídh, a stát Nuadh York. Cuirimíd scéala chum a chéile go minic. Atá sé féin, a bhean agus a chlann go maith." (That letter you forwarded to me – I haven't chanced upon the messenger yet, i.e., Mighcheáll O Néill. He's a hundred miles southwest of me in a big town called Albany in New York State. We send news to each other frequently. He himself, his wife and his children are well): TC Ms. T vii, 69–70.

72 Éamon Brún: PPC to SMG, 1837?: TC Ms. T vii, 70.
See no. 40 above.

73 Séamus de Barra: PPC to TÓB, 1848.
"Cuir chugham scéal ... Stiúruigh do leitir chum Séamus de Barra in Utica, le n-a tabhairt damhsa, agus ar dhruim do leitre abair mar sin." (Send news to me ... Direct your letter to Séamus de Barra in Utica to give to me and say that on the back of your letter): Ó Foghludha, *Pádraig Phiarais Cúndún*, 84.

74 Séan Ó Cachláin: PPC to TÓB, 1849.
"Sin é do chomhursa, Séan Ó Cachláin, ó Fhaithche Bhaile Mhacóda ... tá feirm bhreagh thalmhan ceannaighthe amach go brách anois aige" (Look at your neighbour, Séan Ó Cachláin, from Faithche [*sic*], Ballymacoda ... he has now bought a fine farm of land outright): Ó Foghludha, *Pádraig Phiarais Cúndún*, 85–6.

75 Micheál Ó Maoileanaigh: PPC to TÓB, 1849.
"Micheál Ó Maoileanaigh ó Bhaile Uí Chríonáin, agus a bhean Gobnait Ní Eachtigheirnn, atáid siad go socair sámh annso i gcathair Utica" (Micheál Ó Maoileanaigh from Ballycrenane, and his wife Gobnait Ní Eachtigheirnn, they are settled comfortably here in the city of Utica): Ó Foghludha, *Pádraig Phiarais Cúndún*, 86.

76 Gobnait Ní Eachtigheirnn: PPC to TÓB, 1849: Ó Foghludha, *Pádraig Phiarais Cúndún*, 86.
See no. 75 above.

77 Micheál Ó hEachthigheirnn: PPC to TÓB, 1849.
"Féach Micheál Ó hEachthigheirnn ó Chluain Príost ... Tá sé féin is a mhuinntir uile i bhfochair a chéile in Utica agus iad ag déanamh go maith." (Look at Micheál Ó hEachthigheirnn from Clonpriest ... He himself and all his kin are together in Utica and are doing well): Ó Foghludha, *Pádraig Phiarais Cúndún*, 91.

NOTES

I would like to thank Professor Pádraig Ó Macháin, University College Cork, for his encouraging and insightful supervision of my ongoing doctoral research into the poetry of Pádraig Phiarais Cúndún. Any errors above remain firmly my own. I would also like to acknowledge the encouragement of Dr Máire Ní Iceadha, my colleague in Mary Immaculate College, St Patrick's Campus, Thurles, and the support of the college in the pursuit of my research.

1 Nilsen, "Thinking of Monday," 9; Nilsen, "'The language,'" 301.
2 Nilsen, "Irish Language," 32.
3 Ó Foghludha, *Pádraig Phiarais Cúndún*, x.
4 Nilsen, "Irish Language," 2; Nilsen, "Irish Gaelic Literature," 193.
5 For general accounts of Pádraig Phiarais Cúndún, see Ó Foghludha, *Pádraig Phiarais Cúndún*, vii–xxiv; Ó Floinn, "Pádraig Phiarais Cúndún," 184–94; and Breathnach and Ní Mhurchú, "Cúndún, Pádraig Phiarais." For more detailed accounts and analyses of various aspects of his life and works see Buttimer, "Comhfhreagras Corcaíoch," 15–38; Miller, *Emigrants*, 203, 216, 270–9; Ó Duinnshléibhe, "Aiste na nIarthar," 97–111; and Ó Duinnshléibhe, "Pádraig Phiarais Cúndún," 546–89. Pádraig Phiarais Cúndún is the version of the name used by Risteárd Ó Foghludha as the title for his anthology and by Breathnach and Ní Mhurchú as the title for their biographical sketch. Also used are Pádraig Phiarais, as he was known locally (Ó Foghludha, *Pádraig Phiarais Cúndún*, vii), and Pádraig Cúndún, as he signed his letters (CCCA Ms. G 6, 7). CCCA Ms. G 6 is an 1852 autograph and the only surviving letter from America in Cúndún's hand.
6 Ballymacoda (Baile Mhac Óda) is used here to refer to Cúndún's native locality; the farm he held was located in the townland of Shanakill (an

tSeanchoill). East Cork is used in a more general sense to refer to that part of County Cork in which Ballymacoda is situated and which stretches from the outskirts of Cork city to Youghal.

7 This version of the Irish text is based on NYPL MssCol 1773, 22, which I have edited and translated. The translation and those below aim to express the primary meaning of the Irish original only and do not incorporate literary features; in the interest of brevity, alternative translations are not given, even where they are as valid as those provided. Extracts taken from NYPL MssCol 1773 have been edited, but those from other manuscripts and from Ó Foghludha, *Pádraig Phiarais Cúndún*, have not. NYPL MssCol 1773 is a photostat copy of a late manuscript in Cúndún's hand and contains versions of much of his surviving poetry.

8 For other descriptions of social occasions, some positive and others less so, see "Aiste na nIarthar" (Poem of Faraway Places) (NYPL MssCol 1773, 52–3) and "Atáim re tréimhse i mbrón" (I have been in sorrow for a while) (RIA Ms. 23 B 14, 225–6).

9 Nic Craith, *Malartú Teanga*, 76–77, 84, 87, 100; Ó Duinnshléibhe, "Pádraig Phiarais Cúndún," 546–89.

10 NYPL MssCol 1773, 47–9.

11 Until recently, the most substantial evidence that Cúndún was not monolingual was the existence of English passages in the part of RIA Ms. 23 B 14 (1820s) thought to be in his hand; see Mulchrone et al., *Catalogue*, 826. However, careful comparison with letters known to be in his hand (RL Ms. C 93 and CCCA Ms. G 6) shows that he did not write the English passages. While we cannot entirely rule out that he acquired English from day-to-day usage in Utica, the presence of his cousins' households nearby and of his own sizable family could have allowed him to conduct his business through intermediaries, a proposition that is consistent with the minimal usage of English in his poems and letters from America.

12 No evidence exists that Cúndún wrote to anyone in Ireland outside of east Cork during this time.

13 NYPL MssCol 1773, 22–3.

14 TC Ms. T vii, 65.

15 Ibid., 65.

16 This practice is observed in the letters of the 1830s but not in those of the 1840s and 1850s; this change may be due to postal reforms in 1839–40: Dixon, "Irish Postal History," 131–2.

17 NYPL MssCol 1773, 37.

18 Ibid., 38–9.

19 Ó Foghludha, *Pádraig Phiarais Cúndún*, 79.

20 TC Ms. T vii, 67–8. The letters contain contradictory attitudes toward emigration. While he expresses approval that three of Tomás Stac's daughters have come to America (CCCA Ms. G 6, 3), he sternly admonishes his brother, Tomás Cúndún, not to do likewise as he would surely regret it (TC Ms. T vii, 70).

21 TC Ms. T vii, 69.

22 Ó Foghludha, *Pádraig Phiarais Cúndún*, 100–1. He appears to have been unaware that Tomás Stac was himself working for the society and indeed fully committed to it. Ironically, it seems that Cúndún too had applied to work for the society, having sought and obtained permission from the local Catholic clergy at the time of his lowest ebb, but that he had emigrated before taking it up; see de Brún, *Scriptural Instruction*, 183–4, 460–1. This is the only instance in which Cúndún expresses criticism of one of his correspondents.

23 CCCA Ms. G 6, 5–7. See Nilsen, "Irish Gaelic Literature," 199–200, for a translation of a short excerpt from this passage.

24 As a result, eight of the ten full surviving copies of the poem do not contain the offending lines (121–8): RL Ms. B 20, 6–17; RIA Ms. 24 B 27, 208–20; RIA Ms. 12 O 7, 41–6; NLI Ms. G 662, 33–42; NLI Ms. G 658, 156–64; HL Ms. IR 13, 107–11; NLI Ms. G 871, 232–43; and TC Ms. T vii, 35–46.

25 See Ó Foghludha, *Pádraig Phiarais Cúndún*, 112, for a list of the letters and poems; those composed in America are numbered from eight to thirty-five inclusive, with the exception of numbers twenty-three and twenty-four, which were not composed by Cúndún.

26 Ó Foghludha, *Pádraig Phiarais Cúndún*, ix.

27 "Mo phéin, mo phúir, mo léan, mo lachta-rois" (My suffering, my sorrow, my woe, my flood of tears): NYPL MssCol 1773, 45. The two other poems composed in 1856 are "Im aonar cois abhainn i machaire an áird-os" (On my own by a river in the field of the deer region): NYPL MssCol 1773, 43–4; and "Is caithte dubhach meata an snódh atá orm féin" (My own countenance is spent, grieved and feeble): NYPL MssCol 1773, 46–7. Ó Foghludha presents the latter as being written for Dáibhí Mac Gearailt of Youghal and appends a verse that names Dáibhí Mac Gearailt but does not follow the same metrical pattern as the body of the poem: *Pádraig Phiarais Cúndún*, 105–6. Neither this name nor the verse appears in Cúndún's own version.

28 The household of the third cousin, Piaras Cúndún, is more likely to have been Irish-speaking: TC Ms. T vii, 64; see entries 67–9 in Appendix B.

29 Ó Foghludha, *Pádraig Phiarais Cúndún*, 92.

30 See the 1834 letters to Pártholán Suipéal: TC Ms. T vii, 64; and Mícheághal Ó Glasáin: TC Ms. T vii, 47.

31 TC Ms.T vii, 69–70.
32 He gives an insight into his mentality in this regard in his 1848 letter to Tomás Ó Briain: "Anois chum ná cuirfinn leitir fholamh chughat, tabharfad duit annso na ranna ceóil" (And now so that I wouldn't send you an empty letter, I'll give you here the song verses): Ó Foghludha, *Pádraig Phiarais Cúndún*, 80.
33 Uí Fhlannagáin, *Mícheál Ó Lócháin*, 66, 70; Callahan, "Irish Language," 23; Nilsen, "Irish Gaelic Literature," 200.
34 These are the lament for his wife, "Óm chroidhe mo scread a' teacht go cruaidh" (My cry comes keenly from my heart); and the poem "Do neartuigh go deimhin mo mhisne is mo gháire" (My spirit and my joy have been strengthened indeed), which lauds the achievements of Daniel O'Connell: NYPL MssCol 1773, 30, 37; *Irish-American*, 9 January and 31 July 1858. Coincidently, the year of Cúndún's death (1857) was the same year that an Irish column, or "department," commenced in the *Irish-American*: Nilsen, "Irish Language," 261.
35 Ibid., 259–62; Nilsen, "Irish Gaelic Literature," 200–1.
36 *Nation*, 4 and 11 September 1858.
37 *Gaelic American*, 12 December 1908, 15 January 1910, 23 and 30 April 1910, 7, 14, 21, and 28 May 1910, and 4 June 1910.
38 Ó Duinnshléibhe, "Aiste na nIarthar" and "Pádraig Phiarais Cúndún."
39 Buttimer, "Great Irish Famine," 470–1; Miller, *Emigrants*, 203, 216, 270–9.
40 RL Ms. CF 33, 22.

BIBLIOGRAPHY

Brady, W. Maziére. *Clerical and Parochial Records of Cork, Cloyne and Ross*, vol. 2. London: Longman, 1864.

Breathnach, Diarmuid, and Máire Ní Mhurchú. "Cúndún, Pádraig Phiarais (1777–1857)." In *Ainm.ie: An Bunachar Náisiúnta Beathaisnéisí Gaeilge*. Fiontar: Ollscoil Chathair Bhaile Átha Cliath, 2018. https://www.ainm.ie/Bio.aspx?ID=1062.

Buttimer, Neil. "Comhfhreagras Corcaíoch." In *Séimhfhear Suairc: Aistí in Ómós don Ollamh Breandán Ó Conchúir*, ed. Seán Ó Coileáin, Liam P. Ó Murchú, and Pádraigín Riggs, 1-38. An Daingean: An Sagart, 2013.

– "The Great Irish Famine in Gaelic Manuscripts." In *Atlas of the Great Irish Famine*, ed. John Crowley, William J. Smyth, and Mike Murphy, 460–72, 695–6. Cork: Cork University Press, 2012.

Callahan, Joseph. "The Irish Language in Pennsylvania." In *The Irish Language in the United States*, ed. Thomas W. Ihde, 18–26. Westport: Bergin and Garvey, 1994.

City of Dublin and Hibernian Provincial Directory. London: Pigot and Co., 1824.

A Complete Catholic Registry, Directory, and Almanack, 1837–38. Dublin: W.J. Battersby.

de Brún, Pádraig. *Scriptural Instruction in the Vernacular*. Dublin: Dublin Institute for Advanced Studies, 2009.

Dixon, F.E. "Irish Postal History." *Dublin Historical Record* 23, no. 4 (1970): 127–36.

Griffith, Richard. *The General Valuation of the Rateable Property in Ireland: County of Cork, Barony of Imokilly*. Dublin: HMSO, 1853.

Landed Estates Database. Moore Institute, National University of Ireland, Galway, 18 May 2011. http://landedestates.nuigalway.ie.

Miller, Kerby A. *Emigrants and Exiles: Ireland and the Irish Exodus to North America*. Oxford: Oxford University Press, 1985.

Mulchrone, Kathleen, Elizabeth Fitzpatrick, Lillian Duncan, and Winifred Wulff. *Catalogue of Irish Manuscripts in the Royal Irish Academy*, vol. 2, fasciculi 6–10. Dublin: Royal Irish Academy, 1931–33.

Nic Craith, Máiréad. *Malartú Teanga: An Ghaeilge i gCorcaigh sa Naoú hAois Déag*. Bremen: Verlag für E.S.I.S., 1993.

Nilsen, Kenneth E. "Irish Gaelic Literature in the United States." In *American Babel: Literatures of the United States from Abnaki to Zuni*, ed. Mark Shell, 188–218. Cambridge, MA: Harvard University Press, 2002.

– "The Irish Language in New York, 1850-1900." In *The New York Irish*, ed. Roland H. Bayor and Timothy J. Meagher, 252–74. Baltimore: Johns Hopkins University Press, 1996.

– "'The language that the strangers do not know': The Galway Gaeltacht of Portland, Maine in the Twentieth Century." In *They Change Their Sky: The Irish in Maine*, ed. Michael C. Connolly, 297–339. Orono: University of Maine Press, 2004.

– "Thinking of Monday: Irish Speakers of Portland, Maine." *Éire-Ireland: A Journal of Irish Studies* 25, no. 1 (1990): 6–19.

Ó Conchúir, Breandán. *Scríobhaithe Chorcaí 1700–1850*. Baile Átha Cliath: An Clóchomhar, 1982.

Ó Duinnshléibhe, Seán. "Aiste na nIarthar: An Dán agus mar a Tháinig sé Anuas." In *Sealbhú an Traidisiúin*, ed. Niamh Ní Shiadhail, Meidhbhín Ní Urdail, and Ríonach Uí Ógáin, 97–111. Baile Átha Cliath: Comhairle Bhéaloideas Éireann, 2013.

– "Pádraig Phiarais Cúndún: An Stair agus an Stairsheanchas." In *Séimhfhear Suairc: Aistí in Ómós don Ollamh Breandán Ó Conchúir*, ed. Seán Ó Coileáin, Liam P. Ó Murchú, and Pádraigín Riggs, 546–89. An Daingean: An Sagart, 2013.

Ó Floinn, Tony. "Pádraig Phiarais Cúndún: Fear gur Tháinig an Dá Lá Air." *An Linn Bhuí* 21 (2017): 184–94.

Ó Foghludha, Risteárd. *Pádraig Phiarais Cúndún 1777–1856*. Baile Átha Cliath: Oifig Díolta Foillseacháin Rialtais, 1932.

Slater's National Commercial Directory of Ireland. Manchester: Slater, 1846.

Thom's Irish Almanack and Official Directory. Dublin: Alexander Thom, 1849.

Uí Fhlannagáin, Fionnuala. *Mícheál Ó Lócháin agus An Gaodhal*. Baile Átha Cliath: An Clóchomhar, 1990.

ARCHIVAL COLLECTIONS

Cork City and County Archives (CCCA).

Houghton Library (HL), Harvard University.

National Library of Ireland (NLI), Dublin.

New York Public Library (NYPL).

Royal Irish Academy (RIA), Dublin.

Russell Library (RL), Maynooth University.

Tithe Applotment Books, 1823–37 (TAB). National Archives of Ireland, Dublin. Digital images. titheapplotmentbooks.nationalarchives.ie.

Torna Collection (TC). University College Cork.

5

Irish-Language Folklore in *An Gaodhal*

Tomás Ó hÍde

The first issue of *An Gaodhal* (The Gael) was printed in Brooklyn, New York, in October 1881, thirteen months prior to the appearance of *Irisleabhar na Gaedhilge* (The Gaelic Journal) in Dublin.[1] The bilingual monthly periodical was edited and published by Galwayman Michael Logan (Mícheál Ó Lócháin) until his death on 10 January 1899,[2] after which Geraldine Haverty edited a New Series from March 1899 until 1904.[3] As Ken Nilsen noted, *An Gaodhal* "provided a forum for language enthusiasts, fledgling authors, and collectors of Irish folklore."[4] It is important as one of the few existing sources for "folklore collected from Irish speakers in [the United States]," and as a record of folklore collected in late nineteenth-century Ireland.[5] This chapter pays tribute to Nilsen's interest not only in Irish folklore but also in Irish (and Scottish Gaelic) publishing in North America. Alongside his oral recording activities, Nilsen collected and documented Irish and Gaelic columns across North America, and it is regrettable that the major study we might have hoped to see from this copious labour did not appear. Below I provide an overview of the folklore content in *An Gaodhal*, contributed by Irish speakers resident in both Ireland and the United States, and a transcription and translation of "Eachtra Eoghain Ruadh," one of the folk tales originally published by Logan, which is now not easily accessible.

AN GAODHAL AND IRISH FOLKLORE

Michael Logan desired to share fine examples of Irish-language prose with his readers, who were composed of native Irish speakers learning to read in their mother language and English speakers from Ireland and the United States who were learning Irish as a heritage language.[6] Prose examples include stories that readers collected from Irish speakers, tales that came from manuscript volumes brought to America by immigrants, stories that the editor reprinted from other newspapers and books, and articles written uniquely for the journal.[7] Individuals from both Ireland and America contributed pieces. Edward Lynch Blake (E.L. Blácach) of Ballinrobe, Co. Mayo, for example, wrote to *An Gaodhal* in November 1888 indicating that he had a collection of manuscripts that could be published:

> I have a large collection of MSS [containing] Traditional Stories in the Irish Language. They have been collected from the peasantry of the four Provinces. Some of them were collected by my father, and the remainder I have collected myself. I thought I would be able to get them published in book form but I regret that I am prevented by illness. The stories have never been published, and I think it a great pity that they should be lost. I have altogether 127, besides a lot of poetry, old sayings and nursery rhymes. I will give you the names of some of the stories.

Blake continued by listing the titles of some of the longer tales that would eventually grace the pages of future editions of *An Gaodhal*. The letter is followed by an editor's note that includes this comment: "Mr. Blake states that he will send a story for each issue of *The Gael*. Let each reader try and circulate it that it may be enabled to make Mr. Blake some compensation for the great labor involved in their transcription."[8] Douglas Hyde (Dubhghlas de hÍde) was also a recipient of Blake's collected stories, as can be seen in MS G 1071 in the National Library of Ireland (NLI). Hyde published stories from Blake in *Leabhar Sgeulaigheachta* at the same time that Logan was publishing material from Blake in *An Gaodhal.* Hyde indicated at the end of that book,

> "Cailleacha na fiacla fada" [The hags of the long teeth], "Colann gan cheann" [The headless body], "Cúirt an Chronnáin" [The court of Crinnawn], and "Tobar deire-an-domhain" [The well of D'yeree-in-Dowan],[9] I got, with many more not here printed from Eadbhard Loingseach Blácach, near Ballinrobe, County Mayo, one of the best shanachies in Connacht, or in Ireland."[10]

Others who collected and sent stories from Ireland included Pádruig Ó Laoghaire (1870–1896).[11] Inspired by the collecting activities of Hyde in Connacht, Ó Laoghaire managed to publish his collection of Munster stories in 1895 under the title of *Sgeuluidheacht Chúige Mumhan*.[12] However, in the years leading up to that publication, the readers of *An Gaodhal* were able to experience the riches of Munster folklore with Ó Laoghaire's contributions. One example is the tale "Beagán agus Beannacht nó Mórán agus Mallacht," which appeared in *An Gaodhal* in November 1893.[13] Pádraig Feiritéar (1856–1924) was among the individuals who collected materials on both sides of the Atlantic. He emigrated from Co. Kerry in 1895, and passages of his manuscript were published in *An Gaodhal*.[14] One item he collected before emigrating, the keen "Caoineadh Airt Uí Laoghaire," was printed in *An Gaodhal* a few years after his arrival in New York.[15] Another passage from Feiritéar titled "Sgéalta ó Iarthar Éireann" was published in 1899.[16] Additionally, passages from manuscript volumes from previous generations were included in *An Gaodhal*. Tomás D. de Norradh (Norris) contributed poetry from "láimhsgríobhtha a tá an-aosda go léir" (a manuscript that is really very old).[17] Folklore material from the manuscript of Mícheál Ó Raghallaigh (c.1790–c.1853) was also included in several issues on *An Gaodhal*; see, for example, "An Ceól Síghe" (The Fairy Music), which appeared in February 1902.[18] Ó Raghallaigh's manuscript provided a Kerry version of this legend, which was published with accompanying English translation. Seán Ó Súilleabháin, in *A Handbook of Irish Folklore*, referred to stories involving "fairy dance, music, and song." He asked folklore collectors, "Did dead or living persons take part in these dances as well as fairies? … Was it considered unlucky or of ill-omen to hear fairy music?"[19] Ó Raghallaigh's version has all the expected features of this Irish legend.[20]

As can be seen from the sampling above, a perusal of *An Gaodhal* turns up a fair bit of folklore. Taken more generally, folklore presented includes a variety of Fenian tales, folk stories, local legends, fables, songs, proverbs, toasts, prayers, and riddles. It should be kept in mind that although the folklore that appeared in *An Gaodhal* was published at a time of heightened awareness regarding the value of folklore,[21] the periodical started appearing nearly half a century before methodological expectations for the collection and publication of Irish folklore were standardized.[22] One difficulty with the folklore contained in *An Gaodhal* is that the editor does not always inform the reader as to the provenance of a given piece. Regarding those items for which the editor does not indicate the informant, the possibility exists that translation has taken place from English or French to Irish, or from Irish or Welsh to English, for example.

Fionnuala Uí Fhlannagáin, in the appendices of her 1990 book *Mícheál Ó Lócháin agus* An Gaodhal, included an index of the first three years of *An Gaodhal*. Risteárd de Hae, assistant librarian at the National Library of Ireland from 1929 to 1940 and director thereafter,[23] had already indexed all of *An Gaodhal*, except for the first three years, which were not available to him.[24] In the third volume of his *Clár Litridheacht na Nua-Ghaedhilge 1850–1936*, published in 1940, de Hae focused on prose. Of interest here are the sixty-one items that appeared in *An Gaodhal* that de Hae identifies as "Sgéalta" (stories).[25] It is among these records that we find the folk tales.

Ó Súilleabháin and Christiansen in *The Types of the Irish Folktale* (1963) identified about twenty-five folk tales of note from *An Gaodhal* (see Appendix 1). Similar to de Hae, one needs to search all of the entries in Ó Súilleabháin and Christiansen to identify where *An Gaodhal* is cited. Tales of magic were the most common folklore from *An Gaodhal* cited by Ó Súilleabháin and Christiansen, followed by stories emphasizing jokes and anecdotes. Far less common, though included, were animal tales, religious tales, and romantic tales. Ó Súilleabháin and Christiansen were evaluating each entry to recommend to folklorists as examples of international tale types. In contrast, de Hae was merely indicating all stories published in *An Gaodhal*. To de Hae's credit, he does identify many items that were reprinted from other sources or translated. For example, with the story "Rígh na gCéardaighthe" (King of the Craftsmen), which appeared in the March 1893 issue, de Hae notes, "aisdridhthe ó'n Sacsbheurla le Tadhg Ua Glasáin" (translated from English by Tadhg Ua Glasáin).[26] Likewise, with a few stories attributed to Domhnall Ó Fotharta, de Hae notes that they are reprints from the 1892 book by the same author titled *Siamsa an Gheimhridh* (Winter Entertainment). This information was reproduced from notes in *An Gaodhal* by Logan before or after stories.[27]

It is not possible to make a quick comparison between results reported by de Hae and those reported by Ó Súilleabháin and Christiansen. The authors did not provide complete citations. De Hae omitted page numbers, and Ó Súilleabháin and Christiansen omitted story titles as they appeared in the journal. One therefore has to verify in *An*

Gaodhal whether the two indices are referring to the same story. Additionally, whereas de Hae, in his 1940 index, did report the issues of *An Gaodhal* to which he did not have access, Ó Súilleabháin and Christiansen did not list any limited access to *An Gaodhal* in their 1963 index. However, they were likely using Douglas Hyde's bound collection of *An Gaodhal*, which is still held in the library of the Irish National Folklore Collection (NFC) at University College Dublin. It includes the years 1882–83 and 1890–96, as indicated on page ii of the bound volume.[28] On the third page of the bound collection, in the hand of Seán Ó Súilleabháin, one can read, "Chláraigh mé na märchen san imleabhar seo Deireadh Fómhair 1957" (I catalogued the Märchen in this volume October 1957).[29] It is therefore likely that Ó Súilleabháin and Christiansen's records of international tales in *An Gaodhal* are incomplete, and, of course, they omit notice of other sorts of prose folklore. Nonetheless, in conjunction with de Hae, they are the best guide currently available.

EACHTRA EOGHAIN RUADH

Having carefully sampled *An Gaodhal*, and after considering the suggestions of de Hae, Ó Súilleabháin and Christiansen, and Uí Fhlannagáin, I have chosen one folk tale to highlight the achievement of *An Gaodhal*. "Eachtra Eoghain Ruadh" is a short, realistic tale that was taken down "from the dictation of Mr. Thomas Lannon of Portlaw, Co. Waterford," and appeared in *An Gaodhal* in three parts in 1890 (December) and 1891 (February and May).[30] De Hae notes that the collector was "An Buinneán Aorach" (The Lively Branch).[31] This individual also collected and contributed the popular Irish song "An Spailpín Fánach" (The Wandering Farmhand) to *Irisleabhar na Gaedhilge*, as well as other items to *An Gaodhal*.[32] Perhaps "An Buinneán Aorach" was Rev. Richard Henebry (Risteard de Henebre or Risteard de Hindeberg), whom Uí Fhlannagáin indicates was one of the readers of *An Gaodhal*.[33] Henebry was a native Irish speaker from Portlaw, Co. Waterford. He held academic appointments in the United States and Ireland and is remembered today for his strengths in both Celtic Studies and music.[34] The *Kentucky Irish American* newspaper reported in 1899 that Henebry "picked up many tales and traditions from the Gaelic-speaking workmen around Carrick, and his principal teachers, as he became more advanced, were Seaan Ruadh O'Sheehan and 'Tom' Lannon in Portlaw."[35] Henebry cited Thomas Lannon (Tomás Ó

Leannán) as one of the informants in his doctoral thesis, which was later published in 1898 under the title *The Sounds of Munster Irish*.[36]

In an effort to modernize and standardize the text of the Irish-language tale, the font has been changed from Gaelic to roman, and the dot of lenition has been replaced with the letter <h>. The author has updated the orthography to the standard found in Niall Ó Dónaill's *Foclóir Gaeilge-Béarla* (1977). Although significant standardization of spelling has taken place, little change has been made to the grammar of the sentences; when necessary, grammatical rules indicated in *Foclóir Gaeilge-Béarla* have been followed. An English-language translation follows the standardized Irish version. The English translation is intended to assist in the reading of the Irish; it is not intended to be a literary translation.

Eachtra Eoghain Ruadh
Anseo thíos.
From the dictation of Mr. Thomas Lannon of Portlaw, Co. Waterford.
An Buinneán Aorach

Bhí Eoghan Rua ina gharsún an-aerach cosnochta ag éirí suas dó. Chuaigh sé in airde ar chrann crabaí fiáin a bhí ar thaobh bóthair agus le linn agus é a bheith ag croitheadh na gcrabaí cad a gheobhadh thairis um thráthnóna Dé Sathairn ach sagart agus é ag marcaíocht ar chapall, ag dul ag éisteacht daoine ag an séipéal. Nuair a chuala an capall an crann á chroitheadh tháinig geit ann agus d'fhéach an sagart in airde ar an gcrann a rá, "A gharsúin atá cosnochta, nach ag baint crabaí fiáine atá tú."

"Má tá siad fiáine," arsa an garsún, "is socair a fhanann siad liomsa."

"Tá an diabhal i do phóca, a gharsúin," arsa an sagart.

"Níl an diabhal i mo phóca, mar níl aon bhaint aige liom," arsa an garsún.

"Má théann tú go dtí an tAifreann amárach agus má dhéanann tú amach dom nach bhfuil an diabhal i do phóca tabharfaidh mé péire bróg duit."

D'éirigh an garsún a bhí cosnochta ar maidin Dé Domhnaigh, nigh sé a láimh agus ghlan sé é féin. Níor stad sé ansin go ndeachaigh sé go dtí an séipéal agus rinne sé a shlí suas le hais na haltóra. Léigh an sagart an tAifreann agus ag tabhairt scéil uaidh don phobal d'iarr sé an raibh an garsún cosnochta ansin. Dúirt an garsún go raibh, gairid go leor dó.

"A gharsúin chosnochta," arsa an sagart, "tá an diabhal i do phóca anois."

"Níl an diabhal i mo phóca i dtigh Dé," arsa an garsún.

"Conas a gheobhaidh tú ag déanamh amach dom nach bhfuil an diabhal i do phóca?"

"Gheobhaidh mé go maith," arsa an garsún, "conas a bheadh an diabhal i mo phóca nuair nach bhfuil aon phóca orm?"

"Amárach, an Luan," arsa an sagart leis an ngarsún, "má théann tú go dtí an teach go dtí mé agus cosán a bheith agat agus gan aon chosán a bheith agat, tabharfaidh mé an péire bróg sin duit."

D'imigh an garsún Dé Luain, agus níor stad sé go ndeachaigh sé go dtí geata an tsagairt. Bhí an sagart ag faire air go bhfeicfeadh sé teacht é; bhí cos leis ar an mbán agus cos ar an gcosán. Nuair a chonaic an sagart é, chrom sé ag gáire.

"A gharsúin chosnochta," arsa an sagart, "tar go dtí mé amárach agus bíodh éadach ort agus ná bíodh éadach ort agus tabharfaidh mé an chulaith lena chéile dhuit."

D'imigh an garsún agus chuaigh sé go dtí iascaire ag iarraidh stiall de líon bearránach. Bhain sé gach aon snáithe de na seanéadaí a bhí air de; chaith sé an seanlíon ar a chraiceann, agus bhí éadach air agus ní raibh éadach air ansin.

Thug an sagart an chulaith ar fad dó ina dhiaidh sin.

Tar éis na culaithe nua a fháil, mar a dúramar, tháinig an-taibhse air agus bhí méar mhór aige ar shéan. Bhí file scaitheamh uaidh agus chuaigh sé go dtí é chun a bheadh sé ag caint leis. Lig sé air a bheith an-shimplí go bhfaigheadh fios a rún amach. Nuair chuaigh sé isteach go dtí an teach, bhí an file ag léamh leabhair ag an doras.

"Dia dhuit, a fhir an tí," arsa an garsún.

"Ní fear an tí mé," arsa an file, "ach rí an tí."

"Is breá an leabhar é sin agat," ar sé ansin.

"Ní leabhar a chuige é," arsa an file, "ach éide."

"Is breá an péire bróg iad sin ar do chosa," arsa an garsún.

"Ní bróga iad," arsa an file, "ach socair bhoinn."

Tháinig gadhar a bhí istigh go dtí an doras ar chlos na cainte dó, d'fhéach an garsún air agus a dúirt, "Is breá an gadhar é sin."

"Ní gadhar é a chuige," ars an file, "ach sodaire." Tháinig cailín óg amach.

"Is breá an cailín óg iníon í sin agat," arsa an garsún.

"Ní cailín í," arsa an file, "ach eala an ghrinn."

Bhuail sé isteach san iothlainn agus chonaic sé bó ann.

"Is breágh an bhó í sin agat," ar sé.

"Ní bó ar aon chor í ach each," arsa an file.

"Tá tine bhreá mhóna agat," arsa an garsún.

"Ní tine í," arsa an file, "ach glóir mhór."

"Is breá é an cat sin agat," ar sé.

"Ní cat é," arsa an file, "ach ciúnas."

Bhí bairille beorach faoi bhun an bhalla aige agus dúirt sé nár ba bheoir a bhí ann ach meidhir. Is é suan a thug sé mar ainm ar an leaba agus nuair a ghair sé rí de féin ba cheart go mbeadh a theach ina ríocht agus is amhlaidh a bhí gan amhras.

Tháinig tart ar an ngarsún agus d'iarr sé deoch as tobar fíoruisce ba thíos le hais an tí. D'ól sé deoch agus dúirt,

"Is breá an tobar uisce é seo agat."

"Ní uisce é sin ar aon chuma," arsa an file, "ach iomadúlacht."

Is é an leithéid sin de léann leamh a bhí acu le rith tamaill na hoíche gur imigh an file dá leaba agus dá sheomra féin faoi dheireadh, inar chodail sé go trom gan mheabhair gan mhearbhall intinne go loinnir an lae ghil arna mhárach.

D'fhan an garsún ina shuí scaitheamh maith ina dhiaidh chun go gcuirfeadh sé an teach agus an chuid troscáin trína chéile. Ar dtús, chuir sé smior faoi na bróga agus d'ith an madra iad agus ansin chuir sé an leabhar faoin mbó agus rinne an bhó gnó glan air. Bhuail sé an cat sa tine agus chuaigh an cat sa seomra faoi bhun na leapa. Dhoirt sé an bairille beorach agus, rud níos measa ná gach beart dá rinne go dtí sin, choimeád sé iníon an fhile ina fhochair le rith na hoíche. Níor throm suan de, d'éirigh sé go tráthúil agus chuaigh sé go dtí doras an seomra.

"An bhfuil tú i do shuí, a rí an tí," ar sé. "D'ith sodaire socair bhoinn, shalach an t-each ar éide, chuaigh meidhir faoi thalamh, chuaigh ciúnas i mbun an tsuain agus an ghlóire mhór ina dheireadh, luí mé féin ar an settle le heala an ghrinn i mo fhochair agus mar a bhfuil an iomarca den iomadúlacht agat, tá do ríocht dóite."

"Ó, a bhithiúnaigh," arsa an file, "dá mbeadh a fhios agam gurb é thusa a bhí ann ní bheadh lá eile saoil agat."

D'imigh sé ansin nuair d'éirigh an file chun é a lámhach agus níor stad sé go ndeachaigh sé na mílte ó bhaile. Chuaigh sé ag obair ag feirmeoir agus ní raibh a fhios ag an bhfeirmeoir cérbh é óir bhí sé an-chiúin i rith na haimsire.

An tiarna talún a bhí os cionn an fheirmeora sin, ní thabharfadh sé aon rud do na tionóntaí a dhéanfadh aon seirbhís dóibh. Bhí cráin ag an bhfeirmeoir agus tháinig sí faoi láth. Bhí na fir lá ag ithe a ndinnéar agus dúirt an feirmeoir gurbh fhearr leis ná punt go bhfaigheadh sé teacht ar ál banbh ar an gcollach a bhí ag an máistir. "Cad é an chabhair sin," arsa na fir, "nuair nár thug sé dada d'aon duine riamh chun seirbhís a dhéanamh dóibh?"

Bhí Eoghan ag éisteacht leo ag caint gan aon fhocal aige féin (de cheann a bheith ina choigríoch ina measc) ach nuair a bhí deireadh an tsoiscéil acu ráite thóg sé suas a cheann agus labhair sé leis an bhfeirmeoir a bhí ina shuí ar an *settle*.

"Tabhair domsa an punt agus gheobhaidh mé an collach do do chráin."

"Nach bhfaighinn féin níos luaithe ná thusa; cad é an aithne atá aige ortsa?" arsa an feirmeoir.

"Ambaiste," arsa an garsún, "leagaim punt ar do phuntsa; cuir an dá phunt ar lámh do mhic agus mura bhfaighidh mé an collach do do chráin bíodh an dá phunt agat."

Labhair an mac leis an athair ansin á rá, "Leag an punt agus gheobhaidh tú an dá phunt mura bhfaigheadh sé an collach mar atá mise ag dul leis."

Rinne an feirmeoir mar a dúirt sé agus d'imíodar araon leo.

"Seachain anois," arsa an mac, ag gabháil anonn dóibh go dtí an teach mór, "bíodh *Sir* agat le gach aon fhocal a déarfaidh sé seo."

Chuadar go dtí an geata agus chroith an garsún é chun go ndéanfadh sé glór de. Chuala an duine uasal an torann a bhí amuigh agus tháinig amach go dtí iad agus d'fhiafraigh sé den gharsún cad a bhí uathu. Bhain Eoghan a hata de féin agus labhair sé leis mar seo:

"Chuir *Sir* mise le *Sir* muice go dtí *Sir* collaigh atá ag *Sir* thusa."

"Cé hé thusa?"

"Is mise Eoghan Rua ó Mhóin Rua, buachaill Uilliam Rua *Hatchet*, a tháinig le cráin Rua go dtí collach Rua atá ag Uilliam Rua *Narket*."

"Gheobhaidh tusa an collach," arsa an duine uasal, "agus ní bhfuair aon duine riamh romhat é."

Thángadar abhaile le chéile agus shín an mac an dá phunt chun Eoghan.

Ní fheadair an feirmeoir ansin cad a cheapfadh sé chun a ghabháil arís é. Lá éigin ina dhiaidh sin tháinig an duine uasal go dtí an feirmeoir ag iarraidh airgead a chollaigh. Bhí Eoghan agus an feirmeoir ag oibriú i bhfochair a chéile agus nuair a chonaic sé an duine uasal ag teacht agus an pipe dearg ina bhéal aige; druid sé anonn le hEoghan agus dúirt:

"Sin fear nár thug gal dá phíopa d'aon duine riamh."

"Dar fia!" arsa Eoghan, "cuirimse dhá phunt i gcoinne puint leat go bhfaigheadh mise gal dá phíopa uaidh."

Bhain Eoghan a hata de, dhruid sé ina choinne agus chuir sé caint ar an duine uasal. Labhair Eoghan agus chuir sé ceacht as; an chéad cheacht a chuir sé as stad an duine uasal ag éisteacht leis.

"A fharaire ghroí de shíol na bhfearaibh ab fhearr, a
Scaipfeadh an fíon go fial go fairsing ar chlár;
Ná tagadh ort díth choíche ná galar do bháis,
Ach ó tháinig i do shlí mé cuir an píopa dearg i mo láimh."

Bhí sé ag caitheamh a phíopa i gcónaí agus ag éisteacht le hEoghan ach ní dúirt sé dada an babhta sin agus chuir Eoghan an dara ceacht as:

"A fharaire shéimh i bhféile agus i bhfearadh gníomhartha,
De mhaithe na nGael nach staonfadh ga ná claimhte;
Fad ar an saol faoi réim go maire tú choíche,
Agus tabhairse domsa, más é do thoil é, gal de do phíopa."

Labhair an duine uasal agus dúirt (chun go gcuirfeadh sé in iúl don bhfeirmeoir go ba é airgead an chollaigh a bhí uaidh):

"Duine mise (ar sé) a thuigeann do chursaí an tsaoil,
Is duine mé níl pingin i mo láimh ná réal
Nuair nach dtuigeann tú nó nach miste leat méid mo phéin;
Buaileadh gach duine againn tine ar a phíopa féin."

Labhair Eoghan ansin agus, tar éis an moladh a thug sé dó, chrom sé á cháineadh ar a cheathrú cheacht:

"Donas is duais ort, is minic a chonaic mé
Gan tine, gan aithinne, gan móin ná fraoch,

Bhí do bhríste briste agus clog ar do ghlúin ón ngréin.
Is beagán dúil a bhí i dtobac agat agus nach liomsa nárbh iontas é."

"Ó! Seo duit an píopa," arsa an duine uasal. "Ná tabhair náire dom ar an ngarraí."

Rug Eoghan ar an bpíopa agus chaith sé trí ghal de, óir bhí trí puint curtha as, punt an ghal, agus nuair a bhí na trí gail caite aige, dúirt, "Siúd é an tobac cumhartha ó thóin an mhargaidh – Is fiú punt gach aon tarraingt air, ní hé an toit é ná an teas ná caith ar an iarta é ná caith sa sliabh é.

"Bhainfeadh sé braon ón tsúil,
Bhainfeadh sé sraoth ón tsrón,
Bhainfeadh sé luch as stácaí
agus bainbh as cránacha.
Is furasta é a dheargadh agus is deacair é a mhúchadh;
Is beag a gheobhadh feirmeoirí de, dhéanaidís gol go fiamhach fúthu."

Arsa an feirmeoir, "Dá mbeadh a fhios agam gur tusa a bhí ann ní thabharfainn lá oibre duit go brách."

Thug an feirmeoir punt don duine uasal, agus ghlaoigh an duine uasal ar Eoghan agus dúirt pé fad saoil a bhí aige ba é an fear is cliste a tháinig riamh air é. "Seo duit punt airgead an chollaigh," ar sé, "chomh maith leis an gcuid eile."[37]

The Adventure of Eoghan Rua
Here below.
From the dictation of Mr. Thomas Lannon of Portlaw, Co. Waterford.
An Buinneán Aorach

Eoghan Rua was a very lively barefoot boy growing up. He climbed up on a wild crab-tree that was on the side of the road and as he shook the crabs (wild apples), what happened upon him that Saturday afternoon but a priest who was riding a horse going to hear confessions at the chapel. When the horse heard the tree shaking, he was startled, and the priest looked up to the tree saying, "Oh barefooted boy, aren't you picking wild crab apples."

"If they are wild," says the boy, "they are calm with me."

"The devil is in your pocket, boy," says the priest.

"The devil is not in my pocket, because he has nothing to do with me," says the boy.

"If you go to Mass tomorrow and if you demonstrate that the devil is not in your pocket, I will give you a pair of shoes."

The barefooted boy got up Sunday morning, washed his hands and cleaned himself. He didn't stop then until he reached the chapel and made his way up beside the altar. The priest read the Mass and in giving the homily to the congregants, he asked was the barefooted boy there. The boy said he was, fairly near to him.

"Oh, barefoot boy," says the priest, "the devil is in your pocket now."

"The devil is not in my pocket in the House of God," says the boy.

"How could you figure out that the devil is not in your pocket?"

"I can well figure it out," says the boy, "How could the devil be in my pocket when I do not have any pockets?"

"Tomorrow, Monday," says the priest to the boy, "if you go to my house and you take a path while you take no path, I will give you that pair of shoes."

On Monday, the boy went, and he didn't stop until he went to the gate of the priest. The priest was looking out for him so that he would see him coming; he had a foot on the grass and a foot on the path. When the priest saw it, he bent over laughing.

"Oh, barefooted boy," says the priest, "come to me tomorrow and be clothed and don't be clothed and I will give you the suit together with it."

The boy left, and he went to a fisherman wanting a piece of useless line. He removed every single thread of the old clothes that were on him; he threw the old line on his skin, and he was clothed, and he was not clothed then.

The priest gave the entire suit [of clothes] after that.

After getting the new suit, as we said, he became very proud, and he had his thumb on prosperity. There was a poet a short distance from him, and he went to him so that he could talk with him. He pretended that he was very simple so that he would discover the knowledge of his secrets. When he went in the house, the poet was reading a book at the door.

"Hello, man of the house," says the boy.

"I am not the man of the house," says the poet, "but the king of the house."

"That is a fine book you have," he then said.

"It is not called a book," says the poet, "but armour."

"Those are a fine pair of shoes on your feet," says the boy.

"They are not shoes," says the poet, "but steady of sole."

A dog that was inside came to the door on its hearing the conversation. The boy looked at it and said, "That's a fine dog."

"It isn't called a dog," says the poet, "but a trotting horse." A young girl came out.

"That's a fine young girl of a daughter you have," says the boy.

"She isn't a girl," says the poet, "but the swan of affection."

He entered the farm yard and saw a cow there.

"That's a fine cow you have," says he.

"She isn't a cow at all, but a horse," says the poet.

"You have a fine peat fire," says the boy.

"It is not a fire," says the poet, "but great glory."

"That is a fine cat you have," says he.

"It isn't a cat," says the poet, "but silence."

He had a barrel of beer at the foot of the wall, and he said it wasn't beer but mead. He called the bed slumber and when he called himself king, his house should be his kingdom, and so it was without doubt.

The boy became thirsty and he asked for a drink from a freshwater well that was down beside the house. He drank a drink and said, "This is a fine well of water that you have."

"That's not water at all," says the poet, "but abundance."

That's the kind of foolish learning that they carried on throughout the night until the poet went off to his own room and bed at last, in which he slept heavily, unconscious without mental confusion, until the bright light of day on the morrow.

The boy stayed up a good while after so that he could put the house and the furniture into disarray. First, he put marrow inside the shoes, and the dog ate them, and then he put the book under the cow, and the cow made a complete mess of it. He tossed the cat into the fire, and the cat went into the bedroom under the bed. He poured out the barrel of beer, and one thing worse than everything he had done up until that point, he kept the poet's daughter with him throughout the night. He didn't slumber deeply, he rose punctually, and he went to the door of the room.

"Are you awake, king of the house," says he. "A trotting horse ate steady of sole, the horse soiled the armour, the mead spilled on the ground, silence went under the slumber with great glory after it, I myself laid down on the settle together with the swan of affection and as you have too much of an abundance, your kingdom is burnt."

"Oh, you scoundrel," says the poet, "if I had known that it was you who was there, you wouldn't have had another day of life."

He left, then, when the poet got up to shoot him, and he didn't stop until he had gone miles from home. He went working for a farmer, and the farmer didn't know who he was because he was very quiet at that time.

The landlord who was over that farmer wouldn't give anything to the tenants that would be of any use to them. The farmer had a sow, and she was in heat. The men were eating their dinner, and the farmer said that he would like better than a pound that he should get a litter of pigs from the master's boar. "What good is that," say the men, "when he never gave anyone anything that would be of any help to them?"

Eoghan was listening to them speaking without a word from himself (being a stranger in their midst), but when the discussion came to an end, he lifted his head and spoke with the farmer who was sitting on the settle.

"Give me the pound and I will get the boar for your sow."

"Wouldn't I myself get it sooner than you; does he know you?" says the farmer.

"Indeed," says the boy, "I lay down a pound on your own pound; put the two pounds in your son's hand and if I will not get the boar for your sow, so be the two pounds yours."

The son spoke with the father then saying, "Lay down the pound and you will get the two pounds if he does not get the boar because I am going with him."

The farmer did as he said and they both left.

"Watch out now," says the son as they were going over to the big house, "Say Sir to every word that he will say."

They went to the gate and the boy shook it so that it would make a noise. The gentleman heard the noise that was outside and came out to them, and he asked the boy what they wanted. Eoghan took off his hat and spoke to him like this:

"Sir sent me with Sir pig to Sir boar that you have, Sir."

"Who are you?"

"I am Eoghan Rua from Móin Rua, boy of Uilliam Rua Hatchet, who came with a Rua sow to a Rua boar which belongs to Uilliam Rua Narket."

"You will get the boar," says the gentleman, "and no one before you ever got him."

They returned home together, and the son extended the two pounds to Eoghan.

The farmer didn't know then what he would devise to get it back. Some day after that the gentleman came to the farmer wanting his boar's money. Eoghan and the farmer were working together when he saw the gentleman coming and the lit pipe in his mouth; he moved close to Eoghan and said:

"There's a man who never gave a smoke of his pipe to anyone."

"By Jove!" says Eoghan, "I will put two pounds against your one pound that I would get from him a smoke from his pipe."

Eoghan removed his hat, he moved closer to him and he had a talk with the gentleman. Eoghan spoke and provided him with a quatrain; the gentleman stopped to listen to him at the first quatrain.

"Oh, strong warrior of the best race of men,
Who would dispense wine generously at table;
May deprivation never come on you nor fatal disease,
But since that I happen upon you, place the lit pipe in my hands."

He was still smoking his pipe and listening to Eoghan, but he didn't say a word at that moment, and Eoghan presented him with the second quatrain:

"Oh, gentle warrior in generosity and in the doing of deeds,
Of the gentry of the Irish whom spear, nor swords, would not deter;
Long prosperous life may you enjoy always,
And give to me, if you please, a smoke of your pipe."

The gentleman spoke and said (so that he would let the farmer know that it was the boar's money he needed):

"I am a person (says he) who understands worldly matters,
I am a person who has neither a penny in my hand nor sixpence
When you don't understand, or you don't care about the amount of my pain,
Let each of us light his own pipe."

Eoghan then spoke and, after the praise that he gave him, he started criticizing him in his fourth quatrain:

"Misfortune and gloom on you, I often saw,
Without fire, without spark, without turf nor heather [kindling],
Your pants were with holes and a blister on your knee from the sun.
You had little desire to smoke and wasn't I not surprised."

"Oh! Here is the pipe," says the gentleman. "Don't shame me in the garden."

Eoghan took the pipe and smoked three puffs on it, for three pounds were spent on it, a pound per smoke, and after he took the three puffs, he said, "That's fragrant tobacco from the end of the market – each drag on it is worth a pound, it's not the smoke, nor the heat, nor smoking it at the fireside, nor smoking it in the mountains.

It would extract a tear from the eye,
It would extract a sneeze from the nose,
It would extract a mouse from the stacks,
And piglets from sows.
It is easy to light and difficult to extinguish;
The little that farmers would get of it, they would weep bitterly about."

The farmer says, "If I would have known that it was you, I would never have given you a day's work."

The farmer gave a pound to the gentleman, and the gentleman called Eoghan and said that as long as he had lived, he was the smartest man he had ever come across. "Here is the boar's pound," says he, "as well as the rest."

The eighteenth-century poet Eoghan Rua Ó Súilleabháin was one of the most popular historical figures in Irish-language folklore in Munster.[38] The folk memory of him as a person who often ran into trouble remained strong into the twentieth century, and the *Handbook of Irish Folklore* advised collectors to look out for tales about him.[39] "Eachtra Eoghain Ruadh" is one such tale.

The story contains three parts: Eoghan Rua's dealings with the priest, the poet, and the farmer. Ó Súilleabháin and Christiansen identified the first part as ATU 921, "The King and the Farmer's Son." They provided more than three pages of examples of this popular story in Irish folklore.[40] In this case, the individual in a position of authority, whom Eoghan Rua's clever responses both amaze and amuse, is not the king, but rather a priest.[41] They identified the second part of the story, which concerns the poet's odd and whimsical vocabulary, as ATU 1940, "The Extraordinary Names." Irish examples of this type only take up half a page.[42] While a few versions display minor similarities, such as involving a cat with fire,[43] the most notable one is nearly identical in terms of sequence and lexical items. Collected two generations later from the Uí Chonaill family in An Seanchnoc, Cill Chróch※áin, Co. Kerry, it contains the same unusual names of *sochair bhoinn*, *sodaire*, *ciúnas*, *iomadúlacht*, and *ríocht* for boots, hound, cat, water, and house. Moreover, the daughter in this version, who also spends some of the night with the protagonist, is called *ainnir ghrinn* (maiden of affection) instead of *eala an ghrinn* (swan of affection).[44] A later ATU 921/1940 combination was collected in English in 1938 in Hanstown, Co. Westmeath. As in *An Gaodhal*, cat and fire have contrived names here, and water has a completely different name.[45] The third part of "Eachtra Eoghain Ruadh" illustrates his characteristic, persuasive use of poetry as the tale transforms into a cantefable.[46] While this section is not classified by Ó Súilleabháin and Christiansen, the beginning of the episode, in which Eoghan Rua from Móin Rua takes the sow to the boar, can be read in a tale about Eoghan Rua collected in Co. Limerick four decades later.[47]

CONCLUSION

Although space here does not permit greater examination of "Eachtra Eoghain Ruadh," this tale shows the detail and depth of folklore published in *An Gaodhal*. As a result of the bilingual format of the journal and the interest of Michael Logan in contemporary manuscript collections as well as those from previous generations, *An Gaodhal* proved to be an excellent venue for the sharing of folklore in Irish with a general audience. Even in the final six years under the editorial hand of Geraldine Haverty, when English-language articles outnumbered Irish-language contributions, substantial Irish-language folklore items continued to be published on prominent pages of the journal. From this we can postulate that those reading *An Gaodhal* held in high regard the folklore shared in the pages of this monthly paper. It would likely have been both a source of national pride and a useful resource for Irish instructors, since the vocabulary and structure of the phrases were more colloquial than formal written literature. While the same utility cannot be accorded the folklore in *An Gaodhal* today, given the difficulty the now-archaic font and nonstandard orthography present for modern learners and readers, it ought to be a source of great pride for New York's Irish-language community. Logan and Haverty left us an important record of folklore in Ireland and in the emigrant community at the end of the nineteenth century, and with greater awareness, it is hoped that we see further editions of this valuable material in the years ahead.[48]

APPENDIX I

Listed below are folk tales in *An Gaodhal* (AG) identified by Ó Súilleabháin and Christiansen in *Types of the Irish Folktale*. In most entries, the unedited title of the tale and the provenance of the storyteller, if cited, are followed by the tale type and standard title. Only the number of the first page of each story is given. Tale types have been verified and updated with the ATU index (Uther, *Types*).

AG 5, no. 4 (1886): 585. "Sgeul an Fhir-Feasa Ádh' Mhuil," Ulster. ATU 1641, "Doctor Know-All."

AG 7, no. 8 (1890): 931. "Cailleach na bh-Fiacla Fada agus an Mac Rígh," Co. Mayo, Connacht. Cf. ATU 313, "The Magic Flight" + cf. ATU 316, "The Nix of the Mill-Pond." First published in de h-Íde, *Leabhar Sgeulaigheachta*, 144.

AG 8, no. 2 (1890): front cover. "Mac Righ Caisleán Buidhe Shamhnuigh agus Bainríoghan Tobar Deire 'n Domhain," Connacht. ATU 551, "Water of Life."

AG 8, no. 5 (1890): 52. "Eachtra Eoghain Ruaidh," Co. Waterford, Munster. Cf. ATU 921, "The King and the Farmer's Son" + ATU 1940, "The Extraordinary Names."

AG 8, no. 11 (1891): 124. "An Tobar a Bháin Pádraic," Connacht. ATU 1614*, "Repairing the Well."

AG 8, no. 11 (1891): 129. "Ridire na g-Cleasa," Connacht. Cf. ATU 325, "The Magician and his Pupil."

AG 9, no. 4 (1892): 185. "An Fánuidhe Fíor-Bhocht," Munster. ATU 313, "The Magic Flight."

AG 9, no. 6 (1892): 208. "An Bullán Breac," Co. Cork, Munster. ATU 510, "Cinderella and Peau d'Âne" + ATU 590, "The Faithless Mother."

AG 9, no. 9 (1893): 243. "An Gárlach Coileánach" (two versions), Co. Cork, Munster. ATU 921, "The King and the Farmer's Son"; cf. ATU 920, "The Son of the King and of the Smith."

AG 9, no. 11 (1893): 268. "Nuair is Cruaidh do'n Chailligh Caithfidh Sí Rith," Co. Galway, Connacht. ATU 1791, "The Sexton Carries the Clergyman." First published in Ó Fatharta, *Fuigheall Sgéal*, 9.

AG 9, no 12 (1893): 287. "An Neascóid Chléibhe." Cf. ATU 660, "The Three Doctors."

AG 10, no 4 (1893): 326. "Beagán agus Beannacht nó Mórán agus Mallacht," Co. Cork, Munster. ATU 471, "The Bridge to the Other World."

AG 10, no. 11 (1894): 417. "An Mada-Tighe 7 an Mactíre." ATU 201, "The Lean Dog Prefers Liberty to Abundant Food and a Chain."

AG 11, no. 1 (1895): 5. "An Sionnach agus an Chorr-Ghlas." ATU 60, "Fox and Crane Invite Each Other."

AG 11, no 9 (1896): 100. "Cú Bán an t-Sléibhe," Co. Galway, Connacht. ATU 425A, "The Animal as Bridegroom" + cf. ATU 707, "The Three Golden Children." First published in Ó Fotharta, "Cú Bán," 146.

AG 12, no. 11 (1898): 115. "Uilliam an Chrainn," Co. Mayo, Connacht. ATU 706, "The Maiden Without Hands." First published in de h-Íde, *Leabhar Sgeulaigheachta*, 101.

AG 18, no. 6 (1899): 151. "An Gadaidhe agus a Fhothlainteach," Co. Kerry, Munster. ATU 1525, "The Master Thief."

AG 19, no. 1 (1900): 11. "Ó! A Dhéi go n-Déantar do Thoil air an Talamh mar Dhéantar air Neamh," Connacht. Cf. ATU 759, "Angel and Hermit."

AG 19, no. 2 (1900): 33. "Seamus Gow's Three Chances," Co. Roscommon, Connacht. ATU 750A, "The Three Wishes."

AG 20, no. 9 (1901): 285. "An Bhrúch," Co. Kerry, Munster. ATU 1889 H, "Submarine Otherworld."

AG 21, no. 9 (1902): 289. "The Tinker and the Devil," Co. Galway, Connacht. ATU 330, "The Smith and the Devil."

AG 23, no. 5 (1904): 170. "The Gobhan's Saer's Cow." ATU 934, "Tales of the Predestined Death."

AG 23, no. 11 (1904): 375. ATU 326, "The Youth Who Wanted to Learn What Fear Is."

NOTES

All translations are the work of the author unless otherwise noted. Sincere thanks are given to John Gillen (Hostos Community College) who proofread translations and provided detailed suggestions. The author takes full responsibility for any errors. The author acknowledges the generous access that the New York Public Library provided to *An Gaodhal* from May 2018 to August 2018 by being assigned as a Scholar to the Shoichi Noma and Wertheim Study Reading Rooms. The author also consulted the collection of original *An Gaodhal* issues of Douglas Hyde at the Irish National Folklore Collection (NFC) at University College Dublin on 17 April 2018. Microfilm reels of *An Gaodhal* were additionally viewed at the National Library of Ireland (NLI) on the same Dublin trip, and previously copies of those reels were viewed at Boston College in Massachusetts on 21 October 2017. The author's home library, the Leonard Lief Library at Lehman College, CUNY, purchased copies of the NLI reels in June 2018.

1 The first issue of *Irisleabhar na Gaedhilge* was dated November 1882. See Ní Uigín, "An Iriseoireacht Ghaeilge," 38–9, for general claims of the influence that various Irish-language publications in the United States in the second

half of the nineteenth century had on Irish-language publishing in the first half of the twentieth century in Ireland.

2 Logan took on these duties in addition to his gainful employment as a real estate agent. Various advertisements appear in *An Gaodhal* for his real estate services. See, for example, the advert with the heading, "Real Estate for Sale or to Trade for Brooklyn City Property," which ends: "M.J. Logan, 814 Pacific Street, Brooklyn, NY. Notary public and commissioner of deeds. Loans from 500 up": Logan, "Real Estate," 81. These adverts were often placed in a prominent position, such as at the beginning or end of the journal.

3 The New Series was published in an enlarged format and included much more English-language content than under the previous editor. It began with volume 18, no. 1, in recognition of it being the eighteenth year of publication, even though the previous edition of three months prior was volume 13, no. 3. That is to say, volumes 14 to 17 do not exist.

4 Nilsen, "Irish Language," 272.

5 Nilsen, "Irish in Nineteenth Century New York," 65.

6 Uí Fhlannagáin, *Mícheál Ó Lócháin,* 31.

7 The first issue of *An Gaodhal* contains a popular folk tale about Daniel O'Connell, in which a London waitress warns the politician in Irish of an attempt to poison him. Seán Ó Súilleabháin included this type of O'Connell story in *A Handbook of Irish Folklore*, asking collectors to look out for accounts where O'Connell is "warned by an Irish girl of poison in his drink" (522).

8 Blake, letter to the editor, 839–40.

9 See Hyde's translation, titled "The Well of D'yerree-in-Dowan" (i.e. the well of the end of the world) at https://celt.ucc.ie//published/T307006C/index.html, accessed 11 September 2018.

10 De h-Íde, *Leabhar Sgeulaigheachta*, 240.

11 Uí Fhlannagáin, *Mícheál Ó Lócháin,* 31.

12 Ó Laoghaire, *Sgeuluidheacht*, iii.

13 Ó Laoghaire, "Beagán," 326–8.

14 Ní Úrdail, "Cnósach Luachmhar Seanráite," 63.

15 Feiritéar, "Caoineadh," 120–2.

16 Feiritéar, "Sgéalta," 49–50, 56, 87–9.

17 De Norradh, letter to the editor, 16.

18 Ní Mhurchú and Breathnach, *1782-1881 Beathaisnéis*, 129; Ó Raghallaigh, "An Ceól Síghe," 52–4.

19 Ó Súilleabháin, *Handbook*, 461.

20 See Uí Ógáin, "Music," 197–214.

21 In Ireland, this is evident from competitions at the Oireachtas and substantial Gaelic League publications involving folklore topics; see O'Leary, *Prose Literature*, 96.

22 See Ó Duilearga, "Ó'n Eagarthóir," 417–18.

23 Breathnach and Ní Mhurchú, "Risteárd de Hae."

24 The collection of *An Gaodhal* at the NLI (which now includes the first three years) is presently the most complete. The Brooklyn Public Library does not appear to have holdings of this journal, but the New York Public Library has a collection of original issues covering roughly half of the published volumes.

25 Uí Fhlannagáin only cites one story in the first three years of *An Gaodhal* in the category of *scéalta*: "Tóruigheacht Dhiarmada Agus Ghráinne" in two parts (132). For *fabhalscéalta* (fables), she lists eighteen examples from the first three years (130).

26 De Hae, *Clár Litridheacht*, 966; Ua Glasáin, "Rígh na g-Céardaighthe."

27 De Hae, *Clár Litridheacht*, 860; O'Faherty, "An Chailleach Bheura"; Ó Fatharta, "Nuair Is Cruaidh"; Ó Fotharta, "An Dreoilín."

28 Additionally, the August 1887 *An Gaodhal* issue, though not bound with the other copies, was loosely placed in the volume.

29 This and the previous quotation were standardized and translated by the author. The 1957 date of Ó Súilleabháin's note indicates that *An Gaodhal* was not part of a cataloguing effort of published sources that took place in the 1940s, when NFC manuscripts were moved from their Dublin location during the Second World War in case of bombing: Briody, *Irish Folklore Commission*, 327.

30 "An Buinneán Aorach," "Eachtra Eoghain Ruaidh," 52.

31 De Hae, *Clár Litridheacht*, 695. Pen names were commonly used during this period in Irish-language publishing; see Uí Fhlannagáin, *Mícheál Ó Lócháin*, 32.

32 "An Buinneán Aorach," "An Spailpín Fánach." See de Hae, *Clár Litridheacht*, 695, for an example of an *An Gaodhal* listing for "An Buinneán Aorach."

33 Uí Fhlannagáin, *Mícheál Ó Lócháin*, 37. Rev. Richard Henebry attended Maynooth College starting in 1886 at a time of heated nationalist sentiment in Ireland. The folklore that appeared in *An Gaodhal* in 1890 could well have been collected back home in Waterford during his Maynooth years. It appears that he did not have an Ediphone in his possession until after his time in America at the turn of the century, meaning that folklore taken down in the 1880s would have been by pen and paper. De Hae does not suggest a connection between "An Buinneán Aorach" and Henebry. He lists

stories by "An Buinneán Aorach" and An t-Athair Risteard de Hindeberg separately. See de Hae, *Clár Litridheacht* 695, no. 12311 and 715, no. 12640.

34 Corcoran, *Musical Priest*.

35 "Henebry," *Kentucky Irish American*, 28 January 1899, 3.

36 Henebry, *Sounds*, v; Ní Mhurchú and Breathnach, *1882–1982 Beathaisnéis*, 35.

37 "An Buinneán Aorach," "Eachtra Eoghain Ruaidh."

38 See Ó hÓgáin, *An File*, 132–40, for examples of Eoghan Rua in folklore.

39 Ó Súilleabháin, *Handbook*, 525.

40 Ó Súilleabháin and Christiansen, *Types*, 177–80. In 1963 the story was known as "The King and the Peasant's Son." A variant form of ATU 921 in which "an ill-treated boy gives clever answers to his stingy step-mother" appeared in *An Gaodhal* in February 1893: Ó Laoghaire, "An Gárlach Coileánach": Ó Súilleabháin and Christiansen, *Types*, 177.

41 For another example of the priest claiming that Eoghan Rua is in the grip of the devil, see "Eoghan Ruadh agus an Sagart," unknown collector, Ráithín (Girls) National School, Co. Kerry, 1938, NFCS 457:49.

42 Ó Súilleabháin and Christiansen, *Types*, 330.

43 For example, see the untitled story collected by Betty Feely, An Clochar, Cara Droma Ruisc School, Carrick-on-Shannon, Co. Leitrim, 1938, NFCS 209:429; untitled story told by Mr T. Keohane (70) of Dromsullivan South, Co. Cork, collected by Kitty Sullivan, Ínse Cloch National School, Inchiclogh, Co. Cork, 1938, NFCS 284:210; and "The Poor Scholar," told by the collector's father (60), collected by Máire Ní Ruairc, Mainistir Ó dTórna School, Abbeydorney, Co. Kerry, 1938, NFCS 413:110.

44 "Sgéal," collected by a student at Lóthar National School, Loher, Co. Kerry, 1938, NFCS 466:431–4, 437–40.

45 "A Funny Story" and "Another Funny Story" told by Mr Smyth, Hanstown, Co. Westmeath, collected by a student at Ballinea National School, Ballina, Co. Westmeath, 1938, NFCS 736:46–8.

46 Delargy, "Gaelic Story-Teller," 207.

47 "Eoghan Ruadh agus an Sagart," told by Michael Casey, Martinstown, Co. Limerick, collected by a student at Árd Phádraig School, Ardpatrick, Co. Limerick, 1938, NFCS 509:212.

48 *An Gaodhal* has not entirely faded from memory: *An Gael*, a modern namesake of the monthly journal, began appearing in Summer 2009. The final section in each issue of this quarterly glossy magazine shares one or more items from the past, frequently taken from *An Gaodhal*. Two folktales have been reprinted, "Colann gan Cheann" and "Naomh Pádhraic agus na

hAithreacha Nimhe" (St Patrick and the Snakes); see *An Gael*, Earrach [Spring] 2010, 31–2, Fómhar (Fall) 2010, 29–32, and Earrach 2011, 24–5; Blácach, "Colann gan Cheann" and "Naomh Pádhraic"; de h-Íde, *Leabhar Sgeulaigheachta*, 171–83.

BIBLIOGRAPHY

"An Buinneán Aorach." "An Spailpín Fánach." *Irisleabhar na Gaedhilge* 5, no. 4 (July 1894): 53–5.

Breathnach, Diarmuid, and Máire Ní Mhurchú. "Risteárd de Hae (1902–1976)." In *Ainm.ie: An Bunachar Náisiúnta Beathaisnéisí Gaeilge*. Fiontar: Ollscoil Chathair Bhaile Átha Cliath, 2018. https://www.ainm.ie/Bio.aspx?ID=612.

Briody, Mícheál. *The Irish Folklore Commission 1935–1970: History, Ideology, Methodology*. Studia Fennica Folkloristica 17. Helsinki: Finnish Literature Society, 2007.

Corcoran, Seán. *The Musical Priest*. Waterford Local Radio, 29 December 2013. Audio, 48:48. https://soundcloud.com/rollingwave/the-musical-priest-radio.

De Hae, Risteárd. *Clár Litridheacht na Nua-Ghaedhilge*, vol. 3. Baile Átha Cliath: Oifig Dhíolta Foillseacháin Rialtais, 1940.

De h-Íde, Dúbhghlas. *Leabhar Sgeulaigheachta*. Baile Átha Cliath: Gill, 1889.

Delargy, James H. "The Gaelic Story-Teller: With Some Notes on Gaelic Folk-Tales." *Proceedings of the British Academy* 31 (1945): 177–221.

An Gael. MagCloud. http://www.magcloud.com/browse/Magazine/13595.

Henebry, Richard. *The Sounds of Munster Irish*. Dublin: M.H. Gill and Son, 1898.

Ní Mhurchú, Máire, and Diarmuid Breathnach. *1882–1982 Beathaisnéis*. Baile Átha Cliath: An Clóchomhar, 1986.

– *1782-1881 Beathaisnéis*. Baile Átha Cliath: An Clóchomhar, 1999.

Ní Uigín, Dorothy. "An Iriseoireacht Ghaeilge i Meiriceá agus in Éirinn ag Tús na hAthbheochana: An Cúlra Meiriceánach." In *Iriseoireacht na Gaeilge*, ed. Ruairí Ó hUiginn, 25–47. Léachtaí Cholm Cille 28. Maigh Nuad: An Sagart, 1998.

Ní Úrdail, Meidhbhín. "Cnósach Luachmhar Seanráite as Lámhscríbhinn Feiritéar 1." *Béaloideas* 85 (2017): 63.

Nilsen, Kenneth E. "The Irish Language in New York, 1850–1900." In *The New York Irish*, ed. Ronald H. Bayor and Timothy J. Meagher, 252–74. Baltimore: Johns Hopkins University Press, 1996.

– "Irish in Nineteenth Century New York." In *The Multilingual Apple:*

Languages in New York City, 2nd ed., ed. Ofelia García and Joshua A. Fishman, 53–69. New York: Mouton de Gruyter, 2002.

Ó Dónaill, Niall. *Foclóir Gaeilge-Béarla.* Baile Átha Cliath: Oifig an tSoláthair, 1977.

Ó Duilearga, Séamus. "Ó'n Eagarthóir." *Béaloideas* 1, no. 4 (1928): 416–18.

Ó Fotharta, Domhnall. "Cú Bán an t-Shleibhe [*sic*]." *Zeitschrift für Celtische Philologie* 1 (1897): 146–56.

– *Fuigheall Sgéal ó'n tSean-aimsir*. Baile Átha Cliath: Patrick O'Brien, 1912.

Ó hÓgáin, Dáithí. *An File: Staidéar ar Osnádúrthacht na Filíochta sa Traidisiún Gaelach.* Baile Átha Cliath: Oifig an tSoláthair, 1982.

Ó Laoghaire, Pádruig. *Sgeuluidheacht Chúige Mumhan*. Baile Átha Cliath: Pádruig O Briain, 1895.

O'Leary, Philip. *The Prose Literature of the Gaelic Revival, 1881–1921: Ideology and Innovation*. University Park: Pennsylvania State University Press, 1994.

Ó Súilleabháin, Seán. *A Handbook of Irish Folklore.* Dublin: The Folklore of Ireland Society, 1942.

Ó Súilleabháin, Seán, and Reidar Th. Christiansen. *The Types of the Irish Folktale.* FF Communications 188. Helsinki: Suomalainen Tiedeakatemia, 1963.

Uí Fhlannagáin, Fionnuala. *Mícheál Ó Lócháin agus* An Gaodhal. Baile Átha Cliath: An Clóchomhar, 1990.

Uí Ógáin, Ríonach. "Music Learned from the Fairies." *Béaloideas* 60–1 (1992): 197–214.

Uther, Hans-Jörg. *The Types of International Folktales: A Classification and Bibliography*, 3 vols. FF Communications 284–6. Helsinki: Suomalainen Tiedeakatemia, 2004.

An Gaodhal

"An Buinneán Aorach." "Eachtra Eoghain Ruaidh." *An Gaodhal* 8, no. 5 (December 1890): 52–3; 8, no. 6 (February 1891): 62–3, 70; 8, no. 8 (May 1891): 90.

Blácach, Eadbhard Loingseadh [Edward Lynch Blake]. "Colann gan Cheann." *An Gaodhal* 7, no. 11 (June 1890): front cover–inside front cover, 957; 7, no. 12 (July 1890): front cover, inside front cover, 969; 8, no. 1 (August 1890): front cover, inside front cover.

– "Naomh Pádhraic agus na hAithreacha Nimhe." *An Gaodhal* 7, no. 9 (April 1890): front cover, inside front cover; 7, no. 10 (May 1890): front cover, inside front cover, 945.

Blake, Edward Lynch. Letter to the editor. *An Gaodhal* 7, no. 1 (December 1888): 839–40.

De Norradh, Tomás D. Letter to the editor. *An Gaodhal* 8, no. 2 (September 1890): 16.

Feiritéar, Pádraig. "Caoineadh Airt Uí Laoghaire." *An Gaodhal* 18, no. 3 (June 1899): 54–6; 18, no. 4 (July 1899): 90–1; 18, no. 5 (August 1899): 120–2.

– "Sgéalta ó Iarthar Éireann." *An Gaodhal* 18, no. 3 (June 1899): 49–50, 56; 18, no. 4 (July 1899): 87–9.

Logan, Michael (Mícheál Ó Lócháin). "Real Estate for Sale or to Trade for Brooklyn City Property." *An Gaodhal* 1, no. 8 (May 1882): 81.

O'Faherty, Daniel [Domhnall Ó Fotharta]. "An Chailleach Bheura. *An Gaodhal* 9, no. 8 (January 1893): 230–1.

Ó Fatharta, Domhnall (Domhnall Ó Fotharta). "Nuair is Cruaidh do'n Chailligh Caithfidh Sí Rith." *An Gaodhal* 9, no. 11 (April 1893): 268–9.

Ó Fotharta, Domhnall. "An Dreoilín agus An Liopreachán." *An Gaodhal* 10, no. 11 (December 1894): front cover, inside front cover, 409.

Ó Laoghaire, Pádruig. "Beagán agus Beannacht nó Mórán agus Mallacht." *An Gaodhal* 10, no. 4 (November 1893): 326–8.

– "An Gárlach Coileánach." *An Gaodhal* 9, no. 9 (February 1893): 243.

Ó Raghallaigh, Mícheál. "An Ceól Sighe – The Fairy Music," *An Gaodhal* 21, no. 2 (February 1902): 52–4.

Ua Glasáin, Tadhg, trans. "Rígh na g-Céardaighthe." *An Gaodhal* 9, no. 10 (March 1893): 262.

ARCHIVAL COLLECTIONS

Schools' Manuscript Collection (NFCS). Irish National Folklore Collection, University College Dublin. https://www.duchas.ie/en/cbes.

6

Forming and Training an Army of Vindication: The *Irish Echo*, 1886–1894

Matthew Knight

The work of Ken Nilsen, in particular his studies of the Irish language in the United States, has inspired nearly all of my scholarly research. His exploration of the "virtually neglected" *Irish-American* newspaper, for example, encouraged me to seek out countless reels of microfilm (including the "lost" reel of 1860) to support my dissertation on the paper's Gaelic Department,[1] while a brief mention of the San Francisco *Monitor* served as the motivation for my article on that newspaper's Irish Department.[2] The following chapter also owes its origins to passing references in several of Nilsen's articles, which led me into the wider scholarship on the *Irish Echo* and the Philo-Celtic Societies. I owe Professor Nilsen an overwhelming debt of gratitude for his formative scholarship, and regret that I was never able to meet the man who unknowingly guided my academic career.

In January 1886, the Boston Philo-Celtic Society published the first volume of the *Irish Echo*, a journal that pledged to "assist in the vindication of the character of the Irish race from the foul slanders of centuries by English writers." The newspaper's tagline confirmed its devotion to the language, literature, history, and autonomy of Ireland, and its motto quoted Edmund Burke: "No people will look forward to posterity who do not often look back to their ancestors." A half-column advertisement declared: "If you want to know all about Ireland, the history of the country, its language and literature, the genealogies of its families, its bards and seanchaidhes and its lawgivers and rulers, read the *Irish Echo*." In turn, the prospectus that opened the first issue proclaimed that each subscriber instantly joined an "Army of Vindication" whose objectives were to defend the merits of the Irish language and its literature against the calumnies of English writers who claimed the Irish people had no literature worthy of notice.[3] Although it appeared monthly – with some gaps – from 1886 until 1890, and was revived for a final year in April 1893, the *Irish Echo* has never received a comprehensive treatment in the historiography of the Irish language revival in the United States.[4] This chapter offers a brief documentary history of the Boston Philo-Celtic Society and explores the *Irish Echo* throughout the three major stages of its development, detailing its growth under the editorship of P.J. O'Daly, Michael C. O'Shea, and Charles O'Farrell.

P.J. O'DALY (JANUARY 1886–APRIL 1889)

The first editor of the *Irish Echo* was Patrick J. (P.J.) O'Daly, a founding member of the Boston Philo-Celtic Society, whose mission was to "aid in the cultivation of the Irish language, and in the publication of the copious literature therein."[5] Calls for such a society were made in the Voice of the People column in the New York journal the *Irish World*, beginning in May 1872, with O'Daly among the most passionate advocates, alongside Michael Logan, future founder of the Brooklyn Philo-Celtic Society. Logan promised to offer free Irish lessons in Brooklyn and made good on his word in February 1873 when he announced an Irish class open to all who desired to avail themselves of it, from seven to nine p.m. three nights a week, or as the majority wished. Instruction was free, and the classroom was located thirty minutes from Brooklyn's city hall.[6] Cornelius O'Brien of Buffalo, New York, suggested that classes were not enough, noting that "the Gaelic department in the *Irish-American* [published in New York] was a failure, notwithstanding the editorial erudition and the recognized genius of William Russell, one of the foremost Irish scholars in the country ... The cause of the failure, of course, was the want of support. That support means money, and to raise money it is necessary to have an organization." O'Brien felt that branches of this organization could be established in all the cities in the country and that enough money could be raised to keep a permanent officer at headquarters to issue a monthly journal in the Irish language.[7] A correspondent going by "Leix" added that it would be impossible to "attain any object if a little self-imposed inconvenience and sacrifice are avoided! ... Nothing short of a combined effort on the part of *all* our people can effect a successful result. Organize at once, you who are capable."[8] O'Daly responded with a promise that "Irish will be read and written in Boston before 12 months are to an end by parties who do not now know the alphabet."[9]

O'Daly was true to his word: in a letter titled "Going to Work" and dated 22 April 1873, he announced in the *Irish World* that the first official meeting had been held in Boston for establishing an organization for the revival of the Irish language. Songs and recitations were performed in Irish, and elections were held for officer positions. O'Daly became corresponding secretary, and many members joined at this first gathering.[10] The organization was officially named the Philo-Celtic Society of Boston at its next meeting on 28 April 1873, at which time it was determined that any individual, irrespective of sex, race, creed, or colour, who possessed a good moral character, could become one of four grades of member: Active, Life, Honorary, or Associate. Only the Active members were engaged in the study of the Irish language, however, with classes offered in the "Irish School" at 176 Tremont Street every Sunday afternoon and Thursday evening. The other grades of membership consisted of those who could not devote their time to the study of the Irish language but who were nevertheless anxious to help the movement financially.[11] The Boston *Pilot* reported at this time that the Philo-Celtic Society desired to abandon English, the "jargon of the foe," in order to establish Irish as the national language.[12] Member Thomas F. Carr refuted this claim, however, and subsequently clarified that the Philo-Celtic Society of Boston was not "organized for the purpose of having the Gaelic supersede the English as the national tongue." He continued,

> We are neither radicals nor levelers, nor are we possessed of the wild and chimerical idea of rooting out the English tongue. We have in our society men of intelligence and common sense, who know that the English language is spoken by at least one-third of the civilized inhabitants of the globe … Hence we have never given a passing thought to the silly idea of making Gaelic the national tongue … We saw the rapid decline of the language of our fathers towards oblivion. We saw – and I say it with regret – many who had a knowledge of the language in Ireland as soon as they set foot on the soil of America, recoil from it as if it were tainted by some immorality or forbidden by Divine command … We thought that a society of this kind would help to preserve the vitality of our mellifluous native language, would make it

> respectable so that weak-minded people who knew it would not be ashamed to use it, and "last but not least" to procure copies of all the Gaelic books and manuscripts now mouldering in the libraries and universities of Europe, and form a Celtic library where historian and philologist could have free access to it. These are the aims and objects of the Philo-Celtic Society of Boston, and we expect the cooperation and good wishes of the patriotic and intelligent.[13]

The society grew quite rapidly, reaching one hundred members within months, and those in possession of Irish texts were asked to contact O'Daly, who was compiling a catalogue of Irish manuscripts to be held by the Boston Philo-Celtic Society for future publication.[14] Corresponding Secretary Denis O'Crowley affirmed in a letter to the *Irish World* that after a year and a half, the Philo-Celtic Society of Boston had "done exceedingly well in the way of collecting books in the language and transcribing worm-eaten manuscripts, which have been donated to the society by prominent Irishmen of this city and vicinity."[15] In another letter to the *Pilot*, he singled out several contributors, including Patrick Terry of Somerville, whose donated manuscripts included compositions of poets of the eighteenth century and a copy of the history of the Geraldines written by Dominick O'Daly in 1655; an unnamed gentleman from Woburn, whose donation included accounts of the "Pursuit of Ceallachain of Cashel" (*Tóraíocht Cheallachâin Chaisil*), "The Death of the Children of Tuirreen" (*Oidhe Chloinne Tuireann*), and Fenian poems dated to 1790; and Mr Lovitt of South Boston, who contributed a collection that included the "Battle of Ventry Harbor" (*Cath Fionntrá*).[16] Maurice Ferriter, who had contributed to the *Irish-American*'s Gaelic Department in the past, wrote to the *Irish World* explaining that he had many manuscripts of ancient dates, which he would attempt to circulate as well.[17]

At a business meeting of the Boston Philo-Celtic Society in January 1880, President J.H. Sullivan reported that the society continued to flourish, and had

> established Irish schools in the following places during the last year: in East Boston, South Boston, Boston Highlands, North End, Salem, Weymouth and Quincy; and, although we did not establish the Irish school of Lawrence, yet its numbers got their inspiration from our society … The progress of our society has not been lim-

> ited alone to this state, or to the formation of Irish schools ... but it has gone abroad, sounding from end to end of America, and it has echoed across the Atlantic and vibrated around Dublin Castle in Ireland.

Sullivan further noted that the ladies' class had grown considerably in 1879 and become "the grandest feature of our society. And it gives me great pleasure to state that there are ladies in the class who are advanced enough in the knowledge of the language to assist the regular teachers in giving instructions in the rudiments to those of their sex who are now joining the school." Sullivan also boasted of the many Irish compositions, original and in translation, that had been produced by the Philo-Celtic Society in 1879.[18] One such achievement belonged to O'Daly himself, whose translation into Irish of Robert Emmet's speech from the dock appeared in the *Irish World* of 15 March 1879, and was ornately presented and transcribed by Charles Sprague, a member of the New York Philo-Celtic Society who had allegedly mastered the language after only four months' study.[19] The Philo-Celtic Society appears to have accomplished nearly all of its goals by January 1880; however, it had yet to produce the promised journal devoted to the revival of the Irish language.

A statement from the Philo-Celtic Society of Boston regarding the publishing of Irish literature in roman type had appeared in the *Irish World* in March 1879: "It shall be our duty to treat them [people who use roman rather than Gaelic type] as Anglicised enemies of the Irish language, hardened into West Britons by the contaminating atmosphere of Dublin Castle ... this patriotic revival, through time and space will work and spread, until every book or Irish manuscript throughout the globe will be printed in genuine Irish characters."[20] Given this stance, if the society were to publish a journal, an adequate – and affordable – Gaelic type would be essential. Just months later, James Haltigan's New York–based *Celtic Monthly* published a letter from O'Daly and Sullivan announcing "to all who are interested in the resuscitation of the grand old language of the Celtic race" that the Boston Philo-Celtic Society had obtained matrices for Gaelic type and now had the capability to cast Irish letters in Boston. Most importantly, the Gaelic type could be had for forty-two cents per pound – a price equal to that of the roman. Soon they would be in a position to supply all printers with Gaelic type, and O'Daly and Sullivan respectfully asked the proprietors of newspapers, magazines, periodicals, and books of every kind to send their orders for Gaelic type to the Boston Philo-Celtic Society.[21] Most importantly, they were at last poised to produce a journal of their own.

In January 1881, the Philo-Celtic Society of Boston published the first volume of the *Philo-Celt,* "a monthly miscellany of Irish Literature, partly in the Irish language," issued under the management of the Philo-Celt Publishing Company and edited by O'Daly.[22] While no copies are known to have survived, the *Boston Daily Globe* mentions "very encouraging reports of the success of the January number. Letters of commendation and remittances for annual subscriptions are being received ... it is possible that a second edition of the first issue will be required."[23] The *Irish-American* was less generous in its assessment, noting that "not a word of Gaelic appears in it – which seems rather queer for a magazine which was to be devoted almost exclusively to the propagation of the Irish language movement."[24] On 28 May 1881, the *Pilot* listed the contents of the upcoming issue of the *Philo-Celt,* now including material in Irish, but after that no mentions of the journal occur.[25]

Months later, in October 1881, Michael Logan published the first issue of *An Gaodhal / The Gael* in Brooklyn, and announced that "for the first time in the history of the Irish Nation a newspaper is printed in its language and character."[26] This suggests either that the *Philo-Celt* contained an Irish Department but was not a truly bilingual journal or that its circulation never reached readers in Brooklyn. Perhaps owing to the failure of the *Philo-Celt,* it was not until November 1884 that O'Daly and Irish scholar Michael C. O'Shea once again announced their intention to translate and publish as much ancient Irish literature as survived.[27] Logan welcomed the competition and wished them every success: "We would like to see such journals in every town and city, and would advertise them too ... we shall take as much pride in your success in Boston as if you were a part and parcel of the *Gael* in Brooklyn."[28] One year later, in January 1886, the *Irish Echo,* official organ of the Boston Philo-Celtic Society, appeared in print.

The inaugural issue of the *Irish Echo* presented an attractive although not elaborate masthead featuring an Irish harp garlanded in shamrocks, and ran eight pages with a four-column layout. The prospectus outlined centuries of foul slanders against the Irish people – that their ancestors were barbarians, their language a jargon, and their literature unworthy of notice. All subscribers to the *Irish Echo*

THE
IRISH ECHO.
Devoted to the Interests of the Language, Literature, History, Etc., of Ireland, and to Matters of General and Popular Information.
" No People will look forward to Posterity who do not often look back to their Ancestors."

Irish Echo masthead.

were therefore deemed to be "members of an army for the vindication of the Irish race … By showing the merits of the national language, a reaction is sure to set in and garner widespread support for the revival of the Irish language." Despite this mission to aid in the cultivation of the Irish language, however, the editors also declared, "we will have no Irish department in the columns of our new publication, for some months. We will at first explain to the Irish race, through the medium of the English language (which they now know, better than that of their forefathers) the means … to rebut these slanders."[29]

Immediately following the publication of the first issue, Logan offered a welcome notice of sorts in *An Gaodhal*, saying of the *Irish Echo*:

> It is a lively, interesting English publication, as would be expected from its projectors … but it looks rather strange to us that such a publication coming from such a source wholly ignores the Irish language … [T]he ECHO has not a single word of Irish, even as a specimen … [W]e are surprised at the Boston Philo-Celtic Society where so much superior Irish talent abound[s], and where every convenience exist[s] for turning out Gaelic literature, that the initial number of their journal should appear without a single word in the language whose preservation and cultivation are the ostensible objects of their association![30]

O'Daly replied to the back-handed compliment from Logan with this justification:

> There is no one more anxious than we are to advance the movement in the interest of the Irish language … but unfortunately for

> the language, only a small percentage of our people are so inclined ... There are some, perhaps, who know a little history of the language but not enough to drive them into the movement; these are ashamed at being unable to read it and for that reason will not patronize a publication with Irish in it; others have an unnatural prejudice against such a publication because they cannot read the language ... There is another class ... that think the Irish was no language – that it was only a jargon as represented by English writers ... In order to enlist these classes in this important movement of ours, they must at first be shown in as mild and as tolerant a manner as possible ... to give them some idea now of what was denied them heretofore ... through the medium of the English language, which they, as a rule, only know.[31]

As such, the *Irish Echo* began publishing instructive features in the first issues, with columns on Irish family names taken from the work of John O'Donovan; a full list of the Irish monarchs of the Milesian line down to the Norman invasion; a list of rare books on Ireland available for purchase; and brief passages declaring Irish to be superior to all living languages and older than Latin or Greek. Editorials encouraged readers to join the Boston Philo-Celtic Society and consider attending the Irish classes, and the reports of the society's meetings and monthly entertainments were fully enumerated. To increase circulation, all subscribers were expected to become "recruiting sergeants" to swell the ranks of the vindication army, and members of the Boston Philo-Celtic Society were offered prizes for bringing in the most subscriptions. Top prize was awarded to those who secured at least one hundred subscribers.[32]

In June 1886, O'Shea became the new president of the Philo-Celtic Society of Boston, and the *Irish Echo* promised that "the movement for the language and literature of Ireland will get an impetus now in our city that it has not witnessed for some time."[33] Indeed, O'Shea immediately set a militant tone in his inaugural address: "In your native language alone you have an arsenal and magazine, fully supplied with arms and ammunition for offensive as well as defensive warfare against your implacable enemies ... who, bent upon the total extinction of a nation, considered the destruction of the language and literature of that nation."[34] He also contributed an original poem to the front page of the July issue, titled "The Irish Language," which was to be sung to the air of "The Wearing of the Green":

The Irish language spurned now by hostile Saxon foes,
Shall yet compel them low to bow, as up it proudly goes –
To its imperial eminence as empress of all speech,
The first in vigor, sound and sense, as science soon will teach,
Then speak your native tongue with pride,
And let it now be seen,
That you despise those Saxon foes,
Who call it low or mean.
. . .
The beauteous Deirdre wailed her love, in its heart-melting tones,
For passion such expression not another language owns,
It portrays every feeling that pervades the human heart,
And is rich in ancient terms used in science and in art.
[chorus]
But this noble language long has been by Saxon tyrants banned –
Prescribed and vilely slandered, even in our native land.
To rob us of our learning and to darken our bright fame,
And to lower down beneath their feet the proud old Gaelic name.
[chorus][35]

Alongside O'Daly, the Killarney-born O'Shea soon positioned himself at the heart of the *Irish Echo.* His philological proofs declaring Irish to be the nearest exemplar of the ancient Scythian, dating to ages before the rise of the empires of Assyria and Chaldea, assured readers that the Irish language was worthy not only of their care and regard, but also of the regard of all men dedicated to etymological research and linguistics.[36] O'Shea was fiercely devoted to the revival and often critical of his fellow nationalists. "No Irish language, no Irish Nation," he declared in an editorial: "No nation that lost its language has ever become a nation again. If not to save the language, what are the thousands upon thousands of dollars contributing to the Irish cause for? Is it to free Ireland for West Britons, and English settlers for Durham bulls and bullocks, and for Cheshire sheep?"[37] These words sound powerful but perhaps rang rather hollow to readers of a journal promoting the Irish revival, in which even native speakers like O'Daly and O'Shea wrote solely in the English language. But that was reportedly to change.

The Patrick Terry collection of Irish manuscripts donated previously to the Boston Philo-Celtic Society received notice in the November 1886 *Irish Echo,* accompanied by an editorial, which read in part, "[w]e expect to be in a position next January, the commencement of the second year of publication, to establish an Irish Language Department in the *Irish Echo* … [which], although a body not yet twelve months old, is bursting its swaddling-bands and observes its way to the front, on the philological path."[38] But despite O'Daly's insistence that the journal's income, bills due included, exceeded the outlay and did well for the first year, the first volume of the *Irish Echo* was in fact a financial disappointment.[39] O'Daly was later to admit that sales were much bleaker than he had claimed, acknowledging that "it had 500 in its first issue, and many of its friends were doubtful or lukewarm. Fully 300 of the first volume were given away … and many accounts were in arrears."[40]

Notwithstanding this disappointing first year, the *Irish Echo* made no significant editorial changes to begin 1887. The rhetoric extolling the virtues of Irish remained robust, however, with the March issue claiming that the "Irish language is the most perfectly and philosophically constructed of all known languages," and that "Irish literature is rich and copious, comprising History, Jurisprudence, Botany, Geometry, Genealogy, Astronomy, Logic, Ethics, Theology, Philology, Romance, Poetry and Polite Literature; but this literature is in 'sealed books' in the keeping of the Irish language. The mission of the *Irish Echo* … is to help bring this evidence before the world – to open those 'sealed books' and thereby vindicate the character of the Irish race."[41] In the same issue, O'Shea heaped scorn upon pro-English Americans, addressing them in a column subtitled "An exposure and refutation of English and pro-English wilful slander and malicious misrepresentation, directed against the Irish Nation, against its history, its language, the character of its people, its manners and customs; in short, against everything that could be called distinctively Irish."[42] O'Daly also issued an appeal at this time for a union of all Gaelic societies in the United States. All the Philo-Celtic societies had the same basic aim, which was to promote and revive the Irish language, yet each society functioned independently and there was no centralized management. O'Daly implored the societies to "unite under one head, and with their united efforts raise the language, literature, etc. of the land of our Sires to the proper place."[43] Jealousies and rivalries among the organizations prevented any unification, however, and the idea for a convention to discuss unification never caught on.[44] After more than a year in publication, the *Irish Echo* remained firm in its commitment to the Irish-language revival in all aspects but one: English remained the sole means of communication.

A grand celebration commemorating the fourteenth anniversary of the Boston Philo-Celtic Society was widely advertised in the *Irish Echo* to take place on 5 May 1887, and many songs and recitations in the Irish language were promised. Yet neither O'Daly nor O'Shea could have anticipated the home-grown assault to the dignity of the *Irish Echo* that came only weeks later at the hands of the *Boston Daily Globe*, which ridiculed – intentionally or otherwise – the celebration. "Although in existence all these years," the *Globe* wrote, "this was the first formal celebration of its birth. A peculiar feature was that many of the numbers on the programme were to be delivered in the Celtic tongue … now so little spoken." Thomas O'Neill Russell delivered an address that "must have been interesting, for it was vociferously applauded."[45] On account of this perceived insult a special meeting of the Boston Philo-Celtic Society was held to determine whether the *Boston Daily Globe* had intentionally ridiculed the society and the movement, whose singular goal was to vindicate the character of a slandered people; it was resolved that the *Irish Echo* would publish the report from the *Globe* alongside accounts from other papers to allow the Irish element in America to gauge whether it indeed constituted a serious offense.[46] Although a letter of apology was received the following September from the editor of the *Globe*, who claimed it was only ignorance on the part of the reporter and not intended as burlesque, this incident clearly struck a nerve. As a result, the May issue of the *Irish Echo* declared that "after next month we will have a department in the Irish language."[47]

Following previous patterns regarding such announcements, Irish did not, in fact, appear in the July 1887 issue of the *Irish Echo*; however, the editors did reveal that they had acquired a font of Gaelic type, cast from matrices owned by the Boston Philo-Celtic Society, and that an Irish-language section would appear in the next issue, if the printers agreed to set the type. "They seem to be rather timid about taking hold of it," they explained, "so that it may take another month to break them in."[48] The printers must have continued to struggle through August, for it was not until the September 1887 issue that Irish made its first appearance in the *Irish Echo* – one year and nine months after the founding of the journal. All told, the first and long-awaited Irish language department took up only two columns on the first page of the issue. The alphabet was presented in Gaelic type, followed by a few introductory lessons and the song, "Caitilín Mo Mhúirnín." While readers might confidently say "Tá an rós bog agus an dún mór" (the rose is soft and the fort is large) after reading the lessons, several other passages contained typographical errors that were attributed to the extended absence of O'Daly. In future, assured the editor, no such mistakes would appear.[49] The editors did promise more Irish in successive issues, with material to benefit learners and advanced speakers, although they echoed a former pledge made by O'Daly to "never print the Irish with English characters ... The Irish language was a living language centuries before English was, and at the present day it is ... free from English influences, and we do not propose to put it under English control in this late day."[50]

The front page of the October issue of the *Irish Echo* featured "Ua Dómhnaill A Bú," a translation from the English by O'Shea, followed by a short poem in praise of the Irish language by the same author. A short notice also announced that, owing to the increasing numbers of attendees at the Boston Philo-Celtic Society's Irish school, more spacious quarters would soon be needed. Certainly, all this looked encouraging for the language movement in Boston.[51] Furthermore, despite the November issue not appearing, a letter from Douglas Hyde in Irish in the December issue, which praised the editors of the *Irish Echo* for their efforts in the revival and encouraged readers to take up the learning of their native tongue, only strengthened the resolve of the Philo-Celtic Society.[52]

In January 1888, the *Irish Echo* began its third year of publication with a serialization of *Parliament na m-Ban* (The Women's Parliament), with accompanying English translation. Taken from a manuscript in the Terry Collection, the editors declared that "every person wants to read the proceedings of said Parliament," and newsboys would sell their copies of the *Irish Echo* as fast as they could distribute them.[53] In the same issue, a short poem sent in by Douglas Hyde for the Christmas number was published with an English translation by Michael Cavanagh. The poem ends with hopes for the coming year:

A's cidh atá ar námhaid,
Ag bagairt uile lá,
Le saighdiuribh a's cuirteannaibh,
A's daoinibh dlighe gan fáth,
Tá súil agam go bh-feicfimid,
('S thaithneochadh sé lem' chroídhe),
Na Sacsanaighe gan neart ar bith,
'Sa g-clasanna gan bhrígh.

And though our hateful foemen,
Through tyrant force and guile,
By English laws and "yeomen,"
Should threaten us meanwhile,
(The thought my heart doth lighten),
I think we yet shall see
Our country's future brighten –
The Saxon forced to flee.[54]

Douglas Hyde was not the only prominent Irish-language revivalist to write in support of the *Irish Echo* and its new direction. Thomas O'Neill Russell also wrote a letter in Irish praising the editors for publishing Irish-language material, but exhorting them to be sure to only print proper Irish and avoid corrupting the language. He assured them of his friendship so long as the *Irish Echo* held to his lofty standards.[55]

Six months after the *Irish Echo* began publishing material in Irish, the quantity and quality of the selections began to grow. More poetry was printed in each issue, including selections from celebrated Irish-American poet Patrick O'Byrne (Pádraic); Irish lessons were expanded, and plans were made to publish a textbook; lectures given at other Gaelic societies appeared; and *Parliament na m-Ban* continued its serial run. The editors always had the learner in mind and often included a glossary to the printed material in Irish. As might be expected, the bilingual proceedings of Philo-Celtic Society meetings were also constant features, and the fifteenth anniversary celebration of the Philo-Celtic Society of Boston proved that neither the members of the society nor its president, O'Shea, had wavered in their commitment to the cause of the revival of the Irish language. With Boston mayor Hugh O'Brien presiding, O'Shea gave an address to the society in Irish espousing the *Irish Echo*'s platform: "Gan fios air ár d-teangain dhúchais, ní h-Éirionnaíghe chearta sinn, acht Iar-Breatanaíghe. A sí ár d-teanga léigheanta amháin ár n-arm cosanta a n-aghaidh éitig na n-ughdar Sacson" (In ignorance of our native speech we cannot properly be called Irishmen, but West-Britons. Our learned language alone is our only efficient weapon of defence against the malignant slanders of Saxon authors).[56] The editors also added a new feature to the July 1888 issue, publishing Irish proverbs, with translations, that served to highlight "the elements of the moral notions, customs and manners" of the Irish people.[57] Similarly, Charles O'Farrell of the Philo-Celtic

Society of Boston and Reverend James Keegan from Saint Louis provided columns appealing to the Irish-American community to foster and promote Irish music as well as the language.[58] The *Irish Echo* was evolving into a richer publication and the editors were receiving numerous contributions; they duly informed readers that they were accumulating Irish-language material and would publish it by degrees.[59] Beginning in August 1888, each issue of the *Irish Echo* published "Army Rolls," as they called them, enumerating the subscribers to the journal from various towns and cities around Boston and even into New Hampshire. By September 1888, the *Irish Echo* had received numerous pleas from readers to increase the journal from eight to sixteen pages; the editors began to consider this seriously.[60] One reader, John M. Tierney, wrote from San Juan in the Argentine Republic requesting a full run of the *Irish Echo* from its inception.[61] The journal seemed to be on its way.

As the *Irish Echo* entered its fourth year in January 1889, the editors offered ten thousand thanks, representing its circulation, and wished for twenty thousand subscribers for the following year.[62] The next issue offered a correction, listing the circulation for 1888 at 29,800, the largest for any paper of its kind in the world, and wagering that it could reach fifty thousand the following year.[63] Regardless of the veracity of the claim that the *Irish Echo* had 29,800 subscribers in 1888, the journal had come a long way since its dismal first year and was forced to move its operations to a larger publishing location.[64]

Despite this encouraging news regarding the journal's success, the February 1889 volume was not released, although a double issue was published in March, followed by another sixteen-page volume in April 1889 – an issue that contained a few surprising announcements. The first was a notice that O'Daly would be retiring as editor of the *Irish Echo* and that the "venerable and erudite Michael C. O'Shea" would be succeeding him in that capacity.[65] Perhaps more striking was a new column titled "Instructions for Reading the Irish Language in Roman Characters," which clearly ran counter to the stance of the Philo-Celtic Society of Boston as first expressed by O'Daly sixteen years previously. An editorial explained that "experience has taught us that it is advisable to use said character which is so familiar to all the Irish now, so as to enlist in the cause the thousands who can speak Irish and read it in the Roman characters … but who don't know the old character … [F]or the future a portion of the Irish in the *Irish Echo* will be in the Roman characters."[66] It is difficult to state for certain whether this policy had any effect on O'Daly's decision to resign, but his previous vehement resistance to the roman typeface makes this a strong possibility. Whatever the reason, the May 1889 issue bluntly stated: "Mr. P.J. O'Daly is no longer connected with the *Irish Echo.*"[67]

MICHAEL C. O'SHEA (MAY 1889–MAY 1890)

The *Irish Echo* of April 1889 announced that O'Shea would be its next editor: "[his] thorough knowledge of Ireland's national language and literature, as well as of comparative philology, renders him admirably fitted for the position."[68] O'Shea made assurances that he would sustain the character of the journal, but also noted that the *Irish Echo* had "surmounted a difficulty which seriously threatened the very existence of our paper" and apologized for the long delay in publishing the June issue.[69] No explanation was given regarding the cause of the troubles, however. This same issue commenced *Ceap Craoibhe Gearalthach* (the History of the Geraldines) from the Terry Collection of manuscripts, appearing with facing English translation, and it offered the first selection of poetry in the roman typeface, "Seághan Bán MacGearailt agus a Bhean" (White John Fitzgerald and His Wife), taken from T.R. Howard's manuscript miscellany.[70] The same T.R. Howard contributed an original poem to the November 1889 issue, also in roman type, dedicated to Patrick Kenneally of Malden upon his return to Ireland.[71] By printing the Irish language in roman type, the *Irish Echo* sparked a fiery debate among its readers that would continue for several months.

The first volley supported the Irish font and was initiated by renowned language revivalist Captain Thomas D. Norris in July 1889:

> I am sorry, very sorry, that I see you have decided to have some of our beautiful language appear hereafter in Roman or English type ... I hope you will reconsider and expunge the idea and wipe out from the face of the *Irish Echo* the only dark spot that ever appeared on its beautiful surface. "Burn everything English but its coal!" You know how very easy it is for any reasonable person to learn the Irish alphabet, and how much more easy it is to read Irish with the use of that alphabet than with the English. Our enemies tell us that we never had any literature. Let them not tell our grand-children that we never had any type. A d-tuigeann tú? (Do you understand?)[72]

Norris also enclosed two poems with his letter for publication, but warned, "if you should dress them up in English uniform, for God's sake send them back to me as they are. I want them in Irish or not at all."[73] The other side responded in the following issue, with Joseph Cromien of New York's Bowery branch of the Philo-Celtic Society asking,

> And now shall we build a wall around ourselves and a script brought to us fourteen hundred years ago, and tell the Irish people who speak the language from the cradle that, although they have learned the use of the modern form of the Roman type, they shall be doomed to perpetual ignorance of the beauties of Gaelic unless they consent to learn the use of the ancient script … I implore of you not to turn any person away thirsty who seeks a drink at your fount of Gaelic knowledge: provide for all comers.[74]

O'Shea's reply took up no fewer than four columns in the September issue, and promised that the *Irish Echo* would endeavour to keep its columns clear of all contentious vituperative debate and not insinuate "stubborn pigheadedness" to any gentleman.[75] In November, O'Shea clarified his editorial position and offered a challenge: "We are not averse to Roman characters for the Irish language if we had sufficient patronage to warrant our printing it in said characters … We hear of only a few persons clamoring for the change, let us hear from others if there be any, and if we hear from, say 250 by the New Year, we will guarantee to print one page a month."[76] O'Shea seemed willing to advance the movement in every possible way, but vowed to never abandon the time-honoured Gaelic script. In the end, although only one reader wrote in support of roman type, the *Irish Echo* continued to print the occasional piece in that script, with the majority of material appearing in the Gaelic type.[77]

In January 1890, the new volume of the *Irish Echo* appeared in a sixteen-page, three-column layout, similar to that of Dublin's *Irisleabhar na Gaedhilge / Gaelic Journal* and Brooklyn's *An Gaodhal / The Gael.* This was a format that a large number of subscribers had requested owing to the ease of binding issues together. This first number began publishing *Eachtra Chonaill Golban* (The Adventures of Conall Golban), taken from a manuscript collection donated by Thomas Griffin of Lawrence, Massachusetts, in 1889.[78] Original compositions by Norris, O'Daly, and Boston Philo-Celtic Society member Humphrey

Sullivan also appeared in this issue alongside the opening salvo of a contentious correspondence between Norris and Thomas O'Neill Russell regarding the rules of Irish grammar and proper usage. These two men were known adversaries in the Irish American press, but their feuding had thus far been absent from the *Irish Echo*.[79] Russell had contributed an article about Bishop John Carswell's *Foirm na n-Urrnuidheadh* (Book of Common Order), the first book printed in a Gaelic language, which Russell claimed was free of errors and should be printed without alteration. O'Shea countered that "we would like to make some corrections, but obey his prohibition."[80] O'Shea may have regretted not making the changes, for a three-column letter from Thomas D. Norris, aptly titled "Capt. Norris points out many errors to Mr. Russell," documented dozens of mistakes made by Russell in the allegedly perfect Carswell piece.[81] This type of corrective letter was not uncommon in the press at the time, but Norris – perhaps inadvertently – reopened a debate regarding the proper use of the preposition *chum* (toward, for) that had raged in the pages of the *Irish-American* throughout the year 1888 until it grew so contentious that the *Irish-American* refused to print any further communication on a matter so trifling.[82] Norris's letter fuelled a new chapter in the grammatical feud, however, with multiple columns devoted to usage and savage insult, and with each scholar trying to out-duel the other in matters of syntax. Michael Logan in *An Gaodhal* urged the disputants to cease and desist, but included a jab of his own at Russell, long an adversary of Logan's and oft accused of being a British spy: "There is no more room for discussion of 'chum''s position in the language than there is for the word 'an' [the] … If the lovers of the Gaelic movement knew the motives of the party who originated the discussion they would drop it, for its continuance tends only to promote the end of his questionable purpose."[83] Norris also begged the editors of the *Irish Echo* to end this madness, but not before filling three columns demonstrating that his grammatical prowess was unsurpassed. Mercifully, the editors adopted a new policy: all discussions on Irish grammar must thenceforth be in the Irish language and confined to a length of six hundred words.[84]

Success appeared to have arrived for the *Irish Echo*, for in February of 1890, it ran this notice: "So great is the appreciation of our magazine in New England that a well-known and popular cigar manufacturer is about to start a brand called the 'Irish Echo Cigar' … sure to meet with popular favor among lovers of the Irish language movement."[85] In this same issue the editors boasted that the *Irish Echo* "has now found its way into every state and territory of the Union … we little dreamed that our efforts would be known outside of our immediate friends in New England, or, at the farthest, New York. To-day, San Francisco is up and alive as much as New York, and even the Argentine Republic, England, Germany, and the Canadas have fallen into line, nobly working for the preservation of the old Celtic tongue."[86] This issue also printed an exclusive Irish version of the funeral oration intended to be given by Matt Harris at the grave of John O'Mahony, founder of the Fenian Brotherhood, in 1877. The eulogy was never delivered, as police raided Harris's home and confiscated the document; but the *Irish-American* received a copy and published the address in English in August 1889.[87] Norris translated the speech into Irish for the *Irish Echo*, and a glossary was supplied for learners of the language.[88]

Despite the successes claimed for the journal in February 1890, it soon became clear that it was in financial trouble. The March volume failed to come out, and O'Shea made a point of noting that the *Irish Echo* "will be published promptly on the 15th day of each month, commencing with this, the April number," likely addressing letters of frustration received from subscribers.[89] The May issue then offered to send *Donahoe's Magazine* to subscribers along with the *Irish Echo* for two dollars per year, and also informed readers who suggested the journal procure small Gaelic type for poetry that the *Irish Echo* was not able to spend the necessary $35.[90] The June number also failed to appear, and by July 1890, with no prior announcement, O'Shea was no longer the editor of the *Irish Echo.*

CHARLES O'FARRELL (JULY–DECEMBER 1890; APRIL 1893–MARCH/APRIL 1894)

While no reason was given for O'Shea's departure, it seems that the seventy-eight-year-old was suffering from health problems. In April 1890, Charles O'Farrell wrote to Michael Logan of *An Gaodhal* informing him that "my old friend O'Shea is not getting very good health and my knowledge of the Irish language is not that which would enable me to run the Echo successfully."[91] Regardless of O'Farrell's perceived shortcomings, however, he was listed as the manager of the *Irish Echo* in July 1890. Immediately, he came out in favour of giving more Irish material in roman type, having it and the Gaelic script share equal space: "How are we to please everyone? The only way seems to be to print Gaelic in both Irish and Roman."[92] O'Farrell lacked such diplomacy in his treatment of Scottish Gaelic, however, as a reprinted poem from the *Celtic Magazine* of Inverness, Scotland, was introduced in this way: "The manufacture of what may be called a brand new language by the Scotch about the middle of the last century, is perhaps the most extraordinary linguistic feat ever performed in any age or in any country. It cannot be said, however, that our kinsmen, the Highland Scotch, are to be congratulated on the philological monstrosity they have fabricated."[93] O'Farrell also seemed to favour publishing more prose material in Irish, with more folk tales, legends, and historical writings promised. It mattered little, however, for the financial woes were never settled: an August issue was not produced, nor did an October or December number appear. The November 1890 issue appeared to be the journal's last.

Logan addressed the failure of the *Irish Echo* in *An Gaodhal*:

> The *Irish Echo* has ceased to exist, and more the shame for you, Irish-Americans. Because some of the matter ... did not suit you, you let it die. It published Gaelic, at all events, and when it did it should have been supported by Irishmen, whether its management had been pleasing to them or not ... It was the want of personal responsibility that killed the poor Echo. Like the poor man, it took everyone's advice and got lost."[94]

One of the *Irish Echo*'s major errors, according to Logan, was the decision to publish material in roman type: "The defunct *Irish Echo* of Boston opened its columns to the 'Romano-Keltic' type, and then it died. Gaels will not have it – especially in Éire Mhór."[95] It does appear, however, that O'Farrell and fellow Boston Philo-Celt J.G. Griffin attempted to resurrect the *Irish Echo* under the new name of the *Gaelic Journal.* They claimed that previous subscribers would "have little difficulty in recognizing the old Echo under a new, and we trust, a more appropriate name."[96] The *Gaelic Journal* appeared in January 1891 for a single sixteen-page issue, intended to provide financial support for Griffin's textbook advocating the teaching of Irish by the "natural" (i.e., conversational) method.[97] Although bearing a new title, this journal clearly resembled the *Irish Echo* in layout and content; however, it devoted three pages to full musical scores, which was a new feature.[98] Logan claimed that the *Gaelic Journal* venture was nothing more than a swindle, intent on bilking subscribers without publishing a journal. O'Farrell denied these accusations and denounced "the charges made in the *Gael* as a mendacious and malignant falsehood, a fabrication founded for personal aggrandizement."[99] Wherever the truth lies, no further issues of the *Gaelic Journal* appear to have survived; yet Charles O'Farrell never gave up on the language revival, and he resuscitated the *Irish Echo* in April 1893.

The first issue to appear in more than two years offered a few words of explanation to its readers: "After an unfortunate and somewhat protracted suspension of our little publication, we once more greet our many friends with its revival ... with a vigor and determination never possessed by us before, mainly bought by bitter and costly experience of the past."[100] This latest *Irish Echo* offered a new look, running sixteen pages, but with no columns, making it easier to read yet lighter on content. The April issue was almost entirely in English, featuring a partial translation of Ernst Windisch's "Ancient Irish Legendary Literature and Ossianic Poetry," which originally appeared in French in *Revue Celtique*.[101] The May issue was quite the opposite, with an untranslated version of the Fenian tale *Bruighean Chéise Chorrain* (the Fairy Fort at Keshcorran) followed by a substantial glossary to aid language learners.[102] O'Farrell then chose to begin printing Geoffrey Keating's *Eochair Sgéithe an Aifrinn* (Key to the Shield of the Mass), taken from a manuscript held by the Philo-Celtic Society.[103] Original poetry still appeared in the *Irish Echo*, including offerings from Patrick O'Byrne and many contributions from the venerable Michael C. O'Shea, whose "Comhairle Do Ghaodhalaibh" (Advice to the Gaels) appeared in the September 1893 number alongside his tribute to Douglas Hyde, "Timniughadh Do'n Chraoibhín Aoibhinn." It seems that O'Shea, at this point eighty-one years old, had not given up hope that poetry could stir Irish Americans to take up the cause of the language revival.

The new *Irish Echo* also offered more scholarly essays and book reviews than its predecessor. Thomas O'Neill Russell was the major contributor, and his "Are We Anglo-Saxons or Celto-Saxons?" and "Ancient Irish Literary Remains" showed he had not tempered his enthusiasm for the revival.[104] A good portion of material was also recirculated from the *Gaelic Journal*, *Revue Celtique*, and the *Tuam News*, while a lengthy piece titled "Emblems of Irish Nationality" was taken from the *Dublin Penny Journal* and serialized across five issues. The March–April 1893 issue, the final number of the volume, announced the opening of an Irish school with a hundred students in Providençe, Rhode Island; celebrated the twenty-first anniversary of the Boston Philo-Celtic Society; began publishing "A Key to the Study of Gaelic" by John O'Daly, written exclusively for the *Irish Echo*; and published an original poem by Pádraig Ó Cathasaigh of Malden, Massachusetts. It also announced that the next volume would appear under a "more appropriate cognomen, namely *An Mac-Alla Éireannach*, which means in English 'The Irish Echo'"; however, O'Farrell further noted that receipts for the past volume were far below the expenses occurred.[105] In the end, financial woes overcame enthusiasm, and the *Irish Echo* was no more.

CONCLUSION

Even before the first Philo-Celtic Society was founded in Boston, Patrick Ford contributed an editorial in his *Irish World* addressing the attempted revival of Irish in the United States: "Many able and eloquent arguments are advanced in favor of this project … [but] is this restoration *feasible?*"[106] Michael Logan countered with: "Trying to build a nationality without the language is as vain as trying to build a house in a bottomless swamp … You, Gentlemen, who feel ashamed of your national tongue will never free Ireland. Never."[107] For their part, the editors of the *Irish Echo* were not recruiting for an insurrection; the Army of Vindication was meant to be a cultural rather than a political force: "an army whose members will have no occasion to use or fear a leaden bullet or a ball of dynamite."[108] In this light, was Logan correct when he faulted and shamed the Irish American community for letting the "poor Echo" die, or did the *Irish Echo* fail because its goals were never quite in step with the community it served? Perhaps the best way to answer is to turn the question on its head and consider that the *Irish Echo* never failed at all. While it was not single-handedly responsible for the overthrow of the "foul slanders of centuries by English writers" or the establishment of an Irish Republic, the contributions made by this journal of the Boston Philo-Celtic Society helped forge a new Irish identity in the United States and in Ireland. In the end, the literary revivals in Irish and English, the Gaelic League, and the proponents of physical force all recruited from this Army of Vindication: in reality, the *Irish Echo* created a reserve force for the next generation of Irish cultural nationalists.

APPENDIX I

Index of first lines of poetry in the *Irish Echo*, 1887–1894

The following index contains all the first lines of Irish poetry in the *Irish Echo.* Risteárd de Hae included poems from the fourth and final volume of the *Irish Echo* (1893–94) in his *Clár Litridheacht na Nua-Ghaedhilge 1850–1936*, but he marked the first three volumes "ar iarraidh" (missing). For the sake of completeness, I have included all the poems from 1887 to 1894. Regarding format, I follow the same methodology as Fionnuala Uí Fhlannagáin in her indexes of *An Gaodhal, Irish People, Celtic Monthly, Celtic Magazine,* and *The Emerald.* Where possible, I give the title (T), poet (P), and translator (Tr); I also add notes (N) where applicable. When poets, like Michael C. O'Shea, used numerous versions of their names, I have standardized to the most common spelling.

A bhaintr'each mo chroidhe, ní gan adhbhar do ghruaim: T.: A Bhaintreabhach Mo Chroidhe: Tr.: Pádraic (Patrick O'Byrne): July 1890.

A bh-facadh tú an Chúil-fhionn 's í ag siúbhal ar na bóithri': T.: An Chúil-Fhionn N.: From *The Munster Poets 1st Series*: March 1888.

A bhille ó Éirinn thar sáile, Thug broinniol air bárc do'n domhan t-siar: P.: Michael C. O'Shea: N.: Composed *ex tempore* upon receiving an Irish Blackthorn Stick from Miss E.C. Granger: February 1888.

A Chaitilín mo mhúirnín! Tá 'n mhaidin 'n s'na spéirídh: T.: Cáitilín Mo Mhúirnín: September 1887.

A chaoin teang' ár n-draoithe 's ár n-aos dána aosda: T.: An Teanga Gaedhilge: Tr.: P.J. O'Daly: N.: Published in successive issues. Four lines: April 1888.

A charaid ó thír ghlais mhín Inis sheanda na nGaodhal: T.: Comhairle do Ghaodhalaibh / Advice to the Gaels: P.: Michael C. O'Shea: N.: Accompanying English translation by the author: September 1893.

A Chlanna Gaodhal is mór an náire: T.: An Teanga Gaedhilge: P.: P.J. O'Daly: January 1890.

A Chlanna na h-Éirionn is leun linn bhur n-agair gach lá: T.: Cosnaimh an Ghaedhlig / Preserve the Gaelic: P.: Michael C. O'Shea: April 1889.

A "Chraoibhín Aoibhinn" bhinn ó Éirinn: T.: Timniughadh do'n Chraoibhín Aoibhinn: P.: Michael C. O'Shea: September 1893.

A Chraoibhín Aoibhinn is binn linn do bréithre: September 1889.

A Chraoibhín Aoibhinn ná bí linn mille anach: N.: Four lines: January 1888.

A chreidmhighe 'nois triallaidh: T.: Adeste Fidelis: Tr.: P.H. O'Donnell of Villanova College, PA: December 1888; December 1889.

A chuilm an cheoil bhrónaigh 's an dún dubh thall: N.: Composed by a bard of the last century upon hearing a dove coo from Mothar Uí Roy, the ruin of O'Connor of Corcomroe's mansion in Clare: July 1888.

A Dhiarmuid thréin Uí Dhonnabháin!: P.: Amhlaoibh O'Súilleabháin: N.: An address to O'Donovan Rossa: January 1890.

A g-cualaidh mé guth ag teacht o'n iar: T.: Guth o'n Iar: P.: Pádraic (Patrick O'Byrne): N.: In praise of Father Keegan of Saint Louis, MO. In roman typeface: August 1893.

A Ghaodhal shliucht má thuigean sibh Gaedhilig: T.: President O'Shea's Address: P.: Michael C. O'Shea: February 1888.

A Ghaodhal shliucht uagh Éirin tar saille: T.: Áille na Gaodhailge: P.: Michael C. O'Shea: August 1889.

Air an g-croich ag crochadh bhí: T.: Go Mairidh Éire / God Save Ireland: P.: Father O'Growney: N.: From the *Tuam News*: June 1889.

Air maidin cois leasa air druchd dom: T.: Cailín Deas Crúidhte na M-bó: December 1887.

Air maidin seal am' aonar: T.: Aga na nGaodhal: P.: Seághan O'Dálaigh: February 1890. See also December 1893.

A Mhuintear mo dhúthaigh cia dúbhach linn uagh Éirin: August 1889.

A mhuintir mo dhuthchaigh cia dubhach linn ó Éirinn: T.: Gaodhail agus Gaodhailge / Gaels and the Gaelic: P.: Michael C. O'Shea: N.: With accompanying English translation: September 1893.

An chruit, do scaip trí thallaidh 'n righ: T.: The Harp: P.: Thomas Moore: Tr.: Archbishop MacHale: October 1893.

A ógánaighe Éireann, an eol daoibh an tí: T.: Aindir na Súl Dubh: July 1893.

Ar maidin seal am' aonar: T.: Aga na nGaodhal: P.: Seághan O'Dálaigh: December 1893. See also February 1890.

A sé leónaidh mo chumais: T.: An Bonnaire Fiadha-Phuic: P.: Seághan Clárach (John Clarach McDonald): August 1889.

Atá an t-iarthar a m-bliadhana ag déanamh cúma: T.: An Feart Laoidh Sonn: P.: Micheál Óg O'Longáin: May 1890.

Atá dánta bog searbh dá g-ceapadh le tréimhse: T.: Go M'Fhearr Leigean Dóibh: P.: Séamuis Uí Colmain: September 1890.

Ba h-aoibhinn bheith beo ins an am fad ó: P.: Pádraic (Patrick O'Byrne): N.: With accompanying English translation "Happy it Were to Have Lived Long Ago" by Thomas O'Neill Russell. From the Chicago *Citizen*: March 1889.

Beandacht Dé foraibh uili: T.: "Beannacht Phádruig air Mhuintir na h-Éirionn": March 1888.

Bheirimidh chéudh míle slán leat a's fichid: N.: Address read by Mr T.R. Howard of Malden upon the departure of Patrick Kenneally to Dunallow, County Cork. In roman typeface: November 1889.

Bhí glóire na maidne ag lasadh na spéire: T.: Tobar na Sighe: P.: Pádraic (Patrick O'Byrne): April 1888.

Bidheann focal cáirdis de ghliocas lán: N: Concludes James Keegan's column on Irish Music. 4 lines: September 1888.

Breitheamh ceart comhthrom an t-eug: T.: Smuainte ar an M-Bás: P.: Donnchadh Mór O'Dálaigh: N: From MS. Collection of Dr Murphy, Bishop of Cork: February 1894.

Brón air an t-sneachta, 'gus díbirt: T.: Brón Mór an t-Sneachta: P.: Aindriú Mór Ua Munaoile: N.: Printed in the *Gaelic Journal*'s only issue. Ua Munaoile was from Cnoc an Logha, Co. Mayo, and the poem was submitted by M. O'Gallchabhair of Chicago: January 1891.

Caoin tú féin a dhuine bhoicht: T.: Caoin tú Féin a Dhuine Bhoicht: P.: Donnchadh Mór O'Dálaigh (?): N: From MS. Compiled by William Sheehen of Coolivote, County Cork in 1753: February 1894.

Céad fáilte tar calaith do'n mhasgalaigh mhaorgadh: P.: P.J. O'Daly: N.: Recited upon receiving an Irish Blackthorn Stick from Miss E.C. Granger: March 1888.

Ceird agam féin ort fhir léigheanta dheaghmhúinte: T.: Ceird an Fhile air an Sagairt: September 1890.

Céud slán den oidhche réir sé mo leun nach anocht a tá a tús: T.: Caislean Uí Néill: N: Taken down as recited by Patrick Hennessy from Patrickswell parish in County Galway by J.J. Lyons of Philadelphia, PA, native of Glenamaddy, County Galway: May 1890.

Chaitheas tréibhse mhaith do m' shaoghal, níos mó ná fithche bhliaghain: T.: Éire, Tír mo Dhúthchais: P.: Thomas D. Norris: December 1889.

Cia deir go bh-fuil an t-sean troid thart? P.: Pádraic (Patrick O'Byrne): November 1889.

Cia súd thall aig teacht go d-tí mé: T.: Cómhlabhrádh Idir an "T-Óthar" agus an "Bás" / A Dialogue Between "Death" and the "Patient": N.: From Thomas O'Griffin, Lawrence, MA: November, 1888, January 1889, March 1889, April 1889, July 1889, August 1889, September 1889, November 1889, December 1889.

Cliabhán óir fút, a's tú óg: T.: Cúrsa an Duine Shaidhbhir: P.: An Craoibhín Aoibhinn: August 1889.

Cois na Brice 's me go déigheanach aig déanamh mo smuainte: N.: Contributed by a friend to the *Irish Echo* who has a large collection. N.: De Hae #2124 cites author as Tadhg Ó Donnchadha: January 1889.

Cois taoibh abhan sínnte is mé trath andhé: T.: Dán Aile-Agaireach / Allegorical Poem: P.: Éagán Uí Rathaille: December 1889.

Cread an ríabhradh nímhe-seo air Fhódhla: T.: Tuireamh Dhiarmuda Uí Laoghaire: P.: Aodhgan Ua Rathaighle, 1696: May 1890.

Cread dhéanfamaoid feasda gan adhmad?: T.: Caoine Cille Cais: December 1889.

Do b-fhearr liom féin 'na sparán lann: P.: Pádraic (Patrick O'Byrne): N.: 2 lines: June 1893.

Dob' fhearra liom ainnir chiuin bhéasach: P.: Thomas "Tomás Ruadh" O'Sullivan: N.: Native of Derrynane in County Kerry: August 1888.

Do shiúbhlas a lán gan spás a d-tosach mo shaoghail: T.: Loch Léin: N.: From Munster Poets, 2nd Series: May 1888.

Do shiubhlas a lán lem' dhánta 'sa racaireachd sgeul: T.: Loch Léin: N.: Supplied by Capt. Thomas D. Norris as a more correct and more popular version than that published in May 1888. Committed to memory in his early days: September 1888.

Do thainigh chum na taoide díbearach ó Éirinn: T.: An Díbearach Ó Éirinn: June 1888.

Éire, tá deora 'gus smígeadha do shúl: T.: Erin! The Tear and the Smile in Thine Eyes: P.: Thomas Moore: N.: Identical to MacHale's translation save "Éire" rather than "Eirin": September 1888.

Éistigh sealad, a charaid, lem' bhreithribh grínn: T.: Eachtradh an Bhaitseléara: P.: Diarmaid O'Connell: N.: Sent to the *Irish Echo* by Patrick Stanton of Cork: March 1889.

Fáilte rombat, a thriath!: T.: Patrick Stanton's Welcome to Daniel McCabe: P.: Patrick Stanton: April 1888.

Fer Dána an gilla so siar: N.: By Thaddy O'Higgins, who flourished in the reign of Queen Elizabeth. 4 lines: September 1888.

Fiafruigheann tú ce h-í do fuair mo ghrádh: T.: An Cailín Fuair mo Ghrádh: Tr.: Pádraic (Patrick O'Byrne): September 1893.

Gan bhrigh foraoir! Atá mo chéatfa: T.: Deórchaoineadh na h-Éireann: N.: In roman typeface. Taken from *Revue Celtique:* December 1893.

Ge fada tar tonnaibh ua úr-innis Gaodhal: T.: Fáilte: P.: Michael C. O'Shea: N: Written to the *Irish National Review*, upon seeing Irish in their columns: May 1889.

Gidh an mágh do bhí bláthmhar romham sínte: T.: Laoiḍh Uí Ruairc: Tr.: Deoraidhe Ó Éirinn: May 1890.

Gidh so m'amharc déigheanach air Éirinn a choidhch': T.: Gidh so M'Amharc Déigheanach air Éirinn a Choidhch': May 1893.

Go deigheanach a's Phoebus faoi neoll, ag suidhe dhomh air mhór shleas-aibh Magh: T.: Toireadh air Bhás Sheághain Chláraigh: N.: In roman typeface: April 1888.

Guidhim slán go h-Íobhráthach go bh-fhillidh: T.: Guídhe Filidh do Dhómhnall Ó Chonnaill: P.: Thomas "Tomás Ruadh" O'Sullivan: September 1888.

Inntleacht na h-Éireann na Gréige, 'sna Róimhe: T.: Marbhna Chearb-halláin Air Bás a Mhná, Máire Ní Ghuidhir: July 1890.

Iobhráthach grana na n-dragún liath: N.: Composed by a poet who wished to test Tomás Ruadh O'Súilliobháin's ability at rhapsody; he insults Iveragh and is promptly answered. 4 lines: October 1893.

Iobhráthach na sár-fhear bh-fearamhail bh-fial: N.: Composed by Tomás Ruadh O'Súilliobháin in response to poet insulting Iver-agh, County Kerry. 4 lines: October 1893.

Is aoibhinn a bheith a m-Beinn Eadair: T.: Beann Edear: N: In roman typeface: April 1890.

Is brónach mis' air maidin 'nuair a dhúisíghim as mo néul: T.: Dán Beag air Fhailllighe Mhuintire na H-Éireann 'na Teangain Breágh agus 'na D-Tír: P.: Thomas D. Norris: July 1889.

Is iomadh buille searbh, trom: T.: Mo Phiopa Ghoirid Dhonn: P.: Pádraic (Patrick O'Byrne): June 1888.

Is í seo an teanga do labhair Brian Boróimhe: T.: An Teanga Ghaedhilge a g-Cath Chluana Taird: P.: Amhlaoibh Ua Súilleabháin: April 1890.

Is maighdean 's is baintreabhach do rinn Dia go h-óg díom: T.: An Bain-treabhach 's an Maighdean: July 1888.

Is mór an chreidhill 's an ghreidhim do cheus me: T.: Ar Bás Sheumais

Óig Mhic Coitir: P.: Uilliam (Ruadh) McCoitir / Death of Young James MacCotter: N.: With accompanying English translation: October, November, December 1893.

Is uaibhreach na bh-fuaim tá ár n-adharca mór ghlóradh: T.: Ua Dómhnaill A Bú: Tr.: Michael C. O'Shea: October 1887.

Lá breágh dar éirgheas air maidin: T.: Cúirt Báile Nuadh: N.: Author unknown; ruins of Baile Nuadh still seen south of Belmullet in County Mayo: July 1890.

Maidean mhoch dár ghabhas amach: T.: Faine Geal an Lae: March–April 1894.

Mo chomhairle dhuit a mhic: T.: Comhairle an Bár-Sgollóig: N.: From Maurice Dinneen's Manuscript Miscellany: July 1889.

Mo léun 's mo chrádh gan mé 's mo ghrádh: T.: Máire Maguidhir: P.: Cearbhallán: N.: In roman typeface: March–April 1894.

Mo shlán leat-sa, Éire, mo thír dúchais féin: T.: Cileabradh na N-Imtheachduightheadh N-Gaodhlach / The Irish Immigrants Farewell: June 1888.

Mo shlán lem' dhuthaidh Éire gidh gur fadau aithi a táim: T.: Slán Uí Suilleabháin le Éire: P.: Amhlaoibh O'Suilleabháin: January 1890.

Ná cogaraidh amháin ainm, acht codladh sé faoi sgáth: T.: Ó Na Cogaraidh Amháin Ainim: Tr. Archbishop McHale of Tuam: August 1888.

Ná deun cumann le fear gallda: N.: 4 lines: May 1890.

Ní d'athantaibh na h-Eagailse an fial má's lag: P.: Owen Ruadh O'Sullivan: N.: 4 lines: June 1888.

Ní'l súgaidheacht ná dúil grínn: T.: Lúibín na m-Búclaighe: P.: Uilliam Inglis: N.: From The Munster Poets 2nd Series: March 1888.

Níor chanadh a n-dréachtaibh nuail: P.: Uilliam O'Lionain: January 1890.

Nois bíodh na daoine óga: P.: An Craoibhhín Aoibhinn: January 1888.

O' Bárdaigh Uí Chaoimh is cóir moidheamh air do thréithe: P.: Michael C. O'Shea: N.: Composed for T.R. Howard of Malden, MA, in praise of the O'Keefe's from whom he is descended: July 1893.

Och! Le grádh dhuit níl radharc a'm cheann: T.: Eibhlín a Rúin: September 1890.

"Och ná bodharaigh mé le Gaedhilig!" deir an sclábhuidhe in mo thír: P.: Pádraic (Patrick O'Byrne): July 1888.

Ó! Creid mé dá d-tréigfach sgéimh álain do gnaoí: Tr.: Michael C. O'Shea: September 1889.

O creid mé dá n-eugfadh snas áluinn do ghné: P.: Thomas Moore: Tr.: Pádraic (Patrick O'Byrne): May 1888.

O dhá m-beidheadh a fhios aig d'athair, a Sheághain: T.: Bláth na g-Craobh: N.: Written from the dictation of Grace Ward, a native of Glenties, County Donegal by J.J. Lyons: September 1890.

Oidhe an chuigir, nár chuthail ann digidhe, fann: T.: Oidhe an Chuigir / Fate of the Five [Brothers]: P.: Seághan O'Murchughadh: N.: Taken from MS. Transcribed in 1834 by Denis McCarthy of County Cork. With translation and glossary: June 1893.

Oidhche dhamh go doilg dúbach: T.: Machtnadh an Duine Doilghiosaigh: P.: Seághan Ua Coileáin: N.: Followed by an English translation "The Mourner's Soliloquy in the Ruined Abbey of Timoleague" by Thomas Furlong: April 1890.

Ó pháirc go páirc budh bhreágh mo siúbhal: T.: An Gleann 'nn ár Togadh Mé: P.: An Craoibhín Aoibhinn: May 1890.

O! Tá'n lá ag teacht le cabhair luchd léighin: T.: O! Tá'n Lá ag Teacht: N.: In roman typeface: September 1890.

Séan, a Chriosd, mo labhairt: T.: Invocation from the Féilire Aengusa: N.: Translated into Modern Irish by Thomas O'Neill Russell: N.: R.I.A. fol. 28 a.b.: September 1890.

Sén a Christ, mo labra: T.: Invocation from the Féilire Aengusa: N.: Transcribed by Thomas O'Neill Russell from R.I.A. fol. 28 a.b. With English translation by Whitley Stokes: September 1890.

'Sé Seághan Bán MacGearailt gan dobhat do chuir ceann air: T.: Seághan Bán MacGearailt agus a Bhean: P.: Seán Bán MacGearailt: N.: From T.R. Howard's Manuscript Miscellany. In roman typeface: June 1889.

Shiúbhailfinn féin a g-cómhnuidhe leat, a Eibhlín a ruin!: T.: Eibhlín a Rúin!: N.: In roman typeface: February, September 1890.

Síansach suairc do sgéil: T.: Daniel McCabe's reply to the welcome by Patrick Stanton: P.: Daniel McCabe: April 1888.

'Sí bláth geal ná smear í: T.: Mo Mhúirnín! Tr.: Charlotte Brooke. February 1890.

'Sí cuairt an laoigh ag dul thríd an athbhuaile: T.: Cúairt an Laoigh: April 1893.

'Sí taithneamh mo chroidhe a's croidhe mo chléibh í: T.: Fíor Theanga Éireann Ó: P.: Seághan Ua Dálaigh: May 1893.

Tá cailín deas dam chrádh: T.: Peurla an Bhrollaigh Bháin: N.: In roman typeface; from Petrie's Ancient Music of Ireland: May 1893.

Tá cú air mo chroidh d-taobh a luíghd do fhliucht banaba atá: P.: Michael C. O'Shea: October 1887.

Tá Cúm a Chisde brúidhte brisde: P.: Tomás Ruadh: N.: 4 lines: August 1888.

Táim díbeartha tar sáile: T.: Dóthchus an Díbirthigh: P.: Michael C. O'Shea: October 1893.

Tá'n ghealach ag scapadh a glóire: T.: Cuireadh: P.: Pádraic (Patrick O'Byrne): N.: From the Dublin *Gaelic Journal* No. 40. In roman typeface: February 1894.

Tá sé eugtha 's is mór an truagh: T.: Air Bás Seághain Baoighill Uí Reaghalla: P.: Muiris O'Duinnín: September 1890.

Tá sí sgéitheadh, tá sí sgéitheadh mar na duillibh air an g-crann: T.: Eiséirghe na Gaedhilge: Tr.: Pádraic (Patrick O'Byrne): October 1888.

Tá teampoll annsa Sgeilig mhór: T.: A Curt Reply: N.: Composed by a Kerry bard while travelling abroad. He met his brother who pretended ignorance of his homeland. This angered the poet, who extemporaneously composed this poem using specific localities in Kerry: April 1890.

Tá tréimhse saoghail agam-sa caithte, agus mór agus fada siúmhalta: T.: An Chúilion Dheas Ó Éirinn: P.: Michael C. O'Shea: N.: With accompanying English translation "The Maid of Erin" by the author: August 1888.

Tig, ar duigh suas me a leinbh, tóg me suas beagán níos mó: T.: Dán Beag air Shean Bhean Bhreoite, air Fhéil Lae Phádraic, anns na Stáidibh Aonuighthe: P.: Thomas D. Norris: January 1890.

Timcheall ceud bliadhan tar éis breith mhic Dé: T.: Sgeul na Boramha: Tr.: Thomas O'Neill Russell: July 1888.

Tóg suas arís í, an chláirseach bhriste: T.: Tóg Suas an Chláirseach: P.: Pádraic (Patrick O'Byrne): March 1888.

Tráth agus me air mearaighe: T.: Air an Smaichtín Crón: P.: Seághan Ua Coilleáin: July 1893.

Tráthnóinín déanach is me géin cois na taoide: T.: Síghle Ní Ghadhradh: P.: John Brennan: N.: Poet from Tralee, County Kerry. First stanza only: September 1888.

Trathnona saoire nuair do bhidheas-sa gan cnead: T.: Tionóisg an Fhile: P.: Pádraig Ó Cathasaigh, Malden, MA: March-April 1894.

Truagh liom a chompáin do chor: P.: Bonebhantura O'Heoghusa: N.: For Maolmuire Mac Graith: February, March–April 1894.

Uch is truagh! ó'n uch is truagh! Dá maireann ar lorg na sluagh: T.: Uch is Truagh!: P.: Donnchadh Mór O'Dálaigh: N.: From MS. Compiled by William Sheehan in 1753: February 1894.

NOTES

Research for this article was enhanced by a Short-Term Research fellowship at the New York Public Library, July 2018.

1 Nilsen, "Irish Gaelic Literature," 202. The reel containing the 1860 run of the *Irish-American* in the New York Public Library was catalogued separately from the series of microfilm reels 1849–1915. All copies and digitized editions have a gap between 1859 and 1861.
2 Nilsen, "Irish Gaelic Literature," 213; Knight, "Gaels on the Pacific."
3 O'Daly et al., "Prospectus," 1.
4 For various treatments of the *Irish Echo*, see Ford, "Some Records"; Mac Aonghusa, "An Ghaeilge i Meiriceá"; Mahon, "Ar Thóir na Gaeilge"; Ní Bhroiméil, *Building Irish Identity*, esp. 45–6; Ní Uigín, "Iriseoireacht Ghaeilge"; Nilsen, "Irish Gaelic Literature"; Ó Diollúin, "Micheál Callanánach Ó Séaghdha"; Ó Dochartaigh, "Notaí"; Ryan, "Philo-Celtic Society"; Uí Chollatáin, "Athbheochan"; Uí Fhlannagáin, *Mícheál Ó Lócháin*, esp. 51, 74, 88, 90; and Uí Fhlannagáin, *Fíníní Mheiriceá*, esp. 56, 85, 95, 212–13.
5 O'Daly et al., "Prospectus," 1.
6 *Irish World*, 25 May 1872, 5; 8 March 1873, 7.
7 *Irish World*, 8 February 1873, 7.
8 *Irish World*, 26 October 1872, 5.
9 *Irish World*, 22 March 1873, 6.
10 *Irish World*, 10 May 1873, 6.
11 "Philo-Celtic Society and Irish School," 5.
12 *Pilot*, 12 July 1873, 4.
13 *Pilot*, 19 July 1873, 6.
14 *Pilot*, 12 July 1873, 4; *Boston Daily Advertiser*, 6 November 1882, 1.
15 *Irish World*, 26 December 1874, 6.
16 *Pilot*, 19 December 1874, 6.
17 *Irish World*, 1 February 1873, 7. See Mahon, "Ar Thóir na Gaeilge," for a fuller treatment of the manuscripts acquired by the Boston Philo-Celtic Society.
18 *Pilot*, 24 January 1880, 3. Gaelic Societies were also established in New York (Brooklyn, the Bowery, Harlem), New Jersey, Saint Louis, Chicago, and San Francisco. The *Irish-American* of 28 April 1888 reported that there were even Gaelic classes in Galveston, Texas, and Louisville, Kentucky (1).
19 *Irish World*, 15 March 1879, 9.
20 *Irish World*, 1 March 1879, 6.
21 Sullivan and O'Daly, "Revival of the Irish Language," 174.
22 *Irish World*, 22 January 1881, 7.
23 *Boston Daily Globe*, 10 February 1881, 4.

24 *Irish-American*, 22 January 1881, 2.
25 *Pilot*, 28 May 1881, 6.
26 Logan, Editorial (October 1881), 5.
27 *Pilot*, 22 November 1884, 3.
28 Logan, "Philo-Celts," 416.
29 O'Daly et al., "Prospectus," 1.
30 Logan, Editorial (January 1886), 512.
31 O'Daly, "Our Defence," 4.
32 "Philo-Celtic Society: Prizes," 4.
33 O'Daly, Editorial (June 1886), 4.
34 O'Shea, "Inaugural," 10.
35 O'Shea, "Irish Language," 1.
36 O'Shea, "Re-opening," 8. For a fuller treatment of O'Shea, see Ó Diollúin, "Micheál Callanánach Ó Séaghdha."
37 "No Irish Language," 4.
38 O'Daly, Editorial (November 1886), 4.
39 O'Daly, Editorial (January 1887), 4.
40 "The Echo and Its Future," 4.
41 "Vindicate," 1.
42 O'Shea, "Vindication," 8.
43 O'Daly, "Union," 4.
44 O'Daly, Editorial (September 1887), 4. O'Daly notes that he never heard from the *Irish-American*, the *Citizen* of Chicago, or *An Gaodhal* in regard to a union of Gaelic societies.
45 "Philo-Celtic Society," *Boston Daily Globe*, 6 May 1887, 2.
46 "Has the Boston Daily Globe," 1.
47 O'Daly, Editorial (May 1887), 4.
48 O'Daly, Editorial (July 1887), 4.
49 "Irish Language Department," 1; O'Daly, Editorial (October 1887), 4. The typographical errors consisted of incorrectly placed capital letters in side words, and the absence of marks of lenition, i.e. "mo mac."
50 O'Daly, Editorial (September 1887), 4. This statement was in reply to Father Keegan of Saint Louis, who wrote to the *Citizen* of Chicago suggesting that the *Irish Echo* use the roman typeface. The *Citizen* itself published Irish material in roman type.
51 O'Daly, Editorial (October 1887), 4.
52 Hyde, "Litir."
53 O'Daly, "News Boys," 4.
54 Hyde, "An Craoibhín Aoibhinn," 5.
55 Russell, "D' Fhear-Eagair," 8: "Níl acht aon nidh fíor-thábhachdach agam le

rádh leat, agus so é: go n-deunfaidh tú do dhithchioll deagh-Ghaedhilig d'fhoillsiughadh 'san Mac-Alla, agus truaillighthe cúigeacha do sheachnadh. 'Sí mo chómhairle duit… Do chara cho fhad a's deunair do dhithchioll deagh-Ghaedhilig do chlóbhualadh." (I have only one very important thing to say to you, and it is this: Have the good sense to publish proper Irish in the Echo, and avoid provincial corruptions. That is my advice to you … Your friend as long as you do your best to publish good Irish.) At this time Russell had strained relationships with Michael Logan and *An Gaodhal*, as well as readers of the *Irish-American*.

56 O'Shea, "Dileagra," 5. The Irish is as printed; the translation is by O'Shea.

57 "Irish Proverbs," 4.

58 O'Farrell, "Irish Music," 6; Keegan, "Irish Music," 8.

59 O'Daly, Editorial (August 1888), 4.

60 O'Daly, Editorial (September 1888), 4.

61 Tierney, Letter to the Editor, 7.

62 "The Echo and Its Future," 4.

63 O'Daly, Editorial (March 1889), 8. While Ayer and Son's *American Newspaper Annual* for 1888 and 1889 registered the *Irish Echo*, they offered no circulation numbers (1888: 213, 711, 964; 1889: 1001). In 1890, they list the circulation at 4,000 on pages 304, 944, but at 1,000 on page 1203; 4,000 seems more likely. The circulation of the well-established *An Gaodhal* was listed as 3,000 in 1888 and 2,880 in both 1889 and 1890 (1888: 330, 964; 1889: 801, 1001; 1890: 1008, 1203). The *Irish-American*, one of the flagship newspapers of the Irish in America, had circulation numbers of 25,000, 20,000, and 20,050 in those same years (1888: 353, 779; 1889: 366, 805; 1890: 507, 1012). Furthermore, Rowell's *American Newspaper Directory* gives the *Irish Echo* a circulation of "3000+" in 1891 (37, 323, 857, 992, 1016). 29,800 must be a reporting error.

64 O'Daly, Editorial (March 1889), 8.

65 O'Daly, Editorial (April 1889), 8.

66 Ibid., 5, 8.

67 O'Shea, Editorial (May 1889), 4.

68 O'Daly, Editorial (April 1889), 8.

69 O'Shea, "To the Patrons," 4.

70 O'Daly, "Ceap Craoibhe Gearalthach," transcribed from a 1655 manuscript of Dominick O'Daly; "Seághan Bán MacGearailt," 7.

71 Howard, "Address," 9.

72 Norris, "Pity," 4.

73 Ibid., 4.

74 Cromien, "Modern Protest-Ant," 8.

75 O'Shea, "Mr. J. Cromien," 4-5.
76 O'Shea, Editorial (November 1889), 6.
77 O'Shea, Editorial (January 1890), 1. For more on the Gaelic font controversy, see Ó Conchubhair, "Gaelic Font Controversy," 46–63.
78 "Eachtra Chonaill Golban," 5–8. For an excellent study of Thomas Griffin, his role in the Philo-Celtic Society of Lawrence, MA, his poetry, and his manuscript collection, see Mahon, *Thomas Griffin*.
79 On 4 June 1887 the *Irish-American* printed a letter in which Norris claimed he did not mean to get in a grammatical discussion with Russell, but merely "did it for the public good, and to show that all kinds of guttural gibberish cannot be grafted upon our beautiful language without our knowing it" (3).
80 O'Shea, Editorial (November 1889), 6.
81 Norris, "Capt. Norris," 2.
82 *Irish-American*, 22 December 1888, 3.
83 Logan, Editorial (May 1890), 951.
84 Norris, "Correspondence," 51; O'Shea, Editorial (May 1890), 57.
85 O'Shea, "Irish Echo Cigar," 24.
86 Ibid., 25.
87 *Irish-American*, 24 August 1889, 2.
88 Norris, "Oráid Sochraide," 26–9.
89 O'Shea, Editorial (April 1890), 41.
90 O'Shea, Editorial (May 1890), 57.
91 Logan, "Liar Again," 320–1.
92 O'Farrell, "Correspondence," 67.
93 "Craobh Óir," 77.
94 Logan, Editorial (April 1891), 85.
95 Logan, Editorial (September 1892), 211. Logan often referred to the Irish in America as "Éire Mhór" (Big Ireland), representing their own Irish nation in the United States.
96 Logan, "Irish Echo," 302.
97 Ford, "Some Records," no. 3: 2; Logan, "Irish Echo," 302. See also *Gaelic Journal*, January 1891, 3, in which the method is described as "an imitation of the process followed by nature in teaching a child its mother tongue." Griffin's book was never published.
98 *Gaelic Journal*, January 1891, 6, 7, 12, 15. The scores are for "Ye banks and Braes O' Bonny Doon," arr. Louis Schehlmann (English) and "An Cúilfhinn / The Coulin," (Irish) with words by Archbishop MacHale. Of further interest is a previously unpublished poem by Aindriú Ua Munaoile of Cnoc an Logha, Co. Mayo, on the loss of his cows to the winter snow. I would like to

thank Jay Moschella, Curator of Rare Books at the Boston Public Library, for providing me with a scan of this exceedingly rare volume.

99 O'Farrell, Editorial, 60.

100 "A Few Words," 2.

101 Windisch, "Ancient Irish," 4–16.

102 "Bruighean Chéise Chorrain," 18–27. This was printed from a manuscript text copied by Seághan Ó Múláin of Cork in 1790.

103 O'Farrell, Editorial, 60. The manuscript in question was transcribed in 1731 and belonged to John O'Neill of Tipperary. It was brought to Boston by his daughter, a member of the Boston Philo-Celtic Society.

104 Russell, "Are We Anglo-Saxons," 155–8; Russell, "Ancient Irish Literary Remains," 178–85.

105 O'Farrell, "To Our Readers," 194.

106 *Irish World*, 28 December 1872, 4.

107 Logan, "To Our Readers," 114.

108 O'Daly et al., "Prospectus," 1.

BIBLIOGRAPHY

American Newspaper Annual. Philadelphia: N.W. Ayer and Son, 1888.

American Newspaper Annual. Philadelphia: N.W. Ayer and Son, 1889.

American Newspaper Annual. Philadelphia: N.W. Ayer and Son, 1890.

De Hae, Risteárd. *Clár Litridheacht na Nua-Ghaedhilge 1850–1936*, vols. 2–3. Baile Átha Cliath: Oifig Dhíolta Foillseacháin Rialtas, 1939.

Ford, James J. "Some Records of the Irish Language in the Greater Boston Area." *Bulletin, Éire Society of Boston* 32, no. 2 (November 1973): 1–4; 32, no. 3 (December 1973): 1–4.

Knight, Matthew. "Gaels on the Pacific: The Irish Language Department in the San Francisco *Monitor*, 1888–91." *Éire-Ireland* 54, nos. 3–4 (2019): 172–99.

Logan, Michael. Editorial. *An Gaodhal* 1, no. 1 (October 1881): 5.

– Editorial. *An Gaodhal* 5, no. 1 (January 1886): 512.

– Editorial. *An Gaodhal* 7, no. 10 (May 1890): 951.

– Editorial. *An Gaodhal* 8, no. 7 (April 1891): 85.

– Editorial. *An Gaodhal* 9, no. 6 (September 1892): 211.

– "Irish Echo – Gaelic Journal." *An Gaodhal* 10, no. 2 (August 1893): 302.

– "The Liar Again." *An Gaodhal* 10, no. 3 (September 1893): 320–1.

– "Philo-Celts." *An Gaodhal* 4, no. 1 (November 1884): 416.

– "To Our Readers." *An Gaodhal* 1, no. 11 (August 1882): 114.
Mac Aonghusa, Proinsias. "An Ghaeilge i Meiriceá." In *Go Meiriceá Siar: Na Gaeil agus Meiriceá: Cnuasach Aistí*, ed. Stiofán Ó hAnnracháin, 13–30. Baile Átha Cliath: An Clóchomhar, 1979.
Mahon, William J. "Ar Thóir na Gaeilge: Tionscadal Lámhscríbhinní na Philo-Celtic Society (Bostún) 1873–1893." In *Litríocht na Gaeilge ar fud an Domhain*, ed. Ríona Nic Congáil, Máirín Nic Eoin, Meidhbhín Ní Úrdail, Pádraig Ó Liatháin, and Regina Uí Chollatáin, 155–90. Baile Átha Cliath: Leabhair Comhar, 2015.
– *Thomas Griffin (1829–96) of Corca Dhuibhne and the Irish Community of Lawrence, Massachusetts.* Aberystwyth: Department of Welsh, Aberystwyth University, 2007.
Ní Bhroiméil, Úna. *Building Irish Identity in America, 1870–1915*. Dublin: Four Courts Press, 2003.
Ní Uigín, Dorothy. "An Iriseoireacht Ghaeilge i Meiriceá agus in Éirinn ag Tús na hAthbheochana: an Cúlra Meiriceánach." In *Iriseoireacht na Gaeilge*, ed. Ruairí Ó hUiginn, 25–47. Léachtaí Cholm Cille 28. Maigh Nuad: An Sagart, 1998.
Nilsen, Kenneth. "Irish Gaelic Literature in the United States." In *American Babel: Literatures of the United States from Abnaki to Zuni*, ed. Marc Shell, 177–218. Cambridge, MA: Harvard University Press, 2002.
Ó Conchubhair, Brian. "The Gaelic Font Controversy." *Irish University Review* 33, no. 1, Special Issue: New Perspectives on the Irish Literary Revival (2003): 46–63.
Ó Diollúin, Séamus. "Micheál Callanánach Ó Séaghdha (1812–1901)." In *Litríocht na Gaeilge ar fud an Domhain*, ed. Ríona Nic Congáil, Máirín Nic Eoin, Meidhbhín Ní Úrdail, Pádraig Ó Liatháin, and Regina Uí Chollatáin, 215–32. Baile Átha Cliath: Leabhair Comhar, 2015.
Ó Dochartaigh, Liam. "Notaí ar Ghluaiseacht na Gaeilge i Meiriceá, 1872-1891." In *Go Meiriceá Siar: Na Gaeil agus Meiriceá: Cnuasach Aistí*, ed. Stiofán Ó hAnnracháin, 65–90. Baile Átha Cliath: An Clóchomhar, 1979.
Rowell, George P. *American Newspaper Directory*. New York: Geo P. Rowell and Company, 1891.
Ryan, George E. "The Philo-Celtic Society of Boston." *Bulletin, Éire Society of Boston* 31, no. 3 (December 1972): 1–4.
Sullivan, J.H., and P.J. O'Daly. "Revival of the Irish Language." *Celtic Monthly* 2, no. 2 (September 1879): 174.
Uí Chollatáin, Regina. "Athbheochan Thransatlantach na Gaeilge: Scríbhneoirí, Intleachtóirí, agus an Fhéiniúlacht Éireannach." In *Litríocht na*

Gaeilge ar fud an Domhain, ed. Ríona Nic Congáil, Máirín Nic Eoin, Meidhbhín Ní Úrdail, Pádraig Ó Liatháin, and Regina Uí Chollatáin, 277–309. Baile Átha Cliath: Leabhair Comhar, 2015.
Uí Fhlannagáin, Fionnuala. *Fíníní Mheiriceá agus an Ghaeilge.* Baile Átha Cliath: Coiscéim, 2008.
– *Mícheál Ó Lócháin agus An Gaodhal.* Baile Átha Cliath: An Clóchomhar, 1990.

Irish Echo

"Bruighean Chéise Chorrain." *Irish Echo* 4, no. 2 (May 1893): 18–27.
"Craobh Óir agus Craobh Airgid." *Irish Echo* 3, no. 6 (September 1890): 77.
Cromien, Joseph. "A Modern Protest-Ant." *Irish Echo* 2, no. 19 (August 1889): 8.
"Eachtra Chonaill Golban." *Irish Echo* 3, no.1 (January 1890): 5–9; 3, no. 3 (April 1890): 43–4; 3, no. 4 (May 1890): 55–6.
"The Echo and Its Future." *Irish Echo* 2, no. 13 (January 1889): 4.
"Emblems of Irish Nationality." *Irish Echo* 4, no. 8 (November 1893): 113–17; 4, no. 9 (December 1893): 130–4; 4, no. 10 (January 1894): 152–5; 4, no. 11 (February 1894): 162–3.
"A Few Words to Our Friends." *Irish Echo* 4, no. 1 (April 1893): 2.
"Has the Boston Daily Globe Intentionally Ridiculed the Philo-Celtic Society in the Celebration of Its Fourteenth Anniversary?" *Irish Echo* 1, no. 17 (May 1887): 1.
Howard, T.R. "Address to Patrick Kenneally." *Irish Echo* 2, no. 21 (November 1889): 9.
Hyde, Douglas (an Craoibhín Aoibhinn). "An Craoibhín Aoibhinn ro Chan / Craoibhín Aoibhinn Sang," trans. Michael Cavanagh. *Irish Echo* 2, no. 1 (January 1888): 5.
– "Litir o'n g-Craoibhín Aoibhinn d'Fhear-Curtha-Amach an Mhacalla Eireannaigh." *Irish Echo* 1, no. 23 (December 1887): 1, 5; 2, no. 1 (January 1888): 5.
"Irish Language Department." *Irish Echo* 1, no. 21 (September 1887): 1.
"Irish Proverbs." *Irish Echo* 2, no. 7 (July 1888): 4.
Keegan, James. "Irish Music." *Irish Echo* 2, no. 9 (September 1888): 8.
"No Irish Language, No Irish Nation." *Irish Echo* 1, no. 9 (September 1886): 4.
Norris, Thomas D. "Capt. Norris, Points Out Many Errors to Mr. Russell." *Irish Echo* 3, no. 1 (January 1890): 2.
– "Correspondence." *Irish Echo* 3, no. 4 (May 1890): 51.
– "Oráid Sochraide, air Bás an Tíor-Ghrádhuighttheóra, Sár-Laochamhla .i.

Seághan Ó'Mathghamhna leis an Saoi Onóireach, Matha Thaíris." *Irish Echo* 3, no. 2 (February 1890): 26–9.
– "Pity We Have Not More Like It." *Irish Echo* 2, no. 18 (July 1889): 4.
O'Daly, P.J., ed. "Ceap Craoibhe Gearalthach." *Irish Echo* 2, no. 17 (June 1889): 7; 2, no. 19 (August 1889): 12; 2, no. 20 (September 1889): 6–7.
– Editorial. *Irish Echo* 1, no. 6 (June 1886): 4.
– Editorial. *Irish Echo* 1, no. 11 (November 1886): 4.
– Editorial. *Irish Echo* 1, no. 13 (January 1887): 4.
– Editorial. *Irish Echo* 1, no. 17 (May 1887): 4.
– Editorial. *Irish Echo* 1, no. 19 (July 1887): 4.
– Editorial. *Irish Echo* 1, no. 21 (September 1887): 4.
– Editorial. *Irish Echo* 1, no. 22 (October 1887): 4.
– Editorial. *Irish Echo* 2, no. 8 (August 1888): 4.
– Editorial. *Irish Echo* 2, no. 9 (September 1888): 4.
– Editorial. *Irish Echo* 2, no. 14 (March 1889): 8.
– Editorial. *Irish Echo* 2, no. 15 (April 1889): 8.
– "News Boys, Attention!" *Irish Echo* 2, no. 1 (January 1888): 4.
– "Our Defence." *Irish Echo* 1, no. 3 (March 1886): 4.
– "Union Is Strength." *Irish Echo* 1, no. 16 (April 1887): 4.
O'Daly, P.J., M.T. Gallivan, John O'Neill, Timothy Sullivan, and Wm. M. Murphy. "Prospectus." *Irish Echo* 1, no. 1 (January 1886): 1.
O'Farrell, Charles. "Correspondence." *Irish Echo* 3, no. 5 (July 1890): 67.
– Editorial. *Irish Echo* 4, no. 4 (July 1893): 60.
– "Irish Music." *Irish Echo* 2, no. 8 (August 1888): 6.
– "To Our Readers." *Irish Echo* 4, no. 12 (March–April 1894): 194.
O'Shea, Michael C. "Comhairle Do Ghaodhalaibh." Irish Echo 4, no. 6 (September 1893): 82–4.
– "Dileagra / Address of the President." *Irish Echo* 2, no. 6 (June 1888): 5.
– Editorial. *Irish Echo* 2, no. 16 (May 1889): 4.
– Editorial. *Irish Echo* 2, no. 21 (November 1889): 6.
– Editorial. *Irish Echo* 3, no. 1 (January 1890): 1.
– Editorial. *Irish Echo* 3, no. 3 (April 1890): 41.
– Editorial. *Irish Echo* 3, no. 4 (May 1890): 57.
– "Inaugural of Michael C. O'Shea." *Irish Echo* 1, no. 7 (July 1886): 10.
– "Irish Echo Cigar." *Irish Echo* 3, no. 2 (February 1890): 24.
– "The Irish Language." *Irish Echo* 1, no. 7 (July 1886): 1.
– "Mr. J. Cromien's Double Protest." *Irish Echo* 2, no. 20 (September 1889): 4–5.
– "Re-opening of the Irish School in Boston Last Month." *Irish Echo* 1, no. 10 (October 1886): 8.

– "Timniughadh Do'n Chraoibhín Aoibhinn." *Irish Echo* 4, no. 6 (September 1893): 85.
– "To the Patrons and Readers of the Irish Echo." *Irish Echo* 2, no. 17 (June 1889): 4.
– "Vindication of the Irish Race." *Irish Echo* 1, no. 15 (March 1887): 8.
"The Philo-Celtic Society and Irish School." *Irish Echo* 1, no. 1 (January 1886): 5.
"The Philo-Celtic Society: Prizes for Its Members." *Irish Echo* 1, no. 3 (March 1886): 4.
Russell, Thomas O'Neill. "Ancient Irish Literary Remains." *Irish Echo* 4, no. 12 (March-April 1894): 178–85.
– "Are We Anglo-Saxons or Celto-Saxons?" *Irish Echo* 4, no. 10 (January 1894): 155–8.
– "D' Fhear-Eagair an Mhac-Alla." *Irish Echo* 2, no. 1 (January 1888): 8.
"Seághan Bán MacGearailt agus a Bhean." *Irish Echo* 2, no. 17 (June 1889): 7.
Tierney, John M. Letter to the Editor. *Irish Echo* 2, no. 11 (November 1888): 7.
"Vindicate the Irish Race." *Irish Echo* 1, no. 15 (March 1887): 1.
Windisch, Ernst. "Ancient Irish Legendary Literature and Ossianic Poetry," trans. Thomas O'Neill Russell. *Irish Echo* 4, no. 1 (April 1893): 4–16.

7

Early Use of Phonograph Recordings for Instruction in the Irish Language

William Mahon

Not least among Ken Nilsen's contributions to Celtic studies was his assiduous compilation of an audio and video archive of the living languages. Some of this was done in Ireland, Wales, and Brittany, but the greater part was carried out in North America, where he recorded Irish speakers in Massachusetts and Maine, Scottish Gaelic speakers in Nova Scotia, and Breton restaurant staff in New York City. After moving to Nova Scotia in 1984, his project increasingly became focused on collecting the last remnants of Gaelic speech in Antigonish County, Nova Scotia, not merely because this was the locality in which he had settled, but also because of his sense of the task's urgency. In line with the importance that Ken attached to such records, this chapter is concerned with the use made of recording technology in an earlier era: more specifically, the production of records (on wax cylinders) to assist Irish learners in America in the years 1909 and 1910. The three phonographic correspondence courses discussed below were first advertised between October 1909 and February 1910.[1]

THE FIRST YEARS OF PHONOGRAPHIC INSTRUCTION

Thomas Alva Edison first produced and exhibited his working phonograph in 1877. The following year, in an article in the *North American Review* titled "The Phonograph and Its Future," he discussed the value of the phonograph for "educational purposes" and recommended that it be used to provide recordings of "difficult passages" so that children could memorize school lessons "more correctly." He also advocated it as a means to preserve the voices "of our Washingtons, our Lincolns, our Gladstones," as well as "*the last words* of the dying members of the family."[2] Although he says nothing in this article about the value of the phonograph for the preservation of languages *per se*, he was aware of the possibility, having previously met with an executive member of the American Philological Society who wished to record some Iroquois languages in western New York and Ontario.[3] Edison was delighted with the prospect and boasted in an 1878 interview that "the president of the Philological Society means to travel with it among all the North American tribes."[4]

Edison's early model had proved its worth as a stenographic aid – it was even used in Congress[5] – but recordings using tinfoil as a medium could not be played more than ten times and were mutilated on being removed from the device. The situation changed, however, with the development of wax-medium technology by Chichester Bell and Charles Tainter in 1884–86.[6] After March 1887, the production and marketing of their revolutionary model proceeded apace under the management of the American Graphophone Company. Not to be surpassed, the Edison Phonograph Company produced its own wax cylinder model, the Perfected Phonograph, early in the following year.[7]

With the replacement of tinfoil by wax, the life of a record was substantially increased from about ten replays to forty; and with later wax formulas longevity was improved yet again, although nowhere near to the "thousands of times with undiminished clearness" that Edison outrageously claimed for it.[8]

Edison's improved model had other features that were designed in particular for stenographers: an attachment that could "pare" off a layer of recorded wax in preparation for a new recording; a key "for suspending the reproduction [i.e., the playing] of sounds"; a key that could vary the speed of playback; and a reversing key that could "run the reproducer [i.e., the playing component] back to earlier points on the cylinder." The Edison Phonograph Company also announced that it could make duplicates of cylinders "at slight cost."[9] In many ways, the phonograph was a precursor to the tape or digital recorders of recent times. With these improvements, the potential of the phonograph for language learning was increasingly recognized.

The earliest attested use of the phonograph for that purpose took place at the College of Milwaukee in 1889, where a professor found recordings useful for improving his students' pronunciation of French. A headline in the New York *Evening World* hailed this as a "Novel and Effective Use for the Jersey Wizard's Great Invention."[10] Impressed by this success and publicity, the president of the college decided to purchase more machines.

In February 1891 it was announced that Dr Richard S. Rosenthal, the founder of a highly regarded language school in New York City, had moved to Washington, DC, in order to collaborate with the Columbia Phonograph Company in producing phonograph recordings for his "Meisterschaft" correspondence courses in German, French, Spanish, and Italian.[11] The packages he sold included a phonograph, twenty-four recorded cylinders and the accompanying booklets, "sample cylinders" for students to record on, and a "specimen book" for their written exercises. The phonograph was fixed with an attachment so that words and short phrases could be repeated easily, as well as a ten-way "hearing tube" so that several students could use the "system" simultaneously.[12]

In the mid-1890s, Rosenthal's hegemony in the realm of phonograph teaching was challenged by Rafael Díez de la Cortina, a prominent language teacher who had developed his own variant of the natural method.[13] There is some evidence that he had followed his rival's lead in experimenting with the phonograph as early as 1892.[14] It was not until 1896, however, that he too started selling machines and phonograph media for language instruction.[15]

FURTHER TECHNICAL DEVELOPMENTS

The late 1890s and early 1900s saw another wave of technological developments that made the phonograph much more feasible for language learning. These included a spring motor (in place of wet batteries), harder waxes (which extended the playing life of recordings), and technologies for the mass production of duplicate recordings.[16] In 1902, Edison's National Phonograph Company began to record at high speed (160 rpm) and to use a sophisticated electroplating process for the production of permanent gold-over-silver masters.[17] From each of these, hundreds of "moulded" copies could be turned out with no loss of sound quality. Also produced was a new playing component with a sapphire stylus and variable speed settings (from 70 to 170 rpm). The fidelity was improved to the point that, according to the *Phonogram*, "the Edison Phonograph of 1902 is no more like the Edison phonograph of 1899 or 1900, than a church organ resembles a mouth organ, or a harp resembles a jews-harp."[18]

INTERNATIONAL CORRESPONDENCE SCHOOLS OF SCRANTON

The practical advantages of these improvements for phonographic language learning were recognized, and the Columbia Phonograph Company took advantage of this by recording and supplying records for a new series of language correspondence courses set up by the International Correspondence Schools of Scranton, Pennsylvania.[19] Between May and September of 1902 the *Phonogram* published a series of lengthy articles advertising the ICS's courses and filled with endorsements from teachers and college professors across the country.[20] The standard ICS language "system" consisted of thirty conversational lessons, a complete grammar, a reader, and a lexicon. The elements that were to be used with the recordings included phrases and sentences, remarks, drills, review and conversation, and phonographic exercises.[21] The ICS's courses were rigorous, and it conducted an extensive language school to handle its correspondence component.

THE CORTINA IRISH RECORDINGS (NEW YORK, OCTOBER 1909)

In an advertisement published in the *New York Times* in October 1908 the Cortina Company offered free trials of its "Original Phonographic System," the "complete outfit," which included the machine itself (the Cortinaphone), a textbook, and a set of recordings. More interestingly, it advertised "special records made to order in any language."[22] This offer was taken up, it would appear, by one of the Irish-language groups in New York, and recordings were made. The introduction of phonograph records for learning Irish was noted with great enthusiasm in an article in the *Gaelic American* dated 3 July 1909:

> **Irish by Phonograph: A Great Advance in Facilities for Acquiring Native Speech – Phonographic Records of Lessons in Gaelic.** A few days ago the R.D. Cortina Company, 44 West Thirty-fourth street, made phonographic records of twenty-four Irish lessons. The lessons are from O'Growney's text books. This is the first

> time that lessons in Irish have been prepared for the phonograph, although the Cortina Company has had records for nearly every modern language, as well as for some of the dead languages. Much care has been taken with the Irish records. A native Irish speaker talked into the recording apparatus. This speaker has no taint of provincialism in his speech, and besides he has a very extensive literary knowledge of Irish, Old, Middle and Modern. In listening to the phonograph the student may rest assured that he is listening to the reproduction of the voice of an educated and accurate Irish speaker.[23]

No clue is given as to the identity of the "accurate Irish speaker" whose voice was recorded by Cortina, but the reference to his erudition points to a real need for effective teachers.[24] (There is some irony, it seems, in the advertisement's further claim that the Cortina Company had "made it possible for the student to study Irish without the aid of a native Irish-speaking teacher."[25])

Cortina provided "easy terms" of payment for groups of learners, an arrangement that would have been attractive to the Irish-language societies: "[D]on't overlook the fact that the records and text books can be used by any number of persons, so that if you have a friend who wishes to learn the language you are studying, you may permit him to use them at certain hours or on certain days and share the expense with him; and thus your monthly payments will be divided in half."[26]

The degree to which the exercises in O'Growney's *Simple Lessons* were consistent with the Cortina Method is questionable, and it is not clear if it was truly a correspondence course sponsored by the company. Cortina may have hired the services of a local Irish scholar, but there are no newspaper advertisements to substantiate this. It may be the case that one of the societies simply had the recordings made and then sold them on to their pupils.

THE COLLEGE OF IRISH GAELIC COURSE (SCRANTON, NOVEMBER 1909)

In November 1909 news of a second phonograph course for Irish appeared in the Gaelic Department of the New York *Irish-American*: "The College of Irish Gaelic ... a phonograph-correspondence school that has arisen in Scranton, Ps., the home of correspondence schools."[27]

Its declared aim was to teach Irish "without a grammar and without hard study," phonograph-aided instruction being "the only rational system of learning any language."[28] This article was almost certainly supplied by the designer of the course, John H. Jordan (1866–1934), a part-time real estate agent, tool salesman, and newspaper editor whose parents had settled with a number of famine emigrants in nearby Archbald Blakely Township.[29] In the previous September he had registered four copyrights on behalf of the College of Irish Gaelic: one for a *Complete Course in the Irish Language, in Thirty Lessons without the Use of Technical Grammar*; and three more for booklets containing *Lessons One and Two*, *Lessons Three and Four*, and *Lessons Five and Six* respectively.[30] The first of these copyrighted items was actually an introduction to the course, which Jordan described in the *Irish-American* article as a "valuable treatise on the Irish language and literature, a rich mine of information to be found nowhere else in one book."[31]

Jordan would have heard a lot of Irish as a child, if not from his parents then certainly from settlers from Mayo, Sligo, and Donegal, who made up a substantial portion of the Irish population in and around the mining town of Scranton. His active interest in the language appears to have begun in November 1904, when he joined others in establishing a Gaelic Club in the city.[32] Reporting on this event, the *Scranton Truth* described Jordan as "the brilliant editor of the Sunday Record" and "one of the most accomplished linguists in Scranton." Jordan, as it happens, was already well-versed in Irish literature – albeit in translation – and the paper added that "he will not enter the Gaelic class as a beginner."[33]

Some of this enthusiasm probably came from the anticipation of Douglas Hyde's visit to the United States, which was scheduled for the following year. When Hyde visited Scranton in April 1906 and delivered his speech in the Lyceum Hall, Jordan was among those given a seat of honour on the stage.[34] The Scranton Gaelic Club had been granted permission by the Xavarian Brothers of the College of St Thomas to use classrooms in their main building, College Hall, and this most likely explains Jordan's choice of "College of Irish Gaelic" as the name of the course he was to produce in 1909. The lessons for the course were probably composed in collaboration with the Gaelic Club's teacher, John E. O'Malley, who by then had become interested in the "new methods of linguistry," which did not emphasize the study of grammar.[35]

The *Irish-American* article proceeded to describe the rationale, structure, and layout of the course, which was really a version of the direct method employed by Rosenthal and Cortina:

> The meat of the method lies in the conversation exercises. These are arranged in the form of dialogues, with the Irish sentences on the left hand and their English equivalents on the right hand pages. Each conversation is one connected whole, made up of sentences every one of which [is] a practical, every-day expression. And yet there is nothing in it that goes beyond the language principle taught in the lesson, nothing is anticipated or presented before its time ... This is the way a child learns its mother tongue, or a foreigner learns a new language. He learns entire new phrases, not isolated words. As the phrases are grammatically put together the learner gets his grammar with the phrases ready-made, without recognizing it as grammar. This is the way anybody learns any language, if he would but stop to think the matter over.[36]

Jordan's concern with the ordinary man's fear of grammar is quite tenable, but his expression of this may also provide a glimpse of class mentalities in regard to education:

> Under the new method one does not even need to know what grammar is. He does not even have to know how to read. If he be in a class and the phonograph is set going all that is required is that someone tell him what the sentence pronounced by the phonograph means. This throws the doors of the Irish open to millions, to everybody without exception – doors that up till now have been closed to all but college graduates only.[37]

The only catalogued copy of the printed course material is held in the National Library of Ireland.[38] It is a single printed volume of sixty-eight pages containing Jordan's "Treatise" (pp. 3–46), followed by a new title page and Lesson One (on the present tense of the substantive verb) and Lesson Two (on the past tense). The front cover bears the title of the course as registered in the copyright, a photograph of four men and a woman seated around a phonograph, and the following subtitle: "The Full Phrase Method with the Phonograph, College of Irish Gaelic, Scranton, Pa., 1909." There are no audio recordings for this course listed in the National Library's electronic catalogue.

Jordan's introduction to the *Complete Course* (his "treatise") is a highly pedantic and eclectic mix of history, linguistics, and revivalist ideology.[39] In a discussion of "national individuality" he asks: "Does she [Ireland] wish to attain her national Nirvana by absorption into the divine life of England?"[40] He also floats the bizarre idea that divine providence may have denied Ireland her independence until the time of the "Gaelic Renaissance," after which she could "assemble an Irish-speaking parliament capable of preserving Irish national individuality."[41]

Jordan is clearly enthralled by Rosenthal's progressive approach to language learning, and his rhetorical flourishes frequently borrow from the German linguist's newspaper advertisements.[42] An example of this is his personification of the phonograph: "Prof. Phonograph can instruct one or one hundred with equal facility and felicity. He is always patient and tolerant, never growing tired of repeating any particular phrase or sentence, and can be depended upon to speak nothing but pure grammatical Irish. And he teaches the language perfectly without frightening the student with the ghost of a grim and gruesome grammar."[43] In comparison, Rosenthal declares that his system "enables you to own a native professor. He speaks to you as you will, slowly or rapidly. Day or night he never tires, never fails. Never makes the slightest error." The same advertisement emphasizes the native accuracy of the language on the recordings: "Every accent, every syllable to the minutest modulation is precisely accurate."[44] Again following Rosenthal, Jordan proclaims: "All the Irish words in each lesson are reproduced by a phonographic record in the perfect pronunciation of a native Irish speaker, whose first language is Irish. They are reproduced in exactly the same tone and accent that one hears in an Irish town, and just such phrases as are used by two neighbors when they meet."[45]

The voice on the records, we are told, was that of "Prof. Anthony Kane, a native Irish speaker, and a writer of very graceful Irish verse." In 1910, Anthony Kane was a machine "oiler" employed by the Lackawanna Coal Mine Company. Forty-five years of age and single, he lived with his widowed mother and two brothers at 2129 Rockwell Ave, North Scranton.[46] The remark on his poetic skills may refer to a poem that was published in the Gaelic Department of the *Gaelic American* eight months earlier.[47]

An examination of various federal census records, death certificates, and obituaries associated with him and his family enables us to identify him as a native of Monaghrory (Monach Ruairí), a townland on Blacksod Bay in the parish of Kilmore, County Mayo, about five miles southwest of the town of Belmullet. The family had arrived in America in 1887.[48]

Kane's Belmullet origin is consistent with the dialect evidence presented in Jordan's two extant lessons. In a section on the "Sound of the Letters," examples of Irish words are provided followed by an approximate pronunciation in English orthography: *cinn* : kin, *fionn* : finn, *im* : im, *áit* : awtch, *fán*: fawn, *bád* : bawdh, *dha* [*sic*] : hghaw, *deo* : Joe, *an bhó* : on woe, *pósadh* : poas-oo, *caoineadh* : ko-een-you, *ní'l* : n-yeel, *adharc* : eye-ark.[49]

Lesson One, on "Tá, An bhfuil, Ní fhuil, agam," teaches the present tense of the substantive verb and the idiom for possession.[50] A conversation immediately follows, presumably one that was recorded by Kane. For the most part the Irish is typical Connacht Irish although, interestingly, "How is/are?" is twice rendered by "Cionnas tá …?," an idiom now associated with Munster dialects.[51]

The following extract from Lesson Two (on the past tense of the substantive verb) shows that the conversations could be lively and fairly idiomatic, albeit somewhat stilted because of their efforts to use a restricted vocabulary. The exchanges are numbered here as in the booklet. The translations are Jordan's.

1	Cia an chaoi bhfuil tú, a chara?	How are you, my friend?
2	Ní fhuilim acht mar sin, a dhuine chóir, go raibh maith agat. An bhfuil tú féin i sláinte mhaith?	I am only so-so, my good man, thank you. Are you yourself in good health?
3	Táim, buidheachas le Dia. Bhfuil tú leat féin indiú?	I am, thank God. Are you alone (by yourself) today?
4	Go deimhin; tá mé liom féin indiú, acht ní raibh mé liom féin indé. Bhí mé thíos ag tigh m'athair [*sic*] le cois na farraige.	Indeed; I am alone today, but I was not alone yesterday. I was down at my father's house beside the sea.
5	Bhfuil d'athair slán?	Is your father well?

6	Tá; agus mo mháthair, agus mo shean-athair.	(He) is; and my mother and grandfather.
7	An raibh an fhairrge garbh?	Was the sea rough?
8	Ní raibh sí. Bhí sí ciuin go leor. Tá bád breágh mór ag m'athair. Bhuail Maghnus Mac an Ultaigh bád m'athar le n-a bhád féin, agus bhris sé é.	It was not. It was calm enough. My father has a fine, large boat. Manus McAnulty struck my father's boat with his boat and he broke it.
9	As go bráth liom ins an uisce! Bhí mé beag nach baidhte as bád m'athar!'	Off with me into the water; I was almost drowned out of my father's boat!
10	An gliomach! An raibh sé ar meisce go léir?	The lobster! Was he completely intoxicated?
11	Go deimhin. Bhí Maghnus ar meisce agus mise san uisce!	Indeed. Manus was intoxicated and I was in the water.
12	Bhí sé 'maith go leor,' agus a c[h]liamhain leis.	His son in law was tipsy also.[52]

The implied association of the College of Irish Gaelic with the popular International Correspondence Schools of Scranton gives the impression that there was an established faculty and that there would be an active exchange of lessons and exercises with enrolled students. There is no subsequent newspaper evidence that Jordan's ambitions for the course were ever realized. Indeed, there are no advertisements or copyright applications for the publication of Lessons Three to Thirty. It may be that only a few lessons were ever recorded. In regard to the question of durability and survival, one more feature of the College of Irish Gaelic records deserves mention: they were recorded on hard celluloid (plastic) cylinders produced by the Indestructible Record Company of Albany for Columbia Phonograph in 1908.[53] These were extremely durable, and should any of the College of Irish Gaelic records came to light today, they might prove to be in excellent condition.[54]

THE GAELOPHONE SYSTEM (NEW HAVEN, 1910)

In February 1910 the New York *Gaelic American* published a large advertisement for "The Gaelophone System," a correspondence course using thirty-six phonograph recordings – all recorded in Ireland – of dialogues, recitations, stories, and songs. It was produced by the Gaelophone Company of New Haven, Connecticut.[55] Prospective purchasers were urged to "hear the voice of Dr Douglas Hyde, Father Dinneen, Canon O'Leary, Dr John P. Mac Enri, and John Mac Neill."[56] The songs – seven of them – were sung by Patrick O'Shea (1872–1919), a popular professional singer from Lismore, Co. Waterford, who had won the men's singing competition in the Second National Oireachtas of 1898 and toured in the United States from the fall of 1904 until November 1906.[57]

The advertisement says that the master recordings had been produced by the Columbia Phonograph Company "at Great Expense of Preparation and Manufacture."[58] The three members of the Gaelophone Company were first-generation Irish Americans in New Haven, Connecticut: Louis T. Ready, a clerk, thirty-six years of age; Charles J. Shaughnessy, a salesman for a printing company, forty years of age; and David J. McCoy, unemployed, twenty-eight years of age, but later to become a lawyer.[59]

The advertisement also mentions printed materials. These were to include a reader, a grammar, a collection of prose and poetry, folk tales, proverbs, Irish family names, and "Text Books prepared especially and exclusively for the Gaelophone" by Joseph Dunn (1872–1951), professor of Celtic languages and literatures at the Catholic University of America in Washington, DC.[60] No specific titles are given for these materials, which were obviously produced by other publishers and made available for purchase through the Gaelophone Company. Dunn's "Text Books" refers to the single volume that actually came with the records: *The Gaelophone: Irish Texts and English Translations to Accompany The Gaelophone Records of Irish Dialogues, Folk Tales and Recitations*. The front matter informs us that it was "printed in Ireland by Cahill and Co., Ltd, Dublin, with Irish ink and on Irish paper."

The *Gaelic American* advertisement further declares that "special inducements" and a "special rate" are available to "members of the Founders' class which is now being formed."[61] This suggests that a genuine correspondence course was indeed envisioned by the Gaelophone's originators.

As with Jordan's advertising for the Scranton course, some of the claims made for the Gaelophone are reminiscent of Rosenthal's advertisements: that the "Eye, Ear and Tongue [are] Trained at the Same Time" and that the Gaelophone is the "Most Patient, Tireless Teacher Ever Known, Repeating Words, Phrases and Sentences Thousands of Times."[62] In comparison, Rosenthal states, "Day or night, he never tires, never fails,"[63] and "All functions of language are taught *at the same time.* Eye, ear, tongue and mind are all brought into play."[64]

Joseph Dunn, the author of the course's textbook, was a native of New Haven and a son of Irish parents.[65] After acquiring a PhD in Romance languages from Yale University in 1898, he had been hired as an instructor at Catholic University and there commenced his study of Modern Irish with Dr Richard Henebry, the well-known eccentric cleric who was the first to hold the Ancient Order of Hibernians Chair of Celtic Studies at that university.[66] In 1901, Dunn embarked on a three-year study of Celtic, going to Harvard, Freiburg, and Rennes in turn. Henebry was gone when he returned to Catholic University, and he took over the Celtic course there, albeit as an assistant professor. Dunn spent some of his vacations in Ireland and probably made significant connections with Gaelic League notables there. He was also the director of the Washington Gaelic Society, which held monthly socials where "Celtic subjects" were discussed and "Celtic music" played.[67]

When Douglas Hyde came to give three lectures at Catholic University in May 1906, he was particularly impressed by the "broad-minded" faculty members he met there.[68] Dunn was surely one of these; he and Hyde had lunch at the White House with Theodore Roosevelt, where the three enjoyed a pleasant conversation on the topic of Irish folklore and saga.[69]

It seems likely, then, that Dunn designed the Gaelophone course himself. First, he had the connections and the expertise, and after consultation with his friend Hyde, he could easily have made the recording arrangements with the other Gaelic League luminaries; second, the Columbia Phonograph Company and Catholic University were both in Washington, DC; and third, the three Irish American heads of the Gaelophone Company might well have been parish or school chums of the professor.

Harvard University is fortunate to have in its possession the only complete set of Gaelophone records known to exist.[70] These came to the university from the estate of Fred Norris Robinson, who had taught Joseph Dunn during the latter's time at Harvard in the academic year of 1900–01. Harvard's Gaelophone set also includes Dunn's printed textbook. Only two other copies of this are known to exist: one in the Special Collections department of the James Joyce Library, University College Dublin, and the other in the Yale University Library.[71]

A glance at the arrangement of the dialogues in Dunn's course book will suffice to show that there was an impressive range of twenty-one topics, all but one of which were recorded on cylinder. The G-series of numbers added to the titles below correspond to the numbers on the cylinders.

1 Ag foghluim Gaedhilge / Learning Irish (G-1)
2 An aimsear / The weather (G-2)
3 Ag fiosrughadh fá shláinte / Enquiry about health (G-3)
4 Am agus aois / Enquiring about time and age (G-8)
5 Litreacha / Letters (G-9)
6 Nuaidheachta agus leabhair / News and books (G-10)
7 Ag éirighe ar maidin agus ag cur éadaigh ort / On rising [in the morning] and dressing (no recording)
8 Ag breacfast agus ag suipéar / At breakfast and supper (G-12)
9 Ag dinnéar / At dinner (G-13)
10 Ar fuaid an tighe / About the house (G-14)
11 Taisteal ar an dtraen / Travelling by train (G-15)
12 Ar mhuir / At sea (G-16)
13 Tiomáint ar an mbóthar / Driving (G-17)
14 Ag gabháil an bhóthar / Walking (G-10)
15 Fa'n dtuaith / In the country (G-19)
16 Ar fuaid an bhaile mhóir / Around the town (G-20)
17 Siopuigheachta / Shopping (G-21)
18 Ar cuairt / Visiting (G-22)
19 Ag an séipéal agus ar an sgoil / At church and school (G-23)
20 Cluichthe agus caitheamh aimsire / Games and pastimes (G-24)
21 Mion chomhrádh / Small talk (G-25)

The following two selections will give some indication of the level of sophistication to be found in the dialogues. They are lively and fairly natural, and the device of having a Connacht man speaking with a Munster man was a clever way to introduce dialect differences and to ensure better sales. As with the dialogues in the College of Gaelic course, the conversations are meant to be entertaining; but the Gaelophone exchanges are far more complex and interesting. The impression is given that the topics presented are those that one would expect to be current among young members of the Gaelic League; the speakers discuss the latest book by Hyde (referring to him by his pen name, "An Craoibhín Aoibhinn" [The Delightful Little Branch]) and show some level of interest in fellow *Gaeilgeoirí* (Irish speakers) of the opposite sex. The conversational exchanges are numbered, alternating between the Connacht (C) and the Munster (M) speaker.

Example 1: From the dialogue entitled "Learning Irish"

1.C.	Dia dhuit.	Good morning (God to you).
2.M.	Dia is Muire dhuit, a Sheagháin.	Good morning (God and Mary to you), John.
3.C.	Cé'n sgéal agat faoi an nGaedhilge? Cloisim go bhfuil tú ghá foghluim. A labhrann tú Gaedhilge?	What news have you about the Irish? I hear you're learning it. Do you speak Irish?
4.M.	Ní'l puinn Gaedhling agam fós, agus ní féidir liom i labhairt go maith, acht tuigim a lán de ó sna daoinibh a labhrann í. Is féidir liom beagán de a léigheamh agus a scríobhadh go h-áirithe. Bhfuil aon Gaedhilge agat-sa?	I haven't much Irish yet, and I cannot speak it well, but I understand a good deal of it from the people who speak it. I can read and write it a little, at any rate. Have you any Irish?
5.C.	Ní'l focal in mo phluic, acht labhrann m'athair Gaedhilge go h-an-mhaith.	I haven't a word of it in my mouth, but my father speaks Irish very well.
6.M.	Mo náire go deo thú[!] Cad 'n-a thaobh ná thosnuigheann [*sic*] tú? Budh cheart do gach Éireannach Gaedhling a bheith aige comh maith leis an mBearla [*sic*]. Tá graiméar agus leabhar Gaedhealaighe agamsa 'sa bhaile, agus uaireanta tugaim iarracht ar Gaedhling a labhairt le Nóra Ní Shúilleabháin.	What a pity! Why don't you begin? Every Irishman ought to have Irish as well as English. I have a grammar and Irish book at home, and sometimes I try to speak Irish with Nora Sullivan.

7.C.	Dubhairt sí liom go raibh tú ag dul i bhfeabhas. Ó maiseadh, nach breágh an Ghaedhilge atá agat, bail ó Dhia ort!	She told me that you were improving. O, indeed, what fine Irish you have God bless you![72]

Example 2: From the dialogue entitled "News and Books"

1.C.	Bail ó Dhia ort, a Shéamuis, cé'n sgéal atá agat?	Good morning (God speed you), James. What's the news?
2.M.	Is beag atá. An bhfuil aon sgéal agat-sa?	I haven't much. Have you any news?
3.C.	Tá an-sgéal agam.	I have a great piece of news.
4.M.	Tá súil agam nach droch-sgéal é.	I hope it isn't bad news.
5.C.	Ní h-eadh. Sgéal greann mhar é. Cogair mé leat, eadrainn fhéin, ar chuala tú go raibh Tomás ua Loingsigh agus Áine ní Bhriain an-mhór le n-a chéile?	No; it's a funny story. Whisper; between ourselves, did you hear that Tom Lynch is courting Mary O'Brien?
6.M.	Chuala trácht thairis, acht níor chreideas é.	I heard some talk of it, but I didn't believe it.[73]

The folk tales and recitations are also interesting pieces, and one would hope that a restoration of the cylinders might enable us to hear whether the voices on the recording are truly those promised in the advertisements. In one case, "Árd í Cuain" below, the voice of Eoin Mac Néill is lost to us: there is no corresponding recording in the thirty-six-cylinder set, and it is clear from an examination of their labels that there never was one. The following list of these readings is taken from the contents page in Dunn's textbook. Additional information, provided before or after the texts themselves, is added in the notes.

1 Munster Folktale: An duine bocht agus an leath-amadán / The poor man and the half-fool (G-6).[74]

2 Connacht Folktale: Comhartha na gealaigh / The sign of the moon (G-29).[75]

3 Recitation: An droch-shaoghal / The Bad Times (By the Rev. Patrick S. Dinneen, M.A.) (G-4).[76]

4 Recitation: Bás Ghofradha Uí Dhomhnaill / The death of Godfrey O'Donnell (By John P. Mac Enri, M.D.) (G-5).[77]

5 Recitation: Óid do'n Oireachtas Mór [i mBaile-Áth-Cliath, 1897] / The Oireachtas Ode (by Douglas Hyde, LL.D.) (G-7).[78]
6 Recitation: Árd í Cuain / An Antrim Song (By Prof. John Mac Neill, B.A.) (No recording).[79]
7 Recitation: Agalla[i]mh na Marbh [h-Ermés agus Chárón agus Menippos] / Dialogues of the Dead [Hermes, Charon, and Menippus] (By the Very Rev. Peter O'Leary) (G-35).[80]
8 Recitation: Séadna / Seadna (By the Very Rev. Peter O'Leary) (G-36).[81]

Printed texts of the seven songs sung by Patrick O'Shea were not included in the textbook – an indication, perhaps, that their addition was an afterthought: something to spark up the content. The recorded songs are "The Palatine's Daughter" (G-26), "The Little Red Fox" (G-27), "The Spailpín Fánach" (G-28),[82] "The Fairy Child" (G-31), "Aililiú na Gabhna" (G-32), "Seoithín Seo" (G-33), and "Jimmy Mo Mhíle Stór" (G-34).

Sadly, the Gaelophone course was not to survive the popular changeover from cylinder to disc that was already afoot in the first decade of the century. The longer-playing Victrola discs were rapidly winning over the entertainment market, and it may be that Columbia simply viewed the Gaelophone venture as an opportunity to unload some of its stock of soon-to-be-obsolete two-minute cylinders.[83] The original Gaelophone advertisement warned prospective purchasers that the "system" was only available "to a limited number and for a limited time," an indication perhaps that only one run of sets was ever manufactured. This was borne out in the following year, when some effort was made to market the Gaelophone overseas; the tone of an advertisement in the *Freeman's Journal* does not indicate that sales were going well: "Special offer to purchasers in Ireland and Great Britain. Price reduced to cost of manufacturing. Only 100 sets left. Moulds to be destroyed. No more Gaelic Records to be made. Last chance to buy the Gaelophone."[84] After 1910, no Gaelophone advertisements appeared in the Irish American papers until January 1917, when a small advertisement in the *Gaelic American* announced that the few remaining sets of the Gaelophone were "selling fast," with the original price of $45.00 reduced to $15.00.[85]

CONCLUSION

One would be hard-pressed to conclude that the three phonograph courses discussed above served in maintaining the Irish language in America to any measurable degree. A survey of newspaper articles and advertisements yields no evidence that they sold well or for any length of time. Indeed, the Cortina and the College of Irish Gaelic courses may have failed after the initial run of only a few records. It is worth observing, however, that all three were produced at the end of the cylinder era when the popular market – geared more for entertainment than for education – was demanding disc records and disc players. Phonographs were expensive items, and few would want to waste money on what was deemed to be an obsolete model. It is questionable, also, whether the producers of these courses ever had sufficient staff to supply the correspondence component that learners might have wanted. On the positive side, the cylinder records may have been effective resources for pupils at the first stage of learning Irish, giving them a grounding in the sound system of the language in relation to its orthography. Once past this stage, however, learners would have insisted on real speakers, of whom there were a considerable number a century ago.

The Gaelophone course, unlike the other two, was a completed production and provided recordings suitable for a more advanced level. Its inclusion of songs by a popular Irish tenor would have been an attractive entertainment feature for those whose interests did not extend so far as to learn the language. This may account for some sales five or six years after its debut in 1910.

It was not until the 1920s, by which time the transition to discs was complete, that records for learning Irish re-emerged. These were from the London-based Linguaphone Company: *The Linguaphone Short Irish Course* (1921) by Shan Ó Cuív and Aindrias Ó Muimhneacháin and *Irish in Thirty Lessons* (1929) by Tomás Ó Máille and Mícheál Breathnach. The earlier phonograph courses, however, testify to the thrill of innovation that existed in the American Irish-language movement at the time. One hopes that with the restoration of the Gaelophone cylinders, and the discovery of others, we may yet share the thrill of hearing the living voices of those pioneers.

NOTES

1 The Gaelophone course (but not the others) was also marketed in Ireland.
2 Edison, "Phonograph," 533–4.
3 Feaster, "Origins," 1. Ten years later Edison did in fact comment on the value of the phonograph for teaching the correct pronunciation of foreign languages: Edison, "Perfected Phonograph," 647.
4 Ibid.
5 "The Phonograph in Congress", *Philadelphia Times*, 25 April 1878.
6 "History of the Cylinder Phonograph."
7 Kitao, "History of Language Laboratories," 6; Feastar, "Origins," 3–4; Edison, "Perfected Phonograph."
8 Edison, "Perfected Phonograph," 645; Kitao, "History of Language Laboratories," 5.
9 Edison, "Perfected Phonograph," 645. Prior to the mid-1890s, the manufacture of a duplicate record was crude – nothing more than a purely acoustic recording of an original; see "History of the Cylinder Phonograph."
10 *Evening World*, 10 December 1889. The College of Milwaukee (founded in 1885, now the University of Wisconsin–Milwaukee) was a new institution at the time.
11 Easton, "Meisterschaft System," 53; "Language Instruction," 118. Rosenthal had introduced his Meisterschaft System in 1881; see Rosenthal, *Meisterschaft System*; *Bucks County Gazette*, 13 October 1881; *Middlebury Register*, 14 October 1881; *Nebraska State Journal*, 14 October 1881.
12 "Revolution," 214–16. Rosenthal has a full-page advertisement in the same number of the *Phonogram*.
13 The earliest references to Cortina as a language teacher in New York appear in advertisements in the *New York Times* (23 March 1884, 15 November 1884), at which time he was teaching Spanish and French according to Rosenthal's Meisterschaft System. Cortina first advertised his Cortina Method in December 1888; see "Spanish by the 'Cortina Method,'" *New York Times*, 16 December 1888, 15.
14 Regarding Cortina's early use of the phonograph, it is reported: "Without parade, for the last five years, he has taught various languages by phonograph, in all parts of the world, but especially in South America and in Mexico": "Phonograph as a Teacher," 5.
15 "Teaching by Phonograph," *Sacramento Daily Record Union*, 4 December 1896, 7; "Teaches Language by Mail," *Buffalo Evening News*, 6 January 1897.
16 "History of the Cylinder Phonograph."

17 "Notes," 68–70; "Improvement," 75–7; "Two Great Improvements," 79–80. The National Phonograph Company was formed by Edison and his associates in 1896; see "History of the Cylinder Phonograph."

18 "Notes," 68.

19 Originally established in 1891 to provide advancement through technical education for mine workers, the ICS had discovered a mass market for "practical education" and succeeded in attracting more than 100,000 new enrollments per year in the first decade of the new century: Watkinson, "Education," 348–9.

20 ICS, "Languages Taught by Mail," "French, German and Spanish," and "Modern Languages." In his 1902 article, "Moulding and Mailing the Human Voice," Auld describes his visit to the ICS in terms reminiscent of L. Frank Baum's *The Wizard of Oz*, which had been published two years before.

21 ICS, "Modern Languages," 45–6.

22 "Cortina Language Outfit," *New York Times*, 3 October 1908, 12; 24 October 1908, 12.

23 "Irish by Phonograph," *Gaelic American*, 3 July 1909, 7.

24 Even before Douglas Hyde's visit to America in 1905–06, the interest in Irish was extraordinary. In Scranton, Pennsylvania, the first meeting of a Gaelic Club in 1904 attracted two hundred young Irish-Americans; but they had only one teacher, John E. O'Malley: "Club for the Study of Gaelic," *Scranton Truth*, 3 November 1904, 2.

25 "Irish by Phonograph," *Gaelic American*, 3 July 1909, 7.

26 Ibid.

27 "The College of Irish Gaelic," *Irish-American*, 27 November 1909, 8.

28 Ibid.

29 The article cites the "literature of the college" and draws heavily on Jordan's introduction to his *Complete Course in the Irish Language*: ibid. Jordan's parents were Richard Jordan (born c. 1822) and Bridget Hosie (born c. 1826); see 1850 US Census, Luzerne County, Pennsylvania, Archbald Blakely, p. 78A, family 1705, Richard and Bridget Jordan; 1870 US Census, Luzerne County, Pennsylvania, Archbald Blakely, p. 86B, dwelling 173, Richard and Bridget Jordan. For John H. Jordan in 1910, see 1910 US Census, Lackawanna County, Pennsylvania, Scranton Ward 1, p. 14A, house 1021, family 297, John H. Jordan. Jordan's older brother James was the founder and proprietor of the *Scranton Truth* (1884–1915), a paper that provided an excellent coverage of Irish-American affairs. His obituary is in the *Scranton Truth*, 6 February 1911, 5.

30 *Catalogue of Copyright Entries*, 668. The copyrights are dated 23 September 1909.

31 "The College of Irish Gaelic," *Irish-American*, 27 November 1909, 8.
32 "Club for the Study of Gaelic," *Scranton Truth*, 3 November 1904, 2.
33 "Afternoon Echoes," *Scranton Truth*, 4 November 1904, 4. The "Sunday Record" probably refers to the *Wilkes-Barre Record.*
34 "Gaelic League," *Scranton Truth*, 28 April 1906, 7.
35 "Meeting Night of Prof. O'Malley's Gaelic Class Changed." *Scranton Truth*, 29 October 1906, 7. St Thomas College was renamed the University of Scranton in 1938 and is now administered by the Jesuits.
36 *Irish-American*, 27 November 1909, 8. To this we may compare a Rosenthal advertisement: "[I]t is the natural way in which the mind acquires an unfamiliar language. It is almost exactly as a child learns to talk. Almost unconsciously you glide into *thinking* in a new language. You learn to use sentences rather than isolated words": "Language-Phone," *Brooklyn Daily Eagle*, 3 September 1908, 52.
37 *Irish-American*, 27 November 1909, 8. The same outlook is found in Jordan's "treatise" in which he claims that "terrific terminology and grandiloquent grammatical expressions" were enough "to scare many a stout heart brave enough to stand before the belching cannon's mouth for his motherland": Jordan, *Complete Course*, 5.
38 National Library of Ireland, call number A28035.
39 The topics he discusses are introduced under the following titles: "The Great Awakening," describing the "Irish Renaissance" and heavily quoting an article by Sidney Brooks published in the *North American Review* of August 1908: Jordan, *Complete Course*, 3; "A World-Wide Influence," mostly concerned with the dearth of adequate teachers and textbooks (5); "Competent Teacher of Irish," recommending use of the phonograph (5); "What Is the Irish Language?" (6); "The Seven Languages" (7); "Classification of Languages" (7); "The Indo-European Languages" (8); "The Celtic Group" (8); "Irish a Contemporary of Spoken Latin" (9); "Native Home of the Short Story" (10); "Arrest of Irish Literary Development" (11); "Dr Douglas Hyde's Views" (12); "Dr. Sigerson on Irish Poetry" (13); "The Moderns of the Past" (14); "Ex-President Roosevelt's Opinion," citing Roosevelt's article on "The Ancient Irish Sagas" published in *Century Magazine*, January 1907 (14); "Chairs of Irish in American Universities" (15); "Ireland's Debt to German Scholarship" (16); "The Irish Out-Irished by Strangers" (16); "What is Individuality?" (17); "What is National Individuality?" (19); "An Honest Englishman's Views," quoting Sidney Brooks (20); "Have the Irish the Grit Necessary?" (22); "Faith in Eternal Justice" (23); "The Hand of Providence" (24); "The Structure of the Irish Language" (25); "Its Original Syntax" (26); "Objections to the Learning of Irish" (28); "Shakespeare's Pronunciation"

(29); "Our Method of Learning Irish" (31); "Students Scared Away" (32); "No Grammar in Nature's School" (32); "Self-Consciousness and Awkwardness" (33); "The Phrase, Not the Word, the Unit" (34); "Learned Names for Simple Things" (35); "Why Not Begin with Philology?" (36); "Words When Loose and When in Groups" (36); "Crime of Brain-Breaking" (37); "Law of Association of Ideas" (38); "Teaching by Jerks" (39); "Continuous(!) Thought" (39); "Reduced to an Absurdity," a critique of the "word method" (40); "The Dissection Process" (41); "Men are Only Phonographs" (42); "Our System of Teaching Irish" (42); "There is a Royal Road to Linguistry" (43); "Easy to Think in Irish" (44); "Erin for E'er and Gaelic for Erin!" (46).

40 Ibid., 5.

41 Ibid., 24.

42 This is evident even in Jordan's diction. He refers, for example, to "the meat of the method," while Rosenthal's advertisements refer to "the keynote of the success of this system": Jordan, "College of Gaelic," *Brooklyn Daily Eagle*, 3 September 1908, 52.

43 Jordan, *Complete Course*, 5.

44 "Language-Phone and Rosenthal's Practical Linguistry," *New York Times*, 14 November 1908, 12.

45 Jordan, *Complete Course*, 5.

46 1910 US Census, Lackawanna County, Pennsylvania, Scranton Ward 1, p. 9B, house 2129, family 168, Anthony Kane; 1900 US Census, Lackawanna County, Pennsylvania, Scranton Ward 1, p. 3, house 2129, family 43. Anthony Kane.

47 "Mo Bheannacht Leat go Deo" (My farewell to you forever), *Gaelic American*, 20 March 1909, 7. This poem, beginning "A Éire dheas na gcoillte glas" (O Lovely Ireland of the green woods), describes in some detail the landscape Kane knew as a youth. It is called a "remarkable little poem" in the *Scranton Truth*, 30 March 1909, 6.

48 Anthony Kane was the son of Anthony Kane and Celia Lally (Catholic Parish Registers, Kilmore Erris, Diocese of Killala, baptisms, film 04321/12, p. 20, 3 September 1865, Anth[y] Cain). His mother Celia (alias Cecily, Saly, Sibi) was the daughter of Denis Lally and Sabina Gallegher of Glencastle, on the other side of Blacksod Bay (Catholic Parish Registers, Belmullet, Diocese of Killala, baptisms, film 04231/08, p. 27, 21 December 1846, Saly Lally). His parents were married on 4 September 1860 (Catholic Parish Registers, Belmullet, Diocese of Killala, marriages, film 04231/09, p. 10). Other children of Anthony Kane and Celia Lally were baptized on 30 November 1862, 25 September 1868, 15 April 1871, 21 June 1874, 24 June 1877, and 16 May 1881.

49 Jordan, *Complete Course*, 52–3.

50 Ibid., 54.

51 Ibid., 57.

52 Ibid., 60.

53 *Irish-American*, 27 November 1909, 8.

54 For a description and images of celluloid cylinders, see Jason Curtis, "Indestructible Record (1907–1922)," Museum of Obsolete Media, accessed 17 August 2018, http://www.obsoletemedia.org/indestructible-record.

55 *Gaelic American*, 15 February 1910, 8.

56 Douglas Hyde (Dubhghlas de hÍde) (1860–1945) and John MacNeill (Eoin Mac Néill) (1867–1945), were co-founders of the Gaelic League and leaders of the movement in this period. John P. Henry (Seaghán P. Mac Énrí) (1862–1930) was then a lecturer in Modern Irish in University College, Galway, and the recent author of *A Handbook of Modern Irish* (1903–6) and *An Modh Díreach* (The Direct Method) (1908). Canon Peter O'Leary (Peadar Ó Laoghaire) (1839–1920) was a major figure in the Gaelic League and an outspoken supporter of *caint na ndaoine* (popular speech) as the only practical model for establishing a standard of Modern Irish. Fr Patrick S. Dinneen (Pádraig Ó Duinnín) (1860–1894) was a prolific scholar and creative writer, and the compiler of *Foclóir Gaedhilge agus Béarla* (Irish–English Dictionary) (1904). The voices of Dinneen and Mac Énrí might be unique to the Gaelophone recordings.

57 Catholic Parish Registers, Parish of Lismore, baptisms, film 02467/10, p. 53, 1 September 1872. Some adjudicators objected to O'Shea's Oireachtas prize because he was a professional opera singer: Borthwick, *Proceedings*, 97. During a singing tour in Kerry in 1907, *The Kerry People* reported: "Anybody who has heard him sing a purely Gaelic ballad will admit what singular gifts he can show when dealing with our folk song" (1 June). He was also well-known as one of the first to sing Gaelic songs on the London opera stage: Obituary, *Freeman's Journal*, 8 April 1919. He and his family were settled in Dublin in 1911 around the time the Gaelophone Course was produced: 1911 Census of Ireland, County Dublin, Arran Quay ward, 19 Carnew St, family return, form A, Patrick O'Shea.

58 *Gaelic American*, 15 February 1910, 8. Although the Gaelophone Company had $25,000 in capital, the initial lay-out for immediate production was $1,000: "Corporations Old and New," *Hartford Daily Courant*, 29 January 1910.

59 "To Encourage Language Study," 35. The three members of the company are listed in the 1910 US Census for New Haven County, Connecticut: Orange Township, p. 14A, house 247, family 302, Charles J. Shaughnessy; New

Haven Ward 2, p. 7A, house 124, family 2, Louis Ready; New Haven Ward 9, p. 8B, house 78, family 179, David McCoy.

60 *Gaelic American*, 15 February 1910, 8.

61 Ibid.

62 Ibid.

63 *New York Times*, 7 November 1908, 11; 14 November 1909, 12.

64 *Brooklyn Daily Eagle*, 3 September 1908, 11.

65 1880 US Census, New Haven County, Connecticut, New Haven Ward 9, p. 8B, house 78, family 1, Joseph Dunn. For some brief biographical details, see "Obituary Record."

66 Gerig, "Celtic Studies," 36–7.

67 Ibid., 40.

68 J. Dunleavy and G. Dunleavy, *Douglas Hyde*, 285.

69 Mullhall, "Douglas Hyde in America."

70 For Harvard's catalogue description of the Gaelophone course, visit http://id.lib.harvard.edu/alma/990112934330203941/catalog, accessed 10 June 2018.

71 James Joyce Library, University College Dublin, Special Collections, 34.I.5/9; Yale University Library, Library Shelving Facility, Hax31 D92.

72 Dunn, *The Gaelophone*, 7–8.

73 Ibid., 17.

74 'Diarmuid ua Duibhne' is added after the text: ibid., 50. This was the pen name of Diarmuid Ó Súilleabháin (1872–1952), a noted writer from Valentia Island, Co. Kerry.

75 A note after the text identifies the source as Séamus Ua Dubhghaill (1855–1929), the author of *Cathair Conroí agus Sgéalta Eile* (Cú Roí's Fort and Other Stories): Dunn, *The Gaelophone*, 52; Ua Dubhghaill, *Cathair Conroí*, 55–7. There are some differences between the version of the tale in that book and the one in the *Gaelophone* text. Séamas Ó Dubhghaill, who used the pen name Beirt Fhear (Two Men), was from Cooleanig, near Killarney, County Kerry.

76 A note after the text identifies the source as Dinneen's *Muinntear Chiarraidhe roimh an Droch-Shaoghal* (The People of Kerry before the Famine): Dunn, *The Gaelophone*, 54; Ua Duinnín, *Muinntear*, 79.

77 A note after the text identifies the source as Seaghán Mac Éinrigh's *Bás Ghofradha Uí Dhomhnaill*: Dunn, *The Gaelophone*, 56; Mac Éinrí, *Bás Ghofradha*, 3–4. At the time the Gaelophone course was conceived, Mac Éinrigh had recently published *An Modh Díreach* (1908), an introduction to the direct method of language teaching.

78 A note after the text identifies the source as Hyde's *Úbhla de'n Chraoibh* (Apples from the Branch): Dunn, *The Gaelophone*, 58; Hyde, *Úbhla*, 53–4.

79 A note after the text identifies the source as Eoin Mac Néill's article, "Irish in the Glens of Antrim": Dunn, *The Gaelophone*, 60; Mac Néill, "Irish," 108.

80 A note after the text identifies the source as a portion of Peadar Ua Laoghaire's series, "Agallamh na nDéithe ó Lúcián" (Dialogue of the Gods from Lucian): Dunn, *The Gaelophone*, 64; Ua Laoghaire, "Agallamh," 251–2. Ua Laoghaire (1839–1920) was an outspoken supporter of *caint na ndaoine* (popular speech) as the only practical model for establishing a standard of Modern Irish.

81 A note after the text identifies the source as Ua Laoghaire's *Séadna*: Dunn, *The Gaelophone*, 66; Ua Laoghaire, *Séadna*, 6–7.

82 This recording, digitized by David Giovannoni, may be heard online: Ward Irish Music Archives, Milwaukee, Irish Fest Collection, IF CYL 00-031, audio, 1:54, https://soundcloud.com/ward-irish-music-archives/the-spailpin-fanach-unknown.

83 "History of the Cylinder Phonograph." Columbia was badly affected by a financial depression in 1908 and actually ceased production of additional wax cylinders in that year; see Brooks, *Columbia Master Book*, 11, 13.

84 "What Is the Gaelophone?" *Freeman's Journal*, 4 December 1911.

85 "They Are Selling Fast," *Gaelic American*, 3 January 1917, 3.

BIBLIOGRAPHY

Auld, R.C. "Moulding and Mailing the Human Voice." *The Phonogram*, n.s., 6, no. 1, issue 31 (November 1902): 7–16.

Borthwick, Norma, and Tadhg Ua Donnchadha, eds. *The Proceedings of the Second Oireachtas held in Dublin [Rotunda] on Tuesday, 24th May 1898*. Dublin: The Gaelic League, 1898.

Brooks, Tim, ed. *The Columbia Master Book Discography*, vol. 1. Discographies 78. Westport: Greenwood Press, 1999.

Catalogue of Copyright Entries Published by Authority of the Acts of Congress of March 3, 1891, and of June 30, 1906, part 1, group 2. Washington, DC: GPO, 1909.

Dunleavy, Janet E., and Gareth W. Dunleavy. *Douglas Hyde: A Maker of Modern Ireland.* Berkeley: University of California Press, 1991.

Dunn, Joseph. *The Gaelophone: Irish Texts and English Translations to Accompany the Gaelophone Records of Irish Dialogues, Folk Tales, and Recitations.* New Haven: The Gaelophone Company, 1910.

Easton, Edward. "The Meisterschaft System Taught by the Phonograph." *The Phonogram* 1, no. 2 (February 1891): 53.

Edison, Thomas A. "The Perfected Phonograph." *North American Review* 146, no. 379 (June 1888): 641–50.
– "The Phonograph and Its Future." *North American Review* 126, no. 262 (May–June 1878): 527–36.
Feaster, Patrick. "The Origins of Ethnographic Sound Recording, 1878–1892." *Resound, a Quarterly of the Archives of Traditional Music* 20, nos. 1–2 (January–April 2001): 1, 3–8.
Gerig, John L. "Celtic Studies in the United States." *Columbia University Quarterly* 19, no. 1 (December 1916): 30–43.
"History of the Cylinder Phonograph." Inventing Entertainment: The Early Motion Pictures and Sound Recordings of the Edison Companies. Library of Congress Digital Collections, https://www.loc.gov/collections/edison-company-motion-pictures-and-sound-recordings/articles-and-essays/history-of-edison-sound-recordings/history-of-the-cylinder-phonograph, accessed 28 August 2018.
Hyde, Douglas [Dubhghlas de h-Íde]. *Úbhla de'n Chraoibh: Dánta agus Abhráin*. Baile Átha Cliath: M.H. Gill agus a Mhac, 1900.
"Improvement of the Phonograph." *The Phonogram*, n.s., 4, no. 5, issue 23 (March 1902): 75–7. Originally published in *Literary Digest* 22, no. 12 (January–June 1901): 350.
ICS (International Correspondence Schools, Scranton). "French, German, and Spanish Taught by Mail and Phonograph." *The Phonogram*, n.s., 5, no. 2, issue 26 (June 1902): 28–30.
– "Languages Taught by Mail with the Aid of a Phonograph." *The Phonogram*, n.s., 5, no. 1, issue 25 (May 1902): 12–13.
– "Modern Languages Taught by Mail with the Aid of the Phonograph." *The Phonogram*, n.s., 5, no. 3, issue 27 (July 1902): 44–6; no. 4, issue 28 (August 1902): 60–2; no. 5, issue 29 (September 1902): 74–6.
Jordan, John H. *Complete Course in the Irish Language in Thirty Lessons*. Scranton: College of Irish Gaelic, 1909.
Kitao, Kenji. "The History of Language Laboratories – Origin and Establishment." Educational Resources Information Center, US Department of Education. 1995, https://files.eric.ed.gov/fulltext/ED381020.pdf. Originally published in Japanese: "Gogaku Laboratory no Rekishi – Tanjo to Teichaku." *Doshisha Studies in English* 35 (1984): 86–103.
"Language Instruction by Means of the Phonograph." *The Phonogram* 1, no. 5 (May 1891): 118.
Mac Éinrí, Seaghán P. *Bás Ghofradha Uí Dhomhnaill*. Baile Átha Cliath: M.H. Gill agus a Mhac, 1905.

Mac Néill, Eoin. "Irish in the Glens of Antrim." *Irisleabhar na Gaedhilge* 6, no. 7 (October 1895): 106–10.

Mullhall, Daniel. "Douglas Hyde in America, 1891–1906." *Ambassador's Blog*. Embassy of Ireland, USA. 14 February 2018, https://www.dfa.ie/irish-embassy/usa/about-us/ambassador/ambassadors-blog/douglas-hyde-in-america-1891_1906.

"Notes." *The Phonogram*, n.s., 4, no. 5, issue 23 (March 1902): 68–70.

"Obituary Record of Graduates of the Undergraduate Schools Deceased during the Year 1950–1951." *Bulletin of Yale University* 48, no. 1 (January 1952): 31.

"The Phonograph as a Teacher." *The Phonoscope* 1, no. 8 (July 1897): 5–6.

"Revolution in the Study of Foreign Languages." *The Phonogram* 1, no. 10 (October 1891): 214–16.

Rosenthal, Richard S. *The Meisterschaft System: A Simple and Practical Method, Enabling Any One to Learn, with Slight Effort, to Speak Fluently and Correctly French, German, Spanish, and Italian.* New York: I.K. Funk and Co., 1881.

"To Encourage Language Study." *Talking Machine World* 6, no. 2 (February 1910): 35.

"Two Great Improvements." *The Phonogram*, n.s., 4, no. 5, issue 23 (March 1902): 79–80.

Ua Dubhghaill, Séamus. *Cathair Conroí agus Sgéalta Eile*. Baile Átha Cliath: Connradh na Gaedhilge, 1903.

Ua Duinnín, Pádraig (Patrick S. Dinneen). *Muinntear Chiarraidhe roimh an Droch-Shaoghal*. Baile Átha Cliath: M. H. Gill agus a Mhac, 1905.

Ua Laoghaire, Peadar. "Agallamh na nDéithe ó Lúcián." *Journal of the Ivernian Society* 1, no. 4 (June 1909), 247–52.

– *Séadna*. Baile Átha Cliath: The Irish Book Company, 1904.

Watkinson, James D. "'Education for Success': The International Correspondence Schools of Scranton, Pennsylvania." *Pennsylvania Magazine of History and Biography* 120, no. 4 (October 1996): 343–69.

ARCHIVAL COLLECTIONS

Catholic Parish Registers. National Library of Ireland, Dublin. Digital images. https://registers.nli.ie.

County Dublin. 1911 Census of Ireland, household returns. National Archives of Ireland, Dublin. Digital images. Census of Ireland 1901/1911 and Census Fragments and Substitutes, 1821–51. http://www.census.nationalarchives.ie.

Connecticut. New Haven County. 1880 and 1910 US Censuses, population schedules. Digital images. Ancestry.com. http://ancestry.com.
Pennsylvania. Luzerne County. 1850 and 1870 US Censuses, population schedules. Digital images. Ancestry.com. http://ancestry.com.
Pennsylvania. Lackawanna County. 1900 and 1910 US Censuses, population schedules. Digital images. Ancestry.com. http://ancestry.com.

8

Seán "Irish" Ó Súilleabháin: Butte's Irish Bard

Ciara Ryan

Seán "Irish" Ó Súilleabháin's (1882–1957) journey west to Butte, Montana, at the turn of the last century corresponds to the formulaic reality of his emigrant peers, but his life story is far from commonplace. He became one of the most respected and prominent leaders supporting the Irish language and its cause during a pivotal period in both Butte's and his native country's history, yet his story remains untold. Fortunately, he left behind a rich collection of Irish and English manuscripts that shed light on the cultivation of Irish traditions in Montana, a region of North America beyond the more familiar coastal Irish concentrations in the opening decades of the twentieth century.[1] In honour of Professor Nilsen's important contributions to our understanding of the history of Irish speakers in North America, not least among which was his revelation of the little-known Irish-speaking enclave of Portland, Maine, this chapter examines Seán's life and work in Montana.[2] As we will see, Seán played an important role in Butte's Irish organizations and participated fully in the copying and composing of texts in manuscript form.

FROM BEARA TO BUTTE

Seán "Irish" Ó Súilleabháin was born on 20 June 1882 on the island of Inishfarnard, off the northwest coast of the Beara Peninsula in Kilcatherine Parish, townland of Eyeries, Co. Cork. His father was a fisherman, like the other men on the island.[3] The islanders were dependent on mainland villages for turf and other amenities, and Seán likely received some schooling in a mainland school; according to his own testimony, he attained the American equivalent of eighth grade.[4] In the early 1900s, Inishfarnard's younger generation gradually emigrated – Seán himself departed in 1905 – and the island was abandoned in 1924.[5]

Inishfarnard islanders were not the only people in the region who were leaving. The Beara Peninsula experienced significant emigration beginning in the late nineteenth century, and most Beara emigrants went to Butte, Montana. What was it that enticed them there? The answer has to do with the mining history of the two areas. The townland of Allihies, Beara, 16.7 kilometres south of Eyeries, was a booming mining region in the early nineteenth century. Beginning in the 1860s, however, the industry began to decline, and many of the townland's skilled workers began to look overseas for employment, to American mining towns like Butte. David Emmons highlights the significant movement of people from Beara to Butte in the late 1800s: "Assuming even a measure of accuracy to the name-place association, County Cork in southwestern Ireland supplied a hugely disproportionate share of Butte's Irish population."[6] Of the 1,700 people who left Eyeries between 1870 and 1915, 1,138 went to Butte.[7] As Fr Patrick Brosnan of Butte (1892–1918) wrote in a 1917 letter, "Everyone here is from Castletownbere [in Eyeries] … We have seven fine Catholic parishes all Irish."[8]

The links between Butte and Ireland go back as far as the 1860s when Waterford nationalist and exile Thomas Francis Meagher (1823–1867) was appointed temporary governor of Montana from 1865 to 1867. Gold and silver mining had initially enticed immigrant workers to the area, but copper was most in demand by the end of the century. Entrepreneurs like Irishman Marcus Daly (1841–1900) turned Butte and its neighbouring town, Anaconda, into the world's greatest copper producer. The city's mining companies offered good wages to some ten thousand miners and mine workers.[9] Fr Brosnan succinctly described Daly as "the man that made Butte an Irish town … He did not care for any man but an Irishman and … did not give a job to anyone else."[10] The Irish were one of the first ethnic groups to arrive in significant numbers in Butte, either from other mining camps in Nevada and California or directly from Ireland.[11] When the Irish first arrived, Butte was still a mining camp; they therefore managed to avoid the prejudice of an already established community and were able to mould the city's social structures to their own liking, unlike their compatriots on the east coast.[12] They found employment not just as labourers or miners but as businessmen, foremen, tradesmen, and politicians. Butte was a stop along the way for some transient Irish immigrants, but for others, such as Seán, it became home.

IRELAND'S FIFTH PROVINCE

Seán arrived in a city that former Irish president Douglas Hyde (1860–1949) described as "cathair Éireannach ... beagnach. Is Éireannaigh iad an chuid is mó de na daoinibh atá innti ... agus tá stiúrú gach rud ar láimh na nÉireannach" (essentially an Irish town. Most of the people there are Irish ... and the Irish run everything).[13] Gaelic football was played in Butte as early as 1892, and a branch of the Gaelic Athletic Association was founded in 1913.[14] Beginning in 1895, the Robert Emmet Literary Association held regular Irish lectures, and a local branch of the Gaelic League was formed in 1906. It held dances, *feiseanna* (Irish language and music competitions), and history and language classes. On his inaugural visit to the town in 1906, Hyde collected $2,212.60 from the Irish community to fund the Gaelic League at home,[15] and between 1907 and 1914 Butte's Irish organizations, including the Ancient Order of Hibernians (AOH), sent $600 home annually to support a travelling Irish-language teacher.[16] Fr Michael Hannan (1878–1928), organized Irish history classes at Central High School. These classes were also offered to the Ladies Auxiliary of the AOH.[17] The Irish were proud celebrants of their native heritage in Butte. Today, the remnants of the Irish influence are still imprinted on the mining city. Dublin Gulch, Corktown, and Hungry Hill are some of the town's neighbourhoods, and three of its mines are known as Druid, Hibernia, and Exiles of Erin.[18]

Seán's aunt, Catherine Ní Shúilleabháin, had come to Butte in the late 1800s, and like many other Irish women in America, she saved enough money to fund the further immigration of siblings and family members. Catherine enticed Seán's older brother Michael to come to Butte with the offer of work at the Moonlight Mine, and Seán soon followed. He in turn brought his younger brother Quinn to the city. Seán left no account of his reasons for leaving Beara, but his personal correspondence indicates that he was hungry to escape the economic oppression of his homeland and its lack of educational opportunities.[19] He likely had never left Kilcatherine Parish before he boarded the steamer *Princess Beara* in Castletownbere. The vessel took him to

Queenstown (now known as Cobh), where he boarded the ocean liner *Lucania* that would take him to New York, whence he would join family and friends in Butte.[20]

OCCUPATION

When Seán disembarked in New York on 13 May 1905 his papers listed his profession as an oiler for boats.[21] His uncle-in-law, William Price, gave him his first mining job at the Moonlight Mine. Butte's unstable economy in 1907–08, coupled with his own private regrets about his lack of formal education, likely inspired him to take advantage of the educational opportunities available to advance his literary skills and professional qualifications. He spent the next few years pursuing his goals with quiet determination. Once he finished his mining shift, he would go to the Butte Public library to study and read. Such was his thirst for learning that the librarians regularly gave him any damaged books they had. His love of literature stayed with him all his life, during which time he amassed an impressive personal library.[22]

Seán's studious habits paid off. He soon qualified as a stationary engineer and was hired by the Anaconda Copper Mining Company. However, his career with the organization came to an abrupt end in 1917. The sight of the Union Jack flying above the mine one day filled him with such fury that he tore it down before anyone could stop him. His employers, many of whom were English, were less than pleased with his acute intolerance for displays of Anglophilia. They blackballed him from ever working with the company again.[23] The company bosses, however, did not reckon with his tenacity and resilience, traits instilled in him as a child on Inishfarnard. The Butte City Directories highlight that he continued to work consistently in the city as an engineer, as a health inspector, and later as a janitor in various schools.[24]

FAMILY TIES

Seán's brother and extended family were already settled in Butte by the time he arrived in town, so it appears that he managed to settle relatively easily in the new city. Not long after he arrived, he met Josephine "Bawn" Murphy (1890–1966). Josephine, or "Jose" as she was known, was to be his constant companion for the rest of his life. She became an integral part of his work with Butte's Irish organizations, accompanying him to meetings and helping out on committees. Jose was born in Butte to Timothy "Tade" Murphy and Julia O'Sullivan of Caherkeem, Beara.[25] Photographic evidence of Seán in his wedding portrait reveals a tall, slim, dark-haired, well-dressed man alongside his dark and petite wife.[26] In fact, most photographs show him wearing a three-piece suit, shirt, and tie, as well as a bowler hat. Apart from a mustache, he is clean-shaven in the photos, and he exudes a regal, authoritative mystique.[27] The couple bought their first home at 802 North Wyoming Street, which lies at the junction of two Irish neighbourhoods, Dublin Gulch and Corktown. Their local parish was St Mary's, and one of Sean's great confidants, the aforementioned Fr Michael Hannan – a radical Irish republican – was their parish priest. Seán and Jose lived soberly and respectably in Butte, and in socio-economic terms their American experience was not atypical. The couple sadly lost eight children.[28] The three surviving children were named Mary Veronica ("Verne") (1911–2005), Eamonn de Valera (1919–1966), and John Patrick Sarsfield ("Fr Sars") (1924–2010). There was clearly no subtlety when it came to Seán's political inclinations.[29]

Haunted by his own lack of education, Seán worked tirelessly to make sure his children had the opportunity to graduate from high school. Verne played a central role in Butte's social organizations and even ran for office as a Democrat. She worked at St James Hospital for a time and then opened a bookstore, the O'Sullivan Bookshop, in the 1940s.[30] Imbued with a love of Catholicism, both Fr Sars and Eamonn entered the priesthood. They were scholars in their own right. Eamonn was highly regarded as a sculptor and poet, while Fr Sars was a well-known local historian and genealogist. Documentation in the O'Sullivan Collection in the Butte–Silver Bow Archives, as well as testimonies from family members and friends, indicate that the Ó Súilleabháin household was harmonious and happy.

SEÁN AND LABOUR

When Seán settled in Butte, nowhere in the United States were working conditions more dangerous, corporate capitalists more repressive, and class conflicts more brutal than in the mining towns of the western Rockies.[31] Moreover, the so-called Gibraltar of Unionism, created in the late 1800s by a unique ethnic alliance between Irish mine owners and miners, was disintegrating rapidly in the face of corporate greed, and workers in the city were becoming increasingly frustrated and militant.[32] Fr Sars described his father as "very strong for the unions."[33] Seán's far-left sympathies in the town are revealed in the contents and tenor of his correspondence with some of the leading American labour activists and his lifelong affiliation with Butte's labour unions. From 1914 through the early 1920s, Butte was wracked by strikes. Seán was a member of the Metal Mine Workers' Union in 1917 when they launched a strike in the wake of the Speculator mine fire that killed 165 miners.[34] While Seán's working-class consciousness probably originated in his personal experiences and observations of society in Beara, Butte likely sharpened his political attitudes.

SEÁN'S POLITICAL EFFORTS

Seán was active in various Irish cultural and political societies in Butte. One of the first organizations he joined was the city's branch of the AOH – no doubt for the valuable social connections and sickness benefits it provided its members.[35] He was a member of the Gaelic League by 1908.[36] His membership in the League brought him into contact with some of Butte's most committed supporters of Irish republicanism. Officially as well as by temperament, Seán was a revolutionary republican. He and his brother Quinn were members of Company A of the Irish Volunteers.[37] Company A was a military branch of the local Irish republican and literary society named after the past revolutionary Robert Emmet.[38] Seán was also a member of the Thomas Ashe Council (the local branch of the American Association for the Recognition of the Irish Republic) and the Sarsfield Social Club (the radical branch of Clan na Gael).[39] There is no extant evidence to suggest that he belonged to the radical Pearse-Connolly Workers Club, but considering the involvement of his close friend Fr Hannan in that organization as well as his own proven involvement with Butte's other Irish radical organizations and unions, it would not be surprising if he did participate in their meetings.[40]

Because of Seán's commitment to Irish republicanism, he was chosen to deliver the welcoming address, in Irish, to Éamon de Valera at the Silver Bow Club in Butte on 8 November 1919. De Valera's warm reception is recorded in the following extract: "President de Valera feelingly responded in Gaelic, touching upon the magnificence of the sentiments expressed, and stated that it was the first illuminated address, in Gaelic, that he had received in America."[41] De Valera and Seán soon became professional and political allies. Seán was a key fundraiser for de Valera in Butte and later helped the Irish leader raise money for the Fianna Fáil election fund and for the founding of the party's newspaper *The Irish Press.* It was through his membership in the Thomas Ashe Council that Seán likely came into frequent contact with James E. Murray (1876-1961), an Irish American lawyer, national president of the American Association for the Recognition of the Irish Republic, and future Montana senator. Murray played a pivotal role in Butte's Irish organizations from the 1920s onwards. Correspondence in Seán's collection informs us that the men were close friends and political confidants, frequently collaborating on local Butte matters as well as Irish political issues. Seán also coordinated the visits of the many Irish dignitaries who came to Butte such as Countess Markievicz (1868–1927), Seán Ó Ceallaigh ("an Sceilg") (1872–1957), and Frank Aiken (1898–1983). Ó Ceallaigh later wrote an account of his time in Montana in which he singled out "Seán Ua Súilleabháin, Gaedheal óg ó dhúthaigh Bhéara" (Sean O'Sullivan, a young Irishman from Beara) as "an té ba dhúthrachtaighe d'ar bhuail liom 'san chathair sin" (the hardest-working person I met in that city).[42]

Strikes, mine closures, and a decline in immigration numbers resulted in an exodus of Irish republicans from Butte in the 1920s.[43] Despite the dwindling numbers, Seán continued to work tirelessly for the Irish community until his death in 1957. In terms of influence and longevity, there were few Irish nationalists to match him in Butte. He played a pivotal yet understated role in the Irish organizations; he did not seek the limelight. As a sketch of his character and a testimony to his valuable work with Butte's political organizations, the following Sarsfield Social Club resolutions of condolence to Seán and Jose on the death of their infant Timothy O'Sullivan in 1926 are worth quoting in full: "Sean O'Sullivan is a loyal and faithful member of our club, whose integrity, courage, and high ideals are unexcelled. A lover of liberty and independence for all peoples, and especially the people of Ireland, who are dear to the hearts of Sean and Mrs O'Sullivan who have at all times aided physically, morally and financially in sustaining and upholding the undivided Republic of Ireland."[44]

THE DEAN OF BUTTE'S IRISH BARDS

The leader of the Gaelic revival movement, Douglas Hyde, visited Butte and Anaconda on his tour of the United States in 1906. Hyde's impassioned speeches and his recognition of the traditional culture of the Butte Irish inspired a flowering of cultural consciousness among the Irish immigrants in the city. The community formally established a branch of Connradh na Gaedhilge (the Gaelic League) on 27 January 1907. The organization enabled Seán and many others to lean into their cultural identity and to embrace Douglas Hyde's vision to "cultivate everything that is most racial, most smacking of the soil, most Gaelic, most Irish."[45]

A primary way that the Gaelic League encouraged the cultivation of Irish tradition was by establishing an Irish-language school for its members, including Seán.[46] Instructors like Séamus Ó Muircheartaigh (1877–1927), president of the Butte branch of the Gaelic League and an indefatigable champion of Irish verse, aided Seán in acquiring literacy in Irish.[47] This gave Seán the opportunity to immerse himself in Irish literature, history, and song, and by the time of the 1916 Easter Rising, he was an accomplished reader and writer. Just a few years later, he was teaching Irish-language classes, imparting his rich knowledge of his native tongue to members of the community.[48] Accounts in local newspapers such as *The Anaconda Standard* and *The Butte Independent* demonstrate that Seán was, to the delight of others, an exponent of his Irish traditions, regularly performing songs and recitations at Gaelic League meetings and *feiseanna ceoil* (Irish music competitions).[49]

After the Irish Rebellion of 1916, concerts and meetings that were once dedicated to the preservation of the Irish language in Butte began focusing on achieving an independent Ireland. Seán ardently supported the cause of independence, while continuing to foster his native culture and language. He sang traditional songs at events and meetings throughout Butte and Anaconda, and his home remained a refuge of Gaelic culture.[50] It is no surprise that he earned the nickname Seán "Irish" along the way.

TRANSCRIPTIONS

Seán retained in his memory hundreds of traditional Irish songs from his youth. It is likely that his membership in the Butte Gaelic League inspired him to start writing down this verse soon after his arrival in Montana. He later preserved his repertoire of works for his children.[51] Between 1914 and 1950, Seán produced five notebooks of Irish manuscript material, much of it transcribed from pre-existing sources, but also including original verse and poetry recalled from his childhood.[52] The notebooks are A5 and smaller in size and are written in ink and pencil. Two contain a handful of English songs and translations, but the majority of recorded verse is in Irish. The contents are not organized in chronological or thematic order, and some transcriptions were begun but not completed. In sum, the habits discernible from Seán's writings indicate that unlike contemporary Irish song collectors like Thomas Griffin (1829–1896) and Pádraig Feiritéar (1856–1924), whose texts were prepared for publication in various Irish American newspapers, his transcriptions were intended for private and familial consumption.

Transcriptions of Recollected Works

Seán's library and collection of newspaper clippings reveal his penchant for eighteenth- and nineteenth-century compositions, so it is not surprising that a large proportion of his transcribed works also pertain to this era. In particular, Seán's appreciation for the *aisling* style of poetry is evident.[53] The socio-cultural conditions and political events of the nineteenth century ensured the potency of prophecy in popular culture, and it is reasonable to assume that Seán's family passed on their appreciation of the poetic form to him.

One of the oldest known political allegorical *aisling* works that Seán recorded is the song "An Ros Gheal Dubh [*sic*]" (Fair Black-Haired Rose).[54] The unknown author sings of his country under the similitude of a distressed maiden to whom he is ardently attached. The song is said to date to the time of Queen Elizabeth in the sixteenth century.[55] "Seán Ó Duibhir a' Ghleanna" (John O'Dwyer of the Glen) is another example of a political *aisling* that Seán preserved in his notebooks.[56] The song laments the peaceful Ireland of the past, her exiles, and the destruction of her ancient families. It was popular throughout the country in the eighteenth and nineteenth centuries.[57] Seán transcribed Corkman Piaras MacGearailt's (1709–1781) "An Caol Druimean Óg" (The Young White-Backed Cow) in March 1936, thirty years after he arrived in Butte.[58] Tadhg Gaelach Ó Súilleabháin (1715–1795) was one of the most renowned poets in nineteenth-century Munster. Seán wrote down his poem "An Craoibhinn Aoibhinn Álainn Óg" (The Pleasant Little Branch). Seán's collection also highlights his interest in and familiarity with the compositions of Eoghan Rua Ó Súilleabháin (1748–1782). Eoghan Rua excelled at the *aisling* genre of poetry and was beloved by the people of Munster; Seán wrote down his "Seothó Thoil"

(The Lullaby).[59] In addition, Seán transcribed from memory such well-known anonymous poems as "A Phlúirín na mBan Donn Óg" (Oh Flower of Young Brown-Haired Women), "Síle Bheag Ní Choindealbháin" (Little Celia Connellan), "Seoladh na nGamhna" (Herding the Calves), and "Aisling an Óig-Fhir" (Young Man's Dream).

Seán also recorded poems specific to Beara. One such piece is "Ráiseanna Bhaile Chaisleáin" (Castletown Races). This song is twenty-five verses in length and revolves around an annual boat race held in Beara in the early 1900s. It depicts the fierce rivalry between the competing crews from Beara, Kerry, and Bantry. Seán's grandfather Seana-Mhícheál is frequently mentioned throughout the song.

Acht air druideam doibh,
Tamal óan dtír,
Ní raibh muintir ár n-áite,
Faoi bhreis imnídhe
Mar daithíach gach aon aca sturugadh Mhichíl,
Sé ag g-cómnaighe chun cínn air na badaibh.[60]

But closing in on them,
Out to sea,
Our people were not
Unnecessarily worried
Because they all recognised Michael's outfit,
And he was always ahead of the other boats.

When one compares Seán's American text with the published Irish version below, it is clear that they are strikingly similar:

Ar druidim amach dhóibh
Ró-fhada ón dtír,
Ní bhíodh muintir ár mbaillne
Fé bhreis imnímh,
Mar d'aithníodh ga' haoinne acu feiste Mhichíl
Is é i gcónaí chun cinn ar na bádaibh.[61]

The latter version was given to Tadhg Ó Murchú in 1939 by Diarmuid "Caobach" Ó hÚrdail of Kilcatherine.[62] Ó hÚrdail revealed that a local teacher by the name of Duibhir (Dwyer) composed the song. Seán corroborates this in his own text. There is no definitive proof of when

Seán wrote down his version of the song, but his text is found in the same notebook as "An Caol Druimeann Óg," transcribed in 1936. If indeed Seán transcribed "Ráiseanna" in the mid-1930s, then his version of the song was recorded earlier than the one given to Ó Murchú.

Seán's Political Poetry

Seán's original compositions were heavily influenced by the *aisling* poetry he transcribed. He took inspiration from poets such as Diarmuid 'na Bolgaí' Ó Sé (c.1755–1846), Máire Bhuidhe Ní Laoghaire (1774–c.1848), and Pádraig Phiarais Cúndún (1777–1857), who continued to use the *aisling* form of poetry to illustrate political thought in the nineteenth century. His works reveal a keen awareness of Irish current affairs in the early 1900s. An independent Gaelic Ireland appeared to be within reach, and those circumstances shaped his writings and give them their distinctive quality.

Seán's *aisling* "Cois na Tuinne" (Beside the Wave) chronicles the political developments in Ireland in the lead-up to the 1916 Rising. The piece emulates the structure of an *aisling* poem: while the author-persona is pondering the difficulties faced by the Irish race, he encounters a beautiful woman (Ireland) and questions whether she is the lady in love with Donal Cam O'Sullivan Beare (1561–1618), or perhaps she is Jason's wife (a reference to the Greek hero).[63] Like many *aislingí* of the eighteenth century, Seán's work is replete with historical and literary references to Irish and Classical literary characters. The female interlocutor is distressed about the political climate in Ireland, but ends her conversation with the poet on a hopeful note, foretelling that Ireland's heroes will rise up against their enemy. The following verse is illustrative of the mood at the close of the poem:

> Óig-bhean mhúinte chalma ná bíodh eagla sa tsaoghal ort,
> Is gearaid uait na tréin-fhir atáid a tearnughadh ort arís,
> Is ní fágaid siad aoin-t-Sasanach a m-baile cuain na sléibhte,
> Na scriosfaidh siad le faobhar neart gach smeirle atá thar tinn,
> Beidh ceol is rinnce is rachmus is an t-aifreann da léaghadh dhúinn,
> Is Connradh geal na Gaedhilge in aoinfheacht beid arís,
> Beidh ceol na n-éan cois calaidhthe is a lúib gach coilleadh craobhaighe,
> Sin críoch anois ar mo scéaltha is ar thréan-guth mo chin.[64]

Young courageous woman, do not be at all scared.
The valiant men are drawing near to you once again,
And as they approach you they will not leave an Englishman in port-town or mountain,
Their swords will destroy the strength of every foreign villain
We will have dancing and prosperity, the celebration of mass for us,
And our beloved Gaelic League once again.
Birdsong will be heard by the shore and on every branch of the forest.
So end my stories, told with raised voice.

Seán's corpus includes another *aisling*, "Bánta Mín Éirinn Glas Óg" (The Lush Green Plains of Ireland). The text was written in 1917 and begins like the previous poem; the poet meets a beautiful lady and consoles her on the fate of Ireland, then tries to persuade her to travel with him overseas:

A spéir-bhean dá n-éaluigh thú líomsa,
Thar sáile go tíribh an cheóil,
Is maordha modhamhail béasach a shuidhefin,
Id t-aice go híntinneach óg,
Nó do leighefainsi scéal ar Oisín dut,
Nó air Dhiarmuid nár claoidh riamh dar –nó,
Nó air an d-trean fhear do thaobhaig thar tuínn chugainn,
Do thuit le Oscar in sa ghleo.[65]

Beautiful maiden, if you were to escape with me,
Overseas to the land of music,
I would sit content and happy
At your side in youthful spirit,
Or I would read you a tale about Oisín,
Or perhaps of indomitable Diarmuid, of course,
Or of the courageous man who came to us from abroad,
And who fell with Oscar in battle.

Once the poet promises never to abandon the *spéirbhean*, she agrees to accompany him abroad.

"Dáil Éireann" is the poem that seemed to resonate most deeply with Irish men and women in Montana and in Ireland. The scene was set for the piece when Éamon de Valera was appointed head of the newly formed Irish Parliament in 1919. A profound sense of relief and optimism permeates this work: relief that the English will no longer have the upper hand in Irish affairs, and optimism for the Irish people, who can once again speak their native language freely. As in "Cois na Tuinne," Seán incorporates strong language and images to express his unwavering support of Irish martyrs:

Grá mo chléibh sibh a chlann na nGaedheal-bhocht,
A chuir le chéile is do réidh an glas,
Do bhí air Eirein aige na méirleaig,
An smáil si n-éitheigh na raibh riamh a gceart,
Atá Séoirse ag beicig mar scatha céise,
Do scaoil fá air aonach romhat amach,
Ó scaramh Eirein leis an g-cráin mí bhéasach,
Ba mheasa tréithe is ba thréine smacht.[66]

You are my beloved, oh children of the misfortunate Irish,
Who united together and broke the lock
That the thieves had placed on Ireland,
The lies and sins committed that were never right.
George is screaming like a bunch of young pigs
That you would send before you to the market,
Ever since Ireland broke free from the ill-bred sow
Of the worst character and the most violent rule.

The fact that this work became the most frequently recited and copied of its author's compositions could indicate the extent of the response to it. Seán composed the work in 1919, the same year that de Valera visited Butte. It was during this stay that the Irish leader discovered that Seán was a talented composer of verse. Fr Sars tells the story that de Valera encouraged Seán to submit his poetry to *Féile Craobh Uí Gramhnaigh* (O'Growney's Irish Language Competition) in San Francisco. Seán took his advice and subsequently won first prize and the Gold Medal for his poem "Dáil Éireann." He was awarded second place the following year and third the year after.

Transcriptions of Irish Immigrant Poetry

Seán was also deeply interested in the works of contemporary Irish immigrant poets in the United States, and his papers contain numerous copies of their poetry. One example is "Ar Maidin ar Fáinne an Lae / Amhrán na Mianach" (At the Breaking of the Day / The Mining Song). The six-verse poem lays bare the harsh reality of a miner's life. Seán Ó Dúbhda maintains that Seámus Feiritéar (1897–1919), his brother Mícheál, and their childhood friend Seán Ruiséal ("Jeaicí Claisín"), composed the work in Butte.[67] The following extracts, which discuss the mining machinery in Butte, highlight the minor variations in Seán's handwritten copy of the work in comparison with the published version found in *Duanaire Duibhneach*: "Beidh maisín go hárd ar barra, is í ag obair le cómhacht an aeir" (A machine will be high on top, working with the power of the air) versus Seán's version, "Atá an maisín go h-árd ann ar barra, is é ag obair le *pour* an éir" (The machine is high on top, working with the power of the air).[68]

Butte welcomed many Irish immigrants from Corca Dhuibhne (Corkaguiny), West Kerry, to the city in the early 1900s. One such character was the aforementioned Séamus Ó Muircheartaigh. "An Spailpín" (The Farmhand), as he was called, reached Butte in 1906 and spent several years working in its mines. Like Seán, he never returned home.[69] His song "Beir mo Bheannacht leat, a Nellie" (Bring My Blessing with You, Nellie) is found in Seán's notebooks. Ó Muircheartaigh composed the text in 1910 when his wife Nellie brought their son Oisín home to Ireland so that he could be immersed in Irish language and tradition. That journey inspired the poet to write the eight-stanza song about his fond memories of his youth in Ireland. The following comparison of Seán's version with the printed copy reveals that apart from slight spelling and grammatical variations, the two texts are identical: "Beir mo bheannacht leat go himeall na toinne, chun na bhfaoileán a luíonn ar an dtráig" versus "Beir mo bheannacht leat go h-iomal na toinne, 's chun an fhaoilean a luidheann ar an dtráig" (Bring my blessing with you to the margin of the waves, to the seagulls that lie on the shore).[70]

Seán's Personal Poetry

The work of Seán's contemporaries may have emboldened him to write about his own personal experiences in the United States. For example, we have a handful of extant *ċaointe* (laments) composed by Seán in memory of friends who passed away. One such *caoineadh* was written for Diarmuid Ó Murchú (1907–1931). The short text reflects the young man's early passing. Much like *caointe* of the seventeenth and eighteenth centuries, Seán's poem praises Diarmuid's life and character. He particularly focuses on the invaluable work his friend undertook for the cause of the Irish language:

Clú agus barra san teangan do fúairis féin,
Dá scríobh dá labairt dá teagasc agus fós dá léigh,
Le aois da maire thú mar a mheasaim is dá ba n-dán duit é,
Bheach leabhair agus stártha go fairsing le fághail id dhiaidh.[71]

You achieved excellence in the language and earned respect
In writing, speaking, teaching and reading it.
Had you lived to a ripe age, and if it had been your destiny,
I believe
You would have left a bountiful body of works in your wake.

It is not known for certain when Seán composed the piece, but it was likely soon after Ó Murchú's death in 1931. In the introduction to the poem, we learn that Diarmuid was born in Dún na Mór (likely Donoughmore), Co. Cork, in 1907. He worked as a bank clerk in Butte, and like many of his contemporaries, he contracted tuberculosis and died in the prime of his life.[72] Seán had spent around twenty-six years in Butte when he wrote this piece. One gets the impression that he had adapted to life there, and the composition further illustrates the central role the Irish language still occupied in his life in the 1930s.

This is the last known original poem that Seán composed. However, he did not completely disengage from writing during his remaining twenty-five years; rather, the form of writing changed. Instead of using poetry to express his political views, he focused on corresponding with friends and fellow Irish nationalists in the United States and Ireland about current events. These letters were written in English and Irish.

CONCLUSION

Seán died on 20 June 1957 at the age of seventy-five. His funeral was as modest and self-effacing as his life.[73] The obituaries do not contain any grandiloquent graveside speeches, and his passing did not garner much attention outside of Butte.

Much has been omitted from this short sketch of Seán's life and works. There has been no space to fully examine the contents of his vast library, or his scrapbooks and correspondence. Also, his wife Jose's tireless involvement in Irish cultural and political societies has been largely omitted, as have been the endeavours of Seán's children to preserve their father's heritage and legacy. However, it is hoped that this chapter demonstrates the importance of further investigation of Gaelic manuscript repositories in North America, an area that has not been examined to any great extent so far.

The former Irish ambassador to the United States John J. Hearne (1893–1969), who visited Butte in 1952, described Seán as "one of the noblest Irishmen in America whose love and labour for Ireland all his life have long since become part of the history of Ireland in our time."[74] Seán's devotion to the Irish language, his copying of texts, and his original compositions correct the overriding image of Butte as a rowdy mining frontier town. Instead, they shed light on the cultural richness prevailing among the city's people and their organizations.

NOTES

I am grateful to a number of people for the completion of this chapter. In Butte, and elsewhere in Montana, I would like to thank Ellen Crain and all the wonderful staff of the Butte–Silver Bow Archives for facilitating access to their manuscript collections and for granting me permission to quote from them in this chapter. I learned of the O'Sullivan Collection from Dr Traolach Ó Ríordáin, Director of Irish Studies, University of Montana, Missoula. I am grateful to him for the time, knowledge and assistance he has provided in my completion of this research. In Ireland, I am grateful to numerous members of the Beara community, who spared no efforts whatsoever in assisting me in my research on Inishfarnard. I owe a special debt of gratitude to my PhD supervisor, Dr Cornelius G. Buttimer, Modern Irish, University College Cork, for his wisdom, his guidance, and his support of this research over the years.

1 This chapter is based primarily on papers belonging to the Seán and Josephine O'Sullivan Collection (O'Sullivan Coll), Butte–Silver Bow Archives (BSBA), Butte, Montana. When the last member of Seán's immedi-

ate family (Fr Sars) passed away in 2010, Dr Traolach Ó Ríordáin was instrumental in ensuring that the collection would be housed at the BSBA.

2 See Nilsen, "Thinking of Monday"; Nilsen, "'The language.'"

3 Verling, *Mioscais*, 27.

4 1940 US Census, Silver Bow County, Montana, Butte, enumeration district 47-5, p. 4A, household 89, John Sullivan.

5 Naturalization Records, vol. 4, BSBA; Verling, *Mioscais*, 31.

6 Emmons, *Butte Irish*, 15.

7 Ibid.

8 Fr Patrick Brosnan to his father, 18 February 1917, Patrick Brosnan Letters, David Emmons Collection, BSBA.

9 Emmons, *Butte Irish*, 259.

10 Ibid., 20.

11 Malone et al., *Montana*, 205.

12 On Irish immigrant experiences on the east coast, see Meagher, *Inventing Irish America*; Barrett, *Irish Way*; Miller, "Lost Republics," 117–42.

13 Hyde, *Mo Thurus*, 129–30.

14 "A.O.H. Picnic," *The Anaconda Standard*, 28 June 1892, 3; "Gaelic Football Is to Be Revived Here," *The Anaconda Standard*, 19 April 1913, 4.

15 Ní Bhroiméil, *Building Irish Identity*, 80.

16 Ibid., 90.

17 Diary of Fr Michael J. Hannan (copy), 9 April 1922, David Emmons Collection, BSBA. Hannan was born in Kilcoolen, Co. Limerick, and came to Montana in 1906. He was appointed associate pastor at St Mary's Parish, Butte, in 1910. On his involvement in Butte's Irish political organizations, see Emmons, "Tower of Strength."

18 Hungry Hill is the highest point in the Caha mountain range. The Irish is Cnoc Daod; *cnoc* means "hill" and *daod* means "angry." In an email to a Beara mailing list, author and local historian Riobard O'Dwyer shares the following piece of folklore about how the hill got its name: "It is said that years ago at the time Berehaven Harbour was a base for the British navy, when the sailors broke rules or stepped out of line in any way, their punishment was to walk all the way to the top of the hill … By the time they got back down, they were hungry … Thus the renaming of it as 'Hungry' Hill." RootsWeb (beara@rootsweb.com), 7 September 1999, http://archiver.rootsweb.ancestry.com.

19 Seán Ó Súilleabháin to Pádraig Ó Súilleabháin, n.d., box 4, folder 1, item 13, O'Sullivan Coll, BSBA.

20 O'Sullivan interview, The Gathering; Naturalization Records, vol. 4, BSBA.

21 Naturalization Records, vol. 4, BSBA.

22 While some of the books from Seán's collection have been scattered throughout the United States and Ireland, the majority of his library is contained in boxes 6–18, O'Sullivan Coll, BSBA.
23 O'Sullivan interview, The Gathering.
24 *Butte City Directory*, 1921–49.
25 Josephine Murphy, certificate of baptism from the Church of St Patrick, box 1, folder 7, item 1, O'Sullivan Coll, BSBA.
26 Wedding portrait of Seán and Josephine Ó Súilleabháin, box 5, item B, O'Sullivan Coll, BSBA.
27 Sarsfield O'Sullivan Photograph Collection, BSBA.
28 Sarsfield O'Sullivan, "The O'Sullivan Family History," box 1, folder 11, item 1, O'Sullivan Coll, BSBA.
29 Seán's eldest son was christened in honour of the Irish leader Éamon de Valera; Patrick Sarsfield (*c.* 1660–1693) was one of Ireland's best-known soldiers and Jacobite leaders.
30 *Butte City Directory*, 1945–56.
31 Miller, "Lost Republics," 125.
32 See Emmons, *Butte Irish*.
33 O'Sullivan interview, The Gathering.
34 Emmons, *Butte Irish*, 364.
35 O'Sullivan interview, The Gathering.
36 AOH Ledger, box 17, folder 5, AOH Collection, BSBA.
37 Ibid.
38 Emmons, *Butte Irish*, 311.
39 Seán was a member of the Butte branch of the Friends of Irish Freedom until de Valera split with the organization in 1920 and formed the American Association for the Recognition of the Irish Republic. The Sarsfield Social Club was founded by Seán's good friend Fr Hannan, and Seán was one of its most prominent members. See Emmons, "Tower of Strength," 104–5.
40 The Pearse Connolly Club was formed in Butte at the height of the Irish conflict in 1916. Members of the organization were united in their respect for the poetic nationalism of Pearse and the revolutionary socialism of Connolly. See Emmons, "Tower of Strength," 90.
41 *Proceedings and Activities*, 3. This can be consulted in box 4, folder 8, item 6, O'Sullivan Coll, BSBA.
42 Seán Ó Ceallaigh, "Gaedhil do Casadh Orm i gCéin." *Fáinne an Lae*, 20 March 1926, 2.
43 See Emmons, *Butte Irish*, 398–409.
44 Sarsfield Social Club resolutions of condolence from Pat Murphy, J.H.

O'Meara, and J.M. Raleigh to Seán and Josephine O'Sullivan, 5 November 1926, box 4, folder 7, item 8, O'Sullivan Coll, BSBA.

45 Ó Giolláin, *Locating Irish Folklore*, 117; Connradh na Gaedhilge dues card, box 4, folder 11, item 1, O'Sullivan Coll, BSBA.

46 Gaelic League, *Irish Headline Copy Book*. Seán's copy can be found in box 2, folder 9, items 3 and 4, O'Sullivan Coll, BSBA.

47 NFC 1576:322–3.

48 Diary of Fr Michael J. Hannan (copy), 12 February 1922, David Emmons Collection, BSBA.

49 "Gaelic League," *The Butte Independent*, 10 September 1910, 5.

50 Seán Ó Súilleabháin to Sarse (Sarsfield O'Sullivan), 7 March, year unknown, box 4, folder 5, item 12, O'Sullivan Coll.

51 It is worth noting that more Irish manuscript sources survive for the eighteenth and nineteenth centuries together than for any other era in the Gaelic past. It is reasonable to assume that Seán was aware of scribal activity in Beara. On Gaelic literature of this period, see Buttimer, "Gaelic Literature."

52 Seán Ó Súilleabháin, transcriptions, box 2, folders 1–4, O'Sullivan Coll, BSBA.

53 The allegorical *aisling* or vision poem was one of the most popular forms used by poets in eighteenth-century Irish composition. *Aisling* poems depict an Irish-speaking *spéirbhean* (beautiful woman) offering the poet a message of future deliverance from English rule.

54 Seán Ó Súilleabháin, transcription, "An Ros Gheal Dubh [*sic*]," box 2, folder 2, item 1, O'Sullivan Coll, BSBA.

55 Walsh, *Irish Popular Songs*, 23.

56 Seán Ó Súilleabháin, transcription, "Seán O Duibhir a' Ghleanna," box 2, folder 3, item 1, O'Sullivan Coll, BSBA.

57 Hardiman, *Irish Minstrelsy*, 8–9.

58 Seán Ó Súilleabháin, transcription, "An Caol Druimean Óg," box 2, folder 3, item 1, O'Sullivan Coll, BSBA.

59 Walsh, *Irish Popular Songs*, 27; Seán Ó Súilleabháin, transcription, "Seothó thoil na goil go foil," box 2, folder 2, item 1, O'Sullivan Coll, BSBA.

60 Seán Ó Súilleabháin, transcription, "Raiseanna Bhaile Chaisleáin Bhéara," box 2, folder 3, item 1, O'Sullivan Coll, BSBA. I am responsible for line breaks and capitalization in quoted passages from the transcriptions. I have inserted <h> in place of the Irish *ponc* [dot] to indicate lenition, but I have not otherwise amended the author's spelling.

61 Verling, *Mioscais*, 328.

62 Ibid., 322.

63 Donal Cam O'Sullivan Beare, Prince of Beare, First Count of Berehaven, was

the last independent ruler of the O'Sullivan Beara sept. For further information on Donal Cam, see Sullivan, *Bantry, Berehaven*.

64 Seán Ó Súilleabháin, transcription, "Cois na Tuinne," box 2, folder 1, item 1, O'Sullivan Coll, BSBA.

65 Seán Ó Súilleabháin, transcription, "Banta mhín Eirin ghlas og [*sic*]," box 2, folder 1, item 1, O'Sullivan Coll, BSBA.

66 Seán Ó Súilleabháin, transcription, "An Dáil Eireann, 1919," box 2, folder 1, item 1, O'Sullivan Coll, BSBA.

67 Ó Dubhda, *Duanaire Duibhneach*, 127.

68 Ibid., 131; Seán Ó Súilleabháin, transcription, "Air Meidin le fainne an lae," box 2, folder 1, item 1, O'Sullivan Coll, BSBA.

69 Mac Gearailt, *An Blas Muimhneach*, 3. For further information about Ó Muircheartaigh's life and works, see Breandán Feiritéar's documentary *An Scéal ar Butte* (The Story of Butte).

70 Mac Gearailt, *An Blas Muimhneach*, 4; Seán Ó Súilleabháin, transcription, "Beir mo Bheannacht leat go h-Eirenn," box 2, folder 2, item 1, O'Sullivan Coll, BSBA.

71 Seán Ó Súilleabháin, transcription, "Air bhás Dhiarmuda Uí Mhurc," box 2, folder 1, item 1, O'Sullivan Coll, BSBA.

72 State of Montana, Bureau of Vital Statistics, Standard Certificate of Death for Jeremiah Murphy, 6 March 1931, File no. 37474, Death Records Collection, BSBA; "Jeremiah Murphy Dies," *The Montana Standard*, 7 March 1931, 7.

73 "Sons Celebrate O Sullivan Mass," *The Montana Standard*, 23 June 1957, 7.

74 John J. Hearne to Seán Ó Súilleabháin, 12 June 1957, box 4, folder 4, item 31, O'Sullivan Coll, BSBA.

BIBLIOGRAPHY

Barrett, James R. *The Irish Way: Becoming American in the Multiethnic City*. New York: Penguin, 2013.

Butte City Directory. Butte: Brinck and Malone Advertising Engineers, 1926–27; Salt Lake City R.L. Polk and Co., 1921–25, 1927–49. Published annually.

Buttimer, Cornelius G. "Gaelic Literature and Contemporary Life in Cork, 1700–1840." In *Cork History and Society: Interdisciplinary Essays on the History of an Irish County*, ed. Patrick O'Flanagan and Cornelius G. Buttimer. Dublin: Geography Publications, 1993.

Emmons, David. *The Butte Irish: Class and Ethnicity in an American Mining Town, 1875–1925*. Champaign: University of Illinois Press, 1990.

– "A Tower of Strength to the Movement: Father Michael Hannan and the Irish Republic." *American Journal of Irish Studies* 12 (2015): 77–116.

Gaelic League. *Irish Headline Copy Book.* Dublin: Browne and Nolan, n.d.

Hardiman, James. *Irish Minstrelsy, or, Bardic Remains of Ireland: With English Poetical Translations.* London: Joseph Robins, 1831.

Hyde, Douglas. *Mo Thurus go hAmerice: Nó Imeasg na nGaedheal ins an Oileán Úr.* Dublin: Oifig Díolta Foilseacháin Rialtais, 1937.

Mac Gearailt, Breandán. *An Blas Muimhneach.* Dublin: Coiscéim, 2007.

Malone, Michael P., Richard B. Roeder, and William L. Lang. *Montana: A History of Two Centuries.* Seattle: University of Washington Press, 1995.

Meagher, Timothy J. *Inventing Irish America: Generation, Class, and Ethnic Identity in a New England City, 1880–1928*. Indiana: University of Notre Dame Press, 2002.

Miller, Kerby A. "Lost Republics: The Cashman Brothers in Ireland and America, 1870s–1920s." *American Journal of Irish Studies* 12 (2015): 117–42.

Ní Bhroiméil, Úna. *Building Irish Identity in America, 1870–1915: The Gaelic Revival.* Dublin: Four Courts Press, 2003.

Nilsen, Kenneth E. "'The language that the strangers do not know': The Galway Gaeltacht of Portland, Maine, in the Twentieth Century." In *They Change Their Sky: The Irish in Maine*, ed. Michael C. Connolly, 297–339. Orono: University of Maine Press.

– "Thinking of Monday: Irish Speakers of Portland, Maine." *Éire-Ireland* 25, no. 1 (1990): 3–19.

Ó Dubhda, Seán. *Duanaire Duibhneach.* Dublin: Oifig Dhíolta Foilseachán Rialtais, 1933.

Ó Giolláin, Diarmuid. *Locating Irish Folklore: Tradition, Modernity, Identity.* Cork: Cork University Press, 2000.

Proceedings and Activities of the Thomas Ashe Council of the A.A.R.I.R. Butte: Butte Independent Print, n.d.

Sullivan, T.D. *Bantry, Berehaven, and the O'Sullivan Sept.* Dublin: Sealy, Bryers, and Walker, 1908.

Verling, Máirtín. *Mioscais na gCumar: Béaloideas agus Seanchas ó Bhéarra.* An Díseart, An Daingean: An Sagart, 2010.

Walsh, Edward. *Irish Popular Songs.* Dublin: W.H. Smith, 1883.

ARCHIVAL COLLECTIONS

Death Records Collection, MC0398: Seán and Josephine O'Sullivan Collection (O'Sullivan Coll), Naturalization Records Collection, OC012: AOH Collection, PH212: Sarsfield O'Sullivan Photograph Collection, and SM059: David Emmons Collection. Butte–Silver Bow Archives (BSBA), Butte, MT.

Main Manuscript Collection (NFC) and Schools' Manuscript Collection (NFCS). Irish National Folklore Collection, University College Dublin.

Montana. Silver Bow County. 1940 US Census, population schedule. National Archives. Digital images. 1940census.archives.gov.

The Gathering: Collected Oral Histories of the Irish in Montana. Mansfield Library Archives, University of Montana, Missoula, MT.

9

"Agus cé'n chaoi ar thaithnigh na Canadas leat?" (And How Did You Like Canada?): Irish-Language Canadian Novels from the 1920s and 1930s

Pádraig Ó Siadhail

Kenneth E. Nilsen's posthumously published essay on the Irish language in eastern Canada in the years 1750 to 1900 showcased his extensive research into, and expansive knowledge of, the presence of Irish speakers and their literary footprint in that region.[1] It may seem strange to commence this discussion of early twentieth-century Irish-language novels about Canada by referring to a work noted by Professor Nilsen, namely, a mid-eighteenth-century macaronic poem set in Newfoundland, part of the earliest body of extant work in Irish from North America.[2] In Donncha Rua Mac Conmara's "As I was walking one evening fair / Is mé go déanach i mBaile Sheáin" (And I lately in St John's), the English-language lines relay the narrator's positive experiences of the town and its inhabitants, including the womenfolk, as well as his loyal sentiments toward the British Crown and, particularly, George II and the House of Hanover. But the material in Irish subverts these statements, most tellingly in its pro-Jacobite closing lines, "Is a Chríost go bhfeiceadsa iad dá gcárnadh / Ag an mac seo ar fán uainn ag dul don Fhrainc" (Christ, may I see them pounded / by your son separated from us in France).[3] Key to the poem is the sense that bilingual Irish- and English-speaking insiders would understand the context, the subtext, and the poem's political message, whereas unilingual anglophone outsiders would miss the satire and the poet's true intention. As we will see, this issue of different languages and different messages represents a significant point of divergence between Irish-language novels about Irish immigrants in Canada published in the 1920s and 1930s and similar-themed English-language texts published from the late nineteenth century to the present day. In the former, the main Irish-born characters return to Ireland; in the latter, their counterparts remain in Canada.

In this chapter, I outline and discuss the Canadian content in novels in Irish from the early decades of the twentieth century, compare these with Irish Canadian novels in English, and attempt to explain their contrasting approaches to settling in Canada.[4]

IRISH-LANGUAGE CANADIAN NOVELS

There are two main categories of English-language novels about the Irish immigrating to Canada. The first, historical fiction, has two subgenres. Patrick Slater's *The Yellow Briar* (1933) and Kathleen Coburn's *The Grandmothers* (1949) are examples of what Jason King terms "Irish-Canadian immigrant memoirs," in which the narrators recount their own lives or the lives of their families.[5] A larger group of historical novels is set against the backdrop of the Great Famine and the consequent communal upheaval and emigration of the novels' characters. Prime examples of these texts include Robert Sellar's "The Summer of Sorrow" (1895); Don Akenson's *At Face Value: The Life and Times of Eliza McCormack / John White* (1990); Jane Urquhart's *Away* (1993); and Peter Behrens's *The Law of Dreams* (2006), winner of the 2006 Governor General's Literary Award. There was a lengthy gap – close to a century – between the publication of Sellar's "The Summer of Sorrow," the first Canadian Great Famine novel, and the other novels, all published in the 1990s and 2000s when there was fresh interest in the Great Famine surrounding its sesquicentennial commemoration. But it was Sellar, a Scottish-born Quebec-based newspaperman hostile to the Catholic authorities, who created the template for Canadian Irish Famine works, not least of all by focusing on Grosse Île, the quarantine island in the Saint Lawrence River and burial site for thousands of Irish Catholic Great Famine refugees. In "The Summer of Sorrow," Sligoman Gerald Keegan has kept a diary detailing his community's departure from Ireland, their ocean crossing, and their harrowing experiences on Grosse Île. Keegan dies on the island, but his diary survives and forms the centrepiece of Sellar's story. The rewriting and repackaging of "The Summer of Sorrow," first as *The Voyage of the Naparima: A Story of Canada's Island Graveyard* and later as *Famine Diary: Journey to a New World*, remains a cause célèbre in the world of Irish Studies in Canada and Irish Famine discourse in general.[6] *Famine Diary*, marketed as Keegan's real-life eyewitness journal, was a bestseller in Ireland in the early 1990s.[7]

The second category of English-language novels tells of more recent families or individuals moving to Canada from Ireland in circumstances less traumatic than those of the Great Famine. A leading example is Brian Moore's *The Luck of Ginger Coffey* (1960), winner of the Governor General's Award for Fiction in 1960. The Coffeys, a Dublin family, are newly arrived in Montreal. The father, Ginger, believes himself entitled to easy advancement in their new home, only to learn painfully that, like many other immigrants, he must start at the bottom of the socio-economic ladder. Another example is Emma Donoghue's *Landing* (2007), a same-sex love story about Síle O'Shaughnessy, a Dublin flight attendant, and her long-distance love-interest, Jude, a museum curator in small-town Ontario. At the novel's end, Síle moves to Ontario. In both novels, the Irish characters are independent immigrants unconnected to historic or contemporary Irish communities in Canada.

In all these transnational novels in English, Irish immigrants make their home in Canada, although, in this age of jet travel, Síle in *Landing* plans to make occasional visits back to Ireland. Undoubtedly, the new arrivals will face challenges as they adjust to the host country. But even in the late nineteenth-century "Summer of Sorrow," a work in which the main characters perish, we encounter other Irish who settle successfully in Canada. Ellen brings word to her Canadian-based uncle that their relative, Gerald Keegan, is on Grosse Île. The uncle recounts Ellen's subsequent life: "What came of the colleen? She left us that fall. Her mother's brother in county Kent wrote for her. She married a storekeeper in Chatham, who left her well off."[8] Clearly, Ellen has landed on her feet. Another example from that text draws on the trope of the "peaceable kingdom," which posits that Canada is a place where immigrants can lay aside ancient conflicts from their homelands. Foes from Sligo, Monaghan, a Catholic, and Stanhope, an Orangeman, reconcile as they recover on Grosse Île. Keegan writes in his diary: "The two old enemies are the most cordial of friends and will soon be able to leave. They have agreed to go with the survivors of their families to the London [Ontario] district and take up land together. Both are industrious and steady and having buried their senseless hatred will be of mutual help to one another. Both have money enough to start them."[9] That new start will be in Canada. These characters will never see their homeland again.

In *The Luck of Ginger Coffey*, the Coffeys appear destined to return home, branded as failures for not succeeding in forging a life for themselves in North America. But even as Ginger's world disintegrates, there are hints that the family's circumstances will improve in Montreal. Although the novel's ending leaves their future in Canada undetermined, the one certainty is that they will not return to Ireland. In English-language novels, it is the next generation or their offspring who visit Ireland, as in Maurice Leitch's *Poor Lazarus* (1969), Brian Moore's *The Mangan Inheritance* (1979), and Charles Foran's *Kitchen Music* (1994).

EARLY IRISH-LANGUAGE CANADIAN NOVELS

Surprisingly, perhaps, a cluster of Irish-language novels published in the 1920s and 1930s have Canadian content. Notable examples are Seán Óg Ó Caomhánaigh's *Fánaí* (Wanderer, 1927) and *Onncail Seárlaí* (Uncle Charley, 1930) by "Marbhán," the pen name for Seán Ó Ciarghusa. *Fánaí* is an adventure and love story in the tradition of the dime-store novel. Its author lived in the United States between 1914 and 1922, including a period in the Dakotas, the novel's setting.[10] Seán Ó Lonargáin, *Fánaí*'s peripatetic hero and Oscar Wilde aficionado, arrives in Pembina, North Dakota, finds work on a farm, and quickly falls for and secretly marries the farmer's sister, before falling afoul of two thugs, one of whom is Pinn, a man of European and Native American heritage described in the novel as a *leathfholaíocht* (mixed-blood). After years of forced separation, Ó Lonargáin returns to Pembina to settle scores and reunite with his wife and child.

Pembina is three miles from the Canadian border.[11] It is evident from textual references that Prohibition was in effect in North Dakota at the time. Therefore, when the farmhands wish to celebrate, they head across the border to Tábhairne na hAbhann Deirge (the Red River Tavern) in Emerson, Manitoba.[12] As Manitoba introduced Prohibition in 1916, we can set the novel, whose plot stretches across five years, in the years before 1916. As portrayed in *Fánaí*, Canada is the go-to place for recreation. It is also a handy spot to commit murder without fear of detection. Prior to the novel's dénouement, Pinn schemes to take Ó Lonargáin on a final journey northward: "Mheallfadh sé an leathamadán trasna na teorainn go Ceanada. Ba bheag an nath aige ina ghliocas féin an leathamadán a chur ar stealladh na ngrást ar meisce. Chuirfeadh sé deoch suain nó deoch mhearbhaill agus an chuid eile – b'fhurasta sin"[13] (He would coax the half-wit across the border to Canada. It wouldn't take much to get him drunk. He would drug him and then – the rest would be easy).

Although Canada is never named, significant sections of *Onncail Seárlaí* take place there. Nominally, *Onncail Seárlaí* consists of the lead character's reminiscences of his spell in North America. But the reader quickly learns that it is an extended tall tale. As though the author had compiled his list of the Seven Wonders of North America based on Irish readers' preconceptions, Seárlaí survives encounters with an iceberg, polygamous Mormons, Native warriors, and the 1906 San Francisco Earthquake. The Canadian content commences when Seárlaí prospects for gold in the "Trondiuc" – an approximation of the Indigenous name for the Tr'ondëk River, known to European Americans as the Klondike – before searching for the Northwest Passage and the North Pole. In Seárlaí's hyperbolic narrative, North America is a small place where the novel's characters regularly cross paths. One senses that Ó Ciarghusa drew on printed sources for his descriptions of places such as Dawson City and Herschel Island in Yukon, and for his material on the lives of the Inuit (*na hEscamótaigh* [the Eskimos], according to the convention of the time) above the Arctic Circle. Disappointingly, his portrayal of Indigenous peoples is stereotypically one-dimensional. Nevertheless, there are realistic patches in this cock-and-bull tale that would not be out of place in the celebrated non-fiction account in Irish of the Yukon Gold Rush, Micí Mac Gabhann's *Rotha Mór an tSaoil*, available in English translation as *The Hard Road to Klondike*.[14]

In addition, a handful of translations into Irish from our period are set in Canada. Noteworthy examples include Jack London's Klondike yarns: *The Call of the Wild* (1903), translated by Niall Ó Domhnaill as *Scairt an Dúthchais* (1932), and Tadhg Ó Cúrnáin's translation of *White Fang* (1906) as *Mac an Mhachtíre* (1936). In Louis Hémon's *Maria Chapdelaine* (1933), translated from French by Risteárd Ó Foghludha, the French Canadian heroine must choose between three Québécois suitors: the frequently absent woodsman, the stay-at-home farmer, and the American-based city dweller. Following the death of her true love, the woodsman, Maria rejects the temptations of urban America and settles for the farmer, thereby dedicating herself to her home community's future well-being. The novel celebrates the spirit of

Québécois rural society. Ironically, however, the author was not French Canadian. Louis Hémon (1880–1913), born in Brest in Britanny, only moved to Quebec in 1911. He died prematurely in Ontario a year before his novel was published.[15]

The core of this chapter will focus on three realistic novels in Irish from the 1920s and 1930s, all of them partly set in Canada: *Cúrsaí Thomáis* (Concerning Thomas, 1927) by "M.," the pen name of Éamonn Mac Giolla Iasachta or, as he is better known, Edward MacLysaght, the author of standard reference texts on Irish family names and one-time Chief Herald of Ireland; *Cailín na Gruaige Duinne* (The Brown-Haired Girl, 1932) by Úna Bean Uí Dhiosca;[16] and *Éan Cuideáin* (Strange Bird, 1936) by Pádhraic Óg Ó Conaire, no relation to the acclaimed author Pádraic Ó Conaire. These novels have more in common with English-language works such as *The Luck of Ginger Coffey* and *Landing* than with the historical novels in English. The Irish texts, all of which are set in the early twentieth century, do not mention the Great Famine or Grosse Île. (One striking feature of modern Irish-language literature is the paucity of creative works dealing with the Famine.) The main characters in *Cúrsaí Thomáis* and *Cailín na Gruaige Duinne* originally left Ireland for personal reasons. Emigration is the norm in Connemara in *Éan Cuideáin*, but the novel's protagonist declares that it was a trouncing administered to him by his schoolteacher that caused him to leave home.[17] In the three novels, the characters are not members of recognizable Irish communities in Canada, although they occasionally meet fellow Irish. However, there is one fundamental difference between these works and all the coming-to-Canada novels in English. While the Irish characters in the English-language books remain in Canada, the lead figures in the Irish-language novels return to Ireland.

A close examination of these Irish-language novels brings to light nuances in their individual treatment of immigration to Canada and reverse migration to Ireland. Also, Ó Conaire's *Éan Cuideáin* has a plot twist that separates it from the other novels. All of this sets the scene for a discussion of why the return migration trope was prominent in these 1920s and 1930s novels.

CÚRSAÍ THOMÁIS

In July 1913, while on a world tour, Éamonn Mac Giolla Iasachta and his brother landed on Vancouver Island. In his diary, Mac Giolla

Iasachta described meeting with friends and camping "ag an rinn is faide amach" (on the farthest peninsula). He also met a distant relative who was "ag obair i gceann de na campaí ag glanadh crann – agus chuaigh mé leis ag logáil na gcrann leis na daoine eile" (working in one of the camps clearing trees – and I went with him logging trees with the other people).[18] These autobiographical incidents provide the opening for *Cúrsaí Thomáis* (1927), the earliest of the three Canadian novels under discussion.

The book is a first-person narrative by Tomás Mac Aonghusa of his life from 1905 until the Irish War of Independence. The story begins with Tomás recalling a chance encounter that would change the direction of his life. On furlough from his lumberjack job and from the work camp, he pitches his tent at Lazo Beach outside Comox on Vancouver Island. Like Ó Lonargáin in *Fánaí*, Mac Aonghusa is an educated man. Having quarrelled with his father in Waterford, he left the family farm for North America, where, for three years, he has earned his living by hard manual work. We learn little about those years, while Mac Aonghusa summarizes his experiences in the work camp and his relationships with fellow workers:

> Níor réitigh lucht an champa liom: Rúiseánaigh dhúsmánta, Sorchaigh chúlánta, Albanaigh dhúra, agus clocha reatha gan chúnlach ó gach aon áit sa domhan braonach so. Bhídís róghruama iontu féin agus róshollúnta, fiú amháin agus iad ag gabháil den ragairne deireadh seachtaine – ragairne, slán mar a instear é, ná bíodh aon ní ragairneach ag baint leis ach amháin an méid a d'óltaí.[19]

> I did not get on with the occupants of the camp: morose Russians, reticent Swedes, dour Scots, and drifters from all parts of the world. They were too cheerless and too solemn, even when they were at their weekend revelry – revelry, to be truthful, that had no revelling about it except the amount that they'd drink.

Instead, the focus is on meeting Stiofán Mac Conmara from Co. Clare at Lazo Beach – an encounter that leads to Mac Aonghusa's decision to return with Mac Conmara to farm in Ireland, where the rest of the novel takes place. The Canadian material, one chapter in length, is a prologue for the main action in Ireland, which takes up the next twenty-four chapters.

Unlike the other two Irish-language Canadian novels, Mac Giolla Iasachta's is available in English as *The Small Fields of Carrig* (1929), translated by E. O'Clery. The identity of the translator remains uncertain, though E. O'Clery seems not to be an authorial pseudonym.[20] But one searches in vain for references to Lazo Beach, Comox, Vancouver Island, or even Canada in O'Clery's version of Chapter 1. In the translation, the Irishmen's encounter takes place in an unnamed location in the American West.[21] O'Clery explains in a note: "I have deliberately condensed the first chapter into the very narrow limits of these two pages."[22] The author had given him permission to shorten the chapter and to relegate Chapters 3 and 4 to an appendix. Indeed, according to O'Clery, Mac Giolla Iasachta urged him to excise from his translation several other pages from the original text.[23] O'Clery retains a later reference to Comox but adds an explanatory footnote: "A reference to Tom's first meeting with Stephen – Chapter I of the original."[24] The outcome of these decisions is that Canada is almost completely erased from the translation.

The other direct references to the narrator's time in Canada in the original text and the translation relate to incidents in Vancouver. One occasion is a fight, "nuair a leagas breamhais mór de bhragaire a shíl snáth bán do dhéanamh d'Éireannach ciúin" (when I knocked out a big loutish braggard who had tried to pick on a quiet Irishman).[25] Another is an alcohol-fuelled tryst with a prostitute, revelry apparently more to Mac Aonghusa's delectation than socializing with fellow workers. We learn about this event when Mac Aonghusa and Mac Conmara, in confessional mood, chat in the latter's farmhouse in Co. Clare. This scene reaches its dramatic conclusion when Mac Conmara reveals that he was married to a woman of mixed racial heritage in North America, but that she committed suicide when he rejected their black-skinned child.[26] Mac Aonghusa airs his own skeletons in the cupboard:

> Dúrt leis go raibh mo dhrochthréithe féin ag baint liomsa chomh maith le cách. D'inseas dó rud a thit amach dom i gcathair Vancouver. Is cuimhin liom go raibh rud beag náire orm agus saghas mústar san am céanna agus mé ag insint mo scéil.
>
> "Tuigim," arsa Stiofán, nuair a bhí deireadh agam. "Is beag duine a bhog amach óna thír féin ná fuil an rud céanna le hinsint aige. Ach nach suarach an bheart é ina dhiaidh san is uile. Níos ísle nuair a chuimhnítear a neamhthairbheacht a bhíonn sé. Uch, cá

bhfios duit nach é fear na ngág a ghlan do bhróga cúpla uair a chloig roimhe sin a bhéadh ag teacht amach an doras céanna i do choinne agus b'fhéidir é ar meisce leis."[27]

I mentioned that I had my own share of bad traits as much as anyone. I described an adventure – if I may call it so – that happened to me in Vancouver. I remember the feeling of half-ashamed complacency with which I related it.

"I understand," said Stephen, when I had finished. "There are not many that have knocked around the world a bit who haven't a similar story to tell. But after all, isn't it a poor kind of thing to do – when you consider how ineffectual it is, it places a person on a lower level than Ned's boar beyond. Ugh, how do you know that the man you may meet coming out the door against you, drunk perhaps, isn't the very Chink that cleaned your boots a couple of hours earlier."[28]

Beyond the hints about the narrator's activities, this piece is striking for terminological reasons. In the absence of an Irish-language pejorative for a Chinese person, the author took the English pejorative and worked backwards to fashion an Irish equivalent – *fear na ngág* = man of the chinks = Chink. While the slur is somewhat occluded in the Irish-language text and depends on the reader knowing English, O'Clery's translation makes no attempt to conceal the racist expression.

In the context of Mac Aonghusa and Mac Conmara's shared story, their time together in Canada is short but pivotal. They return home with work skills and life experiences that benefit them in Ireland. But just as they cared little about being in Canada – it is only another temporary location – they have no strong views about leaving it as they have no roots there. Their Canadian soujourn is merely a prelude to the main action back in Ireland.

CAILÍN NA GRUAIGE DUINNE

Éamonn Mac Giolla Iasachta visited Canada while on his world trip. Úna Bean Uí Dhiosca spent a longer time there. According to a biographical sketch, having qualified as a teacher in Ireland, she moved to Canada: "I rith na tréimhse i gCeanada bhí sí ag múineadh inimirceach ón nGearmáin agus ó Shasana i mbothán adhmaid i Sascatchewan. Bhain sí úsáid as a bhfaca sí thall ina húrscéal *Cailín na Gruaige Duinne* (1932). D'fhill sí ar Éirinn arís i gceann trí bliana"[29] (During the time in Canada she taught immigrants from Germany and England in a wooden hut in Saskatchewan. She used what she saw over there in her novel, *Cailín na Gruaige Duinne* [1932]. She returned to Ireland after three years). Regrettably, we cannot confirm that information, including documenting dates spent in Saskatchewan or the specific location where the novelist lived or the school in which she taught.

"Agus ce'n [*recte* cé'n] chaoi ar thaithnigh na Canadas leat?"[30] (And how did you like Canada?). On her return to Ireland, Róisín Ní Bhriain, the narrator and main character, is constantly questioned about Canada. She responds: "D'innsighinn dóibh go raibh dubh-ghráin agam ar an áit sin ach ní innsighinn a thuille"[31] (I told them that I abhorred that place but I told them nothing else). Indeed, Róisín advises her reader: "A léightheóir dhil, b'fhéidir gurbh' fhearr duit gan a thuille a léigheamh"[32] (Dear reader, perhaps it would be better for you not to read any more). Of course, the reader learns directly from Róisín about her Canadian experiences.

Róisín is an interesting character: a Belfast university-educated Protestant from a Unionist background interested in the Irish language. While staying with an Irish-speaking family in Connemara, as the War of Independence raged in the background, Róisín fell in love with one of the sons, Mícheál. But believing that the romance was doomed, she fled to Canada.

She sets the scene for her move:

> Chonnaic mé fógra ón S. P. G. [Society for the Propagation of the Gospel in Foreign Parts] a rádh go raibh múinteoirí uatha le cur amach go dtí na Canadas agus scríobh chucha. Fuaireas sgéala uatha go mbéadh orm sgathamh a chaitheamh i "Normal College" thall. Bhí Céim Ollsgoile agam agus ar an ádhbhar sin ní bheadh ach sgathamh gearr agam san gColáiste iasachta.[33]

> I saw an advertisement from the S.P.G. (Society for the Propagation of the Gospel in Foreign Parts) saying that they needed teachers to send out to Canada and I wrote to them. I got word back from them that I would have to spend a while in "Normal College" out there. I had a university degree and for that reason I would have only a short stay in the foreign College.

When we meet Róisín in Canada in June 1921, she has just disembarked from the train in Aberdeen, Saskatchewan – Aberdeen is a real location, about 40 kilometres northeast of Saskatoon – en route to her teaching position in a school outside the town. We sense Róisín's feeling of being overwhelmed spatially by the prairie landscape. In addition, no one from the school is present to welcome her. In a too-neat coincidence, the first individual Róisín encounters is a fellow-Ulsterperson. He was thriving in Saskatchewan, but, "Níor thaithnigh na Canadas leis" (He did not like Canada), either![34]

Róisín lives in Saskatchewan from mid-1921 to March 1922. She meets fine people, but the bad ones, in the person of Rabhelle, secretary of the school committee, overshadow the good. Róisín recounts their initial meeting:

> Chuir sé fáilte romham go lághach, ach ar an gcéad amharc dá dtug mé air bhí fhios agam nárbh' iontaoibh é. Bhí an braon Indiach ann. Ba iad na Franncaigh an chéad dream a tháinig go dtí an ceanntar sin céad bliadhain roimhe sin ... Rinne na fir cinn riain cleamhnas leis na hIndiachaibh agus ar an gcaoi sin bhí an dá dhuthchas i gcuid mhaith de na daoinibh. Cníopaire críochnuighthe a bhí ins an bhfear san, an fear ba chaime ar dhá chois, d'fhéadfainn a rádh dár bhuail umam ariamh.[35]

> He welcomed me amiably, but from my first look at him I knew that he was not trustworthy. There was a drop of Indian in him. The French were the first people who came to that area a century earlier ... The trappers made matches with the Indians and as a result a fair number of the people were of dual heritage. That man was an out and out wretch, I can say, the most crooked man on two feet I ever encountered.

This negative portrayal of the Métis conforms to the portrayal of characters of mixed European and Native descent as *homo criminalis* in American popular literature of the time – and, indeed, in Irish-language texts from the early twentieth century. Seán Óg Ó Caomhánaigh's *Fánaí* was one such text with its stereotypical presentation of Pinn as a murderous degenerate.[36] Unsurprisingly then, Róisín comes into conflict with Rabhelle, who views her as a suitable match for his son. When Róisín spurns the offer, Rabhelle threatens to have her fired, she consults a lawyer, and Rabhelle plots his revenge. This involves attempting to kill Róisín and, when that fails, burning down the school and blaming the Irish teacher. Róisín's days in Saskatchewan are numbered, but strangely, it is a tragic accident in which Rabhelle has no hand that finally forces her to flee: a young girl's death during a blizzard while she is in Róisín's care. Cleared of wrongdoing or neglect, Róisín retreats to Ireland traumatized by her experiences. It is little wonder that she refuses to comment on her time in Canada. She never wants to hear mention of that cursed country again.

ÉAN CUIDEÁIN

Pádhraic Óg Ó Conaire's *Éan Cuideáin* (1936) provides a twist to the reverse migration theme. The novel begins in Montreal, where a man from Connemara, Colm Ó Donnchadha, is hospitalized after heroically rescuing children in an accident. We soon meet Colm's fiancée, Nanette le Martin, a native Montrealer. Nan is an accomplished woman, a teacher and a linguist. Though never stated explicitly, French is her first language; she acquired Irish (one of her three other languages) from an Irish nun at school and then from Colm. The couple marry and rent accommodation in Griffintown. Colm has been working in Canada for ten years, seven of them in forestry, but at the novel's opening he is an office clerk with a lumber company, and with his happy domestic scene, he is anticipating advancing in the world, raising a family, purchasing a house in the suburbs, and even acquiring a car. He and Nan are content and settled in Montreal, though there are hints that Nan has kept a secret from Colm: as a dare with a childhood friend, the young Nan had climbed a ship's mast, and fallen off it onto the dock. As a consequence, doctors believe that she cannot have children.

News arrives soon after the marriage about Colm's father's death in Connemara. His mother implores her son to return to the family farm. Against Nan's wishes, the couple sell up and move to Ireland, the small family farm, and the mother-in-law from hell. The return home involves significant adjustments for Colm. Using skills and knowledge acquired in Canada, he begins the hard task of improving the house and farm, labour that involves as many failures as successes. Despite that struggle, Colm settles down, looking forward to the day when he can open a shop in which Nan can work. But *bean Cheanada* (the Canadian woman) is unsettled in Connemara. She is the *éan cuideáin* (the "strange bird" of the book's title), the one who arrives in Ireland wearing a fur coat. She is at ease linguistically in Connemara but abhores the relentless struggle for existence and the cramped house she must share with her mother-in-law. Nan cannot and will not contemplate a future for herself in Connemara.

Colm's mother's sudden death removes that irritant. The couple are free to begin afresh on the farm or even in another location in Ireland, but Nan is determined to leave. At novel's end, we see the pair on board a ship to Canada. Though Colm acknowledges that his life in Canada will be easier, he would prefer to stay in Ireland: "Ní dhá dheoin fhéin a bhí sé ag dul thar sáile anonn ath-uair"[37] (It was not of his own will that he was heading across the sea again). He is doing it for his wife, who eases his pain by informing him that – miraculously – she is pregnant. Clearly, Colm will be resuming his upward-moving career in a Montreal office, far removed from the constant slog of farming in the west of Ireland. He admits that he will likely never see his home again. His love for his homeland remains, but, as Pilib Ó Laoghaire notes, his child will grow up as Québécois(e).[38]

There is much more Canadian content – specifically, French Canadian content – in *Éan Cuideáin* than in *Cúrsaí Thomáis* and *Cailín na Gruaige Duinne*. This material falls into three different categories. First, there is Nan's family background. Though we never meet her family, we learn over the course of a few lines that it is a large one: her parents and eight children. The family is moderately prosperous: the father owns a grain store. One sibling is a nun, and two brothers are in the police "amuigh ó thuaidh" (up north).[39] The family has dealt with tragedy: one of Nan's brothers drowned in the Saint Lawrence River. Nan herself received a polished education at a convent school that prepared her for every imaginable possibility – bar subsistence farming in Connemara.

Second, there is the use of Quebec place names, such as Gaspé, Varennes, Carillon, and Lachine. However, there are no actual descriptions of these places. There are regular references to the Saint Lawrence River and the port of Montreal, with hints about its dark side due to Nan's childhood accident – she riffs, "Ó, a dhuganna dorcha doimhne Mhontreál" (O, dark deep docks of Montreal)[40] – and to Mount Royal, which, in Nan and Colm's recollections of strolling there, represents freedom in contrast to their cares in Ireland. One place name mentioned twice is "Griffin Town [*sic*],"[41] where Colm and Nan reside after their marriage: "urlár trí seomra i mbarr tighe i nGriffin Town tóigthe ar cíos acu" (three rooms on one floor at the top of a house in Griffin Town rented by them).[42] Griffintown, on the southwest side of Montreal Island, was the city's Irish enclave. It was "one of Canada's oldest Irish communities, settled long before the Famine – [and] would endure for more than a century after Black '47. In the heart of a French-speaking city dominated by a powerful Anglo-Scots elite, the working-class urban neighbourhood clung stubbornly to its Hibernian character."[43] William Weintraub paints a picture of the Irish Catholic community that settled in Griffintown in the nineteenth century,

> close to the industries along the Lachine Canal – brickyards, foundries, sugar refineries, breweries. As labourers, they helped build much that was important in Montreal, like the Victoria Bridge which, in its time, was the eighth wonder of the world. But they lived in a slum, in wretched housing where four children might share a bed in a tiny room. Streets were prone to flooding, and diphtheria and typhoid were frequent.[44]

The events in *Éan Cuideáin* take place in 1908, so it is worth noting the change in the area's demographics by this time:

> In 1901, only one out of every three Irish Montrealers lived in Griffintown. Large numbers of second- and third-generation Irish had moved into white-collar clerical jobs, many in the railways. Electric streetcars had made the suburbs more accessible and many had moved to Point St Charles, Verdun, or 'over the hill' to Notre-Dame-de-Grâce and other new developments.[45]

Thus, Colm's hope that he and Nan will be able to move from Griffintown to the suburbs accurately captures that neighbourhood's contemporary transformation. Nevertheless, it is surprising that Ó Conaire never references Griffintown specifically as an Irish community – and not all his readers would recognize Griffintown as such – and that he spurns the opportunity and challenge to frame the couple's life there in the context of the wider story of the Irish in Montreal.

The author's approach ensures that the reader learns little about Montreal. Equally, Ó Conaire's treatment of Canada is problematic. After seven years working in forestry, Colm lives in Montreal for another three. Yet back in Ireland, he does not acknowledge his urban experiences when he responds to a neighbour's inquiry about Canada: "'Coillte! coillte! coillte! cnuic, locha, aibhne, sneachta síorruidhe i mbarr na n-árd-bheann, easa cubhracha i ngleannta diamhracha'" (Forests! forests! forests! hills, lakes, rivers, perpetual snow at the top of the high mountains, foamy waterfalls in mysterious valleys).[46]

Again, one encounters similar stereotypes in a nostalgic song about Canada that Colm sings in Connemara. This piece is not in the Irish song tradition, and Ó Conaire likely composed it for the novel. The first verse accurately captures the content and tone of the song:

> A' leagan crann i gCeanada thall ba mheidhreach suairc a bhínn;
> An tuagh im' láimh a' sgoilteadh crann i ngleannta bhí faoi dhraoidheacht.
> ...
> An fiadh is an broc ar chreig is ar chloich 's ealta bán' ar línn,
> Mo bhrón go docht gan mé anocht i dtír an tsneachta mhín![47]
>
> I was happy and content knocking down trees yonder in Canada;
> An axe in my hand chopping trees in enchanted valleys.
> ...
> The deer and the badger on rocks and stones and the white swans in a pool,
> Alas, that I'm not tonight in the land of the smooth snow!

The third and final category of Canadian material consists of French Canadian historical, social, and cultural references that are striking in their specificity. For example, Nan ponders changes she would make if she were to stay in Connemara, "rud nach raibh" (something that she was not going to do):[48]

> Chuirfeadh sí rang cniotála ar bun mar chaitheamh aimsire fhéin. Mhúinfeadh sí do na cailíní óga le baill deas' éadaigh a dhéanamh. Mhúinfeadh sí dhóibh leis an "gcatalogne," brat-urlár a dhéanamh – ceird a bhí go hiongantach aca seo tháinic roimpi. Cá bhfios nach múinfeadh sí dhóibh leis an gcrios iongantach úd, an ceinture flêchee, a dhéanamh, crios nach bhfuil nea-chosúil ar shlí le crios Árann.[49]
>
> She would establish a knitting class as a pastime. She would teach the young girls to make nice items of clothing. She would teach

them to make the *catalonge*, a floor covering – a craft well possessed by those who preceded her. She might even teach them to make that fine belt, the *ceinture flêchée*, a belt not dissimilar to the Aran belt.

St Patrick's statue at the foot of Croagh Patrick in Mayo reminds Nan "[ar] an gCalbharí atá ar an mbealach go Varennes" (of the Calvary on the way to Varennes) in Quebec.[50] And she recalls the feats of Adam Dollard des Ormeaux and Madeleine Verchéres, eminent French Canadian historic personages:

> Thug chun chuimhne íodhbairt uasal Dollard agus a bhuidhine bige ar an 19adh Aibreán, 1659, nuair mhionnuigheadar, 'réis Comaoineach Naomhtha a ghlacadh, go seasfaidís cliú don Fhrainnc go imirt anma. Thug chun cruinnis dealbh gleoite Mhadeleine Verchéres, cailín bhí ionchurtha le Jeanne d'Arc ar gaile is gaisge – cailín a sheas an fód go dána ar feadh seachtaine in aghaidh sluagh Iroquois – gan de chongnamh aici ach a dhá driotháirín óga agus cúpla saighdiúr a raibh meathtacht agus cladhaireacht ina gcroidhe.[51]
>
> The noble sacrifice of Dollard and his small band on April 19, 1659, come to mind when they swore, after receiving Holy Communion, that they would defend the honour of France even if it meant their death. She recalled the exquisite statue of Madeleine Verchéres, a girl who compared with Joan of Arc for intensity and achievement – a girl who boldly stood her ground for a week against a multitude of Iroquois – with the help only of her two young brothers and several thoroughly craven and cowardly soldiers.

Two additional items are particularly conspicuous. In Connemara, at his mother's wake, Colm sings a verse from the French Canadian *voyageur* song, "La fill' du roi d'Espagne" (The daughter of the King of Spain):

> *La fill' du roi d'Espagne,*
> *Vogue, marinier, vogue!*
> *Veut apprendre un metier,*
> *Vogue marinier!*
> *Veut apprendre un metier!*
> *Vogue, marinier!*[52]

The daughter of the King of Spain,
Row, boatman, row!
Wants to learn a trade,
  Row, boatman!
  Wants to learn a trade!
    Row, boatman!

Similarly, Nan recounts in Irish a French Canadian folk tale about the Little Gray Man who protects a secret treasure of gold on the Gaspé coast.[53] The folk tale's inclusion functions to highlight parallels between Irish and French Canadian folk culture. However, it appears that Ó Conaire was primarily seeking to incorporate detailed Canadian content to compensate for the earlier generalizations. What was his source for the tale? Had he composed it, just as he likely composed the lumberjack song? There is no evidence that Ó Conaire had ever been to Canada, never mind Quebec. But both *voyageur* song verse and an English-language version of the folk tale appear in Frank Oliver Call's *The Spell of French Canada*.[54] The first paragraphs of the story in *Éan Cuideáin* and *The Spell of French Canada* provide us with a sense of the tale and – for Irish-language readers – conclusive evidence that Ó Conaire plagiarized Call's work:

> Dhá chnoc mhóra seadh na Sauteux, idir l'Anse-a-Jean agus Cap-aux-Renard. Táid in aon druim amháin, tuairm is trí mhíle ar fad, agus iad beagnach trí mhíle troigh ar aoirde. Nílid ach tuairm is céad slat ón bhfairrge. Tá carraigeacha móra agus sgeirdí in aice an chladaigh. Is iomdha long a cuireadh ó mhaith sa ngiodán seo. Is féidir gunnaí móra a bhí i longa cogaidh fheiceál ag Ruisseau Vallée. Tá fir curtha fá bhun chnoc Sauteux. Oidhche Shamhna feictear soilse aisteacha ag dul soir barr na n-alltracha. Is san áit chéadna ar an gcladach a théighid uilig as. Curtha sa ngiodán sin tá cófra mór láidir, cófra a chuir máirnéalaigh ann fadó. Tá sé lán d'ór. B'eagal leo go mbéarfaí ortha, nó go dtárlóchadh long-bhriseadh dóibh. Dá bhrí sin, chuireadar a gcuid óir i dtalamh ag bun na gcnoc. Bhí ortha annsin crainnte a chaitheamh go bhfeicidís cé air a mbeadh fanacht i gcionn an óir. An máirnéalach ar thuit ar a chrann fanacht, marbhuigheadh é agus cuireadh ar bharr an chófra é. Bhíodh a thaise ghá ghárdáil, ach anois is é an Fear Beag Liath a fhaireas é. B'fhéidir gurb é an máirnéalach é fhéin a chuir cumruíocht duine air féin. Tig le fir chaillte sin a dhéanamh, tá's a'd.[55]

> The Sauteux are two big mountains between l'Anse-à-Jean and Cap-aux-Renards. They form a range about three miles long, the height being nearly three thousand feet. They rise close to the sea at a distance of only a hundred yards. Near the edge of the sea are great rocks and reefs, and here many ships have been wrecked. The cannon of wrecked war-ships are to be seen at Ruisseau-Vallée. At the foot of the Sauteux mountains there are dead men buried. On All Saints' Eve strange lights are seen passing over the cliffs, which always flicker out at the same place on the shore. It is here that is buried a strong box full of gold hidden by some sailors long ago. They feared either capture or shipwreck, so they left their gold buried at the foot of the mountains. When the question of a guardian for the treasure was talked of, they drew lots, and the sailor who had to remain with the gold was killed and buried on top of the casket. His ghost used to guard it, but now it is guarded by the Little Gray Man (*Le petit bonhomme gris*). Perhaps it is the sailor himself who has changed himself into the Little Gray Man. Dead men can do that, you know.[56]

Ó Conaire translated Call's version of the French Canadian folk tale with only the slightest alteration. That was not his sole act of plagiarism. *The Spell of French Canada* was also his source for the other specific Québécois examples: the *catalogne*,[57] the *ceinture flêchée*,[58] and the wayside Calvary shrine near Varennes,[59] as well as details about the historical role models Dollard and Verchéres.[60] Rather than adding authenticity to his work by paraphrasing in his own words material that he had consulted, Ó Conaire directly translated material in Call's book into Irish, presenting it as his own work. Needless to say, *The Spell of French Canada* has no reference to Griffintown.

RETURN MIGRATION

The terms *Poncán* and – even in Irish-speaking areas – *Yankee* were used for returned immigrants from North America.[61] In recent years, scholars have examined the phenomenon of return migration to Ireland from America from the mid-nineteenth to the early twentieth century. However, as Diane Rose Dunnigan notes: "Ascertaining the size of the reverse migration with any precision is problematic due to the inconsistent counting and inaccuracies in record-keeping by shipping lines and government port authorities and because in the records they did keep, they included tourists and business travelers together with departing migrants."[62] Nevertheless, Kerby Miller estimates that around 10 percent of Irish immigrants in the United States returned home in the post-Famine period.[63] Many came home voluntarily. But as Hidetaka Hirota's groundbreaking research about the treatment of the poor in Massachusetts and New York demonstrates, other Irish, including American citizens, were expelled from the United States and forcibly repatriated to Ireland.[64]

Drawing on the work of the Scottish historian Marjory Harper, Dunnigan cites five main reasons why some returned home: "success in the new home, failure, homesickness, a call to return to take over family farm or other property, or a rejection of life overseas."[65] We can relate these to the characters' circumstances in the three Irish-language novels. At the start of *Cúrsaí Thomáis*, Mac Conmara is set to return home having inherited a farm. After his parents' deaths and with no ties in North America, Mac Aonghusa's partnership with Mac Conamara provides a reason to start afresh in Ireland. After her treatment and experiences in Saskatchewan, Róisín in *Cailín na Gruaige Duinne* rejects Canada entirely. Colm returns to take over the family farm in response to his mother's plea. However, Irish popular opinion largely dismissed positive reasons to choose to return, preferring instead to view returnees negatively: "Generally, the Irish at home appear to have viewed the permanent returnees as those who wanted to escape problems; those overcome by serious poor health and unfit for work; those who had failed to make a success in America; or those who were unable to cope with the fast pace and demands of life and work in America."[66]

In *Éan Cuideáin*, Colm and his neighbour, Joe Mhaidhc Ned, were long-time rivals. On meeting Colm after his return home, Joe mocked him:

> "Agus tá an bleitheach sa mbaile arís!" an chéad allagar a chuir sé as, agus tholl sé Colm le amharc. "Há, há! Muid ag dul go Ceanada le bun a dhéanamh … Ní rabhamar le theacht abhaile go Ros na gCloch go deo arís. Há, há," agus chuir cliabhrach air fhéin.[67]
>
> "And the slob is home again!" was the first shout he let out, and he looked right through Colm. "Haha! And we were going to Canada to make good … We were never going to come back to Ros na gCloch again. Haha," and he puffed out his chest.

Mícheál Ó Gaoithín, son of Peig Sayers, the renowned Blasket Island tradition bearer, returned from America. Despite a claim that his health had failed while he was abroad,[68] his memoir confirms that his courage had failed him.[69] If public wisdom deemed Ó Gaoithín a failure, the case of Micí Mac Gabhann serves as a useful counterbalance. He made his fortune prospecting for gold in the Klondike before heading home to Donegal and swapping his thatched cottage for a new slate-roofed two-storey dwelling.[70]

As reverse migration was not so unusual, one would anticipate finding it as a trope in Irish-language literature. Indeed, Aisling Ní Dhonnchadha and Máirín Nic Eoin have published sample texts about return migrants in their anthology of Irish-language writing about the emigrant experience.[71] However, it is surprising to find reverse migration playing a key role in all three Irish-language Canadian novels from the 1920s and 1930s. That omnipresence misrepresents the scale of return migration and distorts the historical record. Of course, one can level a similar charge of misrepresentation and distortion against most Irish Canadian English-language historical novels about the years 1845 to 1871, the decades that cover the Great Famine and Grosse Île (1845–52), the assassination of Thomas D'Arcy McGee in Ottawa (1868), and the Fenian Raids on Canada (1866–71). Whatever the regional variations historically, most Irish Canadians came from Protestant backgrounds and smoothly blended into the Anglo-Scottish mainstream in British North America; indeed, most Irish Catholics adapted relatively easily to their new environment. Contemporary historians view Irish Protestants and Catholics as "part of a *charter group* in the foundation and development of Canadian society."[72] Yet fiction writers focus on the dramatic exceptions rather than the boring norm. Jason King argues that "the narrative design of Irish-Canadian historical fiction and drama is premised upon an imaginative vision of social convulsion and communal tensions that *occasionally* wracked Irish settlements within the Canadas in the nineteenth century."[73] Moreover, apart from Kathleen Coburn's *The Grandmothers* and Don Akenson's *At Face Value*, the main Irish characters in these novels and plays are Catholics.

Thus, fiction writers in Irish and in English are on a par in blithely ignoring the historians. That is how it should be. Fiction sets its own terms of reference and is free to draw on scholarly research, distort it, or merely disregard it. Nevertheless, it is worthwhile exploring the reasons why the reverse migration trope occurs and reoccurs in the three Irish-language novels.

The authors do not present the Ireland to which the characters return in a romanticized way. In *Cúrsaí Thomáis*, one neighbour kills another in a dispute over land; that novel also features unwed mothers and prostitution as well as the local Big House with its Protestant squireen who rules the roost. In *Cailín na Gruaige Duinne*, Róisín is retraumatized by her experiences back in Ireland. After her return, she marries Mícheál, the Connemara man, but the marriage fails, "the first marital breakdown in modern Gaelic fiction."[74] Moreover, Mícheál's pro–Free State brother betrays the anti-Treatyist Mícheál, leading to his capture and extrajudicial execution. Once again, Róisín flees Ireland, seeking temporary refuge in France before returning home. And in *Éan Cuideáin*, Colm's old rival sabotages his attempts to improve the family farm. The Ireland of the returnees is no prelapsarian paradise.

Nor does either linguistic relativism or cultural determinism – in this case, the belief that the Irish language and its speakers have a world view that colours how they see emigration – explain the partiality for reverse migration. Later novels in Irish about coming to North America break away from the return migrant trope. For example, in *Iníon Keevack* (1996), Micheál Ua Ciarmhaic's portrayal of the romantic relationship between an Irishman and an Indigenous woman, the couple remain in North America. Brian Ó Baoill's *Gaistí Geilt* (2013), which combines a post–Irish War of Independence settling-of-scores angle with the real-life story of Albert Johnson, the "Mad Trapper of Rat River" in the Canadian North in the early 1930s, closes in Toronto, with the arrival of the main love interest to meet up with the IRA hitman. It is unclear where the couple will go afterward. Ó Baoill's Fenian yarn *An Taibhse Ghlas* (2013) sees the Canadian-based Fenian return to Ireland after the retreat from Ridgeway in 1866, yet he ends up sailing to the United States to continue the struggle.

The prominence of the return migration narrative twist may reflect a perception that the Irish-reading public in the early decades of the twentieth century was more receptive to stories set in Ireland rather than abroad. In the early 1930s, one commentator claimed that Irish-language theatregoers were not interested in "insipid foreign dramas."[75] Perhaps the novelists believed that, in returning their main characters back home, they were catering to their readers' expectations. Similarly, do not contemporary readers of Great Famine novels, such as Peter Behrens's *The Law of Dreams*, anticipate that the books will contain certain tropes – potato blight and hunger, fever and painful death, bailiffs and eviction, the Poorhouse and coffin ships, and, in Canadian versions, Grosse Île?

However, the most credible explanation for the prominence of the return migrant trope in early twentieth-century novels is that it represented the remnant of Irish-Ireland ideology about "The Emigration Terror," as P.H. Pearse described it.[76] Irish people should remain at home to rebuild the nation as it strived to emerge from the colonial era – or should return, if abroad. Philip O'Leary has explored the negative portrayal of emigration and the emigrant experience in Irish-language prose and drama works from the Irish-language revival period, 1881–1921.[77] It is no coincidence that Éamonn Mac Giolla Iasachta and Úna Bean Uí Dhiosca were not merely converts to, and disciples of, the Irish-language revival but likely compensating for their sense of otherness. Mac Giolla Iasachta's official biography claimed that he was born in a ship off the Cape of Good Hope.[78] In fact, Edward Edgeworth Lysaght was born in Somerset and raised Anglican before moving to Ireland and converting to Catholicism (the Chief Herald position is one in which the ability to mix fact and fiction comes in handy!). The Dublin-born Úna Bean Uí Dhiosca, whose birth name was Elizabeth Rachel Leech, converted from Church of Ireland to Catholicism.[79] As loyal supporters of the Irish Ireland movement, they would have likely accepted negative attitudes about Irish emigration. Unsurprisingly, therefore, their fictional émigrés return home. In contrast, the Connemara man Pádhraic Óg Ó Conaire had a more realistic view of emigration, return migration, and even repeat emigration as normal features of rural life in the west of Ireland. Ironically, as he was apparently the only one of the three novelists who had never been to North America, a small incident in *Éan Cuideáin* perfectly captures the reality of emigration for his home community. No sooner have Colm and Nan arrived in his mother's house from Montreal than neighbours, young and old, crowd in:

> Theastuigh tuairisg uatha ó n-a muintir a bhí thall. Tír-eolas Cheanada agus Mheiriocá ag na gasúir sin i bhfad níos fearr ná tír-eolas a dtíre féin, mar réir mar chítear neithe do mhuintir Ros na gCloch níl ann ach dhá thír 'réis an tsaoghail: Conamara agus Meiriocá."[80]

> They wanted news from their relatives yonder. Those children knew more about the geography of Canada and America than that of their own country because as the people of Ros na gCloch see things, there are only two countries after all: Connemara and America.

CONCLUSION

Cúrsaí Thomáis, *Cailín na Gruaige Duinne*, and *Éan Cuideáin* are works of fiction, not social documents. Nevertheless, Aisling Ní Dhonnchadha and Máirín Nic Eoin are correct in identifying the usefulness of such non-fiction works in understanding aspects of reverse migration: "In their depiction of return migration, these literary texts are particularly valuable for the insights they provide on an under-researched aspect of migrant identity and of migration history."[81] Certainly, the Canadian novels contain such insights. For example, despite the main characters' affinity for Ireland, none is sentimental about his or her homeland. Their views on their host country are determined to a degree by the strength of their relationships there. Mac Aonghusa, a single man, and Mac Conmara, a widower, are drifters. A single woman and a solitary immigrant, Róisín cannot call on the support of an Irish community in her hour of need. These characters have no emotional connection to Canada: they are merely working there and passing through before going home. That is not to say that rootless Irish emigrants inevitably return home. An Ceallach (Kelly) shares a hospital ward with Colm at the start of *Éan Cuideáin*. A minor character who never appears again in the novel, his fate is crystal clear:

> D'fhág sé Éire agus é óg ... Bhí na trí sgóir curtha isteach aige; an chuid is mó dá chuid alluis tugtha. Ariamh ó shoin, agus ó dhubh go dubh, obair, ocras, agus anrógh na clocha ba mhó ar a phaidrín. Nuair a castaí roint [*sic*] airgid ina líon ní bheadh sé sásta mara n-óladh sé é. Agus nuair a bhíodh an phíghinn deiridh caithte, tréimhsí fada cómhnuigheacha agus confadh ocrais.[82]

> He left Ireland when he was young ... He was sixty years old, his best days behind him. Work, hunger and hardship were his daily companions. When he had some money, he invariably drank it. When his last penny was done, there were long spells of institutionalization and ravenous hunger.

Colm is the sole major Irish character in these novels who likes Canada, equating it with freedom and upward mobility. It is no coincidence that he marries there and is relatively settled. But Ireland is still his homeland psychologically, and he would remain there if possible once he returns. Ironically, however, though the main Irish characters in the other novels have freedom of choice to stay or leave, Colm's marriage, especially to a non-Irish woman, compels him to return to Canada, in the same way that earlier Nan believed she had no choice but to accompany her husband to Ireland. At different times in the novel and, no doubt, in their post-novel lives, their marriage bonds have become a yoke. Colm will likely remain in Canada for the rest of his life. Though viewing himself as an exile, he will be successful as a first-generation immigrant. His years abroad will not lessen his affinity for Ireland. But it will be his family who integrate in the New World. In a convergence with one substrand of the Irish Canadian English-language novel, Colm's offspring might even visit Ireland one day in search of their roots.

NOTES

1 Nilsen, "An Ghaeilge."

2 Ibid., 263n3.

3 Mac Conmara, "As I Was Walking," 128. All translations are by the author of this chapter, except where stated otherwise.

4 This chapter is a shorter version of an article first published in Irish in the journal *Léann*: Ó Siadhail, "Agus Cé'n Chaoi."

5 King, "Modern Irish-Canadian Literature," 68. *The Yellow Briar* purports to be a work of non-fiction, recounting the life story of Patrick Slater, an Irish Catholic, from the time of his arrival in Canada during the Great Famine until 1924. In fact, it is a work of fiction by John Wendell Mitchell, a Toronto lawyer and Methodist. See Gnarowski, Introduction, 7–18.

6 Mangan, *Voyage*; Keegan, *Famine Diary*.

7 Jackson, "Famine Diary."

8 Sellar, "Summer," 368.

9 Ibid., 455.

10 Breathnach and Ní Mhurchú, "Caomhánach, Seán."

11 Ó Caomhánaigh, *Fánaí*, 1.

12 Ibid., 70, 143, 145–55.

13 Ibid., 138.

14 Mac Gabhann, *Rotha Mór an tSaoil*; MacGowan, *The Hard Road to Klondike*.

15 Boivin, "Hémon, Louis."

16 The title page of *Cailín na Gruaige Duinne* gives the spelling of the author's name as Úna Bean Uí Dhiosca while the author's entry in *ainm.ie*

gives it as "Uí Dhíosca": Breathnach and Ní Mhurchú, "Uí Dhíosca, Úna."

17 Ó Conaire, *Éan Cuideáin*, 185.

18 Quoted in Ó Ceallaigh, *Éamonn Mac Giolla Iasachta*, 86.

19 Mac Giolla Iasachta, *Cúrsaí Thomáis*, 8.

20 Mac Giolla Iasachta, *Leathanaigh*, 43.

21 MacLysaght, *Small Fields*, 9.

22 Ibid., 10.

23 Ibid., 10.

24 Ibid., 129.

25 Mac Giolla Iasachta, *Cúrsaí Thomáis*, 139.

26 Ibid., 89. In the Irish-language text, Mac Conmara states: "Bhí braon den fhuil ghorm inti. Bhí leanbh dubh aici": ibid., 89. This can be translated as "There was a drop of black blood in her. She had a child who looked black." It is evident that MacLysaght used the adjectives "gorm" and "dubh" respectively to distinguish between racial heritage and skin colour. O'Clery's translation adds a racial slur that is not in the original text: "She had a drop of black blood in her: she had a child as black as any nigger": MacLysaght, *Small Fields*, 71.

27 Mac Giolla Iasachta, *Cúrsaí Thomáis*, 88.

28 MacLysaght, *Small Fields*, 70. The Irish-language quotation does not mention Ned's boar, which, presumably, was rooting around in the field outside. Evidently, O'Clery introduced Ned's boar to provide a point of comparison between the perceived unregulated base instincts of humans and animals. As demonstrated also in note 26, O'Clery was not averse to amending Mac Giolla Iasachta's work for the purpose of effect.

29 Breathnach and Ní Mhurchú, "Uí Dhíosca, Úna."

30 Uí Dhiosca, *Cailín na Gruaige Duinne*, 80.

31 Ibid., 80.

32 Ibid., 48.

33 Ibid., 46–7.

34 Ibid., 49.

35 Ibid., 52–3.

36 Ó Siadhail, "'Is Mise Geronimo,'" 18–21.

37 Ó Conaire, *Éan Cuideáin*, 218.

38 Ó Laoghaire, *Déirc an Dóchais*, 53.

39 Ó Conaire, *Éan Cuideáin*, 168.

40 Ibid., 16.

41 Ibid., 13, 18.

42 Ibid., 13.

43 Doyle Driedger, *An Irish Heart*, 58.

44 Weintraub, *City Unique*, 155.
45 Doyle Driedger, *An Irish Heart*, 251.
46 Ó Conaire, *Éan Cuideáin*, 186–7.
47 Ibid., 150.
48 Ibid., 163.
49 Ibid., 163.
50 Ibid., 166.
51 Ibid., 173–4.
52 Ibid., 193. Italics in original.
53 Ibid., 194–6.
54 Call, *Spell of French Canada*, 291–2, 259–61.
55 Ó Conaire, *Éan Cuideáin*, 194–5.
56 Call, *Spell of French Canada*, 259–60.
57 Ibid., 320.
58 Ibid., 322–6.
59 Ibid., 361.
60 Ibid., 90–1, 96.
61 Mac Gabhann, *Rotha Mór an tSaoil*, 222.
62 Dunnigan, "Irish Return Migration," 6.
63 Miller, *Emigrants and Exiles*, 426.
64 Hirota, *Expelling the Poor*, 2–4.
65 Dunnigan, "Irish Return Migration," 3–4.
66 Ibid., 210–11.
67 Ó Conaire, *Éan Cuideáin*, 43.
68 Breathnach and Ní Mhurchú, "Ó Gaoithín, Micheál."
69 Ó Gaoithín, *Is Truagh ná Fanann an Óige*, 72; O'Guiheen, *A Pity Youth Does Not Last*, 76–8.
70 Mac Gabhann, *Rotha Mór an tSaoil*, 223–6.
71 Ní Dhonnchadha and Nic Eoin, *Ar an gCoigríoch*, 387–415.
72 King, "Modern Irish-Canadian Literature," 68.
73 Ibid., 68.
74 O'Leary, *Gaelic Prose*, 147.
75 "Ball Geal," "The Comhar," 348.
76 Cited by O'Leary, *The Prose Literature*, 141.
77 Ibid., 141–53.
78 Ó Ceallaigh, *Éamonn Mac Giolla Iasachta*, 449.
79 Breathnach and Ní Mhurchú. "Uí Dhíosca, Úna."
80 Ó Conaire, *Éan Cuideáin*, 59.
81 Ní Dhonnchadha and Nic Eoin, "Ar an gCoigríoch," 66.
82 Ó Conaire, *Éan Cuideáin*, 10.

BIBLIOGRAPHY

Akenson, Don. *At Face Value: The Life and Times of Eliza McCormack/John White.* Montreal and Kingston: McGill-Queen's University Press, 1990.

"Ball Geal." "The Comhar Drámuíochta." *The Leader*, 5 November 1932, 348–9.

Behrens, Peter. *The Law of Dreams.* Toronto: Anansi, 2006.

Boivin, Aurélien. "Hémon, Louis." In *Dictionary of Canadian Biography*, vol. 14. University of Toronto / Université Laval, 2003. http://www.biographi.ca/en/bio/hemon_louis_14E.html.

Breathnach, Diarmuid, and Máire Ní Mhurchú. "Caomhánach, Seán (1885–1947)." In *Ainm.ie: An Bunachar Náisiúnta Beathaisnéisí Gaeilge*. Fiontar: Ollscoil Chathair Bhaile Átha Cliath, 2018. https://www.ainm.ie/Bio.aspx?ID=7.

– "Ó Gaoithín, Micheál (1904–1974)." In *Ainm.ie: An Bunachar Náisiúnta Beathaisnéisí Gaeilge*. Fiontar: Ollscoil Chathair Bhaile Átha Cliath, 2018. https://www.ainm.ie/Bio.aspx?ID=738.

– "Uí Dhíosca, Úna (1880–1958)." In *Ainm.ie: An Bunachar Náisiúnta Beathaisnéisí Gaeilge*. Fiontar: Ollscoil Chathair Bhaile Átha Cliath, 2018. https://www.ainm.ie/Bio.aspx?ID=70.

Call, Frank Oliver. *The Spell of French Canada.* Boston: L.C. Page and Company, 1926.

Coburn, Kathleen. *The Grandmothers.* Toronto: Oxford University Press, 1949.

Donoghue, Emma. *Landing.* Orlando: Harcourt, 2007.

Doyle Driedger, Sharon. *An Irish Heart: How a Small Immigrant Community Shaped Canada.* Toronto: HarperCollins, 2010.

Dunnigan, Diane Rose. "Irish Return Migration from America at the Turn of the Nineteenth Century, 1890–1920." PhD diss., National University of Ireland, Maynooth 2011. http://eprints.maynoothuniversity.ie/4735.

Foran, Charles. *Kitchen Music.* Dunvegan: Cormorant Books, 1994.

Gnarowski, Michael. Introduction to *The Yellow Briar: A Story of the Irish on the Canadian Countryside*, by "Patrick Slater" [John Wendell Mitchell], new ed., 7–18. Toronto: Dundurn Press, 2009.

Hémon, Louis. *Maria Chapdelaine*, trans. Risteárd Ó Foghludha ("Fiachra Éilgeach"). Baile Átha Cliath: Oifig Díolta Foillseacháin Rialtais, 1933.

Hirota, Hidetaka. *Expelling the Poor: Atlantic Seaboard States and the Nineteenth-Century Origins of American Immigration Policy.* New York: Oxford University Press, 2017.

Jackson, Jim. "Famine Diary – the Making of a Best Sellar." *The Irish Review* 11 (1991–92): 1–8.
Keegan, Gerald. *Famine Diary: Journey to a New World*, ed. James J. Mangan, FSC. Dublin: Wolfhound Press, 1991.
King, Jason. "Modern Irish-Canadian Literature: Defining the 'Peaceable Kingdom.'" *Canadian Journal of Irish Studies* 31, no. 1 (2005): 67–75.
Leitch, Maurice. *Poor Lazarus*. London: MacGibbon and Kee, 1969.
London, Jack. *Mac an Mhachtíre* [White Fang], trans. an tAthair Tadhg Ó Cúrnáin. Baile Átha Cliath: Oifig Díolta Foillseacháin Rialtais, 1936.
– *Scairt an Dúthchais* [The Call of the Wild], trans. Niall Ó Domhnaill. Baile Átha Cliath: Oifig Díolta Foillseacháin Rialtais, 1932.
"M." [Éamonn Mac Giolla Iasachta]. *Cúrsaí Thomáis: Shíos Seal a's Shuas Seal.* Baile Átha Cliath: Hodges and Figgis, 1927.
Mac Conmara, Donncha. "As I Was Walking One Evening Fair." In *An tAmhrán Macarónach*, ed. Diarmaid Ó Muirithe, 127–8. Baile Átha Cliath: An Clóchomhar, 1980.
Mac Gabhann, Micí. *Rotha Mór an tSaoil*, ed. Seán Ó hEochaidh and Proinsias Ó Conluain. Indreabhán: Cló Iar-Chonnachta, 1996.
Mac Giolla Iasachta, Éamonn. *Cúrsaí Thomáis*. Baile Átha Cliath: An Clóchomhar, 1969.
– *Leathanaigh ó mo Dhialann.* Baile Átha Cliath: Clódhanna Teoranta, 1978.
MacGowan, Michael. *The Hard Road to Klondike*, trans. Valentin Iremonger. London and Boston: Routledge and Kegan Paul, 1973.
MacLysaght, E. *The Small Fields of Carrig*, trans. E. O'Clery. London: Heath Cranton, 1929.
Mangan, James J. *The Voyage of the Naparima: A Story of Canada's Island Graveyard*. Quebec: Carraig Books, 1982.
"Marbhán" [Seán Ó Ciarghusa]. *Onncail Seárlaí*. [Dublin]: Muinntir C.S. Ó Fallamhain, 1930.
Miller, Kerby. A. *Emigrants and Exiles: Ireland and the Irish Exodus to North America.* New York and Oxford: Oxford University Press, 1985.
Moore, Brian. *The Luck of Ginger Coffey*, new ed. Toronto: McClelland and Stewart, 2008.
– *The Mangan Inheritance*. London: Jonathan Cape, 1979.
Ní Dhonnchadha, Aisling and Máirín Nic Eoin, eds. *Ar an gCoigríoch: Díolaim Litríochta ar Scéal na hImirce.* Indreabhán: Cló Iar-Chonnacht, 2008.
– "Ar an gCoigríoch. Migration and Identity in Twentieth-Century and Contemporary Irish-Language Literature." *Irish Review* 44 (2012): 60–74.

Nilsen, Kenneth. "An Ghaeilge in Oirthear Cheanada, 1750–1900." In *Séimhfhear Suairc. Aistí in ómós don Ollamh Breandán Ó Conchúir*, ed. Seán Ó Coileáin, Liam P. Ó Murchú, Pádraigín Riggs, 262–79. An Daingean: An Sagart, 2013.
Ó Baoill, Brian. *An Taibhse Ghlas: Na Fíníní: Ceanada 1866.* Baile Átha Cliath: Coiscéim, 2013.
– *Gaistí Geilt.* Baile Átha Cliath: Coiscéim, 2013.
Ó Caomhánaigh, Seán Óg. *Fánaí*, rev. ed. Maigh Nuad: An Sagart, 1989.
Ó Ceallaigh, Seán. *Éamonn Mac Giolla Iasachta 1887–1986: Beathaisnéis.* Baile Átha Cliath: Coiscéim, 2003.
Ó Conaire, Pádhraic Óg. *Éan Cuideáin.* Baile Átha Cliath: Oifig Díolta Foillseacháin Rialtais, 1936.
Ó Gaoithín, Mícheál. *Is Truagh ná Fanann an Óige.* Baile Átha Cliath: Oifig an tSoláthair, 1953.
O'Guiheen, Micheál. *A Pity Youth Does Not Last*, trans. Tim Enright. Oxford: Oxford University Press, 1982.
Ó Laoghaire, Pilib [Philip O'Leary]. *Déirc an Dóchais: Léamh ar Shaothar Phádhraic Óig Uí Chonaire.* Indreabhán: Cló Iar-Chonnachta, 1995.
O'Leary, Philip. *Gaelic Prose in the Irish Free State 1922–1939.* University Park: Pennsylvania State University Press, 2004.
– *The Prose Literature of the Gaelic Revival, 1881–1921: Ideology and Innovation*. University Park: Pennsylvania State University Press, 1994.
Ó Siadhail, Pádraig. "'Agus Cé'n Chaoi ar Thaithnigh na Canadas Leat?': Úrscéalta Gaeilge 'Ceanadacha' ó na 1920idí agus ó na 1930idí." *Léann* 5 (2018): 75–103.
– "'Is Mise Geronimo': North American Indians in Twentieth-Century Irish-Language Prose." *New Hibernia Review* 20, no. 1 (2016): 14–33.
Sellar, Robert. "The Summer of Sorrow." In *The Summer of Sorrow: Abner's Device and Other Stories. Gleaner Tales: Part Two*, 341–462. Huntington, Quebec: [The Gleaner], 1895.
Ua Ciarmhaic, Micheál. *Iníon Keevack.* Baile Átha Cliath: Coiscéim, 1996.
Uí Dhiosca, Úna Bean. *Cailín na Gruaige Duinne.* Baile Átha Cliath: Oifig Díolta Foillseacháin Rialtais, 1932.
Urquhart, Jane. *Away.* Toronto: McClelland and Stewart, 1993.
Weintraub, William. *City Unique: Montreal Days and Nights in the 1940s and '50s.* Toronto: McClelland and Stewart, 1998.

Scottish Gaels

10

John MacLean's "New World" Secular Songs: A Poet, His Print Editors, and Oral Tradition

Robert Dunbar

Professor Kenneth Nilsen had an abiding interest in the "carrying stream" of the living oral tradition, as well as in the written text, and his many recordings of Gaelic speakers from eastern Nova Scotia and in particular from Antigonish County will be of lasting value to scholars, speakers, and anyone else interested in the language and culture. He was also deeply interested in local Gaelic poets, tradition bearers, and other purveyors of Gaelic culture, including the poet John MacLean (1787–1848) of Tiree and Nova Scotia, whose grave at Glenbard, Antigonish County, Professor Nilsen would visit each year with his students. It may therefore be fitting to consider some issues bearing on the relationship between orality and text – a particularly important relationship in Gaelic Studies – in the context of the life and legacy of John MacLean. One such issue is the role of text as a means of preserving oral tradition: before the advent of sound recording technology in the twentieth century, the transcription and subsequent publication of printed texts was the only option available. A second issue is the role of collectors in transcribing material from the oral tradition and of editors in preparing for publication such transcriptions and other texts that have been reduced to writing. A third issue is the impact of text on the oral tradition. All three of these issues have generated a considerable amount of scholarly attention, although in a Gaelic context somewhat more attention has been focused on the second. This is perhaps partly because of well-known controversies, such as that of James Macpherson and his "Ossianic" texts in the eighteenth century,[1] and more recent debates, for example that with regard to the ways in which Alexander Carmichael chose to present Gaelic texts in the first two volumes of *Carmina Gadelica*.[2] The production of modern scholarly editions of Gaelic texts, and especially of song-poetry – for example, those published under the auspices of the Scottish Gaelic Texts Society – has also required editors to consider how they will treat multiple versions of particular texts and, often, to assess decisions made by earlier editors of such texts.

An examination of some of John MacLean's song-poetry provides a particularly interesting opportunity to explore these issues. First, the poet was himself a collector and publisher of Gaelic verse: he transcribed much of his own poetry, and he committed to writing a large number of song-poems composed by others, later publishing much of this material in two books. Second, the large majority of his poetry was subsequently edited and published by his grandson, Alexander Maclean Sinclair (1840–1924), more than thirty years after John MacLean's death,[3] and some of these versions of his song-poems were subsequently republished in newspapers, journals, and other collections. As we shall see, Maclean Sinclair took considerable liberties with these texts, and in many cases the Maclean Sinclair versions differ dramatically from those which are attributable to the poet himself. Third, many of John Maclean's compositions appear to have been popular during his lifetime, and a significant number have survived to this day among Gaelic singers on both sides of the Atlantic. Given the disparities between the Maclean Sinclair versions and the versions that are more closely associated with the poet, an examination of the surviving song corpus may provide some interesting evidence about the impact of print on oral performance.

John MacLean was perhaps the most important of all the poets who emigrated during the main period of mass Gaelic overseas emigration, which stretched from roughly 1730 to 1860,[4] and he is the author of one of the best-known song-poems concerning the process of emigration, "Òran do dh' Aimearaga" (A Song to America) – also known as "A' Choille Ghruamach" (The Gloomy Forest) – which is still widely known, sung, and recorded. Born at Caolas on the Inner Hebridean island of Tiree, an island that has produced a great deal of Gaelic song-poetry, MacLean is also considered by some to be the greatest of the Tiree bards.[5] He is commonly referred to by Scottish Gaels as Bàrd Thighearna Chola (the Poet to the Laird of Coll) – he was one of the last "family" poets, so honoured by Alexander, the fifteenth chieftain of the MacLeans of Coll – but is known to this day in Tiree by his patronymic, Iain mac Ailein (John, son of Allan).[6] He is known to Nova Scotia Gaels as Bàrd Abhainn Bhàrnaidh (the Barney's River Poet), referring to the location of the poet's homestead in Pictou County, where first he settled after emigrating from Tiree in 1819.[7] He is also known simply as Am Bàrd MacGilleain (the Bard MacLean).[8]

Although not himself a member of the aristocracy, John MacLean had a pedigree that connected him with the Clan MacLean aristocracy: he could trace his pedigree to Eachann Ruadh nan Cath (Red Hector of the Battles), the sixth chieftain of the MacLeans of Duart, the senior MacLean kindred, who was killed at the Battle of Harlaw in 1411.[9] There was also a strong family tradition of poetry: his maternal great-grandfather was Neil Lamont, who had also been appointed poet to the Laird of Coll, and on his father's side, he was related to another significant Tiree poet, Archibald MacLean, known as Gilleasbuig Làidir (Strong Archibald).[10] John MacLean was a shoemaker and a small-scale merchant in Tiree, and like the overwhelming majority of Gaelic-speaking immigrants, was a pioneer farmer in Nova Scotia.[11] He does not appear to have made a great success of these enterprises, based on this account, provided by Maclean Sinclair:

> Nature gave the poet a mind of great capacity; but evidently it did not intend that he should become a wealthy man. He never attended regularly to his work; his mind was not upon it. Poetry occupied his thoughts when pegging sole-leather in Scotland, and cutting down trees in America; it took complete possession of him. He was a good poet; but a poor shoemaker, and a poor farmer. He was very fond of company. He would frequently be away from home. He was clannish, and took pleasure in visiting his friends and acquaintances.[12]

MacLean grew up on an island rich in Gaelic oral tradition, and in addition to being a poet, he was also apparently a tradition bearer of considerable skill. Maclean Sinclair tells us that "his powerful memory ensured that his stores of information connected with the Highland clans and poets were very great," and that he was a *seanchaidh* (tradition bearer) as well as a poet.[13] Maclean Sinclair also notes that his grandfather was well-acquainted with the works of other Gaelic poets, and that he knew many Gaelic poems, including Alexander MacDonald's "Birlinn Chloinn Raghnaill" (The Galley of Clanranald) and

Duncan Bàn MacIntyre's "Moladh Beinn Dòrain" (The Praise of Ben Dorain), by heart.[14] In one elegy composed on his death, another skilled Antigonish County poet, John MacGillivray, makes reference to his deep knowledge of Gaelic tradition: "Chaill sinn tuilleadh 's do bhàrdachd, / Ged a tha sinn 'ga h-ionndrainn, / Chaill sinn t' fhiosrachadh sàr ghasd'" (We have lost more than your poetry, / Though we certainly miss that, / We have also lost your most excellent knowledge).[15] He was particularly esteemed as a singer. Norman MacDonald, an Antigonish County Gael who in 1863 published a version of John MacKenzie's important collection of Gaelic poetry, *Sar-Obair nam Bard Gaelach*, noted that MacLean's conversational powers were excellent, that "the old and the young listened to him with delight," and that "he had a soft musical voice, and was a good singer."[16] In his elegy, MacGillivray also makes reference to John MacLean's skills as a singer: "Gum bu tric e 'm measg uaislean / A' seinn dhuanagan Gàidhlig" (He was often amongst noblemen / Singing Gaelic songs).[17] In another elegy, John Cameron, a friend of the poet, also makes reference to this – "Gheibhte òranan milis / Gu ro phongail bho d' bhilibh, / Dh' fhalbh a' cheòlraidh 's a h-uidheam / Bhon thug an t-eug bhuainn thu" (Sweet songs would be heard / Mostly accurately from your lips, / The muse and the instrument has departed / Since death has taken you away from us)[18] – as does the poet himself, in "Òran do dh' Aimearaga": "Air bheag thoilinntinn 'sa choille chruinn seo, / Gun duine faighneachd an seinn mi ceòl" (With little pleasure in this constricting forest, / And no one asking if I'll sing a song),[19] suggesting that he was accustomed to being asked to sing. However, in addition to being deeply steeped in Gaelic oral tradition, John MacLean was also literate. Maclean Sinclair tells us that he went several years to school; he may well have received instruction at one of the two schools run by the Society in Scotland for the Propagation of Christian Knowledge, which existed in Tiree in his youth.[20] According to Maclean Sinclair, he learned to read and spell both English and Gaelic, to cipher, and to write, proving himself an excellent reader and a good pen-man.[21] He was therefore well-versed in both oral and literary culture.

John MacLean composed forty-four secular song-poems for which we have evidence; my edition of these is due to be published shortly by the Scottish Gaelic Texts Society.[22] Of these, twenty-six were composed in Scotland and eighteen in Nova Scotia. The majority of the secular song-poems are panegyrics. Eight were composed for his patron, Alexander MacLean (1754–1835), the fifteenth Laird of Coll,[23] and two other panegyrics were composed for Alexander's son and heir, Hugh MacLean (1782–1861), the sixteenth and last MacLean Laird of Coll.[24] Three were composed for another significant Highland chieftain, Colonel Alasdair Ranaldson Macdonell, the fifteenth chief of the Macdonells of Glengarry (1788–1828), one of the most controversial figures of the age.[25] Several poems composed in Scotland were panegyrics for more minor members of the Highland aristocracy, notable Highland military figures in the Napoleonic Wars such as Colonel John Cameron of Fassifern (1771–1815), and one was for another poet, Alexander MacKinnon of Morar (1770–1814).[26] Five other poems were in praise of clergymen: two, composed in Scotland, were for Church of Scotland ministers, and three, composed in Nova Scotia, were for Fr Colin Grant (1784–1839), a Catholic priest from Glenmoriston who from 1819 was parish priest in Arisaig, Antigonish County, Nova Scotia, and who befriended and supported the poet.[27] One of MacLean's finest and best-known poems, "Marbhrann do Bhean-Uasail Òig Chliùitich a Bha Pòsta aig Dotair Iain Noble" (An Elegy for a Renowned Young Noblewoman who was Married to Dr John Noble) – apparently the last secular poem he composed, in about 1843 – was a lament for Julia MacNiven, another native of Tiree, who had emigrated to Cape Breton. Another Nova Scotia song-poem was a panegyric to a Gaelic periodical, Rev. Norman MacLeod's *Cuairtear nan Gleann* (Visitor of the Glens), which was published between 1840 and 1843. Most of the rest of John MacLean's Tiree output is comprised of satires or humorous songs about local characters and events, as well as laments on the premature death of young Tiree men. The non-panegyric New World songs included three concerning emigration ("Òran do dh' Aimearaga" among them), some humorous or satirical songs, two of which concerned the temperance movement of the 1830s, some songs to mark local events, and a lament on the death of a child.

John MacLean also composed a significant number of spiritual poems, all several years after emigrating to Nova Scotia,[28] which await a modern scholarly editor. Some of his religious poetry is to be found in Manuscript MG1, volume 2660, Series A (MG1/2660/A), in the Nova Scotia Archives, which also contains an account book kept by the poet, with entries mainly for the period May 1815 to June 1816. More religious poetry, together with some other material, can be found in Manuscript MG15, Series G, volumes 22 to 24 (MG15G/22-24), in the

Nova Scotia Archives. MacLean published twenty of these spiritual poems in an 1835 collection, *Laoidhean Spioradail le Iain Mac Gilleain* (Spiritual Songs by John MacLean), printed in Glasgow. Maclean Sinclair claimed that the poems in this collection "were very inaccurately printed." A manuscript of these poems was acquired by the National Library of Scotland in 2011.[29] The manuscript is in John MacLean's hand and contains all of the poems that appeared in the 1835 collection, as well as six others. This is almost certainly the manuscript from which the Glasgow printer was working, as the poems in the 1835 book are set out in the same order as those in the manuscript. The six additional poems, together with an additional verse for the last song in the 1835 book, all appear after those which were published in the book. Why these poems were not included in the book is unclear, but it may be that the poet had sent some money to fund the printing, and the printer had simply calculated that there were insufficient funds to cover the costs of printing all of the poems, and printed only those which the funds could pay for. Contrary to Maclean Sinclair's assertion, however, the book reproduces almost without fault the versions contained in the handwritten manuscript. Maclean Sinclair indicated that shortly before his death in 1848, John MacLean was considering the publication of a larger second edition of his spiritual poems, but he never accomplished this, and it was Maclean Sinclair who ultimately undertook this task with his 1880 edition of forty-seven of his grandfather's spiritual poems.[30] Given Maclean Sinclair's editorial principles, to be discussed below, a modern scholarly edition of the spiritual poems is badly needed.

Like many literate Gaels of the late eighteenth and early nineteenth centuries, John MacLean understood the utility and indeed the power of the printed word. This was a time of almost cataclysmic economic, social, and cultural change for the Scottish Highlands, and some Gaels perceived print as a means of both preserving an oral culture that was under increasing stress, and bringing aspects of that culture to a wider audience.[31] According to Maclean Sinclair, the poet would compose his songs orally and would only write them down after he had sung them, although Maclean Sinclair also notes that there were some songs which he never committed to writing and which were lost.[32] John MacLean transcribed eighteen of the secular song-poems he had composed in Tiree in a manuscript now identified as MG15, Series G, volume 2, no. 1 (MG15G/2/1), which was one of two manuscripts he brought to Nova Scotia; both manuscripts are now in the

Nova Scotia Archives. Two of the poems he composed in Nova Scotia were added at the end of this manuscript: one appears to be in the poet's hand, and the other, which Maclean Sinclair claims to have added to the manuscript in 1873, is in Maclean Sinclair's hand. John MacLean was, however, also a significant early collector of the work of other Gaelic poets – he had apparently gone on a collecting tour in about 1815 or 1816 – and the bulk of MG15G/2/1, a manuscript of approximately 650 pages, is comprised of MacLean's transcriptions of some 110 song-poems of these poets. A considerable amount of this poetry is the work of other Tiree poets and lesser-known poets from neighbouring inner Hebridean islands. However, MacLean also took down the work of widely known poets such as John MacDonald (Iain Lom) (*c.*1625–post-1707), Màiri nighean Alasdair Ruaidh (Mary MacLeod) (*c.* 1615–*c.* 1707), Mairghread nighean Lachlainn (Margaret MacLean)[33] (*c.*1660–1751), and Alexander MacKinnon (1770–1814), for whom, as was noted earlier, MacLean had composed a panegyric.[34]

In 1818, the year before he emigrated to Pictou County, Nova Scotia, on the ship *Economy*, John MacLean published four hundred copies of *Orain Nuadh Ghaedhlach* (New Gaelic Songs), which contained twenty-two of his own compositions and thirty-four by other poets, including many of the poets just mentioned, and drawn mainly from MG15G/2/1. Sixteen of his twenty-two poems can also be found in MS15G/2/1 and are virtually identical to the manuscript versions. Beginning in 1751, when Alexander MacDonald (Alasdair mac Mhaighstir Alasdair) (*c.* 1695–*c.* 1770), perhaps the greatest poet of the eighteenth century "Golden Age" of Gaelic poetry, published *Aiseiridh na Sean Chánoin Albannaich* (The Revival of the Older Scottish Language), an increasing number of important collections of Gaelic poetry began to be published.[35] John MacLean had copies and had read most of these important early collections.[36]

We get a good sense of his motives for publishing *Orain Nuadh Ghaedhlach*, and perhaps for his collecting project more generally, from the dedication to his patron, the Laird of Coll, who had apparently assisted him with the costs of publication:

> Is iomadh uair a bha mi a' smuaineachadh, mu'n do thòisich mi air an obair so, gu'm bu mhór am beud gu'm biodh na seann òrain, nach robh mi a' faicinn anns na leabhraichean a chaidh a chur a mach roimh so, air an di-chuimhneachadh; is e sin a rinn ro thoileach mi gu an cur air an adhairt.[37]

> Many a time I thought, before I started on this work, that it would be a great pity if many of the old songs, which I do not see in the collections that have been put out before now, were forgotten; and it is that which made me exceedingly happy to put them forward.

This preface offers important evidence of three things. First, it demonstrates that John MacLean knew of and had worked with various collections that had previously been published. Second, it shows that he consciously sought to publish poems and songs that had not previously been published in such collections, thereby filling gaps that had been left by other publishers. Third, it makes clear that he was motivated by a fear that, if not committed to print, many of these song-poems would be lost. In short, like many of the early collectors and publishers of Gaelic verse, MacLean understood that the oral tradition was under increasing pressure from the economic, social, and cultural forces to which reference has already been made, and he saw in print culture a way of preserving that tradition for future generations. He was therefore essentially engaged in what is now referred to as "salvage ethnography."[38] However, as we shall see, print culture can also shape tradition through the editorial choices made in committing the oral tradition to print. It is now difficult to determine the editorial principles that John MacLean may himself have applied to the texts he recorded in manuscripts and published, and therefore the degree to which MacLean himself may have shaped this material.

The second manuscript that John MacLean brought to Nova Scotia and that is now in the Nova Scotia Archives is MG15, Series G, vol. 2, no. 2 (MG15G/2/2). The first part of this manuscript – some 122 pages – was written mainly by Dr Hector Maclean of Grulin, Mull (1704–1783);[39] it was apparently in progress by 1738 and was completed by 1768.[40] Eight years older than the important early collection made by Ranald MacDonald,[41] the majority of the poems in this collection are found nowhere else. The Hector MacLean manuscript had been given to the Bard MacLean by Dr Hector's daughter.[42] Samuel Johnson had met her on his famous tour of the Hebrides in 1773, and wrote of her in complimentary terms.[43] She was apparently an old woman when she passed her father's manuscript to John MacLean.[44] The fact that she entrusted such an important document to the poet indicates the respect with which he was held as both a maker of Gaelic poetry and a custodian of Gaelic tradition. It appears that after the poet's death in 1848, the manuscript passed to the poet's son Charles, and from him to Maclean Sinclair. In addition to the texts that had been transcribed primarily by Dr Hector Maclean, there are a further 104 pages of material, including fourteen song-poems composed by John MacLean. Seven of these are in John MacLean's hand; six of these are song-poems that were composed in Nova Scotia, and one was probably composed while the poet was still in Scotland. Another four song-poems, all composed in Nova Scotia, appear to be in the hand of the poet's son, Charles. The final three, also composed by the poet in Canada, appear to be in Maclean Sinclair's hand;[45] all were added after 1859.

In 1856, John Boyd (Iain Boide) of Antigonish County, the founder and first editor and publisher of the *Casket*, the Antigonish weekly newspaper, which still exists, published eleven of John MacLean's poems in a collection titled *Orain Ghaelach le Iain Mac Illeathain, Bard Thighearn Cholla* (Gaelic Songs by John MacLean, Poet to the Laird of Coll).[46] These eleven poems are the seven in MG15G/2/2 in John MacLean's hand and the four in that same manuscript in Charles's hand; as noted, the three song-poems in Maclean Sinclair's hand in that manuscript appear to have been added after 1859. All eleven poems are essentially identical to the versions in MG15G/2/2. The town of Antigonish, the main centre for the county, is close to Glenbard, where John MacLean's family continued to reside after his death, and it is highly likely that Boyd had access to and was working from that manuscript. In 1863, another Antigonish County Gael, Norman MacDonald, published a Nova Scotian edition of John MacKenzie's hugely influential collection *Sar-Obair nam Bard Gaelach, or the Beauties of Gaelic Poetry and the Lives of the Highland Bards*, which had been first published in 1841 and which would go through seven editions by 1904.[47] MacDonald's edition was essentially a reprint of MacKenzie's, but he added a small number of items, including a profile of John MacLean that Maclean Sinclair, then only twenty-three years of age, had apparently provided him, and four of his song-poems, including "Òran do dh' Aimearaga," all of which had appeared in MS15G/2/2 and in John Boyd's collection, and which were essentially identical to those versions. MacDonald, a native of Moidart, lived in the same community as the poet and had in fact taught Maclean Sinclair in the local school in Beaver Meadow; it is almost certain, therefore, that he would have been working from the manuscript and, perhaps, Boyd's edition of the poems.[48]

Two of John MacLean's song-poems appeared in the 1870s in the periodical *An Gàidheal* (The Gael), which was published between

1871 and 1877 by Angus Nicolson, first in Toronto and then, from 1873, in Glasgow. The first, "An Gàidheal am-measg nan Gall" (The Gael amongst the Lowlanders), appeared in the first issue, in 1871;[49] it is one of the few John MacLean poems for which the Maclean Sinclair versions are essentially the same as the manuscript version and the one published by MacLean himself in 1818. A Nova Scotian composition, "Diteadh Mhic an Tòisich," one of two song-poems composed by John MacLean in the 1830s relating to Prohibition, was also published in *An Gàidheal*, in 1876;[50] this version is identical to the later Maclean Sinclair versions, but it is also one of only four John MacLean song-poems for which we have no sources other than Maclean Sinclair versions. It must have been obtained from Maclean Sinclair, though there appears to be no record of any correspondence between Maclean Sinclair and Nicolson.[51]

Two other song-poems composed by John MacLean, "Òran do dh' Aimearaga" and "Òran a' Bhàil Ghàidhealaich" (Song of the Highland Ball) – the latter is discussed in more detail below – were included by Archibald Sinclair in *The Gaelic Songster / An t-Òranaiche*, published in five parts, between 1876 and 1879, and which, along with *Sar-Obair nam Bard Gaelach*, was the most important collection of Gaelic song-poems of the nineteenth century.[52] Unlike Boyd's 1856 versions of the song-poems, which, as already noted, followed the manuscript versions, Sinclair's versions of these two song-poems resembled the versions published by Maclean Sinclair in 1881 in *Clarsach na Coille* (The Harp of the Forest). It is almost certain that Archibald Sinclair obtained from Maclean Sinclair the versions that he published, and this explains the similarities between the *Òranaiche* versions and those published subsequently by Maclean Sinclair in *Clarsach na Coille*. In a letter from Archibald Sinclair to Maclean Sinclair dated 3 May 1877, Archibald Sinclair referred to having received a copy of "Òran do dh' Aimearaga" – he referred to it as "A' Choille Ghruamach" – when Maclean Sinclair visited Scotland in 1869, but noted that this copy had gone missing, and asked Maclean Sinclair to furnish him a copy "which you consider right, as I would not like to see such a fine song appear in the Oranaiche unless it was correct." He also asked Maclean Sinclair "for any others [i.e., song-poems] you would like to appear."[53] This suggests that Maclean Sinclair had by 1877 settled upon the editorial approach he would employ in respect of the versions of the John MacLean song-poems that appear in 1881 in *Clarsach na Coille*.

The publication by Maclean Sinclair of *Clarsach na Coille* was a watershed in terms of how contemporary and subsequent generations of Gaelic speakers came to understand and interact with John MacLean's poetry. Maclean Sinclair published all but two of his grandfather's forty-four secular song-poems in this collection: one that did not appear was a New World praise poem composed for MacLean's friend, Fr Colin Grant, and the other, "Òran do Dhòmhnaill MacArtair" (A Song for Donald MacArthur), was a skilfully executed satire. It is not clear why the panegyric to Fr Grant was omitted, as it was in both MG15G/2/2 (in John MacLean's hand) and in John Boyd's 1856 collection; it was, however, subsequently published by Maclean Sinclair in *Filidh na Coille* (The Minstrel of the Forest).[54] It appears, however, that "Òran do Dhòmhnall MacArtair" was omitted because of its subject matter. This satire concerned the disastrous journey of a young Tiree Gael to Glasgow, where he got drunk and fell in with a prostitute who stole all his money and gave him a venereal disease. It is highly likely that Maclean Sinclair, a Presbyterian minister, found this subject matter to be objectionable. In his preface to *Clarsach na Coille*, Maclean Sinclair made the following comments: "I have tried to make this collection a work which may be read and sung by all persons, and in any company. I would rather burn all the songs in my possession than publish one which would have a tendency to do harm, or contain indelicate expressions."[55] Maclean Sinclair may well have had the satire of Donald MacArthur in mind when he composed those words. That Maclean Sinclair disapproved of material of a sexually explicit nature is clear from a letter he wrote on 30 January 1915 to Rev. Dr Hugh P. MacPherson, the Rector of St Francis Xavier University in Antigonish, Nova Scotia, in relation to the provision by him to the university's library of his grandfather's copy of Alasdair mac Mhaighstir Alasdair's *Ais-eiridh na Sean Chánoin Albannaich*. Maclean Sinclair had removed several pages from this important early collection, and explained to the rector why he had done so: "The leaves that I cut out between pages 152 and 161 were abominably filthy."[56] These pages had apparently contained mac Mhaighstir Alasdair's "Moladh air Deagh Bhod" (In Praise of a Good Penis) and "Tinneas na h-Urchaid" (The Venereal Disease).[57]

Maclean Sinclair's decision not to publish the poem in *Clarsach na Coille* was honoured by Hector MacDougall (1889-1954), a native of Coll, when he republished the book in 1928.[58] In the preface to this second edition, MacDougall says this about the omission:

> Bha aon òran anns an t-seann leabhar nach do chuir an ceud fhear-deasachaidh anns a' "Chlàrsaich," agus ged nach eil a' bheag ann do am faighte coire smaointich mi gun robh e cho math fhàgail às a' bhualadh so mar an ceudna, agus na bha gu math fhàgail gu math. Is ann do fhear do 'm b' ainm Dòmhnull MacArtair, d' am b' fhar-ainm "Dòmhnull Sealgair," a chaidh a dh' ionnsaidh an fhoghair gu Galldachd is a chaill a chuid airgid an luib "mhnathan-uaisle" Ghlascho a rinn se e.[59]
>
> There was one song in the old book [i.e., *Orain Nuadh Ghaedhlach*] which the first editor did not put in the "Harp," and though there are not a few who could find fault, I thought it just as well to leave it out of this edition all the same, and to leave well enough alone. It is for a man by the name of Donald MacArthur, of the nickname "Donald the Hunter," who went to the harvest in the Lowlands and who lost his money in the company of "gentle-women" of Glasgow that he [i.e., the poet] made it.

MacDougall then gave the chorus and the first three verses of the song – which make reference to the theft of Donald Hunter's money, but not to the prostitute herself or to anything of a sexual nature – prefacing them with the following comment: "Is e seo shios an t-séisd is na ceud tri rannan, ach eagal miothlachd a chosnadh cha teid mi na's fhaide na sin" (Here below is the chorus and the first three verses, but out of fear of causing upset I will not go farther than that). MacDougall was clearly uneasy with Maclean Sinclair's editorial decision effectively to censor the song, but was also clearly conscious of the sensitivities of the potential readership. There may also have been an element of deference to Maclean Sinclair himself, who had died only four years previous to the publication of this second edition.

Clarsach na Coille is the only source for four of John MacLean's secular song-poems; the other thirty-eight that appeared in the collection can also be found in one or more of MG15G/2/1, MG/15G/2/2, MacLean's 1818 collection, or Boyd's 1856 collection. Even a cursory comparison of the Maclean Sinclair versions of these thirty-eight song-poems and those found in earlier sources reveals that MacLean Sinclair frequently changed the earlier versions, in some cases quite radically. These changes went beyond merely tinkering with the orthography and often involved substituting words or phrases. In some cases, they even involved transposing passages and verses, or inserting material for which there is no basis in earlier sources; it must be assumed that this is Maclean Sinclair's own work. Charles Dunn has noted that Maclean Sinclair took "liberties" with the published songs that would "shock … rigorously trained editors of the present age," such as rearranging them "in a more artistic form" and the "smoothing out of grammatical irregularities."[60] Maclean Sinclair himself wrote the following with respect to his editorial principles:

> To prepare a collection of Gaelic poems for the press is by no means an easy work. The first difficulty is the fact that, with a very few exceptions, our Gaelic poets and song-makers were uneducated persons, and consequently frequently violated the rules of grammar and composition, and even the rules of prosody. The second difficulty is that in handing down songs from one person to another, words, lines and verses become lost. The third difficulty is that in the case of old poems one frequently meets with words which he does not understand, and which he cannot find in any dictionary.[61]

The final two difficulties identified by Maclean Sinclair appear to be directed at the older songs in the manuscript sources from which he worked rather than those of John MacLean, although the second difficulty may apply to the small number of John MacLean poems that Maclean Sinclair himself took down from informants (and to those poems transcribed by Charles MacLean, where Charles had been relying on oral sources).

Further evidence of Maclean Sinclair's approach to editing Gaelic verse can be found in a letter he wrote to Counnduillie Morrison, dated 26 January 1898, in reference to the forthcoming publication of *Na Bàird Leathanach / The MacLean Bards*, vol. 1: *The Old MacLean Bards*:

> I have made a few trifling changes in the songs you sent me, partly to remove mistakes in composition, and partly to avoid repetitions in ideas or words. I have also thrown in a verse or two. I have not, however, changed the meaning of the songs. I have weakened the statement about Calum in Mrs MacAskill's lines "Chuir mi suas mo ghùn bainnse."[62] I did not want to make it quite so clear as she made it that she cared nothing for Calum. The sheets are going off to Glasgow this week, where the book will be bound.[63]

In most cases, the changes that Maclean Sinclair made to his grandfather's texts went well beyond the trivial.

After the publication of *Clarsach na Coille* in 1881, several of John MacLean's song-poems appeared elsewhere in print. Twenty-six – nine composed in Scotland, and seventeen composed in Nova Scotia – appeared in another collection edited and published by Maclean Sinclair, *Filidh na Coille*; one, "Òran do dh' Aimearaga," appeared in yet another Maclean Sinclair collection, *The Gaelic Bards from 1775 to 1825*. All of these versions were, unsurprisingly, essentially identical to those published in *Clarsach na Coille*. As has already been mentioned, a second edition of *Clarsach na Coille*, edited by Hector MacDougall, was published in 1928, but the versions of the song-poems that appeared in this collection are essentially the same as those published by Maclean Sinclair in the first edition. All but three of John MacLean's forty-four song-poems were published in the most important collection of Tiree poetry, Eachann Camshron's *Na Baird Thirisdeach* (The Tiree Poets), although in many cases – particularly the panegyrics – only excerpts were published. In all cases, the versions were essentially identical to those published by Maclean Sinclair. Aside from the one panegyric that was published in 1856 by John Boyd, only one other song-poem composed in Scotland appears to have been published in another source, "An Gàidheal am-measg nan Gall," which, as noted earlier, was published in 1871 in the periodical *An Gàidheal*; it also appeared in 1898 in *Mac-Talla* (Echo), a weekly and latterly biweekly newspaper edited and published in Sydney, Cape Breton, between 1892 and 1904 by Jonathan G. MacKinnon, a Cape Breton Gael.[64] As also noted earlier, the Maclean Sinclair and earlier versions of this particular song-poem are, atypically, essentially the same. "Òran do dh' Aimearaga" and "Òran a' Bhàil Ghàidhealaich" also appeared in *Mac-Talla*, and in both cases the versions were essentially the same as those which Maclean Sinclair published in *Clarsach na Coille*.[65] These two are the most widely published John MacLean song-poems. "Òran do dh' Aimearaga" appeared in three Nova Scotia periodicals: the *Sydney Record*, a Nova Scotia newspaper;[66] *Mosgladh* (Awakening), published by the Scottish Catholic Society of Canada between 1922 and 1932;[67] and the Antigonish weekly newspaper the *Casket*, which was founded in 1856 by John Boyd and is still in circulation.[68] It was also published in William J. Watson's highly influential anthology of Gaelic poetry, *Bàrdachd Ghàidhlig* (Gaelic Poetry),[69] in Helen Creighton and C.I.N. MacLeod's important collection *Gaelic Songs in Nova Scotia*,[70] and in

Donald E. Meek's recent important anthology of nineteenth-century Gaelic verse, *Caran an t-Saoghail / The Wiles of the World*.[71] "Òran a' Bhàil Ghàidhealaich," which like "Òran do dh' Aimearaga" had appeared in *An t-Òranaiche* shortly before the publication of *Clarsach na Coille*, was also published in the *Casket*.[72] All of these versions were essentially those of Maclean Sinclair.

The disparities between earlier versions and most of the Maclean Sinclair versions raise the question of which versions were being sung. It should be noted that several versions have appeared on commercial recordings in recent years. In all cases, the performers – most of them renowned contemporary Gaelic singers such as Mary Jane Lamond from Nova Scotia and Arthur Cormack, James Graham, and Mary Ann Kennedy from Scotland – sing Maclean Sinclair's versions.[73] My focus in the following discussion, however, will be on versions of the song recorded from local tradition bearers, mainly from the 1960s to the 1990s, by field workers interested in traditional Gaelic song.

Before turning to such recordings, though, it will be useful to consider the evidence that at least some of John MacLean's song-poems entered the oral tradition nearer the time of composition and well before the appearance of *Clarsach na Coille* in 1881. It is now impossible to know precisely what early singers of MacLean's song-poems might have been singing, but it is certainly possible and indeed likely that their versions would have been closer to MacLean's original compositions. With respect to "Òran do dh' Aimearaga," Maclean Sinclair says the following:

> When the poet sent to Tiree his poem on America, his friends were greatly distressed about him. They offered to send money to bring him back. MacLean of Coll, his old friend, wrote him a kind letter asking him to return, and offering to give him a piece of land free of rent. A more truthful poem than his description of America was never penned; yet it is almost a pity that he sent it home. It was no doubt the means of keeping many persons from emigrating.[74]

From this, it appears that the poem circulated in writing and quite quickly became well-known in Tiree, and perhaps elsewhere in Gaelic Scotland. We also have evidence that the poem was being sung, in this case at a wedding at Tobermory, on the Isle of Mull:

> Tha e air innse gu'n deach an t-oran so a sheinn aig banais ann an Tobair-Mhoire, beagan an deidh do'n bhard a dheanamh 's a chur a nunn gu chairdean. Cha chualas am Muile e gu sin, agus mar chaidh am fear-seinn air adhart, dhruigh an dan air a luchd-eisdeachd air dhoigh 's nach robh suil thioram sa chuideachd n uair a bha e ullamh. Cha'n eil teagamh nach do chuir tilleadh air iomadh duine 's teaghlach bho thighin air imrich do'n duthaich so.[75]

> It is reported that this song was sung at a wedding in Tobermory, a short time after the poet had made it and had sent it over to his friends. It had not been heard in Mull until then, and as the singer proceeded, the song affected its listeners to such an extent that there was not a dry eye amongst those in attendance when it was finished. There is not doubt that it caused many a man and family to reconsider emigration to this country [i.e. Canada].

According to Maclean Sinclair, "Òran a' Bhàil Ghàidhealaich" was composed in response to a gathering organized by David Murray in Merigomish, Pictou County, in 1826, to which only Gaelic speakers were invited. Maclean Sinclair states that the poet repaid his invitation from Murray to attend by composing the song, which he sang at the gathering. The song, which will be explored more closely later in this chapter, is not one of those that MacLean transcribed himself. It appears in MG15G/2/2, the Dr Hector MacLean manuscript, in Maclean Sinclair's hand, and Maclean Sinclair added a note indicating that he inserted it into the manuscript on 30 October 1860. In his preface to the poem in *Clarsach na Coille*, Maclean Sinclair said that he got the song from a man named Archibald MacLean, who lived on "the Big Island," likely Big Island, Pictou County.[76] This indicates that by 1860 the song-poem was in circulation among tradition-bearers in Pictou County. As we shall see below, there are important differences between the manuscript version, written down in 1860, and the version that appears in *Clarsach na Coille*.

At least three other song-poems were in oral circulation well in advance of the publication of *Clarsach na Coille* in 1881. According to Maclean Sinclair, "An Adharc" (The Drinking Horn) was composed in about the year 1827, in recognition of a large, beautiful drinking horn filled with brandy which had been given to the poet by a William Forbes, which the poet then gave to his friend, Fr Colin Grant. The song-poem is found near the end of MG15G/2/1, John MacLean's manuscript. The identity of the scribe is not clear, but it is likely that it was either the poet's son Charles, or Maclean Sinclair. In the preface to the poem in *Clarsach na Coille*, Maclean Sinclair indicates that the song was written down from the singing of Mary Forbes of Beaver Meadow, Antigonish County, in 1873, and that a good portion of the song had already been lost. It is possible that Mary was a daughter or other relation of the unidentified William Forbes,[77] for Beaver Meadow is very close to the poet's final home, in Glenbard, Antigonish County. The manuscript version is not dramatically different from the one published in *Clarsach na Coille*, but the differences are rather significant. The second song-poem for which we have evidence regarding its presence in the oral tradition is "Don Phàrlamaid Ùir" (To the New Parliament), composed by the poet in 1830 during an election campaign in the colony of Nova Scotia. According to Maclean Sinclair, the poet had not taken much interest in the election until he was informed that one of the Liberal candidates had made some insulting references to the Gaels of the colony; in response, he composed the song that very evening and sang it at an election rally the next day. Maclean Sinclair noted that "thousands were present. It had a most exciting effect. It was a real 'brosnachadh-catha' [incitement to battle]."[78] Thus, the poem may have gone into wider oral circulation at the time of composition. The poem is found in MG15G/2/2, the Dr Hector MacLean manuscript, and appears to be in the poet's hand. The other song-poem that was in circulation was "Marbhrann do dh'Alastair Mac-Gilleain, Tighearna Chola" (An Elegy for Alexander MacLean, the Laird of Coll), which was likely composed shortly after the laird's death, in 1835. Maclean Sinclair notes that he learned about this song for the first time on New Year's night, 1880, from his uncle Archibald MacLean. John MacLean had sent the poem forty years earlier to a Hugh McLean, in Cape Breton. Maclean Sinclair contacted Hugh McLean's son, identified as Eòbhan Òg, who replied that the manuscript was lost but that his aunt, Mary McLean, and his niece, Catherine McLean, knew the song by heart, and that Eòbhan Òg had taken it down from their singing and had sent it to him.[79] The only extant version, however, is the Maclean Sinclair one.

From the foregoing, then, we know that a number of John MacLean's songs had entered the oral tradition well in advance of the appearance in print of Maclean Sinclair versions, and that it is likely, and in a few cases certain,[80] that those versions in oral circulation differed from the Maclean Sinclair versions. What, then, of the versions that were recorded from tradition bearers in the second half of the twentieth century? So far, field recordings have been located for nineteen of the forty-four secular song-poems, ten of which were composed in Scotland and nine in Nova Scotia. The single most important informant was the Tiree tradition bearer Donald Sinclair (Dòmhnall Chaluim Bàin), from whom eight of the songs composed in Scotland and three of those composed in Nova Scotia were recorded by field workers of the School of Scottish Studies at the University of Edinburgh.[81] Also recorded by School of Scottish Studies field workers were Rev. William Matheson (1910–1995) of North Uist,[82] Catrìona MacIntyre (Catrìona Dhòmhnaill Ruaidh) (b. 1935) and Mòrag MacIntyre (Mòrag Dhòmhnaill Ruaidh) (b. 1931) of Paisley,[83] Neil MacLean (1870–1954) of Ardtun, Mull,[84] and Nan MacKinnon (Nan Eachainn Fhionnlaigh) (1903–1982) of Barra and Vatersay.[85] As part of the Cape Breton Gaelic Folklore project, conducted between 1977 and 1982, John MacLean's song-poems were recorded by Dr John Shaw from informants such as Joe Allan MacLean of Rear Christmas Island, Cape Breton County, Johnny Williams of Melford, Inverness County, and Mary Ann MacMillan of Beinn Eòin, Cape Breton County.[86] Two of John MacLean's songs were recorded by the American folklorist MacEdward Leach (1897–1967) during a trip to Cape Breton in 1949, one of them from Angus MacIsaac of Giant's Lake, Antigonish County.[87] Maureen Williams (née Lonergan) recorded songs from Archie Alex MacKenzie and his sister, Sister Jane MacKenzie, of Christmas Island, Cape Breton, in 1974.[88] A number of private collectors have also recorded versions of John MacLean songs from Cape Breton informants. The most frequently recorded songs are three song-poems composed in Nova Scotia, "Òran do dh' Aimearaga," "Òran a' Bhàil Ghàidhealaich," and "Marbhrann do Mhrs. Noble" (An Elegy for Mrs Noble), all of which have been recorded from both Scottish and Cape Breton informants. One song composed in Scotland, "An Gàidheal am-measg nan Gall," has also been recorded from informants on both sides of the Atlantic.

In many cases, the informants sing only selected verses of the song-poems, and not infrequently, the order of the verses does not follow the order in any of the manuscript or published versions. In terms of the content, however, only one informant, Neil MacLean of Ardtun, Mull, from whom the lament "Cumha, do Ghilleasbaig MacGilleain,

Fear na Sgurra" (An Elegy, for Archibald MacLean, the Laird of Scour) was recorded, sang a version of a song-poem that more closely resembles the John MacLean version in *Orain Nuadh Ghaedhlach* than the Maclean Sinclair version in *Clarsach na Coille*.[89] In every other case, the version recorded more closely resembles the Maclean Sinclair version. This provides strong evidence not only of the power of print to shape the oral tradition, but also of the power of relatively later, apparently authoritative and widely available print editions to do so.

The song-poem "Òran a' Bhàil Ghàidhealaich," frequently referred to by its first line, "Bithibh Aotrom 's Togaibh Fonn" (Be Light-hearted and Raise a Tune), provides an interesting illustration both of the impact of print and of the ways in which print and the oral tradition interact. Alongside "Òran do dh' Aimearaga," it is one of the two song-poems that have been reprinted in the largest number of collections and recorded most frequently from tradition bearers by field workers; indeed, "Òran a' Bhàil Ghàidhealaich" is still popular amongst Gaelic speakers in both Scotland and Nova Scotia.[90] As noted above, it was composed by John MacLean in 1826 and apparently performed publicly at that time. It was not, however, transcribed in MG15G/2/2 until 1860, when, Maclean Sinclair claimed, he wrote it down from the singing of a Pictou County man, an indication that it was already established in the oral tradition in a form that is reflected in the manuscript version.

The song-poem has a chorus and sixteen verses in the version that appears in MG15G/2/2. In the Maclean Sinclair version published in *Clarsach na Coille* and in all other printed sources thereafter, the chorus and the first seven verses are essentially the same as those in MG15G/2/2; in the remaining verses, Maclean Sinclair makes some obvious changes, although none are as dramatic as those he made to some other texts. He also followed the order of the verses in the manuscript version, but added an additional quatrain after verse ten in the manuscript version, with the result that the Maclean Sinclair versions contain seventeen verses. This is the quatrain added by Maclean Sinclair in *Clarsach na Coille*:

Bha iad fìrinneach gun fhoill
'N àm dol sìos 'us pìob 'ga seinn;
Rùisgte brataichean ri croinn
Aig na saighdeiribh nach mealladh.

They were righteous, without deceit
When advancing to the skirl of pipes;
Banners unfurled on their poles
By the soldiers who wouldn't disappoint.

In the song-poem, John MacLean emphasized in several verses the martial qualities of the Gaels. Maclean Sinclair apparently felt the need to egg the pudding even further, emphasizing the moral as well as the martial virtues of the Highland soldier, something he did repeatedly in his treatment of his grandfather's compositions.

In Scotland, the song has been recorded several times by School of Scottish Studies field workers; informants have included Mòrag MacIntyre,[91] her sister Catriona,[92] and Rev. William Matheson.[93] In Nova Scotia, many recordings have also been made, and informants have included Joe Allan MacLean of Christmas Island,[94] Peter MacLean (Peadar Jack Pheadair Chaluim Ghobha) of Rear Christmas Island,[95] and Sr Jane MacKenzie, also of Christmas Island;[96] the author has also heard a recording of the song made by the late Seumas Watson of Queensville, Cape Breton, from the singing of Angus Rankin of Mabou Ridge, Inverness County.[97] In all cases, although the informants generally do not sing the whole song, and although the order of verses differs from that in the printed sources, the verses that are sung all more closely resemble the Maclean Sinclair versions than the version that was transcribed and added to MG15G/2/2 in 1860.[98] In some cases, we know that the singer was literate in Gaelic and had recourse to printed versions. It has been demonstrated with respect to one such singer, Peter MacLean of Rear Christmas Island, that a printed version is often consulted and acts as a sort of *aide memoire*; the printed version prompts memories of past performances by other tradition bearers, but he does not necessarily defer to it.[99] Nevertheless, versions recorded from Peter MacLean are consistently closer to the Maclean Sinclair versions, and clearly provide a good illustration of the power of a widely available and apparently authoritative printed version to shape performance. With regard to the air, however, there is somewhat more diversity. In the Cape Breton recordings, two closely related but nonetheless distinct airs exist; one is more closely associated with tradition bearers from Christmas Island, the other with tradition bearers from Inverness County such as Angus Rankin. There are also minor but interesting differences in the airs recorded from singers in Scotland, as well as subtle differences in speed of delivery and rhythm.

A particularly interesting recording of "Òran a' Bhàil Ghàidhealaich," for it illustrates many of these points, was made by MacEdward Leach during his 1949 tour of Cape Breton. Unfortunately, the name of the informant was not recorded, but based on the air, which resembles the Inverness County air,[100] the informant may have been from that county. The song is available on the MacEdward Leach website at Memorial University of Newfoundland, where the recordings are held; unfortunately, only an excerpt of it is presently available online, though a transcription has been made of the entire song.[101] The informant sings the chorus and verses one, two, fourteen, nine, sixteen, fifteen and ten, in that order. The version in MG15G/2/2, which Maclean Sinclair had copied down, Maclean Sinclair's published text, and the informant's version are compared below. The chorus and verses one and two differ very little in all three of the versions considered here.

Here are these verses in the version in MG15G/2/2. The ways in which they depart from Maclean Sinclair's published versions are in bold:

Chorus Bithibh aotrom 's togaibh fonn, Cridheil, sunntach gun 'bhith trom, 'G òl deoch-slàinte na bheil thall, Ann an tìr nam beann 's nan gleannaibh.	 Be lighthearted and raise tune, Cheerful and happy, without being sad, Drinking a toast to those over there, In the land of the mountains and glens.
1 Fhuair mi sgeul a bha ro bhinn, Dh'ùraich gleus air teud mo chinn, 'S bidh mi 'nis a' dol 'ga sheinn, Ged tha mi 'sa choill' a' falach. Bithibh aotrom &c.	I got news that was most sweet, And which renewed my poetic muse, I am now going to sing a verse, Though I'm hidden in the forest.
2 Gur h-i sgeul a fhuair mi 'n dràst,' 'S gun a dhùisg i mi gu dàn, 'Bhith 'gam iarraidh 'dh'ionnsaidh bàil 'Th' aig na Gàidheil tùs an earraich.	It is news that I just received, Which inspired me to a song, Being invited to a ball That the Gaels'll have at the start of spring.

14 **Gu tìr** na' Gàidheal **gasta,** treun,
'Rachadh acfhuinneach air ghleus;
Tha **iad** fuasgailte gu feum,
Tha sealgairean air fèidh 'sna beannaibh.

To the land of the excellent, hearty Gaels,
Who'd go well-equipped and prepared;
They are active in time of need,
Hunters chase deer in the hills.

9 **'S gun b' e sin** 'n t-èideadh cuinn',
Breacan **an èileadh** ghrinn,
Osa**i**n **gh**eàrr mun 'chalpa chruinn,
'S boineid ghorm os c**io**nn na mala.

Wasn't that the angled costume,
Tartan of the handsome kilt,
Short hose around their firm calves,
And a blue bonnet upon the brow.

16 Bho nach ruig sinn orra 'n dràst',
Lion **bho ghrunnd a' chuach gu** 'stràc,
'S cuir **man** cuairt i 'nuas gun dàil
Ann an onair àrd nam fearaibh.

Since we cannot reach her right now,
Fill the cup from its bottom to its rim,
And send it around without delay,
In a great tribute to these men.

15 Soraidh bhuam **far chuan** a-null,
Don tìr **ìosal** 'n robh mi 'n tùs,
'S tric a dh'fheuch iad **i** fo 'siùil,
'S iad 'ga stiùireadh 'dh'ionnsaidh cala.

Farewell from me over across the sea,
To the low-lying land where I was young,
Often they'd see her under sail,
As they steer her toward harbour.

10 **Claidheamh cruaidh air chniochdan fìor** [omitted in Sinclair versions]
Stàilinn ghlas mar ealtainn ghèarr,
A' làimh nan gaisgeach nach tais fiamh,
'S nach **bidh** riamalach **gu** 'tarrain.'[102]

A steel sword on true soldiers,
Grey steel, sharp as a razor,
In the hands of the hardy heroes,
And who won't be slow in drawing it.

This is how verses fourteen, nine, sixteen, fifteen and ten appear in *Clarsach na Coille* and Maclean Sinclair's other publications. The ways in which they depart from MG15G/2/2 are in bold:

14 **Òlaibh air** na Gàidhe**il th**reun
Rachadh acfhuinneach air ghleus,
'S a tha fuasgailte**ach** gu feum
Sealgairean air féidh 's na beannaibh.

9 **'S ann ac' féin 'tha** 'n t-éideadh grinn!
Breacan **guaile, fèile cuim**,
Òsan geàrr mu 'n chalpa chruinn,
'S boineid ghorm os ceann na mala.

16 Bho nach ruig sinn orra 'n dràst,
Lìon **a' chuach a suas fo** stràic,
'S cuir **mu 'n** cuairt i nuas gun dàil
Ann an ònair àrd nam fearaibh.

15 Soraidh bhuam **do 'n t-sluagh** a null
'Tha 'san tìr **'s a**n robh mi 'n tùs.—
'S tric a dh' fheuch iad **bàt'** fo shiùil
'S iad 'g a stiùireadh 'dh' ionnsaidh cala.

10 Stàilinn ghlas, mar ealtuinn giar, [line 2 in 1860 version]
Chleachdadh anns na baiteil riamh [new line]
Leis na gaisgich nach tais fiamh
'S nach **biodh** riamalach **a** tarruing.

Finally, here is the transcription of these verses as sung by the unknown Cape Breton informant recorded by MacEdward Leach in 1949. The ways in which they depart from MG15G/2/2 – and accord with Maclean Sinclair's published text – are in bold, and the ways, almost all relatively minor, in which they depart from Maclean Sinclair's published text are italicized:

14 *'S* **òlaibh air** na Gàidheil **th**reun
Rachadh acfhuinneach air gleus[103]
'S a *bha* fuasgailte**ach** gu feum
Sealgairean *na* fèidh *nam* beann*an*.

9 **'S ann aca f*h*èin *b*ha'n** t-èideadh grinn
Breacan **guaile***adh* 's fèile*adh* **cuim**
Òsan geàrr mun chalpa chr*io*nn
'S boineid ghorm os c*io*nn na mala.

16 *'S* bho nach ruig sinn orr' an dràsd'
Lìon **a' chuach** *seo* **suas gu** stràic
Cuir mun cuairt i nuas gun dàil
Ann an ònair àrd nam fearaibh.

15 Sòraidh *bhuan dhan* **t-sluagh a** null
Anns **an tìr** 'san robh mi 'n tùs
'S tric d dh'fheuch iad **bàt'** fo siùil
'S iad *a'* stiùireadh *i gu* cala.

10 Stàilinn ghlas *nan allta* geur
Chleachd *iad* **anns na** *bàtail* **riamh**
Aig **na gaisgich** nach tais fiamh
'S nach **biodh** *dìombanach mun* tarraing.

It is quite apparent that the version recorded by MacEdward Leach is much closer to Maclean Sinclair's published text than to the earlier version added to MG15G/2/2 in 1860, suggesting once again that, at some point, a Maclean Sinclair publication had an impact on the oral tradition. It is suggested that the differences that do exist between the recorded version and Maclean Sinclair's published text are the result of accretions during the process of oral transmission of the song, or are possibly attributable to small lapses in memory of an informant who appears to be older, or perhaps a combination of these factors.

While any conclusions can only be tentative, it would seem that at least two observations can be made based on the evidence presented in this chapter. First, it is clear that the Maclean Sinclair versions of John MacLean's songs have been treated by subsequent publishers and editors as the authoritative versions, as these are the versions that have appeared in print subsequent to the publication of *Clarsach na Coille*. In most cases, it is likely that such publishers and editors would not have had access to the manuscript versions, John MacLean's 1818 collection, or Boyd's 1856 collection, and would have assumed that the versions published by Maclean Sinclair, the poet's grandson, were definitive and reliable. Second, it appears that the publication of the Maclean Sinclair versions has had an impact on the oral tradition. Either the informants themselves, or the singers from whom the informants learned the songs, were influenced by a printed Maclean Sinclair version. Taken together, the power of the printed word seems clear, and the power of later, apparently authoritative and widely available versions is especially great.

NOTES

1 For Gaelic perspectives on the controversy, see Mackenzie, *Report*; Campbell, *Popular Tales*; Thomson, *Gaelic Sources*.

2 See Black, "I Thought He Made It All Up."

3 For an account of the life and work of Maclean Sinclair, see Linkletter, "*Bu Dual Dha Sin*." As we shall see, a smaller amount of MacLean's song-poetry was published shortly after his death by the Antigonish-based publisher John Boyd.

4 For example: "John MacLean was probably the most versatile and renowned of the Highland poets to come out to the New World: Dunn, *Highland Settler*, 60; "Iain MacGhillEathain (John Maclean) is usually regarded as the main patriarch of Nova Scotia Gaelic verse": Thomson, *Introduction*, 220; "undoubtedly one of the greatest Gaelic bards who ever left Scotland": MacDonell, *Emigrant Experience*, 68.

5 "He was, undoubtedly, the ablest, as well as the most productive, of the Tiree bards": Camshron, *Na Baird Thirisdeach*, 38.

6 Sinclair, *Clarsach na Coille*, 132.

7 Ibid., xvii–xviii. In about 1830, he, his wife, and their six children moved once again, six miles east, to what is now Glenbard, Antigonish County (xx).

8 Ibid., xiii.

9 Much of the poet's biographical information was provided by Maclean Sinclair in "Memoir to John MacLean" in *Clarsach na Coille*, xiii–xxvi.

10 One of Neil Lamont's poems and two of Archibald MacLean's poems can be found in Camshron, *Na Baird Thirisdeach*. One of John MacLean's brothers, Donald Cooper (Dòmhnall Cùbair), was also a popular Tiree poet – five of his poems are to be found in Camshron, *Na Baird Thirisdeach* – and one of his sons, Charles, as well as Maclean Sinclair, also composed poetry.

11 Sinclair, *Clarsach na Coille*, xviii–xx.

12 Ibid., xvi.

13 Ibid., xxv.

14 Ibid., xxiii.

15 In "Marbhrann do 'n Bhàrd Mac-Gilleain" in Sinclair, *Filidh na Coille*, 141. All translations are the author's own.

16 MacDonald, *Sar-Obair*, 324.

17 Ibid.

18 John Cameron [Iain Camshron], "Òran Cumha," *Casket*, 3 March 1853, 4.

19 Dunbar, "Secular Poetry," Appendix 1, Poem 28, ll. 135–6.

20 Withers, *Gaelic Scotland*, 129.

21 Sinclair, *Clarsach na Coille*, xiv.

22 Dunbar, "Secular Poetry."

23 For a short biographical account, see Sinclair, *Clan Gillean*, 381–3. For a more detailed discussion of the MacLeans of Coll, see Maclean-Bristol, *From Clan to Regiment*.

24 For a short biographical account, see Sinclair, *Clan Gillean*, 383.

25 Glengarry maintained older chiefly practices such as the patronage of a poet and a piper, while at the same time instigating widespread clearances on his estate. For a detailed biography, see Osborne, *Last of the Chiefs*, and for a more concise account, see MacDonald, *Clan Ranald*.

26 See Dunbar, "Bàrdachd Alasdair MhicFhionghain." John MacLean published two of MacKinnon's poems: Mac Illeain, *Orain Nuadh Ghaedhlach*; and Maclean Sinclair published a collection of them: Sinclair, *Dain agus Orain*. For a brief biographical sketch, and a modern edition of one of his finest poems, "Blàr na h-Òlaind" (The Battle of Holland), see Black, *An Lasair*, 521–3 and 354–61. For a modern edition of another of his finest poems, "Òran air don Bhàrd a Dhol air Tìr san Eiphit" (A Song by the Poet after Going Ashore in Egypt), see Meek, *Caran an t-Saoghail*, 298–303 and 444–5.

27 See Dunbar, "Secular Poetry," Appendix 2, 247–9.

28 Sinclair, *Clarsach na Coille*, xxi.

29 NLS MS.29901, "Spiritual verse in Gaelic by John Maclean."

30 Sinclair, *Dain Spioradail*.

31 Meek, "Gaelic Printing."

32 Sinclair, *Clarsach na Coille*, xxi.

33 There is, however, uncertainty over whether she was a MacLean or a MacDonald: see Ó Baoill, *Mairghread nighean Lachlainn*, 15–18.

34 Ó Baoill, *Maclean Manuscripts*. Ó Baoill gives a comprehensive and detailed catalogue of the contents of both manuscripts.

35 See Dunbar, "Vernacular Gaelic Tradition," 55.

36 Sinclair, *Clarsach na Coille*, xxiii.

37 As reproduced in MacDougall, *Clarsach na Coille*, v.

38 Calhoun, *Dictionary*, 424. For an account of the continuing influence of the "salvage" paradigm in Gaelic scholarship, see MacDonald, "Doomsday Fieldwork."

39 For a summary of the life of Dr Hector Maclean, see Maclean-Bristol, "MacLeans," 86–7.

40 Thomson, *Introduction*, 145; Ó Baoill, *Maclean Manuscripts*, 36.

41 This is known as the Eigg Collection; MacDomhnuill, *Comh-chruinneachidh*.

42 She is identified by Maclean Sinclair as "Màiri nighean an Dotair" (Mary, the Doctor's daughter), though it appears that her name was actually

Christina. See Ó Baoill, *Maclean Manuscripts*, 37; and Sanger and Kinnaird, *Tree of Strings*, 161–2, 239n14.

43 Levi, *Journey*, 132.

44 Sinclair, *Clarsach na Coille*, v; Sinclair, *Na Bàird Leathanach*, 5–6.

45 Ó Baoill, *Maclean Manuscripts*, 37, 49–55.

46 For a profile of Boyd and of the paper he founded, see MacLean, *Casket*, esp. 13–15.

47 MacLean, *Typographia*, 247–8.

48 Donald M. Sinclair, "Some Family History," unpublished typescript dated 1979, Nova Scotia Archives CS90/S616, 10, 46n15.

49 Mac Gilleadhain, "An Gàidheal," 10.

50 Mac-Gill-Eathain, "Diteadh," 262–4.

51 See Linkletter, "*Bu Dual Dha Sin*," Appendix E, "Correspondents in the Maclean, Sinclair Family Fonds, MG 1, vol. 2660, Nova Scotia Archives."

52 Donald MacLean notes that *An t-Òranaiche* "is undoubtedly one of the most popular Gaelic Song Books ever published": *Typographia*, 348.

53 Linkletter, "Alexander Maclean Sinclair Papers," 11; Linkletter, "*Bu Dual Dha Sin*," 252.

54 Sinclair, *Filidh na Coille*, 64.

55 Sinclair, *Clarsach na Coille*, vii.

56 Linkletter, "Alexander Maclean Sinclair Papers," 10.

57 Ibid.

58 See MacCalmain, "Eachann MacDhughaill," 362.

59 MacDougall, *Clarsach na Coille*, ix.

60 Dunn, *Highland Settler*, 80–1.

61 Sinclair, *Clarsach na Coille*, vi.

62 Found at Sinclair, *Na Bàird Leathanach*, 258.

63 Ó Baoill, *Bàrdachd Chloinn Ghill-Eathain*, xxxii–xxxiii.

64 Am Bard Mac Gilleain [John MacLean], "An Gaidheal am measg nan Gall," *Mac-Talla*, 25 February 1898, 280.

65 [John MacLean], "A Choille Ghruamach: Oran do dh-America," *Mac-Talla*, 25 January 1896, 8; Am Bard Mac-Gilleain, "Am Bal Gaidhealach," *Mac-Talla*, 17 October 1896, 112.

66 *Sydney Record*, 23 April 1921, 9.

67 MacGilleain, "Oran."

68 Iain MacGilleathain, "A' Choille Ghruamach," *Casket*, 14 November 1935, 8.

69 Watson, *Bàrdachd Ghàidhlig*, 14-19.

70 Creighton and MacLeod, *Gaelic Songs*, 296–7.

71 Meek, *Caran an t-Saoghail*, 64–73. Meek published a second John MacLean song-poem in this collection, "Òran don 'Chuairtear'" (A Song to the Visi-

tor), in praise of the Gaelic journal *Cuairtean nan Gleann*, which was published between 1840 and 1843 by Rev. Norman MacLeod: ibid., 202–5. "Òran don 'Chuairtear'" and another song-poem, "Am Mealladh" (The Deception), were published by Sr Margaret MacDonell in *Emigrant Experience*, 70–9. For an extended biographical sketch of Rev. MacLeod and a representative sample of his prose writings, see Clerk, *Caraid nan Gaidheal*. Meek also published one of John MacLean's spiritual songs, "Craobhsgaoileadh an t-Soisgeil san Tìr seo" (The Propagation of the Gospel in this Country) in *Caran an t-Saoghail*, 72–9.

72 *Casket*, 25 October 1928, 8. One other song composed by John MacLean in Nova Scotia, an elegy composed on the death of MacLean's good friend, Father Colin Grant, the parish priest of Arisaig, Antigonish County, Nova Scotia, appeared in the *Casket*, 7 October 1926, 8.

73 Mary Jane Lamond performs "An Gàidheal am measg nan Gall" (The Gael amongst the Lowlanders) on *Stòras* (turtlemusik, 2005); Arthur Cormack performs "Òran do dh'Aimearaga" under the title "A' Choille Ghruamach" (The Gloomy Forest) on *Ruith na Gaoithe* (Temple Records, 1989); James Graham performs "Marbhrann do Mhrs. Noble" (An Elegy for Mrs Noble) and Mary Ann Kennedy performs "Bithibh Aotrom (Am Bàl Gàidhealach)" (Be Cheerful [The Highland Ball), both on *The Tiree Songbook* (The Tiree Association, 2017).

74 Sinclair, *Clarsach na Coille*, xix.

75 This is from a column by an anonymous author in the *Sydney Record*, 23 April 1921, 9. Given the similarity of a subsequent passage in this column and the remarks of Maclean Sinclair in *Clarsach na Coille*, it is possible that Maclean Sinclair was the author.

76 Sinclair, *Clarsach na Coille*, 134.

77 There was, however, a William Forbes, identified as a native of Strathglass, Inverness-shire, Scotland, living at Beaver Meadow: MacLean, *History*, 78.

78 Sinclair, *Clarsach na Coille*, 145. The *brosnachadh-catha* is an old genre of Gaelic poetry.

79 Ibid., 125.

80 For example, where Maclean Sinclair collected the song-poem itself and set it down in a manuscript, and then published an altered version in *Clarsach na Coille*.

81 For a profile of Donald Sinclair, see Cregeen, "Donald Sinclair." He was born on 6 August 1885 at Balephuil, Tiree, and died on 3 April 1975. The recordings of him are accessible from the Tobar an Dualchais online database: http://www.tobarandualchais.co.uk, accessed 30 May 2019. He was recorded primarily by Dr John MacInnes, but also by Eric Cregeen. In the Cregeen

recordings, it appears that Cregeen was asking Sinclair about songs published in *Na Baird Thirisdeach*, and was having Sinclair sing aided by the book itself.

82 See http://www.tobarandualchais.co.uk/en/person/482, accessed 30 May 2019. For a profile, see MacDonald, "William Matheson."

83 See http://www.tobarandualchais.co.uk/en/person/328 and http://www.tobarandualchais.co.uk/en/person/319, accessed 31 May 2019. Both Catrìona and Mòrag are daughters of Donald MacIntyre (Dòmhnall Ruadh Phàislig) (1889–1964) of South Uist and Paisley, one of the major traditional Gaelic poets of the twentieth century: see MacMillan, *Sporan Dhòmhnaill*.

84 MacLean was a crofter and forestry worker: http://www.tobarandualchais.co.uk/en/person/42, accessed 31 May 2019.

85 MacInnes, "Nan MacKinnon"; McDermitt, "Nan MacKinnon"; http://www.tobarandualchais.co.uk/en/person/1864, accessed 31 May 2019.

86 These recordings are available on the Gaelstream online database, curated by St Francis Xavier University, where the project was based: http://gaelstream.stfx.ca.

87 "MacEdward Leach: Biography," *MacEdward Leach and the Songs of Atlantic Canada*, Memorial University of Newfoundland Folklore and Language Archive, http://www.mun.ca/folklore/leach/biography/index.html, accessed 31 May 2019. This website is curated by Memorial University of Newfoundland; the recordings are available at "Cape Breton Songs by Title," http://www.mun.ca/folklore/leach/songs/CBsongs.htm.

88 These recordings are included on the cassette accompanying Lonergan, "Canadian Songs," her 1974 MA thesis in Celtic Studies at St Francis Xavier University, completed under the direction of C.I.N. MacLeod. The cassette is held at the Father Charles Brewer Celtic Collection. It appears to me from the recordings that Sister MacKenzie may have been singing aided by *Clarsach na Coille*.

89 SSS SA1953.105.B1.

90 For a recent recording of young Nova Scotia Gaelic singers, see "Bithibh Aotrom 's Togaibh Fonn, Caraman" in the An Drochaid Eadarainn account on YouTube, https://www.youtube.com/watch?v=2FoFvaYOovg, accessed 31 May 2019. The primary singer is Carmen MacArthur.

91 SSS SA1953.09.B1, recorded by Calum Iain Maclean.

92 SSS SA1959.04.B12, recorded by Calum Iain Maclean.

93 SSS SA1975.218.B8, recorded by Ian Paterson.

94 CBFC tapes 209/A02, 246/A04, and 258/A04, recorded by John Shaw.

95 Peter MacLean's version can be heard online: "Siorramachdan Antaiginis is Phiogto: Na h-Òrain: Bithibh Aotrom 's Togaibh Fonn," *An Drochaid Eadarainn*, http://www.androchaid.com/1-bithibh-aotrom-s-togaibh-fonn,

accessed 31 May 2019. He sang a longer version of the song for the CD that accompanied a 2004 republication by Trueman Matheson of Archibald Sinclair's *An t-Òranaiche*.

96 Sr Jane MacKenzie was recorded by Maureen Lonergan (Williams); see the cassette accompanying Lonergan, "Canadian Songs," in the Father Charles Brewer Celtic Collection.

97 The air sung by Carmen MacArthur in the version referred to in note 90 *supra* is essentially the same air that was sung by Angus Rankin.

98 Abridged texts and differently ordered verses are common features of songs that survive in the oral tradition.

99 Conn, "Fitting," 367–9.

100 Care must be taken with such generalizations, as we have only a small number of field recordings, and it is not clear that the same air is or would have been sung throughout Inverness County.

101 "Bithibh Aotrom 's Togaibh Fonn (Be Merry and Raise a Tune)," *MacEdward Leach and the Songs of Atlantic Canada*, Memorial University of Newfoundland Folklore and Language Archive, https://www.mun.ca/folklore/leach/songs/CB/5-05.htm, accessed 31 May 2019. Staff at Memorial University have indicated to the author that they plan to put the full recordings on the website in the near future. I am grateful to the staff for having provided me with a sound file of the entire recording, and the transcription that appears in this chapter is mine; it differs in only minor respects from that which is provided on the website itself.

102 Maclean, Sinclair Family Fonds, Nova Scotia Archives, MG15G/2/2, 226.

103 No aspiration of *gleus* (i.e., *ghleus*), as in the Maclean Sinclair versions.

BIBLIOGRAPHY

Black, Ronald, ed. *An Lasair: Anthology of 18th Century Scottish Gaelic Verse*. Edinburgh: Birlinn, 2001.

– "'I Thought He Made It All Up': Context and Controversy." In *The Life and Legacy of Alexander Carmichael*, ed. Dòmhnall Uilleam Stiùbhart, 57–81. Port of Ness, Lewis: Islands Book Trust, 2008.

Boide, Iain, ed. *Orain Ghaelach le Iain Mac Illeathain, Bard Thighearn Cholla*. Antigonish, 1856.

Calhoun, Craig J., ed. *Dictionary of the Social Sciences*. Oxford: Oxford University Press, 2002.

Campbell, John F., ed. *Popular Tales of the West Highlands, Orally Collected*, vol. 4. Edinburgh: Edmonston and Douglas, 1862.

Camshron, Eachann. *Na Baird Thirisdeach: Saothair ar Co-Luchd-Duthcha aig an Tigh 's bho 'n Tigh / The Tiree Bards: Being the Original Compositions of Natives of Tiree at Home and Abroad*. Stirling: The Tiree Association, 1932.

Clerk, Rev. Archibald, ed. *Caraid nan Gaidheal / The Friend of the Gael: A Choice Selection of the Gaelic Writings by Norman MacLeod D.D.* Edinburgh: John Grant, 1910.

Conn, Stephanie. "Fitting between Present and Past: Memory and Social Interaction in Cape Breton Gaelic Singing." *Ethnomusicology Forum* 21, no. 3 (2012): 354–73.

Cregeen, Eric. "Donald Sinclair." *Tocher* 18 (1975): 41–3.

Creighton, Helen, and Calum Macleod. eds. *Gaelic Songs in Nova Scotia*. Ottawa: National Museums of Canada, 1979.

Dunbar, Robert D. "'Bàrdachd Alasdair MhicFhionghain': An Early Nineteenth Century Panegyric to a Poet." In *Bile ós Chrannaibh: A Festschrift for William Gillies*, ed. Wilson McLeod, Abigail Burnyeat, Domhnall Uilleam Stiùbhart, Thomas Owen Clancy, and Roibeard Ó Maolalaigh, 103–18. Ceann Drochaid: Clann Tuirc, 2010.

– "The Secular Poetry of John MacLean, 'Bàrd Thighearna Chola,' 'Am Bàrd MacGilleain,'" PhD diss., University of Edinburgh, 2007.

– "Vernacular Gaelic Tradition: 16th–19th Centuries." In *The Edinburgh Companion to Scottish Traditional Literatures*, ed. Sarah Dunnigan and Suzanne Gilbert, 51–62. Edinburgh: Edinburgh University Press, 2013.

Dunn, Charles W. *Highland Settler: A Portrait of the Scottish Gael in Cape Breton and Eastern Nova Scotia*. Toronto: University of Toronto Press, 1980.

Levi, Peter, ed. *A Journey to the Western Islands of Scotland and The Journal of a Tour to the Hebrides*, by Samuel Johnson and James Boswell. London: Penguin Books, 1984.

Linkletter, Michael D. "The Alexander Maclean Sinclair Papers in NSARM." *Scotia: Interdisciplinary Journal of Scottish Studies* 27 (2003): 6–21.

– "*Bu Dual Dha Sin* (That Was His Birthright): Gaelic Scholar Alexander Maclean Sinclair (1840–1924)." PhD diss., Harvard University, 2006.

Lonergan, Maureen. "The Canadian Songs of John Maclean (Am Bard MacGilleathain)." MA thesis, University of Glasgow, 1977.

MacCalmain, T.M. "Eachann MacDhughaill." *Gairm* 2 (1954): 362.

MacDomhnuill, Raonuill. *Comh-chruinneachidh Orannaigh Gaidhealach*. Duneidiunn [Edinburgh]: Walter Ruddiman, 1776.

MacDonald, Donald A. "William Matheson." *Tocher* 35 (1981): 283–91.

MacDonald, Fraser. "Doomsday Fieldwork, or, How to Rescue Gaelic Culture? The Salvage Paradigm in Geography, Archaeology, and Folklore,

1955–62." *Environment and Planning D: Society and Space* 29, no. 2 (2011): 309–35.

MacDonald, Norman. *Sar-Obair nam Bard Gaelach, or The Beauties of Gaelic Poetry and the Lives of the Highland Bards*. Halifax: James Bowes and Sons, 1863.

MacDonald, Norman H. *The Clan Ranald of Knoydart and Glengarry: A History of the MacDonalds or MacDonells of Glengarry*, 2nd ed. Edinburgh: Forrest Hepburn and McDonald, 1995.

MacDonell, Margaret. *The Emigrant Experience: Songs of Highland Emigrants in North America*. Toronto: University of Toronto Press, 1982.

MacDougall, Hector. *Clarsach na Coille, a Collection of Gaelic Poetry by the Rev. A. Maclean Sinclair LL.D.* Glasgow: Alex. MacLaren and Sons, 1928.

MacGilleain, am Barde [*sic*] [John MacLean]. "Oran do dh' America," *Mosgladh* 1, no. 9 (1928): 4, 5, 6.

Mac Gilleain, Iain [John MacLean]. *Laoidhean Spioradail le Iain Mac Gilleain; a rugadh ann an eilean Thireadh 'S tha 'n drast ann an America mu Thuath*. Glascho [Glasgow]: Bell agus Bain, 1835.

Mac Gilleadhain, Iain [John MacLean]. "An Gàidheal am measg nan Gall." *An Gàidheal* 1 (1871): 10.

Mac-Gill-Eathain, Am Bard [John MacLean]. "Diteadh Mhic-an-Toisich." *An Gàidheal* 5 (1876): 262–4.

Mac Illeain, Iain [John MacLean]. *Orain Nuadh Ghaedhlach*. Duneudainn [Edinburgh]: R. Meinnearach, 1818.

MacInnes, John. "Nan MacKinnon." *Tocher* 7 (1972): 201–3.

Mackenzie, Henry, ed. *Report of the Committee of the Highland Society of Scotland Appointed to Inquire into the Nature and Authenticity of the Poems of Ossian*. Edinburgh: Archibald Constable, 1805.

Maclean, Donald. *Typographia Scoto-Gaedelica*. Shannon: Irish University Press, [1915]1972.

MacLean, Raymond A., ed. *History of Antigonish*, by Rev. Ronald MacGillivray and Charles J. MacGillivray, vol. 1. Antigonish: Casket-, 1976.

– *The Casket: 1852–1992, From Gutenberg to Internet: The Story of a Small-Town Weekly*. Antigonish: Casket Printing and Publishing, ca. 1992.

Maclean-Bristol, Nicholas. *From Clan to Regiment: Six Hundred Years in the Hebrides 1400–2000*. Barnsley: Pen and Sword Military, 2007.

– "The MacLeans from 1560–1707: A Re-Appraisal." In *The Seventeenth Century in the Highlands*, ed. Loraine Maclean of Lochdarroch, 70–88. Inverness: Inverness Field Club, 1986.

Macmillan, Somerled, ed. *Sporan Dhòmhnaill: Gaelic Poems and Songs by the Late Donald MacIntrye the Paisley Bard*. Edinburgh: Scottish Gaelic Texts Society, 1968.

McDermitt, Barbara. "Nan MacKinnon." *Tocher* 38 (1983): 3–11.

Meek, Donald E., ed. *Caran an t-Saoghail / The Wiles of the World: Anthology of 19th Century Scottish Gaelic Verse*. Edinburgh: Birlinn, 2003.

– "Gaelic Printing and Publishing." In *The Edinburgh History of the Book in Scotland*, vol. 3: *Ambition and Industry, 1800–1880*, ed. Bill Bell, 107–22. Edinburgh: Edinburgh University Press, 2007.

Ó Baoill, Colm, ed. *Bàrdachd Chloinn Ghill-Eathain: Eachann Bacach and Other Maclean Poets*. Edinburgh: The Scottish Gaelic Texts Society, 1979.

– *Maclean Manuscripts in Nova Scotia: A Catalogue of the Gaelic Verse Collections MG15G/2/1 and MG15G/2/2 in the Public Archives of Nova Scotia*. Aberdeen: Aberdeen University Department of Celtic, 2001.

– *Mairghread nighean Lachlainn, Song-maker of Mull*. Edinburgh: Scottish Gaelic Texts Society, 2009.

Osborne, Brian D. *The Last of the Chiefs: Alexander Ranaldson Macdonell of Glengarry 1773–1828*. Glendaruel: Argyll, 2001.

Sanger, Keith, and Alison Kinnaird. *Tree of Strings / Crann nan Teud: A History of the Harp in Scotland*. Temple: Kinmor Music, 1992.

Sinclair, Alexander Maclean. *The Clan Gillean*. Charlottetown: Haszard and Moore, 1899.

– *Clarsach na Coille: A Collection of Gaelic Poetry*. Glasgow: Archibald Sinclair, 1881.

– *Dain agus Orain le Alasdair Mac-Fhionghain*. Charlottetown: Haszard and Moore, 1902.

– *Dain Spioradail, le Iain Mac-Gilleain, maille ri Beagan de Laoidhean Mhic Griogair, Nach Robh gus a So air an Clo-bhualadh*. Edinburgh: MacLachlan and Stewart, 1880.

– *Filidh na Coille: Dàin agus Òrain leis a' Bhàrd Mac-Gilleain agus le Feadhainn Eile*. Charlottetown: The Examiner Publishing Company, 1901.

– *The Gaelic Bards from 1775 to 1825*. Sydney: The Mac-Talla Office, 1896.

– *Na Bàird Leathanach / The MacLean Bards*, vol. 1: *The Old MacLean Bards*. Charlottetown: Haszard and Moore, 1898.

Sinclair, Archibald, ed. *The Gaelic Songster / An t-Òranaiche*, ed. Trueman Matheson. St Andrew's: Sìol Cultural Enterprises, [1876–79] 2004.

Thomson, Derick S. *The Gaelic Sources of MacPherson's "Ossian."* Edinburgh: Oliver and Boyd, 1952.

Thomson, Derick S. *An Introduction to Gaelic Poetry*. Edinburgh: Edinburgh University Press, 1990.
Watson, William J. *Bàrdachd Ghàidhlig: Specimens of Gaelic Poetry 1550–1900*. Stirling: A. Learmonth and Son, 1932.
Withers, Charles W.J. *Gaelic Scotland: The Transformation of a Culture Region*. London: Routledge, 1988.

ARCHIVAL COLLECTIONS

Cape Breton Folklore Collection (CBFC) and Father Charles Brewer Celtic Collection. Angus L. MacDonald Library, St Francis Xavier University.
Maclean, Sinclair Family Fonds. Nova Scotia Archives, Halifax.
National Library of Scotland (NLS), Edinburgh.
School of Scottish Studies (SSS), University of Edinburgh.

11

Two Satires, Three Men, and a Gaelic Newspaper: A Nineteenth-Century Tale

Michael Linkletter

I had the great fortune of being able to call Ken Nilsen both my teacher and my colleague. I studied under him as an undergraduate at St Francis Xavier University (StFX) in the 1990s and kept in touch with him during my graduate career at Harvard, during which time Ken was very much a mentor. It was with great pleasure and honour that I eventually came to work with him in the Celtic Studies Department at StFX. His work on Gaelic in Nova Scotia, among both oral and print sources, was foundational in my early studies. I would like to acknowledge this influence in my present work.

In the autumn of 1898 there appeared in the pages of a small weekly newspaper in Nova Scotia a brief exchange between its editor and a contributor. A contemporary reader might easily take the complaint at the heart of this exchange at face value – that the contributor was simply objecting to the editor's emendations of a recent submission. However, there is a deeper story here that sheds light on the close connections among three men of the Highland diaspora who played significant roles as Gaelic tradition bearers, publishers, and editors. I will endeavour here to tell the interesting story behind the contretemps between the editor and the contributor and two satires that were composed, in the process highlighting important linkages and networks binding members of the Gaelic community of the Canadian Maritimes in the late nineteenth century, as well as the role of satire in connection with a beloved organ of the Gaelic community. The newspaper was the Gaelic periodical *Mac-Talla* (Echo), published in Sydney, Cape Breton, from 1892 to 1904 (540 issues). *Mac-Talla* was entirely in Gaelic, including advertisements, and had subscribers in Canada, Scotland, and the United States as well as among the Gaels of the Highland diaspora in a number of other countries around the world. The three men, a contemporaneous triumvirate sometimes referred to collectively as individuals of import in the Canadian *Gàidhealtachd* of the late nineteenth century, were Jonathan MacKinnon of Sydney, Alexander "the Ridge" MacDonald of Upper South River, Nova Scotia, and Alexander Maclean Sinclair of Belfast, Prince Edward Island.

JONATHAN MACKINNON AND MAC-TALLA

Jonathan G. MacKinnon was born in Stewartdale, Cape Breton, in 1869, a descendant of settlers who had emigrated from Skye to Cape Breton via Prince Edward Island. He was the editor of *Mac-Talla*, which he published out of Sydney, Cape Breton, beginning in 1892, when he was twenty-three. Though *Mac-Talla* had a comparatively long run for an all-Gaelic newspaper, twelve years, MacKinnon struggled with funding the enterprise. He lost a good deal of his advertising income due to a fire in Sydney in 1901 in which many businesses suffered. As prices climbed in the area due to mining and steel production, the costs of the newspaper business became prohibitive, and he issued his last paper in June 1904.[1]

After *Mac-Talla* folded, MacKinnon continued to publish Gaelic-related material. He translated literary classics into Gaelic, including *Am Piobaire Breac agus Da Sgeul Eile* (The Pied Piper and Two Other Tales), *Far am Bi Gradh, Bidh Dia* (Where Love Is, There God Is Also) by Leo Tolstoy, *An Triuir Choigreach* (The Three Strangers) by Thomas Hardy, and *Sgeul an Draoidh Eile* (The Other Wise Man) by Henry Van Dyke. He also published a monthly magazine, *Fear na Ceilidh* (The Visitor), from 1928 to 1930. MacKinnon died in 1944 at seventy-four years of age and is buried in his home community of Stewartdale on Cape Breton Island.

ALEXANDER "THE RIDGE" MACDONALD

Alexander "the Ridge" MacDonald, known variously as Sandy the Ridge, Alex Ridge, or, in Gaelic, Alasdair an Ridse, was born in 1823 in Mabou Ridge, Cape Breton, where his family had settled in 1816 after emigrating from Lochaber. In 1847 the family migrated to Upper South River on the Nova Scotia mainland but continued to use the convenient "Ridge" epithet to differentiate them from the many other MacDonalds in the region. The family boasted a proud lineage as descendants of the MacDonalds of Bohuntin, an important cadet branch of the Clan Donald of Keppoch. MacDonald's father, Allan, was a noted poet and tradition bearer and "was regarded, in Nova Scotia at least, as the *ceann-taigh* or chief representative of this group, a title which his sons ... inherit[ed]."[2]

MacDonald was a prolific informant of Alexander Maclean Sinclair (see below), who said about him: "I took down from [Alex Ridge] 730 lines. He wrote down and sent me 1,120 lines. I thus got from him in all 1,850 lines: all of which, and many more, he had by heart."[3] Maclean Sinclair also gave him a blank notebook and encouraged him to write down his own poetry, which he did. This manuscript is now housed in the Father Charles Brewer Celtic Collection at St Francis Xavier University and has been digitized and placed online.[4] Such was the respect MacDonald had for Maclean Sinclair that he composed a poem in his honour titled "Duanag do'n Mhinisteir A. McL. Sinclair" (A Little Poem for the Minister A. McL. Sinclair).[5] The poet was also a correspondent of Keith Norman MacDonald, who included much of the material Alexander "the Ridge" MacDonald sent him in his own articles in the *Oban Times*. These were collected together in 1900 in his book *MacDonald Bards from Medieval Times*, which includes sections on both Alexander and Allan "the Ridge."[6] Alexander "the Ridge" MacDonald died in 1904 and is buried in South River Cemetery.

ALEXANDER MACLEAN SINCLAIR

Alexander Maclean Sinclair, or Alasdair MacIlleathain Sinclair, as he wrote his name in Gaelic, was born in 1840 in Glen Bard, Antigonish County, Nova Scotia. He spent the first twenty-two years of his career as a Presbyterian minister several miles west of Glen Bard in the East River district of Pictou County. In 1888 he moved to the Belfast district of neighbouring Prince Edward Island, where he resided until his retirement from the church in 1907. He then returned to the mainland to take up a lectureship in Gaelic literature and "Keltic" civilization at St Francis Xavier and Dalhousie universities until 1912; he was awarded an honorary degree of Doctor of Laws by Dalhousie University in 1914.[7] He was the grandson of the well-known poet John MacLean (Iain MacIlleathain), originally from the Scottish island of Tiree, who emigrated to Nova Scotia in 1819.[8] Maclean Sinclair came to be highly regarded by contemporaries on both sides of the Atlantic for his many publications of Gaelic poetry and for his work on Highland history and genealogy, though his editions of poetry are generally not regarded as authorative today due to the heavy hand he employed when editing his texts. He published about twenty books in addition to many articles in magazines, journals, and newspapers, including *Mac-Talla*, to which he submitted almost eighty items over its entire run between 1892 and 1904. Jonathan MacKinnon published three of Maclean Sinclair's books under the *Mac-Talla* publishing company imprint, and the two men corresponded regularly.

THE LETTER

Having introduced the main characters, it remains now to discuss the two satires of our title and the role *Mac-Talla* played in these men's interactions in 1898. The kernel of this story is found in the correspondence between Jonathan MacKinnon and Alexander Maclean Sinclair – in particular, a letter from MacKinnon in which he confides to Maclean Sinclair about a "falling-out" with Alexander "the Ridge" MacDonald:

> I am rather sorry that Alex Ridge and myself are not as good friends as we used to be. But I don't think I was very much to blame. You will find the whole story of our "falling out" on the enclosed slip. You know his writing, that it requires a good deal of correcting before it is fit for publication. His grievance was that in correcting his MSS., I had altered the sense, while all the alterations of which he complained in his letter were typographical errors. I don't know that my reply should give him offence, but it did, and the next thing I got from him was an "Aoir" [satire] of which I of course took no notice. That reply in *Mac-Talla* was all I wrote him. I did not write anything in a private letter or in any other way.[9]

The "enclosed slip" that MacKinnon provided was a clipping from the 25 November 1898 issue of *Mac-Talla* in which MacDonald objected to mistakes that were printed in his father's song "Oran a rinn Ailein an Ridse ann an Deireadh a Laithean" (A Song Composed by Allan "the Ridge" in the End of his Days), which he had sent to *Mac-Talla* for publication. MacKinnon published MacDonald's letter to the editor in which he asked that the song be printed again without emendations:

> **Ag Iomchair a Chlodhadair**
> Fhir-deasachaidh Choir, – Tha beagan fhasal de 'n òran mu dheireadh a chuir mi thugaibh cearr. Anns an t-seachdamh sreath de 'n cheud cheithreamh tha thuirt far am bu choir thuit a bhi. Anns an tritheamh sreath de 'n cheathramh mu dheireadh tha mathadh far 'm bu choir muthadh a bhi. Anns an t-seachdamh sreath de 'n cheathramh sin cha 'n eil an d ris an t-siorruidheachd; agus anns an t-streath mu dheireadh de 'n òran tha sochairt far 'm bu choir siochaint a bhi. Faodaidh duine bhi na sgoilear 's gun e bhi na bhàrd; agus air an aobhar sin an àite an t-òran a dheanamh na b' fhearr 's ann a rinn e na bu mhios' e – a bhi stri ri a cheartachadh. Ma 's e ur toil e, feuchaibh a rithist e seach e bhi na ablach mar sid.[10]

> **Blaming the Printer**
> Dear Editor, – There are a few wrong parts in the last song that I sent you. In the seventh line of the first quatrain *thuirt* [said] is in the place where *thuit* [fell] ought to be. In the third line of the last quatrain *mathadh* [forgiving] is where *mùthadh* [changing] ought to be. In the seventh line of that quatrain the <d> is missing in *sìorruidheachd* [eternity]; and in the last line of the song the word *sochairt* is where *sìochaint* [peace] ought to be. A man may be a scholar without being a poet; and because of that, instead of making the song better he made it worse – wrestling with corrections. If you please, try it again rather than leaving it in that mangled state.

MacKinnon did reprint the song in the same issue of *Mac-Talla*, with this mocking comment:

> Cha d' thugadh ionnsuidh air ceartachadh sam bith a dheanamh air an òran, ach a mhàin air litreachadh nam facal, ni a dh'fheumas sinn a bhi deanamh gu tric, oir tha iomadh aon 'na bhàrd 's 'na sheanachaidh nach eil comasach air facail Ghàilig a

litreachadh ceart. Rinneadh na mearachdan air am bheil ar caraid a gearan leis a chlòdhadair. Cha 'n eil sinn a meas gu bheil iad ag atharrachadh seadh nan sreathan anns am bheil iad gu mor; ach air ghaol a bhi réidh ri Alasdair, (gun fhios c'uin a dh' fhaodas sinn tachairt air a chéile – 's esan cho mor 's sinne cho beag) bheir sinn ionnsuidh eile air an òran mar a tha esan ag àithne dhuinn, agus tha sinn an dòchas nach bi air an ionnsuidh so mearachd sam bith ann. – Am Fear-deasachaidh.[11]

No attempt was made to correct the song in any way, except in spelling the words, something we have to do often, for many is the poet and tradition bearer who is not capable of spelling Gaelic words correctly. The mistakes about which our friend is complaining were made by the printer. We do not think that they change the sense of the lines in which they appear greatly; but to be on good terms with Alexander, (without knowing when we might happen upon one another – he is so big and we are so small) we will give another attempt at the song as he commands us, and we hope there will not be any mistakes in this attempt. – The Editor.

"ÒRAN CÀINIDH DO *MHAC-TALLA*"

The *aoir* (satire) that MacKinnon mentions in his letter to Maclean Sinclair is titled "Òran Càinidh do *Mhac-Talla*" (A Song of Revile to *Mac-Talla*; see Appendix A) and can be found as a loose-leaf insertion in the pages of MacDonald's manuscript at St Francis Xavier University.[12] It consists of twelve stanzas and makes use of colourful imagery that clearly indicates MacDonald's frustration with MacKinnon and *Mac-Talla.* MacDonald is decidedly to the point and lets fly with vituperative verse; he begins by cursing *Mac-Talla* with the disease of death, "galar bàis," and ends by suggesting that MacKinnon put *Mac-Talla* in the outhouse. He scolds him for his very public, sarcastic reply, his "volley," in *Mac-Talla*, which must have embarrassed MacDonald. It is this that surely raised his ire and inspired him to compose his "Òran Càinidh": "Nuair a dh'innis mi dhut gu seòlta / Gun do mhill thu orm an t-òran, / 'S ann a dh'at thu suas le mórchùis / 'S thug thu *volley* 's a' *Mhac-Talla*" (When I told you prudently that you ruined my song, you then swelled up with conceit and fired a volley in *Mac-Talla*). MacDonald's invective peaks when he invokes MacKinnon's own words from his "volley" in *Mac-Talla*, saying, "Bhon a thuirt thu leis a' chonnspaid / Gum bu bheag thu 's gum bu mhór mi, / Cuir a-nis an toll do thòine / Na h-uil' òirleach de *Mhac-Talla*!" (Since you said contentiously that you were small and I was big, now stick up your arse every inch of *Mac-Talla*!).

MacDonald repeatedly berates *Mac-Talla* for calling on its readers to pay for subscriptions and compares *Mac-Talla* unfavourably with the Antigonish *Casket* (to which the poet also contributed material), saying "Faic an *Casket* 's e cho bàigheil. / Tha e modhail 's tha e sàmhach. / Cha chluinn thu e 'g èibheach pàigheadh, / Cleas a ghàrlaich ud *Mac-Talla*" (Look at the *Casket* so friendly. It is polite and it is quiet. You will not hear it yelling for payment, like that rascal *Mac-Talla*). Publishing in Gaelic was a difficult business, as was often bemoaned by its practitioners, including Maclean Sinclair and Archibald Sinclair, the well-known Gaelic publisher based in Glasgow. That *Mac-Talla* was struggling to stay afloat is understandable in the context of the times, according to Donald Meek:

> The creation of a very sizeable printed Gaelic literature was … one of the blessings bestowed by the relocation of the Gaels in the nineteenth century, but this blessing was mixed. It meant that Gaelic literature was increasingly at the mercy of commercial supply and demand. Proximity to the printing press and a body of enthusiastic readers, often in urban environments, regulated output, certainly by the last quarter of the century.[13]

Charles Dunn touches on this topic in *Highland Settler* in relation to *Mac-Talla* with a specific reference to MacDonald's "Òran Càinidh," though without mentioning the poet by name, only that the satire was encountered in an unpublished manuscript at St Francis Xavier University: "one angry subscriber was offended by the editor's reproaches levelled against unpatriotic Gaels. He composed a song in answer to these pleas for money and support."[14]

MacKinnon dealt with the problem of delinquent subscribers through a combination of patriotism and shame by publishing the names of the ones who had fully paid under a column called "Na Gaidheil Dhileas" (The Faithful Gaels) and "Iadsan a phàigh" (Those who paid). This was a subtle way of encouraging those who were in arrears to pay up; however, in many issues he also blatantly asked his readers to pay, stating that it was even their duty to make more people aware of *Mac-Talla* and bring in more subscribers. In several issues in 1898, MacKinnon placed a large, half-page advertisement in his own *Mac-Talla*, stating: "Cha bu choir do Ghaidheal sam bith a bhi as Aonais. Do Dhleas[d]anas. A bhi gabhail *Mhic-Talla*. A bhi leughadh *Mhic-Talla*. A bhi pàigheadh *Mhic-Talla*. A bhi feuchainn ri tuilleadh luchd-gabhail a chur 'na rathad"[15] (No Gael should be without it. Your duty: To subscribe to *Mac-Talla*. To read *Mac-Talla*. To pay for *Mac-Talla*. To try and send more subscribers its way). MacKinnon continues the ad by describing the virtues and benefits of the newspaper. The final paragraph is especially interesting as he makes it very clear how he saw himself as a bastion of the Gaelic community:

> An aon phaipear Gailig a tha air ur-uachdar an domhan. Cha robh a leithid ann roimhe, 's cha 'n eil a leithid eile ri fhaotainn fhathast. Is Gailig gu h-iomlan e. Tha e tigh'n a mach uair 'san t-seachdain. Innsidh e naigheachdan na duthcha agus an saoghal dhut. Bheir e dhut seanachasan taitneach air an am a ta lathair; bheir e dhut sgeulachdan agus eachdraidhean air na h-amannan a dh'fhalbh. A bharrachd air sin bheir e dhut o am gu am: bardachd, litrichean, agus iomadh ni eile a thaitneas riut, agus a bhios a chum buannachd do t' inntinn. Tha aireamh de sgriobhadairean matha Gailig a' sgriobhadh gu daonnan dha, agus tha iad lan chomasach air leughadh taitneach a chumail ri sean agus og. Is abhaist do dhaoine 'nuair a bhios iad a' creic ni nach bi a leithid aig neach sam bith eile, a bhi 'cur pris ard 'na cheann; ach cha 'n eil *Mac-Talla* 'deanamh sin idir. Tha e air son cothrom a thoirt do na Gaidheil, sean agus og, air an cainnt fhein ionnsachadh 'sa chumail suas, agus uime sin cha 'n eil e cosg d'a luchd-gabhail ach dolar 'sa bhliadhna.[16]

> The only Gaelic paper on the surface of the earth. There never was its like and nothing else like it has yet to be found. It is entirely in Gaelic. It comes out once a week. It will tell you the news of the country and the world. It will give you pleasant news of the day as well as stories and history about the past. Besides that, it will give you from time to time: poetry, letters and many other things that will please you and profit your mind. There are a number of good Gaelic writers who continually contribute to it, and they are fully capable of giving pleasant reading to young and old. It is usual for people when they are selling something that no one else has to put a high price on it, but *Mac-Talla* does not do that at all. It wants to give the opportunity to Gaels, young and old, to learn

their own language and keep it up, and moreover it only costs subscribers one dollar a year.

Another interesting and recurring image in the "Òran Càinidh" satire is that of the editor's trousers. MacDonald uses trousers, or pants, as a not so subtle metaphor for his impression of the state of the paper, comparing *Mac-Talla*'s ugly rags with the *Casket*'s new and lovely ones. "Cha bhi thriùsair ann a' fàillinn. / Bidh i ùr air agus àlainn. / Cha bhi clùdan air a' mhàsan / Cleas a' spàgain ud *Mac-Talla*" (His [the *Casket*'s] pants aren't faulty. They're new and lovely on him. There are no rags on his rump like that clubfoot *Mac-Talla*). He goes on in this vein by saying that *Mac-Talla* will never get any money from him even though its pants may be ugly and torn around its rear ("Ged a bhios do thriùsair grànnda / 'S i bhith sracte mu do mhàsan") or patchy and full of holes about its knees ("Ged a bhios do thriùsair clùdach / 'S i bhith tolltach mu do ghlùinean").[17]

The source for this curious motif, used in three verses in the "Òran Càinidh," must surely be a competition that *Mac-Talla* announced in its 16 September 1898 issue seeking the best translation of a particular English-language poem, "The Editor's Pants": "Bheir sinn bliadhna dhe 'n *Mhac-Talla* mar dhuair, do 'n neach a chuireas ugainn, eadar so agus deireadh October, an t-eadar-theangachadh a's fearr air na roinn a leanas" (We will give a year of *Mac-Talla* to the person who sends us, between now and the end of October, the best translation of the following verses):[18]

Lives of poor men oft remind us
Honest men won't stand a chance:
The more we work there grow behind us
Bigger patches on our pants.

On our pants, once new and glossy
Now are stripes of different hue,
All because subscribers linger
And won't pay us what is due.

Then let us all be up and doing
Send your mite, however small,
Or, when the snow of winter strikes us
We shall have no pants at all.[19]

It is at this point that Maclean Sinclair re-enters the picture. Several issues subsequent to MacKinnon's public redress of MacDonald in *Mac-Talla*, there appeared an article titled "Briogais an Fhir-Dheasachaidh" (The Editor's Pants) by regular contributor "Gleann-a-Bhaird" (Glen Bard, that is, the Valley of the Poet), who was almost certainly Maclean Sinclair, given the subject matter (judging a poetry competition) and that Glen Bard was his childhood home. "Gleann-a-Bhaird" / Maclean Sinclair had been the adjudicator of the translation competition, and he now pointed out that the basis for the English-language verses (which he said was not really poetry at all: "Cha bhàrdachd na rannan seo") was Longfellow's "A Psalm of Life": "Lives of great men all remind us / We can make our lives sublime, / And, departing, leave behind us, / Footprints on the sands of time."[20] It would seem that unpaid subscriptions were the bane of many late nineteenth-century newspapers, not just *Mac-Talla*, and "The Editor's Pants" was certainly making the rounds. It appeared in such wide-ranging periodicals as the *American Bee Journal* in 1892 and the *Scottish Canadian* in 1891; Maclean Sinclair was also a contributor and subscriber to the latter.[21] It became known as the "$1,000 poem" and originated with "the editor of the *Rocky Mountain Celt* [who] won the prize of one thousand dollars offered by the syndicate of Western editors for the best appeal poem to newspaper subscribers to pay up their subscriptions."[22] MacKinnon could hardly have been able to resist trying a similar strategy in *Mac-Talla*, perhaps at the suggestion of Maclean Sinclair, and the result was the translation competition.

"Gleann-a-Bhaird" / Maclean Sinclair said that he hoped the translation would bring in more money for *Mac-Talla*, though it would be more appropriate were the editor to have a kilt rather than pants, and he invoked his own grandfather, John MacLean's song in praise of Norman MacLeod's much beloved periodical *Cuairtear nan Gleann* (Traveller of the Glens):[23]

> Nuair théid dàin na briogais' a chur a mach, tha mi an dòchas gu'n dig an t-airgiod a staigh 'na shruth. Ma thig, nach biodh e glic do *Mhac-Talla* feileadh-beag fhaotuinn dha fhéin? 'S e bu fhreagarraiche dha na briogais, agus 's e a b' fhaide a mhaireadh. Nam faicteadh air an t-sràid e na dheise Ghaidhealaich, a sporran làn dhollar, agus a bhata gu h-uallach 'na laimh, 's iomadh fear a bhiodh a seinn oran a *Chuairteir*.

> 'S e 'n *Cuairtear* Ghaidh'lach an t-armunn dealbhach,
> Le 'phearsa bhòidhich an còmhdach balla-bhreac;
> Mar chleachd a shinnsre gu dìreadh gharbhlach,
> 'S e fearail, gleusda gu feum le 'armaibh.
>
> Bidh boneid ghorm agus gearra-chòt' ùr air
> Bidh osan dhealbhach mu 'chalpaibh ùmhail,
> Bidh gartan stiallach thar fiar-bhréid cùil air
> 'Sa bhrògan éille, 's be 'n t-éideadh dùthchais.
>
> Tha cuid nach biodh toilichte le oran a *Chuairtear*; dheanadh iad oran ur fo'n ainm "*Mac-Talla* 'san Fhéileadh-bheag."[24]
>
> When the poems of the pants are published, I hope the money comes streaming in. If it does, would it not be wise of *Mac-Talla* to get a kilt for itself? It would be more suitable than pants and it would last longer. If one saw him on the street in Highland dress, his sporran full of dollars, and his walking stick proudly in his hand, many's the man who would sing the song of the *Cuairtear*:
>
> The "Highland Traveller" is the most comely hero,
> With his beautiful body in a speckled covering,
> Like what his ancestors wore when climbing roughlands,
> And he is manly and skilful in the use of weapons.
>
> He will wear a blue bonnet and new short-coat,
> He will have comely hose about his thick calves,
> And striped garters crossing a slanted back-cloth,
> And his shoes of thongs – the traditional outfit.[25]
>
> There are those who might not be happy with the song to the *Cuairtear*; they can make a new song with the title "*Mac-Talla* in a Kilt."

The focus of "Briogais an Fhir-Dheasachaidh," and the $1,000 poem urging subscribers to pay, almost certainly increased MacDonald's aggravation and undoubtedly provided the basis for the peculiar trouser imagery in his "Òran Càinidh."

"AOIR *MHIC-TALLA*" AND "MOLADH *MHIC-TALLA*"

"Òran Càinidh do *Mhac-Talla*" was, in fact, the second satire MacDonald composed against *Mac-Talla*. The first satire, simply titled "Aoir *Mhic-Talla*" (Satire of *Mac-Talla*; see Appendix B), was published by MacKinnon in *Mac-Talla* in 1893, five years before their falling out in 1898.[26] The "Aoir" was actually published in *Mac-Talla* along with a song in praise of *Mac-Talla*, "Moladh *Mhic-Talla*" (In Praise of *Mac-Talla*; see Appendix C).[27] Both are also located in MacDonald's manuscript at St Francis Xavier University. Going by their placement in *Mac-Talla*, the "Aoir" seems to have been composed first, followed by the praise song. In the manuscript, however, the "Aoir" directly follows the praise song – titled "Òran do'n *Mhac-Talla*" here, but otherwise exactly the same.[28] That MacKinnon felt comfortable in publishing the "Aoir" at all can surely be explained by its relatively innocuous content, but more significantly, its sting is essentially nullified by the accompanying "Moladh." MacKinnon himself explains their inclusion in *Mac-Talla*:

> Air an t-seachdain s'a chaidh thanig thuginn leis a phosta an litir a leanas, a dh-innseas a sgeul fein. A *Mhic Talla*, – Chuir mi oran beag thugad an uirikh [*sic*] s cha dug sibh suil air, agus chuir mi oran beag eile thugaibh am bliadhna s cha dug suil air no bu mhu. Sheall sibh beag orm; agus bho n rinn sibh se sin rinn mise so … Fhreagir sinn an latha sin fein, a gabhail ar leisgeil fein cho math sa dh-fhaodamid, agus a gealltuinn an t-oran a chur an clo an uine ghearr, rud a rinn sinn. Latha no dha an deigh sin fhuair sinn an darra litir bhuaithe, agus 's ann mar so a ruith i, – A Charaid, – Fhuair mi do litir. Tha mi a cur thugad dolar air son bliadhn' eile dhe'n *Mhac-Talla*. Do Charaide Dileas, Alasdair. Agus an sim [*sic*] chuin [*sic*] e sios oran a Moladh *Mhic Talla*.[29]
>
> Last week, the following letter came to us in the mail; it tells its own tale: *Mac-Talla*, last year I sent you a small song and you did not look at it, and this year I sent you another small song and you did not look at it either. You showed me dislike; and because you did, that is why I made this … We replied that very day apologizing as well as we could and promising to print the song in a short time, which we did. A day or two after that, we received the sec-

ond letter from him, and it went like this: Friend, I received your letter. I am sending you a dollar for another year of *Mac-Talla*. Your faithful friend, Alexander. And then he put down[30] a song praising *Mac-Talla*.

It may be that MacDonald did not compose "Moladh *Mhic-Talla*." The manuscript version states that it is by "Iain Chailein."[31] MacKinnon did not explicitly state that it was by MacDonald. This may be implied, however, by its juxtaposition with the "Aoir" in the newspaper and because MacDonald did indeed send it to MacKinnon. MacDonald could have used the praise song as the basis of his "Aoir," and when he felt satisfied with MacKinnon's response, he sent the former to negate the latter. At any rate, MacKinnon clearly felt at ease with publishing both songs together and must have felt satisfied with the resolution achieved through his correspondence with MacDonald and the subsequent praise. Whatever the order of composition, it is obvious that one was the inspiration for the other. They have the same number of syllables per line, similar rhyme schemes, and choruses with a similar number of stanzas (seven in the "Aoir," six in the "Moladh"), and the imagery from one is mirrored in the other. Taking just a few examples, it becomes pretty clear that one was modelled after the other. Both songs use the epithet "talamh a' ghuail" (the land of coal) for Sydney, where *Mac-Talla* was published. Where the chorus of the praise song has "Deoch-slàinte *Mhic-Talla* seo thàinig air chuairt / Thar caolas na mara bho thalamh a' ghuail" (Cheers to *Mac-Talla* that has come round / Over the strait from the land of coal), the "Aoir" has "Bò, bò *Mhic-Talla* bu mhath thu dhol bhuainn / 'S thu dh'fhuireach aig baile feadh talamh a' ghuail" (Bò, bò *Mac-Talla*, get away from us and stay home in the land of coal). The idea of *Mac-Talla* coming over the strait in the chorus of the "Moladh" is repeated later in the third verse of the "Aoir": "Ged thig thu thar caolas" (though you come over the strait). Other similar lines and phrases include "air m' fhìrinn gur math leam" (truly I like it) in the praise song versus "air m' fhìrinn cha ceòl e" (truly it is no music) in the satire. Instead of "Bhith ag éisdeachd ri t' ath-ghuth" (listening to your next word), we see "Chan éisd iad ri t' ath-ghuth" (they will not listen to your next word) in the "Aoir."[32]

There is no mention in the "Aoir" of the complaint that appears in the second satire concerning *Mac-Talla*'s recurring request asking subscribers to pay, though perhaps this is implied in the line "Do bhurral no t' fhuaim" (your whine and your noise). There is only one mention, in the last verse, about altering texts – "milleadh nan òran" (the ruining of the songs) – which was the reason for the "Òran Càinidh," according to MacKinnon's letter to Maclean Sinclair and the 1898 exchange in *Mac-Talla*. MacDonald was known for being touchy about the matter, as an 1892 letter from Father Ronald MacGillivray (known as Sagart Arasaig [the Priest of Arisaig]) to Maclean Sinclair indicates: "[Alex Ridge] composed a song for Sir John McDonald; he sent me a copy. I took the liberty of amending it in a few places, and added two or three verses, and he returned me an answer that he would have none of such work. I did not think much of the song."[33]

MacDonald's relationship with MacKinnon and *Mac-Talla* could be volatile, alternately praising and condemning. It was *Mac-Talla*'s practice of calling out its delinquent subscribers that particularly contributed to MacDonald's annoyance with the paper, especially when he was careful to keep his subscription up to date: "A *Mhic-Talla* nan Creag a bhios a freagairt bron binn: Gheibh thu coig tasdain ann am broinn na litreach so chum 's gu 'm bi thu tighinn g'am shealltuinn fad bliadhna eile" (Oh *Mac-Talla* of the crags that answers sweet sorrow: You will find five shillings [one dollar][34] enclosed with this letter so that you will keep coming to me for another year).[35] And MacKinnon praised him back for always paying on time: "Gu ma slàn do Alasdair an Ridse! Cha leig e an aon latha seachad, ach aig toiseach gach bliadhna cuiridh e an dolair air adhart gus am *Mac-Talla* phàigheadh" (Cheers to Alex Ridge! He does not let a day go by, but at the start of each year he forwards his dollar to pay for *Mac-Talla*. We could not ask for a better subscriber).[36] However, there is almost certainly more to the story behind MacDonald's frustration with *Mac-Talla* that spurred him on to compose his two satires against it. There may have also been political and religious differences that played into his irritation. Despite *Mac-Talla*'s assertions otherwise, it was known for having a certain liberal bias, and while MacKinnon was Presbyterian, MacDonald was Roman Catholic. These are less likely to be factors since MacDonald could easily not have contributed to *Mac-Talla* at all, and he had great respect for the Presbyterian Maclean Sinclair, but it may go some way to explaining the preference he reveals in the "Òran Càinidh" for the Catholic-owned *Casket*. Clan affiliation may be another factor contributing to his rail against *Mac-Talla*. His clan bias is particularly evident in an 1895 letter to *Mac-Talla*. He is positively effusive in thanking MacKinnon for publishing a piece on the MacDonalds at the Battle of Culloden:

> Fhir-deasachaidh ghasda: – Tha mi 'toirt moran taing dhuibh air son gu'n do chlo-bhuail sibh "Eachdraidh Bliadhna Thearlaich," anns am bheil Clann Domhnuill na Ceapaich a faotainn a chliù a choisinn iad cho daor ann am blàr Chòil-fhodair. Dhe na leubh mi riamh mu dheighinn a bhlàir sin, 's i 'n eachdraidh so an aon sgriobhadh anns am faca mi an fhirinn air a cur sios.[37]
>
> Kind editor: I give you much thanks for printing the "History of the Year of Charlie," in which the MacDonalds of Keppoch acquired the fame they won so dearly in the Battle of Culloden. Of what I have ever read about that battle, this history is the only writing in which I have seen the truth put down.

The poet was clearly a proud MacDonald and was quick to defend his clan, especially where old rivalries surfaced, such as with any undue promotion of the Campbells in *Mac-Talla*'s columns. In June 1898, a few months before he composed his "Òran Càinidh," he expressed particular annoyance with the soft *mìn* treatment of the Campbells in an article on Scottish history from an earlier issue:

> 'S fhada bho 'n a chuala sinn gu 'n robh da thaobh air a mhaoil. Tha cuid-eigin a tabhairt dhuinn anns a' *Mhac-Talla*, an taobh min de dh'eachdraidh nan Caimbeulach, ach ma theannas sinn ris bheir sinn dhuibh an taobh molach dhi. Thog na Caimbeulaich iad fein le cealgaireachd us mealltaireachd, agus le bhi cur ceap-tuislidh roimh chinnidhean saor-chridheadh eile, mar a bha na Domhnullaich, na Leathainich agus na Griogairich.[38]
>
> It has been a while since we heard that there were two sides to the headland. Someone in *Mac-Talla* is giving us the soft side of the history of the Campbells, but if we turn to it we'll give you the rough side of it. The Campbells built themselves up by treachery and deceitfulness, and by putting stumbling blocks before other free-hearted clans, like the MacDonalds, the MacLeans, and the MacGregors.

CONCLUSION

The exchange between the three men discussed here, Jonathan MacKinnon, Alexander "the Ridge" MacDonald, and Alexander Maclean Sinclair, was facilitated by a network of correspondence. For many years, *Mac-Talla* itself was at the centre of this triangle and was the catalyst for the falling out and resulting exchange that has been the focus here. The apparent self-confidence exhibited by MacDonald in his satires – the first composed just a year into *Mac-Talla*'s production – must have been reinforced by his awareness of his own role as tradition bearer, a scion of the Bohuntin MacDonalds, and a successor to the old Highland learned classes. His interaction with collectors like Alexander Maclean Sinclair, Keith Norman MacDonald, and others could only have intensified this.

To see a song or poem in praise of *Mac-Talla* is not surprising. Poems in praise of Gaelic newspapers were not uncommon, and *Mac-Talla* had several.[39] According to Sheila Kidd, "the new role which the Highland press was carving out for itself in the 1870s and 1880s had not passed its Gaelic-speaking audience by, with poets including newspapers in their view of events. This was not in itself new as poets had welcomed the first Gaelic periodicals, earlier in the nineteenth century with eulogies."[40] However, it is admittedly surprising to see a satire, let alone two satires of a Gaelic newspaper. Gaelic papers were proponents of the Gaelic language and keystones in building the community, at least as much in the emigrant Gaelic community as at home. Satires tend not to be preserved, perhaps for obvious reasons, and any composed about Gaelic newspapers must be scarce indeed. MacDonald's satires are rare examples of this.

One function of satire is to serve as a social corrective, to reinforce received values of the community. Satires in Gaelic culture were not supposed to be composed without justification, something that MacDonald surely felt he had when he composed both satires. He was quick to recant the first satire with a song praising *Mac-Talla* that overturned the negative imagery from the "Aoir" once he felt that justice had been served by MacKinnon's letter of apology. MacDonald almost certainly felt a catharsis having expressed his frustration; in addition, the corrective implied in his invective is perhaps most evident in his criticism of *Mac-Talla*'s practice of frequently calling for payment. The use of the poem "The Editor's Pants" in a translation competition as a tool to encourage subscribers to pay must have compounded his irritation, and to be publicly rebuked by MacKinnon in the pages of *Mac-Talla* was enough to put him over the edge. All of this provoked his sense of fair play and underscored the irrelevancy of subscriptions in an oral tradition. MacDonald's satires on *Mac-Talla*, then, demonstrate the unease that some Gaels had about the transition from an oral tradition to a printed one. At the same time, the satires are an interesting adaptation of a traditional genre of poetry in a very modern context. This is not satire against an individual, a chieftain, or even another poet; it is dispraise of a newspaper. It would be difficult to find a more appropriate symbol for the period.

APPENDIX A

Edited from CBCC Ms. PB 1633 C612, inserted between pages 136 and 137.

"Òran Càinidh do *Mhac-Talla*"
Le Alasdair an Ridge

Air fonn
"E ho ro mo rùn an Cailin"

Rann 1:
Galar bàis dhut a *Mhic-Talla*.
Canaidh càch nach bi thu maireann
Oir tha 'n deasaiche 'cur gràin oirnn
Ag éibheach pàigheadh a' *Mhic-Talla*.
2:
Tha mi 'n dùil gu bheil e nàr dhut
Bhith cur inisg air na Gàidheil
Le bhith glaganach gun tàmh
Ag éibheach pàigheadh a' *Mhic-Talla*.
3:
Ged is gearanach do chànran
Sìor-chur mearal air na Gàidheil
Gu bheil iomadh fear de 'n àireamh
A tha pàigheadh a' *Mhic-Talla*.
4:
Faic an *Casket* 's e cho bàigheil.
Tha e modhail 's tha e sàmhach.
Cha chluinn thu e 'g éibheach pàigheadh,
Cleas a ghàrlaich ud *Mac-Talla*.

"A Song of Revile to *Mac-Talla*"
By Alexander "the Ridge" MacDonald

To the tune of
"E ho ro mo rùn an cailin"

Verse 1:
The disease of death to you *Mac-Talla*.
People say that you won't last
For the editor disgusts us
Crying for the payment of *Mac-Talla*.
2:
I believe it is disgraceful for you
To be defaming the Gaels,
Ceaselessly rattling,
Crying for the payment of *Mac-Talla*.
3:
Though your grumbling complaint is
Continually disappointing the Gaels,
Many is the man
Who pays *Mac-Talla*.
4:
Look at the *Casket* so friendly.
It's polite and it's quiet.
You won't hear it yelling for payment,
Like that rascal *Mac-Talla*.

5: Cha bhi thriùsair ann a' fàillinn. Bidh i ùr air agus àlainn. Cha bhi clùdan air a' mhàsan Cleas a' spàgain ud *Mac-Talla*.	5: His pants aren't faulty. They're new and lovely on him. There are no rags on his rump Like that clubfoot *Mac-Talla*.
6: Tha e còrr is leth-cheud bliadhna Tighinn gar n-ionnsaidh le deagh riaghailt 'S riamh am pàigheadh cha do dh'iar e Cleas an spiocaire *Mac-Talla*.	6: For over fifty years He has come to us in good order And never did he ask for payment Like that cheapskate *Mac-Talla*.
7: Nuair a thig oirnn ceann na bliadhna Sguiridh mise chur 'gad iarraidh. Tha mi sgìth a' leughadh bhreugan Mar tha sgeulachdan *Mhic-Talla*.	7: When the end of the year comes I will stop getting you. I'm tired of reading lies Like the tales of *Mac-Talla*.
8: Nuair a dh'innis mi dhut gu seòlta Gun do mhill thu orm an t-òran, 'S ann a dh'at thu suas le mórchùis 'S thug thu *volley* 's a' *Mhac-Talla*.	8: When I told you prudently That you ruined my song You then swelled up with conceit And fired a volley in *Mac-Talla*.
9: Bha mi roimhe seo dhut càirdeil, 'Ga do mholadh anns gach àite. Tha mi nise dhut nam nàmhaid, 'S bidh mi 'càineadh a' *Mhic-Talla*.	9: Before this I was friendly to you, Praising you everywhere. I am now your enemy, And I revile *Mac-Talla*.
10: Ged a bhios do thriùsair grànnda 'S i bhith sracte mu do mhàsan, Cha téid dolar bhuam gu bràth A chum a' chràigein ud *Mac-Talla*.	10: Though your pants are ugly And in tatters round your rear, No dollar will ever go from me To that splayfoot *Mac-Talla*.
11: Ged a bhios do thriùsair clùdach 'S i bhith tolltach mu do ghlùinean, Cha téid dolar bhuam 'gad ionnsaidh, 'S cuir nad chùl-taigh' am *Mac-Talla*.	11: Though your pants are patchy And full of holes around your knees, You won't get a dollar from me, And put *Mac-Talla* in your outhouse.
12: Bhon a thuirt thu leis a' chonnspaid Gum bu bheag thu 's gum bu mhór mi Cuir a-nis an toll do thòine Na h-uil' òirleach de *Mhac-Talla*!	12: Since you said contentiously That you were small and I was big, Now stick up your arse Every inch of *Mac-Talla*!

APPENDIX B

Edited from CBCC Ms. PB 1633 C612, 218-9; see also Alexander "the Ridge" MacDonald, "Aoir Mhic-Talla," *Mac-Talla*, 15 July 1893, 6.

"*Aoir Mhic-Talla*"
Le Alasdair an Ridge

Sèist:
Bò, bò *Mhic-Talla* bu mhath thu dhol bhuainn
'S thu dh'fhuireach aig baile feadh talamh a' ghuail.
Bò, bò *Mhic-Talla* bu mhath thu dhol bhuainn.

Rann 1:
Bu mhath leinn do thuineadh
Bhith thall thar a' mhunaidh
'S nach cluinneamaid tuilleadh
Do bhurral no t' fhuaim
2:
Ged dhèanadh iad mór thu
Cha dèan e do chòmhnadh.
'S ann nì e do leònadh
'S do stòr a thoirt bhuat.

3:
Ged thig thu thar caolas
Is imeachd an taobh seo,
Chan fhaigh thu ann daoine
Bheir aonta dhut buan.
4:
Ged dhèanadh tu chleachdadh
Bhith tighinn gach seachdain,
Bu shuarach an eachdraidh
Bhiodh leatsa 'ga luaidh.
5:
Ged thig thu do 'n bhaile
Cha tachair ort caraid.

"The Satire of *Mac-Talla*"
By Alexander "the Ridge" MacDonald

Chorus:
Bò, bò *Mac-Talla*, get away from us
And stay home in the land of coal.
Bò, bò *Mac-Talla*, get away from us.

Verse 1:
We would rather your abode
Be over the mountain
And that we couldn't hear anymore
Your whine or your noise.
2:
Though they would make a big deal of you
It will not help you.
It will hurt you
And take your sources away from you.
3:
Though you come over the strait
To this side,
You won't find anybody
Who will agree with you for long.
4:
Though you would make it a practice
Of coming every week,
Trivial is the tale
You would relate.
5:
Though you come to town
You won't find a friend.

Chan éisd iad ri t' ath-ghuth No caireal do dhuain.	They won't listen to your next word Or the noise of your rhyme.
6: Ged sheinneas tu crònan Le facail neo-chòmhnard Air m' fhìrinn cha cheòl e Thoirt sòlas do 'r cluais.	6: Though you sing a ditty In an uneven way, Truly it is no music To delight our ear.
7: Aon de na h-òighean A rachadh 'gad chòmhnadh Gu milleadh nan òran B' i 'n òinseach gun bhuaidh.	7: Any one of the maidens Who would go to your aid Tampering with songs Would be a fool without success.

APPENDIX C

Edited from CBCC Ms. PB 1633 C612, 216-7; see also Alexander "the Ridge" MacDonald, "Moladh *Mhic-Talla*," *Mac-Talla*, 15 July 1893, 6.

"Òran do'n *Mhac-Talla*" / "Moladh *Mhic-Talla*" Le Iain Chailein	"A Song to *Mac-Talla*" / "In Praise of *Mac-Talla*" By Iain Chailein
Sèist: Deoch-slàinte *Mhic-Talla* seo thàinig air chuairt, Thar caolus na mara bho thalamh a' ghuail. Deoch-slàinte *Mhic-Talla* seo thàinig air chuairt.	Chorus: Cheers to *Mac-Talla* that has come round, Over the strait from the land of coal. Cheers to *Mac-Talla* that has come round.
Rann 1: Nuair thig thu do 'n bhaile, Air m' fhìrinn gur math leam Bhi ag éisdeachd ri t' ath-ghuth 'Ga aithris am chluais.	Verse 1: When you come to town, Truly I like listening to your next word Reporting in my ear.
2: Nuair thig thu gun seachran Mu thoiseach na seachdain, Gur éibhinn gach eachdraidh Bhios leatsa 'ga luaidh.	2: When you come without going astray Around the start of the week, It is a pleasure, Every story you relate.

3:
Nuair thig thu gu d' chàirdean
'S a labharas tu 'n Gàidhlig,
Gur subhach an gàire
Mu d' mhàran grinn suairc.

4:
Nuair sheinneas tu òran
Gu binn fhaclach ceòlar,
Bidh cuan de dh'òighean
'Gad chòmhnadh leis suas.

5:
Gu faighear gun dearmad,
Gach naidheachd neo-chearbach
Mu ghaisgich nan garbh-chrìoch
Bha calma 's an ruaig.

6:
Tha thu eòlach 's gach àite
'N robh clannaibh nan Gàidheal,
Mu 'n cleachdadh 's mu 'n àbhaist
Fo sgàth nam beann fuar.

3:
When you come to your friends
And you speak in Gaelic,
Joyful is the laughter
About your kind, pretty melody.

4:
When you sing a song
Sweetly, wordy, musical
An ocean of maidens
Will help you up with it.

5:
Each clever tale is found
without omission,
About the heroes of the Highlands
Who were brave in the hunt.

6:
You know every place
Where the children of the Gaels have
been,
About their habit and their customs
In the shade of the cold mountains.

NOTES

My thanks to Effie Rankin for her assistance with the satires and for pointing out references in *Mac-Talla* relating to Alexander "the Ridge" MacDonald.

All Gaelic quotations herein are supplied *verbatim et literatim* except the three accompanying songs, which I have regularized for spelling; however, dialectal forms and ellision have been retained. The three songs are supplied at the end of the article for ease of reference. All translations are mine unless otherwise noted.

1 Dunn, *Highland Settler*, 83–7.

2 Rankin, *As a' Bhràighe*, 8.

3 Sinclair, "A Collection," 260–1.

4 CBCC Ms. PB 1633 C612, http://library.stfx.ca/etext/RidgMS1/Ridhome.html.

5 Alasdair an Ridge (Alexander "the Ridge" MacDonald), "Duanag Do'n Mhinisteir A. McL. Sinclair," *Casket*, 25 February 1892, 3. See also "Do an Mhinisteir Shinclair" in CBCC Ms. PB 1633 C612, 183.

6 MacDonald, *MacDonald Bards*, 99–102.
7 See Linkletter, "Bu Dual Dha Sin."
8 Regarding John MacLean, see Robert Dunbar's chapter in this volume and Dunbar, "Secular Poetry."
9 Jonathon MacKinnon to Alexander Maclean Sinclair, 12 December 189[8], MG1/2660/209, Maclean, Sinclair Family Fonds, Nova Scotia Archives. The letter is dated 1899, but this is incorrect; MacKinnon was using predated letterhead for 1899 in December 1898.
10 Alasdair an Ridse (Alexander "the Ridge" MacDonald), "Ag Iomchair a Chlodhadair," *Mac-Talla*, 25 November 1898, 144.
11 Jonathan MacKinnon, "Cha d'thugadh ionnsuidh …" *Mac-Talla*, 25 November 1898, 144.
12 CBCC Ms. PB 1633 C612, inserted between pages 136 and 137.
13 Meek, "Gaelic Literature," 254.
14 Dunn, *Highland Settler*, 85.
15 Advertisement, *Mac-Talla*, 16 September 1898, 63.
16 Ibid.
17 CBCC Ms. PB 1633 C612, inserted between pages 136 and 137.
18 Jonathan MacKinnon, "An Editor's Pants," *Mac-Talla*, 16 September 1898, 64.
19 Ibid.
20 Gleann-a-Bhaird (Alexander Maclean Sinclair), "Briogais an Fhir-Dheasachaidh," *Mac-Talla*, 17 February 1899, 234; Longfellow, "A Psalm of Life," 3, stanza 7.
21 "A $1,000 Poem," *The American Bee Journal*, 22 December 1892, 1; "The Thousand Dollar Poem," *The Scottish Canadian*, 29 October 1891, 14.
22 Ibid. 14.
23 See Rev. Dr Norman MacLeod's *Cuairtear nan Gleann*, published 1840–43.
24 Gleann-a-Bhaird (Alexander Maclean Sinclair), "Briogais an Fhir-Dheasachaidh," *Mac-Talla*, 17 February 1899, 234.
25 These are the fifth and seventh stanzas of John MacLean's "Òran don 'Chuairtear," translated by Meek, *Caran an t-Saoghail*, 203.
26 Alasdair (Alexander "the Ridge" MacDonald), "Aoir *Mhic-Talla*," *Mac-Talla*, 15 July 1893, 6. See also CBCC Ms. PB 1633 C612, 218–19.
27 Alasdair (Alexander "the Ridge" MacDonald), "Moladh *Mhic-Talla*," *Mac-Talla*, 15 July 1893, 6.
28 CBCC Ms. PB 1633 C612, 216–17.
29 Jonathan MacKinnon, "Am Bard 's *Mac-Talla*," *Mac-Talla*, 15 July 1893, 6.
30 "Chuir e sios" could be interpreted in the sense that MacDonald put/wrote down and included or sent the song, but it does not explicitly imply that he necessarily composed the piece.

31 I have so far been unable to determine exactly who Iain Chailein is, if not MacDonald himself.

32 Alasdair (Alexander "the Ridge" MacDonald), "Moladh *Mhic-Talla*," *Mac-Talla*, 15 July 1893, 6; and "Aoir *Mhic-Talla*," *Mac-Talla*, 15 July 1893, 6.

33 Ronald McGillivray to Alexander Maclean Sinclair, 27 March 1892, MG1/2660/256, Maclean, Sinclair Family Fonds, Nova Scotia Archives.

34 See Campbell, "Scottish Gaelic," 132: "For many years the settlers clung close to their old monetary nomenclature, based upon the Scots coinage in use before the Union with England in 1707 worth a twelfth of the corresponding English denomination … A dollar was *cóig tasdan* [five shillings]. This curious survival is going out of use, and *dollars* and *cents* (*sentaichean*) are the terms now nearly always used."

35 Alasdair an Ridse (Alexander "the Ridge" MacDonald), "Alasdair an Ridse," *Mac-Talla*, 4 July 1896, 2.

36 Jonathan MacKinnon, "Gu ma Slàn do Alasdair an Ridse!" *Mac-Talla*, 4 July 1896, 2.

37 Alasdair an Ridse (Alexander "the Ridge" MacDonald), "Litir o Alasdair an Ridse," *Mac-Talla*, 31 August 1895, 4.

38 Alasdair an Ridse (Alexander "the Ridge" MacDonald), "Na Duimhnich," *Mac-Talla*, 24 June 1898, 416. See also Dunn, *Highland Settler*, 103.

39 See, for instance, "An Ciaran Mabach" (Gilleasbuig Ruadh MacDhomhnaill), "Oran do *Mhac-Talla*," *Mac-Talla*, 6 February 1897, 1.

40 Kidd, "Burning Issues," 293–4.

BIBLIOGRAPHY

Campbell, John Lorne. "Scottish Gaelic in Canada." *American Speech* 11, no. 2 (April 1936): 128–36.

Dunbar, Robert D. "The Secular Poetry of John MacLean, 'Bàrd Thighearna Chola,' 'Am Bàrd MacGilleain.'" PhD diss., University of Edinburgh, 2007.

Dunn, Charles W. *Highland Settler: A Portrait of the Scottish Gael in Cape Breton and Eastern Nova Scotia*. Wreck Cove: Breton Books, [1953]1991.

Kidd, Sheila. "Burning Issues: Reactions to the Highland Press during the 1885 Election Campaign." *Scottish Gaelic Studies* 24 (2008): 285–307.

Linkletter, Michael. "*Bu Dual Dha Sin* (That Was His Birthright): Gaelic Scholar Alexander Maclean Sinclair (1840–1924)." PhD diss., Harvard University, 2006.

Longfellow, Henry Wordsworth. "A Psalm of Life." *The Complete Poetical Works of Henry Wadsworth Longfellow*, 2–3. Boston and New York: Houghton Mifflin, 1922.

MacDonald, Keith Norman. *MacDonald Bards from Medieval Times*. Edinburgh: Norman MacLeod, 1900.

Meek, Donald, ed. *Caran an t-Saoghail / The Wiles of the World: Anthology of 19th Century Scottish Gaelic Verse*. Edinburgh: Birlinn, 2003.

— . "Gaelic Literature in the Nineteenth Century." In *Edinburgh History of Scottish Literature*, vol. 2: *Enlightenment, Britain and Empire (1707–1918)*, ed. Ian Brown, Thomas Clancy, Susan Manning, and Murray Pittock, 253–66. Edinburgh: Edinburgh University Press, 2006.

Rankin, Effie. *As a' Bhràighe / Beyond the Braes: The Gaelic Songs of Allan the Ridge MacDonald (1794–1868)*. Sydney: Cape Breton University Press, 2004.

Sinclair, Alexander Maclean. "A Collection of Gaelic Poems." *Transactions of the Gaelic Society of Inverness* 26 (1904–7): 235–62.

ARCHIVAL COLLECTIONS

Father Charles Brewer Celtic Collection (CBCC). Angus L. Macdonald Library, St Francis Xavier University.

Maclean, Sinclair Family Fonds. Nova Scotia Archives, Halifax.

12

"Rachainn Fhathast air m'Eòlas" (I'd Go Yet by My Experience): (Re)collecting Nineteenth-Century Scottish Gaelic Songs and Singing from Prince Edward Island

Tiber F.M. Falzett

In this offering of research in memory of a man who was for so many, the current author included, a beloved educator, mentor, and friend, it is fitting to delve further into the subaltern yet vibrant realm of Gaelic literary expression in the North American diaspora. Professor Nilsen passionately dedicated his life's work to giving voice to these underrecognized minority-language groups in the United States and Canada, and inspired, trained, and warmly encouraged many scholars and language activists to continue his noble pursuit. This chapter will explore emergent nineteenth- and early twentieth-century networks for the performance, documentation, and recollection of Gaelic song within its wider aesthetic, religious, and social domains in the Scottish Gaelic-speaking diaspora of Canada's Maritime provinces, New England, and beyond.

SCOTTISH GAELS IN BOSTON'S MULTICULTURAL CITYSCAPE

Religious devotion, like kinship and *dùthchas* (the intergenerational relationship to the land of one's ancestors), plays an important role not only in the spiritual lives of the Gaels but also in the transmission and documentation of vernacular traditions in both religious and secular contexts. As Professor Nilsen recalled in 1986 in "The Nova Scotia Gael in Boston," the diasporic Gaelic-speaking communities in the United States established by Scottish Gaels from Canada's Maritime Provinces from the mid-nineteenth through the twentieth centuries were often centred upon the church:

> As the number of Nova Scotians in Boston increased they gradually established various institutions and social organizations. Two Protestant churches, the Scotch Presbyterian Church and the United Presbyterian Church, had large Gaelic-speaking congregations. The former of these, founded in 1887 and often referred to as the Old Scotch Church, had weekly services in Gaelic for several decades. These services included the precenting of psalms in the traditional Highland fashion. Over the years this church also sponsored a number of Gaelic plays. It continues to foster Gaelic activities, and its Gaelic choir still meets on a monthly basis.[1]

The presence of Scottish Gaelic-speaking Presbyterian congregations in the Greater Boston metropolitan area, founded by a secondary wave of migration from Canada's Maritime provinces (then colonies in British North America), goes back as early as the first half of the nineteenth century.[2] On 6 March 1846 the aforementioned United Presbyterian Church opened its doors for worship at 36 Washington Street in Boston, with the vast majority of its clergy and congregation hailing from Canada's rural Maritime *Gàidhealtachd* (Scottish Gaelic-speaking region).[3] Immigration was at the forefront of these communities' identities, with the bulk of the church's members having arrived in Boston from Canada within living memory of their ancestors' emigration from Scotland's Highlands and Hebrides, or having undertaken the Atlantic crossing themselves. With the United Presbyterian Church moving its location to the corner of West Brookline Street and Warren Avenue and the founding of a second Gaelic-speaking Presbyterian congregation at the "Old Scotch Church" nearby on Emerald Street in 1887, Scottish Gaels formed a conspicuous group within the ethnolinguistic patchwork of Boston's nineteenth- and early twentieth-century immigrant population. As one commentator noted in 1891, "the Clyde and Saint Lawrence empty into Boston harbor; if one doubts this, let him attend the Scotch Church and hear 700 people sing the old psalms in Gaelic. There are more

Canadians in this country than in Canada, and Canada is Presbyterian."[4] By the mid-twentieth century these churches' intergenerational presence on Boston's cityscape had created a wider sense of belonging for the city's diasporic Scottish Gaelic-speaking community. According to Harvard Celtic scholar Charles Dunn, who conducted important fieldwork among Scottish Gaelic speakers throughout their North American diasporas,

> a street intersection between the two churches became so popular as a meeting place for the members of both congregations that they named the place "Scotch Corner." There the subject of their conversation was usually news from the old home, and the language they spoke, as often as not, was Gaelic. The Gaels have merged into the stream of North American city life, but they still retain a feeling of individuality, a love for their own traditions, and a memory of their own unique origin.[5]

In our contemporary circumstances of the unsettling resurrection of nativist discourse and open hostility toward immigrants, it is useful to remind ourselves of the reception afforded these Scottish Gaelic-speaking immigrants from Canada's Maritimes by New England's centuries-old English Congregationalist hegemony, bearing in mind its formidable social stratification, and the pressure to conform to the expectations of this dominant cultural, religious, and linguistic juggernaut. Indeed, these immigrants were among countless others who were often met with, at best, a silent suspicion rooted in a deep-seated and intergenerationally fostered antipathy toward the Other going back to the establishment of the Massachusetts Bay Colony.[6]

THE MACDONALDITES

Along with the two prominent Boston congregations founded by Gaelic-speaking migrants from Cape Breton Island and the Eastern counties of Nova Scotia, other, later Presbyterian congregations were established in the surrounding communities by Gaelic-speaking Prince Edward Islanders.[7] These included the First Presbyterian Church of Quincy, Massachusetts, founded in 1894 and first attended by the Prince Edward Island–born Reverend D.B. MacLeod, described by Rev. Malcolm Campbell (Calum Caimbeul), then of Strathalbyn (Srath Alba), PEI, as having "lann a chinn do Ghàidhlig" (a head full of Gaelic).[8] The other congregation with connections to Prince Edward Island's *Gàidhealtachd* was founded in 1895 across the Charles River in Cambridge as a satellite of the Church of Scotland's Prince Edward Island Presbytery. This sect was referred to popularly as the "MacDonaldites," and it attracted members from as far afield as Quincy, Massachusetts, and Providence, Rhode Island.[9]

Both in their New England diaspora and at home in Prince Edward Island, the MacDonaldites were followers of the charismatic Perthshire-born messianic latter-day prophet Rev. Donald MacDonald (Dòmhnall Dòmhnallach mac Dhòmhnaill) (1783–1867), who established his ministry among the Highland and Hebridean Gaels on Prince Edward Island in 1827 after an unsuccessful mission in Malagawatch, Cape Breton Island, that began in 1824.[10] During his lifetime, MacDonald's flock grew into the thousands – comprising predominantly Scottish Gaelic–speaking Prince Edward Islanders – and he oversaw two revivals or *dùsgaidhean*, the first between 1829 and 1830 and the second in 1861.[11] In 1895 the Cambridge MacDonaldites requested a visit from Rev. MacDonald's successor, the Nova Scotia–born Scottish Gaelic–speaking Rev. John Goodwill, who had been serving the MacDonaldite congregations of Prince Edward Island since 1875 and who had led the third and final island-wide MacDonaldite revival around 1890.[12]

In 1897, thirty years after Rev. MacDonald's death, the new Church of Scotland congregation in Cambridge founded by Prince Edward Island emigrants outbid a Swedish immigrant organization to purchase the old Baptist Church on 171 Hampshire Street as a permanent house of worship for its members. This acquisition was the source of a great deal of highly opinionated consternation and unreserved animus in the established community, as revealed in Boston and Cambridge broadsheets of the period.[13] The *Cambridge Chronicle* reported on Saturday, 4 September 1897, under the headline "The McDonaldites Are at It Again. They Have a Church of Their Own and Hold Disgusting Services Each Week – Complained of as a Nuisance":

> They began their services, if that word expresses it, immediately, and for two months they have "played to crowded houses." They meet Tuesday evenings at 7.30 o'clock, Sunday mornings at 10.30 and Sunday afternoons from about 5 to 7 o'clock. The scenes in the church at these times are almost beyond description. The meetings open well enough. There is singing of Psalms, such as it

is, in doleful, nasal, funeral notes. Then somebody gets up and reads a passage in such "hell-deserving" tones that the dismal singing which follows seems as jolly as a snatch from De Koven. All this medley of misery is manufactured by twenty men on the platform. The audience of fellow MacDonaldites sits just in front of the platform, the women occupying the central section of seats and the men at each side. After the singing and reading have seemed to tire everybody out, the visitor sees where the fun comes in. If he watches closely, he will see some young woman have a twitch and a shudder in her left shoulder. Then she has a shudder and a twitch in her right shoulder. This is a sign that the MacDonaldites are approaching the interesting part of the meeting. Some of the other female followers of MacDonald will have the same symptoms of the on-coming whirlwind of religion, then another and another, man, woman and child, till the wriggling, screaming, shouting, dancing, jumping, stamping, convulsed and confused mass of rattled and raving men and women sink back into their seats, one by one out of sheer exhaustion, and the doleful cadences from the platform rise and fall till another wave of excitement rolls in and breaks higher than the one before …

Call this thing religion or by any other name, it would be equally as bad. No one objects to the MacDonaldites holding their meetings, if only they will not disturb people. While their religious fervor is rising, real estate in the vicinity of the church on Hampshire street is going down. An informant, a prominent employee of the West End road, says that several tenants have moved away from the locality already. He thinks it good reason for asking Chief Cloyes to interfere in the interests of the neighborhood. People cannot sleep with this racket going on. Real estate owners will have to work to find tenants for their houses, if this noise and excitement with all the attending noisy crowds, are to be kept up. If any one lay critically ill within hearing of this disturbance, it might be a serious matter. Those who object to the MacDonalites' style of worship, object in strong language. Their minds are made up that the sect ought to go and leave the community to its naturally quiet and peaceful state.[14]

In many ways, such external criticism of the MacDonaldites was nothing new. The uninitiated and largely anglophone witnesses were quick to comment negatively on the expressive aesthetics of evangelical worship as engaged in by Reverend Donald MacDonald and his followers.[15] Such discourse sought to undermine the authority of these forms of evangelical worship from the outside in, and in this regard it is important to note the use of external aesthetic criteria. Beyond the aesthetic sphere of the ornamented polyphonic performance of the metrical psalms by these Church of Scotland congregations (a performance style once found throughout early-modern Calvinist worship in northwestern Europe and today afforded an iconicity of style in Scottish Gaelic contexts) is the adaptation of vernacular forms of expression as part of the communication of their faith.[16] For example, a later column appearing in Montreal's *Gazette* on Monday, 4 February 1935 includes a description of the singing of a hymn prior to the commencement of a MacDonaldite service in Charlottetown, PEI through acoustic simile with other forms of Scottish Gaelic musical expression:

> The service started in a simple manner with an announcement by the clergyman: "I think we had better sing a hymn."
>
> There was no tuning fork but one of the elders started the eulogy of 21 verses and as many choruses to the tune of the Gaelic hymn, "Air Irin Arin u Hero" [*irin àirin ù horo*]. The congregation swelled into the chorus and slurred from high to low note giving the effect of the skirl of the bagpipes.[17]

In addition to the sonic experience of worship, and as detailed in the above newspaper commentaries, particular attention was frequently given to the physical manifestation of worship referred to popularly as "the work" and "the power," as found among MacDonaldite congregations.[18] These terms appear to be linked semantically to concepts of *obair* / *oibreachadh* (work, working) and *cumhachd* (power) as expressed in Reverend MacDonald's and church elder Ewen Lamont's compositions of *laoidhean spioradail* (spiritual hymns), and as noted above were often equated by the outside observer with dance.[19] MacDonald himself encouraged this form of expressing one's devotion, which he saw as being rooted in several passages from scripture that he enjoyed quoting from the pulpit,[20] including Jeremiah 31:13: "An sin ni an òigh gàirdeachas anns an dannsa, na daoine òga, agus na seann daoine le chèile: oir tionndaidhidh mise am bròn gu h-aoibhneas, agus bheir mi dhoibh comhfhurtachd, agus ni mi sòlasach iad an déigh an àmhghair" ("Then shall the virgin rejoice in the dance, both young men and old together: for I will turn their mourning into joy, and will comfort them, and make them rejoice from their sorrow"); and Psalm 47:1: "Buailibh bhur basan uile shlóigh; togaibh iolach do Dhia le guth gairdeachais" ("O clap your hands, all ye people; shout unto God with the voice of triumph").[21]

In the cycle of anecdotal narratives that circulated about the Reverend MacDonald during his lifetime and long after his death, it is noted that when he emigrated from Glengarry, Scotland, he brought with him little else than the clothes on his back and his fiddle.[22] Eyewitnesses would recall that shortly after he arrived in Prince Edward Island, they saw him dancing what appears to have been *an ruidhle ceathrar* (the foursome reel, or "Scotch Four") at a wedding:

> There were present a few who had been attending dancing school in Charlottetown. These began to sneer at what they regarded as awkward capers of the country folk. On noticing this Mr. McDonald, with a warm feeling for the sons of toil, stood up, buttoned his coat and asked the fiddler to play a certain tune. He took the hostess as partner and with another chosen couple danced a reel. "There," said a gentleman who was present, "is what you may call dancing."[23]

The blurring between these secular forms of Scottish Gaelic vernacular cultural expression and the emergent evangelical approaches to worship throughout the nineteenth-century revivalism that was afoot during and after Donald MacDonald's ministry on Prince Edward Island is worthy of note; indeed, it likely rests at the heart of the movement's success, in that it spoke to popular forms of worship within the bounds of wider local aesthetic criteria.[24] Furthermore, it appears that the innovations in worship linked to popular cultural expression were in many ways a unique development within these Church of Scotland congregations in Prince Edward Island's early nineteenth-century diasporic *Gàidhealtachd*. As Domhnull C. Friseal noted in his brief review of Rev. Donald MacDonald's life and work, his approach to composing spiritual verse was more utilitarian than that of his forebears: "Cha ruigeadh e an inbhe aig Padraig Grannd no idir Dùghall Bochanan ach tha na laoidhean aig Dòmhnul Dòmhnullach siubhlach reidh agus a' freagairt air a' chrioch airson gun deachaidh an deanamh: 's e sin teagasg sgriobtuireil a thoirt seachad agus brosnuchadh anama"[25] (He didn't reach the level of Patrick Grant or indeed Dugald Buchanan but Donald MacDonald's hymns are fluid and steady, suiting the purpose for which they were made: to teach scripture and stir the spirit).

Outsiders' perceptions of these seemingly unorthodox approaches to religious devotion and of the aesthetics of MacDonaldite evangelical expression can also be traced in the emergent mid-nineteenth-century attitudes of internal derision and hostility held by some of the more pervasive evangelical movements in Gaelic Scotland toward popular forms of vernacular and secular expression of music, dance, and storytelling. This included the Great Disruption (*Briseadh na h-Eaglaise*) of 1843 that resulted in the founding of the Free Church (*An Eaglais Shaor*)[26] alongside the mass burning of bagpipes and fiddles, as often remembered by the infamous proverb "Is feàrr an teine beag a gharas la beag na sìthe, na'n teine mòr a loisgeas la mòr na feirge" (Better is the small fire that warms on the little day of peace, than the big fire that burns on the great day of wrath).[27] As the Reverend Murdoch Lamont recounted, probably from his father Ewen's first-hand experience, these changes to worship in Scotland's *Gàidhealtachd* are likely what led later Calvinists arriving on the island in the early 1840s – primarily from the isles of Skye and Raasay – to view the stylistics of the singing of Rev. Donald MacDonald's spiritual verse with suspicion. As a retort, these "newcomers" were labelled *seicealaran* (hacklers/hecklers) by the initiated.[28]

Some of these divisions were rooted in MacDonaldite congregations' unorthodox performance of choral hymns, known popularly as "big songs" or *òrain mhòra*, which was seen as markedly similar to the singing of *òrain luaidh* (waulking songs):

> The hushed silence of the place before the services began was not the gaping drowsiness of frigid formalism, but a silence of expectation – of temporary restraint like a calm before a storm. When "McDonald's big songs," as they called the hymns, began to peal out and to "thrill the air with quick vibration" like the chorus at a "thickening" [i.e. *luadh* or waulking]; when the *threller* of real emotion, which art can but faintly imitate, enriched the strong voices of many sons of youth who as arrows were; when tears of joy trickled down the tanned cheeks of aged men; and when women young and old sprang to their feet with a voice of praise amid clapping of hands; the evidence of supernatural power, be it from above or from beneath, became too evident and most of the

"new comers" rushed out in panic, without waiting to hear enough of the preacher to judge him or his gifts. But this did not end the matter; they came again and yet again and the panic at the appearance of the dreaded work grew less on each occasion.[29]

The "thickening" or *luadh* held a prominent place in the social life of Prince Edward Island's nineteenth-century *Gàidhealtachd*,[30] serving as a foundation for a wider aesthetic system for the performance and composition of vernacular verse, whether devotional or secular. In a devotional context, the airs to popular *òrain luaidh* were well-suited to winning over converts.[31] Collective choral singing, whether of hymns or of waulking songs, fosters a sense of togetherness and the forging of group unity. For example, Peter Jack MacLean of Christmas Island, Cape Breton, perceived the shared singing of a song's chorus as "tighinn o'n cridhe" (coming from a singular and shared beating heart).[32] Such sentiments are echoed by singers of hymns in the Old Regular Baptist congregations in the Appalachians of southeastern Kentucky and southwestern Virginia as being "tuned up" by "singing from the heart."[33] The song aesthetics adopted by the MacDonaldites thus functioned within a wider system of "traditional referentiality," which, according to John Myles Foley, is capable of "evoking a context that is enormously larger and more echoic than the text or work itself, that brings the lifeblood of generations of poems and performances to the individual performance or text" through engaging and comparing the texts, anecdotes, sources, and contexts for these locally made songs alongside associated narratives about their composition.[34]

THE LAMONT FAMILY

Rev. Murdoch Lamont (Murchadh mac Eòghain 'ic Caluim 'ic Mhurchaidh Bhuidhe 'ic Iain 'ic Dhunnchaidh 'ic Dhòmhnaill 'ic Mhurchaidh 'ic Dhunnchaidh 'ic Coinnich) (1865–1927), a first-generation Prince Edward Island–born Gael, was a product of these multiple diasporas. It is within the wider aesthetic realms of secular and religious forms of Scottish Gaelic expression described above that he developed his own understanding of, and appreciation for, his various communities' rooted approaches to communicating their experiences through verse. In a small, vanity-published booklet printed in Quincy, Massachusetts, in 1917 titled *An Cuimhneachan: Òrain Céilidh Gàidheal Cheap Breatuinn agus Eilean-an-Phrionnsa* (The Remembrance:

Ceilidh Songs of Cape Breton and Prince Edward Island Gaels), we have some of the most complete records afforded of vernacular verse composed in Scottish Gaelic during the nineteenth century in Prince Edward Island.[35] He went on to furnish a comprehensive biography of Rev. Donald MacDonald and his followers titled *Rev. Donald MacDonald: Glimpses of his Life and Times*, published by Murley and Garnhum in Charlottetown in 1902. When he was well into his forties, he enrolled as a student of Divinity at the University of Glasgow, which he attended from 1908 to 1911 and where he won the essay prize in Professor James Cooper's Church History class. By 1912, he had been licensed by the Presbytery of Glasgow.[36]

Murdoch's great-grandfather Murchadh Buidhe (Yellow Murdoch), who, according to family tradition, was born *c.*1725 in Valtos, Trotternish, Skye (Bhaltos, An Taobh Sear, An t-Eilean Sgitheanach), was remembered as a boat-builder and violin-maker by trade who had served in an unofficial Jacobite contingent during the 1745 Rising.[37] His grandfather Malcolm (b. *c.*1760), a prosperous cattle drover who operated between Skye and the Scottish mainland, moved from Valtos to Lyndale in Bernisdale, Loch Snizort Beag (Liondal, Beàrnasdal, Loch Snìosart Beag) and married Isabella MacDonald (Iseabal ni'n Aonghais a' Phìobaire), daughter of Angus MacDonald, a renowned local bagpiper.

Murdoch's father, Ewen Lamont (Eòghan 'ic Caluim 'ic Mhurchaidh Bhuidhe) (1817–1905) was born to Malcolm and Isabella in Lyndale, Skye, as the seventh of seven sons. Around the age of twelve, Ewen emigrated with his parents on the *Mary Kennedy*, arriving in Charlottetown harbour on Monday, 1 June 1829. The Lamonts settled in Orwell Head (Bràigh Orwell),[38] Lot 57, Prince Edward Island, which in 1880 was, according to Murdoch's brother Rev. Donald MacDonald Lamont, renamed Lyndale after their father's Skye birthplace.[39] From the 1840s to the 1860s, Ewen Lamont was listed as a teacher administering to four schools in the Uigg and Orwell districts straddling the boundary between Lots 50 and 57 in Eastern Queens County, PEI. These communities were an extension of the wider Belfast district first settled by Scottish Gaels primarily from the Isle of Skye in 1803 under the leadership of Thomas Douglas, the Fifth Earl of Selkirk. Remarkably, Ewen Lamont included instruction in Scottish Gaelic literacy as an integral part of his successful pedagogical approach toward the education of his predominantly Scottish Gaelic–speaking pupils in both Scottish Gaelic and English.[40]

Self-admittedly "more at home in Gaelic than in English,"[41] Ewen Lamont was also a renowned composer of Scottish Gaelic hymns, which were published alongside others composed by Rev. Donald MacDonald in *Laoidhean Spioradail*, which first appeared in 1858 and was reprinted in 1870 and 1887.[42] It was also Ewen who recovered the nearly lost verses composed by emigrant bard Calum Bàn MacMhannain (Malcolm Buchanan, "the Polly Bard") of "Òran an Imrich" (The Song of Emigration) "o bheul seann duine, aois ceithir fichead 's a còig, a dh'ionnsaich e an làithean òige o'n ùghdar" (from the recitation of an old man, age eighty-five, who learned it in his youth from the composer),[43] detailing the circumstances of the bard's departure from Flodigarry (Flòdaigearraidh), Skye, with the Selkirk settlers to Prince Edward Island in 1803.[44] This desire to document and maintain knowledge of local verse within the wider repertory of Scottish Gaelic literary inheritance was part of the ethos of nineteenth-century Prince Edward Island Gaels, serving as an integral part of a wider cosmology. As Ewen Lamont noted in his biographical sketch of the Reverend Donald MacDonald, "Some of the old people could read their Gaelic Bibles, and most of their young folks were well versed in Gaelic literature."[45]

Ewen's sons, Angus, Donald, and Murdoch, having benefited from their father's tuition, were inheritors of Gaelic traditions carried over from the Isle of Skye, as well as locally composed verse that vividly captures the experience of Gaels on Prince Edward Island. Each was remembered as an active bard in his community, as noted in 1987 by the then one-hundred-three-year-old Margaret MacLeod of Little Sands, PEI, a granddaughter of Ewen and niece of the Lamont brothers.[46] Margaret also recalled a humorous locally composed song, "Òran a Mhaorach" (Song to Mussel-Mud), which she attributed to her uncle Murdoch Lamont, concerning an eventful afternoon harvesting Prince Edward Island's iconic marine fertilizer.[47]

REV. MURDOCH LAMONT

Rev. Murdoch Lamont's multiple and diverse careers over his lifetime reveal an extraordinary trajectory for a first-generation Scottish Gael born in the North American diaspora. In an obituary appearing in *Life and Work: The Church of Scotland Magazine and Mission Record* in October 1927, he was remembered as follows:

> By the sudden death of the Rev. Murdoch Lamont, minister of Rothiemurchas, on 13th August, the Church lost a man of unusual gifts, of independent mind, and of marked personality. Born of Highland stock in Prince Edward Island, Canada, he followed the occupation of an engineer in the States till middle age, when he entered Glasgow University to study for the ministry. In 1912, he was appointed minister of Oa [An Obha, Islay] where he practically rebuilt the church with his own hands; in 1916 he was translated to St Mark's, Glasgow, where he toiled with equal enthusiasm and acceptance; and in 1925 he was called to Rothiemurchas. Mr. Lamont, who was 62 years of age, was an attractively unconventional type, and will be long held in remembrance by all who knew him.[48]

Murdoch's life began in 1865 on his parents' Orwell Head homestead along the Murray Harbour Road. First-hand accounts of his early adult life in this community are given in his diaries, kept between 1885 and 1888.[49] Then, as today in Prince Edward Island, the *céilidh* was such an integral part of the social life of Islanders that even local livestock partook in the action, as Lamont noted in an entry from Tuesday, 1 December 1885: "Cloudy, cold – When I went to see the cattle this morn the horses were nowhere to be found. I guess they are off *ce[i]lidhing*[50] – Ang[us] was down this morn – I found the horses at Malcolm Gillis' barn. Father went to Mal[colm]'s – I wrote to Don[ald]. I went to the P. Office."[51] It seems that such winter pastimes as visiting and singing were at the forefront of twenty-some-year-old Murdoch's mind in his entries during the 1885–86 holiday season, and that he was then nurturing a keen interest in Scottish Gaelic song, as he went on to note in an entry from Sunday, 20 December 1885: "Snowed, Rained last night, cold and windy today, Don went up to Ang[us] this noon. I spent most of the day binding and reading McKenzie['s] B-of-G.P. [*Sar-Obair nam Bard Gaelach / The Beauties of Gaelic Poetry*]."[52] Murdoch's commentary gives a unique insight into the popularity of Gaelic song and the oral and literary frameworks for its transmission and performance in the late nineteenth-century island *Gàidhealtachd*. He concluded his entry for Friday, 22 January 1886 with another note on MacKenzie's popular anthology:

> Snowing, I went to R[oderick] McLeod's to help haul saw wood – I brought home MacKenzie[']s ["]B. of G. Poetry"[.] I had it for a

> good while. I learned one tune on its account ~ Don learned it from Ang[us.] It is the tune of "Òran Don Mhisg."[53] I left R[oderick]'s for home about ½ of 8 but it was when I got this side of R[oderick]'s woods[,] I thought of the axe, so I had to turn back for it. It rained heavy this eve and night.[54]

His keen interest in tracing the airs to songs by engaging in sources from locally maintained oral tradition, supplemented by published texts, is echoed in a note he provided decades later in *The Prince Edward Island Magazine* concerning the melody to Calum Bàn MacMhannain's "Òran an Imrich":

> Although the beautiful air to which the song was composed comes within the compass of the bagpipe's limited gamut of nine tones, and has its principal notes on the favourite E and A of that instrument, still the supposition that it had a McCrimmons [*sic*] for its author may be considered fanciful. When an Old Highlander told me that the same air was sung to McCodrun's [*sic*, read MacCodrum's] "Song to Old Age" [Òran na h-Aoise], and when, upon examining McKenzie's "Beauties of Gaelic Poetry" I found that the said song to old age was to be sung to the air of "The Pearl of the Irish Nation," I confess I felt a little apprehension in case this fine old tune, like some more of our best melodies might be traced to the Emerald Isle. But what of it? If the first McCrimmon was, as they say, an Italian, is it not better to keep the tune within our Empire?[55]

Despite his prejudicial Empire-nationalist views, his commentary highlights a carefully fostered knowledge of Gaelic song tradition, which laid the foundation on which he built his own dedicated interest in documenting local Prince Edward Island Gaelic song composition that would have otherwise been lost.

On 21 April 1891, Murdoch Lamont was enumerated in that year's census as being twenty-five and living with his wife Effie Ann and their ten-month-old son Samuel at his parents' home along with his younger siblings, Donald and Margaret Ann.[56] Two and a half years later, on 2 September 1893, Murdoch was first listed in the "Iadsan a Phaigh" (Those Who Paid) subscriber list to *Mac-Talla* with an address in Liontal (Lyndale, formerly Orwell Head), PEI. However, from 1894 until 1903 Murdoch was regularly listed as a paid *Mac-Talla* subscriber in Quincy, Massachusetts. Indeed, it appears that by his mid-thirties, Murdoch had left Lot 57 with his young family along with his mother and father and was living intermittently between Quincy, Massachusetts, and the settlement of Stanchel in the Strathalbyn district of Lot 67, Western Queens County, PEI, an area that shared strong kinship with the Skye and Raasay communities of the Kings and Queens County line.

In 1901, Murdoch, his growing family, and his parents were all enumerated in that year's census in the same household in Lot 67, with Murdoch and his parents being listed as Scottish Gaelic mother-tongue speakers and the children and his wife as English mother-tongue speakers.[57] Nearby, Murdoch's older brother Angus and his sister-in-law Catherine (née Macpherson), as well as their children born prior to 1890, were also enumerated as Scottish Gaelic mother-tongue speakers; however, children born after 1890 were listed as having English as their mother tongue.[58] Taken as a whole, roughly six hundred residents of Lot 67 in 1901 were recorded as mother-tongue speakers of Scottish Gaelic, making up over 60 percent of the population.[59]

MURCHADH CAM

Other Lamont relations had been established in the Strathalbyn district for nearly sixty years, having emigrated from the Isle of Skye in the 1840s. Included among them was a generational contemporary and cousin of Ewen Lamont, Murdoch Lamont (Murchadh mac Aonghais 'ic Iain 'ic Mhurchaidh Bhuidhe 'ic Iain 'ic Dhunnchaidh 'ic Dhòmhnuill 'ic Mhurchaidh 'ic Dhunnchaidh 'ic Coinnich) (1822–1902),[60] who emigrated from Bernisdale, Skye, aboard the *Nith*, arriving in Charlottetown harbour on 14 September 1840 and taking up land in Springton (Bail' an Tobair), Lot 67.[61] As this Murdoch later recalled in *Mac-Talla*, "Cha robh duine air bòrd gun charaide ga choinneachadh. Cuid gu Strath Alba 's cuid eile gu Valleyfield, 's mar sin sìos. Bha sinn gu math dheth seach iadsan a thàinig romhainn"[62] (There was not one person on board without a relation meeting him at port. Some went to Strathalbyn and others to Valleyfield, and so forth. We were well off compared to those who came before us). Murdoch later went on to comment on the state of the Scottish Gaelic language in the Strathalbyn district in Lot 67 in the final decade of the nineteenth century:

> Tha suas ri dà cheud taigh anns a' sgìre seo, 's gun taigh Goill na measg ach a ceithir, agus 's i mo bheachd nach eil deichnear dhiubh 'gabhail a' Mhic-Talla. Ud! Ud! Na innseadh Gall a Ghàidheal e. Cha 'n eil coire sam bith agamsa air na Gàidheil, ach an dìmeas a tha pàirt dhiubh 'deanamh air a' Ghàidhlig … Cha'n urrainn mi mòran coire 'chur air an òigridh ged nach biodh Gàidhlig aca. Ach luchd nan ceann liatha, 'mablaich Beurla, gun fhios carson! … 'S ann a thoill iad le chéile bogadh crochaidh; iadsan a' bruidhinn Beurla 's gun i idir aca. An Gàidheal a nì dìmeas air a Ghàidhlig, cha chreid mi gu robh meas aig' air a mhàthair, a thàlaidh e le ceòl binn na Gàidhlig.[63]
>
> There are upwards of two hundred homes in this district, and only four non-Gaelic-speaking homes among them, and it's my estimate that there aren't ten subscribing to *Mac-Talla.* Tsk! Tsk! Don't let a non-Gael tell it to a Gael. I find no fault with the Gaels, except with those who disdain the Gaelic language … I can't place much blame on the youth despite their not speaking Gaelic. But the grey-haired folks, maiming their English, without knowing why! … They deserved to be swinging while hanging; speaking English without having it. The Gael that despises the Gaelic language, I believe that he didn't love his own mother who cradled him to the melodious music of the language.

During his lifetime the elder Murdoch Lamont served as the Commissioner of Roads and Bridges as well as a Clerk of the Commissioner's Court in Prince Edward Island, and he was a frequent contributor to *Mac-Talla* under the pen name "Murchadh Cam" (One-Eyed Murdoch).[64] He was well-liked by its readers and contributors; its editor, Jonathan G. MacKinnon, described him in his obituary, which appeared on 3 October 1902:

> Bha litir uaithe uair is uair anns a' *Mhac-Talla*, agus bu mhath a chòrd iad ris na leughadairean, ged nach robh iad idir ri 'n coimeas ri e-fhèin a chluinntinn a' còmhradh. Bha eòlas air fad is farsuing anns an Eilean, agus far an robh eòlas air bha meas air. Bha e na Ghàidheal cho dìleas 's a b'aithne dhuinn riamh; bha 'chridhe 'n dlùth-cheangal ri 'dhùthaich 's ri cainnt a shinnsear.[65]

> Time and again his letters appeared in *Mac-Talla*, and they were well enjoyed by the readers, although they never had the opportunity to hear him speak. He was known far and wide on the Island, and where they knew him they cherished him. He was as faithful a Gael as we've ever known; his heart was closely linked to his homeland and the language of his ancestors.

It is evident that *Mac-Talla* often served as a social network among Scottish Gaelic speakers internationally in what had often become the increasingly anglicized and minoritized reality of their daily lives. The younger Murdoch was likely inspired by his elder cousin's frequent contributions to *Mac-Talla*, and shortly after his passing in 1903, Murdoch began writing letters to the paper from Quincy, Massachusetts.

MAC-TALLA AND *AN CUIMHNEACHAN*

The situation in Quincy among secondary Gaelic-speaking immigrants was similar to the language shift from Scottish Gaelic to English then under way in Prince Edward Island's intergenerational *Gàidhealtachd*, as Murdoch noted:

> Tha mòran de chlann nan Gaidheal 'san àite so, ach cha 'n 'eil spéis ro mhòr aig a chuid as motha dhiubh do 'n Ghàidhlig. Cha 'n 'eil iad a' cumail suas an aon phàipeir Gàidhlig a tha againn. Bha là eile ann – là anns an robh na Gàidheil glé dhìleas d' an cànain agus da chéile. Ar leam gu 'n robh iad anns na tìmannan ud a' cur aithne an Abstoil an gnìomh, a' dèanamh "gàirdeachas maille riùsan a tha ri gàirdeachas, agus caoidh maille riùsan a tha ri caoidh."[66]

> There are many descendants of the Gaels in this place, but most of them don't hold the Gaelic language in high regard. They are not maintaining the only Gaelic paper we have [*Mac-Talla*]. There was another day – a day in which the Gaels were very loyal to their language and to each other. I think that during those times they were aware of the Apostles through their deeds, "rejoicing with those who rejoice, and weeping with those who weep."

In the same letter, we get further insight into Murdoch's desire to engage *Mac-Talla* as a means of both sharing and retrieving items of

Scottish Gaelic verbal art, for he thanks the Cape Breton contributor "Peigidh Phabach" (Shaggy Peggy), the pen name of Dan MacPherson,[67] for providing a version of "Òran a' Mhathain" (The Bear's Song).[68] He then goes on to request from Peigidh a copy of the song "Òran a' Mhagain" (The Frog's Song), giving a verse to aid others' memory in hopes of it later appearing in the paper.[69] Murdoch's exchanges with Peigidh began in 1903, when the former first wrote in offering some versions of Scottish Gaelic mouth music he had heard during his youth in Prince Edward Island,[70] and the latter contributed a variation to one of the *puirt* (tunes) in response.[71] The exchanges between Murdoch and various other *Mac-Talla* contributors recalling items of oral tradition and song allowed for the retrieval of local Prince Edward Island poetic output through the collective memory maintained by Scottish Gaels in the North American diaspora.

In his first letter to *Mac-Talla*, published on 9 January 1903, Murdoch also provided fragments of songs composed locally in the Prince Edward Island community of his youth to see if more could be recalled by other readers:

> Bha duine còir anns an nàbachd an d'rugadh mi – Ruairidh Mòr Mac Leòid – a rinn iomadh òran gasda. Chuala mi aon dhiubh aig Murchadh Mac Mhanainn, am Beinn 'ic Mhanainn, E.P.I. 'S còir do Mhurchadh a chur anns a' Mhac-Talla dhuinn. Sheinn Ruairidh:
>
> Na'm faighinn air m' òrdugh / Soitheach diongmhalt a sheòladh, / Rachainn fhathast air m'eòlas / 'S ruiginn Troternis chaomh.
>
> Rinn Callum bàn Mac Mhanainn marbh-rann do dhithis nighean eireachdail a thuit le tinneas a bhrist am mach am measg an luchd-imrich a thàinig air an soitheach Polly. So sreath dheth:–
>
> Chuir mi iad an cill nam Frangach, / 'S cha chuir fuachd a gheamhradh as iad [*sic*].
>
> Tha mi cinnteach gu'm bheil an t-òran so aig Murchadh. Bidh mi nis a sgur.
>
> Do charaid, Quincy, Mass. M. MAC LAOMUINN.[72]

> There was a dear man in the community where I was born – Big Rory MacLeod – that made many fine songs. I heard one of them from Murdoch Buchanan, in Mount Buchanan, PEI. Murdoch should send it into *Mac-Talla* for us. Rory sang:

If I could get under my command / A steadfast vessel to sail, / I would go by my knowledge / And I would reach beloved Trotternish.

Fair Malcolm Buchanan made a eulogy for two beautiful girls who were struck down with the disease that broke out among the immigrants that came on the *Polly*. Here is a line from it:

I placed them in the French chapel, / And winter's cold will not put an end to them.

I am certain that Murdoch has this song. I will stop now.

Your friend, Quincy, Mass. M. Lamont.

Although no information was received concerning either song from Murdoch Buchanan of Mount Buchanan, Murdoch Lamont did receive an answer regarding the first song fragment in the 20 February 1903 issue of *Mac-Talla*:

> Fhuair sinn an t-òran a leanas o Chalum Mac Leòid ann a' Vancouver, B.C. Rinneadh le 'athair, Ruairidh Mac Leòid, a bha an Eilean a' Phrionnsa. Chuir M. Mac Laomuinn ann an Quincy, Mass. ceathramh dheth ann an litir bheag a sgrìobh e ugainn o chionn ghoirid.[73]

> We received the following song from Malcolm MacLeod in Vancouver, B.C. It was composed by his father, Rory MacLeod, who was in Prince Edward Island. M. Lamont in Quincy, Massachusetts sent a verse of the song in a short letter he wrote to us a little while back.

Could Ruairidh Mòr (Roderick MacLeod) (*c.* 1797–1887) be the same neighbour R. MacLeod who loaned young Murdoch Lamont his copy of MacKenzie's *Sar-Obair nam Bard Gaelach* in the winter of 1886 to be rebound, and who ultimately served as a source of inspiration to young Murdoch as a burgeoning documenter of Gaelic song?[74] The five additional verses to the song provided by the bard's son, Capt. Malcolm MacLeod of Vancouver, in response to Murdoch's request constitute an extraordinary instance of *Mac-Talla*'s role in the documentation of nineteenth-century Scottish Gaelic literature that otherwise would have been lost.

Such exchanges likely set the stage for the 1917 appearance of the booklet *An Cuimhneachan* in Quincy that contained several pieces of material gleaned from *Mac-Talla*, as Murdoch Lamont (by then a reverend) notes in the foreword:

> Gheibhear anns an leabhran so beagan de òrain nach robh gus an so air an clò-bhualadh. Chan eil am fear-deasachaidh ag ràdh gur iad an roinn a b'fheàrr de òrain Gaidhlig Cheap Breatuinn, 's Eilean-an-Phrionnsa a tha fathast air cuimhne anns na tìrean sin.
> Tha mi an comain *Mac-Talla* air son nan òrain "C'ait an caidil an nionag," "òran imrich" &c. Mar chuimhneachan air na làithean a dh'fhalbh; tha mi an dòchas gum bith an oidheirp so feumeil.[75]
>
> Found in this booklet are a few songs that have not been printed until now. The editor does not claim that they are the best of the Gaelic songs of Cape Breton and Prince Edward Island as still remembered in those districts.
> I am indebted to *Mac-Talla* for the songs "Càit' an Caidil an Nighneag" [Where Will the Lass Sleep] and [Calum Bàn Buchanan's] "Òran Imrich" among others. I hope this endeavour will be a suitable memorial for days gone by.

Of the fourteen song-texts presented in the volume, six are attributed to Prince Edward Island sources, two are from Cape Breton, and the remainder are popular nineteenth-century compositions from Scotland or oral traditions found in Scottish Gaelic–speaking communities on both sides of the Atlantic. The Scottish Gaelic verse contained within is currently being edited by the author of this chapter for an anthology of Scottish Gaelic song and narrative from Prince Edward Island. Several of the songs compiled by Lamont in *An Cuimhneachan* are compositions by Skye settlers in Prince Edward Island and, in contrast to the poetry composed at the time of emigration or initial settlement, naturally highlight an emerging locus centred upon their new island home.

"ORAN LE RUARAIDH MACLEOID"

Roderick MacLeod (Ruairidh Mòr) was remembered as a local bard in the Belfast District of Queen's County, Prince Edward Island; he was also a renowned strongman.[76] Malcolm MacQueen in his *Skye Pioneers* remembers Ruairidh Mòr as follows:

> The strength of some of these Highlanders was prodigious. Rory McLeod, of Pinette, father of Capt. Malcolm McLeod, who died in Vancouver in 1924, was recognized as one of the strongest men in Canada ... He was frequently compared with Angus MacAskill [aka "The Giant MacAskill"], one of the world's greatest giants ... This man only, would the Belfast people admit, was more powerful than Rory McLeod of Pinette, their hero. [77]

The emerging Gaelic heartland of Prince Edward Island in the shared imagination of the community's strongman and bard can be seen particularly well in MacLeod's only attributed contribution in *An Cuimhneachan*, "Oran le Ruaraidh MacLeoid (Ruaraidh Mór Belfast), Eilean-an-Phrionnsa" (A Song by Roderick MacLeod [Big Rory Belfast] of Prince Edward Island).[78] In the song, Ruairidh Mòr commemorates the completion, fitting, and launching of a vessel built in the local shipyard, voicing his desire to take the helm and sail it back to Skye, the land of his birth, relying solely on his *eòlas* (knowledge, discernment, experience) to make the journey.[79]

In the edition of the song that appears in Rev. Murdoch Lamont's anthology, *An Cuimhneachan* (See Appendix A), two additional verses are added to the beginning, the first of which names the boat "[an] diùlnach aig Sandi" (Sandy's hero).[80] In a footnote, Lamont identifies "Sandy" as "Alasdair MacGilleain ('an Goisteadh')" (Alexander MacLean ["The Godfather"]) and indicates that he built "soitheach mòr air Abhainn Pinette aig an àm. Chaidh i do'n Fhraing a' cheud turas" (a large vessel on the Pinette River at the time. It sailed to France on its maiden voyage).[81] Alasdair MacGilleain, "an Goisteadh," may perhaps be the same person as Alexander Maclean, "Alasdair Gasda" (Gallant/Brave Alexander), of Portage, Belfast.[82] Maclean was the Conservative running mate of land agent William Douse and the opponent of Reform candidates John Little and John MacDougall in the infamous election of 1 March 1847.[83] In an audit of the annual *List of New Vessels Registered in Prince Edward Island* between the years 1823 and 1850, the following vessels were registered by one A. / Alexander M'Lean / MacLean: *Portree* (1838), *Isle of Skye* (1843), *Highland Chief* (1846), and *Ben Nevis* (1847).[84]

Although Lamont gives no air to the song, the melody to the well-known eighteenth-century love panegyric "Bothan Àirigh Am Bràigh Raithneach" (The Sheiling in Brae Rannoch) well aligns with Ruairidh Mòr's *luinneag* (chorus) and quatrains.[85] Ruairidh Mòr's metrics are similar to, though not as faithfully executed as, those employed by the anonymous female bard. The loose syllabic construction of each line of his quatrains and his frequent use of assonance in end-rhymes as well as in internal rhymes offer a free vernacular adaptation of the stricter *rannaigheacht*-type metres of Classical Gaelic.[86] Also, Ruairidh Mòr echoes the earlier composer's pastoral imagery in his fifth verse, in which he too praises the *àirigh*. Although there is a longing (*cianalas*) within Ruairidh Mòr's lines for a return to the land of one's *dùthchas*, his allegorical voyage of the diasporic imagination runs full circle with a return to his new and prosperous Prince Edward Island home, echoing the sentiments of well-known compatriots like Calum Bàn Mac Mhannain, who famously extolled it as "Eilean an Àigh" (the Island of Prosperity/Joy).[87]

CONCLUSION

Taken together, the *eòlas* of each generation discussed here was not only one of rooted contentment fostered by a spiritual sense of *dùthchas* (belonging) to a particular place and its people, but also one of restlessness, given the shared experience of near perpetual motion, as maintained in the living memories of concurrent generations of Scottish Gaels belonging to multiple primary and secondary diasporas. Like the MacDonaldites' successful adaptation of popular secular forms of expression for religious purposes, these various, seemingly contradictory oppositions, according to our current taxonomies of understanding, formed an integrated cosmology that served as a consistent backdrop to these Gaelic diasporas. Beginning with his own birth in a MacDonaldite elder's home in Orwell Head, Prince Edward Island, and following his multiple migrations, Rev. Murdoch Lamont's determined efforts, through written text, to retrieve from collective oral memory nineteenth-century Scottish Gaelic songs composed in Prince Edward Island bore fruit. The bonds of memory and kinship maintained between Gaels scattered throughout North America are revealed in his engagements with other Gaelic speakers in the pages of *Mac-Talla* at the turn of the twentieth century. His *An Cuimhneachan* appeared at a point of crisis that witnessed the dismantling of rural communities, outward migration to urban centres, and the attrition of the Scottish Gaelic language. As a result, it represents a significant harvest reaped from the collaborative recollection of shared forms of communal expression once rooted in the everyday experience of Prince Edward Island's vibrant nineteenth-century *Gàidhealtachd*.

APPENDIX A

"Oran le Ruaraidh MacLeoid, (Ruaraidh Mór Belfast) Eilean-an-Phrionnsa," in Mac Laomuinn, *An Cuimhneachan*, 15–16.[88]

Hithill iu, hill o ró ho,
Hithill iu, hill o ró ho,
Hithill iu, hill o ró ho,
Hogaidh ó hó ró hì.

'S ann tha diùlnach aig Sandi,
Chaidh a thogail sa gheamhradh,
Nuair a gheibh iad air sàl i,
Théid i [dh]an Fhraing a dh'aoin sgrìob.

Sandy has got a hero,
That was built in the winter,
When they launch her on the salt-sea,
She'll head to France on a mission.

Nuair a thig a cu[i]d iaruinn,
'S acfhuinn ri cliathaich,
Théid i dh'ionnsa[i]dh an iasga[i]ch;
'S bheir i [']bhliadhna dhan Rìgh.

When her irons
And ropes are fitted onboard,
She'll head toward the fishing grounds;
And she'll give the year in service to the King.

A rìgh' gur muladach thà mi,
'S mi na m' aonar an dràsda,
'S tric mo smaointean air mo chàirdean
O'n lath' dh'fhàg mi Portrìgh.

Lord, I am woeful,
And alone now,
My thoughts often turn to my relations,
Since the day I left Portree.

Na'm faighinn air m'òrdugh
Soitheach diongmhalt a sheòladh,
Rachainn fhathast air m'eòlas
'S ruiginn Tròternis chaoimh.

If I could get under my command
A steadfast vessel to sail,
I would go by my own experience
And I would reach beloved Trotternish.

Rachainn na b'fhàid' ann air m'eòlas,
Ruiginn dùthaich nan Leòdach,
Far an d'fhuair mi m'òg àrach,
'S tric a dh[']òl às a['] chìch.

I'd venture further by my knowledge,
I'd reach MacLeods' country,
Where I was brought up,
Often drinking from the breast.

B'e sin dùthaich mo mhàthar,
Far an d'fhuair i òg àrach,

That was my mother's country,
Where she was brought up,

Bhiodh an crodh ac' air àiridh 'S iad ag àrach nan laogh.	They'd have cattle on the shieling And they'd be grazing the calves.
Mìle beannachd gu bràth Do'n àite [']bheil sinn an dràsda! Their na mnathan gu stàtail, Lìonte làn a' phoit-tì.	A thousand blessings forever To the place we are now! The women speak proudly, With the teapot filled to the brim.
Bidh iad 'g iarraidh an t-siùcair Gus a fàgail na's cùbhraidh, 'S mur bi uachdar glè ùr innt' Cha bhi diù aca dhith.	They'll desire sugar, To enhance its fragrance, But for the lack of the freshest cream, They'll have no reason to be ashamed.

NOTES

1 Nilsen, "Nova Scotia Gael," 87–8.
2 Dunn, "Gaelic Church"; Nilsen, "Collecting," 58–9n15.
3 Ibid.
4 Scott, "Eight Years," 403.
5 Dunn, *Highland Settler*, 134–5. For relevant oral histories, see Burrill, *Maritimers*, 98–106.
6 See Bailey, *Race and Redemption*; and Bendroth, *Fundamentalists*, for further relevant discussions.
7 Linkletter, "Island 'Gàidhealtachd,'" 231.
8 C.C., "Litir à Srathalba," *Mac-Talla*, 27 October 1899, 124. Rev. Malcolm Campbell contributed frequently to *Mac-Talla* under the abbreviation C.C. (Calum Caimbeul). I am currently editing and translating his and other Prince Edward Islanders' contributions to *Mac-Talla*. For the sake of clarity in quoting Scottish Gaelic texts here, I have made some revisions to various orthographic inconsistencies and errors contained in the original texts.
9 Bishop, *Church of Scotland*, 15–17.
10 Although little is known of MacDonald's origins in Scotland's *Gàidhealtachd* it is widely believed that he was born in Drumcastle on the border of Rannoch, Perthshire, on 1 January 1783, and that these MacDonalds were known locally as MacKays: Lamont, *Rev. Donald McDonald*, 2–4. This was the same district that would have witnessed in living memory crowds of more than five hundred individuals assembling to hear the open-air preaching of the evangelist, teacher, and composer of spiritual verse Dugald Buchanan (Dùghall Bochanan) (1716–68); see Meek, *Laoidhean Spioradail*.

For descriptions of MacDonald's failed ministry in Cape Breton see Lamont, *Rev. Donald McDonald*, 21–30.

11 For detailed discussions of MacDonald's ministry in Prince Edward Island, see Lamont, *Rev. Donald McDonald*; Weale, "Ministry"; Weale, "The Time Is Come!"; Friseal, "Ministear agus Bàrd."

12 Weale, "Ministry," 242.

13 See "A Strange Revival: New Sect Introduces Dancing," *Boston Sunday Post*, 31 January 1897, 1; "The McDonaldites Are at It Again. They Have a Church of Their Own and Hold Disgusting Services Each Week – Complained of as a Nuisance," *Cambridge Chronicle*, 4 September 1897, 1; "In Defence of the McDonaldites. The Other Side Presented by a Member of the Sect," *Cambridge Chronicle*, 11 September 1897, 7.

14 "The McDonaldites Are at It Again."

15 It is also worthy of note that MacDonaldite religious practices were the focus of an unpublished paper titled "The Religious Customs of the MacDonaldites of Prince Edward Island" read at a local meeting of the Iowa Branch of the American Folk-Lore Society held 26–27 November 1909 by Mr John F. Kelly of Iowa City; see "Local Meetings," 434.

16 For specific consideration of the role of hymnody among the MacDonaldites, see Whytock, "Gaelic Hymnody"; Campbell, "Giving Out the Line." I am very grateful to Rev. Jack C. Whytock for gifting me a copy of the English-language edition of Rev. Donald MacDonald's *Hymns*, as is still used prior to worship in Prince Edward Island's Free Church of Scotland congregations.

17 "Kirk Edict Defied in Charlottetown – MacDonaldite Preacher Disregards Attempt to Oust Him," *Gazette*, 4 February 1935, 10. The hymn in question is likely MacDonald's twenty-one-verse "Eulogy" set to the air "Irin, arin, u horo": MacDonald et al., *Hymns*, 9–12). Elder Ewen Lamont translated nineteen of these verses "o Bheurla Mhinisteir Dhonullaich" (from Rev. MacDonald's English) into Gaelic as, "Dan Emmanuel," with the chorus, or *cosheirm*: "Seinnibh dan a chliu bhibhuan, / Le cridh aoibhneach ceol is duan; / Crunaibh 'n ceol le cliu do'n Uan / Ar Tighearn Ios' Emmanuel": Donullach and MacLaomuinn, *Laoidhean Spioradail Feumail*, 132–4, rendered from MacDonald's English chorus: "Sing the song of endless praise, / Sing with cheerful hearts your lays, / Crown your anthems with the praise / Of Jesus Christ Emmanuel": Donullach and MacLaomuinn, *Laoidhean Spioradail Feumail*, 132–4; MacDonald et al., *Hymns*, 9. See Ross, *Elizabeth Ross Manuscript*, 139; and MacDonald, *Gesto Collection*, 45 for versions of the melody. In School of Scottish Studies SA1975.219.B6, Rev. William Matheson discusses various applications and forms of this air (also set to the chorus "Èirich agus Tiugainn O" [O, Rise and Come Along]).

18 Pratt, *Dictionary*, s.vv. "McDonaldite" and "works."
19 Donullach and MacLaomuinn, *Laoidhean Spioradail Feumail*, passim.
20 Lamont, *Rev. Donald McDonald*, 79.
21 *Leabhraichean an t-Seann Tiomnaidh*; King James Bible.
22 Lamont, *Rev. Donald McDonald*, 20.
23 Ibid., 34.
24 Meek, "Saints and Scarecrows," 17–20.
25 Friseal, "Ministear agus Bàrd," 99.
26 In 1929 the Church of Scotland dissolved its affiliation with the Prince Edward Island MacDonaldite Section, and by 1954 the remaining MacDonaldite congregations of Prince Edward Island had joined the Free Church of Scotland; see Bishop, *Church of Scotland*, 21.
27 Carmichael, *Carmina Gadelica*, xvi. The translation is Carmichael's.
28 Lamont, *Rev. Donald McDonald*, 110–11.
29 Ibid., 110–11; for further, often entertaining, discourse on the aesthetics of MacDonaldite worship and hymnody, see Macphail, *Master's Wife*, 126–35.
30 The iconicity of the "thickening" or *luadh* in Prince Edward Island's nineteenth-century *Gàidhealtachd* was remembered by one Mrs Alexander Gillis (née MacLeod, nighean Dhòmhnaill Bhàin Òig, b. *c.*1850) for Malcolm A. MacQueen in his *Skye Pioneers and "The Island"* as follows: "When recently questioned about amusements in the Orwell district of her youth, she declared without hesitation that … the waulking, or 'thickening frolic' was the happiest day of the year … This was accompanied by a Gaelic song, the rhythm of which lent itself to the movement. The hilarity produced by the singing robbed the task of any appearance or sense of labour … Songs were composed to commemorate striking events in the district. Some were in Gaelic, others in English" (30–1).
31 Cf. Meek, "Saints and Scarecrows," 20.
32 This usage is explained in Falzett, "Tighinn o'n Cridhe," 236–52. The phrase means literally "coming from their heart."
33 Titon, "Tuned Up," 329–30.
34 Foley, *Immanent Art*, 7–8.
35 Mac Laomuinn, *Cuimhneachan*. I am most grateful to Dr Michael D. Linkletter for generously giving me a copy of this work, which he informs me was given to him by Professor Nilsen.
36 Ibid.; "Reverend Murdoch Lamont," The University of Glasgow Story, accessed 20 September 2017, https://www.universitystory.gla.ac.uk/biography/?id=WH25312&type=P.
37 This and subsequent information on Lamont family tradition was gleaned from an online family genealogy, www.linneberg.com, accessed in 2016,

that is no longer available. Further information on this branch of Lamonts can be found in MacLeod, *Lamonts of Lyndale*, as well as The Island Register, accessed 20 September 2017, http://www.islandregister.com.

38 "Braidh Orwell" is given as the Scottish Gaelic for Orwell Head by Rev. Donald MacDonald in *Plan of Salvation*, 206.

39 Douglas, *Place-Names*, 35.

40 MacLennan, *From Shore to Shore*, 55.

41 Lamont, *Biographical Sketch*, 38.

42 Nilsen, "Some Notes," 129.

43 Murchadh Laman, "A Eilean a Phrionnsa," *Mac-Talla*, 13 April 1895, 1. The verses were sent into *Mac-Talla* by Ewen's cousin, the elder Murdoch Lamont (Murchadh mac Aonghais 'ic Iain 'ic Mhurchaidh Bhuidhe) (1822–1902) of Springton (Bail' an Tobair), PEI; cf. Callum Ban Mac Mhanainn, "Oran Imrich," *Mac-Talla*, 14 November 1902, 79. Lamont's oral source was likely Roderick MacLeod; see Irwin, "Selkirk Settlers," 400.

44 See MacDonell, *Emigrant Experience*, 106–13; and her "Bards on the Polly," 34–9.

45 Lamont, *Biographical Sketch*, 23.

46 See the field recording made by Dr John W. Shaw for the Prince Edward Island Gaelic Field Recording Project Collection, tape 4, recorded on 25 August 1987, Robertson Library, UPEI. I am very grateful to Dr Shaw for permission to use these recordings.

47 Ibid.; see Falzett, "Oran a Mhaorach."

48 *Life and Work*, 223. I am grateful to Dr Andrew Wiseman for locating and providing a copy of this obituary.

49 Photocopies of the Murdoch Lamont Diary are held in the Prince Edward Island Collection at UPEI's Robertson Library.

50 Pratt, *Dictionary*, s.v. "ceilidh," defines the use of the word as a verb in Island English, citing similar examples to Lamont's usage with the addition of the 'ing' English verbal suffix to the Scottish Gaelic noun.

51 Murdoch Lamont Diary, 1 December 1885.

52 Murdoch Lamont Diary, 20 December 1885.

53 "Òran do'n Mhisg" (A Song to Inebriation) by the blind bard and fiddler Allan MacDougall (Ailean Dall) (*c.*1750–1829) of Glencoe, Argyll: MacKenzie, *Sàr-Obair*, 305.

54 Murdoch Lamont Diary, 22 January 1886.

55 Irwin, "Selkirk Settlers," 401. For "Òran na h-Aoise," see Matheson, *Songs*, 325–6.

56 1891 Census of Canada, Queen's County, Prince Edward Island, Township [Lot] 57, division no. 2, p. 28, family 103, Ewen Lamont et al.

57 1901 Census of Canada, Prince East, Prince Edward Island, Township [Lot] 67, division no. 1, p. 4, family 27, Murdoch Lamont et al.

58 1901 Census of Canada, Prince East, Prince Edward Island, Township [Lot] 67, division no. 1, p. 5, family 32, Angus Lamont et al.

59 There were 595 mother-tongue Scottish Gaelic speakers in Lot 67 enumerated out of a total of 965 individuals, making up 61.6 percent of the population: 1901 Census of Canada, Prince East, Prince Edward Island, Township [Lot] 67.

60 See his *sloinneadh* (patronymic) as given in Murchadh Laman (Murdoch Lamont), "A Eilean a Phrionnsa," *Mac-Talla*, 13 April 1895, 1.

61 Ibid.

62 Mec Laomuinn (Murdoch Lamont), "Na h-Eilthirich," *Mac-Talla*, 4 August 1894, 6.

63 Murchadh Cam (Murdoch Lamont), "A Eilean a' Phrionnsa," *Mac-Talla*, 21 January 1898, 238.

64 For a description of the origins of the pen name "Murchadh Cam" see C.C. [Rev. Malcolm Campbell], "Litir a Baile-nan-Seobhag," *Mac-Talla*, 12 December 1902, 90–1 at 91.

65 Jonathan G. MacKinnon, "Bàs Mhurchaidh Mhic-Laomuinn," *Mac-Talla*, 3 October 1902, 50.

66 M. Mac Laomuinn ([Rev.] Murdoch Lamont), "Litir a Quincy," *Mac-Talla*, 11 December 1903, 90.

67 MacPherson is identified by *Mac-Talla*'s editor, Jonathan G. MacKinnon, as "a young man who is foreman in my office"; see Linkletter, "*Bu Dual Dha Sin*," 251.

68 See "Oran a' Mhathainn," *Mac-Talla*, 18 September 1903, 48. The song, which circulated in oral tradition in Cape Breton until the end of the twentieth century, is attributed to Alexander Maclean (Alasdair mac Eòghainn Bhàin) of Judique, Cape Breton; see MacLellan, *Brìgh an Òrain*, 409.

69 See "Oran mar gum b'ann eadar am Bard agus Magan" (A Song as if between the Bard and a Frog) by Angus MacDonald (Aonghas mac Alasdair), of Mabou, Cape Breton, in MacLellan, *Failte*, 73–4.

70 M. Mac Laomuinn ([Rev.] Murdoch Lamont), "Litir a Quincy," *Mac-Talla*, 9 January 1903, 112.

71 "Peigidh Phabach" (Dan MacPherson), "Litir a Lag an t-Slocain," *Mac-Talla*, 6 February 1903, 127.

72 M. Mac Laomuinn ([Rev.] Murdoch Lamont), "Litir a Quincy," *Mac-Talla*, 9 January 1903, 112.

73 Mac Leoid, "Oran," *Mac-Talla*, 20 February 1903, 136.

74 Irwin, "Selkirk Settlers," 400. It is also possible that this Roderick MacLeod

of Portage was Ewen Lamont's oral source for Calum Bàn MacMhannain's "Òran an Imrich," according to supplementary notes attributed to Rev. Murdoch Lamont that appeared in *Prince Edward Island Magazine*.

75 Mac Laomuinn (Rev. Murdoch Lamont), *Cuimhneachan*, 3.

76 Cf. Stanley-Blackwell and MacDonald, "Strongman."

77 MacQueen, *Skye Pioneers*, 114.

78 Mac Laomuinn, *Cuimhneachan*, 15.

79 Ibid., 16.

80 Ibid., 15.

81 Ibid.

82 MacQueen, *Skye Pioneers*, 112.

83 This is the same election that resulted in the infamous "Belfast Riot," which pitted the majority of Belfast's Presbyterian Scottish Gaelic-speaking residents against their Roman Catholic, English-speaking Irish neighbours. The latter were emigrants from County Monaghan in Ireland, who had settled in Belfast between the 1830s and the Great Famine. See O'Grady, *Exiles and Islanders*, Chapter 9: "A Storm Over Belfast: An Irish Retrospective."

84 See "The Island Register Shipping Stories, Info, and Folklore," *Island Register*, accessed 20 September 2017, http://www.islandregister.com/ships.html.

85 Kerrigan, *Anthology*, 24–7, 336; Mac Laomuinn, *Cuimhneachan*, 15.

86 Watson, *Bàrdachd Ghàidhlig*, 314.

87 MacDonell, *Emigrant Experience*, 112–13.

88 Thanks to Griogair Labhruidh for highlighting several Skye idioms in the song's text.

BIBLIOGRAPHY

Bailey, Richard A. *Race and Redemption in Puritan New England*. Oxford: Oxford University Press, 2011.

Bendroth, Margaret Lamberts. *Fundamentalists in the City: Conflict and Division in Boston's Churches, 1885–1950*. Oxford: Oxford University Press, 2005.

Bishop, J.H. *Church of Scotland in Prince Edward Island (MacDonaldite Section)*. [Charlottetown?], [1991?].

Burrill, Gary, ed. *Maritimers in Massachusetts, Ontario, and Alberta: An Oral History of Leaving Home.* Montreal and Kingston: McGill-Queen's University Press, 1992.

Campbell, Norman. "'Giving Out the Line': A Cross-Atlantic Comparison of Two Presbyterian Cultures." *Scottish Reformation Society Historical Journal* 1 (2011): 241–65.

Carmichael, Alexander. *Carmina Gadelica / Ortha nan Gàidheal: Hymns and Incantations.* Edinburgh: T. and A. Constable, 1900.

Donullach, Donull, and Ewen MacLaomuinn. *Laoidhean Spioradail Feumail ri'n Seinn am measg nan Gael, Cumtadh ri Teasgasgan Eglais na h-Alba.* Baile-Shearlot, Eilean Phrionsa Eduard [Charlottetown, PEI]: Deorsa Bremner, 1870.

Douglas, R. *Place-Names of Prince Edward Island with Meanings*. Ottawa: F.A. Acland, 1925.

Dunn, Charles. "A Gaelic Church in Boston, Massachusetts." *An Teangadóir* 4 (1957): 24.

– *The Highland Settler: A Portrait of the Scottish Gael in Cape Breton and Eastern Nova Scotia.* Halifax: Formac, 1968.

Falzett, Tiber F.M. "'Oran a Mhaorach': The Mussel Mud Song by Rev. Murdoch Lamont (Murchadh mac Eòghain 'ic Caluim ic Mhurchaidh Bhuidhe, 1865–1927)." *Island Magazine* 82 (2017): 29–34.

– "'Tighinn o'n Cridhe' ('Coming from the Centre'): An Ethnography of Sensory Metaphor on Scottish Gaelic Communal Aesthetics." PhD diss., University of Edinburgh, 2014.

Foley, John Miles. *Immanent Art: From Structure to Meaning in Traditional Oral Epic.* Bloomington: Indiana University Press, 1991.

Friseal, Domhnull C. "Ministear agus Bàrd: Dòmhnull Dòmhnullach." *Transactions of the Gaelic Society of Inverness* 52 (1980–82): 90–101.

Irwin, Archibald. "The Selkirk Settlers in P.E. Island. – III. Notes to Emigration Song." *Prince Edward Island Magazine* 4, no. 11 (January 1903): 399–402.

Kerrigan, Catherine, ed. *An Anthology of Scottish Women Poets*. Edinburgh: Edinburgh University Press, 1991.

Lamont, Ewen. *A Biographical Sketch of the Late Rev. Donald McDonald.* Charlottetown: John Coombs, 1892.

Lamont, M. *Rev. Donald McDonald: Glimpses of His Life and Times*. Charlottetown: Murley and Garnhum, 1902.

Leabhraichean an t-Seann Tiomnaidh agus an Tiomnaidh Nuaidh: Air an Tarruing o na Ceud Chanuinbh chum Gaelic Albanaich. London: The British and Foreign Bible Society, 1829.

Life and Work: The Church of Scotland Magazine and Mission Record 49 (October 1927): 233.

Linkletter, Michael D. "*Bu Dual Dha Sin* (That Was His Birthright): Gaelic Scholar Alexander Maclean Sinclair (1840–1924)." PhD diss., Harvard University, 2006.

– "The Island 'Gàidhealtachd': The Scottish Gaelic Community of Prince

Edward Island." *Proceedings of the Harvard Celtic Colloquium* 16–17 (2003): 223–43.
"Local Meetings." *Journal of American Folklore* 22, no. 86 (October–December 1909): 434–5.
MacDonald, Rev. Donald. *Plan of Salvation*. Charlottetown: Bremner Brothers, 1874.
MacDonald, Rev. Donald, and Elders. *Hymns for Practice Not to be used in the Solemn Worship of the Sanctuary*. N.p.: Church of Scotland, Province of Prince Edward Island, 1999.
MacDonald, Keith Norman. *The Gesto Collection of Highland Music*. Leipzig: Oscar Brandstetter, 1895.
MacDonell, Margaret. "Bards on the Polly." *The Island Magazine* 5 (1978): 34–9.
– *The Emigrant Experience: Songs of Highland Emigrants in North America*. Toronto: University of Toronto Press, 1982.
MacKenzie, John. *Sar-Obair nam Bard Gaelach, Or, The Beauties of Gaelic Poetry: With Historical and Critical Notes, and a Comprehensive Glossary of Provincial Words*. Glasgow: Macgregor, Polson, & Company, 1841.
Mac Laomuinn, M. *An Cuimhneachan: Òrain Céilidh Gàidheal Cheap Breatuinn agus Eilean-an-Phrionnsa*. Quincy: printed by the author, 1917.
MacLellan, Lauchie Dan N. *Brìgh an Òrain / A Story in Every Song*, ed. and trans. John W. Shaw. Montreal: McGill-Queen's University Press, 2000.
MacLellan, Vincent, ed. *Failte Cheap Breatuinn: A Collection of Gaelic Poetry*. Sydney: Island Reporter, 1891.
MacLennan, Jean M. *From Shore to Shore: The Life and Times of the Rev. John MacLennan of Belfast*. Edinburgh: Knox Press, 1977.
MacLeod, Harold C. *The Lamonts of Lyndale*. Montague, PEI, 2003.
Macphail, Sir Andrew. *The Master's Wife*. Charlottetown: Institute of Island Studies Press, 1994.
MacQueen, Malcolm. *The Skye Pioneers and "The Island."* Winnipeg: Stovel Company Ltd., 1929.
Matheson, William, ed. *The Songs of John MacCodrum, Bard to Sir James MacDonald of Sleat*. Edinburgh: Scottish Gaelic Texts Society, 1938.
Meek, Dòmhnall Eachann, ed. *Laoidhean Spioradail Dhùghaill Bhochanain*. Glasgow: Comann Litreachas Gàidhlig na h-Alba (Scottish Gaelic Texts Society), 2015.
Meek, Donald. "Saints and Scarecrows: The Churches and Gaelic Culture in the Highlands Since 1560." *Scottish Bulletin of Evangelical Theology* (Spring 1996): 3–22.

Nilsen, Kenneth E. "Collecting Celtic Folklore in the United States." In *Proceedings of the First North American Congress of Celtic Studies*, ed. Gordon MacLennan, 55–74. Ottawa: Chair of Celtic, University of Ottawa, 1988.

– "The Nova Scotia Gael in Boston." *Proceedings of the Harvard Celtic Colloquium* 6 (1986): 83–100.

– "Some Notes on Pre-*Mac-Talla* Gaelic Publishing in Nova Scotia (With References to Early Gaelic Publishing in Prince Edward Island, Quebec and Ontario)." In *Rannsachadh na Gàidhlig 2000*, ed. Colm Ó Baoill and Nancy R. McGuire, 127–40. Obar Dheathain: An Clò Gaidhealach, 2002.

O'Grady, Brendan. *Exiles and Islanders: The Irish Settlers of Prince Edward Island*. Montreal: McGill-Queen's University Press, 2004.

Pratt, Terry Kenneth, ed. *Dictionary of Prince Edward Island English*. Toronto: University of Toronto Press, 1988.

Ross, Elizabeth Jane. *The Elizabeth Ross Manuscript: Original Highland Airs Collected at Raasay in 1812 by Elizabeth Jane Ross*, ed. Peter Cooke, Morag MacLeod, and Colm Ó Baoill. Edinburgh: University of Edinburgh, School of Celtic and Scottish Studies, 2011. https://www.ed.ac.uk/files/imports/fileManager/RossMS.pdf.

Scott, J.L. "Eight Years in New England." *The Church at Home and Abroad* (May 1891): 402–3.

Stanley-Blackwell, Laurie, and Shamus MacDonald. "The Strongman, the Storyteller, and Eastern Nova Scotia's Scots." In *Rannsachadh na Gàidhlig 5*, ed. Kenneth E. Nilsen, 253–66. Sydney: Cape Breton University Press, 2010.

Titon, Jeff Todd. "'Tuned Up with the Grace of God': Music and Experience among Old Regular Baptists." In *Music in American Religious Experience*, ed. Philip Vilas Bohlman, Edith Waldvogel Blumhofer, Edith L. Blumhofer, and Maria M. Chow, 311–34. Oxford: Oxford University Press, 2006.

Watson, William J., ed. *Bàrdachd Ghàidhlig: Specimens of Gaelic Poetry, 1550–1900*. Sterling: A. Learmonth & Son, 1932.

Weale, David. "The Ministry of the Reverend Donald McDonald on Prince Edward Island, 1826–1867: A Case-Study Examination of the Influence and Role of Religion within Colonial Society." PhD diss., Queen's University, Kingston, 1976.

– "The Time Is Come! Millenarianism in Colonial Prince Edward Island." *Acadiensis* 7, no. 1 (1977): 35–48.

Whytock, Jack C. "Gaelic Hymnody: An Auld World Beat with a New World Tempo." Paper presented to the Canadian Society of Presbyterian History, 2005, http://www.csph.ca/assets/csph2005_whytock.pdf.

ARCHIVAL COLLECTIONS

Gaelic in Prince Edward Island: A Cultural Remnant (Gaelic Field Recording Project) and Murdoch Lamont Diary, 1885–1888. Prince Edward Island Collection, Special Collections, Robertson Library, University of Prince Edward Island.

Prince Edward Island. Queen's County. 1891 Census of Canada, population schedule. LAC, Ottawa. Digital images. https://www.bac-lac.gc.ca/eng/census/1891.

Prince Edward Island. Prince East. 1901 Census of Canada, population schedule. LAC, Ottawa. Digital images. https://www.bac-lac.gc.ca/eng/census/1901.

School of Scottish Studies, University of Edinburgh.

13

Gaelic Heroes of the True North: Alexander Fraser's Literary Interventions in Canadian Gaeldom

Michael Newton

Benedict Anderson's classic study *Imagined Communities* highlighted the role of the printed word in the formulation and unification of national identities during the emergence of modern nation-states.[1] It has long been argued that literary professionals and activities have served a vital and active role in the creation and maintenance of Gaelic culture and identity in Scotland,[2] although this approach to understanding the social role of Gaelic literature (in oral tradition and written form) has not been applied systematically in diasporic contexts. I investigate here how Alexander Fraser, a prominent Gael who left the Scottish Highlands for Canada, contributed to reconstituting a *Gàidhealtachd* in exile through the exercise of the literary imagination. To that end, I examine in detail his most ambitious work, *Leabhar nan Sonn*. This chapter commemorates Ken Nilsen's significant contributions to the recovery of Scottish Gaelic literature in Canadian periodicals.

ALEXANDER FRASER: A BIOGRAPHICAL SKETCH

Alexander Fraser – known in his native tongue as Alasdair Friseal – was born in Kiltarlity, Scotland, in 1860. He emigrated to Toronto in 1886 to work as a journalist with *The Toronto Mail* for fourteen years. He edited other periodicals, or columns within them, in Toronto, most with a Scottish focus. Fraser became the first provincial archivist for the Province of Ontario in 1903, serving in that capacity until 1935. He passed away the following year, in 1936.[3]

During Fraser's lifetime, Gaels were a large, if culturally marginalized, ethnic group scattered across the provinces. Indeed, it has been estimated that at the time of Confederation (1867), Gaelic was the third-most common language of European origin in the country.[4]

Despite the poor educational provision for Gaelic in Scottish schools, and the general animosity of formal institutions toward the language, Fraser could not only speak but also read and write his native tongue. His work as a journalist and involvement in heritage organizations allowed him to position himself in the international network of Gaelic print culture of the era, one that spanned several continents.

Fraser served for many years as an editor for the *Scottish Canadian* newspaper and produced several volumes of *Fraser's Scottish Annual.* Both venues offered Gaelic texts. He transcribed Gaelic oral tradition from tradition bearers he chanced upon and sought out in Canada, and he collected texts from other field workers.[5] He utilized his literacy in his official roles in Scottish and Gaelic organizations around Ontario and taught a Gaelic course at Knox College for three years (teaching people who already had some knowledge of Gaelic to read the Bible). In 1904, he advanced a proposal for a lectureship in Celtic Studies at the University of Toronto, and in 1913 he taught several introductory Celtic Studies courses at McMaster University.[6] He was thus a native Gael steeped in his hereditary tradition, and in addition, he had sufficient education and self-confidence to promote Gaelic language, culture, and history in a formal manner in institutional contexts.

FRASER'S LITERARY PRODUCTIONS

In a wide-ranging article about Scottish organizations in Canada, Michael Vance contends that Fraser's vision of the Scot in Canada was an ethnically chauvinistic one that had the effect of marginalizing other ethnic groups:

> Fraser understood that organized Scottishness, in the form of societies and celebrations, had assisted the Scots in promoting their political, economic, and cultural influence in the Dominion. He was eager to reinforce this organization as the means of maintaining the Scottish influence that he viewed as being so

> beneficial to his adopted country. Ultimately, though, claiming a special status for the Scots in Canada rested on a "racial" premise that has also had the ability to marginalize or exclude other groups in the country.[7]

Vance's claim is problematic, given that Scots are not a singular ethnic or racial group: the anglophones (of England and the Scottish Lowlands) had been "othering" Gaels as an inferior race for generations.[8] Although there were pan-Scottish organizations in Canada at the turn of the twentieth century, many others had been created for the specific linguistic, social, and cultural needs of Gaels or even more specific regional communities within the Highlands.[9] Texts written by Gaels reflected a range of values and agendas, employed distinct rhetorical codes, and catered to different audiences, depending on whether they were written in Gaelic or English.[10] Fraser's writings offer a cautionary warning that conclusions based solely on anglophone texts, to the exclusion of Gaelic sources, can be incomplete and misleading in terms of fully understanding the Scottish immigrant experience and how it intersected with those of other ethnic groups.

Fraser does not acknowledge or explore the Highland–Lowland divide in his anglophone texts; his agenda is to legitimate the participation of *all* Scots in nation-building, giving Highlanders a free ride on Lowland coattails. It is fair to say that Fraser's anglophone texts often resort to clichés about Scottish traits and virtues, and reinforce contemporary forms of racialism; that said, Highlanders were quite aware that they had been racially categorized as "lower" than the Anglo-Saxons, who were at the top of the hierarchy (to which Lowlanders argued they belonged as well). Fraser sometimes appears to be reassuring his Scottish audience that they are, in fact, valuable assets to the British Crown and worthy of an honoured place in the imperial order, perhaps also pressing that message to other listeners to reassure them of the loyalty and capacity for service offered by all Scots, both Lowlanders and Highlanders.

Regardless, Fraser's Gaelic texts are quite different in tone and context from his English ones. They affirm the value of the Gaelic language and tradition and the central role played by both in transmitting and embodying identity, in contrast to the premises of racial essentialism. He urges Gaels to be loyal to their heritage, depicting Canada as a haven for his fellow countrymen who wish to nurture

Title	*Year*	*Number of pages*
Leabhar nan Sonn (Book of the Heroes)	1897	115 long pages
Cànan agus Cliù ar Sinnsearan (The Language and Renown of our Ancestors)	1901	16 short pages
Machraichean Móra Chanada (Canada's Great Prairies)	1907	56 long pages
Sir Seòras Uilleam Ros (Sir George William Ross)	1915	58 long pages

their culture on their own terms instead of acquiescing to the demands of anglophones.

Fraser produced at least four Gaelic volumes of various lengths that were printed in Canada.[11] The first of these, *Leabhar nan Sonn*, was by far his most ambitious and sustained effort to elucidate a vision, in literary form, for a Gaelic ethnic subculture in Canada. I will be subjecting the content, rhetoric, and structure of that text to close reading in order to argue that Fraser was engaging in a social engineering project, promoting literature, oral and written, as the means by which Gaels could validate and foster their native language and culture, as well as maintain the unique capacities that would enable them to make specifically Gaelic contributions to nation-building in their adopted home.

Fraser's 1902 address to the Caledonian Society of Montreal, printed as "The Mission of the Scot in Canada," presents key assertions and objectives that help to interpret his work. First, he contends that Scottish society nurtures traits and values that can benefit Canada. These capacities are to be valued not for their own sake or even for that of the Scottish community alone, but rather for what they can contribute to the nation:

> If patience ever be a virtue it is in the erecting of a national structure from such complex material as is embraced in our population … to do what in us lies to advance the common weal, to strengthen the ties which bind us to the land we left and the land we live in, by every worthy means available, and in this way hold up a national ideal which our offspring can pursue. In this work the Scot has not only a place, and an important one, but also a peculiar one; indeed, every race and people has its own peculiar work to do. It can do it better itself than if helped by others.[12]

Fraser enumerates specific characteristics that he claims Scots manifest and should be encouraged to sustain. These positive characteristics relate not only to Canadian nation-building but also to the project of creating a nation that is different from and indeed better than the United States, in order to reduce the lure of economic opportunities available across the border. A study of the migration of Canadians in the late nineteenth and early twentieth centuries summarizes the demographic trends: "Migration by Canadians to the U.S. was substantial through this period regardless of language spoken. We note that odds of migration to the U.S. by English-speakers was even greater than was the odds of their moving interprovincially. In other words, even during a period of substantial western settlement, the U.S. proved to be a larger draw to English-speaking Canadians."[13]

Fraser explicitly acknowledges the American elephant in the room in his address, but asserts Canada's moral superiority against American secular materialism. He first quotes Sir Charles Dilke on the issue: "Just at present the example of the United States cannot have a very wide influence on other countries … Materialistic civilization never will have much influence on thought, for the whole idea is to get rich. The Americans used to influence people at one time, but in the last few years has [*sic*] ceased to do so, because the development of materialism has nullified their high moral power."[14]

Fraser then asserts that the virtues brought by Scottish immigrants can help the new nation of Canada resist American influence. Scottish religious tradition and its standards, he argues, impart an impeccable moral compass to individuals and their institutions: "One Scottish ideal which stands eminently forth among others is that of public conscience – high honour in public life."[15] Canadian communities, moreover, can withstand the temptations of out-migration by drawing from "the intense love of the Scot for his native soil."[16] The love of home, as a geographical site of attachment, has its social correlative in the "Scot's profound respect for the sanctity of the family relation."[17] Fraser does not expand on the reasons why this trait is important, although his quotation from the poetry of Allan Ramsay used to substantiate it suggests that it is crucial for social cohesion and the cultivation of kindliness in broader contexts.[18] He alludes in passing to other positive qualities of the Scottish character: mercy, hospitality, and national solidarity.[19]

Fraser also expresses concern that while the pioneers exercised heroic acts of strength and vigour in felling the forest, the physical hardiness of the current generation seems to be in decline. He adds that Scottish tradition offers an antidote to degeneration for men in the form of athletic games, as "they are clean, manly, robust, and lend themselves to generous rivalry in the field or ring."[20] All people, however, young and old, male and female, can benefit from the exercise of Scottish dance tradition.[21]

In his Gaelic texts, language loyalty is a pervasive theme. The Gaelic conviction that cultural identity has a linguistic basis contradicts the credo of racial essentialism dominant in anglophone discourse of the time. In *Cànain agus Cliù ar Sinnsearan*, for example, he states:

> Oir a dh'easbhaidh an canain aosda sin … c'aite 'm biodh clanna nan Gaidheal? Cha bhiodh iad air am faotainn air feadh cinnich an t-saoghail. Nach eil dearbhadh againn air a so 'n ar tir fein? Air gach taobh amhainn mhor St. Lawrence … Tha na h-ainmean ann an sin, ach an iad Gaidheil a tha 'g an giulan? Loire, cha'n iad, ach muinntir a thionndaidh gu bhi nam Frangaich, 'nan canain, 'nan cleachdaidhean, 'nan creideamh, agus 'nan cridheachan … 'n uair a chromas a Ghaidhlig a ceann aosda, urramach, liath 'sa bheir i suas an deo, cha'n fhag i 'n a deigh sluagh ris an abrar na Gaidheil, oir bithidh na ginealaichean a leanas sinn air an slugadh suas ann an cuan marbhtach di-chuimhne an t'saoghail.[22]

> In the absence of that ancient language … where would the Gaels be? They would not be able to be found throughout the peoples of the world. Don't we find evidence of this in our own country? On every side of the great St. Lawrence River … The names are there, but are they Gaels who bear them? Alas, they are not, but people who became French in their language, traditions, religion and hearts … When Gaelic bows its grey, aged, honourable head, and gives its last breath, it will not leave a people who will be called Gaels in its wake, since the generations who will follow us will be swallowed up in the fatal, forgetful ocean of the world.

Similarly, in the emigrant propaganda tract *Machraichean Móra Chanada*, he laments the assimilative pressures to which Gaels who emigrated to the Scottish Lowlands were subjected, and contrasts it unfavourably with the ability of Canadian immigrants to sustain communities on their own ethnolinguistic terms:

> Dh'fhag mòran Ghaidheil tir an athraichean. Chaidh cuid diubh gu Galldachd – do na bailltean mòra, do na h-obraichean mòra far an robh a chuid bu mho dhiubh air an slugadh suas am measg choigreach. Dh'fhas, mar bu tric, an clann suas ann an aineolas air canain, 's air gné nan Gaidheal agus, an diugh, cha'n 'eil dad ri fhaotainn diubh ach na h-ainmean a chi neach thairis air dorsainn nam buth air an t-sraid. ... Sin agaibh coimeas eadar iadsan a dh'fhag a Ghaidhealtachd airson na Galldachd agus airson Canada dha no thri linntinn roimhe so. Co dheth'n dithis a rinn an taghadh a b' fhearr? Tha mi fein a' creidsinn gu'n d'rinn iadsan a thainig gu Canada.[23]

> Many Gaels left the land of their fathers. Some of them went to the Lowlands – to the big cities, for substantial careers where the majority of them were swallowed up by a foreign people. Most often, their children grew up ignorant of the language and character of the Gaels, and today there is nothing left of them but the names you see over the doors of shops on the street ... There you have the difference between those who left the Highlands for the Lowlands and for Canada two or three generations ago. Which of them made the better choice? I myself believe those who chose to come to Canada made the better one.

Fraser urges Scottish organizations to take responsibility for honouring, nurturing, and harnessing those virtues in Canadian society, suggesting that a nationwide federation be established whose main purpose would be "instilling into the minds and hearts of young Scottish Canadians of a love for the history, literature, music and songs of Scotland."[24] Literature was to be the primary vehicle for the transmission of Scottish identity and for the maintenance of Scottish attributes at the individual level:

> There are many great qualities, other than those mentioned, bound up in the Scottish character, which are revealed in Scottish history and literature ... The Scottish love for literature is almost as strong as that for the home ... No nation has been more deeply

influenced by her minstrelsy, which, indeed, reflects the character of the people.[25]

These, then, are the concerns that inform Fraser's Gaelic tracts and provide a lens through which to understand his rhetoric and aims.

LEABHAR NAN SONN

Leabhar nan Sonn has seven chapters:

1 A summary of a book about the ancient Gaelic ballads of Ulster and a description of the scholar behind the work.
2 A biographical account of the Gaelic poet Eóghann MacColla.
3 A biographical account of Gilleasbaig MacEalair.
4 A biographical account of Daibhidh Speinse.
5 A biographical account of Domhnull Catanach.
6 A fictional description of a *céilidh* in Canada.
7 A reminiscence of Sabbath traditions in Fraser's home community.

Each of these chapters elaborates elements of Fraser's "imagined community," providing role models who embody aspects of Scottish ideals or depicting the values and functioning of the idealized social order. The book's foreword explains that the texts that comprise the volume were initially published as columns in newspapers that Fraser edited. A second print run of this volume was made the same year as the first, suggesting that it found a receptive audience.

I summarize the content of each chapter below and explore connections between Fraser's social agenda and his literary representations of individual Gaels and the Gaelic community.

Duain Ultach

The first chapter begins by introducing us to the island of Islay and to a host of prolific Gaelic scholars who were raised on the island in the nineteenth century. Islay is in a number of respects – geographic, linguistic, genealogical, and so on – a bridge between Gaelic Scotland and Ireland. Fraser quickly homes in on Eachann MacIlleathain (Hector MacLean), a schoolmaster, and his recently published volume

Duain Ultach / Ultonian Hero-Ballads (1892). MacIlleathain gathered together written and oral sources from Ireland and Scotland to assemble what he believed to be the most archaic stratum of Gaelic literary tradition, the Ulster Cycle. Rather than repeat this material, Fraser provides a prose summary in modern Scottish Gaelic with occasional snatches of verse.

The Ulster Cycle consists of a set of narratives, in prose and verse, that revolve around the characters whose power centre was at Emain Macha in Ulster. The infamous Cú Chulainn is explicitly identified by Fraser as a *sonn* (hero),[26] although I believe that the purpose of including this material at the outset of the volume is not to provide paragons of human conduct or cultural exemplars for contemporary society, but rather to establish a prestigious literary lineage for Gaeldom. It also allows him to discuss the social role of Gaelic poets and literati in perpetuating the deeds and memories of heroes.[27]

Some of the events of these narratives actually take place in Scotland, particularly the tales of Conlaoch and Deirdre. The summary of the concluding narrative, that of Fraoch, is extremely brief, and although Fraser does not discuss its setting, it has been localized in at least three spots in the Scottish Highlands.[28]

Fraser mentions that variants of the narratives about Deirdre had been collected from oral tradition around the Scottish *Gàidhealtachd* in the eighteenth and nineteenth centuries,[29] and observes that the names of some of the characters continue to be familiar to Gaels in Scotland and Ireland in his own time.[30] This helps underscore the cultural continuity of Gaeldom, despite catastrophic disruptions in recent generations.

Fraser prefaces the first ballad, "Duan a' Ghairbh" (Lay of Garbh), with the note that it is very old but of uncertain age, set in the time before the Viking invasions.[31] He says of the ballad "Na Cinn" (The Heads): "Tha e air a chreidsinn le daoine foghluimte ar la-ne gu'm buin an duan so do'n chuairt-uine is aosmhoire do sheann eachdraidh na h-Eirionn air am bheil aithris ann an litreachas na duthcha sin"[32] (It is believed by the learned people of our time that this ballad belongs to the oldest period of the ancient history of Ireland which is described in the literature of that land). In other words, this corpus establishes the historical horizon of a distinctly Gaelic literature, a Classical native canon. It is clear that Fraser sees this material as the shared literary inheritance of Scotland and Ireland that should be cherished by all Gaels.[33]

I have one other conjecture about the significance of the Ulster Cycle in Fraser's text: it may be that the narrative's geographical structure of a north–south rivalry, which locates heroic action and lasting fame in the north, is meant to be analogous to the contemporary rivalry between Canada and the United States. Fraser does not explicitly comment on such parallels, however.

Eóghann MacColla

Fraser quickly moves into the present in the following chapter with a biographical sketch of the poet Eóghann MacColla (Evan MacColl) (1808–1898). The first two pages of this account outline the functions, responsibilities, and privileges of the Gaelic bard in holding together the fabric of society and in upholding traditional values. Fraser thus underscores the notion (generally accepted by Celtic scholars to the present) that the native literati were responsible for helping to perpetuate the stability of the Gaelic social and moral order. Literature had a centuries-old precedent of serving the purpose of social engineering.

Notwithstanding Fraser's prefatory comments declaiming his qualifications, MacColla was in the mould of a new generation of poets who generally kept to lighter subjects (especially love and local community anecdotes) and who eschewed controversial issues and political stances. Fraser actually defends MacColla several times from charges that his poetry did not support fellow Gaels vigorously enough in times of trial, and that he received preferential treatment from elite Highlanders, who seem to have done him special favours.[34] Fraser doubtlessly overemphasizes MacColla's qualities in order to create a kind of charter myth for Gaelic literary production in Canada, to demonstrate how the practice of Gaelic poetry could flourish in a new environment.

Most of Fraser's biographical account is adapted from John Mackenzie's *Sar-Obair nam Bard Gaelach / The Beauties of Gaelic Poetry* (1841) and MacColla's own volume of poetry, *Clàrsach nam Beann / The Mountain Minstrel* (1836), although there are occasional additions. Some of these relate to his early life in Scotland, but most are from his career in North America. Fraser emphasizes that MacColla's parents were deeply rooted in Argyllshire families and tradition. Despite the light, contemporary nature of his own compositions, MacColla was heir to a wealth of literary and historical material, a fact borne out by his correspondence with Fraser and several contemporary Gaelic periodicals.[35]

Fraser represents MacColla as a generous host with an open home for all who wished to learn about Gaelic tradition from him. He served as official poet for several different organizations in Ontario.[36] Tensions between loyalties to Canada and the United States appear in this profile: MacColla's son had moved to New York, and although the poet (supposedly) had no interest in leaving British soil, he finally submitted to his son's request to come to live with him in the United States, prompting a farewell celebration that drew people from across the region. This sojourn did not last long, however. When MacColla returned to Toronto, a song of praise was performed for him by the local Gaelic Society.[37]

MacColla was a boon not just to Gaels in Ontario in a narrow ethnocentric sense, says Fraser, but to all Canadians. Immediately after discussing the poet's response to the injustices of the Clearances, he states:

> Cha'n e amhain gu bheil cridhe a Bhaird 's an aite cheart 's a chuis so; tha e mar an ceudna a' bualadh le comh-fhulangas do mhuinntir sharaichte gach cinneach fo'n ghrein, agus dh'fhuiling e airson nam beachdan saorsail a shearmonaich e 'na bhardachd, an aghaidh ainneart agus, mar a bha esan a creidsinn, droch riaghladh na duthcha.[38]

> It's not just that the poet's heart is in the proper place in this matter; it also beats with compassion for the oppressed people of every race in the world, and he has suffered for the liberal opinions he has preached in his poetry against injustice and, as he saw it, the misrule of the country.

The community for whom Gaelic poets could be concerned in the New World was no longer limited to just his kin group or the *Gàidhealtachd*, but could be extended to humanity as a whole, especially fellow immigrant groups seeking refuge.

Gilleasbuig MacEalair

The third chapter offers a sketch of Sheriff Gilleasbuig MacEalair (Archibald MacKellar) (1816–1894) as a paragon of socio-political success in Canada. He is portrayed from the outset as a thorough Gael, born in Argyll, yet also a man whose life and deeds had been woven into the fabric of Ontario.[39]

MacEalair had boasted that it would be hard to find a site more beautiful, even in the Highlands, than that of his adopted home – Hamilton, the *lios Ontario* (garden of Ontario).[40] Fraser gives Gaels such as the Sheriff credit for helping to create the bounty and order of the area, recounting the heroic deeds of the pioneer settlers:

> Is tric tha cuimhne an t-Siorraim dol air a h-ais a dh'ionnsuidh nan laithean ud, 'n uair a bha athair 's a choimhearsnaich a gearradh sios na coille dhomhail, 's a ruamhradh, 's a glanadh an fhearainn a chum gu a bhi g'a thoirt fo chuing do'n duine. Bha iad 'nan daoine treun sgairteil, a chuireadh an aghaidh ri cruadal, 's nach tugadh geill fhad 's bu bheo iad. Agus bha na mnathan de'n smior cheudna. Cha bu bhoirionnaich lag-chridheach, no lag-dhruimeach iadsan. B'e taghadh ar duthcha iad.[41]

> The Sheriff's memory often harkens back to those days of yore, when his father and neighbours were cutting down the dense forest, breaking up the soil and cleaning up the land in order to domesticate it for humans. They were brave, robust people who would confront hardship head on, and would never surrender as long as they lived. And the women had the same grit. They were not soft-hearted or weak-backed women. They were the cream of our country's crop.

Fraser describes MacEalair as a leader like a chieftain of old. He had a solid educational grounding and was with a company of men defending the British Crown during the Rebellion of 1837. His primary accomplishments were not in the cause of war, however, but in peace, particularly as a political leader. He enjoyed strong support from his fellow Gaels, and started his career in government by being elected to the governing board of Kent County, where he served for fifteen years. He channelled all of his energy to support those who fought for justice, and in return, the population trusted in his honour and virtue.[42]

His career is further outlined as a member of the Canadian Parliament and the Ontario provincial assembly. For his widespread achievements and social networks, his star shines brightly in the Gaelic firmament:

> Ach 's ann mar Ghaidheal, am measg a luchd-duthcha, a tha 'n Siorram Mac-Ealair aig a neart. Tha gradh aige do Chanada mar bu dual do neach a rinn na h-uiread air a son, ach tha a chridhe a' plosgartaich le teas-ghradh do Thir nam Beann. Tha e min-eolach air eachdraidh na duthcha sin anns an d' araicheadh athraichean. Tha e cuimhneachail air a luchd-cinnidh, agus cha'n 'eil ni sam bith cho taitneach leis ri bhi cosnadh an deagh-ghean 's an run. Tha e 'na dhuine fialaidh agus is tric a lamh 'na phoca d'a luchd an uireasbhuidh. Tha e 'na bhall urramach agus 'na ard cheann-iuil do Chomunn Gaidhlig Thoronto, 's an ni ceudna do Chomunn Hamilton. Aig na coinneamhan bliadhnail, tha e daonan comhla riu g'am misneachadh, 's g'an comhairleachadh a bhi cumail suas cliu an sinnsre. Cha'n 'eil moran d'a leithid air am fagail 'n ar measg, ach ged a tha an aois a laidhe air, 's a chiabhagan liath air tanachadh, 's e durachd agus dochas Gaidheil Chanada gu 'm bi e fada air a chaomhnadh gu bhi mealtainn solas agus toil-inntinn am measg a chairdean 's a luchd eolais.[43]
>
> But it is as a Gael, among his compatriots, that Sheriff MacEalair is at his strongest. He loves Canada, as is natural for someone who has done so much for its sake, but his heart beats with warm affection for the Land of the Mountains. He is intimately familiar with the history of that country in which his forefathers were reared. He is mindful of his kinsfolk, and there is nothing that he enjoys more than to earn their goodwill and affection. He is an honorary member of and high counselor to the Toronto Gaelic Society and likewise of the Hamilton [Gaelic] Society. At the annual meetings, he is always in their company, encouraging and counseling them to maintain the good reputation of their ancestors. There are not many like him remaining among us, but even though old age is lying on him, and his grey locks growing thin, it is the sincere wish and desire of the Gaels of Canada that he will be spared for a long time in order to enjoy solace and happiness amongst his friends and family.

Fraser emphasizes here that there is no inherent conflict or incompatibility between love of the Highland motherland and loyalty to Canada, and that MacEalair was a respected member of a substantial community of Gaels who celebrate both.

Daibhidh Speinse

The fourth chapter provides a biographical account of Daibhidh Speinse (David Spense) (born *c.* 1829), who seems to represent an intermediary facilitating the integration of immigrant Gaels into Canadian society, as well as a role model for the rewards of benevolence. If anyone in Canada deserves to be titled *Caraid nan Gàidheal* (Friend of the Gael), we are told, it is this man.[44] As Fraser reminds us, the nickname *Caraid nan Gàidheal* had been first coined a couple generations earlier for the prolific writer Rev. Norman MacLeod in Scotland. This thus seems to be another example of a conscious strategy of transferring Scottish concepts and precedents to a Canadian cultural setting to convey a sense of familiarity for Gaelic emigrants.

Speinse had shown kindness to hundreds of Gaels in Canada and had defended them when they needed help:

> Ag amharc air ais da fhichead bliadhna 'us corr, anns an duthaich so, b' urrainn d'a naigheachd innseadh air na rinn na Gaidheil a chum na coilltean a reiteachadh agus an tir fhosg[l]adh suas, a bhiodh eibhinn ri cluinntinn, oir tha e min-eolach air na h-aitean anns an do shuidhich iad, air dhoibh Canada a ruigsinn, bho thoiseach gu meadhon na ceud bliadhna so, ciud diubh gun sgillinn ruadh 'n an sporrann, 's gun dad 'n an cridhe ach gamhlas 'us mi-run do na daoine cruaidh-chridheach leis an robh iad air am fogradh gun iochd, thar a chuan. Cha robh caraid a thachair orra air an taobh so do'n fhairge a b'fheumaile dhoibh na esan, a thagair an cuis 's a sheas air an ceann 'n uair nach robh comas aca moran a dheanadh air an son fein.[45]

> Looking back over forty years and more, in this country, he could tell stories about what the Gaels have accomplished in order to clear the forests and open up the landscape that would be exciting to listen to, for he is intimately acquainted with the places where they settled after they reached Canada, from the beginning to the middle of this century, some of them without a penny in their wallet, and with nothing in their hearts but resentment and ill-will towards the hard-hearted people who dispossessed them mercilessly across the ocean. He was the most helpful friend they encountered on this side of the ocean, who pleaded their case and

defended them when they did not have the ability to do very much for themselves.

Gaels leaving the Highlands without skilled job training or with very little knowledge of urban, English-speaking life would have been particularly encouraged to know that they would encounter kind and sympathetic people such as this.[46]

Speinse was born in Islay. Fraser discusses the education he received on the island and the excellent teachers and peers from whom he benefited, including Eachann MacIlleathain (editor of *Duain Ultach / Ultonian Hero-Ballads*). Fraser emphasizes the influence of MacIlleathain's teaching on Speinse and the subsequent interest he took in Gaelic linguistic and literary matters. To underscore the "brain drain" from the Scottish *Gàidhealtachd* flowing into Ontario, Fraser mentions that Speinse's old schoolmaster was then living in Bruce County.[47]

All but two of Speinse's siblings emigrated and settled in Ontario. He opened a shop in a community full of Gaels and found himself engaged in an array of tasks on behalf of his compatriots, particularly those undertakings that drew from his strengths in literacy, communication, and administration. Fraser, no doubt hoping to buoy the hopes of potential emigrants, describes Speinse throwing himself gladly into these efforts, which brought him and his family to Toronto in 1871. Here he found other like-minded folk: "Ann an Toronto bha buidheann do Ghaidheil a bha laiste le gradh do'n duthaich 's do na h-uile ni a bhuineadh dhi"[48] (In Toronto, there was a group of Gaels who were burning with the love of their homeland and everything that belonged to it).

It was to be regretted that Speinse had not yet committed his vast store of Gaelic tradition to writing, but it was hoped that he would complete such a volume in the near future.[49] This assertion underscores the utility of literature in offering a shared sense of community and culture, as well the promise that Canada could fulfill the potential of Gaels and their inherited tradition.

Domhnull Catanach

Domhnull Catanach (Donald Cattanach) (1799–1883), born in Badenoch, Scotland, is extolled by Fraser as a role model for religious leadership. His character sketch thus delineates the prospects for a spiritual community for Gaelic emigrants in Canada. His father, Iain Catanach, an accomplished *seanchaidh* (tradition bearer), died in Canada at the age of eighty-four.[50] This detail provides strong Gaelic credentials for Domhnull and pre-emptively dispels any potential tension between the sacred and secular dimensions of immigrant life. Such issues had been particularly divisive throughout the nineteenth century in the Highlands.[51]

Domhnull arrived in Glengarry County, Ontario, in 1826, which prompts Fraser to discuss the state of the landscape at that time and the hardy constitution of the pioneers who rose to the challenge of converting it into arable land. Thus he implicitly counters the stereotype of Gaels as lazy:

> Bha Gleann a Garadh air ur aiteachadh agus bha an roinn mhor deth fo choille gun rathadan mora, gun drochaidean agus gun moran do na goireasan a tha a nis aig doras gach tuathanach air fad na siorramachd. Ach bha an sluagh bho'n Ghaidhealtachd. Bha iad turail, toigheach air an cuid, agus iarrtanach gu bhi deanadh a ni a b' fhearr a b' urrainn daibh do'n chrannchur, direach an t-seorsa air an tric le cuibheal an fhortain tionndadh le soirbheas ... Cha robh an gnothach soirbh; cha b' ionnan na h-amanan sud 's an la'n diugh ... Bha a' choille domhal, tiugh, ri gearradh sios leis na tuaghan, craobh an deigh craoibh, na muillionan diubh.[52]

> Glengarry was newly settled and a great deal of it was still forested, without good roads or bridges, and without the conveniences that are now at the door of every yeoman throughout the county. But the population was from the Scottish Highlands. They were sensible, desirous of their fortune, and willing to accomplish the best thing that they could for their future, exactly the sort that the Wheel of Fortune favours so often ... The matter was not easy; those days were very different from the present day ... The forest was dense and thick, and had to be felled with axes, tree by tree, millions of them.

This emphasis on the muscular, manly fortitude of the pioneers is balanced by compelling portraits of Gaelic women. Iain Catanach was Domhnull's son with his first wife, Ceit NicDhomhnuill, who was a widow with three children from a previous husband. In an excerpt from a song-poem by Eóghann MacColla, Iain, the president of the

Toronto Gaelic Society at the time that Fraser wrote, is described as devoted to his mother tongue.[53]

Domhnull married Fionnghuala NicCoinnich in 1839 following the death of his first wife. Fraser expands upon her illustrious Highland lineage, which connects her closely to the celebrated Flora MacDonald of Jacobite fame. Her immediate family, moreover, are celebrated for their heroism in defending the British Crown during the Rebellion of 1837. Fionnghuala is praised as a pillar of her community in her own right:

> 'N a dachaidh aig Lagan bha i 'n a mathair do'n chlann a dh'fhagadh gun mhathair, – "is blath anail na mathar" – 'n a cul-taice d'a fear-posda, 'na deagh bhana-charaid do'n fheumach 'sna bean taighe aoidheal, fhialaidh, mor-chridheach, nach do leig a h-aon riamh seachad air a dorus, a bha feumach, gun a riarachadh, 's nach d'fhailnich riamh ann a bhi toirt toilinntinn d'a cairdean 's d'a luchd-daimh a bhiodh a' tional aig taobh a cagailt. Bha i 'na deagh bhan-sgeulaiche, 's bha buadhan-conaltraidh eireachdail aice a bha thar tomhas ann an geiread, 's ann an deisealachd. Bha sean-fhacail a duthcha aice air barr a meoirean, bha i min-eolach air orain nam bard, bha i ionnsaichte 's na sgriobtuiribh, agus bha a cuimhne cho math 's gu robh e furasda dhi briathran ughdair, no rann, a ghabhail gun mhearachd. Bhiodh e duilich toilinntinn bu mho fhaotainn na oidhche a chur seachad 'na teaghlach.[54]

> In her home at Lagan, she was a mother to those children who were left without a mother, – "A mother's breath is warm" – a pillar of support to her husband, a great friend to the needy, and a generous, hospitable, great-hearted homemaker, who never let anyone who was needy pass her door without bestowing something on them, and who never failed to give pleasure to her friends and family who would gather around her hearth-side. She was an excellent storyteller, and she had expressive powers of communication that were beyond compare in intelligence and eloquence. She had the proverbs of her homeland memorized, she was intimately knowledgeable about the song-poems of the poets, she was learned in the Scriptures, and her memory was so good that it was easy for her to recite the words or verses of an author. It would be difficult to find any greater mental enjoyment than to spend an evening in the company of her family.

Notable in this complimentary depiction of the female hero is the emphasis on the traditional Gaelic virtues of hospitality, a prodigious memory, and engagement with literature.

The Catanach family named their property in Kenyon "Lagan" after Domhnull's birthplace in the Highlands[55] – another symbolic statement about the continuity of the Gaelic community. Fraser is at pains to emphasize, however, that this was not an enclave seeking ethnic purity. To the contrary, Domhnull had a number of francophones in his service; he was kind to them, and many settled around Lagan. Thus it was not unusual to hear young people in the community speaking fluent Gaelic, English, and French.[56]

Cross-community bonds are also highlighted in religious terms. Domhnull realized that the area did not have an adequate spiritual ministry, and he took up the call "mar rìgh air an ceann" (like a king over them).[57] He taught the scriptures and organized worship services, which were attended by people of all denominations. Domhnull was also a champion of the Temperance cause.[58]

Fraser gives a short account of the children born at Lagan, praising their Highland make-up: "Tha gne an fhior-Ghaidheil ri faicinn annta uile. Tha an gaol air Gaidhealtachd na h-Alba cho laidir 's ged a b'i aite am breith"[59] (The character of the true Gael could be seen in all of them. Their love for the Scottish Highlands was as strong as if they had been born there). He substantiates this by recounting that one daughter named the property in the northwest to which she relocated "Loch Earrachd" after another place name in Badenoch, Scotland.[60]

A Céilidh *in Canada*

The penultimate chapter in the book presents an archetypal Hogmanay *céilidh*, held on the night appointed by the old traditional calendar. The *céilidh* was the social gathering par excellence for embodying and transmitting Gaelic culture, and at its most basic reading, the staging of this ritual in the volume asserts the survival of one of the fundamental institutions of Gaeldom, one central to social cohesion and the transmission of tradition and communal memory.[61]

Fraser presents the *céilidh* as a *còmhradh* (dialogue), one of the most popular prose genres in nineteenth-century Gaelic literature. This format was particularly well-suited to a population making a long, slow transition from orality to written literature and often appeared in periodicals, which were then read aloud at *céilidhs*. Fraser's *còmhradh* shares many features with those that had been so prominent in the popular press, but it also makes some radical departures. His text has no explicit expository or polemical function, it does not feature a voice of authority intending to educate, inform, or convert the readership,[62] and it does not aspire to reform Gaelic society as a whole.[63] A close reading of the constituent members of the *céilidh*, the interactions between them, and the materials shared suggest that this *céilidh* is instead an extended analogy for an idealized egalitarian immigrant Gaelic community; it illustrates the rooting of Gaelic tradition in a Canadian context in ways that enable the participation of all members according to their own particularized inheritance.

We are told that after supper is over, the man of the house (the de facto master of ceremonies) arises to begin the *céilidh* with a toast to the queen and to the country in which they reside. The drink is then offered to *am pìobaire ruadh* (the red-haired bagpiper), who is nearly a century old and has the gift of prophecy, thus embodying a continuous tradition. To underscore this point, the man of the house declares:

> Is taitneach leam a bhi cumail suas nan doighean a chunnaic mi aig m' athair 's aig mo sheanair. Leanamaid riutha fhad 's a bhitheas sinn beo ... Gu ma fada 'mhaireas an cliu 's an cleachdaidhean ann an tir morh [*sic*] Chanada![64]
>
> It gives me pleasure to keep up the traditions that I saw my father and grandfather practicing. Let's stick to them for as long as we live ... May their renown and their traditions live long in the great land of Canada!

The man of the house asks the bagpiper for a tune, but the latter suggests that Sìne, a young woman in the company, sing a song. The man of the house instead insists that Niall Sgoilear (Neil the Scholar) tell a story.

Niall begins by recounting how Gaelic traditions sustained the early pioneers in Canada. He recalls an elderly woman in Bruce County who was valued by her neighbours for her store of songs and stories. When she failed to appear at the Hogmanay *céilidh*, a group of boys went by her house and found that a nearby tree had fallen during a storm that night. They cut it up into firewood without telling her. The next day, the old woman joined her neighbours and expressed her gratitude after offering a dramatic interpretation of those events. Neil's contribution confirms that kindliness and oral tradition reinforce each other in Gaelic life.

Sìne then sings a popular Gaelic song, "Bruthaichean Ghlinn Braoin" (The Banks of Loch Broom), with the company singing on the chorus. The song is in the voice of a soldier imprisoned in France and recalls the woman he loves and the place of their courtship. The man of the house discusses the author of the song and the two melodic variants, stating his preference for the Ross-shire melody in a non-judgmental way. This acknowledges that Gaelic tradition exists in variation, and that while individuals may have biases, it is not necessary to denigrate the predilections of others. Local rivalries have often flared between immigrant Highland communities and undermined pan-Gaelic solidarity.[65]

The bagpiper then plays "Cabar Féidh" (Deer Antlers) and passes the floor to Alasdair Dhruim a' Chnuic (Alasdair of Hillbank),[66] who explains the origins of the place name Creag an Spioraid (Rock of the Spirit) in Bruce County. His narrative reflects the vernacular Gaelic *dinnsheanchas* (place lore) genre,[67] but what is particularly interesting here is that the story is about Indigenous history: the characters belong to two rival nations embroiled in a bitter feud. Although the portrayal of violence is not flattering to those groups, the tale is not dissimilar to clan sagas and local legends in Gaelic tradition, including ones about the haunting of a location by a restless and vengeful spirit. Alasdair states that he has received this from oral tradition, thus indicating that the immigrant community is capable of absorbing traditions from Indigenous neighbours in a manner that is natural for Gaels. The man of the house explicitly states: "Tha iomadh sgeul, neonach air innseadh mu na h-Innseanaich, 's tha sinn ag earbsa gu'n cluinn sinn tuille dhiubh mu'n teid a bhliadhna so seachad"[68] (There are many strange tales told about the Indians, and we trust that we'll hear more of them before this year is over).

Sìne then asks Gilleasbuig to sing a song, but Lachlann scolds her for being too pushy. This is one of several occasions during the *céilidh* when men hold this self-confident woman in check, thus implying, albeit in playful tones, that social conventions require the primacy of male authority. In fact, while the women sing (and we are told which songs), none of them recite tales or hold extended dialogue during the *céilidh*.

The man of the house then announces that Gilleasbuig Saor (Archibald the Carpenter) will tell the story of the changeling of Glenquoich. This is a lengthy variant of a very well-known folk tale.[69] The only noteworthy aspect of the tale is that the father of the changeling is a member of the Highland gentry, rather than a farmer, as in most variants. This makes his reliance on the tailor – at the bottom rung of the social ladder – for the recovery of his heir all the more significant in terms of the web of relations and interactions between the upper and lower classes. Gilleasbuig concludes by saying he has repeated the tale as he heard it in Tiree, but "tha i air a h-innseadh air caochladh dòigh ann an caochladh aitean" (it is told in differing ways in different places), again highlighting the variation of tradition in the Gaelic world without favouring one faction over others.

The man of the house comments that although traditional Gaelic narratives about fairies and witches are strange, the ideas of many contemporary youth are more foolish than these ancestral superstitions. Although he does not elaborate, we can infer that he is disparaging secular materialism.[70] He then asks another young woman, Ciorstaidh, to sing the popular song of unrequited love, "Fhir a' Bhàta" (O Boatman).

Lachlann an t-Srath (Lachlann of the Strath) concludes with a variant of a very common tale about the evil eye.[71] A female neighbour comes to a home to ask for an ember from the fire to restart her own. After her visit, the woman of the house, who is busy making butter, notices that her churn has stopped being productive. A visiting tailor suspects that the neighbour has the evil eye and takes preventative measures. The tale has strong misogynistic overtones, especially at the end when the tailor threatens to brand the shape of the cross on the forehead of the neighbour with a hot tong if she makes another attempt to steal from the home.

Even setting aside the misogyny, this is a sour note on which to end the *céilidh*, given that it illustrates social tensions and jealousies in communities.[72] It may be that Fraser was not consciously aware of the negativity of the tale. Alternatively, he may have been using the narrative to imply that a strong, proactive hand can be effective in containing disruptive, selfish, and antisocial forces in communities and in protecting the interests of the collective.

The man of the house then clears the floor, the bagpiper strikes up a tune, and the two young women, Niall, and Gilleasbuig dance the "Reel of Tulloch." This illustrates that Gaelic tradition offers the means of maintaining the physical well-being of members of the community. After this, they all drink a toast, and the company departs.

A Sabbath Afternoon in the Highlands

In the final section of the book, Fraser gives a nostalgic description of an archetypal Sunday afternoon from his childhood. These short six pages portray a family at home after church in terms that emphasize the strong bonds of kin and community, the stability and security resulting from the exercise of hierarchical authority, and the discipline and contentment imparted to individuals as a result of these conditions. As in the previous chapter, Fraser implies that this ritual offers a socio-political model from a Gaelic context that can be transferred to and extended in Canada:

> Air an latha araid so, shuidh an teaghlach sios gu bi[a]dh, gu modhail, ordail, mar bu ghnath, an clann bheaga le 'a lamhan paisgte, 's an suilean duinte; an fheadhainn mhora le'n cinn cromta, a' feitheamh gu foistinneach air a bheannachd. Bha 'n comhradh aig a bhord freagarrach do'n la 's do'n am, stolda, gun bhi ro-sholuimte. Cha robh na h-igheanan ag innseadh do chach a 'cheile ciod na srolagan riomhach a bha am ban-choimhearsnaich a caitheamh; ni mo thuirt Anna ri Mairi gu robh boineid ur air ceann Pheigidh Bhride. Cha robh guth air gnothaichean na seachdain, no air sgeulachdan faoine an t-saoghail. Bha e soilleir gu robh urram air a chuir air La an Tighearna leis an teaghlach so.[73]

> On this particular day, the family sat down to a meal, in a mannerly and orderly fashion, as usual, the small children with their hands folded and their eyes shut; the adults with their heads bent, waiting calmly for the blessing. Their conversation at the table was appropriate for the day and time, dignified without being too serious. The girls were not talking to each other about the beautiful ribbons that their neighbours were wearing; nor did Anna tell Mary that Peggy Bridget was wearing a new bonnet on her head. There was no mention of the business of the week, or of the vainglorious secular news. It was clear that this family respected the Day of the Lord.

It is noteworthy that Fraser depicts worldliness and vanity in specifically female terms in this passage. He also describes a son as nearly breaking a family rule by speaking irreverently about the foibles of old men at church; he is stopped, however, by his mother with a stern look.

At seven in the evening, the community gathers at the house of a neighbour for continued discussion of spiritual matters. The religious discussion resembles a *céilidh*, rebutting any inherent incompatibility between sacred and secular spheres: it is held in the same room used for *céilidh*s; the man of the house offers the first prayer; songs and stories are shared;[74] and after the theme of the morning sermon is read by an elder, each of the youths is asked to reiterate, from memory, a portion of the morning's sermon, receiving feedback from others.

Following this, the group reviews the current section of the Shorter Catechism for that week. Each person in attendance must provide the verbatim answer to one or two questions from the section. After this, the group sings one of the psalms, a prayer is offered, another chapter is read by an elder, and a final prayer brings the meeting to a close.

Fraser concludes this chapter and the book by remarking on the relationship between the exodus of the Highland people and an apparent decline in religiosity:

> Mar 'eil aireamh an luchd-eisdeachd aig na coinnimhean cho lionmhor 's a b'abhaist, cha'n ann a chionn gu bheil tograidhean an t-sluaigh air an tarruing o nithean siorruidh, ach a chionn gu bheil clann nan Gaidheal a cosnadh am beo-shlainte fad air falbh bho achaidhean uaine tir an duthchais, 'n am fogarraich ann an tiribh chein; 's mar 'eil luchd-aideachaidh cho comasach, deasbhriathrach, ann a bhi togail fianuis air taobh na firinn 's na coireachd, 's a bha an athraichean leth-cheud bliadhna roimhe so; mar eil gibhtean cinn Phoil aca, guidhemid gu'm biodh tomas iomchuidh do ghradh Bharnabhuis 'n an cridheachan.[75]

> If the size of the audience at the meetings isn't as large as they used to be, it's not because the population's devotions have been drawn away from eternal matters, but because the Highland people are making their living far from the green pastures of their ancestral land, as exiles in foreign countries; and if adherents aren't as capable and well-spoken as their forefathers were fifty years ago – if they do not have the intellectual talents of Paul – let us pray they might have an appropriate measure of the love of Barnabas in their hearts.

Fraser is implying that Gaelic communities in Scotland would find in Canada the security and stability they need for their religion to take root and thrive; in other words, their social vulnerability in the Highlands does not allow them to acquire and transmit the practices of a healthy moral and spiritual regime. Emigration would offer them religious as well as economic salvation.

CONCLUSIONS

Fraser's book was speaking directly to its Highland audience in the language they understood, using the literary genres and tropes that conveyed meaning to them, as well as the oral narratives, songs, and elements of tradition that were the stuff of their life experience, world view, and social interactions. *Leabhar nan Sonn* was a compelling vehicle for reimagining the contemporary circumstances of his audience as an immigrant community in Canada that had something valuable to offer as Gaels, despite having been stigmatized as a racially inferior and socially undesirable ethnic group in Scotland.

Leabhar nan Sonn presents Canada as welcoming Gaelic immigrants, not least because of the groundwork of early pioneers from the Highlands, who are extolled as heroes. Inserting Gaels into the pre-Confederation story of Canada offered the immigrant community a sense of investment in its future prosperity. Fraser's text presents verbal portraits of settlers who embody success in different fields of endeavour, including literature, education, politics, commerce, religion, community leadership, and the military. His description of their high moral character, generosity, and goodwill toward fellow Gaels suggests that he hoped to minimize doubts about relocating to Canada due to the anticipated challenges. These themes echo the texts of other Canadian Gaels, who used literature to reframe their communal history from a narrative of defeat and humiliation to one of ultimate triumph and fulfillment.[76]

Leabhar nan Sonn manufactures a semblance of continuity for Gaelic culture and tradition, from the ancient Caledonian past to the Canadian present. Tradition bearers and culture heroes like MacColla represent the replanting of Gaelic heritage in Canada, where it has the freedom to realize its potential. These creative renderings of Gaeldom minimize the traumatic disruptions and dislocations of Highland experience so as to alleviate collective self-doubt and strengthen the resolve of Gaelic immigrants to maintain a distinctive identity and culture, which had been disenfranchised by the anglophone hegemony that was also dominant in Canada.

Fraser's favourable presentation of Gaelic society and of the strong familial and social bonds of Highland life suggests that he sincerely believed in the value of these traits and thought they could be transplanted to Canada to benefit the nation as a whole. He implies that religious life serves as the cornerstone of a moral conscience and he advocates for synergies between church, family, and community such as he had experienced in his youth in the Highlands. The physical fitness of human beings also deserves attention, and he asserts that Gaelic tradition provides a means of maintaining healthy bodies while also facilitating social interaction.

Fraser's Gaelic texts emphasize loyalty to language but also indicate receptiveness to multicultural inclusivity, contradicting the notion that he promoted an ethnocentric and racialist agenda. To the contrary, he recounts relations between Gaels and other ethnic groups in Canada in explicitly positive and symbiotic terms. On the other hand, his loyalty to empire and adherence to a patriarchal hierarchy do not sit well with modern progressive sensibilities.

It is just, fitting, and crucial that we come to a reckoning with the consequences of colonization, racism, and ideologies of conquest and domination and see them clearly as the crimes that they were and continue to be. But it is also important to read the remains of the past, in all their contradictions and ambiguities, with empathy and nuance if we are to understand how those caught up in these tumultuous transformations attempted to navigate and negotiate the range of flawed options available to them.

NOTES

1 Anderson, *Imagined Communities*, 44–6.
2 The seminal study is John MacInnes, "The Panegyric Code in Gaelic Poetry and Its Historical Background" in *Dùthchas nan Gàidheal*, 265–319.
3 MacLeod, "Quaint Specimens."
4 Dembling, "Gaelic in Canada."
5 Newton, "Alexander Fraser as Ethnographer."
6 Newton, "Alexander Fraser's Efforts."
7 Vance, "Brief History," 105.
8 Newton, *Seanchaidh na Coille*, 3–8; Stroh, *Gaelic Scotland*, 185–211.

9 Newton, *Seanchaidh na Coille*, 421–62; idem., "Gaelic Organizations."
10 Newton, *Seanchaidh na Coille*, 8–28.
11 Dunn, *Highland Settler*, 89, says that Fraser produced eight Gaelic volumes, but I have not been able to identify more than these four. In a copy of Dunn's notes left with the Celtic Collection of St Francis Xavier University, the other four volumes are listed as *An Gàidheal ann an Canada*, *Linn an Àigh*, *Òrain Dùthcha nan Eilean*, and *Sir. S. MacCoinnich am Fear-Tagraidh Fuileachdach*. Barron, "Some Notes," 55, also claims that Fraser wrote at least eight books in Gaelic, but he does not name them.
12 Fraser, *The Mission*, 10, 11.
13 Lew and Cater, "Canadian Emigration," 24.
14 Fraser, *The Mission*, 19.
15 Ibid., 18.
16 Ibid., 20.
17 Ibid., 21.
18 Fraser quotes from Act 1, Scene 2, of Ramsay's *The Gentle Shepherd.*
19 Fraser, *The Mission*, 26–7.
20 Ibid., 25.
21 Ibid., 25.
22 Fraser, *Cànain agus Cliù*, 9–11. All translations into English are my own.
23 Fraser quoted in Newton, *Seanchaidh na Coille*, 180.
24 Fraser, *The Mission*, 16.
25 Ibid., 22, 23.
26 Fraser, *Leabhar nan Sonn*, 15.
27 Ibid., 25.
28 Meek, "Place-Names and Literature," 162–5.
29 Fraser, *Leabhar nan Sonn*, 25–6.
30 Ibid., 14.
31 Ibid., 9.
32 Ibid., 17.
33 Ibid., 9.
34 Ibid., 53–6.
35 For MacColla's correspondence with Fraser, see folder F-1015-6-2-2, Alexander Fraser Fonds, Archives of Ontario.
36 Fraser, *Leabhar nan Sonn*, 48–9.
37 Ibid., 50–1.
38 Ibid., 56.
39 Ibid., 66–7.
40 Ibid., 66–7.
41 Ibid., 69. As noted earlier, *Leabhar nan Sonn* was based on newspaper articles

that Fraser had previously published. Fraser did not update his text to reflect MacEalair's passing in 1894 and continued to describe him in the present tense in the 1897 book.

42 Ibid., 67, 72–3.
43 Ibid., 75.
44 Ibid., 76.
45 Ibid., 76–7.
46 This point is made explicitly on page 79.
47 Ibid., 77–8.
48 Ibid., 81.
49 Ibid., 83–4.
50 Ibid., 85.
51 The Disruption of 1843 is mentioned on page 90.
52 Ibid., 85, 86.
53 Ibid., 87–8. To my knowledge, this poem is not preserved anywhere else.
54 Ibid., 93–4.
55 Ibid., 88.
56 Ibid., 89.
57 Ibid., 90.
58 Ibid., 89–90.
59 Ibid., 94.
60 It is not stated whether this property was in the northwest of Ontario or the Northwest Territories of Canada.
61 Newton, *Warriors of the Word*, 102–6, 119–21.
62 Although one of the characters is called Niall Sgoilear (Neil the Scholar), he does not utilize his learning for didactic purposes in the dialogue.
63 Kidd, *Còmhraidhean nan Cnoc*, 39–49.
64 Fraser, *Leabhar nan Sonn*, 97–8.
65 Dunn, *Highland Settler*, 100–2, 141–2.
66 This character is given a territorial style, but it is never indicated where the place named Druim a' Chnuic is located.
67 Newton, *Warriors of the Word*, 298–301.
68 Fraser, *Leabhar nan Sonn*, 104–5.
69 Bruford and MacDonald, *Scottish Traditional Tales*, 345–51.
70 In a letter written near the end of his life, Fraser noted that he had "defend[ed] the superstitions of my native parish" as a teenager. See Barron, "Some Notes," 56.
71 Ibid., 401–4.
72 Ní Dhuibhne, "'The Old Woman as Hare.'"

73 Fraser, *Leabhar nan Sonn*, 110–11.

74 Fraser mentions the use of a Bible and Book of Psalms, thus highlighting Gaelic literacy. For extended discussion of literacy in the Gaelic communities of Quebec, see Bennett, *Oatmeal and the Catechism*, 134–6.

75 Fraser, *Leabhar nan Sonn*, 115.

76 Newton, *Seanchaidh na Coille*, 144–5, 187–9, 508–10.

BIBLIOGRAPHY

Anderson, Benedict. *Imagined Communities*. London and New York: Verso, 1991.

Barron, Hugh. "Some Notes on the Parish of Kiltarlity." *Transactions of the Gaelic Society of Inverness* 50 (1979): 40–59.

Bennett, Margaret. *Oatmeal and the Catechism: Scottish Gaelic Settlers in Quebec*. Montreal and Kingston: McGill-Queen's University Press, 2003.

Bruford, Alan, and Donald A. MacDonald. *Scottish Traditional Tales*. Edinburgh: Polygon, 1994.

Dembling, Jonathan. "Gaelic in Canada: New Evidence from an Old Census." In *Cànan agus Cultar / Language and Culture: Rannsachadh na Gàidhlig 3*, ed. Wilson McLeod, James E. Fraser, and Anja Gunderloch, 203–14. Edinburgh: Dunedin Academic Press, 2006.

Dunn, Charles W. *Highland Settler: A Portrait of the Scottish Gael in Cape Breton and Eastern Nova Scotia*. Wreck Cove: Breton Books, [1953] 1991.

Fraser, Alexander. *Cànain agus Cliù Ar Sinnsearan*. Toronto: n.p., 1901.

– *Leabhar nan Sonn*. Toronto: William Briggs, 1897.

– *The Mission of the Scot in Canada*. Toronto: R.G. McLean, 1903.

Kidd, Sheila. *Còmhraidhean nan Cnoc: The Nineteenth-Century Gaelic Prose Dialogue*. Edinburgh: Scottish Gaelic Texts Society, 2016.

Lew, Byron, and Bruce Cater. "Canadian Emigration to the U.S., 1900–1930: Characterizing Movers and Stayers, and the Differential Impact of Immigration Policy on the Mobility of French and English Canadians." Paper presented at the Canadian Network for Economic History Conference, Banff, Alberta, October 2012. http://www.economichistory.ca/pdfs/2012/lew-cater.pdf.

MacLeod, Donald. "'Quaint Specimens of the Early Days': Priorities in Collecting the Ontario Archival Record, 1872–1935." *Archivaria* 22 (1986): 12–39.

MacInnes, John. *Dùthchas nan Gàidheal: Selected Essays of John MacInnes*, ed. Michael Newton. Edinburgh: Birlinn, 2006.

Meek, Donald. "Place-Names and Literature: Evidence from the Gaelic Ballads." In *The Uses of Place-Names*, ed. Simon Taylor, 147–68. Edinburgh: Scottish Cultural Press, 1998.

Newton, Michael. "Alexander Fraser's Efforts to Establish Celtic Studies in Ontario." *The Virtual Gael* (blog), 13 February 2017. https://virtualgael.wordpress.com/2017/02/13.

– "Alexander Fraser as Ethnographer in Gaelic Ontario." *The Virtual Gael* (blog), 4 April 2017. https://virtualgael.wordpress.com/2017/04/11.

– "Gaelic Organizations in Nineteenth- and Early-Twentieth Century Ontario." *International Review of Scottish Studies* 41 (2016): 37–71.

– *Seanchaidh na Coille / Memory-Keeper of the Forest: Anthology of Scottish Gaelic Literature of Canada.* Sydney: Cape Breton University Press, 2015.

– *Warriors of the Word: The World of the Scottish Highlanders*. Edinburgh: Birlinn, 2009.

Ní Dhuibhne, Éilis. "'The Old Woman as Hare': Structure and Meaning in an Irish Legend." *Folklore* 104 (1993): 77–85.

Stroh, Silke. *Gaelic Scotland in the Colonial Imagination: Anglophone Writing from 1600 to 1900*. Evanston: Northwestern University Press, 2017.

Vance, Michael. "A Brief History of Organized Scottishness in Canada." In *Transatlantic Scots*, ed. Celeste Ray, 96–119. Tuscaloosa: University of Alabama Press, 2005.

ARCHIVAL COLLECTIONS

Alexander Fraser Fonds. Archives of Ontario, Toronto.

14

Betraying Beetles and Guarding Geese: Animal Apocrypha in Scottish and Nova Scotian Gaelic Folklore

Kathleen Reddy

I am greatly indebted to the late Professor Kenneth Nilsen, who provided my first introduction to Scottish Gaelic *seanchas* (oral tradition) in its original language through his use of material gathered from Nova Scotian tradition bearers in his Gaelic classes at St Francis Xavier University. This introduction led to a continuing fascination with Gaelic oral tradition and eventually to research concerning apocryphal folklore.

There are many apocryphal tales in Gaelic *seanchas* that feature Biblical figures and episodes. This chapter explores a selection of related etiological apocryphal tales featuring animals, which were collected from *seanchaidhean* (tradition-bearers) in Catholic and Presbyterian Gaelic communities in the Western Isles of Scotland and Cape Breton, Nova Scotia, Canada, in the nineteenth and twentieth centuries. Such tales are presumed to be primarily found in Catholic communities, where they were accepted as part of community members' religious understanding of the world, whereas it is commonly understood that they were not preserved in modern Presbyterian communities, where non-scriptural and folkloric elements of religious belief were not valued in the same way. Through an examination of the ways ideas about religious belief affected both how these tales are framed and how they were collected, this prelimary investigation will test these common assumptions about apocryphal *seanchas* in Catholic and Presbyterian Gaelic communities. It will address the claim that Catholic communities have served as a richer collection ground for these tales and reveal complex attitudes toward these tales in both Catholic and Presbyterian communities.

APOCRYPHAL TALES

Apocryphal folk tales often serve an etiological function. As religious studies scholar Marion Bowman explains, "their attraction lies in using a biblical setting ingeniously and explaining familiar aspects of human behaviour or the natural world," usually in a way that incorporates an element of moral judgment.[1] In this respect, the Gaelic apocryphal tales collected in the nineteenth and twentieth centuries are not unusual. Many of these concern animals that come to the aid of Christ or that inhibit his progress when he is fleeing the authorities. The creatures' actions are seen in a moral light and have long-lasting physical effects; as we will see in the tales examined below, the way the animals either aid or hinder Christ affects their descendants' appearance to the present day.

The interplay between Christ and the natural world in apocryphal tales is highlighted by Irish folklorist Dáithí Ó hÓgáin, who states that "folklore tends to reflect philosophical ideas in its own physical way. Thus the Christian theory of history, which has the birth of Jesus ushering in a new era, gives rise in European folklore generally to the notion that the physical and cultural environment was reshaped in many ways during the life of the Saviour."[2] A similar interplay with the natural world can be perceived in medieval *exempla*, which were used as teaching tools in sermons and were spread throughout Europe by medieval religious orders.[3] John Shaw notes a connection between these medieval moral tales, which draw upon religion, and modern Gaelic apocryphal folklore.[4] He argues convincingly that some of the Gaelic apocryphal tales were brought from Ireland to the Scottish Highlands as *exempla* by Irish missionary priests after the Reformation.[5] To Shaw's evidence, Sìm Innes adds an earlier instance of transmission. Innes shows that the miracle of the instantaneous harvest in the Classical Gaelic poem "Fuigheall beannacht brú Mhuire" (Overflowing of blessings is Mary's womb) in the sixteenth-century Book of the Dean of Lismore traces its origins at least as far back as the fourteenth century.[6] The same miracle features in several versions of the apocryphal tale of Christ and the beetles explored below. This evidence that apocryphal tales were circulating in both pre- and post-

Reformation Gaelic Scotland suggests that apocryphal lore has long been established in Scottish Gaelic oral tradition.

SCRIPTURE IN PRESBYTERIAN AND CATHOLIC THEOLOGY

Given the position of scripture in Presbyterian theology, we might expect members of late nineteenth- and early twentieth-century Gaelic-speaking Presbyterian communities not to have valued stories of Christ that come from the oral tradition rather than from biblical sources. The Church of Scotland, the Free Church of Scotland, and the Free Presbyterian Church of Scotland, all of which had representation in the Scottish Highlands during this time, adhered to the 1648 Westminster Confession of Faith.[7] This doctrinal summary includes the statement: "The whole counsel of God concerning all things necessary for His own glory, man's salvation, faith, and life, is either expressly set down in Scripture, or by good and necessary consequence may be deduced from Scripture: unto which nothing at any time is to be added, whether by new revelations of the Spirit, or traditions of men."[8] Therefore, theological authority is found in scripture alone [*sola scriptura*].[9] In keeping with this doctrine, scholars have noted the reverence with which Presbyterian communities in the Scottish *Gàidhealtachd* (Gaelic-speaking Highlands) held scripture as late as the twentieth century. In an anthropological study of a Lewis crofting community in 1970 and 1971, for example, Susan Parman attests that the Presbyterian island of Lewis was then known as "Tìr an t-Soisgeul" (the Land of the Gospel).[10] Moreover, Maighread Challan describes the morning and evening ritual, lasting into the twentieth century in North Uist, of "a' gabhail an Leabhair" (taking the Book), in which the head of the household would read a chapter from the Gaelic Bible to assembled family members.[11]

Members of twentieth-century Gaelic-speaking Catholic communities would also have revered scripture, but this reverence would not have been to the exclusion of other ways in which their faith could have been informed. The Catholic understanding of the role of scripture places it in tandem with tradition and church teaching in informing Catholics' faith. As the Catechism of the Council of Trent, originally issued in 1566 and still considered authoritative in the twentieth century, states, "[n]ow all the doctrines in which the faithful are to be instructed are contained in the Word of God, which is found in Scripture and tradition."[12] Additionally, the importance of the authority of the Catholic Church's teaching can be seen in a Gaelic context in a short catechism published in Antigonish, Nova Scotia, during the 1912–50 episcopate of Bishop James Morrison. The catechism includes the question, "Ciamar a bhios sinn cinnteach ciod a thaisbean Dia?" (How can we be sure of what God revealed?). The following answer is given: "Le teisteanas na h-Eaglaise, o na 'si steidh agus carradh na firinne" (From the testimony of the Church [i.e., church teaching], as she is the foundation and pillar of truth). The answer is supported by a reference to 1 Timothy 3:15, in which the Church is referred to in the same terms.[13]

The close relationship between scripture and church teaching in Catholic theology contrasts with the Presbyterian emphasis on scripture alone, *sola scriptura*. Despite the Presybterian embrace of *sola scriptura*, however, it appears that apocryphal tales about Christ were told in Presbyterian communities in the Scottish *Gàidhealtachd* (Gaelic-speaking Highlands). As Alan Bruford and D.A. MacDonald note, "The cycle of stories about Christ and his pursuers … includes origin legends told in various parts of Scotland, by Protestants as well as Catholics."[14]

CHRIST AND THE BEETLES

It is not difficult to find examples of apocryphal tales in the oral record in Gaelic-speaking Catholic areas in the nineteenth and twentieth centuries. Versions of an apocryphal tale concerning two types of beetles and their encounter with Christ as he flees from authorities were recorded by School of Scottish Studies fieldworker Elizabeth Sinclair in Barra and Vatersay in the mid-twentieth century. Sinclair recorded the following version in 1965 from the well-known Vatersay tradition bearer, Nan MacKinnon (Nan Eachainn Fhionnlaigh) (1903–1982).[15]

Mar a Ghlèidh an Ceàrr-Dubhan Crìosta Nuair a Bhrath Daol E
Bhiodh iad ag ràdh, uaireigin dhen t-saoghal, gun robh bruidhinn aig a h-uile creutair. Agus nuair a bhathar an tòir air Crìosta, an fheadhainn a bha a' falbh, chan fhaiceadh iad e, thachair iad air daol a' seo, agus ceàrr-dubhan. Agus dh'fhaighneachd iad am faca iad Mac Dè.

'S thuirt an daol, "An-dè, dè," ars' e fhèin. "Chaidh Mac Dè seachad."

'S thuirt an ceàrr-dubhan, is a' freagairt, "Fhichead latha gus an dè, chaidh Mac Dè seachad."

Is bha iad ag ràdh, ged a gheibheadh duine ceàrr-dubhan, nach eil còir aige ri mharbhadh idir. Ach air an… cur air a dhruim dìreach, air tàilleabh 's nach do bhrath e Crìosta. Ach air tàilleabh 's gun do bhrath an daol Crìosta, tha iad ag ràdh gum bu chòir dhut a marbhadh.[16]

How the Dung Beetle Protected Christ when the Chafer Beetle Betrayed Him

They would say, a long time ago, that every creature had the power of speech. And when they were in pursuit of Christ, the ones who were in pursuit, they couldn't see him. They met this chafer beetle, and a dung beetle. And they asked had they seen the Son of God.

And the chafer beetle said, "Yesterday, yesterday," he said, "the Son of God went past."

And the dung beetle said, in response, "It's twenty days since yesterday that the Son of God went past."

And they used to say, if a person were to find a dung beetle, that he shouldn't kill it, but put it on its back, since it didn't betray Christ. But because the chafer beetle did betray Christ, they say that you should kill it.

Sinclair recorded another version of the same tale in 1962 from Kate Gillies (Ceit Mhìcheil Fhionnlaigh) (1891–1979), who, like MacKinnon, was born in Barra but raised in Vatersay.[17] This version differs in that the *ceàrr-dubhan* (dung beetle) is the betrayer of Christ and punished accordingly, while the *caille-chòsag* (wood louse) remains loyal. This version also features the miraculous growth of a crop in order to conceal Christ, a motif previously noted in the Classical Gaelic poem "Fuigheall beannacht brú Mhuire" and present, too, in other versions of the tale of Christ and the beetles. Gillies's account is as follows:

Ìosa Crìosta agus an Ceàrr-Dubhan

Cha toigh le duine sam bith an ceàrr-dubhan, agus gu h-àraid airson dè bhathar a ràdh ris nuair a bha cainnt aig a h-uile creutair. Nuair a bha iad an tòir air Crìosta, bha e a' falbh an latha a bha seo, agus bha e a' dol seachad air feadhainn a bha a' cur talmhann aig taobh an rathaid.

Agus thuirt e riutha, "Ma chì sibh duine a' tighinn air mo thòir-sa," ors' esan, "Canaibh sibh riutha, gum faca sibh mo choltas a' dol seachad an latha a bha sibh a' cur an talmhann-sa. Agus a-màireach, nuair a thig sibh," ors' esan, "Bidh fochann air."

Seo mar a bha. Thàinig iad an làrna-mhàireach agus bha fochann air an talamh. Agus thàinig an luchd-brath. 'S dh'fhaighneachd iad dha na daoine a bh' aig an talamh, am faca iad coltas Chrìosta a' dol seachad. Agus thuirt na daoine gum faca, an latha a bha sinn a' cur an talmhann-sa.

Is fhreagair an ceàrr-dubhan, is thuirt e, "An-dè, an-dè," thuirt esan, "a chaidh Mac Dè seachad."

Is thuirt a' chaille-chòsag, "Trì Dihaoine an deoghaidh a chèile, cuimhnich ort fhèin an-dè, a bhradag."

Is an uair sin, cha toigh le daoine an ceàrr-dubhan.[18]

Jesus Christ and the Dung Beetle

Nobody likes the dung beetle, and especially what is said of him from when every creature had the power of speech. When they were pursuing Christ, he was fleeing on this day, and he was going past some men who were planting a field beside the road.

And he said to them, "If you see anyone coming after me," he said, "Say to them, that you saw someone of my likeness going by the day you were planting the field. And tomorrow, when you come," he said, "The corn will be in blade."

So it was. They came the next day and the field was in blade. And the traitors came. And they asked the men who were in the field, had they seen someone of Christ's appearance going past. And the men said that they had, the day they were planting the field.

And the dung beetle answered, and he said, "Yesterday, yesterday," he said, "Christ went past."

And the wood louse said, "Three Fridays, one after the other since the day, recollect yourself, woman."

And from that time, no one likes the dung beetle.

As well as being collected in Barra and Vatersay in the twentieth century, the tale of Christ and the beetles appears to have been well-known in the Uists in the late nineteenth century. The following unattributed version was collected by Fr Allan MacDonald (1859–1905), probably in his Daliburgh parish in the south end of South Uist in 1887:[19]

> It is said that the [chafer] beetle (daol) tried to betray our Lord in his flight to Egypt. Herod's men were in pursuit of him and came to Egypt and were enquiring of the people if they had observed the Holy Family pass by that way. The person particularly addressed said he observed a group pass that would correspond to the description given. Being further asked when they had passed, he replied that they passed when the corn which was now yellow in his field had been sown. The seed had been sown only the previous day, but a miracle had been wrought in favour of the owner of the field on account of some kindness shown to the Holy family. As the soldiers were departing on the furtherance of their search a black beetle crept across the path & said "An dè, an dè, chaidh Mac Dhè seachad" [Yesterday, yesterday, the Son of God went past]. The sharded beetle called "Ceardobhan" [dung beetle] with less regard for truth than for charity said "Briag, Briag, a bhradaig! Seachd bliadhna thun an dè chaidh Mac De seachad" [A lie, a lie, woman! It's seven years since the day that the Son of God went past].[20] The daol is universally detested and trampled to death when seen, but the "ceardobhan" is a favourite.[21]

Fr Allan's version of the tale reveals a marked consistency with the later versions given by Nan MacKinnon and Kate Gillies, suggesting that the tale did not vary greatly as it was told in the Catholic islands in the nineteenth and twentieth centuries.

Alexander Carmichael also gathered items related to this tale in the Western Isles. In the second volume of *Carmina Gadelica*, he includes an unattributed prose version of the tale with the statement that "there are many curious legends and beliefs current in the Isles about the 'cearr-dubhan,' or sacred beetle," perhaps indicating that the account printed is a composite text.[22] He then provides a verse version titled "Duan nan Daol" (Poem of the Beetles) in which the *ceàrr-dubhan* is again the protector of Christ, while the *daol* (translated by Carmichael as the "black beetle," cf. Fr Allan's text above) is the betrayer.[23] The ambivalent character of the *ceàrr-dubhan* is also indicated in Carmichael's notes in the same volume, in which he states: "Co ard 's gu'n seol an cearr-dubhan, / Is ann 's a ghlar a thuiteas e." This is translated by Carmichael as "However high the [dung] beetle soars, / It is in the filth it falls."[24]

Significantly, in Carmichael's published list of contributors, the reciter of "Duan nan Daol" is given as "Aonas Iain MacRury, Calf-herd, Scolpaig, North Uist."[25] This indicates that the item was collected in Presbyterian North Uist, countering Carmichael's own claim that it was difficult to obtain folkore items in Presbyterian areas due to the devaluation in these areas of traditional folklore.[26] Further biographical research would be needed to definitely determine MacRury's religious affiliation, although it is very likely he was a Presbyterian.[27] Regardless, this item is evidence that a geographical religious divide demarcating where folklore material of this nature was to be found was perhaps not as marked as has been assumed.

In addition to its presence in a wider area of the Scottish *Gàidhealtachd* than may first be presumed, it should be noted that the tale of Christ and the beetles is an international tale with a particularly strong Irish connection.[28] The tale's instantaneous harvest motif can be found in medieval Irish poetry, and there is a possible Irish ecclesial origin for tales of this sort, as put forward by Shaw; in addition, the tale of Christ and the beetles has been collected by Irish folklorists in an almost identical form.[29] These connections may help explain the tale's prevalence in Gaelic-speaking Catholic communities, where a more continuous connection to medieval *exempla* and Irish religious folklore have been noted. However, the collection of a related verse in Presbyterian North Uist suggests that echoes of the tale remained in at least one Presbyterian Gaelic community until the late nineteenth century.

CHRIST AND THE HENS

A related apocryphal etiological tale concerning creatures protecting and betraying Christ – in this case, domestic fowl – was collected from Catholic and Presbyterian tradition bearers in Cape Breton and North Uist. Individual examples of this tale further suggest a need to question assumed differences between Catholic and Presbyterian communities in regard to Gaelic apocryphal tales.

A version of this tale was collected in 1967 by School of Scottish Studies fieldworker Angus John MacDonald from Roderick MacDonald (Ruairidh na Càrnaich) (1883–1970) of Carnach, North Uist, which was a Presbyterian community.[30] Roderick MacDonald's father Angus (Aonghas na Càrnaich) was a noted local bard, and his childhood home was a well-known *taigh-cèilidh* (ceilidh house) where community members would gather in the evenings.[31] As Linda NicLeòid states about Roderick MacDonald: "Bho aois uabhasach òg, fhuair e oideachadh prìseil ann an Gàidhlig gu làitheil tro bheul-aithris, ann an iomadach sgil agus cuspair, eadar an dachaigh, an cèilidh agus a' chroit sa Chàrnaich"[32] (From a very early age, he received valuable instruction in Gaelic daily through folklore, in various skills and topics, between the home, the *cèilidh*, and the croft in Carnach). Although he was not highly literate in Gaelic, he was able to read the Gaelic Bible. Like his father, he was a bard who composed numerous songs. He was also a well-regarded storyteller. He held many stories of the supernatural in his repertoire, and it appears that he believed in the *droch shùil* (evil eye) and the *dà shealladh* (second sight).[33]

In MacDonald's version of the story of Christ and the hens, the adult Christ is being pursued by Roman soldiers:

> Chuala sibh mu dhèidhinn sgeulachdan faoine seanna bhan agus seo té dhiùbh dhuibh. Bha na saighdeirein Ròmananch air tòir Chriosda aig an ám a bha seo agus a h-uile h-àite thigeadh iad air cha robh ach – "An fhaca sibh colas Mac Dhé a' dol seachad ann a sheo?" Cha robh duine ann a dh'innseadh an fhìrinn dhaibh agus chanadh a chuid bu mhutha nach fhaca no 's dòcha gu faca bha chionn seachduinn ged a bhiodh E air a bhi ann an dé. Ràinig Criosd an latha bha seo daoine a bha càthadh shìl agus dh'innis e dhiùbh [*sic*] gu robh na saigdeirein Ròmanach air a thòir 's gun iad fad air deireadh air. "O gu ta," ars àsan, "cha'n fhaigh iad thu air an turus seo idir," agus chuir iad e 'na shìneadh air a bheul fodha agus thòisich iad air càthadh an t-sìl air uachdar.
>
> Bha tòrr mór bireach de shiol air a mhullach ar a thàinig na saighdeirein 'sa dh'fhaighneachd iad, "Am faca sibh Mac Dhé a' dol seachad ann a sheo?" "Chunnaic," ars àsan, "tha trì Diar-daoin as déigh a chéile bho chaidh Mac Dhé seachad." Thàinig a seo na tunnagan is thòisich iad air ith' an t-sìl aig iomall an tòirr ach thàinig an uair-sean na cearcan is ghabh iad dìreach a mhuallach an tòirr is thòisich iad ri sgapadh le'n casan. Bha iad a sìor sgapadh is eagal mòr air na daoine gu nochdadh iad Criosda fo shùilean na saighdeirein ach mu dheireadh dh'fhalbh iad agus shàbhail Criosda 's cha robh an còrr ann.
>
> Tha e coltach gu d' thàinig peanaist air na cearcan airson cho faisg 's a chaidh iad air Criosda a chuir an làmhan a dhearg nàmhaid an lath' ud. 'S e 'n pheanaiste sean gun drùdhadh gach meal a thigeadh as an adhar orra, ach chon an latha diugh cha

dean na meallan ach sleamhnachadh far itean nan tunnagan 's cha dhrùdh iad idir orra.

You have heard about the old wives' tales and here is one of them for you. The Roman soldiers were in pursuit of Christ at this time and every place they used to come to there was nothing but – "Did you see the likeness of the Son of God passing here?" There wasn't anyone who would tell them the truth and the greater part used to say that they didn't or, perhaps, that they did a week ago, though He would have been there yesterday. This day Christ came on men who were winnowing grain and He told them that the Roman soldiers were pursuing him and that they weren't far behind Him. "O, but they certainly won't find You this time," said they, and they put him lying face down and they started winnowing grain over Him.

There was a large conical heap of grain on top of Him when the soldiers came, and they asked, "Did you see the Son of God passing here?" "Yes," said they, "The Son of God passed three Thursdays ago." Now the ducks came and they started to eat the grain at the edge of the heap, but then the hens came and they proceeded straight to the top of the heap, and they started to scatter it with their feet. They were scattering more and more, and the men were much afraid that they would uncover Christ before the soldiers' eyes, but at last they left and Christ just escaped and no more.

Apparently the hens were punished for how near they came to delivering Christ into the hands of his greatest enemy that day. That punishment is that every shower that might come down from the sky would drench them to the skin, but to this day the showers will only slip off the ducks' feathers and they won't drench them.[34]

This tale was published in the School of Scottish Studies journal *Tocher* with a note that the "original recording [was] erased after transcription."[35] However, another telling recorded from MacDonald in 1958 includes significant contextual information for placing the tale in a social and religious framework. In the 1958 recording, MacDonald prefaces the tale by explaining to the collector, John MacInnes:

Tha cuimhn' agam, nuair a bha mi na mo ghille bheag, mo sheanmhair, bha i na seann bhoireannach, a-staigh – bha i ma cheithir

> fichead bliadhna agus a seachd-deug nuair a dh'eug i. Agus bhiodh i a' dèanamh – ag innse cus de stòraidhnean dhuinn, gu h-àraid air feasgar Sàbaid. Bhiodh stòraidhnean beaga aice, agus stòraidhnean a bh' air an toirimeasg leinn, às a' Bhìobla, sgeulachdan faoine sheana-bhean, nach bu chòir a bhith ag èisteachd riutha. Agus chan eil dùil a'm nach innis mi tè dhuibh.[36]
>
> I remember, when I was a little boy, my grandmother, she was an old woman, in the house – she was about ninety-seven when she died. And she would do – tell lots of stories to us, especially on Sunday afternoons. She had little stories, and stories which were forbidden to us, from the Bible, old wives' tales, that shouldn't be listened to. And I think I'll tell you one of them.

MacDonald then recites the tale, with no major differences from the version recorded in 1967, and concludes, "agus sin agad tè dha na sgeulachdan faoine sheana-bhan" (and there you have one of the old wives' tales).

It is significant that MacDonald bookends the 1958 version of the tale by calling it *sgeulachd fhaoin sheana-bhean* (an old wives' tale, literally a foolish old women's tale) – the same statement he makes about it in the 1967 recording. In one sense, this is factual; he heard the tale from his grandmother when she was an old woman. However, it can also be heard as a dismissive statement, a form of hedging he employed to distance himself from the tale. This is not surprising considering the official religious views of his Presbyterian community. Yet the fact that he recorded the tale for two different collectors over the course of a decade also indicates that he recognized some value in the tale, despite his admission "nach bu chòir a bhith ag èisteachd [rithe]" (that it shouldn't be listened to).

As may be expected, a much less ambivalent relationship between the storyteller and the tale is found in a version recorded from a member of a Gaelic-speaking Catholic community in Cape Breton, Michael MacNeil (Migi Bean Nìlleig Ruairidh Eòin a' Phlant) (1917–1995). A version of the tale of Christ and the hens was collected from MacNeil by Jim Watson and published in the Cape Breton-based periodical *Am Bràighe*.[37] MacNeil was separated from MacDonald by the North Atlantic, yet the two storytellers share some significant similarities in their acquisition of Gaelic community knowledge and role as community tradition bearers.

MacNeil was from Rear Iona on Lake Bras d'Or in central Cape Breton. His ancestors were from the Isle of Barra, as were most of the Scottish Gaels who settled in the area.[38] The rural area in which MacNeil was born and raised was predominately Catholic, with the local population proudly aware of their Barra roots. As Michael Kennedy states, "these old world regional and religious affiliations were strongly maintained in Cape Breton."[39] Significant to note is that most of the Gaels who settled in Cape Breton from the end of the eighteenth century to the middle of the nineteenth were Catholics, originating from mainland districts, Barra, and South Uist.[40] This gave Cape Breton Gaelic culture, particularly in areas such as Iona, a distinctly Catholic flavour. In 1932, when MacNeil was a working teenager, it was noted that the population of the Iona area was "all Catholic and nearly all Gaelic speaking."[41]

Like MacDonald in North Uist, MacNeil was known as an exceptional storyteller who was very knowledgeable about Gaelic traditions in his area.[42] He gained this knowledge at a young age, as he had to go to work at the age of eight in order to support his family after his father's death. He worked as a postman, and as a result, instead of obtaining a formal school-based education, he learned traditional Gaelic ways through time spent with community elders on his mail route.[43] Watson gives an account of how MacNeil placed this traditional knowledge in a philosophical framework: "For Mickey, all subject matter was connected. Songs couldn't be sung without understanding their stories: dreams, forerunners, spirits, the evil-eye and divination were all based in philosophical explanations and reported on with examples of their significance to everyday life."[44]

Watson's description of MacNeil indicates that he can be considered a "star informant," a term coined by Kenneth Goldstein in 1964. A star informant is someone who is "knowledgeable, eloquent, and willing to help with the task of elucidating their culture." Star informants also "often occupy a somewhat distant or peripheral position in society" and therefore are "in a genuinely good position for detached observation."[45] It is certainly true that MacNeil was known as a local "character." In the article written in tribute to MacNeil after his death, Watson includes a picture of MacNeil with the caption: "Migi Bean Nilleig, standing beside his famous 'lemon' car. In 1993, Migi painted lemons on his car after a dispute with a local car dealer over servicing, an incident given national media coverage."[46] In an interview with Watson published in the tribute article, MacNeil expresses a keen awareness of language and cultural change in his community and the forces behind it. When asked for his opinion about the cause of the sharp decline of Gaelic in Cape Breton, he replies: "Uell, tha mi creidsinn a' rud a thug oirr' a dhol sios gur e dìreach nach do thuig 'ad cho prìseal 's a bha i an toiseach" (Well, I believe that the thing that has made it [Gaelic] go down is that in the beginning they didn't understand how valuable it was).[47] Implicit in this comment is that MacNeil appreciates the value of his native language and is therefore eager to share his repertoire of local Gaelic *dualchas* (tradition) with a sympathetic listener such as Watson. MacNeil's loyalty to and preference for his native Gaelic is also demonstrated in his answer to Watson's question: "Dé 's fhearr leibh fhéin, stòiridh a chluinnteil anns a' Ghàidhlig na anns a' Bheurla?" (Which would you prefer, hearing a story in English or Gaelic?). MacNeil replies: "O, a' Ghàidhlig, a' Ghàidhlig, a' Ghàidhlig, a' Ghàidhlig, a' Ghàidhlig. Dè blas? Dè blas?" (O, Gaelic, Gaelic, Gaelic, Gaelic, Gaelic. What taste? What taste?).[48] The word *blas* (taste) has connotations of quality and positive aesthetic judgment.[49]

The following version of Christ and the hens is one of a number of apocryphal Gaelic tales recorded from MacNeil.[50]

> Mar bu trice, bhiodh ise [Muire] a' toirt leathse Crìosda, bha e 'na phàisde, ann am bascaid mar gum biodh 'tighinn o 'n stòr. Ach anisd, chuir i [Muire] triop a' falach e ann an coirce, 's thàinig na cearcan 's sgrìob 'iad far a' robh an coirce 's leig iad faicinn. Ach dè rinn na geòidh, thàinig 'ad sin anuas 's sgaoil 'ad an ìtean amach 's chuir 'ad a' sin mu chuairt. An fheadhainn a bha lagh aca 'son marbhadh a dhianamh, uell, cha rachadh aca air fhaicinn 's cha deach Crìosda bho na geòidh.
>
> Uell anisd, a' rud a chaidh a dhianamh … Dh'fhàg Crìosda seo mar shùileachan. Ged nach tigeadh ach a' fras a bu shuaraich' agus a' chearc – bi i muigh – toisichidh i ruith, ach nuair a bhuaileas beagan dheth oirre, tha i 'stad. 'S ma tha i 'dol a stad an àite sam bith, stadaidh i far am bi an t-uist' a' doirteadh oirre. Stadaidh i aig ceann an taighe no fo 'n t-sruth far am bi an t-uiste. Bi i na gioban truagh gu siorraidh nuair a shileas i. Ach gun dug e seo dha na geòidh, ged a bhiodh e air a' chuan geamhradh no samhradh nach biodh e fluich no fuar.
>
> The Blessed Virgin Mary would usually take Christ with her, when he was an infant, in a basket, as though she were coming from the store. Now, one time she hid him in [a pile of] oats, and the chick-

> ens came and scratched where the oats were, and revealed him. But what did the geese do but come down and spread out their wings around him. Those enforcing the law couldn't see him, and Christ stayed put with the geese.
>
> Well, the thing that was done ... Christ left this as a warning. Even though the slightest shower should come when the chicken is outside, the chicken will start running. But when a little rain strikes her, she will stop. And if she's going to stop any place at all, she'll stop where the rain pours on her. She'll stop at the corner of the house, or anywhere the rain is flowing. She will always be a bedraggled heap when it rains. But he gave this to the geese, although he should be on the ocean in the winter or summer, he wouldn't be wet or cold.[51]

Although the content of MacNeil's tale is almost identical to that of MacDonald's version, the context in which the two storytellers place the tale is very different. While MacDonald distances himself and his community from the tale by labelling it an old wives' tale and explaining that apocryphal tales of its kind were forbidden, MacNeil connects the tale with the everyday experiences of his contemporaries through the homely detail of the infant Christ being carried in a basket by his mother "as though she was coming from the store."[52]

RELIGION AND DIFFERING ATTITUDES TO APOCRYPHAL TALES

MacNeil's and MacDonald's differing approaches, as well as MacNeil's comments about his perception of the value of Gaelic language and culture, reflect the accepted understanding of the different approaches members of Catholic and Presbyterian Gaelic communities took to Gaelic cultural expression in the nineteenth and twentieth centuries. As Kennedy asserts:

> Where the two churches differed most significantly from the early 19th century on was in the treatment of Gaelic secular culture – the songs, stories, folk beliefs, and most especially, the music and dance pastimes of the Gaels. Regrettably, a vast array of Gaelic tradition was identified as sinful in this era of heightened religious sentiment and very actively discouraged, especially in Protestant communities.[53]

However, a further account collected on the Catholic island of Eriskay reveals that Catholic and Presbyterian Gaels did not always adhere to the accepted dichotomy in their attitudes toward apocryphal tales.

The tale of Christ and the beetles is discussed in a recording of Donald MacInnes (Dòmhnall MacAonghais) (d. 1956) made by Calum Iain MacLean (1915–1960) of the School of Scottish Studies in 1953.[54] MacLean prompts MacInnes with a summary of a version of the story in which the *daolag* (beetle) betrays Christ's whereabouts but the *dealan-dè* (butterfly) remains loyal. MacInnes responds that he has heard the tale, but rather than retelling it in full, he gives a seemingly candid opinion of tales of this kind: "Ò, chuala mi an stòiridh a bha sin, math gu leòr. Agus 's ann aig seann daoine a chuala mi i cuideachd. Tha iad cho *stupid* 's cho *nonsen*[*s*]*ical* ged dh'innseadh iad na stòiridhean a bha sin, tà, co-dhiù. Ach na dhèoidh sin, bha fios aca gun robh Crìosta ann"[55] (Oh, I heard that story, all right. And it was from the old people that I heard it too. They're so stupid and nonsensical, but they would tell those stories anyway. But despite that, they knew that Christ existed). It appears that MacInnes was referring to stories such as this as "stupid," rather than to the people who told them. His commentary may be considered to be out of keeping with the accepted view of attitudes toward apocryphal tales in Catholic communities, in that it suggests that a Catholic storyteller's relationship to apocryphal tales was not always a straightforwardly credulous one.

Rather than a strict, religiously aligned model of differing attitudes toward apocryphal tales, what is needed is a nuanced understanding of the relationship between the storyteller, the story, the audience, and the community in which the storyteller is based. Margaret Read MacDonald explains that "the story format provides a vehicle for talking without owning one's words" and that this can be seen as one of the primary functions of storytelling.[56] MacInnes, in his commentary, explicitly distances himself from the tale through a derogatory evaluation of it, much like Roderick MacDonald in North Uist does. However, Margaret Read MacDonald also highlights additional factors that come into play during the storytelling event: that stories may serve to express a world view and that the telling of a tale is affected by the audience's response.[57] It may be that in telling the tale to a university-educated collector, originally from a Protestant background, who was recording the tale for a similarly educated audience of outsiders, MacInnes gauged his audience's possible evaluation of the tale as "stupid" and endeavoured to disassociate himself from the world view that such a tale implies. MacInnes's evaluation of the tale might have been quite different had he been telling it in the setting of a local *taigh-cèilidh*, with an audience of community members whose understanding of the tale would be similar to his own. It is impossible to say this for certain, of course, but few twentieth-century Gaelic speakers would have been unaware of the educated elite's long history of deriding Gaelic culture. This may have coloured MacInnes's responses, even to a sympathetic interlocutor like MacLean, and predicated his use of English terms to denigrate the tale.

The widely accepted dichotomy of attitudes toward Gaelic cultural expression in Catholic and Protestant communities appears also to have influenced scholars' patterns of collecting, which has resulted in apocryphal tales mainly being recorded in Catholic communities. Maighread Challan highlights the self-fulfilling pattern of mid-twentieth-century folklore collecting in the Outer Hebrides. When tradition bearers who could be deemed star informants were discovered in South Uist and Barra, collectors tended to remain in these communities, and as a result, limited collecting was done in North Uist.[58] Challan also suggests that this pattern of collecting was influenced by the idea that Presbyterian evangelism had extinguished what remained of traditional folklore in the Protestant islands.[59] She cites a 1988 recording of North Uist native and School of Scottish Studies collector Donald Archie MacDonald (1928–1999): "We had been more or less fed by the doctrine that tradition had survived in the Catholic islands and not on the Presbyterian islands and here was all that stuff lying, not as immediately accessible on the surface, but just below the surface from the Presbyterian communities."[60] This investigation has borne out MacDonald's comments. It does appear that Gaelic apocryphal *seanchas* was more prevalent in nineteenth- and twentieth-century Catholic communites than in Presbyterian ones. However, apocryphal *seanchas* did exist in Presbyterian communities during this time period, and although it may be harder to locate, this material is significant and should not be passed over. The prevalence of apocryphal *seanchas* in Catholic communities in comparison to their Presbyterian counterparts may also be exaggerated due to accepted notions of where material was to be found and subsequent folklore collecting patterns.

CONCLUSION

Through this investigation of a selection of Gaelic etiological apocryphal tales concerning betraying beetles, guarding geese, and drenched hens collected from twentieth-century Gaelic tradition bearers in the Uists, Barra, and Cape Breton, it has been shown that it is important to consider both the content of Gaelic apocryphal tales and how they are framed by the storytellers. What a *seanchaidh* says about apocryphal tales may reveal attitudes toward a community's beliefs about religion and folklore that may or may not support established narratives. The relations among the storyteller, the tale, community religious belief, the audience, and folklore collection practices is a complicated one, yet careful investigation of each aspect of these relations may reveal important insights into the Gaelic oral tradition in both Catholic and Presbyterian communities.

NOTES

Many thanks to Dr Sìm Innes and Mr Gillebrìde Mac 'IlleMhaoil of Celtic and Gaelic, University of Glasgow, for their assistance with this chapter. I would also like to acknowledge the invaluable work of collecting and sharing Cape Breton Gaelic *seanchas* undertaken by Jim Watson (1949–2018) of Baile nan Gàidheal / the Highland Village Museum.

1 Bowman, "Folk Religion," 91, 93. See also Utley, "Bible," 12.
2 Ó hÓgáin, *Lore of Ireland*, 299–300.
3 Shaw, "Dà Exempla," 115.
4 Ibid.
5 Shaw, "Sgeulachd," 101–3; Shaw, "Dà Exempla," 116.
6 Innes, "Cràbhachd," 139–47; McKenna, *Aithdioghluim Dána*, 112.
7 Joseph D. Small asserts that the Westminster Confession of Faith (1647) is "the most widely embraced confession among Presbyterian churches": "Presbyterian Churches," 980. In an account of nineteenth-century Highland evangelicalism, Allan MacColl states that "every ordained minister and lay office-bearer in both the Established and Free Churches in this period was obliged to subscribe to the Westminster Confession of Faith": *Land*, 59. A description of the role of the Westminster Confession of Faith in the Free Presbyterian Church of Scotland can be found in the *Catechism of the History and Principles of the Free Presbyterian Church of Scotland*, 9–11. For an

account of Presbyterianism in Nova Scotia in the nineteenth and twentieth centuries, see Campbell and MacLean, *Beyond the Atlantic Roar*, 193–236.

8 *Confession of Faith*, 5.

9 As Ted Campbell explains, "it is characteristic of historic Protestant churches to insist that the Bible is the sole, final authority for faith and for the reform of the church (thus *sola scriptura*, 'by scripture alone')": "Protestantism," 989.

10 Parman, *Scottish Crofters*, 133, 150.

11 Challan, *Air Bilean an t-Sluaigh*, 55.

12 *Catechism of the Council of Trent*, 8. See also *Catechism of the Catholic Church*, paragraphs 74–90.

13 *Aithghearradh an Teagasg Chriosda*, 5.

14 Bruford and MacDonald, *Scottish Traditional Tales*, 464.

15 For biographical information about Nan MacKinnon, see MacKinnon, *Tales*, 2–9.

16 SSS SA1965.18.B4. Unless otherwise stated, all Gaelic transcriptions and English translations are by the author.

17 See http://www.tobarandualchais.co.uk/en/person/3135, accessed 4 September 2018.

18 SSS SA1962.06.A18b.

19 The place and date of collection are suggested by the surrounding material in Fr Allan's notebook. The preceding two pages contain a Gaelic religious verse, "Duan an Dòmhnaich," collected in 1887 and attributed to a Mrs McCormack of North Lochboisdale: CW 58A, 18v–19r; Flòraidh Komori, "Pàipearan Mhgr Ailein (16)," *Am Pàipear*, October 2003, 14. Following Fr Allan's version of the tale of Christ and the beetle are blessings collected from Smercleit, South Uist, in 1887: CW 58A, 20r; Flòraidh Komori, "Pàipearan Mhgr Ailein (17)," *Am Pàipear*, November 2003, 14.

20 MacDonald includes an alternative version here as well: "Tri di-haoine an deigh cheile, cuimhnich an de a bhradag" (Three Fridays after another, since the day; remember, woman): CW 58A, 19v.

21 CW 58A, 19v.

22 Carmichael, *Carmina Gadelica*, 188. Questions have been raised about the reliability of material found in *Carmina Gadelica*. See Black, "I thought he made it all up."

23 Ibid., 188–91. The evidence Carmichael found in Barra of belief of the salvific efficacy of killing beetles is also similar to Fr Allan's account. In a note dated 1901 he writes that "boys from the Isle of Barra/Barraigh believe that if they take 'nine nines of heads' off a beetle then they will not

go to 'the aite s miosa [the worst place, i.e. Hell] with teeth'" (CW 110/35, 14r).

24 Carmichael, *Carmina Gadelica*, 248. Here, as throughout this chapter, the original Gaelic and English orthography of written sources has been preserved.

25 Ibid., 381.

26 Carmichael illustrates this in an account of the challenges he faced when collecting information in the Ness area of Lewis: "It was with extreme difficulty that I could obtain any information on the subject of my inquiry, because it related to the foolish past rather than to the sedate present, to the secular affairs rather than to the religious life of the people": *Carmina Gadelica*, xxxiii.

27 Although the informant was from Protestant North Uist, the surname MacRury does not clearly indicate a religious affiliation. Parish marriage records from the 1820–55 period in North Uist, Benbecula, and South Uist list the majority of marriages involving a party with the surname MacRury as occurring in Protestant churches, although there are three MacRurys from Torlum, Benbecula, who married in the Catholic parish of Ardkenneth, South Uist, during this period: Lawson, *Index*, 19 (North Uist); 32 (South Uist).

28 See ATU 750E, "The Flight into Egypt," a subset of the "God Rewards and Punishes" tale type, for mention of the beetle as a betrayer of the Holy Family, as well as references to other versions of the tale documented in areas throughout Europe and featuring various persons and creatures as helpers or betrayers: Uther, *Types*, 399–400.

29 See M'Clintock, "Beasts," 78–9. Seán Ó Súilleabháin gives a version of an apocryphal tale concerning insects and the miraculous growth of corn that is strikingly similar to the Hebridean versions above, with the added variation of the earwig betraying Christ along with the cockroach: *Miraculous Plenty*, 37. Ó Súilleabháin notes that this version was collected from a County Mayo informant and that "this story is very common in Ireland and in other countries in Europe": ibid., 255. A similar regional English tradition concerning a species of beetle is cited by Anthony Swindell: "In Derbyshire, the killing of the devil's-head beetle is adjured, as it was the creature that betrayed Jesus' whereabouts in the garden to Judas": "British and Irish," 190. Swindell's source is Hope, "Some Derbyshire Proverbs," 280. The association of Christ with the scarab beetle (another name for the *ceàrr-dubhan* [dung beetle]) in the writings of several early Christian authors suggests that the tale of Christ and the beetles may be rooted in earlier Christian traditions. According to Yves Cambefort, authors such as Saint Ambrose and Saint Augustine referred to the scarab beetle as a type of Christ, based

on the Greek version of the Old Testament Book of Habakkuk 2:11: "For the stone shall cry out of the wall, and the beetle out of the timber shall answer it": "Beetles."

30 MacDonald, "Criosda," 14–15.

31 NicLeòid, "Ruairidh na Càrnaich."

32 Ibid.

33 Ibid. There are forty items from Roderick MacDonald in the *Tobar an Dualchais* online sound archive, including stories, songs, and traditional cures. These were collected in the 1950s and '60s by John MacInnes and Donald Archie MacDonald of the School of Scottish Studies. See http://www.tobarandualchais.co.uk/en/person/7846, accessed 4 September 2018.

34 MacDonald, "Criosda," 14–15; translated by Angus John MacDonald.

35 Ibid., 15.

36 SSS SA1958.171.A3.

37 Watson, "How the Geese," 25.

38 Watson, "Migi Bean Nìlleig," 14; Dunn, *Highland Settler*, 25.

39 Kennedy, *Gaelic Nova Scotia*, 25. Kennedy cites an anecdote from Rod C. MacNeil of Barra Glen (near Iona), who, when visiting the Isle of Barra for the first time, was asked how long he had been away from Barra. His answer was "two hundred years" (131).

40 Ibid., 24–5. Barra people first settled around Lake Bras d'Or in 1802 (24).

41 Campbell, *Songs*, 29.

42 Watson, "Migi Bean Nìlleig," 14. There are six items from Migi Bean Nìlleig in St Francis Xavier University's Cape Breton Folklore Collection; these consist of songs and supernatural tales collected by John Shaw: CBFC tapes 331.3/A, 332/A02, 332/A03, 332.3/A, 333/A02, and 342/A03.

43 Watson, "Migi Bean Nìlleig," 14.

44 Ibid.

45 Cashman et al., Introduction, 11–12.

46 Watson, "Migi Bean Nìlleig," 14.

47 Ibid., translated by Watson.

48 Ibid., translated by Watson.

49 These connotations of the word *blas* have been explored in Falzett, "Tighinn o'n Cridhe."

50 MacNeil's apocryphal tales feature Biblical figures and Catholic saints. See, for example, "An Duais a Thug Crìosda dha 'n Bhoireannach Bhochd" (How Jesus Rewarded the Poor Woman) and "Nuair a Rinn Iosa Céilidh air Calum Cille" (When Jesus visited St Columba), in Watson, "Bloigheagan," 13.

51 Watson, "How the Geese," 25, translated by Watson.

52 This ambivalent use of a traditional tale has been noted before. See, for instance, Joan Radner's examination of the tale "The Woman Who Went to

Hell" as told by the famous Irish storyteller Peig Sayers and by her son Michael, which demonstrates that the same story can be used to carry two directly opposing messages, depending on who is telling it: "Woman," 112.

53 Kennedy, *Gaelic Nova Scotia*, 126.

54 SSS SA1953.38.A4. MacInnes was born in Eriskay and lived in North Glendale, South Uist. For biographical information about Calum MacLean, see Henderson, "Calum MacLean."

55 SSS SA 1953.38.A4.

56 MacDonald, "Fifty Functions," 409.

57 Ibid., 413, 414.

58 Challan, *Air Bilean an t-Sluaigh*, 5–6.

59 Ibid., 6.

60 Ibid., 6. For biographical information, see Ian A. Fraser, "Donald Archie MacDonald," *The Herald* (Glasgow), 27 July 1999, 16. Donald Meek also states that "the collection of oral traditional material was more actively pursued in the Catholic communities than the Protestant ones in the earlier part of this [the twentieth] century" and that this imbalance has contributed to the notion that Gaelic oral tradition is more prevalent in Catholic areas: *The Scottish Highlands*, 53.

BIBLIOGRAPHY

Aithghearradh an Teagasg Chriosda. Diocese of Antigonish, n.d.

Black, Ronald. "'I Thought He Made It All Up': Context and Controversy." In *The Life and Legacy of Alexander Carmichael*, ed. Dòmhnall Uilleam Stiùbhart, 57–81. Port of Ness: Islands Book Trust, 2008.

Bowman, Marion. "Folk Religion in Newfoundland: The Unauthorized Version." *London Journal of Canadian Studies* 9 (1993): 87–97.

Bruford, Alan, and Donald A. MacDonald. *Scottish Traditional Tales*. Edinburgh: Polygon, 1994.

Cambefort, Yves. "Beetles as Religious Symbols." *Cultural Entomology Digest* 2 (February 1994). https://www.insects.orkin.com/ced/issue-2/beetles-as-religious-symbols.

Campbell, D., and R.A. MacLean. *Beyond the Atlantic Roar: A Study of the Nova Scotia Scots*. Toronto: McClelland and Stewart, 1974.

Campbell, John L. *Songs Remembered in Exile*. Aberdeen: Aberdeen University Press, 1990.

Campbell, Ted. "Protestantism." In *Christianity: The Complete Guide*, ed. John Bowden, 987–92. London: Continuum, 2005.

Carmichael, Alexander. *Carmina Gadelica*, vol. 2. Edinburgh: Oliver and Boyd, [1900] 1928.

Cashman, Ray, Tom Mould, and Pravina Shukla. Introduction to *The Individual and Tradition: Folkloric Perspectives*, ed. Ray Cashman, Tom Mould, and Pravina Shukla, 1–26. Bloomington: Indiana University Press, 2011.

Catechism of the Catholic Church. Ottawa: Canadian Conference of Catholic Bishops, 1994.

Catechism of the Council of Trent for Parish Priests, trans. John A. McHugh, O.P. and Charles J. Callan, O.P. New York: Joseph F. Wagner, [1934] 1947.

A Catechism of the History and Principles of the Free Presbyterian Church of Scotland, 1942–43, rev. ed. Religion and Morals Committee of the Free Presbyterian Church of Scotland, 2013.

Challan, Maighread. *Air Bilean an t-Sluaigh: Sealladh air Leantalachd Beul-Aithris Ghàidhlig Uibhist a Tuath*. Belfast: Cló Ollscoil na Banríona, 2012.

The Confession of Faith. Edinburgh: Blackwood, 1928.

Dunn, Charles W. *Highland Settler: A Portrait of the Scottish Gael in Cape Breton and Eastern Nova Scotia*. Wreck Cove: Breton Books, [1953] 1991.

Falzett, Tiber. "'Tighinn o'n Cridhe' – 'Coming from the Centre': An Ethnography of Sensory Metaphor on Scottish Gaelic Communal Aesthetics." PhD diss., University of Edinburgh, 2015.

Henderson, Hamish. "Calum MacLean 1915–60." *Tocher* 39 (1985): 81–8.

Hope, R.C. "Some Derbyshire Proverbs and Sayings." *Folk-Lore Journal* 2, no. 9 (1884): 278–80.

Innes, Sìm Roy. "Cràbhachd do Mhoire Òigh air a' Ghàidhealtachd sna Meadhan-Aoisean Anmoch, le Aire Shònraichte do Leabhar Deadhan Lios Mòir." PhD diss., University of Glasgow, 2010.

Kennedy, Michael. *Gaelic Nova Scotia: An Economic, Cultural, and Social Impact Study*. Halifax: Nova Scotia Museum, 2002.

Lawson, Bill. *Index to the Marriages (Recorded and Unrecorded) in the Parish of South Uist (including Benbecula) Inverness-shire 1820–1855*. Northton: Bill Lawson, 1995.

– *Index to the Marriages (Recorded and Unrecorded) in the Parish of North Uist 1820–1855*. Northton: Bill Lawson, 1998.

MacColl, Allan, W. *Land, Faith and the Crofting Community*. Edinburgh: Edinburgh University Press, 2006.

MacDonald, Angus John. "Criosda 's na Cearcan 's na Tunnagan / Christ and the Hens and the Ducks." *Tocher* 1 (Spring 1971): 14–15.

MacDonald, Margaret Read. "Fifty Functions of Storytelling." In *Traditional Storytelling Today: An International Sourcebook*, ed. Margaret Read MacDonald, 408–15. Chicago: Fitzroy Dearborn, 1999.

MacKinnon, Nan. *Tales, Songs, Tradition from Barra and Eriskay*. Castlebay: Comunn Eachdraidh Bharraidh, 1993.

McKenna, Lambert, S.J. *Aithdioghluim Dána: A Miscellany of Irish Bardic Poetry, Historical and Religious, Including the Historical Poems of the Duanaire in the Yellow Book of Lecan*, vol. 2. Irish Texts Society 40. Dublin: Irish Texts Society, 1940.

M'Clintock, Letitia. "Beasts, Birds, and Insects in Irish Folk-lore." *The Eclectic Magazine of Foreign Literature, Science and Art*, n.s., 31, no. 1 (1880): 78–82.

Meek, Donald E. *The Scottish Highlands: The Churches and Gaelic Culture*. Geneva: World Council of Churches Publications, 1996.

NicLeòid, Linda. "Ruairidh na Càrnaich (1883–1970): Seanchaidh, Seinneadair agus Eòlaiche-Sprèidh Ainmeil à Uibhist a Tuath." *Seanchas Gaelic Jukebox Blog*. Dachaigh airson Stòras na Gàidhlig (DASG), University of Glasgow. 26 April 2016. https://dasg.ac.uk/seanchas/ruairidh-na-carnaich-1883-1970-seanchaidh-seinneadair-agus-eolaiche-spreidh-ainmeil-a-uihist-a-tuath-le-linda-nicleoid-uibhist-a-tuathglaschu.

Ó hÓgáin, Dáithí. *The Lore of Ireland: An Encyclopedia of Myth, Legend, and Romance*. Cork: Collins, 2006.

Ó Súilleabháin, Seán. *Miraculous Plenty: Irish Religious Folktales and Legends*, trans. William Caulfield. Dublin: Comhairle Bhéaloideas Éireann, 2011.

Parman, Susan. *Scottish Crofters: A Historical Ethnography of a Celtic Village*. Fort Worth: Holt, Rinehart and Winston, 1990.

Radner, Joan. "'The Woman Who Went to Hell': Coded Values in Irish Folk Narrative." *Midwestern Folklore* 15 (1989): 109–17.

Shaw, John. "Dà Exempla à Ceap Breatainn." In *Atlantic Currents: Essays on Lore, Literature and Language*, ed. B. Almqvist, L. MacMathuna, S. MacMathuna, S. Watson, and C. MacCarthaigh, 115–23. Dublin: University College Dublin Press, 2012.

– "'Sgeulachd a' Chait Bhig 's a Chait Mhóir': A Gaelic Variant of 'The Two Travellers.'" *Scottish Studies* 30 (1991): 93–106.

Small, Joseph D. "Presbyterian Churches." In *Christianity: The Complete Guide*, ed. John Bowden, 979–81. London: Continuum, 2005.

Swindell, Anthony. "British and Irish." In *The Bible in Folklore Worldwide*, ed. Eric Ziolkowski, 183–210. Berlin: de Gruyter, 2017.

Uther, Hans-Jörg. *The Types of International Folktales: A Classification and Bibliography*, vol. 1. Helsinki: Academia Scientiarum Fennica, 2004.

Utley, Francis Lee. "The Bible of the Folk." *California Folklore Quarterly* 4, no. 1 (1945): 1–17.

Watson, Jim. "Bloigheagan do Sheanachas o Mhigi Bean Nìlleig." *Am Bràighe* 5, no. 3 (Winter 1998): 11, 13.
– "How the Geese Saved Jesus." *Am Bràighe* 3, no. 4 (Spring 1996): 25.
– "Migi Bean Nìlleig: Mar Chuimhneachan 1917–1995." *Am Bràighe* 2, no. 4 (Spring 1995): 14–16.

ARCHIVAL COLLECTIONS

Cape Breton Folklore Collection (CBFC), Angus L. MacDonald Library, St Francis Xavier University.
Carmichael-Watson Collection (CW), University of Edinburgh Library.
School of Scottish Studies (SSS), University of Edinburgh.

15

Annie Johnston and Nova Scotia

Lorrie MacKinnon

Ken Nilsen was a dear friend and collaborator. We often spoke about "doing something" about Annie Johnston and her Nova Scotia connections. I offer this in tribute to Ken.

Annie Johnston (Annag Aonghais Chaluim Bhàin 'ic Dhòmhnaill 'ic Chaluim) (*c.* 1889–1963) was one of the great Gaelic tradition bearers of the island of Barra, Scotland.[1] She spent much of her life sharing traditional stories and songs with anyone and everyone who was interested in Gaelic, including academics, students of Gaelic, and collectors such as Marjorie Kennedy-Fraser, John Lorne Campbell, and Alan Lomax. Many of her stories and songs were published, and she presented some of them at the 1953 International Gaelic Conference in Stornoway.[2] She also had deep and abiding connections with the Gaels of Nova Scotia. These connections spanned from the 1920s until her death in 1963 and resulted in numerous letters to Nova Scotian correspondents and contributions to Nova Scotian publications. In 1954, Annie made the journey across the Atlantic Ocean, where she visited widely, was received into many homes, and even took on the role of folklore collector, making audio recordings of some of the stories and songs of the Canadian Gaelic tradition bearers she met. It is my intention in this chapter to trace Annie's transatlantic journey and shine some light on her Nova Scotian correspondents, hosts, informants, and friends.

NOVA SCOTIAN CONNECTIONS

The earliest connection seems to date from 1928, when the Clan MacNeil Association of North America sent assistance to the

Annie Johnston, Fr Roddy MacDonald, Margaret Fay Shaw, Sheila Lockett (secretary), and John Lorne Campbell at Canna House (© Canna Archives, National Trust for Scotland).

agricultural fair in Barra. This prompted a Gaelic letter in thanks from Annie.[3] John A. MacDougall (1861–1944) of Glace Bay, Nova Scotia, was a member of the executive of the Clan MacNeil Association and also very involved in Gaelic activities in Nova Scotia; this included playing an active role in the Scottish Catholic Society.[4] This is likely how Annie's letter came to be published on the front page of the January 1929 issue of *Mosgladh,* the society's journal. Thus began a correspondence that lasted until MacDougall's death in 1944,[5] during which time several contributions by Annie appeared in *Mosgladh*.[6]

In 1941, with the encouragement of John Lorne Campbell (1906–1996), Annie wrote a letter to Msgr P.J. Nicholson (1887–1965), originally from Beaver Cove, Nova Scotia, but then a professor of physics at St Francis Xavier University (StFX) in Antigonish. He was also the editor of the Gaelic column in the Antigonish weekly newspaper, the *Casket*, titled "Achadh nan Gaidheal," which ran from 1920 until 1944, when he became president of the university.[7] This column was a mix of previously published items, stories and songs collected by Nicholson, and contributions from readers. Msgr Nicholson published several items sent to him by Annie.[8] They believed there was a family connection between them, as Msgr Nicholson's mother was a Johnston with roots in Barra, but they never determined exactly what the relationship was.[9]

In several of her letters to Msgr Nicholson, Annie references Canadians whom she met in Barra during the Second World War and with whom she continued to correspond; for example, there are references to Gregory MacKenzie of Christmas Island, Alasdair MacKenzie (who was related to Msgr Nicholson and visited Barra on his two days' leave), and Henry MacNeil (*c.* 1917–1982) from Sydney (whose mother was a Johnston from Beaver Cove).[10] She also maintained a correspondence with well-known Gaelic scholar and bard Angus Y. MacLellan (1878–1960), as Msgr Nicholson acknowledges in a 1948 reply: "It is interesting to know that Gregory MacKenzie is keeping in touch with you. Two weeks ago I dropped in on another of your correspondents, Angus Y. MacLellan. I found him in good health and spirits. He retired as lighthouse keeper on Margaree Island a few years ago because of ill-health. His memory has been quite impaired, but he remains a delightful host at a ceilidh."[11] The correspondence between Annie and Angus Y. would have been quite interesting, steeped as both were in traditional Gaelic culture, but it has not been archived and may no longer be extant. Angus Y. was best known for his song, "An Innis Aigh" (The Happy Island).[12]

In 1948, Msgr Nicholson and StFX history professor Fr Malcolm MacDonell (1919–2015) received a grant from the Carnegie Corporation to attend the Conference of Empire Universities at Oxford in July of that year.[13] They took the opportunity of this transatlantic journey to visit Annie in Barra, and had tea at her home, Taigh a' Ghlinne (the Glen House). They had also hoped to visit her brother Calum in Edinburgh, where he was then residing, but when they stopped in on a Saturday night, he had gone to confession. In a rare English-language letter dated 7 March 1949, Annie notes, "I was delighted to get your letter with all your interesting news. I knew from the Radio and from letters from different people of your 'adventures' after leaving Barra. My brother Calum was devastated with grief at having missed you. He could talk of little else while he was home for his annual holiday in August."[14]

ANNIE JOHNSTON IN NOVA SCOTIA

Over the years Annie must have expressed a desire to visit Nova Scotia, as we see this mentioned in the correspondence between Campbell and Msgr Nicholson.[15] Annie's wish was fulfilled in 1954. The genesis of her own trip was one taken by three MacNeil relatives from Grand Narrows, all living in the United States – Dan MacNeil, an engineer in Boston, Rod MacNeil (1900–1973) in Pittsburgh, and Dan's son Dr Donald MacNeil – to Barra in 1951.[16] They must have met up with Annie there, perhaps having tea at Taigh a' Ghlinne, as Msgr Nicholson had done. Subsequently, Dan invited Annie to come to Nova Scotia and Boston. He had done very well in his profession, so he offered to pay for her trip.[17] Msgr Nicholson mentions the invitation in a letter to Annie dated 9 March 1954:

> A note just received from Canna states that the MacNeils are inviting you to Nova Scotia. I do hope you will be able to come. By this time you probably know that I shall be a pastor in Sydney on the last day of March and unfortunately my rectory has no guest room … Father MacKenzie whom you met in Barra years ago is situated about ten miles from my new rectory and he has lots of room. In fact I am sure we could easily find a dozen places where they will consider it a real privilege to have you call and stay just as long as it will suit you.[18]

Annie travelled by boat to Halifax and then made her way to Antigonish. As her letters show, she stayed at StFX's Gilmora Hall, which was a female students' residence as well as the home of the Congregation of Notre Dame. She was a guest of Sr St Veronica MacDonald (1888–1973), a professor of history at StFX and one of the early promoters of Gaelic there.[19] As a consequence of Sr St Veronica's vision for the future of the language, the first Chair in Celtic Studies at StFX, held by Professor Kenneth Nilsen, was established in her name. Annie had a great fondness for her, noting in her letters, for example, "nach i tha gasda da rireabh!" (isn't she kind!).[20]

From Antigonish Annie made her way to Cape Breton, driven by Fr John Angus Rankin and Sr Marion Power,[21] and stayed in Grand Narrows at the home of Dan MacNeil. She had a marvellous time, as she later relayed to Campbell in a letter to Canna dated 6 August 1954: "Cha robh a leithid de uine thoilichte aig duine riamh an aite s a bh'agamsa an Ceap Breatuinn, cha robh mionaid de uine agam le m'fhein on dh'eirinn moch air maduinn gus an rachainn don leapaidh moch an ath mhaduinn" [22] (No one ever had such a happy time as the time I had in Cape Breton, I never had a moment to myself from the time I awoke in the morning until the time I went to bed early the next morning).

Annie had opportunities to visit many Gaelic speakers while staying in Grand Narrows. Likely at the suggestion of Campbell, she accepted the loan of a tape recorder in Antigonish and recorded traditional material from some of the people she met.[23] One such visit was to Benacadie Glen, where she recorded Mrs Patterson (Ceiteag Ailean Bhragaidh) (1872–1964) singing the waulking song "A' Bhean Iadaich" (The Jealous Woman).[24] This is the only song that Annie mentions by name in her letters describing her trip, and she had a great interest in it. In fact, in 1939 she had helped American folklorist Paul Brewster, who was a doctoral student at that time, with his research into the story communicated in the song (ATU 780 "The Singing Bone"), sending him the verses that her mother had (seven couplets), as well as those held in manuscript by Keith Norman MacDonald (thirteen couplets).[25] She would have been interested that Mrs Patterson knew so many verses of the song (likely twenty-six couplets), as she noted to Brewster that "the story is still known in Barra but only fragments of the song."[26]

In her letter to Campbell of 6 August 1954, Annie also states that she taped Hugh MacKenzie (Eoghann Archie Sheumais 'ic Dhomhnaill 'ic Eachainn 'ic Gilleasbuig 'ic Fhionnlaidh 'ic Iain Buidhe nan Saighead) (1896–1971), who was from the Rear of Christmas Island but living at Grand Narrows at that time – Ken Nilsen would collect from Hugh's younger brother Archie Alec in 1993 in Halifax. She goes on to say that she hopes to record Frans Eachainn MacNeil (Frans Eachainn Ruaraidh Mòr 'ic Dhòmhnuill 'ic Ruaraidh) (1867–1954) the next week.[27] Frans was from Iona, Cape Breton, but had lived for thirty-two years in New Waterford, where he worked as a contractor.[28] He was noted for his store of genealogy and old stories. Annie recorded from him the story of how Calum Caimbeul of Barra came to Ceap Breatuinn.[29] Msgr Nicholson later noted to Campbell that "Annie Johnston brought him [Frans Eachainn] a hand-woven cravat when she came this way."[30]

Annie travelled to the Sydney area to meet with Frans Eachainn, and her stay in Sydney was memorable not only for her, but also for the people she encountered. Shortly before departing Grand Narrows, she explained to Campbell how she intended to get there: "bha duin' uasal coir a Sidni a coimhead orm agus thuirt e rium nan tiginn a dh'fhuireach do a thaigh-san gu'n toireadh France do m'ionnsaidh" (A lovely gentleman from Sydney came to see me and said that if I would come to stay with him that he would bring Frans to see me).[31] That man was James MacNeil (Jim Hughie mac Stephainn 'ic Alasdair 'ic Eachainn) (1889–1956) from Grass Cove. He was very active in the Scottish Catholic Society and had worked at Sydney Steel for forty years, starting as a clerk and ending as the Supervisor of Costs. He and his wife Elizabeth hosted Annie for over two weeks in late August. His grandson Vince MacLean remembers being kicked out of the house so that Annie could have his bed. Vince would take her to go shopping on the bus, and he recalls that there were many ceilidhs with good fiddlers, including his father Joe MacLean and Bill Lamey home from Boston. StFX Celtic professor and Gaelic folklore collector Major C.I.N. MacLeod (1913–1977) also came several times to visit her, as she was friends with his father Alasdair Mòr in Scotland.[32] This may be where MacLeod learned he ought to visit Hugh MacKenzie, Mrs Patterson, and Mr and Mrs Frank MacNeil (Big Frank), as Annie visited and recorded from all of these people.[33]

On 27 August 1954, Annie wrote again to Campbell from the MacNeil family home on Yendys Street in Sydney, telling him how she was getting on: "the kindness of the folk here is unwavering. It has to be experienced in order to be understood. My host and hostess Mr and Mrs Jim Hugh MacNeil – no connection – but they treat me as if I belonged here. Sr St Veronica at Antigonish was the same." She goes on to comment on the latest recordings she has made:

> I have been fortunate since coming to Sydney in meeting a grand family at Big Pond who have a wonderful store of "old country" songs. Mr and Mrs Frank MacNeil – great friends of Fr Stanley. I spent two evenings there and recorded some 7 or 8 songs. Fr

> Stanley was at the recordings and was so interested that he himself asked to be given the microphone and was as pleased as a baby with a new toy to hear his own voice coming back.[34]

In a subsequent letter dated 30 August 1954 she says, "Did I tell you how well I got along with Fr Stanley? I was shy about meeting him but he expressed such an interest in me so Frank MacNeil and his wife asked him to meet me when I was down there."[35] The family remembers that visit very clearly, especially that Annie arrived in a green car – likely Jim Hughie's car.[36]

All three of these new informants were located in Big Pond. Fr Stanley MacDonald (1882–1970) – Sr St Veronica's brother – was the parish priest there. Frank MacNeil (Big Frank; Frank Micheal) (1881–1961) was born at Big Pond and later moved to Sydney, where he worked as a tram car operator. After meeting and marrying his wife, Mary Ann MacIntyre (1878–1974), who was also working in Sydney, the couple moved back to Big Pond and farmed on land owned by her people. In addition to farming, Big Frank worked on the roads and as a flagman on the Bras d'Or Lakes in the winter, going across the ice and marking the way with felled trees. Frank and Mary Ann's house was a community gathering place, particularly on Sundays, when it would be full of people singing.[37]

Frank learned many of his songs from Mary Ann's aunt, who lived in Boston. Mary Ann didn't often sing the verses, but she knew all of the songs and if Frank made a mistake, she would correct him. Annie says of Mary Ann, "I found that Mrs Frank MacNeil knew nearly every Barra Oran Luaidh (waulking song) that I ever knew – some of them I'd forgotten."[38] Considering the large number of songs Annie knew, her praise of Mary Ann is high indeed.[39]

Annie also socialized with others while staying with Jim Hughie and Elizabeth MacNeil in Sydney. In a letter written to Msgr Nicholson after her return to Barra, she states:

> And who says I did not meet your sister? I had one of the happiest evenings of my life in the home of Mr and Mrs Hector MacLean, and I was told she was your sister. I was staying at the house of Mr and Mrs Jim Hughie MacNeil Sydney and one evening Mr Hector MacLean and his son-in-law Mr Gillis came to see me, and asked Mr and Mrs MacNeil and myself to ceilidh in their house. And

> what a ceilidh! There was "food in the eating place, drink in the drinking place and music in the listening place" and I could have stayed there forever.[40]

Hector MacLean (Hector Mick 'ic Dhomhnaill 'ic Eachainn 'ic Aonghais 'ic Iain 'ic Lachlainn 'ic Eoghainn 'ic Leathain) (1887–1972) was from Boisdale, Nova Scotia, but left there at the age of thirteen to work in the coal mines in Glace Bay. He initially boarded with a woman from Boisdale parish who told him about the Thompson and Sutherland Foundry in North Sydney, and so he moved there to work and kept working until the age of seventy-two. He married Msgr Nicholson's sister Catherine (Catherine nighean Sheorais mac Alasdair 'ic Iain 'ic Phadruig 'ic Iain 'ic Sheorais) (1881–1969) in 1913. Their home on Archibald Avenue in North Sydney was a regular ceilidh-house, full of visitors and music and Gaelic songs. "Mr. Gillis" was Ambrose Gillis (Ambrose mac Chaluim Eoghain 'ic Aonghais 'ic Chaluim 'ic Dhomhnaill 'ic Dhunnchaidh) (1913–1957), the son of the bard Calum Eoghain. That evening there were people there who had come up on the train from Boisdale, and one can imagine the house full of music and Gaelic songs.[41]

In early September, Annie travelled from Nova Scotia to Boston via Connecticut with Rod MacNeil.[42] She expressed her anticipation in a letter to Campbell dated 27 August 1954:

> From the news I get, the social "swirl" amongst Cape Bretoners living there will be as great as here. It seems that Boston is to Cape Breton what Glasgow is to the Highlands. If I can manage at all I'll go to Pittsburgh. Rod MacNeil, with whom I am to travel to Boston, works in Pittsburgh and may ask me to visit him there, though he has not yet done so. Mrs Byron, a niece of France Eachainn who lives in Connecticut has asked me to come and stay a week. She is arranging to have Ninian a Choddie and his family for me to meet them.[43]

Ninian a' Choddie was the youngest son of the Barra tradition bearer known as "the Coddy" (John MacPherson) (1876–1955).[44] A sailor, Ninian had gone ashore in the United States and married there.[45] The opportunity to meet with him would have been special for Annie, for they could visit after his long absence, and she could then carry news back to his father in Barra. Annie's time in the United States was not without sadness, however, as she learned of the death of Frans Eachainn while there:

> I heard before I left Boston about Frans Eachainn's death. I need not tell you how sorry I was about that, nor how much I felt I owed to those who had made it possible for me to meet him. Mrs Byron, his niece, told me that her sister, who had visited him in hospital, wrote her and told her that he had spoken about me there. I think he got some pleasure out of meeting someone from Barra. God rest him! He was a wonderful person.[46]

Annie did not arrive home from her trip until November 1954. She was supposed to come home by boat via Liverpool, but ended up travelling by plane due to a problem with the boat's engines.[47] The trip had been very meaningful to her, as she expressed in a letter to Msgr Nicholson on 1 December 1954:

> Chord mo chuairt rium na b'fhearr na rud sam bith a thachair orm riamh nam bheatha. Nuair bha mi an Caolas Nam Barrach, bhithinn uairean a cur na ceiste rium fhein, "Saoil an anns an t-Sithean a tha mi?" Bha mi cho sona sin! Bha a h-uile duine a thachair orm cho cairdeal is cho coibhneil is cho baigheil is ged thogteadh mi na measg chan iarrainn an t-aite fhagail.[48]

> I enjoyed my trip more than anything that had ever happened in my life. When I was at Grand Narrows I would be sometimes asking myself, "Do you think that I am in a fairy mound?" I was so content there! Everyone that came to see me was so friendly and so kind and so respectful that had I been raised among them I would not want to leave the place.

She kept up a wide correspondence after her 1954 trip and was planning to return in 1960, but she never got the chance. She had not seen the last of her Cape Breton friends, however. In 1958, Sr St Veronica and Sr Margaret MacDonell (b. 1920) made a lengthy trip to Scotland. Likely due to the hospitality received from Sr St Veronica in Antigonish, Annie came from Barra to Canna to meet them and escorted them over to South Uist. Sr Margaret, a native Gaelic speaker from Judique, Cape Breton, who would later become a professor of

Celtic at StFX, fondly remembers Annie sitting in the back seat of the car singing Gaelic songs with Scottish folklore collector Calum MacLean (1915–1960).[49]

After Sr Margaret's visit, she and Annie corresponded regularly, and when Dan MacNeil, who funded Annie's North American trip, passed away unexpectedly in 1959, Annie expressed her sorrow to Sr Margaret:

> Fhuair mi buile ghoirt nuair fhuair mi naigheachd bais Daniel MacNeil Boston a c[h]aochail gu grad air 1st Sept is e a cluich "golf" comhla ri cairdean. Is e Daniel a thug dhomhsa cothrom air a chuairt a ghabh mi gu Ceap Breatunn agus na Staitean Aonaichte agus a rinn iomadh coibhneas eile rium on am sin. Agus bha gach gnothach deiseil aige gus mi dhol thairis air an ath shamhradh, gus a bhi an lathair aig banais-tighe a bha e a dol a dheanamh anns an tigh bheag a bha e a cur air doigh dha fhein aig na Narrows.[50]

> I received a painful blow when I got the news of the death of Daniel MacNeil, Boston, who died suddenly on September 1st while playing golf with friends. It is Daniel that gave me the opportunity to come to Cape Breton and the States and he has done many other kindnesses for me since that time. And things were ready for me to go across next summer to be present at a house-wedding that he was going to have at the little house that he was getting ready for himself at the Narrows.

The cancelation of Annie's planned second Nova Scotian visit brought an end to thoughts of transatlantic journeying. She was likely unable to finance such a trip on her own. The responsibilities of home and her own failing health were also contributing factors.

CONCLUSION

It is hoped that a broader collection of Annie Johnston's correspondence and other writings will one day be published, either online or in book form, for her letters show the beauty of her Gaelic, her activity in the Gaelic world, and her sense of humour. Her observations about the people she met in Nova Scotia – some of whom later became correspondents – also merit further attention than I have been able to give them here. She noted many things in addition to their kindness and generosity, such as how people danced what seemed to her like Irish jigs and how they would come great distances to visit with her.[51] Her appreciation of all that the Gaelic world in Nova Scotia had to offer is worth consideration and reflection.

The following reminiscence by her niece, Annie Pheadair Kearney of Barra, nicely sums up Annie Johnston's relationship with the many Nova Scotia Gaels that were part of her life for thirty-five years:

> She spoke of her delight at the way those second and third generation Barra / Canadian / Americans had in many cases retained the Gaelic language and culture of the old country they had left in the 1920s and earlier. She wasn't one to wallow in sentimentality, but was touched by her meetings with those new Canadian and American emigrants and how they had held on, in difficult circumstances, to the roots of their early upbringing. Her Canadian and American trips made a lasting impact on Annie, creating vivid, happy memories for her which she talked about till her dying days.[52]

NOTES

I presented a version of this chapter at a symposium on 22 August 2018 at the twenty-eighth annual Féis an Eilein, the Gaelic cultural festival in Christmas Island, Nova Scotia. The symposium has been held every year since 2003 and has covered many different topics. The evening includes a mix of formal presentations and contributions by local tradition bearers. In 2008, for instance, the evening was a "mini-Rannsachadh" (research conference) that drew from the speakers at Rannsachadh na Gàidhlig 5, organized by Ken Nilsen at St Francis Xavier University in Antigonish that July. Ken was one of the participants in the symposium, speaking about Msgr Nicholson and his *Achadh nan Gaidheal* column, and he thoroughly enjoyed the event. I extend my deepest thanks to the organizers of Féis an Eilein for their support of these evenings. I also wish to thank the families of those whom Annie visited in 1954 for their help, Sr Margaret MacDonell for her interest and encouragement, Tony Kearney for his enthusiasm for the project, Fiona MacKenzie at Canna House, and Kathleen MacKenzie at the St Francis Xavier University Archives. I have not modified the text of transcriptions in any way. Unless otherwise stated, all translations are my own.

1 Annie styled herself this way in her first letter to Msgr Nicholson; see A. Johnston to Msgr P.J. Nicholson, 20 November 1941, RG 5/11/25517, Office of the President Fonds, StFX Archives. She was one of eight children born to Catrìona Aonghais 'ic Dhòmhnaill Mhòir MacNeil, originally of Sanntraigh, and Aonghas Chaluim Bhàin Johnston: Campbell, "Anna and Calum," 162–3. Her date of birth has been reported as 10 February 1886: "Contents," 210. This appears to be inaccurate, since she indicated in letters to Msgr Nicholson that she was twelve when her father died in 1901; see A. Johnston to Msgr P.J. Nicholson, 20 November 1941, RG 5/11/25517, and 7 March 1949, RG 5/11/25529, Office of the President Fonds, StFX Archives. Additionally, her grand-nephew Tony Kearney confirmed in a letter to the author dated 12 August 2018 that she was five years older than his grandmother, who was born in 1894.

2 *Tocher* 13 (Spring 1974) is a tribute to Annie and her brother Calum (also a respected tradition bearer). In the opening essay, J.L. Campbell outlines many of the collectors who were helped by Annie and Calum: "Anna and Calum," 162–5; see also Campbell, "Anna Nic Iain," 313–14. As an acknowledgment of the great help that Annie and Calum were to him, the second volume of his *Hebridean Folk Songs* is dedicated to them (as well as to tradition bearers Roderick MacKinnon and Mrs Neil Campbell). Annie's songs and tales appear in this and other collections, and she also submitted material to publications including *Béaloideas*, *Gairm*, and the *Casket* (Antigonish); see, for example, NicIain, "Toimhseachain"; NicIain, "Baird"; and Annag NicIain, "Murchadh Mac Bhria[i]n Garaidh," *Casket*, 6 November 1941, 8 (learned from Ealasaid Eachainn 'Illeasbuig of Castlebay, Barra). Annie's participation in the 1953 International Gaelic Conference in Stornaway is referenced in a letter to Msgr Nicholson: A. Johnston to Msgr P.J. Nicholson, Latha Nan Tri Righrean (Feast of the Three Kings, i.e., 6 January), 1954, MG 2/1/105, Patrick J. Nicholson Collection, StFX Archives.

3 NicIain, "Letter."

4 "Convention," 4; "News of the Councils," 1; "Notes," 50–1.

5 In a letter to Msgr Nicholson dated 15 May 1944, Annie notes "B'abhaist dhomh a bhi a faotainn fios an drasd agus a rithist o John A. MacDougall, Glace Bay – ach is fhada o nach cuala mi fios sam bith. An aithne dhuibh a bheil a beo fhathast? no bheil e tinn" (I used to be getting word now and again from John A. MacDougall, Glace Bay – but I haven't heard anything in a long time. Do you know if he is still alive? Or is he ill?): RG 5/11/25520, Office of the President Fonds, StFX Archives. MacDougall's death is acknowledged in a letter from Msgr Nicholson to J.L. Campbell: "You probably

know that [he] died this fall after months of acute suffering": 20 October 1944, RG 5/11/1603, StFX Archives.

6 See, for example, NicIain, "Second Letter"; "Poet Priest." Although the latter is unattributed, it is quite likely that Annie either contributed it or shared the contents in a letter to one of her correspondents, given her interest in Father MacMillan and his songs; see NicIain, "Baird."

7 Nilsen, "P.J. Nicholson," 315.

8 See, for example, Annag NicIain, "Murchadh Mac Bhria[i]n Garaidh," *Casket*, 6 November 1941, 8.

9 In a letter to Msgr P.J. Nicholson dated 20 November 1941, Annie elaborates how they are connected: RG 5/11/25517, Office of the President Fonds, StFX Archives; but in a subsequent letter to him dated 7 March 1949 she indicates that this is not correct: RG 5/11/25529, Office of the President Fonds, StFX Archives. In his letters to Msgr Nicholson, J.L. Campbell often refers to her as "your cousin Miss Annie Johnston"; see, for example, 24 August 1962, MG 2/1/49h, StFX Archives.

10 See, for example, A. Johnston to Msgr P.J. Nicholson, Latha nam Marbh (Day of the Dead, i.e., 1 November) 1944, RG 5/11/25521; and 18 November 1946, RG 5/11/6235, Office of the President Fonds, StFX Archives.

11 Msgr P.J. Nicholson to A. Johnston, 26 March 1948, RG 5/11/6237, Office of the President Fonds, StFX Archives.

12 This song has been published many times. See, for example, Creighton and MacLeod, *Gaelic Songs*, 46–7.

13 Msgr P.J. Nicholson to A. Johnston, 26 March 1948, RG 5/11/6237, Office of the President Fonds, StFX Archives: "A Conference of the Empire Universities will be held at Oxford between the 19th and 22nd [of July]. I had no thought of going until two weeks ago when an announcement came to me that most of the expense of the trip would be borne by a grant from the Carnegie Corporation, and now it looks as if this were a rare opportunity." Fr Malcolm MacDonell joined the history faculty at StFX in 1957: Cameron, *For the People*, 271.

14 A. Johnston to Msgr P.J. Nicholson, 7 March 1949, RG 5/11/2552, Office of the President Fonds, StFX Archives.

15 See, for example, Msgr P.J. Nicholson to J.L. Campbell, 29 May 1950, RG 5/11/25424, StFX Archives: "It is very interesting to hear that Miss Johnston is planning on coming to Nova Scotia. We shall do anything within reason to make her stay pleasant."

16 Msgr P.J. Nicholson notes to J.L. Campbell that they will be going to Scotland in late June: 9 May 1951, RG 5/11/25456, StFX Archives.

17 A. Johnston to Sr M. MacDonell, 24 November 1959, MG 116/2017-24-

2200/Annie Johnston, 1957–1963, Margaret MacDonell Fonds, StFX Archives; Rory MacNeil, nephew of Dan, in conversation with the author, 23 August 2018.

18 Msgr P.J. Nicholson to A. Johnston, 9 March 1954, MG 2/1/106, Patrick J. Nicholson Collection, StFX Archives.

19 Sr M. MacDonell in conversation with the author, 19 August 2018. Sr St Veronica was sister to Angus L. MacDonald (1890–1954), the former premier of the province, who had died suddenly that spring, and Fr Stanley MacDonald (1882–1970), parish priest in Big Pond when Annie visited.

20 A. Johnston to J.L. Campbell, 6 August 1954, CH2/2/1, NTS Canna Collection.

21 Sr M. MacDonell in conversation with the author, 19 August 2018.

22 A. Johnston to J.L. Campbell, 6 August 1954, CH2/2/1, NTS Canna Collection. Annie wrote this letter from Antigonish.

23 The tapes are in the NTS Canna Collection at Canna House. A list of all of the Nova Scotian material in the Canna Collection was prepared by Neil Fraser in 2004 and provided to me at that time by Canna House archivist Magda Sagarzazu. Cape Breton University's Beaton Institute also holds one tape of folklore collected by Annie: Sound and Moving Image Collection, Tape T-1646. This was donated by the family of Frank MacNeil, who had received it, at their request, from J.L. Campbell in the 1980s: Gordon and Patsy Gillis in conversation with the author, 10 August 2018.

24 A. Johnston to J.L. Campbell, 6 August 1954, CH2/2/1, NTS Canna Collection.

25 Brewster, "Two Gaelic Variants," 187; Uther, *Types*, 439–40.

26 Brewster, "Two Gaelic Variants," 187. The probable length of Mrs Patterson's version can be observed in Creighton and MacLeod, *Gaelic Songs*, 158–60. See also fourteen couplets from Mrs Patterson on Tape T-18 (collected 1963) at the Beaton Institute.

27 A. Johnston to J.L. Campbell, 6 August 1954, CH2/2/1, NTS Canna Collection. Ken Nilsen recorded the story of Iain Buidhe nan Saighead on video from Hugh's younger brother Archie Alec in 1993; see Nilsen, "Air Chéilidh," 14. A copy of the video was given to me by Archie Alec.

28 Written information from the obituary in the *Sydney Post-Record* of 27 September 1954, provided by Vince MacNeil (Frans Eachainn's great grandson) to the author on 31 May 2018.

29 Neil Fraser, "A Complete List of Materials from Cape Breton as Found in the Canna Collections," 2004, NTS Canna Collection, 10.

30 Msgr P.J. Nicholson to J.L. Campbell, 26 March 1956, MG 115/4, John Lorne Campbell Fonds, StFX Archives. Calum Caimbeul was one of the early Barra settlers in Cape Breton. See MacNeil, *All Call Iona Home*, family 281, which states that he came from Scotland to Cape Breton in 1817.

31 A. Johnston to J.L. Campbell, 6 August 1954, CH2/2/1, NTS Canna Collection.

32 Vince MacLean in conversation with the author, 10 August 2018. Annie's friendship with Alasdair Mòr is noted in several letters she wrote to Msgr Nicholson. On Ash Wednesday, 23 February 1955, for example, she states: "And Alasdair Mor! He was a very dear friend of mine. Sr Veronica was thrilled when I told her that the 'Mac Neill' whom Alasdair always quoted (in Catholic matters) was myself. We were regular Gaelic correspondents for more than twenty years": MG 2/1/110, Patrick J. Nicholson Collection, StFX Archives. Annie is referring to the book *Litreachean Alasdair Mòr*, which started as a column in the *Stornaway Gazette*. Sr St Veronica was very fond of that book. StFX Professor Emerita Sr Margaret MacDonell retains Sr St Veronica's copy – a treasured possession: Sr M. MacDonell in conversation with the author, 19 August 2018.

33 Thirty-two of the ninety-three songs in *Gaelic Songs in Nova Scotia* were contributed by C.I.N. MacLeod from Mrs Patterson, Mr and Mrs Hugh MacKenzie, Frank MacNeil, and Jim Hughie MacNeil. Unfortunately, the recording Helen Creighton Fonds CR-216, which is referenced as the source for most of these informants' songs, is of MacLeod singing them. I am therefore unable to verify that the verses were in fact sung by these informants: Creighton and MacLeod, *Gaelic Songs*, 108–15, 120–88, 284–5, 290–2. Many of Jim Hughie MacNeil's songs derive from his unpublished manuscript, the location of which today is not known: ibid., 143, 146, 151, 181, 211, 222.

34 A. Johnston to J.L. Campbell, 27 August 1954, CH2/2/1, NTS Canna Collection.

35 A. Johnston to J.L. Campbell, 30 August 1954, CH2/2/1, NTS Canna Collection.

36 Patsy and Gordon Gillis (grandson of Frank) in conversation with the author, 17 August 2018.

37 Ibid. Fr Stanley had great affection for Big Frank. When Big Frank died, he wrote the following: "A man of fine physical presence, he was endowed with gifts of mind and heart which fully matched his bodily stature. His hospitable home was rarely found without visitors and whether one or many, all were made heartily welcome and entertained with true Highland prodigality. Possessing a magnificent singing voice, and a really extraordinary repertoire of the old Gaelic songs, his guests never lacked entertainment of the best quality, while his keen sense of humour added its share of brightness and jollity. He had the simple and tender but deep-rooted and unswerving faith of his Highland ancestors, a faith that, while never obtrusive, manifested itself in his everyday life. A chuid de Pharras

dha – may he have his share of heaven as the old Gaelic saying has it. He gave a great deal of innocent pleasure to many during his life and to such, surely, a due reward is given." Handwritten by Fr Stanley; in possession of Patsy and Gordon Gillis.

38 A. Johnston to J.L. Campbell, 30 August 1954, CH2/2/1, NTS Canna Collection.

39 Forty-six unique songs in the Tobar an Dualchais online archive were recorded from Annie Johnston; see http://www.tobarandualchais.com, accessed 23 January 2019. It is likely that she knew many more than that.

40 A. Johnston to Msgr P.J. Nicholson, Ash Wednesday, 23 February 1955, MG 2/1/110, Patrick J. Nicholson Collection, StFX Archives. Annie is quoting from "Duan na h-Aoigheachd" (the Rune of Hospitality), which demonstrates hospitality to the stranger because "Gur minig, minig, minig / A theid Criosd an riochd a' choigrich" (Often, often, often / Goes Christ in the stranger's guise): MacLeod, "Two Gaelic Runes," 51–2. The translation is Kenneth MacLeod's. MacLeod collected this verse in Eigg from Janet MacLeod.

41 Letter from Catherine Gillis (granddaughter of Hector MacLean) to the author, 17 August 2018.

42 A. Johnston to J.L. Campbell, 30 August 1954, CH2/2/1, NTS Canna Collection: "next week I go to Boston."

43 A. Johnston to J.L. Campbell, 27 August 1954, CH2/2/1, NTS Canna Collection.

44 MacPherson, *Tales*, 10.

45 Letter from Oighrig Keogh to the author, 10 August 2018. Oighrig's sister was at school with Ninian.

46 A. Johnston to Msgr P.J. Nicholson, Ash Wednesday, 23 February 1955, MG 2/1/110, Patrick J. Nicholson Collection, StFX Archives.

47 A. Johnston to Msgr P.J. Nicholson, 1 December 1954, MG 2/1/103, Patrick J. Nicholson Collection, StFX Archives. Annie comments about the plane trip: "da uair dheug a thug mi a' tilleadh, an àite an da-latha dheug a bha dùil agam a thoirt anns a bhàta" (it took twelve hours returning instead of the twelve days that I expected in the boat).

48 Ibid. The spelling of "thogteadh" is original.

49 Sr M. MacDonell in conversation with the author, 19 August 2018.

50 A. Johnston to Sr M. MacDonell, 24 November 1959, MG 116/2017-24-2200/ Annie Johnston, 1957–1963, Margaret MacDonell Fonds, StFX Archives.

51 Sadly, she also noted what was happening with Gaelic at that time: "Tha smior na Gaidhlig air an t-seann linn ach cha' n'eil smid aig an oigridh" (The old people have the marrow of Gaelic but there isn't a speck in the

young people): A. Johnston to J.L. Campbell, 6 August 1954, CH2/2/1, NTS Canna Collection.

52 Letter from A. Kearney to the attendees of the Féis an Eilein symposium, 19 August 2018, in the author's possession.

BIBLIOGRAPHY

Brewster, Paul G. "Two Gaelic Variants of 'The Two Sisters.'" *Modern Language Notes* 56, no. 3 (1941): 187–92.

Cameron, James D. *For the People: A History of St. Francis Xavier University*. Montreal and Kingston: McGill-Queen's University Press, 1996.

Campbell, John Lorne. "Anna and Calum Johnston." *Tocher* 13 (Spring 1974): 162–5.

– "Anna Nic Iain." *Gairm* 43 (1963): 313–14.

Campbell, John Lorne, and Francis Collinson, eds. *Hebridean Folk Songs*, vol. 2. Oxford: Clarendon Press, 1977.

"Contents." *Tocher* 13 (Spring 1974): 210.

"The Convention." *Mosgladh*, n.s., 1, no. 1 (February 1928): 4, 6.

Creighton, Helen, and Calum MacLeod. *Gaelic Songs in Nova Scotia*. Ottawa: Department of the Secretary of State, 1964.

Macleoid, Iain N. *Litreachean Alasdair Mòr*. Steornabhagh: Oifis Cuairtear Steornabhaigh, 1932.

MacLeod, Kenneth. "Two Gaelic Runes." *Celtic Review* 7, no. 25 (February 1911): 50–1.

MacNeil, Stephen R. *All Call Iona Home: 1850–1950: The Genealogy of the Founders of Iona and Their Descendents*. Antigonish: Formac, 1979.

MacPherson, John. *Tales of Barra told by the Coddy*, ed. J.L. Campbell. Edinburgh: W. and A.K. Johnston and G.W. Bacon, 1960.

"News of the Councils." *Mosgladh*, n.s., 1, no. 2 (March 1928): 1.

NicIain, Anna (Annie Johnston). "Baird a' Bhaile Againn." *Gairm* 8 (1954): 309–14.

– "Letter from Barra." *Mosgladh*, n.s., 1, no. 12 (January 1929): 1, 8.

– "A Second Letter from Barra." *Mosgladh*, n.s., 2, no. 2 (March 1929), 1–2.

– "Tóimhseachain o Innse Gall." *Béaloideas* 4, no. 2 (1933): 173–7.

Nilsen, Kenneth. "Air Chéilidh aig Mac Archie Sheumais." *The Clansman* 7, no. 6 (December 1993–January 1994): 14.

– "P.J. Nicholson and 'Achadh nan Gaidheal.'" In *Bile ós Chrannaibh: A Festschrift for William Gillies*, ed. Wilson McLeod, Abigail Burnyeat, Domhnall Uilleam Stiùbhart, Thomas Own Clancy, and Roibeard Ó Maolalaigh, 315–28. Ceann Drochaid: Clann Tuirc, 2010.

"Notes." *Mosgladh* 1, no. 4 (An Geamhradh 1923–4): 50–1.
"A Poet Priest." *Mosgladh*, n.s., 3, no. 4 (February 1931): 4.
Uther, Hans-Jörg. *The Types of International Folktales: A Classification and Bibliography*, vol. 1. FF Communications 284. Helsinki: Suomalainen Tiedeakatemia, 2004.

ARCHIVAL COLLECTIONS

Helen Creighton Fonds. Canadian Museum of History Archives, Gatineau, Quebec.
John Lorne Campbell Fonds, Margaret MacDonell Fonds, Office of the President Fonds, and Patrick J. Nicholson Collection. St Francis Xavier University (StFX) Archives.
National Trust for Scotland (NTS), Canna Collection. Canna House, Isle of Canna.
Sound and Moving Image Collection. Beaton Institute, Cape Breton University.

16

"Togaidh an Obair an Fhianais" (The Work Bears Witness): Kenneth Nilsen's Gaelic Columns in the *Casket*, 1987–1996

Catrìona NicÌomhair Parsons

Gaelic proverbs so often encapsulate in a few rhythmical, sinewy, poetic words the essence of what is meant; so, as I ruminated over a title for this chapter, it seemed to me that the proverb that would best express my sense of Professor Nilsen's important body of work was "Togaidh an obair an fhianais." My focus will be on that part of his work that is revealed in the articles he submitted for publication in the local Antigonish newspaper, the *Casket*, based on fieldwork he did with one of the region's last speakers of Gaelic. Without the research he undertook of his informant's stock of Gaelic stories and local history, a large amount of information pertaining to the Gaelic of Antigonish County, Nova Scotia, would have been lost.

GAELIC IN THE *CASKET*

In a 2010 essay, Nilsen describes how the *Casket* – whose title refers to a casket containing jewels – came into being and outlines some of its history:

> *The Casket* was founded by John Boyd in 1852, a year before the establishment of St Frances Xavier College. The previous year Boyd had published an all-Gaelic monthly *An Cuairtear Òg Gaelach*, or *The Gaelic Tourist* as it was called in English. This

> venture was apparently not a success, so Boyd started *The Casket*, which at first had four pages in English and four pages in Gaelic. Eventually, the Gaelic section became smaller and smaller and for years it would appear only as a single Gaelic column. For much of the 1880s Gaelic disappeared completely from the paper, but it reappeared on an occasional basis in the 1890s and in the first two decades of the twentieth century. Then in 1920 [P.J. Nicholson's *Achadh nan Gàidheal* column] started … and it continued basically unbroken until 1944. In the 1950s Major Calum MacLeod became a fairly regular Gaelic contributor to the paper and continued to do so on an occasional basis until his death in 1977. From 1987 to 1996 I published approximately sixty Gaelic pieces in the paper consisting of material I recorded from one of the last Antigonish Gaelic speakers. A few Gaelic articles appeared in the paper in 2008 and this was continued in 2009.[1]

Copies of the *Casket* are now archived in the Angus L. MacDonald Library at St Francis Xavier University. The first of Nilsen's Gaelic columns appeared on 14 October 1987 under the header *Suas leis a' Ghàidhlig!* [Up with the Gaelic!]. He contributed Gaelic columns to the *Casket* first on a biweekly basis, then monthly, with an occasional hiatus particularly in summer months. These columns continued through the first halves of 1995 and 1996, amounting to sixty-one altogether. (See the Appendix for a full list of Nilsen's columns.)

DANNY CAMERON AND THE GAELIC COLUMNS

Most of Nilsen's Gaelic columns were drawn from the many interviews he recorded, first on audiotape and later on videotape, of Donald (Danny) Cameron of Beaver Meadow, Antigonish County. Nilsen writes that Cameron was "exceptional in several ways":

> First of all he was born in Jamaica Plain, Boston, in 1898; but due to family circumstances [i.e., his mother's death] he was sent to Beaver Meadow, Antigonish County, mainland Nova Scotia at the age of five months, where he was raised in a Gaelic-speaking milieu by his maternal grandparents [Donald and Christine (Fraser) MacRae], whose ancestors were from Strathglass and Kintail. Gaelic declined in mainland Nova Scotia several decades earlier than in Cape Breton. Today [May 1986] there is only a handful of

> speakers of mainland Nova Scotia Gaelic, and I have met none who is as fluent as Mr. Cameron. Furthermore, the fact that comparatively little Gaelic material has been collected in mainland Nova Scotia makes Donald Cameron's oral traditions all the more important. He has what seems to be an inexhaustible fund of folk-narratives. They include episodes set in Scotland and tales of Scottish settlers in Nova Scotia, as well as anecdotes that cover all periods of his life: his early days in Beaver Meadow, his work in lumber camps, his travel on the harvest train to western Canada, and his return to [the Boston area] at age thirty-seven.[2]

Boston had been a popular destination for migrant Gaelic Nova Scotians since the late nineteenth century; in fact, Danny told Nilsen that his mother had emigrated there from Antigonish in 1890.[3] When Danny returned in the late 1930s, "he actually increased his fund of Gaelic stories as he met and conversed with many Gaelic speakers from both Antigonish and Cape Breton." It was at the Cape Breton Gaelic Club of Boston that Nilsen met him in 1979. Nilsen recalls the occasion in a *Casket* article he penned shortly after Danny's death in Malden, Massachusetts, on 26 March 1995:

> Danny was regaling the audience with his Gaelic jokes. Bill Lamey, then president of the club, introduced me to Danny. Danny invited me to his house for dinner, and I had been visiting him ever since. He and his wife [Elizabeth MacPherson, originally of Black River, Cape Breton] were delightful hosts and were eager to share their knowledge of Gaelic culture ... I owe a great debt to Danny because of his willingness to share his knowledge with me and to let me record his reminiscences.[4]

We, in turn, owe a debt to Professor Nilsen for his efforts over sixteen years (1979–95) to preserve Danny Cameron's valuable store of mainland Gaelic folklore for posterity.

Gathered below is a selection of Danny's oral traditions excerpted from Nilsen's Gaelic columns. The stories Nilsen printed fall into various categories: anecdotes of local characters, often ending with a witty retort; fairy stories; psychic phenomena; *ròlaistean* (tall tales); tales involving priests, usually ending with a quip at the priest's expense; and an etiological tale, which explains why something is the way it is. In addition, Danny describes life in eastern Nova Scotia (playing the fiddle at dances in the late 1920s and 1930s), customs at Christmas, the New Year, *Latha nan Trì Righrean* (The Feast of the Three Kings, i.e., 6 January), and Halloween. Nilsen usually began his articles with a brief Gaelic greeting and introductory comments, adding an English summary after the Gaelic tale. He occasionally included translations, but generally he did not.

Unless otherwise indicated, the translations below are by the author. Folklore notes contributed by Gregory R. Darwin are included at the end of the chapter.

I A FAMILY HISTORY STORY

The inaugural *Suas leis a' Ghàidhlig!* column on 14 October 1987 presents a family history story concerning Danny's great-great-grandfather Murdoch MacRae, who emigrated from Kintail, Scotland in 1811.[5] Nilsen recorded the account on videotape on 27 April 1986.

Murchadh nan Ciad agus Muinntir Mhic Rath

Murchadh nan Ciad, se sin a' chiad Mhac Rath a thàinig anseo as Albainn agus se mo shinn-sinn-seanair a bh'ann. Thàinig e a nall, e fhéin agus Eoghann Mór, Dòmhnallach a bh'ann, agus stad iad far a bheil Beaver Meadow no Lòn an Dòbhrain Duinn. Agus cheannaich e ceithir ciad acair air son deich *cent* an acair. Cha robh sian ann ach a' choille. Bha a h-uile rud ri ghearradh air a' bhaile. *Well* e fhéin is Eoghann Mór, *chlear* iad an t-àit' co-dhiu. A' chiad rud a rinn iad, na craobhan a ghearradh sìos agus seors bothan de thigh logaichean a dhèanamh dhai' fhéin. (Agus nam bithinn aig an tigh, dh'fhiachainn dhut far a' robh am bothan beag a thog iad dar a thàinig iad as Albainn.)

Donnchadh, Alasdair is Dòmhnall na gillean a bh'aig Murchadh. Agus Ceiti, Màiri agus Iseabal, na h-ìghnean. Ach co-dhiu, dar a dh'fhàs na gillean suas, rinn e dà leth de'n bhaile. Air an taobh deas dhe'n abhainn, chuir e mo shinn-seanair, Donnchadh Mac Rath. Fhuair e a' chuid sin dheth. Is dh'fhuirich Alasdair air an taobh eile.

... Phòs [Donnchadh] ban-Sisealach is bha deichnear aige. Agus se a mhac mo sheanair-sa, Dòmhnall ...

Sin agad an dòigh a bha muinntir Mac Rath. Chan eil gin dhiubh beò an diugh. Chan eil gin dhiubh ann tuillidh. Is mise an aon duine a bhuineas dhai.'

KN: Ciamar a fhuair Murchadh nan Ciad an t-ainm a tha sin?

DC: Fhuair e an t-ainm sin bho'n a bha ciad dollar aige 'na phòc' dar a thàinig e a dh' ionnsaidh Albainn Ùr. Cha robh móran airgid ac'. Bha ciad, bha e coltach ri mìle an diugh, no dà mhìle an diugh. A bharrachd air a' *fare* a bh'aige tighinn a nall air a' chuan, bha ciad dollar 'na phòc' a bharrachd air a' siod agus fhuair e an t-ainm "Murchadh nan Ciad."[6]

Murdoch of the Hundreds and the MacRae Family

Murdoch of the Hundreds, that's the first MacRae who came here from Scotland and he was my great-great-grandfather. He came over, himself and Big Ewan, who was a MacDonald, and they stopped where Beaver Meadow is. And he bought four hundred acres for ten cents an acre. There was nothing there but the forest. Everything on the homestead had to be cut. Well, himself and Big Ewan, they cleared the place anyway. The first thing they did was to cut down the trees and make a bothy-like house of logs for themselves. (And if I were at home, I would show you where the little bothy was that they built when they came from Scotland.)

Duncan, Alasdair, and Donald were the boys that Murdoch had, and Katie, Mary, and Isobel were the girls. But anyway, when the boys grew up, he made two halves of the homestead. On the south side of the river, he put my great-grandfather, Duncan MacRae. He got that portion of it. And Alasdair stayed on the other side.

... Duncan married a Chisholm woman and he had ten children. And his son Donald was my grandfather ...

There you have the circumstances of the MacRae folk. There's none of them alive today. Not one of them is here anymore. I'm the only one who is related to them.

KN: How did Murdoch of the Hundreds get that name?

DC: He got that name since he had a hundred dollars in his pocket when he came to Nova Scotia. They didn't have much money. A hundred, it was like a thousand today, or two thousand today. Besides the fare he had coming over the ocean, he had a hundred dollars more than that in his pocket and he got the name "Murdoch of the Hundreds."

2 A FAIRY STORY

For his second column on 4 November 1987, Nilsen printed Danny Cameron's version of the popular story "Di-luain, Di-màirt" (Monday, Tuesday). It was recorded on videotape on 15 November 1983. The English translation is Nilsen's.

Di-luain, Di-màirt

Is ann ann an Albainn a bha e. Bha duine a'sin agus cha robh e gu math idir agus bha cuma gàbhaidh droll air, fhios agad, agus bha croit mhór air an druim aige. Agus bha e faireachdainn dona, bheil fhios agad, nach robh e coltach ri duine sam bith eile. Ach co-dhiù, chaidh e mach aon latha, chaidh e sìos dh'ionnsaidh na beanntaichean. Is bha e coiseachd. Chuala e crònan ann an cnoc far a' robh na sìthean. Bha e ag éisneachd. Is bha boireannach astaigh, té dhe na sìthean is bha i cur ponach a chadal is bha i seinn:

"Di-luain, di-màirt, di-luain, di-màirt, di-luain, di-màirt."

Agus thuirt am bodach, an duine air an taobh amuigh, "Di-ciadain."

Stad i tacan beag is thuirt i:

"Di-luain, di-màirt, di-luain, di-màirt, di-luain, di-mairt, di-ciadain. Di-luain di-màirt, di-luain, di-màirt, di-luain, di-màirt, di-ciadain."

Agus thàinig i mach, leum i mach, "Bhon a dh'fhàg thusa an t-òran agam-as math, tha mise dol a chur leigheas ort."

Thug i gi'faighear dhan an duine is dh'fholbh am ploc bho'n an druim aige is bha e cho dìreach ri slat.

Ach co-dhiù, thàinig e dhachaidh dh'ionnsaidh a' bhaile far a' robh e fuireach. Is choinnich e fear eile ann is an aon trioblaid air. Choimhead a' fear eile air is thuirt e, "Càite robh thu, a Dhòmhnaill? Dé dh'éirich dhut? Tha thu cho dìreach ri slat iasgaich."

Well, dh'inns e a' rud a thachair dha ... *Well*, dh'fholbh am burraidh eile, dh'fholbh e an ath latha. Bha esan a' dol a dh'fhaighinn leigheas cuideachd. Chaidh e suas is dar a ràinig e an cnoc far a' robh a' sìthean, bha i gabhail an t-òran:

"Di-luain, di-màirt, di-luain, di-màirt, di-luain, di-màirt, di-ciadain."

Is thuirt am burraidh air an taobh amuigh, "Di-ardaoin."

Mhill e am port. *Well, start* i e co-dhiù:

"Di-luain, di-màirt, di-luain, di-màirt, di-luain, di-màirt, di-ciadain, di-ardaoin."

O, cha do chòrd sin idir rithe. Ghabh i an fhearg is thàinig i mach.

"Mhill thusa am port agam-as. Tha mise dol a mhilleadh thusa."

Is thug i gi'faighear dha is an àite am ploc a chur dhe'n an druim aige, chuir i am ploc eile air is bha dà phloc air.[7]

Monday, Tuesday

It was in Scotland. There was a man there and he wasn't quite right. He had an awfully odd appearance, you know, he had a hump on his back. And he was feeling bad, you know, that he wasn't like everyone else. But anyway, he went out one day, he went down to the mountains. He was walking along. He heard crooning in a hill where the fairies were. He listened and there was a woman in there, one of the fairies and she was putting a baby to sleep and she was singing:

"Monday, Tuesday, Monday, Tuesday, Monday, Tuesday."

And the old man, the man who was outside said, "Wednesday."

She stopped a while and said:

"Monday, Tuesday, Monday, Tuesday, Monday, Tuesday, Wednesday, Monday, Tuesday, Monday, Tuesday, Monday, Tuesday, Wednesday."

And she came out, she jumped out, "Since you improved my song, I'm going to cure you."

She gave the man a blow (?) and the hump left his back and he was as straight as a rod.

But anyway, he came home to town where he lived. And he met another man who had the same trouble. The other man looked at him and said, "Where were you, Donald? What happened to you? You're as straight as a fishing rod."

Well, he told him what had happened to him … Well, the other fool went off the next day. He was going to get cured also. He went up and when he reached the hill where the fairy was, she was singing the song:

"Monday, Tuesday, Monday, Tuesday, Monday, Tuesday, Wednesday."

And the fool outside said, "Thursday."

He ruined the tune. Well, she started it, anyway:

"Monday, Tuesday, Monday, Tuesday, Monday, Tuesday, Wednesday, Thursday."

Oh, she didn't like that at all. She got angry and came out.

"You ruined my tune. I'm going to ruin you."

She gave him a blow and instead of taking the hump off his back, she put the other hump on his back and [then] he had two humps.[8]

This tale, transcribed as Nilsen heard it, exemplifies his informant's dialect and quality of Gaelic very well. One of my graduating Gaelic classes liked it so much that when we formed a team named *Spòrs* (Fun) to bring Gaelic to local schools, it was transformed into a skit for the young students to enjoy. Nilsen states elsewhere that "Mr. Cameron's version … is the only Scottish Gaelic rendition known in which the words 'Di-luain, Di-màirt' are sung to a definite tune."[9]

3 A TALL TALE

In the 10 February 1988 article, Danny tells a *ròlaist* (tall tale) about Doimhgean Oighrig (Donald Effie), "one of the colorful figures who lived in the Keppoch" in Antigonish County.[10] The story was recorded on 24 June 1986.

Doimhgean Oighrig

Doimhgean Oighrig, o, se briagadair gàbhaidh a bh'ann. Cha b'urrainn dhut creidsinn sian a bhiodh e ag ràdhainn. O, bhiodh ròlaisdean aige bha diabhalta. Chan innseadh e briag air duine sam bith ach air fhéin is na rudan a rinn e.

Bha e ag inns' aon uair a bha e ag obair air *building* shuas ann an New Brunswick. Bha e ag innse cho àrd is a bha am *building*. "Agus bha sinn air son c[r]ìoch a chur air. Bha sinn ag obair air anns an oidhche. Bha sinn airson crìoch a chur air mus tigeadh an t-uisge. *Well*," thuirt e, "a Dhòmhnaill, innsidh mi a nis dhut cho àrd is a bha e. Dh'fheum sinn dol air ar bial fodha 'nar sìneadh gus a' ghealach a leigeil seachad." Bha sin àrd.

O, Doimhgean Oighrig, se duine gàbhaidh a bh'ann. Bha e shuas anns a' choille ag obair ann am Miramichi. Is chaidh e amach aon latha, bha an t-uisge ann, agus chaidh e amach is thug e leis an gunna còmh' ris. Cha robh aige ach aon pheilear agus bha e air son *moose* fhaighinn. Ràinig e an abhainn bha seo is choimhead e seachad air an abhainn, thuirt e, is bha creag a'sin. Is an diabhal bha *moose* air aon taobh dhen a' chreag is bha mathan air an taobh eile.

Ach co-dhiu cha robh fhios aige ciamar a gheobhadh e an dithis dhiubh le aon pheilear. Chuimhnich e air rud-eigin a dheanadh e. Loisg e air a' chreag is sgoilt e am peilear. Chaidh an darna taobh sa' mhathan agus an taobh eile anns a' *mhoose*. Fhuair e an dithis dhiubh.

"Ach," thuirt e, "*bhust* an gunna orm agus, o, thug e buille gàbhaidh dhomh is thuit mi san abhainn. Agus chaidh am baraill aig a' ghunna, chaidh e suas an abhainn is mharbh e dà fhichead tunnag. Thuit mi san abhainn is bha bòtuinnean mór' àrd' orm. Dar a thàinig mi as an abhainn bha na bòtuinnean, bha iad làn bric agus dà *mhink*!"[11]

Donald Effie

Donald Effie, O, he was a terrible liar. You couldn't believe anything he would say. O, he would have tall tales that were diabolical. He wouldn't tell a lie about anyone at all but himself and the things he did.

He was telling one time that he was working on a building up in New Brunswick. He was telling how high the building was. "And we wanted to finish it. We were working on it during the night. We wanted to finish it before the rain came. Well," he said, "Donald, I will tell you now how high it was. We needed to stretch face down in order to let the moon go past." That was high.

O, Donald Effie, he was a terrible man. He was up in the woods working in Miramichi. And he went out one day, it was raining, and he went out and he took the gun with him. He only had one bullet and he wanted to get a moose. He reached this river and looked beyond the river, he said, and there was a cliff there. And damn it, there was a moose on one side of the cliff and a bear on the other side.

But anyway, he didn't know how he would get the pair of them with one bullet. He remembered something he could do. He fired on the cliff and he split the bullet. One half went in the bear and the other half in the moose. He got the two of them.

"But," he said, "the gun broke on me and, o, it gave me a terrible blow and I fell in the river. And the barrel of the gun, it went up the river and it killed forty ducks. I fell in the river and I had big high boots on. When I came out of the river, the boots, they were full of trout and two minks!"

4 ANOTHER TALL TALE

Another *ròlaist* features in the column for 22 November 1989, this time about an exceptional dog. (No collection date is given.) Danny appears to have enjoyed this story form; two additional tall tales appeared in the Gaelic column on 7 December 1988 and 15 March 1989 (see Appendix).

Cù Glic
Bha cù agam-as, cha robh a leithid riamh ann. Innsidh mi dhut cho glic 's a bha e. Bha *clock* againn air a' sgeilp os cionn a' *stove* agus thigeadh an cù astaigh feasgar an àm gus an crodh fhaighinn agus choimheadadh e air a' *chlock* is bhiodh fhios aige dé'n uair a bha e is dh'fholbhadh e ag iarraidh a' chrodh is thoireadh e dhachaidh iad.

Ach co dhiubh, air son beagan spòrs, chuir sinn an *clock* a' falach air. An diabhal mura thàinig e astaigh is cha robh an *clock* idir ann. Chaidh e mach. Thàinig e staigh a rithist. Cha robh an *clock* idir ann.

Chaidh e mach air cùl an taigh' is chuir e 'spòg suas ri bhathais mar seo is e coimhead dìreach cho àrd 's a bha 'ghrian is bha fhios aige an uair sin dé'n uair a bha e. Is dh'fholbh e a dh'iarraidh a' chrodh. Se cù math bha sin![12]

A Wise Dog
I had a dog, there never was the like of him. I will tell you how wise he was. We had a clock on the shelf above the stove and the dog would come in in the evening when it was time to get the cattle and he would look at the clock and he would know what time it was and he would go to fetch the cattle and he would bring them home.

But anyway, for a little fun, we hid the clock on him. The devil if he didn't come in and the clock wasn't there at all. He went out. He came in again. The clock wasn't there at all.

He went out to the back of the house and he put his paw up to his forehead like this looking [to see] just how high the sun was and he knew then what time it was. And he went to fetch the cattle. That was a good dog!

5 AN ETIOLOGICAL TALE

In the story printed on 30 March 1988, Danny explains why the blacksmith is never tired. Nilsen recorded this story on audiotape on 2 July 1979.

Crìosd agus an Gobhainn
Bha iad ag ràdhainn a's an t-seann dùthaich nach biodh gobhainn sgìth gu bràch air sàilleabh rud a rinn e aon uair dar a bha Crìosd air talamh.

Bha Crìosd is a mhàthair, bha iad a' dol ro'n a' bhaile bha seo. Cha robh e (ach) 'na ghille bìodach, beag. Stad i aig taigh duine fiach a' faigheadh i deoch do dh'uisge dha'n a' ghille bheag is dhiùlt iad an t-uisge dha.

Chaidh i gu leth dusan de dh'àitean is chan fhaigheadh i deoch dha'n uisge. Thàinig iad gu gobhainn mór is bha e ag obair anns a' cheàrdach.

Is dh'fhoighnich iad dheth a' faigheadh iad deoch dhe dh'uisge. Is chaidh an gobhainn, stad e obair, is chaidh e dh'ionnsaigh an tobair is fhuair e soitheach mór de dh'uisge is thug e dha'n an fhear bheag e agus dha'n mhàthair. Is thionndaidh a' fear beag is thuirt e ris:

"Cho fada 's a bhios gobhainn beò gu deireadh an t-saoghail cha bhi sgìos air a' ghobhainn."[13]

Christ and the Blacksmith
They were saying in the old country that a smith wouldn't ever be tired as a consequence of a thing he did one time when Christ was on earth.

Christ and his mother were, they were going through this town. He was only a tiny, little lad. She stopped at someone's house to see if she would get a drink of water for the little boy and they refused the water for him.

She went to a half dozen places and she couldn't get a drink of water. They came to a big smith and he was working in the smithy.

And they asked of him if they could get a drink of water. And the smith went, he stopped his work, and he went toward the well and he got a big container of water and he gave it to the little one and to the mother. And the little one turned and said to him:

"As long as there is a smith alive, until the end of the world, the smith will not be weary."

6 A "PRIESTLY" STORY

Suas leis a' Ghàidhlig! on 25 May 1988 contains Danny's story about Fr Kenneth J. MacDonald (1821–1910), "one of the best-known figures in Gaelic traditions of Antigonish and Inverness counties." As Nilsen tells us, Fr MacDonald "served as parish priest of Mabou from 1865 to 1894 and is remembered as a hard-working priest, a strict disciplinarian and a staunch supporter of temperance. He was also a firm believer in the need for education."[14] No collection date is given.

Maighstir Coinneach

Bha Maighstir Coinneach bochd, bha e coltach ri Maighstir Anndra. Cha robh esan ach a' trod is a' faighinn coire.

Bha càraid a' fuireach ann am M[a]bou. Cha robh clann idir ac' ach thog iad gille a thàinig as Halifax. Cha robh e dol 'na sgoil idir is bha e mu dheidhin naoi no deich bliadhna de dh'aois.

Is Maighstir Coinneach, chaidh e suas aon latha is chunnaic e an gille beag.

"Bheil an gille tha siod a' dol 'na sgoil?"

"Chan eil."

"*Well*, feumaidh tu chur 'na sgoil."

"*Well*, cha d'fhuair mi-fhìn sgoil is fhuair mi air adhart."

"*Well*, cha dean sin an gnothach an diugh. Coimhead seo. Cuir thusa an gille tha sin 'na sgoil. Dar a dh' éireas e suas 'na dhuine, chan fhaigh e sian nas fheàrr na 'spaid is a' phiocaid is cha bhi tùr ann. Tha sgoil, sin a' rud math."

"O, tha mi creidsinn gum beil, ach chan eil fhios 'am. Chan urrainn dhomh chur 'na sgoil."

"Carson nach urrainn dhut a chur 'a sgoil?"

"*Well*, tha tuilleadh's fada aige ri coiseachd."

"Dé cho fada's a tha aige ri dhol?"

"[O], teann air trì mìle."

"Huh, chan eil sin fada," thuirt Maighstir Coinneach. "Bheil fhios agad, a Dhòmhnaill, am Pàp a th'againn an diugh, dar a bha e 'na ghille òg gun coisicheadh e seachd mìle 'na sgoil? Dé do bharail air-a-sin?"

"Hm," thuirt a' fear eile. "*Well*, cha robh dùil againne Pàp a dheanamh dhen fhear seo ann!"[15]

Father Kenneth

Poor Father Kenneth, he was like Father Andrew [MacGillivray, parish priest of Lismore, Pictou County, 1871–97[16]]. He was only scolding and finding fault.

There was a couple living in Mabou. They didn't have any children at all but they raised a lad who came from Halifax. He wasn't going to school at all and he was about nine or ten years of age.

And Father Kenneth, he went up one day and he saw the little lad.

"Is the lad there going to school?"

"No."

"Well, you must send him to school."

"Well, I myself didn't get schooling and I got ahead."

"Well, that won't do the job today. Look here. You send the lad there to school. When he grows up into a man, he won't get anything better than a spade and pickaxe and he'll have no understanding. School, that's the good thing."

"O, I believe that's so, but I don't know. I can't send him to school."

"Why can't you send him to school?"

"Well, he's got too far to walk."

"How far does he have to go?"

"Oh, close to three miles."

"Huh, that's not far," said Father Kenneth. "Do you know, Donald, the Pope we have today, when he was a young lad, that he would walk seven miles to school? What's your opinion of that?"

"Hm," said the other man. "Well, we didn't expect to make a Pope of this one anyway!"

7 AN ENCOUNTER WITH A MERMAID

In the 1 February 1989 issue, Danny recounts a short tale about a man who saw a mermaid near Cape George, Antigonish County. Danny's source is named only as MacAonghais (MacInnis). Nilsen recorded this story on videotape on 5 January 1989.

A' Mhaighdean Mhaireannach

Bhiodh iad a' bruidhinn air a' mhaighdean mhaireannach, is thuirt MacAonghais gu' faca a té dhiubh aon uair anns a' Chape. Cha robh fhios aige dé dheanadh e.

Bha i 'na suidhe air creag, thàinig i as an uisg.' Is bha cìor aic' is bha i cìoradh a' falt aic.' [Is] thuirt e gu robh falt oirre cho briagha is a chunnaic e air duine riamh. Se iasg a bha 'na leth dhi [agus] fos cionn sin bha a h-uile cuid eile dhi, bha i direach coltach ri boireannach sa bith eile.

Well, chuir e iongatas gàbhaidh (air). Chual e mun déidhinn ach cha do chual e gu faca duine iad. Ach chunnaic e gun i bh'ann agus thuirt e gu robh is briagha cuideachd, boireannach briagha. Choisich e cho socair is a b'urrainn dha fiach a' faigheadh e teann oirre.

By gosh, chual i e is thionndainn i mun [cuairt] is choimhead i air is chunnaic i gu robh e tighinn is dìreach chaidh i astaigh anns an uisg' agus chan fhaca e tuillidh i.

Well, se a mhac a bha ag innse dhomhs, bha e pòsda ann an Allt a' Bhàilidh, ach dh'inns e siod dhomh, thuirt e, "ach cha[n] eil mise ga chreidsinn co-dhiù," thuirt e, "dh'inns am bodach e co-dhiù, dar a bha mi beag."[17]

The Mermaid

They used to speak about the mermaid, and MacInnis said that he saw one of them in the Cape. He didn't know what he would do.

She was sitting on a rock, she came out of the water. She had a comb and she was combing her hair. And he said that she had hair as beautiful as he had ever seen on anyone. Half of her was fish and above that was every other part of her, she was just like any other woman.

Well, it astonished him greatly. He heard about them but didn't hear that anybody saw them. But he saw that it was she and he said that she was beautiful too, a beautiful woman. He walked as softly as he could to see if he could get close to her.

By gosh, she heard him and turned around and looked at him and she saw that he was coming and right away she went into the water and he didn't see her any more.

Well, it was his son who was telling me, he was married in Bailey's Brook, but he told that to me, he said, "but I don't believe it anyway," he said, "the old man told it anyway, when I was small."

8 A DEVILISH TALE

The following, published 21 February 1990, is a story that Danny heard some eighty-five years before he told it to Nilsen on 8 June 1989.

Triùir Gillean agus an Donas
Bha e mu dhéidhinn triùir de ghillean, daoine, bha iad sa choille. Rug an oidhch' orra. Fhuair iad *camp* agus chaidh iad astaigh. Agus bha dà leabaidh air an ùrlar ach bha an treasamh té, cha robh i idir ann. Bha a' fear eile, bha e deanamh leabaidh dha fhéin. Fhuair an dithis eile sa leabaidh 's,

"*Well*," thuirt fear dhiubh, "truagh nach robh dà nighean bhòidheach againn còmh ruinn a nis anochd bho'n a tha sinn sa choille annaseo."

'S thuirt an treasamh fear, "*Well*, tha mi cur Dia eadar rium 's iad sin. Chan eil iad bhuam idir."

Well, cha robh e fad' gus a dh'fhosgail an doras. Thàinig triùir dhiubh astaigh a'san doras.

Leum dithis dhiubh sa leabaidh còmh ris na gillean. Dh'fhuirich an té eile 'san doras. Agus chaidh a' fear eile amach, (ach) cha leigeadh i amach idir e. A nis,

"Cha thill thu."

"Tillidh mi, tillidh mi," ghabh e an t-eagal. "Tillidh mi. *Well*, innsidh mi dhut, cum thusa greim air a' bhreacan agam is dar a thig mis' amach cum e 'nad làmh is beir tarraing air is bidh fhios agad gu bheil mi amuigh a'sin."

"Hm," thuirt an nighean, "gabh amach matà." Is dhùin i an doras is chum i greim air a' bhreacan.

Is dar a fhuair esan amach, thug e am breacan dheth agus cheangail e ann an craogh e agus dh'fholbh e mar gum biodh an donas ann.

Thòis is' air tarraing am breacan dar nach robh e tighinn astaigh. 'S thàinig am breacan is cha robh e idir ann. Is chaidh i mach is cha robh e ann. Ghabh i fearg an diabhail is thug i as a dhéidh, ag éigheach 's a' sgiamhail as a dhéidh. Se an donas a bh'ann, fhios agad.

Well, bh'esan a' ruith is bha e ruith is bha e ag ùrnaigh ri Dia gu rachadh a shàbhaladh is nach marbhadh i siod e. Ach chaidh e seachad air pairic mhor is bha i làn de dh'eich òg. Is bha stàlainn ann. An duine òg, leum e astaigh miosg na searraich is chaidh na h-eich man cuairt air mar sin is dh'fhuirich a' stàlainn air an taobh amuigh is bha e *gallop* fad na h-oidhch' man cuairt air an t-sorcal, fhios agad.

Thàinig is' agus cha b'urrainn dhi dhol seachad air na lorgan mar chruthaich Dia e, tha fhios agad, is cha b'urrainn dhan an nighean faighinn seachad. Bha a' stàlainn, chum e suas fad [na] h-oidhch' a' *gallop* man cuairt gu sàbhaileadh e a' fear a bha astaigh eadar riu. Thàinig a'sin a' latha is theich i.

Agus leig e a'sin a' stàlainn seachad is chaidh esan air n-ais dh'ionns' a' champ is fhuair e an dithis a bha còmh ris, an dithis dhiubh, bha iad marbh anns a' champ. Sin an dòigh a bha a' stòraidh. Se'n donas a bha san triùir dhe na h-igheanan.

KN: Se seann sgialachd a tha sin.

DC: O, cho sean ris a' cheò. Dh'fhaodte gun tug Murchadh MacRath as an t-seann dùthaich e, tha fhios gun tug, no fear dhe na Frisealaich, chan eil fhios agam-as co dhiubh.[18]

Three Lads and the Devil

It was about three lads, men, they were in the wood. The night caught them. They found a camp and they went inside. And there were two beds on the floor but the third one, it wasn't there at all. The other man, he was making a bed for himself. The other two got into bed and

"Well," said one of them, "a pity that we didn't have two beautiful girls now tonight since we are in the wood here."

And the third fellow said,

"Well, I am putting God between me and those. I don't need them at all."

Well, it wasn't long until the door opened. Three of them came in at the door. Two of them jumped into bed along with the lads. The other one remained in the door. And the other man went out, (but) she wouldn't let him out at all. Now,

"You won't come back."

"I will come back, I will come back," he got frightened. "I will come back. Well, I'll tell you, you keep hold of my plaid and when I come out keep it in your hand and take hold of it and you will know that I'm out there."

"Hm," said the girl, "go out then." And she closed the door and she kept hold of the plaid.

And when he got out, he took off the plaid and tied it in a tree and went off as if the devil were there.

She began pulling the plaid when he wasn't coming in. And the plaid came and he wasn't there at all. And she went out and he wasn't there. The anger of the devil took hold of her and she took off after him, shouting and screaming after him. The devil was there, you know.

Well, he was running and he was running and he was praying to God that he would be saved and she would not kill him. But he went past a big field and it was full of young horses. And there was a stallion there. The young man, he leapt in among the foals and the horses went around him like that, and the stallion waited on the outside and he was galloping all night around the circle, you know.

She came and she couldn't go past the [stallion's] tracks as God brought it about, you know, and the girl couldn't get past. The stallion was, he kept up galloping around all night so that he would save the man that was inside between them [the tracks]. Then the day came and she fled.

And he let the stallion [go] aside then and he went back toward the camp and he found the two who were with him, the pair of them, they were dead in the camp. That's the way the story was. The devil was in the three of the girls.

KN: That's an old story.

DC: O, as old as the mist. It might be that Murdoch MacRae brought it from the old country, surely he did, or one of the Frasers, I don't know anyway.

9 A CHILDREN'S RHYME

In the 9 October 1991 column we find a children's rhyme that Danny learned from his grandparents in Beaver Meadow approximately eighty-eight years earlier. The English translation is by Nilsen and accompanies the rhyme in the column. No collection date is given.

Mise chunnaic an t-iongantas	I saw a wonder
Nach fhaca duine riamh	That no one ever saw:
Gunna air gualainn tarbh	A bull with gun on his shoulder
Is e dol a mharbhadh fiadh,	Going to kill a deer,
Tromb aig an fhitheach	A crow with a jew's harp,
Is fidheall aig a' ròcais	A rook with a fiddle
Dag caol aig an uiseag	A lark with a pistol
Is musgaid aig a' smeòrach,	A robin with a musket,
Am bradan a' treabhadh	A salmon plowing
'S a' seabhag a' cliathadh,	A hawk harrowing
An dreathan donn ag uisgealadh	A wren watering
'S a' luch a' cur gu fiadhaich!	And a mouse sowing wildly![19]

In 2008 the *Casket* Gaelic column was resurrected, this time with other members of the St Francis Xavier University Celtic Department – as well as community members – also participating, with eight articles contributed through the year. In more recent years, even as the *Casket* newspaper came under the control of Halifax's *Chronicle Herald* and began to be offered as a free publication, I have made a point of continuing to contribute the occasional article (Gaelic with English translation), and I am glad to say the new régime, aware of the historical imperative, has continued to be receptive. It was Professor Nilsen who led the way, however, by his dedicated example. As he himself expressed it, the *Casket* Gaelic columns from 1987 to 1996 form "the most extensive collection of mainland Nova Scotia Gaelic in print."[20]

Although he is no longer with us, Nilsen's work continues to bear witness not only to his love of the Gaelic language and his respect and fondness for those who opened their homes and hearts to him, but also to his dedication and diligence in collecting important cultural material that would have gone unrecorded otherwise. I would like to conclude with a brief cameo. Often, when a group of Gaels was present before him, he would greet people with a smile and begin speaking with the words: "A dhaoine mo ghaoil!" (My beloved people!).

FOLKLORE NOTES

Gregory R. Darwin

1 "Murchadh nan Ciad agus Muinntir Mhic Rath"

Accounts like this one – a family history concerning an immigrant ancestor – are extremely common among diaspora communities such as the Nova Scotian Gaels. Danny Cameron's account demonstrates what Zeitlin, Kotkin, and Baker refer to as the "character principle" and the "transition principle" of family stories: such stories highlight the distinctive traits and qualities of the persons involved – here, Murchadh's wealth and his work ethic – and focus on periods of transition and crisis, establishing a community in the new land.[21]

Nicknames or epithets such as *nan Ciad* are also extremely common in Gaelic- and Irish-speaking communities, as they provide, along with patronymics, a way of differentiating individuals of the same name in communities with a relatively small number of permitted personal names. Patronymics identify someone by the name of their parent, or another ancestor: Eoghann Mór is a *Dòmhnallach*, a descendant of Dòmhnall, while Murchadh's descendants, including Danny, are collectively referred to as *muinntir Mhic Rath*, the descendants of Mac Rath. Nicknames, on the other hand, are typically derived from obvious physical features, professions, or other distinguishing traits. The nickname *nan Ciad* refers to Murchadh's noteworthy wealth upon arriving in Nova Scotia; as Nilsen noted, a hundred dollars was greater than what "the average pioneer" would have had upon reaching North America.[22]

2 "Di-luain, Di-màirt"

This is a version of ATU 503, "The Gifts of the Little People," which is known across Europe, the Middle East, India, Japan, the Caribbean, and in English, French, and Spanish-speaking parts of the Americas.[23] It is well-known in Ireland and Gaelic Scotland, where, as in Danny Cameron's version, the hero is most often a hunchback whom the fairies reward for completing their song by removing his hump, while his companion (another hunchback) is given the first man's hump in punishment for unartfully attempting to do the same. In many Irish versions, the fairies' song (consisting of the days of the week) is accompanied by a simple melody; as Nilsen notes, the melody is not common in Scottish Gaelic versions.

3 "Doimhgean Oighrig"

The *ròlaist* is a genre found in both Gaelic Scotland and Nova Scotia, although far more examples have been collected in Nova Scotia. Like other "tall tale" traditions, *ròlaistean* are mostly realistic, with certain elements exaggerated for comic effect; much of their entertainment value comes from the attempt to tell such an obvious falsehood with a straight face. The second episode is an example of motif X1122.2, "Lie: person shoots many animals with one shot," which is known in many North American storytelling traditions.[24] A similar story was collected from Angus MacDonald of Mabou in 1982 by John Shaw and appears as "Mar a Chaidh Aonghus Bàn a Shealgaireachd" (Fair-haired Angus goes Hunting) in *Na Beanntaichean Gorma*.[25]

4 "An Cù Glic"

Another version of this story was collected from Joe Neil MacNeil of Middle Cape, Cape Breton, by John Shaw in 1982, and was published as "An Cù Glic" (The Wise Dog) in *Na Beanntaichean Gorma*.[26] MacNeil's version includes a second episode, in which the dog leads a stray calf and her mother home by dipping his tail in milk, and, unlike Cameron's version, is not related as a personal experience.

5 "Crìosd agus an Gobhainn"

This is a version of a story that is common in Ireland, where it is often connected with the expression "tuirse na ngaibhne ar na buachaillí bó" (the exhaustion of the smiths on the cowherds). Seán Ó Súilleabháin and Reidar Christiansen classified it as AT 750*, "Hospitality Blessed," in *The Types of the Irish Folktale*.[27] In most Irish versions, the Virgin Mary rewards the smith for providing her with a pin or brooch (*biorán*) for her cloak or her infant son's clothing, rather than for giving them a drink of water, after many others had refused her. These other people may be identified as representatives of other professions, explaining why they suffer exhaustion from their duties while smiths do not.[28] In some Irish versions, the smith has this exemption because Mary or Christ blesses the water of the forge with the power to cure fatigue.[29] This is a possible, albeit loose, parallel for the role played by water in Danny Cameron's story.

6 "*Maighstir Coinneach*"

As Nilsen noted in an earlier column containing a story about Fr Andrew MacGillivray, "Anecdotes about ministers and priests form a large part of the repertoire of many Gaelic raconteurs."[30] Danny Cameron's repertoire was replete with such material; as Nilsen states elsewhere, "Of the 250 anecdotes I have collected from him nearly 100, or roughly 40%, involve the Catholic clergy."[31] This story belongs to a category Nilsen calls "stories relating to a specific personality."[32] Further details about and examples of such lore collected from Danny Cameron and others can be found in his article, "The Priest in the Gaelic Folklore of Nova Scotia."

7 "*A' Mhaighdean Mhaireannach*"

Accounts of seeing mermaids, whether given as personal experience narratives or, like here, as second-hand accounts delivered with varying degrees of belief or skepticism, are common throughout Gaelic Scotland and Ireland.[33] The ordinary word for "mermaid" in Gaelic is *a' mhaighdean mhara* (the maiden of the sea), which is used in both Scotland and Nova Scotia. The term used here, *a' mhaighdean mhaireannach* (the ever-lasting [?] maiden), might be a malapropism. The description of the mermaid – a beautiful woman, combing her long hair, whose lower half is a fish – is consistent with the description of such beings in similar accounts from Scotland and Ireland, as well as the depiction of mermaids in various other legends and tales from these countries.[34] Other stories involving mermaids are known in Nova Scotia,[35] but as far as I can determine, no versions of the legend about a man who marries a mermaid by stealing her tail or cloak (ML 4080, "The Seal Woman") have been collected in Canada, despite the fact that the story is well-attested throughout Gaelic Scotland.[36]

8 "*Triùir Gillean agus an Donas*"

This is a version of a legend that the School of Scottish Studies classified as F112, "Wish for Female Company."[37] It is relatively well-known in the Highlands, mostly in Argyll and the Outer Hebrides, but apparently unknown outside of Scotland and Nova Scotia; Nilsen references an Argyllshire version collected in the 1880s and published by James MacDougall.[38] Cameron's version is atypical in that it explicitly identifies the women as the devil or agents of the devil; more typically they are referred to as fairies, *glaistigs*, or similar supernatural beings. In a number of versions from the Outer Hebrides, the young man who refuses the companionship of the strange women is identified as a MacPhie of Colonsay, and a black dog is instrumental in saving his life.

9 "Mise Chunnaic an t-Iongantas"

Another version of this rhyme was published in October 1954 in *An Gàidheal Òg*, where it is attributed to Dòmhnall MacPhàil of Gleann Urchadain (Glenurquhart). The first two and last four lines of each version are identical except for minor variations (e.g., "is iomadh rud a chunnaic mi" versus "Mise chunnaic an t-iongantas"; "ag uirsgeuladh" versus "ag uisgealadh"), which seems to indicate oral transmission. The two versions differ the most in their middle section: MacPhàil's rhyme is much shorter, but preserves the same pattern of short prepositional or verbal noun phrases describing wild animals linked by the conjunction *is* (and):

Is iomadh rud a chunnaic mi	Many's the thing I've seen
Nach fhac' duin' eile riamh:	That no one else ever saw:
Craobh a' fas gun bhàrr gun duilleig	A tree growing without crown, without leaves
'S i gun bhun gun fhriamh;	Without base, without roots;
An iolaire a' treabhadh,	An eagle plowing,
'S an fheannag trang a' cliathadh,	And a busy crow harrowing,
An dreathann-donn ag uirsgeuladh,	A wren spreading dung,
'S an luch a' cur gu fiadhaich.	And a mouse sowing wildly.[39]

APPENDIX

The following is a summary of the *Suas leis a' Ghàidhlig!* column in the *Casket*, 1987–96. Dr Ken Nilsen is noted as KN and Danny Cameron as DC. Audiotape or videotape recording dates are provided when given in the column.

1987

14 October	Story of "Murchadh nan Ciad agus Muinntir Mhic Rath" told by DC, videotape, 27 April 1986.
4 November	Story of "Di-luain, Di-màirt" told by DC, videotape, 15 November 1983.
25 November	Fiddling in A' Cheapach (the Keppoch) and Beinn a' Bhrùnaich (Brown's Mountain) by KN. DC's reminiscences of Aonghas Fìdhlear, his five fiddler sons, and the new priest, audiotape, 29 April 1980.
9 December	"Gaelic Placenames of Eastern Nova Scotia" by KN.
23 December	A song and customs of "Oidhche Nollaig" (Christmas Eve), "Oidhche Chulainn" (Hogmanay), and "Oidhche nan Trì Righrean" (The Night of the Three Kings; the Eve of the Epiphany) from DC.

1988

27 January	Story of "An Sneachda Mòr" (the Great Snow) of 1904–5, told by DC, 17 January 1980.
10 February	DC's *ròlaist* of local character Doimhgean Oighrig, with English summary, recorded 24 June 1986.
24 February	Two brief stories from DC that involve priests: "Maighstir Anndra agus am Ponach" (Father Andrew and the Lad) and "Leigheas an Déididh" (Healing of the Toothache), with English summary, videotape, 12 September 1987.
16 March	Psychic Phenomena: *bòcain*, *taibhse*, *taighsearachd*, *an dà shealladh*, *tathasg*, *manadh* (spectre, ghost, second sight, second sight, apparition, omen). DC's experience with such phenomena, with English summary, videotape, 2 March 1988.
30 March	"Crìosd agus an Gobhainn": an etiological tale by DC explaining why the blacksmith is never tired, with English summary, audiotape, 2 July 1979.
4 May	"A'Cluich aig na Dannsaichean" (Playing at the Dances): DC describes what it was like fiddling at Giant's Lake and elsewhere in the Antigonish area in the 1920s and '30s; brief English explanation in advance of the Gaelic account.

25 May	DC's story about Maighstir Coinneach (Father Kenneth J. MacDonald) (1821–1910), with English summary.
21 September	"Iain 'ain 'ic Ailein" (John, son of John, son of Alan): this individual's witty comment on Boston's hot summer, by DC, with English version.
5 October	"Raonull, an Gobhainn": DC tells a story he had heard from Ronald the Smith of Bailey's Brook, Pictou County, Nova Scotia, some fifty years before. KN starts off this time in Gaelic. English summary.
19 October	"Calum Sheumais agus a' 'Fenian Raid Money'" (Malcolm, son of James, and the "Fenian Raid Money"): a long story by DC. One-sentence English summary.
9 November	"Am Barrach agus am Mathan" (The Barraman and the Bear): a story about a settler from Barra in the Lakevale area, heard by DC in Boston from the late Ralph MacGillivray. English summary.
30 November	"A' Ghàidhlig ann an Eureka" (Gaelic in Eureka): a story by DC about visiting a Gaelic-speaking couple in Eureka, Pictou County, Nova Scotia, audiotape, 21 September 1988.
7 December	"Mar a Fhuair am Barrach MacNìll a Bhean" (How Barraman MacNeil Got His Wife): another *ròlaist* about the Barra settler, with a brief explanation at beginning, audiotape, 21 September 1988.
28 December	DC tells about the cold Christmas of 1914. Reference to Gates of Heaven being open at Christmas time; witty end to story. Brief English introduction.

1989

18 January	KN sends greetings to DC on reaching his ninetieth birthday. "Domhnall Camaron is Ronald Reagan" (Donald Cameron and Ronald Reagan): a story from when DC was working in the General Electric plant in Lynn, Massachusetts, during the early days of the Second World War, with English introduction, videotape, 5 January 1989.

1 February	DC tells of the MacInnis who met a mermaid, videotape, 5 January 1989.
22 February	"Bruadal" (A Dream): a story by DC about a dream visit from a ghost with an unpaid bill.
15 March	St Patrick's Day greeting in Irish. *Ròlaist* by DC about *an tàillear paraisdeach* (the parish tailor) from the Keppoch who got swallowed by a whale sailing to Pictou from Scotland, audiotape, 8 March 1989.
5 April	KN writes about winter in Gaelic. Two short, humorous pieces from DC, "Am Màgan" (The Frog) and "Aonghas Crùbach agus am Mathan" (Lame Angus and the Bear); no English summary.
12 July	"An t-Easbuig Friseal agus Ailean Mór" (Bishop Fraser and Big Alan): a story told by DC about Bishop Fraser, introduced by KN in English; no English summary. Ailean Mór Dòmhnallach gets the better of the Bishop. DC's grandmother was the bishop's niece.
13 September	"Dunnchadh Mhìcheil agus am Pamphlet" (Duncan, son of Michael, and the Pamphlet): a story DC heard over sixty years earlier in Bailey's Brook involving Maighstir Anndra MacGillebhràth and Dunnchadh Mhìcheil, with a brief English introduction; recorded 28 August 1989.
11 October	DC tells about one of the early pioneers in South River, known as Aonghas Gòrach or Aonghas Casruisgt, videotape, 22 September 1988.
25 October	"Oidhche Shamhna ann a' Morristown" (Halloween in Morristown): an account by DC, briefly introduced in English, videotape, 14 September 1988. KN starts by questioning DC in Gaelic.
8 November	"Òran a' Mhadaidh Ruaidh" (The Song of the Red Fox): DC heard this song in Bailey's Brook many years earlier and sings it to the tune of "An Tè a Chaill a' Ghàidhlig" (The Woman Who Lost the Gaelic). He attributes it to Iain am Pìobaire MacGille Bhràth. KN prints the song from *An Cuairtear Òg*, July 1851.
22 November	"Cù Glic": a short *ròlaist* by DC.

1990

24 January	A conversation between KN and DC about the situation of Gaelic in Beaver Meadow, Antigonish County, at the turn of the century, audiotape, 3 January 1990.
21 February	DC's story "Triùir Gillean agus an Donas" with brief words in Gaelic between KN and DC at the end, recorded 8 June 1989.
14 March	St Patrick's Day greeting in Irish. "A' Fear a Chunnaic Duine Marbh" (The One Who Saw a Dead Man): a story DC heard in Bailey's Brook in the 1920s about a bill forty years unpaid; the one who saw the dead man was a MacDonald (Seumas mac Alasdair) and the dead man was a Chisholm; recorded 27 February 1990.
4 April	Three Gaelic verses by KN in praise of the Antigonish Gaelic Choir, at that time going under the name of "Togamaid Fonn" (Let's Raise a Tune), directed by Eilidh MacKenzie of Scotland. Sr Margaret MacDonell introduced the group at an Immaculata Hall Concert, which included Cape Breton fiddler Natalie MacMaster and the Scotia Dancers.
25 April	KN greets the spring, and the readers, in Gaelic. "Na Dannsaichean ann am Boston" (The Dances in Boston): DC speaks of fiddlers he knew in Boston and a little about the world he knew fifty to sixty years earlier. KN interviews him. Recorded 15 November 1983.

1991

9 October	A Gaelic children's rhyme that DC learned about eighty-eight years earlier in Beaver Meadow from his grandparents. KN: "At 92+, Danny is doing well and sends his greetings from Boston to all his friends in Antigonish."

1992

29 January — DC's account of an encounter between Rev. Andrew MacGillivray, parish priest at Lismore before the turn of the twentieth century, and Rev. Iain Fraser. Recorded 26 August 1991.

12 February — A little Gaelic *duanag* (ditty) about the *Faoillich* (the harsh time of winter), followed by DC's reminiscence about Brown's Mountain. Recorded 26 August 1991.

18 March — KN gives an Irish toast for St Patrick's Day, "Sláinte agus Saol" (Health and Long Life). "Beinn a' Bhrùnaich II": DC continues his recollections of Brown's Mountain. Recorded August 1991.

20 May — Reprint of two short pieces from 5 April 1989, "Màgan" and "Aonghas Crùbach agus am Mathan."

28 October — DC reminisces about *Oidhche Shamhna* (Halloween) of sixty or seventy years ago.

1993

17 March — St Patrick's Day greeting in Irish. "An Carghas" (Lent): DC reminisces about Lenten customs in rural Antigonish in the early decades of the twentieth century.

7 April — DC on "a few interesting farm items": *an dùdach* (the sounding horn) and the horse-fiddle.

8 December — KN greets local piper Allan J. Cameron on his ninetieth birthday. A short conversation with him in Gaelic about the Camerons' experiences when they first arrived in the area.

1994

19 January — "Na Seann Làithean ann a' Siorramachd Antigonish" (The Old Days in Antigonish County): traditions from DC's grandmother Ciorstaidh Dha'i Fhriseil, niece of Bishop Fraser. Recorded 24 July 1988.

23 February	"Cha Ghabh e Inns" (It won't Take Telling): a short Gaelic anecdote that DC heard in Boston many years prior from Alec MacVarish, a native of Cape Breton. Recorded 18 August 1988.
16 March	St Patrick's Day again and KN begins with the Irish greeting: "Beannachtaí na Féile Pádraig!" DC has an anecdote titled "Am Biadh ann am British Columbia" (The Food in British Columbia), featuring "the nineteenth-century local character 'Dòmhnall Mhàmaidh,' who was noted for his witty repartees," recorded 10 January 1991.
27 April	A short anecdote from DC concerning "an incident that took place many years ago in St. Joseph's, Antigonish County on Là Bealltainn (May Day)."
12 October	KN: "We recommence the Gaelic column this week with a short comical anecdote DC told me back in July 1979": "Leig sìos creagan is maidean air mo cheann" (Let down rocks and sticks on my head), recorded 2 July 1979.
16 November	"Lòn an Dobhrain Duinn" (Beaver Meadow): KN and DC converse in Gaelic about Beaver Meadow. Recorded 21 September 1988 when DC was back in Antigonish for a visit.
7 December	In this story, "Tha Fiaclan gu Leòr Aice" (She Has Enough Teeth), DC builds on a witty remark made by a man who was not invited to his neighbour's wedding. Recorded 2 July 1979.

1995

25 January	DC tells a story that explains the expression "Cho Teth ri Gaol Tàilleir" (As Hot as a Tailor's Love), recorded June 1985.
22 February	"A' Tarraing Guail gu Loch Abar" (Hauling Coal to Lochaber): DC's Uncle Duncan took a load of coal from the James River Station to Lochaber where Fr MacCormick was parish priest back around 1913.
15 March	St Patrick's Day again and KN gives his greeting of "Beannachtaí na Féile Pádraig" once more. In the

	story, "An t-Easbuig Friseal agus am Pìobaire" (Bishop Fraser and the Piper), DC tells about Bishop Fraser's response to a recent immigrant's piping, recorded 3 June 1985. See Dunn, *Highland Settler*, 55 for a different version in English (KN).
19 April	"Latha Chùil-lodair, Cnòideart, Alba Nuadh" (Culloden Day, Knoydart, Nova Scotia): a poem by Catrìona NicÌomhair Parsons, introduced by KN, unfortunately printed without the last line. (Perhaps this is why KN repeated it for Culloden Day, 1996.)
26 April	"Bàs Dhòmhnaill Chamarain" (The Death of Donald Cameron) by KN in Gaelic and English.

1996

3 January	A few reminiscences from the late Danny Cameron of what the Christmas and New Year celebrations were like in Beaver Meadow, Antigonish County, eighty or ninety years earlier. Recorded December 1987.
13 March	KN opens with his customary St Patrick's Day greeting in Irish. DC recounts an anecdote about "Ailein Mór agus a Bhean" (Big Alan and his Wife), who lived in Upper South River in the nineteenth century. Recorded December 1985.
10 April	Repeat of Catrìona NicÌomhair Parsons's poem "Latha Chùil-lodair, Cnòideart, Alba Nuadh" with English translation.
12 June	An anecdote DC heard about Fr MacIsaac, the first parish priest of Glendale, Cape Breton, recorded 24 February 1987.
10 July	A column appropriate for Antigonish Highland Games Week as DC talks about his maternal grandmother's family, the Frasers, and a stone throwing event in Scotland back in the 1800s. Recorded May 1987.

NOTES

Grateful thanks to Special Services librarian Susan Cameron and archivist Mary Rose Laureys at the Angus L. MacDonald Library, St Francis Xavier University, for giving me invaluable assistance in retrieving Professor Nilsen's *Casket* articles. Thanks also to Gregory R. Darwin for his valuable Folklore Notes.

1 Nilsen, "P.J. Nicholson," 315; cf. Nilsen, "A Ghàidhlig sa Chasket / Brief Notes on Gaelic in the Casket," *Casket*, 5 March 2008, 13B.
2 Nilsen, "Nova Scotia Gael," 90–1; cf. Nilsen, *Casket*, 26 April 1995, 2A.
3 Nilsen, "Nova Scotia Gael," 83.
4 Nilsen, *Casket*, 26 April 1995, 2A.
5 Ibid.; Nilsen, "Priest," 191.
6 Nilsen, *Casket*, 14 October 1987, 2.
7 Nilsen, *Casket*, 4 November 1987, 2.
8 Nilsen, "Nova Scotia Gael," 100–1n19.
9 Ibid., 91.
10 Nilsen, *Casket*, 10 February 1988, 2
11 Ibid.
12 Nilsen, *Casket*, 22 November 1989, 2A, 7A.
13 Nilsen, *Casket*, 30 March 1988, 4B, 8B.
14 Nilsen, *Casket*, 25 May 1988, 2B; cf. Nilsen, "Priest," 185
15 Nilsen, *Casket*, 25 May 1988, 2B.
16 Nilsen, *Casket*, 24 February 1988, 2; Nilsen, "Priest," 185.
17 Nilsen, *Casket*, 1 February 1989, 2A.
18 Nilsen, *Casket*, 21 February 1990, 3A, 9A.
19 Nilsen, *Casket*, 9 October 1991, 2A.
20 Kenneth Nilsen, curriculum vitae, kindly shared by Marty Nilsen; cf. Nilsen, "Recording," 26.
21 Zeitlin, Kotkin, and Baker, *Celebration*, 14–15.
22 Nilsen, *Casket*, 14 October 1987, 2. Nilsen references MacLean, *History*, 1:77, 2:70–1.
23 Uther, *Types*, 288.
24 Thompson, *Motif-Index*, 523.
25 Shaw, *Na Beanntaichean Gorma*, 122–5.
26 Ibid., 128–9.
27 Ó Súilleabháin and Christiansen, *Types*, 147.
28 Ó Héalaí, "Tuirse na nGaibhne," 87.
29 Ibid., 98–101.

30 Nilsen, *Casket*, 24 February 1988, 2.
31 Nilsen, "Priest," 181.
32 Ibid.
33 See, for example, Fomin and Mac Mathúna, *Stories*, 47–8; and Mac Giollarnáth, "An Dara Tiochóg," 83–6.
34 Darwin, "Seal Woman," 83–8, 114–17.
35 See, for example, Shaw, *Na Beanntaichean Gorma*, 2-29.
36 Darwin, "Seal Woman," 21–2, 252–85, 287–8.
37 MacDonald, "Migratory Legends," 28–9.
38 Nilsen, *Casket*, 21 February 1990, 3A. See "An Ceathrar Shealgair is an Ceathrar Ghlaistig" (The Four Hunters and the Four *Glaistigs*) in MacDougall, *Folk Tales*, 259–62.
39 "Seadh, Am Faca," 40, trans. Gregory R. Darwin.

BIBLIOGRAPHY

Darwin, Gregory R. "'Mar gur dream sí iad atá ag mairiúint fén bhfarraige': The Seal Woman in Its Irish and International Context." PhD diss., Harvard University, 2019.

Dunn, Charles W. *Highland Settler: A Portrait of the Scottish Gael in Cape Breton and Eastern Nova Scotia*. Wreck Cove: Breton Books, [1953]1991.

Fomin, Maxim, and Séamus Mac Mathúna. *Stories of the Sea: Maritime Memorates of Ireland and Scotland*. Berlin: Currach Bhán Publications, 2015.

MacDonald, Donald Archie. "Migratory Legends of the Supernatural in Scotland: A General Survey." *Béaloideas* 62–3 (1994–5): 29–78.

MacDougall, James. *Folk Tales and Fairy Lore in Gaelic and English*. Edinburgh: John Grant, 1910.

Mac Gillarnáth, Seán. "An Dara Tiachóg as Iorrus Aithneach." *Béaloideas* 10 (1940): 3–100.

MacLean, Raymond A., ed. *History of Antigonish*, by Rev. Ronald MacGillivray and Charles J. MacGillivray, 2 vols. Antigonish: Casket, 1976.

Nilsen, Kenneth E. "The Nova Scotia Gael in Boston." *Proceedings of the Harvard Colloquium* 6 (1986): 83–100.

– "P.J. Nicholson and 'Achadh nan Gaidheal.'" In *Bile ós Chrannaibh: A Festschrift for William Gillies*, ed. Wilson McLeod, Abigail Burnyeat, Domhnall Uilleam Stiùbhart, Thomas Owen Clancy, and Roibeard Ó Maolalaigh, 315–28. Ceann Drochaid: Clann Tuirc, 2010.

– "The Priest in the Gaelic Folklore of Nova Scotia." *Béaloideas* 64–5: 171–94.

– "Recording Scottish Gaelic Folklore and Oral History in the United States." *Scotia: Interdisciplinary Journal of Scottish Studies* 27 (2003): 22–33.

Ó Héalaí, Pádraig. "'Tuirse na nGaibhne ar na Buachaillí Bó': Scéal Apacrafúil Dúchasach." *Béaloideas* 53 (1985): 87–129.

Ó Súilleabháin, Seán, and Reidar Th. Christiansen. *The Types of the Irish Folktale*. Helsinki: Academia Scientiarum Fennica, 1963.

"Seadh, Am Faca?" *An Gàidheal Òg* 6, no. 10 (An Damhar [October] 1954): 40.

Shaw, John. *The Blue Mountains and Other Gaelic Stories from Cape Breton / Na Beanntaichean Gorma agus Sgeulachdan Eile a Ceap Breatainn*. Montreal and Kingston: McGill-Queen's University Press, 2007.

Thompson, Stith. *Motif-Index of Folk Literature*, vol. 5. Bloomington: Indiana University Press, 1955.

Uther, Hans-Jörg. *The Types of International Folktales: A Classification and Bibliography*, vol. 1. Helsinki: Academia Scientiarum Fennica, 2004.

Zeitlin, Steven J., Amy J. Kotkin, and Holly Cutting Baker. *A Celebration of American Family Folklore: Tales and Traditions from the Smithsonian Collection.* New York: Pantheon, 1982.

Publications by Kenneth E. Nilsen

1973 "A New Third Person Plural Subject Pronoun in the Irish of Bun a' Cruc, Sraith Salach, Conamara." *Éigse* 15, no. 2: 114–16.

1983 "Some Features of the Irish of Bun a' Cruc, Recess, Co. Galway." *Proceedings of the Harvard Celtic Colloquium* 3: 91–106.

1984 "An Irish 'Life of St. Margaret.'" *Proceedings of the Harvard Celtic Colloquium* 4: 82–104.

1985 "Three Irish Manuscripts in Massachusetts." *Proceedings of the Harvard Celtic Colloquium* 5: 1–21.

1986 "Down among the Dead: Elements of Irish Language and Mythology in James Joyce's *Dubliners*." *Canadian Journal of Irish Studies* 12, no. 1: 23–34.

"The Nova Scotia Gael in Boston." *Proceedings of the Harvard Celtic Colloquium* 6: 83–100.

"Readings and Singings from the Irish." Review. *Aisteoirí na Mainistreach ag Léamh*, 2 cassettes, produced by Máire Ní Ghráinne. Dublin: Paycock Publications, 1985; and *Blas Meala: A Sip from the Honey-Pot: Gaelic Folksongs with English Translations*, by Brian O'Rourke. Blackrock: Irish Academic Press, 1985. *Irish Literary Supplement* 5, no. 2: 36.

1987 Suas leis a' Ghàidhlig! *Casket* (Antigonish NS). 14 October, 2; 4 November, 2; 25 November, 2; 9 December, 2; 23 December, 2.

1988 "Collecting Celtic Folklore in the United States." In *Proceedings of the First North American Congress of Celtic*

Studies, ed. Gordon W. MacLennan, 55–74. Ottawa: The Chair of Celtic Studies, Ottawa University.
Suas leis a' Ghàidhlig! *Casket*. 27 January, 2; 10 February, 2; 24 February, 2; 16 March, 2; 30 March, 4B, 8B; 4 May, 4B, 15B; 25 May, 2B; 21 September, 2B, 9B; 5 October, 2B; 19 October, 2A, 8A; 9 November, 2A, 16A; 30 November, 2A, 4A; 7 December, 2A, 12A; 28 December, 2A, 13A.

1989 Suas leis a' Ghàidhlig! *Casket*. 18 January, 2A, 13A; 1 February, 2A; 22 February, 2A, 10A; 15 March, 2A, 7A; 5 April, 2A, 10A; 12 July, 2A; 13 September, 2A, 7A; 11 October, 2A, 6A; 25 October, 2A, 4A; 8 November, 2A, 9A; 22 November, 2A, 7A.

1989–90 "The Gaelic Place-Names of Mainland Nova Scotia – a Preliminary Survey." *Ainm: Bulletin of the Ulster Place-Name Society* 4: 220–3.

1990 Suas leis a' Ghàidhlig! *Casket*. 24 January, 2A, 3A; 21 February, 3A, 9A; 14 March, 2A, 6A; 4 April, 2A, 7A; 25 April, 2A, 7A.
"Thinking of Monday: Irish Speakers of Portland, Maine." *Éire-Ireland* 25, no. 1: 3–19.

1991 "Le Gaélique en Nouvelle-Ecosse." *Bretagne Linguistique. Cahiers du Groupe de Recherche sur l'Économie Linguistique de la Bretagne* 7: 79–91.
"Mícheál Ó Broin agus Lámhscríbhinní Gaeilge Ollscoil Wisconsin." *Celtica* 22: 112–18.
Review. *Douglas Hyde: A Maker of Modern Ireland*, by Janet Egleson Dunleavy and Gareth W. Dunleavy. *Celtic Studies Association Newsletter* 10, no. 2: 6–7.
Suas leis a' Ghàidhlig! *Casket*. 9 October, 2A.

1992 Suas leis a' Ghàidhlig! *Casket*. 29 January, 2A, 8A; 12 February, 2A, 14A; 18 March, 2A, 8A; 28 October, 2A, 3A.

1992-93 "Scéalaíocht Chois Fharraige." Review. *Tom Bheairtle Tom Ó Flatharta ag Scéalaíocht* and *Tom Pheaidí MacDiarmada ag Scéalaíocht*, Cló Iar-Chonnachta, 1992. *Béaloideas* 60–61: 323–4.

1993 Suas leis a' Ghàidhlig! *Casket*. 17 March, 2A, 9A; 7 April, 2A; 8 December, 2A, 3A.

1993–94 "Air Chéilidh aig Mac Archie Sheumais." *The Clansman* 7, no. 6 (December–January): 14.

1994 "The Celts and Their Languages." *The Clansman* 8, no. 1 (1994): 12–13.

Suas leis a' Ghàidhlig! *Casket*. 19 January, 2A; 23 February, 2A; 16 March, 2A; 27 April, 2A; 12 October, 2A; 16 November, 2A; 7 December, 2A.

1995 Suas leis a' Ghàidhlig! *Casket*. 25 January, 2A, 3A; 22 February, 2A; 15 March, 2A; 19 April, 2A; 26 April, 2A.

1995–96 "'Se (Shay) Versus 'Se (Say)." Gaelic Notes. *Celtic Heritage* 9, no. 6 (December–January): 16.

1996 "A Brief History of the Department of Celtic Studies, Saint Francis Xavier University, Antigonish, Nova Scotia." *Journal of Celtic Language Learning* 2: 78–80.

"Le Gaélique en Nouvelle Écosse. Survivance d'une Langue Orale au Nouveau Monde." *Bretagne Linguistique. Cahiers du Groupe de Recherche sur l'Économie Linguistique de la Bretagne* 10: 97–103.

"The Irish Language in New York, 1850–1900." In *The New York Irish*, ed. Ronald H. Bayor and Timothy J. Meagher, 252–74. Baltimore: Johns Hopkins University Press.

"The Origin of Lenition (aka Aspiration)." Gaelic Notes. *Celtic Heritage* 10, no. 2 (April–May): 24.

"The Past Tense." Gaelic Notes. *Celtic Heritage* 10, no. 5 (October–November): 16.

"Some Notes on the Gaelic of Eastern Nova Scotia." *Scottish Gaelic Studies* 17, ed. Donald MacAulay, James Gleasure, and Colm Ó Baoill. *Festschrift for Professor D.S. Thomson*: 292–4.

Suas leis a' Ghàidhlig! *Casket*. 3 January, 2A; 13 March, 2A; 10 April, 2A; 12 June, 2A; 10 July, 2A.

"Trì Bliadhna, Ceithir Bliadhna, Cóig Bliadhna, Sia Bliadhna ..." Gaelic Notes. *Celtic Heritage* 10, no. 1 (February–March): 27.

"The Vocative Case." Gaelic Notes. *Celtic Heritage* 10, no. 3 (June–July): 22.

1996–97 "The Priest in the Gaelic Folklore of Nova Scotia." *Béaloideas* 64–65: 171–94.

1997 "Irish in Nineteenth Century New York." In *The Multilingual Apple: Languages in New York City*, ed. Ofelia García and Joshua A. Fishman, 53–69. Berlin: Mouton de Gruyter.

"Nasalizing Particles." Gaelic Notes. *Celtic Heritage* 11, no. 2 (April–May): 12.
Review. *An Introduction to the Celtic Languages*, by Paul Russell, London: Longman, 1995. *Journal of Multilingual and Multicultural Development* 18, no. 5: 433–6.
"The Twenty-Third Psalm." Gaelic Notes. *Celtic Heritage* 11, no. 5 (October–November): 27.

1998 "The Passive in Scottish Gaelic (Part 1)." Gaelic Notes. *Celtic Heritage* 12, no. 1 (February–March): 18.

1999 "Ais-éiridh na Gàidhlig – Gaelic Revival." *Chronicle-Herald* (Halifax), 14 February, C2. Reprinted as "A Reminiscence." *Proceedings of the Harvard Celtic Colloquium* 31 (2012): 337–41.
"Irish Language in the U.S." In *The Encyclopedia of the Irish in America*, ed. Michael Glazier, 470–4. Notre Dame: University of Notre Dame Press.

2000 "Living Celtic Speech: Celtic Sound Archives in North America." In *6th Annual Conference of the North American Association for Celtic Language Teachers: The Information Age, Celtic Languages and the New Millenium* [*sic*], ed. Richard F.E. Sutcliffe and Gearóid Ó Néill, 89–94. Limerick: Department of Computer Science and Information Systems, University of Limerick.
"The Passive in Scottish Gaelic (Part 2)." Gaelic Notes. *Celtic Heritage* 14, no. 2 (May–June): 18–19.

2001 "Beannachtaí na Féile Pádraic / Blessing of the Feast of St. Patrick." Gaelic Notes. *Celtic Heritage* 15, no. 1 (March–April): 16–17.
"Saoghal Tubaisteach / A Calamitous World." Gaelic Notes. *Celtic Heritage* 15, no. 5 (November–December): 22–3.
"Se Duine Math a Th'ann." Gaelic Notes. *Celtic Heritage* 14, no. 6 (January–February): 28–9.
"Suas Leis a' Ghàidhlig! Gaelic is on the Move." Gaelic Notes. *Celtic Heritage* 15, no. 2 (May–June): 36.
"That: Demonstrative Pronoun, Relative Pronoun, and Conjunction." Gaelic Notes. *Celtic Heritage* 15, no. 3 (July–August): 14–15.

2002 "Irish Gaelic Literature in the United States." In *American Babel: Literatures of the United States from Abnaki to Zuni*, ed. Marc Shell, 188–218. Cambridge, MA: Harvard University Press.

"More on Tuilleadh, Barrachd, and Còrr." Gaelic Notes. *Celtic Heritage* 16, no. 1 (March–April): 18–19.

"Some Notes on Pre-*Mac-Talla* Gaelic Publishing in Nova Scotia (with References to Early Gaelic Publishing in Prince Edward Island, Quebec, and Ontario)." In *Rannsachadh na Gàidhlig 2000: Papers Read at the Conference "Scottish Gaelic Studies 2000," Held at the University of Aberdeen, 2-4 August* 2000, ed. Colm Ó Baoill and Nancy R. McGuire, 127–40. Aberdeen: An Clò Gaidhealach.

"So Many / Many / As Much / Many." Gaelic Notes. *Celtic Heritage* 16, no. 3 (July–August): 16–17.

"Tuilleadh, Barrachd, agus Còrr: Use of 'More' in Gaelic." Gaelic Notes. *Celtic Heritage* 15, no. 6 (January–February): 20–1.

2003 "Compound Prepositions I: An Déidh." Gaelic Notes. *Celtic Heritage* 16, no. 6 (January–February): 38, 43.

"Recording Scottish Gaelic Folklore and Oral History in the United States." *Scotia: Interdisciplinary Journal of Scottish Studies* 27: 22–33.

2004 "'The language that the strangers do not know': The Galway Gaeltacht of Portland, Maine in the Twentieth Century." In *They Change Their Sky: The Irish in Maine*, ed. Michael C. Connolly, 297–339. Orono: University of Maine Press.

2005 s.v. Sinclair, Alexander MacLean. In *Dictionary of Canadian Biography*, vol. 15, ed. Ramsay Cook and Réal Bélanger, 949–51. Toronto: University of Toronto Press.

Review. *An Haicléara Mánas: A Nineteenth-Century Text from Clifden, Co. Galway*, by Nancy Stenson. *Journal of the Galway Archaeological and Historical Society* 57: 213–17.

2006 "Celtic Languages in North America," s.vv. (1) Irish, (2) Scottish Gaelic, and (5) Breton. In *Celtic Culture: A Historical Encyclopedia*, vol. 1, ed. John T. Koch, 376–9, 379–81, 383–4. Santa Barbara: ABC-CLIO.

Liam Ó Caiside. "Agallamh: Coinneach Nilsen aig Naomh FX / An Interview with Ken Nilsen of Saint Francis Xavier University." *An Naidheachd Againne: Newsletter of An Comunn Gàidhealach, America* 23, no. 2–3: 5.

2007 Review. *Caint Ros Muc. Imleabhar I: Téacs. Imleabhar II: Foclóir*, by Arndt Wigger. *Journal of the Galway Archaeological and Historical Society* 59: 193–6.

2008 "A' Ghàidhlig sa Chasket / Brief Notes on Gaelic in the Casket." Suas leis a' Ghàidhlig / Up with the Gaelic. *Casket*. 5 March, 13B.

"John Ford's Use of Gaelic in *The Quiet Man*: An Interview with Nora Folan." In *John Ford in Focus: Essays on the Filmmaker's Life and Work*, ed. Kevin L. Stoehr and Michael C. Connolly, 122–7. Jefferson: McFarland.

"Latha Bealltainn – May Day." Suas leis a' Ghàidhlig / Up with the Gaelic. *Casket*. 7 May, 13B.

Trans., "John Ford: A Memorial" by Maidhc P. Ó Conaola. In *John Ford in Focus: Essays on the Filmmaker's Life and Work*, ed. Kevin L. Stoehr and Michael C. Connolly, 68–74. Jefferson: McFarland.

2009 "Leabharlann Gàidhlig / A Gaelic Library." Suas leis a' Ghàidhlig / Up with the Gaelic. *Casket*. 18 November, 6B.

2010 Ed., *Rannsachadh na Gàidhlig 5: Fifth Scottish Gaelic Research Conference, St. Francis Xavier University, Antigonish, Nova Scotia, July 21-24, 2008*. Sydney: Cape Breton University Press.

"A' Ghàidhlig an Canada: Scottish Gaelic in Canada." In *The Edinburgh Companion to the Gaelic Language*, ed. Moray Watson and Michelle Macleod, 90–107. Edinburgh: Edinburgh University Press.

"P.J. Nicholson and 'Achadh nan Gaidheal.'" In *Bile ós Chrannaibh: A Festschrift for William Gillies*, ed. Wilson McLeod, Abigail Burnyeat, Domhnall Uilleam Stiùbhart, Thomas Own Clancy, and Roibeard Ó Maolalaigh, 315–28. Ceann Drochaid: Clann Tuirc.

"Sgrìob dhan t-Seann Dùthaich ~ A Trip to Scotland." Suas leis a' Ghàidhlig / Up with the Gaelic. *Casket*. 29 September, 6B.

2012 "James Cullinan and Some Items of South Tipperary Seanchas." In *Atlantic Currents: Essays on Lore, Literature and Language / Sruthanna an Aigéin Thiar: Aistí ar Sheanchas, ar Litríocht agus ar Theanga*, ed. Bo Almqvist, Críostóir Mac Cárthaigh, Liam Mac Mathúna, Séamus Mac Mathúna, and Seosamh Watson, 150–62. Dublin: University College Dublin Press.

s.vv. Celtic Languages in North America, Breton; Celtic Languages in North America, Irish; and Celtic Languages in North America, Scottish Gaelic. In *The Celts: History, Life, and Culture*, vol. 1, ed. John T. Koch and Antone Minard, 164–5, 165–7, 167–8. Santa Barbara: ABC-CLIO.

2013 "An Ghaeilge in Oirthear Cheanada, 1750-1900." In *Séimhfhear Suairc: Aistí in Ómós don Ollamh Breandán Ó Conchúir*, ed. Seán Ó Coileáin, Liam P. Ó Murchú, and Pádraigín Riggs, 262–79. An Díseart, An Daingean: An Sagart.

Contributors

GREGORY R. DARWIN is a recent graduate of the Department of Celtic Languages and Literatures at Harvard University, with a doctoral dissertation on the Seal Woman legend. His research interests include supernatural belief and oral narrative, the relationship between folklore and literature, cultural exchange between the Gaelic and Norse spheres, and the digital humanities. His work has appeared in *Folklore*, *Éigse: A Journal of Irish Studies*, *The Parish Review: Journal of Flann O'Brien Studies*, and elsewhere.

AIDAN DOYLE is a lecturer in Irish in University College, Cork, Ireland. His research focuses on the grammatical structure and sociolinguistics of Irish. He is the author of *A History of the Irish Language* (2015).

ROBERT DUNBAR is professor and chair of Celtic languages, literature, history, and antiquities at the University of Edinburgh. He is currently completing a scholarly edition of the secular song-poems of John MacLean, which will be published by the Scottish Gaelic Texts Society. His research interests include Gaelic literature, language, and culture in Canada, eighteenth- and nineteenth-century Gaelic literature and society, and language policy and planning for Gaelic and other Celtic languages. He is also currently completing a monograph on legislation and policy for Gaelic in Scotland, Welsh in Wales, and Irish in the Republic of Ireland and Northern Ireland, supported in part by a British Academy fellowship.

TIBER F.M. FALZETT is a lecturer/assistant professor in folklore and ethnology in the School of Irish, Celtic Studies, and Folklore at University College Dublin. From 2018 to 2020 he was the inaugural visiting lecturer in Scottish Gaelic studies at the University of North Carolina at Chapel Hill. He holds his PhD in Celtic and Scottish studies and MScR in Scottish ethnology from the University of Edinburgh as well as a BA Hons (First) in Celtic from St Francis Xavier University in Antigonish, Nova Scotia. He has conducted more than a decade of fieldwork among Scottish Gaelic speakers in Cape Breton Island, Nova Scotia, and the Outer Hebrides. His research explores the survival of locally composed song verse in the Maritime Gàidhealtachd along with communally maintained aesthetics concerning language, verbal art, and music as expressed through embodied experience and sensory metaphor.

MATTHEW KNIGHT is an associate librarian at the University of South Florida Libraries in Tampa. He teaches "The Irish in America," "Irish Rebels and Revolutionaries," and "Modern Ireland" through the USF Department of History. A graduate of Harvard's Celtic Languages and Literatures program, his major research involves the revival of the Irish language in nineteenth-century Irish American newspapers and the University of South Florida's Dion Boucicault Theatre Collection.

MICHAEL LINKLETTER is the Sister Saint Veronica Professor of Gaelic Studies and head of the Department of Celtic Studies at St Francis Xavier University in Antigonish, Nova Scotia. He was awarded a PhD in Celtic languages and literatures from Harvard University in 2006. With Seonaidh Ailig Mac a' Phearsain, he published *Fògradh, Fàisneachd, Filidheachd / Parting, Prophecy, Poetry* about the writings of Duncan Black Blair in the Gaelic newspaper *Mac-Talla*. He has most recently been working in the area of death and dying among Highland immigrants to the Maritimes and, with Laurie Stanley-Blackwell, co-authored the article "Inscribing Ethnicity: A Preliminary Analysis of Gaelic Headstone Inscriptions in Eastern Nova Scotia and Cape Breton" in *Genealogy* (2018).

LORRIE MACKINNON has published articles in *Celtic Heritage*, *Am Braighe*, and *Rannsachadh na Gàidhlig 5: Fifth Scottish Gaelic Research*

Conference. She is responsible for the annual symposium at Féis an Eilein, the Gaelic cultural festival in Christmas Island, Nova Scotia. She met Ken Nilsen in 1991 and they worked on many projects together, including visiting and recording several native speakers.

WILLIAM MAHON, a native of Paterson, New Jersey, received his doctorate in Celtic languages and literatures from Harvard University in 1987. From 1995 to 2015 he was a lecturer in Modern and Early Modern Irish in Aberystwyth University's Department of Welsh and Celtic Studies. Since retirement in 2015 he has continued to do research in the history of the Irish Language in America, post-classical Modern Irish prose (1650–1850), and nineteenth-century East Galway manuscripts.

MICHAEL NEWTON earned a PhD in Celtic studies from the University of Edinburgh. He was an assistant professor in the Celtic Studies department of St Francis Xavier University in Nova Scotia from 2008 to 2013 and the technical lead of the University of North Carolina Digital Innovation Lab from 2013 to 2017. He has written several books and numerous articles about many aspects of Scottish Gaelic culture and history, with particular emphases on the diaspora, Gaelic literature, ethnic identity and exchange, human ecology, and dance tradition. In 2018 he was recognized with the International award at the annual Scottish Gaelic awards in Glasgow, Scotland. His 2015 publication *Seanchaidh na Coille / Memory-Keeper of the Forest: Anthology of Scottish Gaelic Literature of Canada* is the first extensive collection of Gaelic Canadian literature and analysis of it.

CATRÌONA NICÌOMHAIR PARSONS is a long-time Gaelic language teacher, most especially in the Celtic Department of St Francis Xavier University in Antigonish, Nova Scotia, and at the Gaelic College in Cape Breton. Her chief areas of research include linguistics, Gaelic pedagogy, North American Gaelic literature, and Gaelic song. Her publications include the Gaelic course *Gàidhlig troimh Chòmhradh* (1989–93) in three volumes with accompanying CDs, commissioned by the Gaelic College Foundation, and *Seallagain* (2016), a handbook on Scottish Gaelic structure, with sound files, for the University of Otago in New Zealand.

TONY Ó FLOINN lectures in Roinn na Gaeilge on the Thurles Campus of Mary Immaculate College, Limerick. His current research focuses on the lives and literary works of east Cork natives Pádraig Phiarais Cúndún (1777–1857) and Dáibhí de Barra (1757/8–1851). He also has a particular interest in the late manuscript tradition in Waterford County and surrounds as well as the experiences and literary output of native Irish and Scottish Gaelic speakers in North America.

TOMÁS Ó HÍDE is professor of languages and literatures at Lehman College of the City University of New York where he lectures in the Irish language section. He has served as director of the CUNY Institute for Irish-American Studies and president of the North American Association for Celtic Language Teachers. He is the primary author of the books *The Irish Language in the United States* (1994), *Colloquial Irish* (2008), and *Seáinín Tom Sheáin: From Árainn to the Silver Screen* (2019).

PÁDRAIG Ó LIATHÁIN is an assistant professor in Fiontar agus Scoil na Gaeilge, Dublin City University. His research interests include Irish language literature from the seventeenth century to the present, including Irish connections with Newfoundland and New England. His latest book is an annotated critical edition of Donncha Rua Mac Conmara's eighteenth-century poem "Eachtra Ghiolla an Amaráin." He is editing and preparing for publication the complete diaries of the twentieth-century Irish poet Seán Ó Ríordáin.

PÁDRAIG Ó SIADHAIL is a professor in Irish studies and holder of the D'Arcy McGee Chair of Irish Studies at Saint Mary's University, Halifax, Nova Scotia. His publications include a history of Irish language theatre and critical full-length biographies of Piaras Béaslaí (1881–1965), the Liverpool-born journalist and Irish Revolution-era activist, and Katherine Hughes (1876–1925), the Canadian-born writer and Irish Republican organizer and propagandist in the post-1916 period. In recent years, Ó Siadhail's scholarly research has focused on aspects of transnationalism, including representations of, and encounters with, North America's Indigenous peoples in Irish language writing and a survey of Irish language literature from and about Canada.

KATHLEEN REDDY has a background in Gaelic education in Nova Scotia and Scotland. She is currently working toward a PhD in Celtic and Gaelic at the University of Glasgow. Her research concerns connections between local religious practice and Gaelic language and culture in twentieth-century Gaelic-speaking Catholic communities.

CIARA RYAN is a PhD candidate at University College Cork. She is currently based in Montana, where she teaches Irish language at Carroll College and Spanish and French at Helena College, University of Montana.

NANCY STENSON is professor emerita of linguistics at the University of Minnesota. She was a scholar in the Dublin Institute for Advanced Studies in 1976–77 and has returned there as a visiting professor on several occasions. In 2012–15, she was a Fulbright Fellow and a Marie Curie Incoming International Fellow in the School of Psychology at University College Dublin. Her research has included Irish language learning, Irish syntax, and various aspects of Irish–English language contact.

NATASHA SUMNER is an associate professor of Celtic languages and literatures at Harvard University. Her research focuses on the Gaelic narrative corpus about the hero Fionn mac Cumhaill in Ireland, Britain, and North America. She is the principal investigator on the Fionn Cycle Folklore Project to create an online database of Fenian folklore, and she is an adviser to the Boston and the Irish Language Project to collect oral histories of Boston area Irish speakers. She teaches courses on Irish and Scottish Gaelic language, post-medieval literature, and folklore.

Index

Page numbers in italics refer to tables.